History

GOES TO THE

Movies

A Viewer's Guide
to the Best
(and Some of the Worst)
Historical Films
Ever Made

MAIN STREET BOOKS

Doubleday

New York ★ London ★ Toronto
Sydney ★ Auckland

History

GOES TO THE

Movies

Joseph Roquemore

A Main Street Book

PUBLISHED BY DOUBLEDAY
a division of Random House, Inc.
1540 Broadway, New York, New York 10036

MAIN STREET BOOKS, DOUBLEDAY, and the portrayal of a building with a tree
are trademarks of Doubleday, a division of Random House, Inc.

Book design by Maria Carella

Library of Congress Cataloging-in-Publication Data
Roquemore, Joseph H.
    History goes to the movies: a viewer's guide to the best
    (and some of the worst) historical films ever made / Joseph
    Roquemore.
        p.   cm.
    Includes bibliographical references and index.
    1. Historical films—History and criticism.   I. Title.
PN1995.9.H5R67   1999
791.43′658—dc21   99-29079
                                                CIP

ISBN 0-385-49678-8

December 1999

First Edition

10   9   8   7   6   5   4   3   2   1

For My Parents

Kathryn Brown Roquemore
and
Joseph Harmon Roquemore *(in memoriam)*

Contents

Preface   xv

1
Ancient, Classical,
and Medieval History

Alexander the Great   7

Becket   8

    The Lion in Winter   10

Braveheart   10

The Egyptian   12

    Land of the Pharaohs   14

    Cleopatra (1934)   14

The Fall of the Roman Empire   15

    Spartacus   19

    Barabbas   19

    Ben-Hur   19

Sign of the Pagan   20

    Attila   20

Jesus of Nazareth   20

    Peter and Paul   22

King David   23

    The Story of David   24

    David and Bathsheba   24

Masada   25

Quest for Fire   26

Robin Hood, Prince of Thieves   28

    The Adventures of Robin Hood   29

    Robin and Marian   29

The Ten Commandments   29

    Moses   31

The Vikings   32

The War Lord   33

    The Crusades   36

Excalibur 36

El Cid 37

2

Early American History

Amistad 43

Black Robe 44

The Buccaneer 45

Christopher Columbus 46

    1492: Conquest of Paradise 48

The Crucible 48

    Maid of Salem 49

The Howards of Virginia 49

    John Paul Jones 51

    The Madness of King George 51

The Last of the Mohicans 51

Plymouth Adventure 52

3

U.S. Civil War

The Birth of a Nation 59

Dark Command 60

    Kansas Raiders 61

Drums in the Deep South 61

    Shenandoah 62

    Friendly Persuasion 63

Gettysburg 63

Glory 64

Gone with the Wind 65

The Horse Soldiers 66

Ironclads 67

The Red Badge of Courage (1951) 68

    The Red Badge of Courage (1974) 70

Springfield Rifle 70

    The Raid 72

Young Mr. Lincoln 73

    Gore Vidal's Lincoln 74

    The Prisoner of Shark Island 74

4

The American West

Broken Arrow 81

Butch Cassidy and the Sundance Kid 82

Cheyenne Autumn 83

Conagher 85

    Lonesome Dove 88

    Monte Walsh 88

    Will Penny 88

Drum Beat 88

The Far Country 90

Geronimo: An American Legend 91

The Grey Fox 92

Heaven's Gate 93

    The Big Country 95

I Will Fight No More Forever 95

Jeremiah Johnson 96

    Man in the Wilderness 97

    The Mountain Men 98

The Last Command 98

    The Alamo 100

    The Alamo: 13 Days to Glory 100

The Last Day 100

The Lawless Breed 102

   The Gunfighter 103

Lawman 103

   The Tin Star 104

   High Noon 104

The Long Riders 105

   The Return of Frank James 106

Pony Express 107

   Western Union 108

The Searchers 108

   Two Rode Together 110

Son of the Morning Star 110

   Dances With Wolves 114

   They Died With Their Boots On 115

   Custer of the West 115

Stagecoach 115

   Wells Fargo 116

Tom Horn 117

Ulzana's Raid 118

   The Stalking Moon 119

   Apache 120

Union Pacific 120

   The Iron Horse 121

Wagon Master 122

   Bend of the River 123

The Westerner 124

   The Life and Times

      of Judge Roy Bean 125

Wild Times 125

Winchester '73 126

Wyatt Earp 128

   Tombstone 129

   Gunfight at the O.K. Corral 130

Young Guns 130

   Young Guns II 131

   The Left-Handed Gun 132

5

World War I

All Quiet on the Western Front (1979) 137

   All Quiet on the Western Front

      (1930) 139

   Paths of Glory 139

The Blue Max 140

   Aces High 141

A Farewell to Arms (1957) 141

   A Farewell to Arms (1932) 143

Gallipoli 143

   The Lighthorsemen 146

   Anzacs: The War Down Under 146

Sergeant York 146

   The Fighting 69th 149

6

1920–1940: Gangsters, the Roaring Twenties, and the Great Depression

Al Capone 155

   The Untouchables 156

Bonnie and Clyde	*156*	A Time to Love and	
Bugsy	*157*	a Time to Die	186
Dillinger	*158*	*The Desert Fox*	*186*
Young Dillinger	160	*The Desert Rats*	*188*
The Front Page (1931)	*160*	Tobruk	189
The Front Page (1974)	161	Five Graves to Cairo	190
King of the Hill	*161*	*Escape from Sobibor*	*190*
Places in the Heart	*163*	Judgment at Nuremberg	193
The Grapes of Wrath	165	Schindler's List	193
Of Mice and Men (1981)	165	The House on Garibaldi Street	194
Of Mice and Men (1992)	165	Operation Eichmann	194

7

World War II

		Fat Man and Little Boy	*194*
		5 Fingers	*196*
		The Great Escape	*197*
		The Captive Heart	199
Anzio	*172*	49th Parallel	199
To Hell and Back	172	*The Halls of Montezuma*	*200*
Battleground	*173*	The Thin Red Line (1964)	201
Battle of the Bulge	174	The Thin Red Line (1998)	201
Battle of Britain	*175*	Battle Cry	202
Hope and Glory	177	*Hiroshima: Out of the Ashes*	*202*
The Boat (Das Boot)	*177*	*The Longest Day*	*204*
The Enemy Below	178	Breakthrough	206
Run Silent, Run Deep	178	Saving Private Ryan	206
The Bridge on the River Kwai	*179*	The Big Red One	207
Empire of the Sun	181	*The Man Who Never Was*	*207*
Back to Bataan	181	One Against the Wind	208
Prisoners of the Sun	181	*Memphis Belle*	*209*
The Court-Martial of Billy Mitchell	*182*	Twelve O'Clock High	210
Cross of Iron	*183*	*Midway*	*211*
Stalingrad	186	In Harm's Way	212

Mission of the Shark	*213*
Objective, Burma!	*214*
Merrill's Marauders	215
O.S.S.	*215*
Decision Before Dawn	217
Patton	*217*
The Last Days of Patton	219
The Sands of Iwo Jima	*219*
Sink the Bismarck!	*221*
Pursuit of the Graf Spee	222
In Which We Serve	222
Tora! Tora! Tora!	*222*
From Here to Eternity	223
A Walk in the Sun	*224*

8
Korean War

The Bridges at Toko-Ri	*231*
Men of the Fighting Lady	232
The Manchurian Candidate	*232*
The Rack	234
Sergeant Ryker	234
Men in War	*234*
The Steel Helmet	235
Pork Chop Hill	*236*
Retreat, Hell!	*238*
Fixed Bayonets	239

9
Unity and Upheaval:
USA, 1950–1975

American Graffiti	*245*
Apollo 13	*246*
The Right Stuff	247
Blackboard Jungle	*248*
JFK	*249*
Fatal Deception:	
Mrs. Lee Harvey Oswald	251
Medium Cool	*252*
Woodstock	254
Easy Rider	254
The Graduate	254
Mississippi Burning	*255*
Malcolm X	257
Nixon	*257*
All the President's Men	260
Kissinger and Nixon	260
Quiz Show	*261*

10
Vietnam War

Bat 21	*269*
Flight of the Intruder	*270*
The Hanoi Hilton	271
Full Metal Jacket	*272*
Go Tell the Spartans	*273*

Hamburger Hill	274	**12**	
Indochine	276	**Social History, Period**	
The Iron Triangle	278	**Pieces, and Biography**	
The Killing Fields	279		
Platoon	280	The Age of Innocence	318
Casualties of War	282	The Bounty	319
The Deer Hunter	282	Mutiny on the Bounty (1962)	321
A Rumor of War	282	Mutiny on the Bounty (1935)	322
Apocalypse Now	282	Damn the Defiant!	322
		Cal	322
11		Shake Hands with the Devil	326
Cold War		Far and Away	326
		Michael Collins	326
The Beast	291	Patriot Games	326
The Big Lift	292	In the Name of the Father	327
Berlin Tunnel 21	294	The Charge of the Light Brigade (1968)	327
The Falcon and the Snowman	295	The Charge of the Light Brigade	
Family of Spies	297	(1936)	328
Gulag	298	Citizen Kane	329
Sakharov	299	Doctor Zhivago	331
The Heroes of Desert Storm	300	Nicholas and Alexandra	333
The Hunt for Red October	302	The Duellists	333
Stalin	303	Barry Lyndon	335
Burnt by the Sun	305	Fire Over England	335
The Inner Circle	305	The Sea Hawk	338
Strategic Air Command	306	The Virgin Queen	338
By Dawn's Early Light	308	The Private Lives of Elizabeth	
On the Beach	308	and Essex	338
To Kill a Priest	308	Elizabeth	339
Crisis in the Kremlin	311	Lady Jane	339

Gandhi   340

Ike: The War Years   341

Khartoum   342

Land and Freedom   343

    For Whom the Bell Tolls   345

The Last Emperor   346

Lawrence of Arabia   347

Lost Command   349

    The Battle of Algiers   351

MacArthur   351

A Man for All Seasons   353

    The Private Life of Henry VIII   354

    Anne of the Thousand Days   355

A Night to Remember   355

    Titanic (1997)   357

    Titanic (1953)   357

Raid on Entebbe   358

Rob Roy   359

Shadowlands (1985)   361

    Shadowlands (1993)   362

The Spirit of St. Louis   363

A Tale of Two Cities (1935)   364

    The Scarlet Pimpernel (1982)   368

    Waterloo   369

Zulu   369

    Zulu Dawn   373

    Mountains of the Moon   373

    Breaker Morant   373

Acknowledgments   375

Preface

Asked in 1993 to comment on charges that *In the Name of the Father* grossly mangles contemporary British and Irish history, female lead Emma Thompson fumed, "I don't give a damn!" (Director Jim Sheridan's politically correct movie exalts Irish thief Gerry Conlon, convicted by British courts—on solid evidence—of conspiring to kill five persons in a 1974 terrorist bombing.) Ever since *The Birth of a Nation*'s 1915 premiere, feature-film makers have rewritten history to fashion top-dollar entertainment, but this was wholesale contempt for the truth: what mattered the most for Thompson and Sheridan was their fierce anti-British ideological agenda, not entertainment—and certainly not history.

In the Name of the Father is high-octane feature-film propaganda, ham-fisted if you're familiar with Conlon's case—but effective (moderately, at least) if you're not. This is nothing new. Movies have always made superb political weapons. Hitler commissioned many documentaries for public consumption, and Stalin—partial to feature films—hung banners blaring Lenin's famous pronouncement "Of all the arts, Cinema is the most important" in countless Moscow movie theaters (see *The Inner Circle*). The Soviet Central Film Industry Directorate reviewed every single movie produced in Russia, and the bureau's director had instant, direct access to Stalin.

Feature films pack great persuasive power, because viewing them is like witnessing crimes or automobile accidents: well-made movies hold your interest continuously, riveting all of your attention on "what happens next" and pulling you forward—pell-mell, with no time to reflect on individual scenes—until the final credits roll. The result: you don't remember much about a film after watching it for the first time. Very few people have memories muscular enough to recall even half the plot, in reasonably accurate sequence, of an absorbing movie, and still fewer can remember facial expressions or voice intonations associated with specific dialogue sequences (including politically and morally loaded conversations). For this reason, films have extraordinary power—unmatched by any other medium—to leave you with a strong sense of what is right and what is wrong, of who is bad and who is good, even though critical details presented in the movies may be slanted or false.

Well, so what? They're just movies. In fact, they're *not* just movies. Millions of Americans are fanatical history-lovers—their number grows each year—and they pack theaters every time new films on historical figures or events come to town. *Saving Private Ryan* (1998) and *Titanic* (1997) raked in viewers and cold cash for months. One of the History Channel's most popular programs, *Movies in Time*, airs twice daily—morning and afternoon—five days a week. Many high school teachers screen movies in the classroom: a couple of years ago, I saw a list of 100 film titles (students could pick and choose, apparently) used in a world history course at an area school. Clearly, countless Americans get most of their history from television and the big screen. But what, exactly, are they getting?

Not enough, much of the time: the odds are very high that most movies, at some point, will lead you away from history unless they send you to the library. For example, "I don't remember everything the Nez Percé fugitives did in *I Will Fight No More Forever,* but soldiers hunted them down, relentlessly, for no reason at all" is the near-universal reaction to Richard T. Heffron's moving 1975 film, and it's sadly wrongheaded. The U.S. Army went after the Nez Percés because several drunken braves had slaughtered, without provocation, 19 settlers in Oregon. Heffron presents the incident so briefly and superficially that it seems trivial (some viewers don't remember it at all), simplifying a maddeningly complicated moral situation—most Nez Percés were law-abiding, solid citizens—and leaving audiences with an incomplete version of a tragic episode in Native American history.

Similar historical "flattening" occurs in countless films and—in relatively recent movies—with annoying frequency. Some of the industry's finest historical and period films (*A Man for All Seasons, The Duellists, Black Robe, Ulzana's Raid, Go Tell the Spartans, The Age of Innocence*) premiered during the past three and a half decades. But the 1960s also triggered a flurry of politically charged, history-based movies humming with factual distortions and, occasionally, outright lies (*The Battle of Algiers, Lost Command,* Tony Richardson's 1968 remake of *The Charge of the Light Brigade*). Today, the trend continues on a larger scale: many films released in the 1990s reflect blatant disdain (at least as intense as Ms. Thompson's) for solid, reliable history.

History Goes to the Movies is a source of information and, it is hoped, entertainment for everyone interested in the actual history behind a wide selection of movies grouped into 12 sections—11 covering historical periods and events (early U.S. history, World War II) and a twelfth containing biographies and period films (*A Man for All Seasons, The Age of Innocence*). Each film review includes an essay on the history covered in one or more movies, a brief plot summary, an assessment of each film's historical accuracy and entertainment value, and a list of books for readers interested in learning more about the history framing the movie. Several reviews include a "For Further Viewing" section for movies about the same—or related—subjects covered by the film listed as the main title in the Contents. This doesn't mean that movies recommended for further viewing are less entertaining or less "significant" for movie fans and history buffs than the book's main titles. I've listed *Saving Private Ryan,* for example, as further viewing for *The Longest Day*—but Spielberg's blockbuster is certainly as important as Lean's film chronicle of the Allied assault on "Fortress Europe" (my assessment of *Saving Private Ryan* is, in fact, longer than my remarks on *The Longest Day*). *The Longest Day* simply covers more ground than *Saving Private Ryan*: it delivers a broader historical overview of the D-Day landings and the planning behind them. (Occasionally, other historical considerations such as period accuracy determine a film's place in reviews including two or more movies.)

In style and approach, *History Goes to the Movies* is familiar and informal: I've tried to make the background essays lively and thorough enough to engage movie fans and general readers, and wherever possible I've included well-documented, funny, offbeat, and occasionally horrific anecdotes germane to the essay's historical material. The background essays form the heart of *History Goes to the Movies*—plot summaries are necessarily brief, and, obviously, they can't highlight every error (or historical bull's-eye) in each film. Omissions include less significant factual blunders and mistakes transparent to common sense. In *Saving Private Ryan,* for example, Wehrmacht machine-gun nests atop steel-and-concrete-reinforced earthworks rake American D-Day landing craft mercilessly, gunning down hordes of GIs before they hit the water. In fact, German machine gunners always stayed *inside* their bunkers—especially on heavily bombarded Omaha Beach—unless they wanted to go home in shoeboxes. (For attacking Allied infantry, deadly Wehrmacht machine guns were almost always the number-one, kill-them-at-all-costs targets—wherever the action unfolded.) And throughout the film, Spielberg's Americans shoot virtually every surrendering German: obviously, soldiers on both sides did this, but not 100% of the time—and the Allies were eager to take prisoners during the Normandy campaign. I've ignored these mistakes in my review of *Saving Private Ryan* to focus on other, more serious errors in the film. Star ratings reflect each movie's historical accuracy (five stars: don't miss it; no stars: tell your in-laws to rent it) and—to a far less degree—its power to amuse.

Obviously, expecting textbook accuracy from films (or any form of entertainment) would be ridiculous—and producers have delivered a remarkable number of historically faithful movies. They risk millions of dollars on films every year, then count viewers' votes—week after week—as they pour in from ticket booths around the country: it's no surprise that filmmakers reshape the past as often as they do. But some of them get far too much of their history wrong. *History Goes to the Movies* is a guide, however imperfect, for readers and viewers aiming to get it right.

History
GOES TO THE
Movies

chapter 1

Ancient, Classical, and Medieval History

(Overleaf)
Braveheart
(Photofest)

Chronology

B.C.

1,500,000
Homo erectus appears.

1,400,000
First use of fire by hominids.

300,000–200,000
Homo sapiens sapiens appears in Africa.

150,000
Neanderthal man appears.

45,000–35,000
Cro-Magnons colonize Europe.

9000
City of Jericho settled; grain cultivation begins.

3100
Unification of Upper and Lower Egypt.

2000–1500
Patriarchal narratives of Hebrew Bible.

1755
Babylonian king Hammurabi establishes Law Code.

1600
Phoenicians develop alphabetic (Canaanite) script.

1280
Israelite Exodus from Egypt.

1005
David becomes king of Israel and Judah.

973–932
Reign of Solomon. Israel develops legal system, external trading relationships.

933
Solomon's sons Jeroboam and Rehoboam divide kingdom into Israel and Judah.

776
First Olympic Games.

700–500
Greek city-states formed.

586
Nebuchadnezzar II captures Jerusalem, exiles Israelites to Babylon. Babylonian captivity ends gradually between 538 and 445.

559–530
Cyrus the Great establishes Persian Empire.

510–508
Cleisthenes introduces democracy in Athens.

509
Roman Republic founded.

490
Athenians defeat Persians at Marathon.

477–405
Athens' "Golden Age": Parthenon built;

careers of Socrates and Plato; Pericles heads
Athens' democratic government.

431–404
Peloponnesian War: Sparta defeats Athens.

390
Gauls sack Rome.

356–338
Philip II of Macedon unites Greek states.

336
Alexander the Great succeeds Philip II. Rules
until death in 323.

264–241
Rome wins First Punic War against Carthage.

250
Hebrew scriptures translated into Greek (the
Septuagint).

218–201
Second Punic War: Hannibal invades Italy
across Alps. After early victories, he loses
Battle of Zama, surrenders battle fleet and
Spanish territories to Rome.

196
Rosetta Stone written in Egyptian hieroglyphs,
Greek.

149–146
Rome wins Third Punic War, destroys
Carthage.

60
Crassus, Pompey, and Julius Caesar form
Rome's first ruling Triumvirate.

58–51
Caesar's campaigns in Gaul.

49–44
Julius Caesar wins civil war, becomes dictator
of Rome. Caesar assassinated in 44; Mark
Antony seizes power.

31
Octavian defeats Cleopatra and Antony at Actium.

30
Rome sacks Athens, absorbs Egypt after
Cleopatra's suicide.

5–4 (?)
Birth of Christ.

A.D.
28
John the Baptist beheaded.

30(?)
Crucifixion, resurrection of Christ.

32
Saul of Tarsus converted to Christianity, name
changed to Paul.

34–67
Paul's missionary activity. Romans execute him
in 67.

50–80
Synoptic Gospels written.

54
Nero becomes Roman emperor. Launches first
widespread persecution of Christians in 64,

blaming them for great fire that destroys half of Rome. He commits suicide in 68 A.D.

64
Apostle Peter crucified.

66–73
Great Jewish revolt; Vespasian's son Titus captures and destroys Jerusalem in 70.

69
"Year of the four emperors" (Nero's successors): Servius Galba, Marcus Salvius Otho, Aulus Vitellius, and Caesar Vespasian. Vespasian rules ten years, builds Colosseum, brings unprecedented prosperity, stability to empire.

100
John's Gospel written.

114
Hadrian succeeds Trajan; Rome at height of its power.

200
Bishop of Rome (Pope Zephyrinus) recognized as head of western church.

313
Edict of Toleration allows Christianity in Roman Empire.

325–337
Constantine rules Roman Empire. Converts to Christianity, baptized on deathbed in 337.

370
Mongols invade Europe.

410
Visigoths sack Rome.

420
Anglo-Saxons invade Britain.

434–53
Attila rules Huns; invades Italy in 452, spares Rome when supplies dwindle and disease decimates his army.

455
Vandals sack Rome.

476
Romulus Augustus, Rome's last western emperor, deposed, ending Western Empire.

546
Goths take Rome.

800
Charlemagne becomes first emperor of Holy Roman Empire.

800–850
Germanic nobles—the "Franks"—begin feudal agricultural system; it flourishes for centuries.

1066
William the Conqueror leads Norman invasion of England.

1096–99
First Crusade.

1147–49
Second Crusade.

1154
Henry II accedes to English throne, appoints Thomas à Becket chancellor in 1155.

1162
Appointed archbishop of Canterbury, Becket clashes with Henry over civil and canon court jurisdictions.

1170
Becket murdered by Henry's knights.

1189–92
Third Crusade.

1202–4
Fourth Crusade.

1215
England's King John signs Magna Carta.

1217–21
Fifth Crusade.

1218
Genghis Khan completes Persian conquests.

1225
Thomas Aquinas born.

1228–29
Sixth Crusade.

1248–54
Seventh Crusade.

1270
Eighth Crusade.

1298
Edward I defeats William Wallace at Falkirk, reconquering Scotland.

1337–1453
Hundred Years War between England and France.

1348
"Black Death" decimates Europe.

1430
Joan of Arc captured in Burgundy. Convicted of heresy and witchcraft in Rouen, she burns at stake on May 30, 1431.

1436–37
Gutenberg invents printing press.

Alexander the Great ★★★

(1956) 141 Minutes

Director: Robert Rossen

Cast: Richard Burton, Fredric March, Claire Bloom, Stanley Baker, Danielle Darrieux

Historical Background: July 332 B.C.— Phoenician Alexander III's Macedonian shock troops and League of Corinth allies closed their dreadful six-month assault on Tyre (Persia's top ally) with a bedlam of nonstop, profligate murder: as soon as they breached the island city's fortifications, they raged through streets, public buildings, and homes, hacking everyone they found to pieces. Butchering 7,000 civilians on-the-spot, they sold 30,000 more into slavery, then crucified 2,000 military-age men. Savagery had marked the campaign from the start—arrogant, well-provisioned Tyrians set the bloodbath's ugly course, murdering several Macedonian envoys under a flag of truce. Every day, crackling red-hot sand dumped from high battlements blanketed screaming attackers (the searing, powder-fine clouds penetrated breastplate crevices, sifting under corselets and dealing slow, agonizing death). Alexander's combat engineers countered with marvelous siege technology—floating torsion-driven catapults, collapsible assault towers, huge battering rams—and an 880-yard causeway linking mainland staging areas to the city.

Tyre was Alexander's greatest victory—in one stroke, he neutralized Persian king Darius III's Mediterranean fleet, freeing him to launch a breathtaking eastward drive all the way to the Indian frontier. Fighting in wedge-shaped phalanxes, highly disciplined Macedonians had clobbered the hated Persians on the Issus plain in 333. Outnumbered four to one, they did it again near Arabela (331), then rolled eastward, scattering opponents every step of the way and renaming at least 70 captured towns for Alexander. In six years they drove all the way to the Hindu Kush and invaded modern Pakistan, winning their final major engagement on the Hydaspes River (326 B.C.).

It was an incredible performance, sealing Alexander's first place position among ancient strategists and field commanders. Brilliant, iron-willed, hot-tempered, and ruthless, he was a consummate survivor—many contemporaries thought that he plotted his father Philip's murder, and Alexander himself weathered a 330 B.C. assassination attempt. He studied under Aristotle. He was an eccentric world-class athlete, shunning the Olympics because all of its contestants weren't kings. Supremely practical, he was also an idealist determined to build a "Brotherhood of Man" (homonoia) by bringing conquered adversaries into a worldwide fraternity of allies. (Some historians dismiss this notion as hagiographic propaganda.) Rome built an empire on Alexander's legacy. His tiny army wrecked Persia's gigantic, moribund kingdom. He pioneered vast trade networks, extending Hellenistic culture throughout the Near East. With it went the linguistic roots of Koine Greek, the common language spoken by Paul of Tarsus on his first-century missionary journeys. (See *Peter and Paul.* Alexander's cities also gave the apostles densely populated urban bases for spreading Christianity across the Mediterranean basin.) On June 13, 323 B.C., Alexander's epic career ground to a dreary, prosaic halt: he died in misery—at age 32—after a ten-day stretch of gluttony and heavy drinking in Babylon.

Alexander the Great is a feast for amateur historians—and a soporific ordeal for movie fans. An all-world cast labors gamely to manage cumbersome dialogue littered with ancient quotations and laughable throw-outs ("Alexander, what thoughts drive through your storm-tossed brain?"). But Rossen accurately covers most of Alexander's major exploits (omitting his fits of brutality and fatal drinking binge). Minor blunders surface throughout: for example, Alexander's wife, Roxane, appears as Darius' daughter (Soghdian baron Oxyartes was her real father); Alexander (Burton) executes his father's assassin and cuts the fabled Gordian knot with a sword (in fact, Macedonian noblemen killed Philip's murderer, and Alexander yanked a hidden peg securing the huge knot's loose end). A tedious, oddball film—but worthwhile for patient viewers.

Recommended Reading:
Peter Green, *Alexander of Macedon, 356–323 B.C.;* Robert Payne, *Ancient Greece: The Triumph of a Culture.*

Becket ★★★★

(1964) 148 Minutes

Director: Peter Glenville

Cast: Richard Burton, Peter O'Toole, John Gielgud, Donald Wolfit, Martita Hunt, Pamela Brown

Historical Background: December 29, 1170—Kent, England: Reginald FitzUrse, Hugh de Moreville, Richard le Breton, and William de Tracy—barons fiercely loyal to Henry Plantagenet (King Henry II)—thundered into Canterbury Cathedral's great palace hall, crashed Archbishop Thomas à Becket's vespers hour, and ordered him to revoke papal excommunications of seven rogue bishops (all chief counselors to the king) or submit to arrest. Not likely, replied the primate. FitzUrse seized him roughly, drawing an instant, furious rebuke: "Let go of me, Reginald. . . . Let go of me, you pimp!" Jolted by the blistering malediction, FitzUrse unsheathed his sword and swept it forward in a wide, sibilant arc, grazing Becket's head and driving him to his knees. In a heartbeat, Breton and Tracy bolted forward and hacked the archbishop to death with four more crushing strokes. It was a dark, sorry end to a story illuminated, at first, by bright prospects for an enlightened Christian society under a just, capable king.

Fifteen years earlier, Becket had completed a breathtaking rise from merchant-class Norman roots to England's royal chancellorship. He performed brilliantly in office for seven years, conducting diplomatic missions, dominating receptions with glittering, courtly wit, and spearheading the king's successful 1159 Toulouse military campaign. (Henry was a superb monarch. He extended Norman rule all the way to the Pyrenees. He launched stunning legal reforms, founding England's system of common law and trial by jury. But epic-scale infidelities wrecked his marriage to Eleanor of Aquitaine and uncaged snarling familial rancor hot enough to ignite a brief war. Prodded by their mother, Henry's four restless, power-starved sons—Richard, Henry, John, and Geoffrey—launched a bloody 1173 revolt against the crown. Desperate battle raged until October 1174, ending in victory for Henry, pardons for his sons, and imprisonment for Eleanor. The king reigned, but he lived in misery until his death on July 6, 1189.) As chancellor, Becket became Plantagenet's most trusted political ally. Then Henry engineered his friend's election as archbishop, and everything began to unravel under the pressure of two muscular personalities waylaid by misunderstanding, bad timing, and choking doses of their own black bile. (Henry's temper was legendary: a fit of anger once drove him to stuff his mouth with straw and chew the stalks into pulp.) Immediately after his consecration in June 1162, Becket innocently—but tactlessly—returned the chancellor's Great Seal to Henry. He might as well have flung a gauntlet into the king's face. Hoping to build harmony between church and state, Henry had quietly secured a special papal dispensation permitting the new archbishop to keep his chancellor's post. Wrongly construing Thomas' resignation as a formal shift of loyalty, Henry took the gloves off and waited for his friend's next move.

It came quickly enough. Without warning, the flamboyant, prosperous Becket made a stunning personal about-face. He gave most of his money to the poor. He fasted regularly and wore hair shirts beneath his vestments. Above all, he labored mightily to become Europe's fairest canon-court judge, setting a potential collision course with Henry. Throughout medieval Europe, two great systems of jurisprudence—civil law and canon (or ecclesiastical) law—existed side by side. Each had its own hierarchy, its own financial machinery, and its own courts. Each had its own jurisdictions, as well: Church courts settled cases involving marriage, divorce, and heresy, but clerics charged with grave crimes could demand trials in ecclesiastical tribunals, often drawing lighter sentences there than civil courts imposed. (Canon law forbade punishing criminals by mutilation, for example—a common sentence in secular courts.) Because most Europeans were Christians, the system usually worked smoothly, thanks to flexible administrators—on both sides—with high diplomatic skills and sharp noses for serviceable compromise.

But a bizarre, anomalous flurry of clerical crime struck England between 1157 and 1163, and Thomas ignored Henry's order to send several "criminous clerks" to civil courts. (The rebuff wasn't as unreasonable as it sounds: in some cases, civil trials would have amounted to double jeopardy.) Henry responded with the Constitutions of Clarendon (1164), expanding royal power over ecclesiastical courts. Becket wouldn't sign them, Henry charged him (absurdly) with misappropriating public funds, and the archbishop fled into a six-year Continental exile. A shaky reconciliation returned him to England in 1170, but bitter conflict flared again with his refusal to lift excommunications of several bishops loyal to Henry. The king was furious: "[Becket] ate my bread and mocks my favors," he roared. "Can no one free me of this lowborn priest!" Incredibly, FitzUrse and his fellow barons took the spontaneous detonation literally and galloped to Canterbury, finally bringing medieval England's most celebrated public quarrel to a bloody end. News of the murder flattened Henry: sick with grief, he locked himself in his chambers, eating nothing for three days and eventually submitting to public penance at the great cathedral. In 1173, Pope Alexander III canonized Becket, and his tomb became England's greatest shrine.

Becket bristles with factual blunders. Exercising a sixties-style social consciousness, Glenville makes Becket a Saxon (Thomas and Saxon England vs. Norman oppressor Henry = intimations of Vietnam laced with smoldering racial tension). Burton rightly plays Becket as a man of high principle and towering courage—but Glenville ignores the archbishop's impetuous bullheadedness and makes him a libertine until his consecration (Becket took a vow of chastity as a young man and never broke it). Worst of all, O'Toole's Henry, badly shortchanged, deliberately orders his barons to murder Becket. Still—a literate film, expertly directed and well acted by all.

For Further Viewing:
The Lion in Winter ★★★ (1968) 135 Minutes (Peter O'Toole, Katharine Hepburn, Anthony Hopkins, Nigel Terry, Jane Merrow, Timothy Dalton, John Castle, Nigel Stock): Anthony Harvey's adaptation of James Goldman's play excels in spots, but flops badly on the facts. In 1183, Henry II assembles John, Richard, Geoffrey, Eleanor (on furlough from prison), and Alais Chapet—Richard's fiancée

and Henry's mistress—for Christmas Court at Chinon Castle. Schemes and power plays swarm like cockroaches, sparking a volcanic family brawl. Between emotional eviscerations, Eleanor and Henry reminisce copiously (they're still in love); the queen views Alais with sophisticated detachment; at film's end, all convene to clear the air, and Eleanor gamely returns to captivity. In fact, the Chinon Christmas Court came in 1172, Eleanor loathed Alais, her affections for Henry had chilled to permafrost by 1183, etc., etc. But wonderful period detail and fine performances by O'Toole and Hepburn make the film well worth watching.

Recommended Reading:
Richard Winston, *Thomas Becket;* Richard Barber, *Henry Plantagenet: A Biography;* Marion Meade, *Eleanor of Aquitaine: A Biography.*

Braveheart ★★★★★

(1995) 177 Minutes

Director: Mel Gibson

Cast: Mel Gibson, Sophie Marceau, Patrick McGoohan, Catherine McCormack, Brendan Gleeson, James Cosmo, David O'Hara, Peter Henly, Alun Armstrong, Ian Bannon

Historical Background: March 1296—Berwick, Scotland: Unarmed and frozen with terror, Berwick's freemen watched Edward Plantagenet's English troops sprint through a shallow ditch and level the flimsy breastworks guarding their borough. Too stunned to resist, the burgesses retreated through town, then surrendered. On Edward's orders, swordsmen in chain mail hacked away at the bewildered Scots for hours, stopping only when Plantagenet (King Edward I, commonly called Longshanks) gagged at the sight of a crying infant seated next to its slaughtered mother. Edward remained in Berwick, sending the Earl de Warenne northward to take Dunbar's redoubtable castle. After a brief siege, Dunbar fell. Garrisons at Edinburgh and Roxburgh soon followed, and by the time Edward's legions reached Stirling—the tactical gateway to the Highlands—its defenders had vanished. Longshanks' soldiers, it seemed, could have conquered Scotland with their bare hands.

Edward had poured four years of sweat and intrigue into conceiving and hatching the perfect opportunity to strike northward: in 1292, Scotland was a volatile disunion of greedy nobles, each smoldering with ambition and eager to fill his country's vacant throne. But none of them held clear, undisputed title to the crown. Fearing all-out civil war, the bishop of St. Andrews asked Edward to settle the matter, assuring him that the nobles and their new king would accept his decision, then bow to his sovereignty. (This was nothing new; for years, Scottish rulers had held great tracts of land in England in exchange for their loyalty to English kings and submission to English law.) Plantagenet—eager for years to unite and rule all of Britain—met the nobles at Norham on the Tweed, naming John Balliol (a compliant, easily dominated man) king of Scotland. Three years later, Balliol tired of Edward's bullying and refused to march with him against Philip IV in Gascony. Edward happily mustered an army, trampled his way

to Stirling virtually unopposed, imprisoned Balliol, and removed the Stone of Destiny from Scone Abbey (where Scottish kings traditionally received their crowns). Certain that he'd won complete victory, Longshanks proclaimed himself ruler of Scotland and led his army across the Channel to make short work of the detested French.

But the victory was not total: from utter obscurity, two Highland patriots, William Wallace and Andrew of Moray, took the field against Edward's occupation force in southern Scotland. Wallace and 30 men routed the English garrison at Lanark in May 1297. Small landowners and their clans helped drive the English out of Perth, then retired with Wallace to Selkirk Forest. Determined to take advantage of Edward's absence, Moray soon joined them. On September 11, Wallace and Moray led their raw army against Warrene—now vice-regent of Scotland—at Stirling. From Stirling Castle's gates, a field of hillocks and knolls tumbled downward to a narrow bridge crossing the River Forth, then rose steeply to a ridge called the Abbey Craig. Concealing most of their troops on the craig's reverse slope, Moray, Wallace, and a small clot of infantry approached the Forth to lure Wallene's army from the castle. It worked. As soon as half the Englishmen had crossed the bridge, hundreds of howling Scots bolted over the ridge's summit, roared down its forward slope, and cut them to pieces. Countless soldiers in heavy English armor plunged from writhing chaos on the bridge into the turbulent waters below, while Wallene could do nothing but watch helplessly from the river's southern bank. In terrified disarray, the vice-regent's army broke into pell-mell retreat toward the English border and safety. Wallace—quickly named Guardian of the Kingdom—invaded northern England and sacked several towns before returning to the Highlands. (The gravely wounded Moray had died in the field at Stirling.)

With Edward's return from France in 1298, Scotland's nobles again fragmented into bickering factions. Most of them refused to ride with Wallace against Longshanks, one of the premier tacticians and great commanders in all of Europe. He had legions of armored cavalry, and Wallace had none—an enormous disadvantage, equivalent to fighting a modern desert war without tanks. On July 22, Edward led 2,000 cavalry and 12,000 infantrymen against Wallace at Falkirk. Fighting from four concentric defensive rings ("schiltrons") and protected by a line of bowmen, the Highlanders stood fast until furious onslaughts by English cavalry overwhelmed their archers and freed Longshanks' Welsh bowmen to pick off Wallace's infantry piecemeal. The schiltrons soon broke apart, and Edward's army swept the field. Wallace escaped, and the war continued—guerrilla-style—until Scotland's maverick nobles surrendered to Longshanks in 1304. A year later, Sir John Menteith captured Wallace near Glasgow and turned him over to Edward. Tried and convicted of treason—an absurdity, since he'd never sworn allegiance to Plantagenet—Wallace was brutally executed on August 23, 1305. But Scotland's struggle for autonomy wasn't over. Inspired by Wallace's example and led by Robert Bruce, resurgent Highlanders won de facto independence by destroying an enormous English force at Bannockburn in 1314. (Edward III formally recognized the Scottish monarchy in 1328.) Finally, 175 years later, Scotland's James IV married the daughter of England's Henry VII, uniting the two crowns.

This sweeping biography of the legendary Wallace won Gibson an Academy Award (Best Director) and took Oscars for Best Picture, Cinematography, Sound Effects, and Editing. *Brave-heart* doesn't claim infallibility for historical accuracy—as it shouldn't, since scholars are uncertain about many details of Wallace's life. But it gives us the next best thing: stunning period detail, great battle scenes, finely drawn characters, and magnificent performances—especially by McGoohan (Edward) and Gibson (Wallace). Curiously, elements of Wallace's two decisive battles are wrong (no narrow bridge at Stirling and no schiltrons at Falkirk), but who cares? *Braveheart* is a terrific movie, filled with small fictions, but true to the spirit of William Wallace and his grand enterprise.

Recommended Reading:
Erik Linklater, *The Survival of Scotland: A Survey of Scottish History from Roman Times to the Present Day;* R. L. Mackie, *A Short History of Scotland;* Andrew Fisher, *William Wallace;* James McKay, *William Wallace: Braveheart.*

The Egyptian ★★★

(1954) 140 Minutes

Director: Michael Curtiz

Cast: Victor Mature, Jean Simmons, Edmund Purdom, Peter Ustinov, Gene Tierney, John Carradine

Historical Background: A single strip of fertile land 12 miles wide, more than 1,000

miles long, bisected from end to end by the Nile River, and flanked on either side by vast desert wastes housed and sustained an entire civilization—ancient Egypt—for 2,700 years. The Nile gave Egypt's first king, Menes (3000 B.C.) a military supply route for unifying Upper and Lower Egypt. For the empire that followed, everything depended on the orderly, ever-recurring dynamics of the river: each July, heavy rainfall and melting snows in central Africa and Ethiopia sent water cascading into the Nile, causing it to overflow its banks in September. Annual inundations left thick layers of fertile silt cultivated by farmers to grow flax, grains, and abundant varieties of fruits and vegetables (The Nile could deal death as well as life: floods five feet below normal meant drought and famine, and waters cresting three feet too high demolished irrigation ditches and devastated villages.) Egypt's taxation system reflected the link between national prosperity and the river: every year, government officials used "Nilometers" to measure flood levels, estimate the probable harvest from each field, and set taxes from their calculations.

Egypt's polytheistic religion—the source of its social and political stability—also grew from the river's annual cycles. Thoroughly dependent on nature's whims, the Egyptians worshiped countless gods residing in the natural world and controlling its movements. Osiris, for example, was the god of vegetation whose capricious temper dictated annual agricultural yields. Earth, air, water—all of the physical elements—had their own deities, as did every activity associated with life in the Nile River Valley. Because their universe teemed with jealous, easily angered gods whose volcanic personalities—once provoked—might disrupt nature's vital rhythms, the Egyptians feared change of any kind. They nurtured hierarchy and stability

and never rocked the boat: Osiris was Osiris, Pharaoh was Pharaoh, his word was law, and that was that.

The Egyptians' animistic beliefs extended with special force to the realm of death: nothing, for them, ever perished—animals and human beings simply passed into other states or "appearances" at the moment of expiration. Ancestral spirits wielding magical powers roamed the world and shaped the course of human events. Ancestor worship drove Third Dynasty pharaohs to build the first pyramids honoring the cult of the dead. (Scholars divide Egypt's history from Menes' reign to 332 B.C. into three major eras, the Old, Middle, and New Kingdoms, incorporating 31 ruling dynasties. The Third Dynasty began in 2800 B.C.) Early pyramids, called step pyramids, rose from square bases to flat, rectangular peaks in a series of stages progressively decreasing in size. By 2600 B.C., pharaohs were building true, smooth-sided pyramids ending in pointed summits. Each pyramid's triangular sides faced the four compass points, sloping from base to apex at an angle of 50°. Pyramid entrances—usually located on the north wall—led to royal sepulchers after traversing several lesser chambers (some of them decoys). Many pyramids housed a maze of small, winding passages leading away from burial vaults or to secondary chambers. Most pyramid complexes included adjacent mortuary temples and pavilions linked to the Nile by canals. Eighty royal pyramids still stand in Egypt, most of them built by the end of the Sixth Dynasty (2200 B.C.).

In 1300 B.C., the 19th Dynasty began with the rise of Horemheb, whose grandson Seti I shaped the early trajectory of western history by enslaving Israel. Events recorded in the Book of Exodus probably unfolded during the reign of Ramses II, the dynasty's greatest pharaoh: he expanded Egypt's empire southward from Syria to the fourth cataract of the Nile in present-day Sudan. With his death in 1225, ancient Egypt settled into long, fatal decline. Eight consecutive rulers (all called Ramses) battled invasions by Libyans, Assyrians, Babylonians, Persians, and migrating Indo-Europeans called Sea Peoples. In 332 B.C., Alexander the Great overran the country and named himself pharaoh, opening Egypt's Macedonian Ptolemaic period. Cleopatra VII, last of the Ptolemaic sovereigns and antiquity's most legendary heroine, lost Egypt to the Romans in 30 B.C. The daughter of Ptolemy XII, she became queen at age 18, ruling jointly with two brothers and eventually with her son, Ptolemy XV. Charming—but not a great beauty—she was a master of intrigue, captivating Julius Caesar and Mark Antony in two amorous campaigns to increase her own power and Egypt's autonomy. (She "attacked Rome," according to one writer, "by using Romans.") Eventually, she married Mark Antony, but Octavian—later the emperor Augustus—defeated them in the Battle of Actium on September 2, 31 B.C. Eleven months later, Cleopatra killed herself, bringing ancient Egypt's long history to a close.

The Egyptian traces the rise of Horemheb (Mature) and the changing fortunes of an idealistic young physician (Purdom, in the title role). For period detail, the film literally is a cinematic museum: producer Daryl F. Zanuck persuaded several prestigious museums to lend 20th Century Fox priceless Egyptian clothing, jewelry, furniture, weapons, and vases for reproduction by studio craftsmen and artists. Zanuck spent $600,000 of a $5 million budget on sets alone. The result is a faithful re-creation of Egyptian culture (or at least its trappings) in 1300 B.C. Ustinov steals the show as a literate beggar, and scenes of Egyptian street life are fine—but *The*

Egyptian barely drags along, and much of its dialogue is silly ("For a cheesemaker he has bold eyes"). Still, it's a great set piece and eccentric enough to entertain aficionados of antiquity.

For Further Viewing:

Land of the Pharaohs ★★★ (1955) 106 Minutes (Jack Hawkins, Joan Collins, Dewey Martin, James Robertson Justice): Co-scripted by William Faulkner, *Land of the Pharaohs* casts Hawkins as Pharaoh, whose obsession with building his pyramid blinds him to hostile intrigue orchestrated from all sides by his ambitious, scheming secondary wife (Collins). Top billing should go to sets, terrific special effects, and convincing speculation on techniques for constructing the great pyramids.

Cleopatra ★★★★ (1934) 100 Minutes (Claudette Colbert, Henry Wilcoxon, Warren William, C. Aubrey Smith): Few spectacles on film—or in nature—can rival Colbert's scintillating Cleopatra rolling out of a carpet at the feet of William's stunned Julius Caesar. Director Cecil B. DeMille is reasonably faithful to history, even though he elevates romance over politics (and his sets often resemble Flash Gordon's Planet Mongo more than Ptolemaic Egypt or ancient Rome). Wilcoxon makes an excellent womanizing, pugnacious Antony. Better fare than the lumbering, interminable Richard Burton–Elizabeth Taylor version (1963).

Recommended Reading:

Margaret Oliphant, *The Atlas of the Ancient World;* Michael Grant, *Cleopatra;* Cyril Aldred, *The Egyptians;* Nicholas Reeves, *The Complete Tutankhamun.*

The Fall of the Roman Empire ★★★★

(1964) 153 Minutes

Director: Anthony Mann

Cast: Stephen Boyd, Alec Guinness, Sophia Loren, Christopher Plummer, James Mason, Anthony Quayle, John Ireland

Historical Background: In 180 A.D., Lucius Aelius Aurelius Commodus—Marcus Aurelius' sadistic heir, Rome's newly crowned monarch, and over-the-top nut case supreme—took eight additional names, bringing his title count to a grand total of 12. (Before his paramour Marcia murdered him in 192, Commodus ordered every month of the Roman calendar renamed for himself.) Title-gathering by Roman emperors began with Octavian in 27 B.C.: crowned Augustus Caesar by a Senate packed with loyal allies, Rome's first full-blown emperor used ten different names to sign official documents during his long reign. Persisting for more than five centuries after Augustus' death—and peaking with Aurelian, collector of more titles than any other Roman sovereign—this bizarre practice reflects a cancerous "given" born with the infant empire: Rome's emperors, recorded history's most powerful men, had no idea in whose name—by what legitimate authority higher than raw, naked power—they ruled 70 million souls in virtually every province of the civilized world. As soon as the Senate opened impartial, republican law to encroachment by Octavian's singular will, Rome's vibrant "body politic" began to atrophy, leaving a gigantic artifact—the empire—sustained by brute force and destined to wither slowly and ingloriously away.

Founded (according to legend) in 753 B.C. by Latin prince Romulus, Rome grew from a dreary clot of ramshackle mud huts on the Tiber River's east bank to a realm so vast that a second-century vagrant could plod from Hadrian's Wall in Britain all the way to Egypt on Roman roads, speaking nothing but Latin and spending imperial coinage every step of the way. Meagerly documented and shrouded in mystery, the Romans' "regal period" ended in 509 B.C. with a revolt against their despotic seventh king (Lucius Tarquinius Superbus). Victorious nobles banished Superbus for life and replaced him with two consuls (annually elected executive magistrates), forging a republic—complete with a robust patrician Senate—that would stand for 500 years. In 471 B.C., the Concilium Plebis, an assembly acting for peasants, farmhands, laborers, artisans, and small landholders—most of the state's poor and middle-class citizens—formed. Rome's earliest written law code (the Lex XII Tabularum) came two decades later: engraved on bronze tablets and displayed in the Forum, the Law of the Twelve Tables gradually flowered into a legal canon covering every area of jurisprudence and completing one of antiquity's greatest legacies to western civilization—the classic model for representative government based on impartial law and secured by a system of checks and balances incorporating every layer of society.

With the Republic came breathtaking territorial growth. Roman troops crushed a large Latin army near Lake Regillus in 499 B.C. and took Fidenae in 426. Thirty years later, Veii—a key Etruscan city—fell. (Stunning military reversals came in 390 B.C. with an invasion by Gallic charioteers ferocious enough to smash crack Roman legions near the Allia River, drive reeling survivors ten miles southward to Rome, and attack the embattled city—all within three days. For seven months, towering blond Gauls occupied the area, finally leaving after pocketing copious tribute from cowed city officials.) By 338 B.C., Rome had taken Latium and Etruria, and five decades later, relentless legionaries finally throttled the tough, stubborn Samnites. Italy's Greek cities came next, falling one by one until King Pyrrhus of Epirus fled for his life with remnants of an army battered mercilessly for five bloody years (280–275 B.C.). With that, Italy belonged to the Romans. In three bitterly contested conflicts—the Punic Wars of 264–241, 218–201, and 149–146 B.C.—Rome reduced Carthage to smoking rubble, then launched onslaughts in every direction, overrunning the entire Mediterranean, most of Spain, and all of Gaul by the end of the first century. At its height, Roman rule reached the eastern shores of the Caspian Sea.

For centuries, the Republic's might turned on citizen armies manned by dedicated volunteers, led by hard-eyed aristocrats, built on iron discipline and smash-mouth training—and demobilized as soon as final victory came. Military life was grueling business for new recruits. Hour after hour, they whaled away at one another with double-weight wooden replicas of their bread-and-butter armaments, the tough shoulder-to-ankle-length *scutum* shield and the *gladius,* a short stabbing sword that left thousands of luckless enemies stiff in the dust. Rigorous conditioning bred soldiers able to mount crushing assaults or build massive fortifications after marching 20 miles—with 80-pound battle kits—through desert or mountain terrain. Grouped into 6,000-man legions incorporating highly disciplined companies of 50 to 100 men ("centuries"), the army was mobile and incredibly flexible in the field. Legionaries advanced

in tightly packed, staggered ranks capable of changing direction on a dime to mass their forces suddenly for devastating strikes against smaller enemy troop concentrations. Before closing with their adversaries, legionaries hurled *pila*—javelins with long iron points designed to pierce the toughest shields, then bend sharply under the weight of heavy wooden shafts. Unable to extract the *pila*'s barbed tips, enemy soldiers had two choices: drop their gear and run or slug it out with crack Roman troops protected by iron cuirasses and huge *scuta.*

By 100 B.C., growing demands for troops forced Rome to build a professional standing army, and with it came a fatal dilemma: as the Republic pushed its borders ever outward, widely dispersed legions developed fierce loyalties to ambitious generals, fragmenting the army politically. In January, 49 B.C.—two years after crushing the last Gallic revolts—Julius Caesar led his legions across the Rubicon River, ignited a civil war, drove rival Pompey and his allies out of Italy, then ended the conflict with a bloody victory at Pharsalus in August 48. Handed supreme power for a decade in 46 B.C. and named dictator for life two years later, he fell to more than 50 republican assassins in the Senate on March 15, 44 B.C. For the conspirators it was too late—Julius Caesar had killed the glorious Republic. In 42 B.C., Octavian, Lepidus, and Marc Antony partitioned Rome's dominions, but their Triumvirate quickly fell apart: civil war flared again, finally ending in Octavian's victory and enthronement as Augustus Caesar.

One of antiquity's finest and most popular sovereigns, Augustus enjoyed a glittering 40-year reign, but his lasting legacy—the dynastic empire—smoldered with ugly, corrosive toxins, some inherited, some endemic to rule by decree grounded in military might. Chief among them was illegitimacy: the question "Why does Claudius (or Nero, or Carcalla, or Severus) rule?" always had the same answer—"Because he controls the army." No matter how powerful or capable Rome's ruler of the day might be, the empire was constantly up for grabs, and everybody knew it: between 238 and 253 A.D., stupefied Roman citizens watched ten different emperors take the throne, then vanish without a trace (average tenure: 1.5 years).

The empire's sheer size and economic processes fueled other quandaries. Insular local trade dominated Roman commerce: Rome never built an industrial base to offset expensive imports (silks, spices, precious stones) with high end domestic products for foreign markets. Imperial prosperity turned on wealth looted from newly vanquished provinces, and as Rome's conquests multiplied, the cost of maintaining its military machine mushroomed: by 250, emperors began devaluing the currency, launching inflationary spirals and, eventually, wrecking their monetary system. Worse still, new territory for Roman expansion grew more remote every year and finally disappeared, leaving an empire financed by staggering taxes and strangling on a huge internal bureaucracy recruited to collect and spend the money. Government regulation gradually throttled freedom of movement and vocation: by 300 A.D., Rome had made compulsory universal membership in urban trade unions (*collegia*) hereditary, forbidding ordinary city dwellers to change occupations and shackling them to a gigantic economic treadmill going nowhere. From Italy's southern tip to the outer fringes of Gaul, angry malcontents littered the Roman world.

This was nothing new—throughout Rome's history, rebellions and slave uprisings flared regularly. Fuming, stiff-necked Jews launched three of the hottest provincial revolts: the bloodiest detonated in 66 A.D., peaked with Jerusalem's destruction by Titus in 70, and raged into 73. (See *Masada*. Jewish guerrilla-style rebels—"Zealots"—began sniping away at legionaries the moment Rome took direct control of Jerusalem in 6 A.D. Freed from prison by Pontius Pilate just before Jesus' execution, the outlaw Barabbas might have been a Zealot.) Legionaries battled for two years to suppress another insurrection in 117, then leveled 50 rebel strongholds and hundreds of villages in a furious struggle (132–35) against Bar Kokhba's forces from Judea and Galilee. (Notable provincial uprisings also erupted in Egypt, Sardinia, Sicily, Epirus, and Cyrenaica.) The last great slave rebellion devastated southern Italy in 73 B.C.: led by Thracian slave and army deserter Spartacus, 70 fierce gladiators escaped from Capua's training school, brawled their way through town, fled to Mt. Vesuvius, raked in thousands of fugitive slaves, and forged an enormous fighting force (120,000 strong, by some accounts). They clobbered two Roman columns sent to recapture them, then quickly overran most of southern Italy. In the spring of 72 B.C., they split into two armies—one under Spartacus, one under the Gaul Crixus—and began caviling over what to do next. Spartacus launched a run for the Alps, but Crixus' forces stayed put and eventually fell to legionaries near Monte Gargano. After winning two battles in Picenum, Spartacus reversed his decision to cross the mountains and turned south again, this time aiming for Sicily. It was too late. In 71 B.C., eight legions under Marcus Licinius Crassus overtook and crushed the rebels in Lucania, killing Spartacus and crucifying 6,000 surviving slaves along the Appian Way.

More than any other feature of Roman civilization, institutionalized slavery drove the empire's long decline and ruinous collapse. By

100 A.D., Rome itself housed half a million slaves—30% of the city's population. Throughout Italy and the provinces, slaves toiled away at every conceivable task: they cooked, cleaned, tutored children, attended ladies in their toilets, worked in government offices, manned road-building gangs and construction crews, assisted physicians, labored on great plantations, and died by the thousands in imperial mines. All of this muscle power left the Romans utterly indifferent to any kind of labor-saving technological innovation. Paul Johnson calls the Romans' approach to technology "comatose," noting their failure to develop water mills for processing raw grain and their indifference to newly developed machines for hauling stone columns to building sites. Worst of all, unlike their enemies, the Romans never invented—or adopted—saddles fitted with stirrups to make horses stable (and devastating) platforms for expert, athletic riders wielding swords, lances, and short bows. (The army always meant "infantry" to Roman generals, anyway—they used cavalry for reconnaissance and other secondary missions.) Wars against mounted invaders equipped with stirrups were no contest, in the end: Rome's foot soldiers and bareback cavalry were sitting ducks for thundering, highly trained horsemen.

In 180, large-scale Roman expansion died with Marcus Aurelius on the Danube frontier (a brawling campaign against Germanic tribes raged there)—for legionaries, three centuries of bloody defensive warfare lay ahead. In 220, Goths invaded Asia Minor and the Balkans. Fifty years later, they routed the legions from Dacia. During the fourth and fifth centuries, the empire reeled under successive waves of Franks, Burgundians, and Ostrogoths, and Rome itself fell twice—to Alaric's Visigoths in 410 and to raging Vandals 45 years later. But the Romans

hated and feared Attila's Huns more than all of his predecessors combined. Howling at the top of their lungs and mounted on quick, barrel-chested, stubby-legged horses, sharpshooting Hun bowmen in wedge-shaped formations rode circles around enemy infantry and cavalry, decimating their ranks with bone-tipped arrows before closing in with swords. In 370 A.D., Hun armies poured across the Volga into southeastern and central Europe, routing every barbarian tribe they found and reaching the Alps by 430. Attila and his brother Bleda jointly inherited the Hun crown in 434, mounted a furious assault on the Eastern Empire seven years later, and withdrew with a mountain of gold tribute in 443. (First partitioned into eastern and western realms by Diocletian [284–305], the empire reunited under Constantine [325–37], divided again after his death, reunited briefly under Theodosius I in 392, then split permanently in 395 under his sons Arcadius and Honorius.) In 445, Attila murdered Bleda, then drove all the way to Thermopylae in a second campaign (447) against the Eastern Empire. Five years later, Roman general Aetius—leading a combined army of legionaries and Visigoths—stopped a Hunnic invasion of Gaul in the Battle of the Catalaunian Plains. Attila regrouped and invaded Italy in 452, forcing a meeting with Pope Leo to negotiate fat ransom figures for prominent Christian and Jewish captives. In less than a year, famine and disease forced the Huns out of Italy, and Attila died in 453—of a nosebleed, according to some speculators. The Western Empire unraveled at warp speed, ending with a whimper in 476 with the ouster of Romulus Augustulus by Germanic mercenaries. Their coup was little more than a gesture: barbarians had manned Rome's provincial armies for years, and benefits of Roman citizenship had long since vanished, especially for foreign provincials with no inherent loyalty to their distant rulers (many had no idea, from year to year, who the emperor was). The eastern realm fared better, surviving as the Byzantine Empire and finally passing with the fall of Constantinople to the Ottoman Turks in 1453.

The Fall of the Roman Empire makes good viewing for history buffs, even though it hums with anachronisms and factual errors. Mann begins on the Danube frontier shortly before the death of Marcus Aurelius (Guinness), then follows the fortunes of Commodus (Plummer) and Livius (Boyd), the dead emperor's handpicked successor—a fictional character and curious blunder: Commodus was Marcus' only designated heir (and unlike Plummer he didn't press Rome's policies on the northern frontier). His sister Lucilla was hardly the cluster of classical virtues portrayed by Loren: she was a notorious adulteress, and in 182 she hatched an abortive plot to murder Commodus. But Mann's period detail is excellent, his battles authentic, and the dreary, near-desperate atmosphere surrounding his remote Germanic garrisons on-target. Best of all, the sheer size and diversity of Rome's dominions drench the movie from start to finish.

For Further Viewing:

Spartacus ★★★★ (1960) 184 Minutes (Kirk Douglas, Jean Simmons, Laurence Olivier, Tony Curtis, Charles Laughton, Peter Ustinov, John Gavin, John Ireland): Despite smothering obstacles—bickering superstars, script-related conflicts, a long search for the right actress (Simmons) to play the fictional Varinia—director Stanley Kubrick finally sent *Spartacus* to the editing room in spring 1959. The result: a riveting mix of accurate history and Hollywood hokum. Rigorous training at Capua's gladiatorial school, butchery and spectator bloodlust in the arena, the awful mayhem of ancient hand-to-hand combat, and meticulous period detail throughout all ring true. Among the movie's glaring errors: Julius Caesar (Gavin) helps suppress the slave revolt (pure fiction); Kubrick's Spartacus doesn't divide his army; Crassus (Olivier) arrests and crucifies Spartacus (Douglas). Worst of all, Dalton Trumbo's script makes Spartacus a noble revolutionary opposed to slavery everywhere—hardly surprising, but utter nonsense. Spartacus and Crixus were brutal enough to murder hundreds of innocent Romans, and their only goal was getting out of Italy—not ending Roman oppression.

Barabbas ★★★★ (1961) 134 Minutes (Anthony Quinn, Silvana Mangano, Jack Palance): One of history's great enigmas, Barabbas vanished forever after his release from prison. With consummate skill and well-informed speculation, director Richard Fleischer fills in the blanks, producing one of the finest historical films ever made on everyday life in Rome's eastern provinces. Barabbas (Quinn, in a magnificent performance) leaves Jerusalem after the crucifixion, rejoins his old outlaw band, falls into Roman hands, and lands in a penal sulfur mine. (A grim segment on life in the mines will make your skin crawl.) He later becomes a gladiator, then a Christian convert—all in entertaining, convincing fashion. Fleischer delivers great renditions of arena fighting, life in the Christian catacombs, and the burning of Rome. Based on Pär Lagerkvist's Nobel Prize–winning novel—and a winner all the way.

Ben-Hur ★★★★ (1959) 212 Minutes (Charlton Heston, Stephen Boyd, Jack Hawkins, Haya Harareet, Hugh Griffith): Director William Wyler's adaptation of Lew Wallace's novel traces the fortunes of a first-century-A.D. Judean aristocrat unjustly sentenced to the galleys (and later freed) for crossing an ambitious Roman tribune (Boyd). Among the film's musts for amateur historians: Wyler's spectacular chariot race, his stark picture of galley-slave life, and his meticulous rendition of an epic sea battle. (The imperial navy—always a second-string service—policed Italy's coast from bases at Misenum and Ravenna and transported troops and supplies to provincial garrisons. Roman fleets patrolled the Danube, the Rhine, and the English Channel, targeting pirates and supporting the legions.) The realistic, wildly staged chariot race unfolds in a perfect replica of the Circus Maximus, Rome's huge U-shaped amphitheater (seating capacity: 250,000)—but Wyler puts the stadium in Jerusalem, not Rome!

Sign of the Pagan (1954) 92 Minutes (Jack Palance, Jeff Chandler, Rita Gam, Ludmilla Tcherina, Alexander Scourby): Director John Sturges names his characters for real fifth-century leaders, then trashes history completely in this awful spectacle. In the movie, Marcian (Chandler—a "centurion of [western emperor] Valentinian's Guard") visits Constantinople to keep eastern emperor Theodosius II from bribing Attila (Palance) to lead an alliance of Huns, Scythians, and other barbarians into Rome. Pulcheria, Theodosius' sister, implores the Huns to join Valentinian instead, then overthrows her brother when Attila refuses. Cowed by Pope Leo at the Eternal City's gates, Attila retreats, then falls in a Roman ambush. In fact: Theodosius died two years before Attila's Italian campaign; Theodosius' daughter married Valentinian III (no plots there); the Scythians vanished from history more than 300 years before Attila's western onslaughts; Marcian served in the Eastern Empire's army; Pulcheria mounted no intrigue against Theodosius—etc., etc., etc. Fun in spots, but rated "X" for history lovers.

Attila ★ (1954) 83 Minutes (Anthony Quinn, Henri Vidal, Sophia Loren, Irene Papas): Director Pietro Francisci's low-camp classic features Quinn as Attila, mouthing awful dialogue and lapsing often (and oddly) into a South Side Chicago brogue. Inferior dramatically to *Sign of the Pagan*, *Attila* is more faithful to history (no stretch there), at least in spots: Bleda doesn't survive, Roman general Aetius actually makes an appearance, and Valentinian's sister Honoria (Loren) lands in a scheme to marry Attila—some historians believe that this actually happened, others write it off as Byzantine court rumor. Read about it—and skip the movie.

Recommended Reading:
Robert Payne, *The Horizon Book of Ancient Rome* and *The Roman Triumph;* Justine Davis Randers-Pehrson, *Barbarians and Romans: The Birth Struggle of Europe, A.D. 400–700;* Otto Manchen-Helfen, *The World of the Huns: Studies in Their History and Culture;* José Ortega y Gasset, *An Interpretation of Universal History;* Paul Johnson, *Enemies of Society* (Chapter 2, "Cancers of the Ancient World"), Keith R. Bradley, *Slavery and Rebellion in the Roman World, 140 B.C.–70 B.C.*

Jesus of Nazareth ★★★★
(1977) 371 Minutes

Director: Franco Zeffirelli

Cast: Robert Powell, Olivia Hussey, Anne Bancroft, James Mason, Rod Steiger, Laurence Olivier, James Farentino

Historical Background: In 30 A.D., history's most famous public encounter, Jesus of

Nazareth's Jerusalem trial, quickly reeled into a paroxysm of indecision by Roman procurator Pontius Pilate. Inflaming a riotous mob demanding Jesus' execution, Pilate insisted—again and again—that he could "find no evil in the man." It was baffling behavior. Pilate had nothing to gain by freeing Jesus and every reason to convict him on the spot. The trial unfolded during Passover, an eight-day festival celebrating Israel's liberation from a foreign power (Egypt)—and a yearly nightmare for the Romans. The fifth imperial power to occupy Palestine, Rome (like its predecessors) found the Jews virtually ungovernable. They were insolent, mulish, fanatically independent, and incredibly brave, and during Passover thousands of them—in high mettle—flooded Jerusalem. (Worse still, by 30 A.D., Judea rumbled frightfully with bloody insurrectionist attacks on legionaries and Jewish collaborators.) For the Romans, barely keeping the lid on made a successful Passover week, and in Jerusalem suspicious-looking Jews could land in jail (or on crosses) for breathing too deeply.

Judea's Roman governors were ruthless, brutal, hard-eyed men, and Pilate was harsher than most: Herod Agrippa remembered his "vindictiveness," calling him "inflexible, a blend of self-will and relentlessness." He was capable of lynching perfectly harmless Jews and forgetting about it within seconds; he did so many times, in fact, ordering several "executions without trial" (Philo Judaeus) during his Judean tenure. Pilate sneered at absolute standards of any kind: "What is truth?" he asked Jesus at one point—not what is *the* truth (restricting the query to specific evidence or facts), but what is truth with a capital T. Pontius Pilate is history's premier self-proclaimed moral relativist; right and wrong, guilt or innocence,

meant nothing to him. Expediency was everything, and condemning Jesus would be a splendid career move, diffusing volcanic Jewish passions and enhancing Pilate's reputation for toughness in Rome. Instead, he waffled under the defendant's white-hot gaze and heavy silence (in the Synoptic Gospels, Jesus utters one four-word sentence during his trial; in John, he speaks three times). At one point, Pilate tried to dump the case altogether, dispatching Jesus to Herod Antipas' court (the king sent him back). Fear—unanticipated and enervating—is the only possible explanation for Pilate's dithering performance, and he certainly wasn't afraid of the Jews (he forced them over angry protests—to fix the sign proclaiming Jesus "King of the Jews" to his cross).

The whole affair, especially Pilate's famous self-exculpatory handwashing ritual, was bizarre, chilling, almost hallucinatory. In this the Gospel accounts are perfectly consistent: laced with paradox and mystery, much of Jesus' public career was eerie, strange, dreamlike. By traditional Jewish standards, his messianic claims came straight out of deep left field: first-century Jews expected the long-awaited Messiah to be a regal warrior intent on building a perfect earthly kingdom. Instead, they got an apolitical, absolute nobody—an itinerant carpenter born in a stable and based for three decades in a remote, nothing town (Nazareth was so superfluous that highways to the Sea of Galilee bypassed it). Many of his proclamations—"I am the way, the truth, and the life. . . . He who has seen me has seen the Father"—were staggering: under normal circumstances, only a delusional clown or demonic megalomaniac would say such things (Charles Manson, considered Christ reincarnate by his followers, made similar claims). But clearly, Jesus was neither: no one took him lightly, and non-Christians still endorse his moral teachings (Muslims consider him a great prophet). Throughout the New Testament, his beatific aphorisms (blessed are the meek, love your neighbor, forgive your enemies) mingle strangely with dark, terrible pronouncements ("Brother will deliver up brother to death . . . and you will be hated by all for my name's sake"). And despite the great rigor of his demands ("You must be perfect, as your heavenly Father is perfect"), his followers persevered doggedly, turning their tiny sect—Jesus' ministry covered an area smaller than Vermont—into a full-fledged religious movement.

With a small core of believers, Peter (first among Jesus' 12 original disciples) and Paul of Tarsus (a Pharisee committed, before his conversion, to destroying Christianity in Damascus) laid the foundations of world Christendom. Peter pioneered the embattled Church in Jerusalem. (Unlike Gentile converts, his "Jewish-Christian" congregation retained many Mosaic Law observances; their church died with Titus' destruction of Jerusalem in 70 A.D.) Around 40 A.D., he and Paul met—for the first time—to streamline their apostolic work: Peter would lead Christian missions to the Jews, Paul would carry the new faith to Gentiles. (According to Acts, Paul's conversion came during a blinding encounter with the risen Christ on the Jerusalem–Damascus road. The experience galvanized him: he rarely slept afterward, pouring himself into his missionary work by day and earning money as a tentmaker at night. He completed four apostolic journeys covering thousands of miles to cities throughout the Mediterranean Basin.) Eventually, Rome martyred both men, crucifying Peter in 64 A.D. and beheading Paul three years later. Their long, harrowing

struggle paid off spectacularly: in the fourth century, Christianity became the Roman Empire's official religion, and by 1996 Christian churches counted more than 1.5 billion members worldwide.

A fine script, excellent period detail, and great work by a huge ensemble cast make this the best film version of Jesus' life. Powell excels in the lead, but lacks the Messiah's daunting physical presence: according to some sources, Jesus was six feet tall (towering, in those days), and he was sufficiently powerful to mop the temple floor with moneylenders trafficking there, then rout them into Jerusalem's teeming streets. (They must have been terrified, offering no resistance to his onslaught.) A very good film—scrupulously faithful to scripture and comprehensive enough to make a fine introduction to the Gospels.

For Further Viewing:
Peter and Paul ★★★ (1981) 200 Minutes (Anthony Hopkins, Robert Foxworth, Raymond Burr, Jon Finch, Jean Peters): Director Robert Day's long chronicle of the Church's early years is reasonably accurate—with a few glaring exceptions. Day absurdly makes Luke the physician a near-agnostic. Paul (Hopkins) resembles a New Age radical, objecting to Jerusalem's insistence that Gentile converts "avoid immorality": give them "full Church membership without rules," he shouts, "any requirement [implies] that faith is not enough." Paul's mission downplayed Mosaic rules and rituals (circumcision, dietary restrictions)—but not laws governing morality: in many letters and homilies, he warned the Corinthians against promiscuity. Hopkins' outburst suggests that for Paul, believing the Gospels guaranteed salvation and that right conduct ("good works") was superfluous. For

all of the apostles, "faith" and "works" were inseparable ("By works is faith made perfect. . . . Faith without works is dead"—James 2:20–22). Still, a hard-hitting account of the obstacles facing first-century apostles.

Recommended Reading:
The Navarre Bible in the Revised Standard Version and New Vulgate (with detailed commentary by the University of Navarre Faculty); Robert Payne, *The Christian Centuries: From Christ to Dante;* Paul Johnson, *A History of the Jews.*

King David

(1955) 114 Minutes

Director: Bruce Beresford

Cast: Richard Gere, Edward Woodward, Denis Quilley, Niall Buggy, Alice Krige, Cherie Lunghi

Historical Background: 1010 (?) B.C.—Elah Valley, Judah: Under the rules of single combat, gigantic Philistine champion Goliath was thoroughly outgunned in his one-on-one proxy brawl with Israelite herdsman David—their dazzling skills with the sling ranked Hebrew shepherds with the most dangerous characters stalking Judah's wild, tumbling hills. Fashioned from cords attached to a leather

pocket, slings were long-range herding tools: in skilled hands, they sent 18-ounce stones rocketing past distant strays at 100-mph speed, loudly smacking the ground and quickly driving the animals back to their flocks. Slings made fearsome weapons—Benjamin's army recruited 700 soldiers able to "sling a stone at a hair and not miss" (Judges 20:16). Unsupported by archers, Goliath was nothing, for David, but a fat, slow target.

The Biblical tale of David's triumph isn't pure legend—packed with eyewitness accounts, First and Second Samuel form the world's first comprehensive, reliable narrative histories. (Late 20th century archaeological digs confirm the historicity of many Old Testament books: even parts of Genesis contain real historical figures—Abraham, for one. The Jews' passion for presenting a full view of their past in orderly, written texts was unique among ancient cultures. Determined to record the progress of their relationship with God, they were obsessed with accuracy: even though Hebrew texts overstate Goliath's size (height: 9′9″), Josephus mentions him (height: 6′9″), and his brother Elhanan surfaces in Chronicles. Clearly, David won some sort of titanic duel in northern Judah. (Single combat between champions was a well-known Philistine custom. One of history's fiercest predatory cultures, the Philistines mounted a crushing 12th-century-B.C. drive from the Aegean basin to the Mediterranean Sea. Only Egypt withstood the onslaught, barely winning two bloodbaths in 1190.) By 1050 B.C., Philistine legions had built a five-city military alliance on Palestine's southern coast, threatening the Israelites with annihilation.

Grimly scrapping their decentralized tribal confederation, the Jews united under Benjamite guerrilla Saul for a no-quarter campaign against Philistia and other long-standing enemies. He scored several minor triumphs, then routed Ammon's occupation force at Jabesh-gilead. Anointed Israel's first king by the prophet Samuel, Saul routed Philistine garrisons at Gibeah and Michmash, but he never crushed the hated invaders decisively. Eventually rebuked by Samuel for offering unauthorized religious sacrifices and looting Amalek (Yahwist law forbade pillaging), the king drifted into black despair. Worse still, as nonstop warfare raged, David won battle after battle, driving his popularity among common folk through the ceiling. Saul fell to rock-bottom levels of homicidal jealousy, trying twice to kill his finest commander with spears. After the second incident, David fled to a desert stronghold, built a 600-man fugitive army, and—incredibly—joined ranks with Gath's Philistine king Achish. Walking a diplomatic highwire, he fought many battles for Achish, memorizing Philistine tactical doctrine—and always avoiding Israelite forces. In 1005, swarming Philistines slaughtered Saul's army at Mt. Gilboa, killed his three sons, and left the king to commit suicide. David returned to Hebron, earning the crowns of Judah (in the south) and Israel (kingdom of the northern tribes) before his thirty-first birthday.

Author of at least 80 psalms, David submitted personal ambition to his faith's rigorous demands, building a monarchic theocracy—not a traditional oriental dictatorship. He crafted profitable trading agreements with Tyre. He established a centrally located government in Jerusalem, uniting Israel and Judah. He dismembered Philistia's rapacious legions, driving them onto a narrow sliver of Mediterranean coastline and keeping them there. Routing other predatory enemies, David pushed Israel's dominions all the way to Damascus in the north and southward to

the Red Sea. Morally, he stumbled more than once. Second Samuel immortalizes his worst lapse—an adulterous liaison with Bathsheba, wife of virtuous Hittite officer Uriah. David sent Uriah on a suicidal combat mission, then married his widow. Drowning in bitter remorse, he eventually wrote scripture's third-longest penitential psalm, the 51st. Antiquity's greatest monarch, David died in 966 B.C. To this day, only Moses holds a higher place in Israel's history.

Before *King David*'s premiere, a producer described its "treatment" of David (Gere) for critic Michael Medved: "We could've played to the Bible Belt . . . but we don't see David as some Holy Joe, praise-the-Lord kind of guy. We wanted to make him a richer, deeper character." (Righteous, dude. By the way—what's a "psalm"?) From start to finish, Beresford slings flatulent nonsense. Gere's deathbed counsel to Solomon is typical: "Don't follow the prophets, follow your own heart," a full reversal of the real king's charge to his heir ("Keep God's commandments; walk in his paths; observe his customs, his judgments, and his statutes, as they are written in the Law of Moses"—1 Kings 2). Hold your nose—tightly—and view at your own risk.

For Further Viewing:

The Story of David ★★★★ (1976) 250 Minutes (Anthony Quayle, Timothy Bottoms, Jane Seymour, Keith Michell): Accurate, realistic, and thorough, this long chronicle of David's entire career is one of the best Biblical epics ever made. Directors David Lowell Rich and Alex Segal emphasize character, not action or spectacle, but the film never drags. Well acted by all, but Quayle (a rugged, willful Saul drifting slowly into mad paranoia) walks off with the movie.

David and Bathsheba ★★★★ (1951) 116 Minutes (Gregory Peck, Susan Hayward, Raymond Massey):

An excellent rendition of the legendary scandal, despite sluggish pacing and scattered historical distortions. Hayward's Bathsheba is too compliant—a real pushover—on first meeting the king (Peck); to downplay David's guilt, director Henry King wrongly makes Uriah a high-stomached fanatic (he volunteers for his fatal mission). Still, a faithful adaptation of Second Samuel, with topnotch performances by Peck and Massey (as the prophet Nathan).

Recommended Reading:
Geoffrey de C. Parmiter, *King David: Shepherd and Psalmist;* Thomas Cahill, *The Gifts of the Jews.*

Masada ★★★★

(1984) 131 Minutes

Director: Boris Sagal

Cast: Peter O'Toole, Peter Strauss, David Warner, Anthony Quayle

Historical Background: Spring, 73 A.D.—southern Judea: As they breached Fortress Masada's second defensive wall, battle-hardened shock troops from Roman governor Flavius Silva's Tenth Legion expected a hand-to-hand brawl, with no quarter asked or given, against tenacious Jewish Zealots. Instead, they encountered only the silence of death. Scattered around them lay the corpses of 960 men, women, and children who—exhorted by their leader, Eleazar ben Ya'ir—had preferred suicide to imprisonment or slavery. According to Jewish historian Josephus, the Romans were staggered by the Jews' "courage, resolution, and immovable contempt of death." After an exhausting two-year siege, the grisly finale was a bitter pill for Flavius to swallow.

Organized into a guerrilla army by Judah the Galilean when Rome occupied Jerusalem in 6 A.D., the Zealots opposed any kind of foreign influence or power over Israel. They ignited the Jewish Revolt of 66 A.D. by seizing the Roman garrison on Masada and killing its occupiers. Set atop a mesa towering 1,300 feet above the desert and ringed by a 4,600-foot double wall, the 20-acre fortress boasted two luxurious palaces built by Herod the Great in 31 B.C., large weapons caches, huge storehouses filled with dried food, aqueducts that carried rainwater to multiple 200,000-gallon storage cisterns, and 37 defensive towers. Masada seemed impregnable, but Jewish veterans of the war against Rome weren't fooled. Thoroughly familiar with the logistical capabilities of their enemy, they must have known from the start that building an assault ramp on the mesa's western slope would be a routine job for Roman battlefield engineers.

And so it was. First they built siege camps at eight strategic locations around Masada and sealed off eastern approaches to the mesa with a long fortified barrier. Then they fashioned a 330-yard assault embankment crowned with a stone tower. Bombarding the Zealots with catapults, the Romans hauled a battering ram to the stone tower and smashed through Masada's outer wall on May 2, 73 A.D. The next day, they burned their way through a wooden wall sealing the initial breach and found the fallen Zealots. (Two women and five children survived the mass suicide.) Today, Masada is a national shrine of Israel and one of the country's most popular tourist sites.

As entertainment, *Masada* is excellent; as history, it is flawed. Period detail is superb, and portrayals of first-century Mediterranean daily life couldn't be better. But Sagal absurdly portrays Ya'ir as an agnostic (the Jews at Masada were intensely orthodox in their beliefs, as were most first-century Zealots). And O'Toole's Silva exudes sympathy for the Zealots—a notion that Roman commanders would have found incomprehensible. Still, *Masada* is an accurate recreation of the siege and is well worth a look.

Recommended Reading:
Yigael Yadin, *Masada: Herod's Fortress and the Zealots' Last Stand;* Flavius Josephus, *The Great Roman-Jewish War: A.D. 66–70.*

Quest for Fire ★★★★

(1981) 97 Minutes

Director: Jean-Jacques Annaud

Cast: Everett McGill, Rae Dawn Chong, Ron Perlman, Nameer El Kadi

Historical Background: Human beings are the only creatures on earth possessing language and the ability to control fire. Without fire, prehistoric men were marginal brutes limited to warm-weather regions and revolting diets of tough, uncooked meat and edible roots. Denied shelter in caves occupied by predators, tiny clans roamed Africa's open savanna, scavenging food by day and hiding from foraging beasts at night. Early man's management of fire captured from lightning-ignited blazes fully reversed nature's balance of power. Using fire to scatter predators and provide warmth, entire communities spread into Asia and northern Europe. Their number increased dramatically because cooking killed food-borne bacteria and parasites. Fewer people starved: torch-waving hunters stampeded animal herds into ravines, then harvested as much meat as they could carry. With fire its primary weapon, human intelligence displaced—once and for all—the superior motor skills of lower animals. For centuries, tribes nursed smoldering flames around the clock, passing precious embers from family to family. No one knows precisely when people mastered reliable fire-starting techniques, but experts agree that *Homo erectus* began using fire 1.4 million years ago.

Language is a different story: no issue has provoked hotter scholarly disputes than the origin and early history of language. (In 1866, colliding theories ignited debates so volcanic that the Linguistic Society of Paris banned discussions on the subject at meetings.) Language sets modern humans apart, because using it requires highly developed brains and vocal tracts missing in early hominids. For decades, Neanderthal man's mysterious disappearance drove furious controversy—turning partly on early-human linguistic capabilities—over the genesis of modern *Homo sapiens*. Stocky, weak-chinned, and beetle-browed, Neanderthals drew sharp ridicule as wordless, knuckle-dragging near-apes after workers unearthed the first Neanderthal skeleton in 1856. Scholarly assessments gradually moderated: by the 1960s, everyone agreed that Neanderthals controlled fire and used stone tools—but opinions on their linguistic skills varied wildly. Then, in 1983, diggers in northern Israel discovered a Neanderthal hyoid bone virtually identical to its modern counterparts. (The free-floating, horseshoe-shaped hyoid anchors the tongue's base, linking major muscles of the neck and lower jaw. Without it, articulation nuanced enough to produce spoken language is impossible.) It was a sensational find: clearly, the Neanderthals could speak. But their larynges lay too high in the throat to produce clear, nonnasal sounds, and their long, uncurved tongues could barely control voice-box movements and shapes, limiting their repertoire of consonants and critical vowels.

For 100,000 years, the Neanderthals flourished, surviving most of Europe's last Ice Age. Then, around 35,000 B.C., they simply vanished, partly because their truncated vernacular severely checked their ability to transmit technological know-how and organize collective activities as adroitly as waves of invading Cro-Magnons. The first modern humans, Cro-Magnons fanned out from Africa, colonizing vast territories by 45,000 B.C. and launching a sudden outburst of sophisticated technological and artistic activity. Cro-Magnons had bows and arrows and spear-throwers (grooved three-foot sticks capable of flinging short projectiles 150 yards). Some of their wall paintings include perspective drawing techniques first used by modern Europeans in the 14th century. Old-school "multiregional" theories of global colonization assume that Cro-Magnons assimilated the Neanderthals through interbreeding, but many scientists dismiss the notion. Based on mitochondrial-DNA analysis, their research traces modern human origins back to a single woman—a "mitochondrial Eve" living in Africa 200,000 years ago and representing an entirely new species. Armed with modern linguistic capabilities, "replacement-theory" Cro-Magnons built intricate, flexible social systems and steadily elbowed primitive Neanderthals toward civilization's fringes, eventually supplanting them. Despite hard genetic evidence and recent South African excavations yielding modern human remains dating from 100,000 B.C., multiregionalists furiously reject the replacement theory. A new controversy—volatile enough to end friendships—has driven anthropologists into warring camps, just as language-related disputes did in 19th-century Paris.

A wild-and-woolly adaptation of J. H. Rosny-Aîné's popular novel: 80,000 years ago, McGill, Perlman, and El Kadi (presumably Neanderthals—they live in caves, control but can't make fire, and speak a primitive language) search for burning tinder after apelike raiders extinguish their clan's source of fire. Annaud's obvious aim, cramming as much information as he can into his movie, inevitably produces anachronisms: Neanderthals mingle with Chong's Cro-Magnon clan, for example, 35,000 years before modern humans colonized Europe. But the film's essentials—Anthony Burgess' "special languages," the awful menace of hungry predators, the knockout impact of emerging technology (spear-throwers, fire drills, man-made shelters)—ring true throughout. A fine, riveting movie.

Recommended Reading:
Peter Farb, *Humankind;* Michael J. Behe, *Darwin's Black Box: The Biochemical Challenge to Evolution;*

Göran Burenhult, ed., *The First Humans: Human Origins and History to 10,000 B.C.;* Erik Trinkaus and Pat Shipman, *The Neanderthals: Changing the Image of Mankind.*

Robin Hood, Prince of Thieves ★

(1991) 138 Minutes

Director: Kevin Reynolds

Cast: Kevin Costner, Morgan Freeman, Mary Elizabeth Mastrantonio, Christian Slater, Alan Rickman

Historical Background: Robin Hood— Today's Standard Version: While King Richard I fights the Third Crusade, the Sheriff of Nottingham steals Robert ("Robin") of Locksley's estate. Determined to prevail, Robin assembles a band of outlaw bowmen in Sherwood Forest. (His top gun, Little John, signs on after besting Robin in a brawl with staves, and Maid Marian—in flight from randy Prince John—soon joins them.) They poach deer, steal from the rich, give to the poor—and Robin eventually lands in jail. His men rescue him, Richard returns and pardons everybody, the sheriff goes down hard, and Robin gets the girl.

Parts of the tale might be true. After centuries of scholarly digging, Robin Hood—prob-

ably a real outlaw—remains a tantalizing riddle. Lettered musings on his identity collate medieval church records, court proceedings, and estate genealogies with exploits chronicled in the *Gest of Robyn Hode,* a 15th-century narrative poem liberally embellished in Renaissance folk ballads. Mountainous research answers many questions surrounding the legend. Robin was a yeoman, not an earl. He stole for himself, not for the poor. His men fought with swords— never staves—and most were capable archers. (Welsh huntsmen fashioned the first longbows from six-foot lengths of yew. Pulling the weapons to a full draw took 100 pounds of force, enough power to drive 37-inch arrows through armored breastplate.) Richard died a century before Robin prowled the woods: the only king mentioned in the *Gest,* Edward II, ruled 1307–27. Robin's forest refuge was Barnsdale (well north of Sherwood), and Maid Marian was a stock figure in May festivals and 16th-century ballads—not Robin Hood's girlfriend.

Stubborn mystery still shrouds Robin's true identity: medieval documents swarm with Robert Hoods, Robyn Hodes, Robert Hood Hills, and Robynhouds, and even if you drop law-abiding candidates, so many contenders remain that the name might as well be Tom Smith. Some modern scholars assign Robin to the 1290s. Others date him later because the *Gest* stresses archery so heavily. (The longbow's great age came in the 14th century, peaking with the battle of Crécy-en-Ponthieu: in 1346, British bowmen rained thousands of arrows onto charging French knights, slaughtering an incredible 1,500 horsemen and rendering armor-based military technology obsolete.) Meanwhile, Robin's legend still grows: discovered in 1936, documents dated long after

Richard died and before Edward reigned mention the fugitive Robert Hod—he could easily be Robin Hood II.

Reynolds glumly nails medieval England's par-for-the-course violence and austere, grimy "look"—the film's only credible elements. Mastrantonio's Marian is a weird Eleanor Smeal/Snow White combo, and transplanted Moor Freeman oozes political correctness (his comment—it's not a joke—on Christmas mistletoe: "In my country we talk to our women, we don't trick them with plants"). Worst of all is Reynolds' airheaded rendition of Catholicism as the mother of all villainy—in most of the medieval sources, Robin Hood is a devout Marian Catholic (his main reason for loathing corrupt clerics). No surprise there; this pretentious dirge wallows in ignorance. Freeman, for example, carries a refracting telescope—300 years before its invention in 1608.

For Further Viewing:
The Adventures of Robin Hood ★★★★ (1938) 102 Minutes (Errol Flynn, Olivia de Havilland, Basil Rathbone, Claude Rains, Alan Hale, Melville Cooper): History buffs and teachers should stick with this vintage Sherwood Forest spectacle: it's perfectly faithful to the rollicking spirit of the *Gest of Robyn Hode* and the content of ballads and expanded versions of the folk legend *(Robin Hood and Little John, Robin Hood and the Curtal Friar, The True Tale of Robin Hood)*. Packed with grand pageantry, super dialogue ("What's the matter, Gisborne? Run out of hangings?"), and dynamite performances, especially by Rains (Prince John), Hale (Little John), and Cooper (the sheriff).
Robin and Marian (1976) 112 Minutes (Sean Connery, Audrey Hepburn, Nicol Williamson, Robert Shaw, Richard Harris): Director Richard Lester's

stupid "update" of the folktale belongs in yesterday's trash. Middle-aged and exhausted, Robin (Connery) and Little John (Williamson) return from the Crusades, find a hypocritical Marian (Hepburn) in a nunnery, and renew their battle with the sheriff (Shaw). Laced with sophomoric nihilism, James Goldman's script wrecks the legend and fizzles after King Richard (Harris) dies. Where history intrudes, it's usually bogus: the king, for example, implies that he tried to have children with Queen Berengaria—in fact, their marriage was purely formal and probably remained unconsummated (see *The Crusades*). Worst of all is Lester's depraved version of Robin's death: traditionally, his cousin poisons him, but here, Marian does it, then kills herself. She should've burned the master print first.

Recommended Reading:
J. C. Holt, *Robin Hood.*

The Ten Commandments ★★★

(1956) 220 Minutes

Director: Cecil B. DeMille

Cast: Charlton Heston, Yul Brynner, Anne Baxter, Edward G. Robinson, Yvonne De Carlo, John Derek

Historical Background: Bristling with "sacred discontent," Moses and his successors openly insisted that the religious and cultural practices of antiquity's most powerful men were fictions, illusions, monstrous lies. A favorite target was Egyptian polytheism: binding countless gods, and the people serving them, to nature's rumbling mechanical cycles, Egypt's religion was implacably hostile to the faculty of free will, and, therefore, to the rigors of moral choice. For the Jews, nature worship also withered under the hard scrutiny of reason (see Jeremiah 10): how, for example, could "gods" mighty enough to control natural processes—the sun's movements, the Nile's flood levels—be buried themselves in nature's manifestations and subject to its laws? Ritual prostitution, animal worship, epic-scale slavery, child sacrifice, fertility cults—Israel's prophets took a long, scorching look at pagan culture and walked away fuming: backbreaking conscript labor was just one of many abominations left behind during the Hebrews' long flight from Egypt.

Few historians still consider the Exodus story pure legend. Spectacular late-20th-century archaeological finds—legal documents, administrative records, and the metropolitan ruins of Ur, Pithom, and Pi-Ramesse—confirm the historicity of many Old Testament books. Exodus, Numbers, Judges, and even parts of Genesis mix history with myth and include real historical figures—Abraham, for one, and certainly Moses. Born in Egypt to Levite parents, Moses is Jewish history's pivotal figure. Before his rise, "Israel" amounted to scattered groups of Semitic outcasts ("Habiru") toiling on Egyptian construction projects for food, water, and squalid shelter. Between 1280 and 1220 B.C., Moses—a visionary, dynamic personality marked by high intelligence, fits of ruthlessness, and fearful self-doubt—rallied and led a chaotic mob of human debris (numbering 15,000 at least) on a white-knuckle getaway into the Sinai wilderness. (Merneptah—not Ramses II—was probably Pharaoh.) Hours ahead of Egypt's legions, the Jews fled south along the Sinai Peninsula's western edge, stopped and received the Tables of the Law at Mt. Sinai, wheeled northward again, and slogged all the way to Kadesh-barnea. From there they skirted Edom's western border, crossed the Arnon River, brawled their way through waves of bellicose Amorites to the Dead Sea's northern shore, and crossed the River Jordan into Canaan (the Promised Land).

It's a great story, but the Bible doesn't stop there. Throughout the long journey, an inscrutable God (Yahweh) performs astonishing miracles, feeding his people and shielding them from calamity again and again; at one point, he parts the "Sea of Reeds" (probably the Gulf of Suez or Lake Timsah), marshals the Israelites across, then drowns thousands of pursuing Egyptian soldiers. Commentaries dismissing the miracle stories as embellishments by post-Exilic scribes to lend authority to Mosaic Law are wrongheaded in their assessment of ancient Hebrews. Down-to-earth realists, most Hebrews were far too skeptical—too practical and grounded in the here-and-now—to swallow any sort of scribal hocus-pocus. An aging Sarah, for example, laughs derisively at God's news of her coming pregnancy: "After I am worn out and my husband is old, will I now have this pleasure?" (Gen. 18:12). Hermeneutics, archaeology, even plausible naturalistic explanations of the miracle stories will never fully explain the Jews' stunning transformations in the wilderness. The Hebrews were nothing but bickering, unlettered rabble—the scum of the earth—before leaving Egypt. Thirty-nine years later, they'd formed a unified society full of purpose, backed by a disciplined army, inspired by a strange new monotheistic faith (utterly without precedent), and ordered by antiquity's most sophisticated legal code—the first based on human rights and obligations and not on property ownership.

Clearly, something extraordinary happened in the Sinai. The miracle stories stubbornly retain their ancient implications, especially if you read them figuratively or "symbolically," because the core of Biblical monotheism—a single, universal God able to make entire worlds from scratch—turns on concepts ("eternity" and "creation") incomprehensible to finite creatures and beyond the powers of language to express literally. Both notions were radically new: many ancient religions had formation myths, but before Genesis, concepts of one God creating everything—matter, energy, the works—from absolutely nothing simply didn't exist (the Hebrew word *bará*— "creation *ex nihilo*"—has no equivalent in many languages, including English). More baffling still is Yahweh's eternal nature: we can easily imagine a "world without end," but God has no beginning, either (this baffling, essential fact generates his name: "I AM," he tells Moses—not "I was," "I will be," or "I have been for a million years"). Try to explain how, precisely, anything can exist without beginning, and you'll quickly fall silent or lapse into gibberish—but the prophets linked everything they wrote to their relationship with a creator existing outside of time. This accent on an eternal realm without genesis or sequence saturates ancient Hebrew itself; the language has no tenses, only loose conjugations for perfect or imperfect, almost encouraging Biblical authors to mix temporal planes: "Before Abraham was, I am" (John 8:58), declares Jesus, pointing beyond history toward categories that we can sense, but never understand—just as the Exodus miracles point

beyond nature toward the strange, impenetrable mystery at the heart of the Hebrew Bible.

DeMille's blockbuster hums with anachronism and factual errors: Ramses—not Merneptah—is Pharaoh; Moses is his brother by adoption; Joshua meets Moses before the flight from Egypt (in Exodus, Joshua surfaces later); worse still is Moses' grasp of ethical monotheism before his first encounter with Yahweh. And worst of all, there's a nutty subplot featuring the "throne princess" Nefretiri (Baxter—she carries a sizzling torch for Moses throughout). Apparently, DeMille doctored the name of Ramses' first queen, Nefertari, for the film. Historians know little about Nefertari, but she certainly didn't vamp Moses. Entertaining—but slim pickings for history buffs.

For Further Viewing:

Moses ★★★ (1975) 141 Minutes (Burt Lancaster, Ingrid Thulin, Anthony Quayle, Irene Papas): A reasonably accurate, authentic survey of the Pentateuch, from rag-wrapped slaves and the grimy, exhausting drudgery of seminomadic desert life to Moses' wonderful last-ditch efforts to squirm out of God's commission to lead the Exodus (his lamest argument: "I'm slow of tongue"—i.e., he's a lousy public speaker!). Beware of several puzzling flaws: confused geography has liberated Hebrews shouting, "To the east!"—then heading southward to the Sinai; director Gianfranco DeBosio's take on the miracles is inconsistent, presenting some as divine intervention and offering modern naturalistic explanations—by Moses, of all people—for others. Lancaster's contrived closing monologue makes the final boring hour more tedious.

Recommended Reading:

Herbert N. Schneidau, *Sacred Discontent: The Bible*

and *Western Tradition;* Paul Johnson, *A History of the Jews;* Peter Kreeft, *You Can Understand the Old Testament;* Edmund Wilson, *Israel and the Dead Sea Scrolls;* Thomas Cahill, *The Gifts of the Jews.*

The Vikings ★★★★

(1958) 114 Minutes

Director: Richard Fleischer

Cast: Kirk Douglas, Tony Curtis, Ernest Borgnine, Janet Leigh, Alexander Knox, Frank Thring

Historical Background: "From the fury of the Norsemen deliver us, O Lord": medieval Christians in Europe's coastal villages and river towns murmured the same prayer thousands of times between 800 and 1100 A.D., when Viking raiders ruled the high seas and inland waterways from Greenland to the Caspian Sea. (Russia, in fact, owes its name to the Vikings, who called their eastern trading partners the Rus. To this day, many residents of Novgorod and Kiev have Scandinavian names.) There is evidence—though no conclusive proof—that the Vikings also reached Newfoundland on Canada's northeastern coast. Even if this proves untrue, it is certain that the areas they traversed stretched for thousands of miles in all directions.

The enormous range of Viking military

and commercial expeditions confirms the superior design of their famous longships. The elegant, nimble warships drew very little water and proved remarkably versatile: unmatched for river fighting, coastal raids, and battle on the open seas, they were trim enough for portage around fortifications, inland shallows, and waterfalls. Early longships carried 80 men, but much larger complements manned the great vessels of the 11th and 12th centuries. Viking shipwrights often bound parts of their vessels together with tough spruce roots, creating a sinuous flexibility that left the longships all but indestructible in even the worst weather. Steered with a huge side rudder and powered by oars and a single sail, Norse warships could manage ten-knot speeds on the open sea.

Viking raiders repeated proven tactical moves on every foreign incursion. Once ashore, they beached their ships and built camps fortified with earthworks and log barricades. Protected by conical iron helmets, leather vests, and wooden shields, they fought with spears, heavy swords, and battle-axes. They attacked in tight phalanxes or from large, wedge-shaped formations called "swine arrays." Every eyewitness account dwells on the ferocity of Viking assaults. The English adjective "berserk" derives from *berserksgangr,* Old Norse for "bearshirts"—a subgroup of Viking warriors clad only in wild animal skins and stoked for battle by massive doses of psychotropic muscarine toadstools. According to the ancient *Ynglinga Saga,* the *berserksgangr* fought "like mad dogs or wolves, immune to fire or iron, biting their shields, and mowing down everything in their path." The bearshirts were fearsome, but by all accounts only slightly more fanatical than run-of-the-mill Norse warriors.

At home, it was a different story. Near-maniacal Viking killers returning from raiding expeditions assumed the plodding existence of European farmers. They lived in sod-roofed houses and raised cattle. They minted their own coins. And they obeyed their wives—always. Viking women, in fact, lived lives of wildly conflicting extremes. Unmarried girls and spinsters were virtually invisible, making little imprint on Norse village life. But after marriage, women wielded considerable influence in the community. Wives controlled domestic matters with stern, silent determination so severe that historians describe Viking warriors as utterly docile before the intense practicality and indomitable will of the Norse female. (Noted often in Icelandic literature, their daunting behavior served Viking women splendidly in the humdrum daily business of marriage—and in its dissolution: more than one burned-out Viking wife donned an ill-fitting pair of men's trousers and sauntered lewdly around the village to shame her husband into granting a quick divorce.)

A final paradox of history matches the strange incongruities of Viking culture: though they are ranked with the most barbarous warriors of all time, the Norsemen's only lasting contribution to European civilization was literary. By the end of the 11th century, their assimilation into indigenous populations throughout Europe had ended the Vikings' reign of terror. Awful memories of their raids gradually faded, surviving only as plot elements for long narrative sagas written in the ancient runic alphabet—a quaint relic of the distant past.

A rare, reasonably convincing Hollywood portrait of Viking culture and warfare. Douglas is a Viking prince and Curtis his illegitimate half brother, the offspring of an illicit liaison between their father (Borgnine) and a Saxon queen. Leigh plays the lovely princess who becomes a point of contention between the two. (Snarling fiercely all the way, Douglas dominates the movie from start to finish.) Filmed in and around Norway's majestic fjords, *The Vikings* delivers epic battles and authentic period detail—including full-scale replicas of ancient longships—and drips with a cold, foggy atmosphere that takes you straight back to medieval Scandinavia. A very good movie for amateur historians.

Recommended Reading:
Rudolf Poertner, *The Vikings. The Rise and Fall of the Norse Sea Kings;* A. W. Brøgger and Haakon Shetelig, *The Viking Ships;* Magnus Magnusson, *Viking: Hammer of the North.*

The War Lord ★★★★

(1965) 123 Minutes

Director: Franklin Schaffner

Cast: Charlton Heston, Rosemary Forsyth, Richard Boone, Guy Stockwell, James Farentino

Historical Background: Spring 1177—Marne River Valley: spectators looking for William Marshall, newly crowned champion of

Europe's premier chivalric competition, found their man on his knees in a local forge, his head resting atop a large anvil. During the final event, opponents had hammered Marshall's helmet into a shapeless lump, jamming it in place and handing the tournament blacksmith a ticklish challenge: pound and rip the headgear apart without deafening (or killing) his client. He succeeded, and Sir William went on to become one of England's finest cavaliers, clobbering more than 100 adversaries in a crushing ten-month competitive onslaught.

First staged by ninth-century Frankish nobles, medieval tournaments gradually developed standard formats: cavalry duels ("jousts") preceded bruising slugfests featuring knights battering opponents into exhausted oblivion with maces and swords, then holding them for fat "ransoms" at day's end. By the 12th century, a competitive knightly "tour" flourished, filling a key economic niche for war-torn Europe's toughest horsemen: medieval society's ravenous appetite for armored cavalry bred a huge knightly class, but most knights could count on 40 days' guaranteed employment, at best, in traditional military service to kings or mighty lords. Europe teemed with impecunious "knights-errant" able to make a living only by selling their services to warring manors—or excelling in tournament competition.

Norman duke William the Conqueror's victory over Britain's King Harold Godwinson near Hastings capped the knight's rise to battlefield supremacy. On October 14, 1066, 7,000 fierce Saxon infantrymen assembled on Caldbed Hill—shield to shield, shoulder to shoulder, in ranks so closely packed that casualties had nowhere to fall—and waited for Armageddon. At 9 A.M., William struck hard, hurling waves of sprinting infantry straight at the heart of Harold's army. Saxon warriors cut them to bits with five-foot battle-axes, sending mangled survivors reeling downhill in a pell-mell rout. William quickly released his knights: 1,000 horsemen raced forward, crashing thunderously into Harold's stout phalanx. Fighting like wild men, Saxon defenders unhorsed knight after knight and hacked them to death as soon as they hit the ground. Awful slaughter raged through the afternoon. By dusk, the crushing power of William's cavalry finally prevailed, putting the duke on England's throne and opening the door for land-hungry Norman immigrants (200,000 by 1087).

It was a high-water mark for one of history's great cultures. Descended from pugnacious Vikings, Norman pirates forged permanent settlements along the lower Seine River around 900 A.D. By 1150, they'd pushed through Normandy, building the most deftly governed state in Europe. They were flexible, disciplined, and imaginative: Normans invented the exchequer—and they wrote the book on medieval warfare. Adapted by every western military power, their equipment and fighting techniques prevailed on battlefields throughout Europe. For more than two centuries, armored cavaliers thundered into battle shrouded in tough chain-mail "hauberks" fashioned from thousands of tiny steel rings. (Jointed plate-armor suits with visored helmets surfaced 300 years after Hastings.) Norman knights carried kite-shaped shields and eight-foot lances held under the arm for shock assaults against enemy infantry formations. Forged from layered steel strips, medieval swords could easily sever limbs and—in the hands of exceptionally powerful knights—split lightly armored torsos completely in two. (Few knights practiced sophisticated fencing techniques: thrust, slash, parry—

with maximum force and no fancy footwork—completed the medieval swordsman's fighting repertoire.)

Normans built Europe's first castles—complexes incorporating single fortified towers ringed by ditches and timber palisades. With dizzying speed, castles mushroomed in size and sophistication, and by 1400, thousands of vast, elaborate citadels dotted Europe's landscape. Linked by subterranean passages, massive concentrically set walls with flanking towers formed multiple defense lines. Gatehouse "murder-holes" gave crossbowmen interlocking fields of fire. Tower floors incorporated chutes with camouflaged trapdoors to swallow charging invaders whole, plunging them into dank underground dungeons. For months—even years—attacking armies hammered away at defenders with huge siege engines: basic arsenals included battering rams, ballista (gigantic crossbows), mangonels (heavy catapults), and trebuchets (mighty slings loaded with stones large enough to kill several men at once). To storm castle walls, raiding parties built siege towers fitted with gangplanks. Besieging armies would do just about anything to reduce enemy garrisons: they practiced history's first systematic biological warfare, catapulting tons of revolting animal carrion over battlements to spread disease among defenders. In spite of all this, well-provisioned garrisons usually prevailed.

For medieval knights, the main battle theaters lay in Spain and the Holy Land. In 718, Asturian mountaineers campaigned to retake Spain from fanatical Moorish invaders. Fighting flared sporadically for 300 years, then raged hotly during 11th-century drives by Christian armies to unseat the Muslims once and for all. Spain's long "Reconquista" produced one of Europe's greatest knights—the brilliant commander Rodrigo Diaz de Vivar (popular name: El Cid, "the Lord"). From day one, swashbuckling military feats and murky intrigue marked Rodrigo's career. A tough opportunist, he fought for Castile's Sancho II in a fraternal feud with Alfonso VI of León. Incredibly, Vivar switched sides after Sancho's death, married Alfonso's niece (Jimena), gradually fell out of favor at court, then joined ranks with al-Mu'tamin—monarch of Saragossa's hated Muslim dynasty. For a decade, Vivar flourished as a free-lancing mercenary, inflicting defeat after defeat on Saragossa's enemies. In 1086, he rode south to build an independent province around Valencia, a fortress city on the Mediterranean coast. Rodrigo won a long, bloody brawl for the town in 1094 and gave French bishops jurisdiction over its mosques, drawing waves of Christian colonists to Spain. The Cid governed Valencia until his death in 1099; three years later, a Muslim force reoccupied the city and held it for more than 135 years.

Knightly warfare's long, bloody high noon came 35 years after invading Seljuk Turks devoured more than half of the Byzantine Empire, seizing Jerusalem, sealing its holy sites, and butchering countless European pilgrims. Eastern emperor Alexius I called for help, and Pope Urban II sounded the appeal in a ringing oration at the 1095 Council of Claremont. Aiming to retake Jerusalem and protect Christian pilgrims, legions of the faithful launched the first of eight major crusades (and countless lesser ventures) a year later. For two centuries, a steady tide of humble knights, brutal mercenaries, devout civilians, selfless clerics, land-hungry nobles, and vagrant oddballs rolled eastward toward the Holy Land. Their opening salvo came in two waves. Peter the Hermit—a strange, monklike visionary—orchestrated the

First Crusade's tragic overture, leading a huge civilian "army of the poor" to swift annihilation by raging Turks in June 1096. The Crusade proper was a different story: led by Norman, French, and Flemish knights, a muscular army flattened Antioch's Muslim garrison in June 1098, recaptured Jerusalem a year later, and returned to Europe.

In 1187, the city changed hands again, igniting the legendary Third Crusade (1189–92), pitting Christendom's greatest knight, Richard I of England, against the finest warlord of Islam, Saladin, sultan of Syria and Egypt (before occupying Jerusalem, he'd slaughtered 15,000 Crusaders in a terrible battle near Hattin, Galilee). Richard overran Cyprus, Jaffa, and Acre in 1191, then launched bitter, inconclusive forays against Saladin at Jerusalem. A year later, agreements freezing the European onslaught and opening Jerusalem to western pilgrims ended the stalemate. Crusading warriors fought on for another century, grimly holding the line in towering, isolated strongholds. Always short-handed, western commanders could never garrison castles and field attacking armies simultaneously. Islam's mounted archers—the heart of their fighting forces—gave Crusaders fits in open terrain, seldom closing for European-style brawls with sword and mace. In 1291, Acre, the last Christian stronghold, collapsed, ending the Great Crusades. Organized pilgrimages to the Holy Land ended in 1489: by then, history's first firearms had rendered armored knights obsolete.

In 11th-century Normandy, ace knight Heston commands an occupation force protecting villagers from "Frisian raiders." (Early Frisians were ferocious pagans, but they never formed the military monolith portrayed here: by 785,

Charlemagne had conquered and Christianized them.) Smitten by a village girl, he arbitrarily exploits an obscure law—the *Maritagium*—forcing her to sleep with him on her wedding night. The result: bloody mayhem without quarter. Fine filmmaking, but based on misconceptions about the *Maritagium*. (It applied only when bridegrooms failed to pay marriage fees. A canonical variation affected newlyweds enjoined by the Church to postpone honeymoons for 24 hours: at certain times, the *jus primae noctis* returned "right of the first night" to petitioning grooms.) Still, a fine castle set, a knockout performance by Boone (Heston's snarling lieutenant), and a grim final siege make this a must-see film for amateur historians.

For Further Viewing:
The Crusades ★ (1935) 123 Minutes (Henry Wilcoxon, Loretta Young, Ian Keith, C. Aubrey Smith): Cecil B. DeMille's Third Crusade cartoon showcases hot romance between Young (Navarre's Princess Berengaria) and Wilcoxon (Richard I), leaving history in tatters on the studio floor. Richard, for example, marries Berengaria to get beef cattle from her father (Richard's mother really arranged the match to secure Aquitaine's southern border). Worse still are DeMille's farcical wedding (Berengaria marries the absent king's sword!) and Richard's growing passion for his bride: in fact, the marriage probably remained unconsummated (Richard was a practicing homosexual—he publicly confessed this outside a Messina church in 1191). Crusader history also flops: Peter the Hermit appears a century too late, and on-screen cavalry combat is all wrong (Muslims fight only with swords, never as mounted archers). The upside: a fine rendition of the Acre siege and Keith's robust Saladin.
Excalibur ★★★ (1981) 140 Minutes (Nicol Williamson, Nigel Terry, Helen Mirren, Gabriel

Byrne, Nicholas Clay): Medieval records offer few solid facts about King Arthur. Welsh ruler Uther Pendragon was probably his father; Arthur led local resistance to Germanic invaders, defeating them in 516 at Mt. Badon (native Britons' last victory over the Anglo-Saxons), and he died between 538 and 542. Correctly setting his gory version of the Camelot legend "in the Dark Ages" (476–800 A.D.), director John Boorman makes Merlin the magician his key character and incorporates many elements from Arthurian legend: the doomed marriage to Guinevere; her adultery with Launcelot; Arthur's homicidal illegitimate son Mordred; the satanic enchantress Morgana. *Excalibur* convincingly re-creates the period's violence and wild-eyed superstition, but history buffs will gag on its worst blunders. Round-table cavaliers, for example, wear plate armor centuries before its invention—and they wear it around the clock (at meals, in meetings, during afternoon naps; in one segment, Uther copulates in it). An interesting—but downbeat and very strange—movie.

El Cid ★★★ (1961) 184 Minutes (Charlton Heston, Sophia Loren, Herbert Lom, Michael Hordern): Director Anthony Mann fills the screen with traditional Spanish legend: Vivar reluctantly kills Jimena's father in a duel; she hates him for it, then forgives him; Alfonso is impetuous, egotistical, jealous of others' successes (wrong on all counts); and Valencia's chamber of commerce couldn't top Heston's saintly Rodrigo. Worst of all, in a fabricated finale, the Cid's corpse—strapped on a galloping horse—leads Valencia's army to victory over besieging Moors. Even so, Mann has crafted a fine epic on subjects opaque for most audiences, earning top marks for authentic sieges, smash-mouth duels, and fine work by Lom (a pitiless Moorish commander).

Recommended Reading:

Raymond Rudorff, *Knights and the Age of Chivalry;* Frances and Joseph Gies, *Marriage and the Family in the Middle Ages;* Robert Payne, *The Dream and the Tomb: A History of the Crusades;* Richard Fletcher, *The Quest for El Cid.*

chapter 2

Early American
History

(Overleaf)
The Crucible
(Photofest)

Chronology

1492
OCTOBER 12: Columbus reaches San Salvador.

1565
SEPTEMBER: Spanish establish St. Augustine, Fla., oldest city in U.S.

1607
MAY: British found Jamestown, Va.

1620
NOVEMBER 21: *Mayflower* Compact.

DECEMBER 26: *Mayflower* lands at Plymouth, Mass.

1629
JUNE 27: Massachusetts Bay Colony established.

1630
Boston founded.

1692
MAY–OCTOBER: Salem witchcraft trials.

1718
New Orleans founded.

1754–1763
French and Indian War.

1765
MARCH 22: British pass Stamp Act.

1767
JUNE 29: England's Townshend Act places

import duties on goods shipped to American colonies.

1770
MARCH 5: Boston Massacre.

1773
APRIL 27: England passes Tea Act.

DECEMBER 16: Boston Tea Party: colonists disguised as Indians throw British tea shipments into Boston Harbor.

1774
MARCH 31: British Parliament passes first of four "Intolerable Acts" punishing colonists for Boston Tea Party.

SEPTEMBER 5–OCTOBER 26: First Continental Congress convenes in Philadelphia.

1775
APRIL 19: First skirmishes between British troops and American irregulars (Lexington and Concord, Mass.).

JUNE 17: British win Battle of Bunker Hill.

1776
JULY 4: Declaration of Independence.

SEPTEMBER 22: British hang Nathan Hale for espionage.

1777
OCTOBER 17: Colonists defeat British at

Saratoga, wrecking Britain's plan to split colonies in two along Hudson River.

NOVEMBER 15: Continental Congress adopts Articles of Confederation.

DECEMBER 17: Continental Army winters in Valley Forge, Pa.

1778
FEBRUARY 6: France recognizes U.S. independence.

1779
SEPTEMBER 23: John Paul Jones defeats British frigate *Serapis.*

1781
OCTOBER 19: British general Cornwallis surrenders to Washington at Yorktown, Va.

1783
SEPTEMBER 3: Treaty of Paris ends Revolutionary War.

1787
MAY 25: Constitutional Convention opens in Philadelphia.

1789
MARCH 4: Constitution goes into effect.

APRIL 30: Washington inaugurated president.

1790
DECEMBER 6: Capital moved from New York to Philadelphia.

1791
DECEMBER 15: Bill of Rights becomes part of Constitution.

1792
DECEMBER 5: Washington reelected. Runner-up John Adams becomes vice president.

1796
SEPTEMBER 17: Washington's Farewell Address. Adams elected president in December.

1800
JUNE: Washington, D.C., becomes permanent U.S. capital. President Thomas Jefferson sworn in there March 4, 1801.

1808
DECEMBER 7: James Madison elected president.

1812
JUNE 4 AND 8: Congress votes for war with Great Britain.

JUNE 18: Madison declares war on Great Britain.

1814
DECEMBER 24: War of 1812 ends with the Treaty of Ghent.

1815
JANUARY 8: Battle of New Orleans, fought after war has ended.

Amistad ★★

(1997) 152 Minutes

Director: Steven Spielberg

Cast: Djimon Hounsou, Anthony Hopkins, Morgan Freeman, Matthew McConaughey, Stellan Skarsgård, Nigel Hawthorne

Historical Background: Nineteenth-century slave-trafficking was big business on a global scale: by 1795, slaves formed 20% of America's population, and 50 years later the entire federal budget totaled only 10% of the cash value of American slaves. Arab slavers brutally harvested and sold slaves from the Ivory Coast to the far side of the Indian Ocean. For Barbary pirates, everyone was fair game: at one point, Algiers held 25,000 enslaved white westerners. Even native West Africans practiced slavery: many built (and filled) coastal holding depots for big-spending Arab traffickers. (For this reason, few American slaves—17,000 between 1819 and 1845—returned to Liberia, an American-established African colony for freedmen: they knew that local traders would probably enslave them again.)

England finally stood up and said no to all of this. An 1807 abolition bill outlawed slave-trading (but not slaveholding) in English dominions worldwide, and aftershocks from Dutch slaveowner atrocities in England's newly won Demerara colony (in present-day Guyana) eventually killed British institutionalized slavery. An 1823 crown dispatch banned flogging in Demerara, but the planters ignored it, igniting a slave revolt. Quickly regrouping, the Dutch slaughtered 200 slaves and murdered John Smith, a Congregational missionary and slave sympathizer. Ordinary Brits were furious, hounding Parliament until it abolished slavery entirely in 1834.

There were many other rebellions. One of the most exotic peaked in America and turned, in part, on Britain's landmark legislation. In 1839, 52 Sierra Leone prisoners led by Singbe Pieh (renamed Cinqué in Cuban captivity) mutinied on the *Amistad,* captured the slave schooner, killed its captain, and ordered surviving crewmen to head for Africa. They sailed east during the day but covertly changed course at night, and the ship ended up near Long Island 60 days later. Authorities jailed 43 surviving slaves on murder and mutiny charges, and the Spaniards—insisting the mutineers were Cubans born into slavery—demanded their return. Led by New York entrepreneur Lewis Tappan, Evangelical abolitionists publicized the affair, recruited eminent lawyer Roger Baldwin, and defended the slaves in the Hartford, Connecticut, district tribunal, eventually taking the case to the U.S. Supreme Court. (For political reasons, President Martin Van Buren intervened for the Spaniards, unconstitutionally merging executive and judicial functions—and failing miserably, in the end.) Former president John Quincy Adams joined Baldwin in Washington, eloquently reprising his argument that the mutineers were Africans taken illegally from a British protectorate. On March 9, 1841, the Court ruled for the mutineers, and ten months later they were back in Sierra Leone.

Amistad scores several bull's-eyes: a fine performance by Hounsou (Cinqué), a bravura segment on the terrible transatlantic passage, and an accurate presentation of the affair's legal trappings. Many errors are harmless enough: at film's end, Spielberg all but sanctifies Jefferson (a slave-holder); he reduces Adams' two-day Supreme Court oration to brief invocations of everyone's ancestors; he concocts a closing Cinqué–Adams conversation that never took place.

But Spielberg's overall presentation of the *Amistad* story badly falsifies history, ridiculing the Evangelicals and obscuring their key role in the case. (Without them, the mutineers would have been back on the trading block immediately.) He misrepresents Baldwin, and by extension the community that at its own expense returned the mutineers to Sierra Leone. During a meeting, for example, Tappan (Skarsgård) says, "Christ went to the cross to make a statement," and Baldwin (McConaughey) replies, "Christ lost." The fatuous, anachronistic dialogue is bad enough; far worse is its trivialization of Baldwin's religious beliefs: like Tappan, Baldwin was a Christian abolitionist and would have insisted that Christ *was* the statement ("In the beginning was the Word . . . and the Word was God," John 1—a favorite passage of Evangelicals). Tappan was severe, overly decorous, authoritarian, and aloof—but like it or not, he launched the mutineers' rescue and kept it alive. *Amistad* should have been a great film—unfortunately, Hollywood got in the way.

Recommended Reading:
Mary Cable, *Black Odyssey: The Case of the Slave Ship* Amistad; Bertram Wyatt-Brown, *Lewis Tappan and the Evangelical War Against Slavery;* Paul Johnson, *The Birth of the Modern: World Society, 1815–1830.*

Black Robe ★★★★

(1991) 101 Minutes

Director: Bruce Beresford

Cast: Lothaire Bluteau, August Schellenberg, Aden Young, Tantoo Cardinal, Sandrine Holt, Yvan Labelle

Historical Background: On March 17, 1649, Father Jean de Brébeuf finally died after enduring the most sadistic torments ever inflicted on a New World missionary. The revolting catalog of horrors meted out by his Iroquois captors ended in an orgy of ritual cannibalism (the Indians cut large pieces of flesh from his body and ate them while he was still alive). Brébeuf had pioneered a 23-year Jesuit mission to the Hurons in New France, the largest North American colony (it covered most of eastern Canada as well as the area between the Appalachian Mountains and the Missouri River in the U.S.). Numbering 20,000, the Hurons lived in 18 permanent villages located between Lake Simcoe and Georgian Bay on the southern Ontario Peninsula. They built sophisticated agricultural systems, growing tobacco, squash, beans, and corn. Suspicious at first, they gradually warmed to the Jesuits and their projects (Ontario's first hospital and school, the region's first European-style farm, and the New World's first canal system). Missionaries also brought the Indians of New France hatchets, steel knives, and highly prized bolts of woven cloth.

The Hurons were far more advanced

than their traditional enemies, the five tribes of the Iroquois League (the Mohawk, Oneida, Cayuga, Seneca, and Onondaga). Often called an "enlightened" political system, the confederation was a military alliance breeding arrogance and igniting Iroquois wars of conquest against other Canadian tribes for the sole purpose of taking and enslaving prisoners—or killing them by ritual torture. French missionary Jacques Bruyas, appalled by the Iroquois' bloodlust, noted that they would gladly travel 900 miles— the distance from Quebec City to the Ste. Marie Mission—to take scalps. By midcentury, the scalps they wanted most were Huron and French. (In 1615, explorer Samuel de Champlain had helped a Huron raiding party fight off a band of Mohawks, making the entire Iroquois League France's implacable enemy.)

Iroquois armies launched an all-out war of extermination against the Hurons and "black robes" in July 1648. By 1650, fewer than 300 Hurons remained alive: the Iroquois had killed most of them, though many had died from diseases brought to New France by Europeans. On June 10, the last of 12 Jesuit missions burned to the ground. The Iroquois had murdered 20% of the Roman Catholic priests in Huronia by then, and it would be 150 years before Europeans ventured into the vast Canadian interior again.

A moving, evenhanded look at European and Native American cultures divided by mutual incomprehension and struggling to survive the daily rigors of life on Canada's early-17th-century Indian frontier, based on Brian Moore's fine novel of the same name. Bluteau excels as Father Laforgue, a young Jesuit leading a 1,500-mile expedition to New France's Ste. Marie Mission. Equally outstanding are Holt (a

Huron girl attached to the expedition) and Labelle, who revels wildly in his role as Mestigoit, a strange, hyperkinetic Montagnais holy man. Deliberately paced, loaded with period detail, and beautifully filmed in Canada's northern woodlands.

Recommended Reading:
Brian Moore, *Black Robe;* Glenn Kittler, *Saint in the Wilderness: The Story of St. Isaac Jogues and the Jesuit Adventure in the New World;* Robert M. Utley and William E. Washburn, *The American Heritage History of the Indian Wars.*

The Buccaneer ★★★

(1958) 121 Minutes

Director: Anthony Quinn

Cast: Yul Brynner, Charlton Heston, Claire Bloom, Charles Boyer, Inger Stevens

Historical Background: In August 1813, a large force of British-allied Creek Indians murdered 553 people in Samuel Mims' southern Alabama stockade, disemboweling the pregnant women and leaving them to broil in the smothering Gulf Coast heat. Well before the War of 1812, Britain had sponsored Indian attacks to rout American border settlers from territories claimed by both countries. Even worse:

at war with France, England interdicted U.S.-French maritime trade and forced 5,000 Americans—at gunpoint—to serve on British warships. Infuriated, Congress declared war on June 18, 1812.

Manning bigger, faster ships, the tiny U.S. Navy fought well on the high seas and Great Lakes. America's ground troops fared worse, losing battle after battle; in August 1814, British forces marched into Washington, firing the Capitol, White House, and Treasury buildings. The only significant Yankee victories belonged to Andrew Jackson's 5,000 brawling volunteers. In 1813, they'd crushed Creek armies at Tallushatchee and Talladega, then slaughtered 900 warriors at Horseshoe Bend, taking the Indians completely out of the conflict. The war's most critical battle raged hotly two weeks after the Treaty of Ghent formally ended hostilities. By January 1815, Jackson had occupied New Orleans. On the eighth, a veteran British army launched frontal assaults at the city's Rodriguez Canal against 5,100 Yankee sharpshooters and pirate skipper Jean Laffite's cannoneers (commanded by his brother Alexandre). Under withering Kentucky-rifle fire, the British got close enough to shoot their anemic smooth-bores for a grand total of five minutes. Jackson's Americans lost 23 men, flattening an incredible 2,036 enemy soldiers. It was a stunning knockout punch—had Jackson lost, Britain would have controlled the Mississippi and occupied (temporarily, at least) a daunting chunk of North America.

Accurate in spirit, Quinn's entertaining chronicle of the New Orleans battle slings ample fiction: its romantic entanglements are claptrap; Heston's Jackson is far too old; Brynner's Laffite is too volatile and impolitic; and one of his

brothers—Pierre, a key figure—never appears. But *The Buccaneer* is worth a look, if only for its spectacular, accurate rendition of the battle.

Recommended Reading:
Robin Reilly, *The British at the Gates: The New Orleans Campaign in the War of 1812.*

Christopher Columbus ★★★

(1985) 135 Minutes

Director: Alberto Lattuada

Cast: Gabriel Byrne, Faye Dunaway, Oliver Reed, Eli Wallach, Nicol Williamson

Historical Background: October 12, 1492: In rapt wonder, Christopher Columbus fell to his knees on San Salvador Island's northeastern shore, finally ending a blind, harrowing journey into the absolute unknown. Piloting three 80-ton ships, he and 90 men had taken 70 days to complete the first European transatlantic voyage, changing forever the historical trajectory of an entire planet. It was a triumph of perseverance, dazzling nautical skills, and eleventh-hour good luck. Born in Genoa in 1451, Columbus had spent most of his life at sea by his 30th birthday. Determined to pioneer westward commercial sea lanes to Cathay, he moved to Castile in 1485, spent seven years hawking exploration proposals in Spain's royal court, and—with Queen Isabella's keen support—acquired, provisioned, and rigged two caravels (*Niña* and *Pinta*) and the flagship *Santa María* for a long, rough ride: all of this despite stern warnings by experts that Columbus had gravely underestimated the 38,830,000-square-mile Atlantic's width. They were all too correct (and none of them held flat-earth theories: virtually all literate late-medieval Europeans understood that the planet was spherical).

On August 3, 1492, Columbus' tiny fleet left Palos, cruised down Africa's northwestern coast, turned due west at the Canary Islands, and spent five pressure-packed weeks at sea (a brief mutiny ignited and fizzled 48 hours before landfall). Thirty-one days into the voyage, lookouts spotted massive bird concentrations to the southwest, and Columbus—on a hunch—changed course, trailing them all the way to San Salvador. Convinced they'd reached Cathay's offshore islands, the Spaniards befriended local Taïnos natives, weighed anchor, launched a groping search for mainland Asia, and found Cuba (October 24) instead. Six weeks later they reached Haiti (christened Hispaniola by Columbus), left 39 men to build Europe's first settlement in the Americas (Navidad), and returned to Barcelona in March 1493, dazzling everyone with exotic spices, native jewelry, and several Indian captives. A large colonizing venture (1493–96) and two more explorations (1498–1500 and 1502-4) by Columbus ranged from Hispaniola to Venezuela's Trinidad Island. (Internecine melees and Indian warfare rocked the second and third voyages: on November 27, 1493, advance elements of the second expedition found Navidad's colonists butchered by Carib raiders. Savage reprisals led by homicidal loose cannons Alonso de Ojeda and Mosen Margarit escalated the violence. Between the two voyages, Francisco Roldán and Adrián de Muxica led revolts against Columbus' brother Bartolomé—acting *adelantado* during the admiral's absence. Both insurrections fizzled, and Columbus—back from Cádiz in 1500—executed seven rebels.)

Brilliant, overconfident, insubordinate, and incredibly tenacious, Columbus was no saint, but he certainly wasn't the leering demon drawn by many quincentenary authors. He did enslave a number of Indians, and embattled colonial troops killed others. On both sides, it was ugly business, but it wasn't state-sponsored European genocidal oppression: Ferdinand and Isabella detested slavery, hotly censuring Columbus for the practice more than once. And Columbus—a genius at sea—was a lousy administrator, blind to certain subordinates' simmering ambitions and thinly cloaked taste for violence: this encouraged sporadic—not systematic—atrocities by brutal freelances such as Ojeda. Columbus died in Valladolid, Spain, on May 20, 1506—unaware of what, precisely, he'd discovered in 1492.

Byrne is dynamic in the lead, and Lattuada usually sticks to the facts (Columbus' long battle for first-voyage state backing, his feud with Roldán, the San Salvador landing, and dealings with Taïnos natives). But history suffers more than once: condemned criminals form most of Byrne's crew—in fact, only three first-voyage crewmen ever logged jail-time; to keep Columbus squeaky-clean, the film shifts responsibility for slave-taking to the crown (utterly false).

Worst of all, Lattuada demonizes the Church for systematically "exploiting . . . the Indians for revenue"—an appalling historical falsification: Pope Paul III's *Sublimis Deus* encyclical sternly forbade enslaving or disenfranchising Indians, and the Dominican Order fiercely resisted mistreatment of Native Americans. Still, a reasonably faithful, absorbing overview of Columbus' career.

For Further Viewing:
1492: Conquest of Paradise ★★ (1992) 145 Minutes (Gerard Depardieu, Sigourney Weaver, Armand Assante, Angela Molina, Fernando Rey): Director Ridley Scott's epic crazily scrambles Columbian hagiography with politically correct anti-Catholic/European nonsense: everyone but Columbus buys the flat-earth fallacy; in a florid performance, Rey weirdly inflates Muxica's importance, cramming every conceivable Evil European Oppressor cliché into a single character; Depardieu's mumbling Columbus idealizes the navigator but guts his walloping personality; etc., etc., *ad nauseam.* Lovely to look at, but historically off-course.

Recommended Reading:
Robert Royal, *1492 and All That: Political Manipulations of History;* Felipe Fernández-Armesto, *Columbus;* William D. Phillips, Jr., and Carla Rahn Phillips, *The Worlds of Christopher Columbus;* Samuel Eliot Morison, *The European Discovery of America.*

The Crucible ★

(1996) 123 Minutes

Director: Nicholas Hynter

Cast: Daniel Day-Lewis, Winona Ryder, Paul Scofield, Rob Campbell, Bruce Davison

Historical Background: The 17th century produced empirical science, modern society's technological foundations, and a near-universal obsession with witchcraft. In England, for example, Robert Boyle pioneered the study of ordinary air's role in sound transmission—but witchcraft and hoodoo therapeutics fascinated him (he touted the "medical virtues" of stewed earthworms and believed that "subterranean demons" infested British coal mines). Black magic's zenith came before midcentury: between 1600 and 1650, more than 5,000 witches in France's Alsace region burned at the stake. Unlike organized religion, witchcraft has no formal doctrines, only a moldy grab bag of charms, spells, incantations—all offering fertility, health, or soothsaying. Three degrees codify "the Craft": white magic (benevolent, featuring rabbit's feet and love potions), black magic (malicious, aided by Lucifer), and "pact" (Satan worship—the third, horrific degree). Image magic—melting wax figurines, burning or stabbing goat's-hair dolls—dominates black-magic ritual.

History's oddest witch-hunt came at century's end in Salem Village in the royal colony of Massachusetts. In February 1692, Betty Parris (age nine) and Abigail Williams (age 11) sickened physically, then lapsed into convulsive fits marked by amnesia, deafness, bloating, hallucinations, tongue contracture, and involuntary cryptic prattle. Medical examinations drew charges of witchery tutelage—against Sarah Osburn, Sarah Good, and Tituba (a Carib Indian slave)—from the girls. On March 1, village magistrates arrested the three women. Tituba soon confessed to third-degree witchery, describing a "Devil's Book" signed by nine Salem women. Off-the-chart panic swept Salem: in May, colonial governor William Phillips arrived, opened a special court, and launched a series of trials, eventually convicting 150 people of sorcery. Nineteen died on the gallows, and a 20th was crushed to death for refusing to testify. Many familiar bromides about the affair collapse under cursory scrutiny. Puritanism, for example, caused nothing—Lutherans, Anglicans, Catholics, and Quakers also prosecuted witches. Some victims may have lied—but not all of them: like other towns, Salem hosted practicing witches, and their power probably relied on collective fear intense enough to ignite pathological hysteria (the clinical symptoms match). And most New England clergymen tried to temper (not aggravate) Salem's witch mania. In October, moderation finally triumphed with the summary dissolution of Phillips' special court.

This leering rendition of Arthur Miller's attack on McCarthyism features knockout location filming and period detail (courtroom, chapel, and household sets, picture-postcard farms, hand-sewn linen costumes). Otherwise, Hynter peddles benighted cliché throughout, trashing Salem's clergy and blaming everything on repressed sexuality—had that been the case, half the world's teenagers would have dabbled in sorcery. Even worse: Ryder—an overage, panting Abigail—ignites intermittent, unintended low comedy, groping Lewis roughly (and often) enough to qualify him for multiple purple-heart nominations.

For Further Viewing:

Maid of Salem ★★★ (1937) 86 Minutes (Claudette Colbert, Fred MacMurray, Gale Sondergaard, Louise Dresser): Director Frank Lloyd's aging gem is reasonably solid, despite many fictions and anachronisms: a girl harboring grudges against Tituba, for example, ignites witchcraft hysteria after reading Cotton Mather's *Wonders of the Invisible World*—actually published much later. Lloyd delivers a balanced view of the Puritans—all aren't moping, superstitious killjoys—and makes the witch-hunt's protracted fury flow more from rumor and popular frenzy than calculated theocratic persecution. Fine work by Colbert (a witch-hunt casualty) and witty, realistic dialogue. (Fish in school-house etiquette: "Speak not, sing not, hum not, and spit only in the corner").

Recommended Reading:

Chadwick Hansen, *Witchcraft at Salem.*

The Howards of Virginia ★★★

(1940) 122 Minutes

Director: Frank Lloyd

Cast: Cary Grant, Martha Scott, Cedric Hardwicke, Richard Carlson

Historical Background: In May 1775, Benjamin Franklin, John Adams, and George

Washington prepared to lead one-third of America's colonists in bloody revolt against history's largest empire. (More than 30% of the colonial population—including Franklin's son William—backed England; most lived in Georgia, South Carolina, and New York. Loyalists suffered terribly throughout the war, losing homes, employment, and all of their money. Eventually, 80,000 resettled in Canada or returned to England.) Colonial anti-British rage dates from the Seven Years War: groaning under a huge national debt, victorious England bled its colonies for revenue, slapping an internal tax (the 1765 Stamp Act) on newspapers and legal documents. Duties on tea, paint, glass, and lead came in 1767. Indocile Yankees fumed: for a century, they'd practiced advise-and-consent self-government—colonial assemblies passed laws, representatives presented them to the crown for approval, and that was that. Suddenly, all this was history: angry, powerless colonists began boycotting British imports and trashing customs warehouses.

Despite warnings from prudent diplomatic veterans, Britain's King George escalated, packing Boston with jittery British regulars. (A tragic figure, George III blindly drove his colonies toward revolt. Intelligent, but relentlessly inflexible and unschooled in colonial affairs, he surrounded himself with mediocre political hacks contemptuous of American leaders and colonial representatives. In 1788, he weathered a temporary fit of madness caused by porphyria, an inherited metabolic disorder. The awful attacks recurred at least three times before his death in 1820.) By 1775, Massachusetts was a powder keg. On April 19—a year after Parliament closed Boston's port to retaliate for 1773's infamous "Tea Party"—Yankee militiamen gunned down 275 redcoats near Lexington and Concord.

The war was on. Chronically outmanned, the Continental Army faced 42,000 British regulars and 30,000 German mercenaries. (At Valley Forge, disease and hunger temporarily reduced George Washington's 20,000-man hibernating force to 3,000 able-bodied soldiers.) But Washington waged a brilliant eight-year war of attrition, whittling away at his adversaries piecemeal. (British soldiers carried wildly inaccurate smoothbore muskets: to hit anything at all, they had to fire thundering volleys from close ranks. Packing powerful, accurate flintlock hunting rifles, American sharpshooters usually stayed out of musket range, riddling massed British formations at will.)

In 1778, France joined the fight, making the Revolution a full-fledged international conflict and fueling the colonial war effort—heavily reliant on weaponry and provisions shipped from Nantes—by keeping Atlantic sea-lanes open. (Scottish-born John Paul Jones became the war's maritime legend. Facing murder charges, he fled to America in 1774, joined the skeletal Continental Navy, and in 1776 skippered the *Providence.* In one two-month rampage, he captured eight British ships and sank eight others. His finest hour came in 1779: piloting the sluggish 40-gun *Bonhomme Richard,* Jones defeated England's redoubtable *Serapis* in a four-hour, no-quarter North Sea brawl.) In September 1781, French warships ferried 15,800 French and American troops to Virginia's York–James Peninsula and blockaded Chesapeake Bay, trapping Charles Cornwallis' 8,000 redcoats in Yorktown. They surrendered on October 19, virtually ending the ground war. On September 3, 1783, the Treaty of Paris formally closed the American Revolution.

Grant and Scott (Hardwicke's sister) build a profitable Shenandoah plantation, then revolution splits the family (Grant revolts, Hardwicke remains loyal), taking a heavy toll on everyone. Lloyd's look at rural colonial life excels, and his flickering mid-film catalog of British outrages, the war's opening salvoes, and a grimly tenacious Continental Army is accurate. But Lloyd's Jefferson loves commoners (the real Jefferson called them "the swinish multitude"), his Loyalists are all highborn snobs (not true), and his ordinary Englishmen are rebel sympathizers (most Brits were apathetic). Still, a rare, decent wire-to-wire chronicle of Revolutionary America.

For Further Viewing:

John Paul Jones ★★★★ (1959) 126 Minutes (Robert Stack, Charles Coburn, Peter Cushing, Bette Davis): Director John Farrow's remarkably accurate account of Jones' career, opening with his first voyage (at age 12) and chronicling his brilliant Revolutionary War performance. Farrow compresses history occasionally and tweaks a few facts for dramatic purposes: Jones, for example, never owned a colonial farm, and his brother's estate went to a sister in Scotland, not to him. Nevertheless, great fare for history buffs, with wonderful nautical sets, Coburn's superb Franklin, and a rousing *Serapis–Bonhomme Richard* shootout.

The Madness of King George ★★★★ (1994) 107 Minutes (Nigel Hawthorne, Helen Mirren, Ian Holm, Rupert Everett, Julian Rhind-Tutt): Nicholas Hytner's knockout version of Alan Bennet's play about the king's first illness is on target historically most of the time. Highlights include George's harrowing 1788–89 confinement in Kew's Old Palace; Everett's overfed, hedonistic Prince of Wales; Rhind-Tutt's cold, efficient, book-balancing William Pitt the Younger; and barbarous 18th-century medical "remedies." Best of all, Hawthorne's marvelous George isn't a weak, neu-

rotic monarch—a common modern misconception, especially in the U.S.

Recommended Reading:

George F. Scheer and Hugh F. Rankin, *Rebels and Redcoats;* Robert McCluer Calhoon, *The Loyalists in Revolutionary America, 1760–1781;* Samuel Eliot Morison, *John Paul Jones: A Sailor's Biography;* Ida Macalpine and Richard Hunter, *George III and the Mad Business.*

The Last of the Mohicans ★★

(1992) 122 Minutes

Director: Michael Mann

Cast: Daniel Day-Lewis, Madeleine Stowe, Russell Means, Eric Schweig, Wes Studi, Jodhi May

Historical Background: August 9, 1757—Fort William Henry, New York: Defeated and paroled by Louis de Montcalm's French–Abenakis Indian assault force, British colonel George Monro's garrison—2,000 strong, including women and children—began a 16-mile march to Fort Edward, leaving their sick and wounded behind. After the evacuation, Abenakis braves swarmed into the fort's hospital and murdered convalescents where they lay. Another Indian contingent ambushed Monro's column, butchering more than 200 men, women, and children. Immortalized by James Fenimore Cooper, the engagement remains the most famous action—for Americans—of the 1754–63 French and Indian War.

The conflict opened with France's schemes to block British colonial expansion west of the Appalachians. By midcentury, French fortifications dotted the Ohio Valley, stretching from the St. Lawrence River to the Mississippi. Initial salvoes came in 1754–55: Lt. Col. George Washington led a combined force of Virginia volunteers and Native American warriors on a fort-building mission near the Monongahela–Allegheny river confluence. Both sides had Indian allies: the Iroquois League (see *Black Robe*) backed England, and the Abenakis and Huron fought with France. Replacing no-show Iroquois scouts in 1756–57, the Mohicans—a Massachusetts Algonquian tribe—served brilliantly with British and colonial troops on the Lake Champlain front. Crack French regulars from Fort Duquesne routed Washington's Virginians, then slaughtered Scottish major general Edward Braddock's return expedition in 1755. For three years, the French hammered their adversaries into the ground, but British industrial might and naval power held, and in 1758–59, Anglo-colonial forces prevailed at Louisbourg, Fort Frontenac, Crown Point, Fort Niagara, and Quebec (Montcalm died there), virtually ending the war. On February 10, 1763, the Treaty of Paris gave England all of North America—and the world's greatest empire.

Great action, period detail, and cinematography—but awful history. Mann makes the British bumbling fools, demonizes the Hurons, drops the Fort William Henry hospital slaughter, and kills Monro during the fatal evacuation (he survived the real engagement). Mann's Montcalm is a brave, saintly gentleman—in fact, he did nothing to stop the sick-bay massacre. What could have been great fact-based filmmaking is instead a reasonably entertaining fantasy unrelated to history.

Recommended Reading:
Francis Jennings, *Empire of Fortune;* Patrick Frazier, *The Mohicans of Stockbridge.*

Plymouth Adventure ★★★★

(1952) 105 Minutes

Director: Clarence Brown

Cast: Spencer Tracy, Gene Tierney, Leo Genn, Dawn Addams, Lloyd Bridges

Historical Background: New Plymouth Colony's *Mayflower* religious separatists began dying methodically in late December 1620. Praying for an early spring, most spent the winter crammed into a hastily built 20-foot-square "Common House." The rest lived outside in dugouts—large foxholes shielded from howling New England winds by sod roofs seated on rickety wooden posts. They were begging for pestilence, and in January they got it: for three months, pneumonia and scurvy leveled the community—one death at a time—killing half the original company by March 31. The winter had been mild, but awful shipboard conditions and a grueling 65-day slog through mountainous seas had driven everyone's resistance through the floor.

An old wine transport worth £129, the *Mayflower* was about 90 feet long—only four yards longer than a tennis court—and 26 feet wide amidships. On September 16, she weighed anchor, groaning with 102 pilgrims, 47 officers and crewmen, and copious provisions: dogs, chickens, pigs, dried food—the works. (An unseaworthy consort ship, the *Speedwell*, turned back.) Smothering "'tween decks" quarters with five-foot ceilings crammed passengers into individual bed-sized living spaces. Aware that storms raked the Atlantic each fall, skipper Christopher Jones braced for a perilous voyage. The first squalls hit almost immediately, soaking everything on board—clothing, bedding, passengers, food. Seasickness raged—soon, unventilated passenger holds stank of bilge, human waste, and cooking-brazier smoke. On November 21—before the community unraveled—41 men signed William Bradford's *Mayflower* Compact, agreeing to build a "Civil Body Politic" and abide by its

laws. It was modern history's first social compact, a flat-out proclamation of the right to self-government stronger than anything yet seen in the colonies. A month later, the Pilgrims landed at Plymouth. In 1643 their representatives signed the Articles of Confederation for the United Colonies of New England, launching America's first experiment in constitutional government.

A terrifying mid-Atlantic storm and textbook-accurate history make this a superb Hollywood period piece. Brown mangles facts occasionally: Tracy's Jones irrationally detests the Pilgrims. In fact, they delayed launching for six weeks, guaranteeing a stormy autumn voyage and infuriating Jones; Tierney's Dorothy Bradford commits suicide (unconfirmed speculation); the Tracy–Tierney romance and his intentional off-course navigation are hokum. Otherwise, a terrific version of the epic voyage.

Recommended Reading:
Kate Caffrey, *The* Mayflower.

chapter 3

U.S. Civil War

(Overleaf)
Glory
(Photofest)

Chronology

1820

MARCH: "Missouri Compromise" prohibits slavery north of latitude 36°30′.

1854

MAY 30: Kansas–Nebraska Act.

1859

OCTOBER 16: John Brown seizes Harpers Ferry Arsenal.

1860

NOVEMBER 6: Lincoln elected president.

DECEMBER 20: South Carolina secedes.

1861

JANUARY 9–26: Mississippi, Florida, Alabama, Georgia, and Louisiana secede.

FEBRUARY 4: Confederate States of America formed; Jefferson Davis elected president.

FEBRUARY 23: Texas secedes.

APRIL 12: Confederates bombard Fort Sumter.

MAY 23: Virginia secedes.

MAY 6–JUNE 8: Arkansas, North Carolina, and Tennessee secede.

JULY 21: Confederates win First Battle of Bull Run.

1862

MARCH 9: Ironclads *Virginia* and *Monitor* fight to stalemate at Hampton Roads.

APRIL 6–7: Union wins Battle of Shiloh.

MAY 1: New Orleans falls to Union troops.

JUNE 1: Robert E. Lee named Army of Northern Virginia commander.

JUNE 26–JULY 1: The "Seven Days" of battles between Lee and McClellan wrecks McClellan's Peninsular Campaign.

AUGUST 29–30: Confederacy wins Second Battle of Bull Run.

SEPTEMBER 17: Battle of Antietam.

DECEMBER 13: Lee wins Battle of Fredericksburg.

1863

JANUARY 1: Emancipation Proclamation.

MAY 1–4: Lee wins at Chancellorsville. Stonewall Jackson killed.

MAY 3: U.S. Congress requires men between ages of 20 and 45 to register for draft.

JULY 1–3: Union wins at Gettysburg.

JULY 4: Vicksburg falls.

JULY 13–15: New York City draft riots.

NOVEMBER 23–25: Grant wins at Chattanooga.

1864
MARCH 9: Grant made Union Army commander.

MAY 5–6: Wilderness Campaign begins, continues into June.

MAY 8–19: Battle of Spotsylvania. Grant disengages, races for Cold Harbor.

MAY 11: Jeb Stuart killed at Yellow Tavern, Va.

JUNE 3: Lee wins at Cold Harbor.

SEPTEMBER 2: Atlanta falls.

NOVEMBER 8: Lincoln reelected.

NOVEMBER 16: Sherman begins march to sea.

DECEMBER 21: Savannah falls.

1865
APRIL 2: Richmond evacuated.

APRIL 9: Lee surrenders to Grant at Appomattox Courthouse, Va.

APRIL 14: John Wilkes Booth assassinates Lincoln.

APRIL 26: Booth killed in Virginia.

DECEMBER 18: Thirteenth Amendment prohibiting slavery ratified.

The Birth of a Nation ★★

(1915) 159 Minutes

Director: D. W. Griffith

Cast: Lillian Gish, Mae Marsh, Henry B. Walthall, Miriam Cooper

Historical Background: Abraham Lincoln's plans for rebuilding the shattered Confederacy died with him in April 1865, clearing the way for a 12-year power struggle between the Old South's landed aristocracy and Radical Republicans in Congress. Determined to create a new Southern power base, Lincoln's successor, Andrew Johnson, disenfranchised all former Confederate officers and opened much of the South's private property to confiscation. (As much as anything else, this period of "Congressional" and "presidential" Reconstruction, 1865–77, proved that fanatics on both sides of any issue are likely to be ruthless, greedy, and corrupt.)

Under provisional governors appointed by Johnson in 1865, most Southern state legislatures ratified the 13th Amendment, freeing black Americans. But fearing that 4 million newly freed, vengeful slaves would dominate state legislatures and fill governor's mansions throughout the region, Southerners illegally elected many former Confederate leaders to public office and passed "Black Codes" limiting the civil rights of former slaves. Led by Thaddeus Stevens, Radical Republicans retaliated with the 1867 Reconstruction Act—passed over Johnson's veto—establishing five Southern military districts and imposing *de facto* martial law throughout the entire region. Radicals then passed the Tenure of Office Act—again over Johnson's veto—blocking presidential dismissal of any cabinet member without Senate consent. (Protecting Secretary of War Edwin M. Stanton and preserving the Southern military occupation were the Republicans' true aims. Johnson fired Stanton anyway, and Congress impeached—but couldn't convict—him in 1868.) Passage of the 15th Amendment in 1870 guaranteed blacks the right to vote, but terrorist groups such as the Ku Klux Klan gained solid local support by keeping former slaves away from the polls. During the next seven years, Radical power shrank, and President Rutherford B. Hayes recalled all Federal troops from the South in 1877, ending Reconstruction.

Based on Thomas Dixon's *The Clansman,* Griffith's epic of apartheid remains popular among film buffs willing to ignore its tasteless bigotry. Many "facsimile" scenes are striking (accurate restagings of Lincoln's assassination, battle scenes modeled on Mathew Brady photographs). *The Birth of a Nation* delivers a harshly Confederate perspective on Reconstruction commonly held throughout much of the United States until the 1950s. Many historians have softened Griffith's fuming view of the era, describing it instead as a botched opportunity to deliver on promises won at enormous cost during the Civil War.

Recommended Reading:
James M. McPherson, *Ordeal by Fire: The Civil War and Reconstruction.*

Dark Command

(1940) 94 Minutes

Director: Raoul Walsh

Cast: John Wayne, Walter Pidgeon, Roy Rogers, Claire Trevor

Historical Background: In September 1864, "Bloody Bill" Anderson—William Quantrill's top lieutenant and the war's number-one homicidal psychopath—led 200 mounted "Bushwhackers" (proslavery guerrillas) to grisly triumph over Federal regulars near Centralia, Mo. Suddenly surrounded, 115 Union infantrymen fired a few shots, dropped their weapons, and surrendered. Minutes later, all were dead on the ground, their bloody scalps festooning Bushwhacker bridles. Racked by mayhem long before Fort Sumter fell, the Kansas–Missouri inferno saw more remorseless savagery than any other Civil War theater.

The 1854 Kansas–Nebraska Act opened both territories for settlement, allowing residents to choose or reject slavery by referendum. Nebraskans quickly went free-state, but Kansas was up for grabs. Envisioning an abolitionist juggernaut on their western flank, Missourians flooded Kansas with proslavery voters, and Kansas free-staters battled to keep them out. (In 1854, Radicals founded Lawrence, loading it with armed abolitionist settlers financed by the New England Emigrant Aid Co.) By 1857, "Bleeding Kansas" had produced more than 200 mangled corpses. Matching Anderson's blood mania death-for-death were Kansas' pro-Union "Jayhawkers," mustered by Jim Lane—

a power-mad, dissolute, gaunt fanatic. On September 22, 1861, Lane's "Red Legs" (1,500 "diseased, mutinous rabble," according to a camp follower) thundered through Osceola, Mo., plundering banks, stores, and homes, killing nine civilians, then torching the town. By January 1862, they had sacked Morristown, Independence, Pleasant Hill, West Point, and Harrisonville.

Organized and led by Quantrill, raging Bushwhackers retaliated. They burned bridges and sank Union boats on the Blue River. They hijacked Federal mail, gunned down Federal patrols, ransacked Union trains, and terrorized abolitionist towns along the 270-mile Kansas–Missouri frontier. Their bloodiest raid came on August 21, 1863: aiming to kidnap and execute Lane, 450 Bushwhackers tore into Lawrence, guns blazing. They wrecked the town, stole everything they could carry, and murdered 150 men and boys—all while Quantrill ate breakfast at a local hotel. (Lane scurried into a cornfield, surviving unscathed.) Border-state violence didn't end with the war: on May 10, 1865, Union soldiers killed Quantrill in Kentucky; three of his men—Cole Younger and the James brothers—formed history's most celebrated outlaw gang. In 1866, Lane sank into madness and shot himself with a revolver, lingering for days before dying. His last words: "Bad, bad."

Republic Pictures hawked this potboiler as solid history to Kansas and Missouri secondary schools. Pidgeon plays an overage, cultured "Will Cantrell": this is all you need to know before changing channels or finding a good book. Wayne—elected marshal of Lawrence (over Pidgeon!)—chases sore loser Cantrell all over Kansas, finally killing him in a pulp-fiction finale. A tedious, intrusive Wayne–Trevor–Pidgeon triangle flops badly. A wire-to-wire, inaccurate catastrophe: even Walsh's version of the Lawrence bloodbath is wrong (the town wins).

For Further Viewing:
Kansas Raiders ★★ (1950) 80 Minutes (Audie Murphy, Brian Donlevy, Scott Brady, Tony Curtis): A few facts gamely surface in this obscure B movie: Lane's men are "Red Legs"; Quantrill (Donlevy) inducts recruits under a black flag (a venerated—but unverified—tradition in Quantrill lore); Brady plays a lethal Bloody Bill. But fiction usually prevails: led by Jesse (Murphy), the entire James gang—actually formed after the war—joins the Bushwhackers; a contrite, middle-aged Quantrill dies heroically to save Jesse's life; and the James boys are honorable, misled idealists. Entertaining—but not for Civil War purists.

Recommended Reading:
Duane Schultz, *Quantrill's War: The Life and Times of William Clarke Quantrill.*

Drums in the Deep South ★★★

(1951) 87 Minutes

Director: William Cameron Menzies

Cast: Barbara Payton, James Craig, Guy Madison, Barton MacLane, Craig Stevens

Historical Background: The Civil War saw greater civilian participation, grimmer civilian suffering, and more internecine bickering than any other American conflict. Throughout the war, virtually every state housed full-throated dissenters on the great issues—slavery and secession. In the North, simmering opposition to the conflict—strong from the start in Illinois, Michigan, Ohio, and Indiana—gathered steam and spread with Lincoln's Emancipation Proclamation, flaring into pitched battle on New York City's teeming streets in mid-July 1863: conscription riots took more than 100 lives there before 40 infantry regiments finally restored order. Northern antiwar groups—the Copperheads, Knights of the Golden Circle, and Sons of Liberty—thrived. Many Southern civilians just wanted to be left alone. To feed its troops, Richmond ordered farmers to fork over 10% of their crops, infuriating everyone—especially small, nonslaveholding planters. Many upland Virginia farmers resented the squeeze: their state didn't secede until May 23—three months after other Southerners formed the Confederate government responsible for burdensome impressment laws. Civilians in nine Southern states formed battalion-size infantry units, marched north, and fought for the Union.

Raging across the invaded Confederacy, bitter fighting muted local antiwar factions and visited awful suffering on Southern noncombatants. Their worst hardships came with Union general William Tecumseh Sherman's barbarous 1864 sweep from Chattanooga to the Atlantic. On May 6, his crushing 98,000-man juggernaut rolled into Georgia, driving straight for Atlanta and laying waste to 120 miles of mineral and agricultural resources vital to the Confederate war effort. Opposing him were 60,000 tenacious rebels under

Joseph E. Johnson. Waging a torrid fighting retreat, Johnson hammered away at Sherman's legions, hoping to cut their communication and supply lines and bleed them down to size before they overran Atlanta. It didn't work. Sherman countered with a series of quick, bloody flanking thrusts, driving the rebels all the way to the Chattahoochee River by midsummer. On July 18, John Bell Hood replaced Johnson; he fought engagements at Peachtree Creek, Decatur, and Ezra Crossing between the 20th and 28th, then withdrew to Atlanta's stoutly fortified trenchworks. Under heavy siege, Hood's tattered garrison held out for a month, finally evacuating the city on September 1.

The Federals occupied Atlanta, wrecked its central railyard, leveled every public building in town, and torched most of the city, all by early November. Aiming to crush civilian support for rebel armies in the Deep South, Sherman launched a 62,000-man southeastward onslaught through the heart of Georgia on November 16. Rumbling toward Savannah in two massive columns flanked by hundreds of "bummers" (deserters from both sides bent on stealing everything they could), Union troops burned crops, confiscated far more food than their army could possibly eat, shot hundreds of animals, and looted countless homes—including slave cabins—along a smoldering 60-mile front. Despite standing orders to run them off, 25,000 fugitive blacks (Sherman called them "useless mouths") trailed the columns. The nightmare continued for 425 miles. Savannah fell on December 21, and the only Confederates able to fight on waited in the Carolinas and lower Virginia for the end. It came three and a half months later—on April 9, 1865, Robert E.

Lee's starving army surrendered at Appomattox Courthouse.

West Point grad Madison leaves Georgia to fight for the Union, returning three years later with Sherman's Atlanta-bound army. His orders: defend a Chattanooga–Atlanta rail line against rebel saboteurs led by former Academy classmate Craig. Secretly informed of Yankee plans by old flame Payton, Craig and his men dig in and start shelling the tracks. Menzies' fictional story unfolds in an authentic setting: throughout the war, both sides relied heavily on railroads for troop and supply transport, and rebel efforts to block Sherman's march to Atlanta were at least as stubborn as the film suggests. Definitely an offbeat movie, but historically faithful—in spirit, at least—to a critical phase of the war neglected by Hollywood.

For Further Viewing:
Shenandoah ★★★ (1965) 105 Minutes (James Stewart, Doug McClure, Glenn Corbett, Patrick Wayne, Katharine Ross, Philip Alford): Director Andrew McLaglen's look at a cantankerous Virginia widower (Stewart) determined to keep his family out of the war. Union troops imprison his youngest son (Alford) and scavengers further decimate his clan while he's off searching for the boy. McLaglen draws a vivid picture of the conflict's violent encroachment on civilian life. (And the war did snare many children: 11-year-old Charles Hab was the youngest Confederate trooper, and Curtis Black, age nine, the youngest Yank.) Entertaining, but liberally peppered with factual lapses: *Shenandoah* insists that slavery caused the war (emancipation wasn't an official Federal objective until 1863), ignoring Southern contempt for remote centralized government.

Friendly Persuasion ★★★★ (1956) 140 Minutes (Gary Cooper, Dorothy McGuire, Anthony Perkins, Marjorie Main, Robert Middleton, Richard Eyer): Cooper, McGuire, and Perkins shine in William Wyler's terrific film about southern Indiana Quakers rocked by the war despite their efforts to stay on the sidelines. Torn between Quaker pacifism and commitment to the Union, Cooper's son (Perkins) joins a home-guard unit to fight rebel general John Hunt Morgan's invading cavalry—and Cooper sets out to find him. More period drama than war chronicle, but basically on-target historically: Morgan's raids in Indiana and Ohio marked the Confederacy's northernmost thrusts into Union territory. Wyler's sudden shift, at film's end, from deliberately paced segments on Midwestern rural life to violent battle scenes delivers a walloping view of the war's capricious impact on civilians.

Recommended Reading:
Corydon Edward Foote, *With Sherman to the Sea: A Drummer's Story of the Civil War.*

Gettysburg ★★

(1993) 248 Minutes

Director: Robert Maxwell

Cast: Jeff Daniels, Sam Elliott, Richard Jordan, Tom Berenger, Stephen Lang, Martin Sheen

Historical Background: Despite its glittering military record, the Confederacy faced near-desperate circumstances in May 1863. Confronting vastly outnumbered rebel forces were huge Union armies dotting a 1,000-mile front from the Mississippi River to Richmond. Grant's 47,000-man army surrounded Vicksburg, cutting the city off from resupply and reinforcement. The Union's naval blockade had severely cut shipment of basic goods to Southern civilians. Something had to be done, and Robert E. Lee devised a bold plan: he would invade the Union for a second time, forcing a negotiated settlement of the war by drawing Grant away from Vicksburg, smashing Union forces between Harrisburg and Washington, and threatening to overrun the Northern capital.

The Army of Northern Virginia crossed the Potomac on June 15 at Williamsport, Md. By June 24, the rebels had moved all the way to Chambersburg, Pa. Unknown to Lee, Union forces shadowed every move he made, carefully staying between his army and Washington. On July 1, two Federal cavalry brigades under General John Buford ran smack into forward elements of Lee's invasion force north of Gettysburg, and the largest battle ever fought in the western hemisphere began. Day one established both armies' positions. Union general George Meade held the high ground running south from Culp's Hill along Cemetery Ridge to the summit of Little Round Top. On lower ground to the west, Confederate troops faced the Federals at every point along the line. On the second day, Lee attacked the entire Union front *en echelon,* striking first at Little Round Top. As Meade dispatched reinforcements toward the rocky hill, rebel soldiers launched phase two of their attack on the weakened Federal center, then assaulted the front's opposite end (Meade's right flank). They reached the summit of Cemetery Ridge and nearly took Little Round Top before falling back. The battle raged for a third and final day, ending after Pickett's disastrous charge collapsed in bloody failure. Twenty-eight thousand Confederates and 23,000 Federals had fallen—a casualty rate of more than 30%. (Found among the Southern dead was the corpse of a woman who had followed her husband into battle.) The South never recovered from the defeat.

Based on Michael Shaara's *The Killer Angels* and a major disappointment despite wonderful performances by Elliott, Jordan, Daniels, and hundreds of reenactors fighting like wild men to re-create the three most critical days in American history. After opening well, *Gettysburg* slides into a cataract of clichés about the Old South, the "burden of leadership," and major issues driving the war. Sheen (badly miscast as Lee) and Berenger (Longstreet) are unconvincing. Sloppy editing, a pompous score, and superficial understanding of the battle turn what should have been a great film into a made-for-TV potboiler.

Recommended Reading:
Shelby Foote, *The Civil War: A Narrative* (Vol. 2); W. L. Storrick, *Gettysburg: The Place, the Battle, the Outcome.*

Glory ★★★★★

(1989) 122 Minutes

Director: Edward Zwick

Cast: Matthew Broderick, Denzel Washington, Morgan Freeman, Andre Braugher, John Finn

Historical Background: July 18, 1863—Charleston, S.C.: As Col. Robert Gould Shaw's all-black 54th Massachusetts infantrymen sprinted toward Fort Wagner's hostile guns, marshes and seaward approaches to Charleston Harbor blocked their flanks, funneling them into densely packed concentrations impossible to miss for Confederate artillerists and riflemen. Hissing minié balls, high-explosive shells, and antipersonnel canister ripped 25-foot gaps in the advancing blue line. But the 54th kept moving. Leaving a ghastly trail of corpses behind them, Shaw's men drove over Wagner's earthworks, swarming into its forward sectors before rifle and cannon shot rolled them downward onto the beach. Half the regiment, including Shaw, perished, and Fort Wagner stood fast until war's end.

A stirring performance by the 54th—but not the first by black Federal troops. On June 7, 100 white soldiers and two "freedmen" regiments defending an outpost at Milliken's Bend had mounted desperate bayonet charges to repulse 2,500 rebel attackers: it was a bloody victory—the first for Union Army blacks in a major battle. Federal policymakers waited until late 1862 to form black infantry units. Lincoln had been an abolitionist for years, but declaring war on slavery in 1861 was out of the question: he had to preserve the Union to free Confederate slaves; that meant keeping troops from Delaware, Maryland, Kentucky, and Missouri—all slave states—in the Federal camp and leaving black men on the sidelines.

But a year later, Confederate armies seemed unbeatable. To win the war, Lincoln needed man-power, and the March 1863 Enrollment Act opened the Army of the Potomac's ranks to black volunteers and conscripts. Few Union veterans be-lieved that they would perform well in combat: un-derequipped and underpaid at first, blacks drew the army's worst assignments (latrine-digging, fatigue duty). But Milliken's Bend changed everything: be-fore war's end, 180,000 black soldiers—10% of the Union Army's head count—fought in 450 engage-ments. More than 37,000 died in battle, and 17 earned the Congressional Medal of Honor.

Zwick's hard-hitting account of the 54th is Hol-lywood's best film on the Civil War, despite ample factual slippage. Shaw (Broderick) is *Glory*'s only history-based major character; Freeman's Sgt. Rawlins, Washington's fiery Trip, Finn's salty Sgt. Mulcahy—all are fictional. Few of the 54th's re-cruits were former slaves, and Congressional sanc-tion for more black regiments came before the Fort Wagner brawl (not because of it). Still, a terrific, highly accurate film, with in-your-face combat choreography and incredible period detail.

Recommended Reading:
James M. McPherson, *The Negro's Civil War.*

Gone with the Wind ★★★★

(1939) 222 Minutes

Director: Victor Fleming

Cast: Clark Gable, Vivien Leigh, Leslie Howard, Olivia de Havilland, Hattie McDaniel

Historical Background: In 1794, Amer-ica's Industrial Revolution overtook the Old South: Eli Whitney's cotton gin so accelerated separation of the plant's lint and seeds that slaves running a gin could cull cotton 50 times faster than they could by hand. Whitney's mar-vel drove prices down and profits up, whetting a limitless worldwide appetite for cotton: by 1860, 55% of America's foreign-trade rev-enue—$190 million—flowed from sales of short-staple cotton. Driven by market demand, gigantic economies of scale—the great planta-tions—began dominating Southern industrial output and changing Southern demographics: during the early 1800s, big growers shunned hilly Atlantic Coast states for the Deep South's sprawling flatlands. Thousands of small farms flourished, but plantations fueled the machine, harnessing the muscle power of more than 3.5 million slaves to plant, cultivate, harvest, and haul enormous annual yields to the South's rav-enous gins (in 1860, England alone bought 1 billion pounds of Southern cotton).

Insular and self-sufficient, plantations maintained their own stockyards, dairies, veg-etable gardens, smokehouses, livestock, and slaughter pens. Their owners hosted lavish fetes and balls, attended military academies, developed an elaborate code of honor, and bred splendid horses. A tiny minority, the great planters still survive in popular notions of antebellum Southern life, but their political and economic inflexibility eventually destroyed the Confederacy. As cotton production rocketed, prices fell, and most planters sank into debt. During the 1850s, some Southerners supported economic diversification and immigration from Northern cities. The planters ignored them. Stagnant population levels eroded Southern strength in the House of Representatives, and slavery—for the planters—became a power issue. (Five slaves raised a state's head count by three in population surveys determining Congressional representation—small wonder that big growers fought emancipation tooth-and-nail and favored bringing slave-ridden Cuba into the Union.) By 1861, a staggering number of slaves labored on a few plantations: 75% of the Confederacy's households and 90% of its men-at-arms owned no slaves and had nothing to gain from secession. But the planters' extraordinary clout in secessionist conventions (legislatures, not voters, picked delegates) dragged 11 states from the Union—and the Old South to ruin.

Gone with the Wind has taken many hits for stereotyping blacks and whitewashing their squalid lot as chattel slaves. No argument there—but its reputation as pure nostalgic fantasy is off the mark. MGM spent millions on authentic sets and costumes (Fleming's rebel uniforms are awful, but most of his period detail is excellent), and the film's portrait of nuts-and-bolts plantation operations—including Mrs. O'Hara's key administrative role—is on the money. So are Gable's blockade-running Rhett Butler (a moderate Southerner out in the cold)

and Scarlett's postbellum scramble to survive. Inferior to *Glory* for accuracy—but far better than *The Birth of a Nation*.

Recommended Reading:
William C. Davis, *The Cause Lost: Myths and Realities of the Confederacy.*

The Horse Soldiers ★★★

(1959) 119 Minutes

Director: John Ford

Cast: John Wayne, William Holden, Constance Towers, Ken Curtis

Historical Background: From day one, Southerners dominated the cavalry war. Superior Confederate commanders—Nathan Bedford Forrest, John Hunt Morgan, Jeb Stuart—had better raw material than their Federal counterparts: few Union recruits rode well, but rebel cavalrymen had spent half their lives on horseback, and they supplied their own mounts—highly trained, top-of-the-line animals, infinitely better than the government-issue scrags dumped on most green Federal horsemen. Worse still, Confederate tactics were light-years ahead of antiquated Union cavalry doctrine built on massed charges—unsupported by infantry—against positions bristling with rifled muskets. Rebel horsemen mounted lightning hit-and-run attacks, blowing enemies apart with pistols, carbines, and sawed-off shotguns. Southern infantry, cavalry, and artillery fought together, and whenever they could, rebel cavalrymen dismounted and fought on the ground, concealed from long-range Union ordnance. For three years, they thoroughly outclassed their adversaries.

In 1863, the gap began closing, thanks to the unlikeliest candidate for mounted heroics in either army: Col. Benjamin H. Grierson, a 36-year-old Illinois music teacher terrified of horses since childhood—a pony had kicked him in the face, leaving permanent scars—and assigned, over steaming protests, to cavalry duty in the West. On April 17, Grierson left La Grange, Tenn., leading 1,700 troopers all the way to Baton Rouge on a raid through rebel-infested Mississippi countryside. His objectives: to divert Southern resources from Grant's upcoming thrust against Vicksburg and destroy railroad facilities linking the city and its Eastern suppliers. In two weeks, Grierson destroyed telegraph wires and bridges, torched Confederate warehouses, captured 1,000 horses, killed 100 enemy soldiers, wrecked two locomotives and 36 fully loaded boxcars, and demolished 60 miles of track. (Much of the wreckage came at Newton Station, a pivotal railroad town near Meridian.) Hunted every step of the way, Grierson launched several small-unit feints in different directions, confusing everyone on his trail. On May 2, he entered Baton Rouge, and Union sympathizers eager to reward his performance gave him the one thing he least wanted—a Thoroughbred horse.

Ford fictionalizes Grierson (Wayne, as "Marlowe"), links him with Towers in a silly romantic subplot (pure Hollywood: Grierson was happily married), concocts a feud between Wayne and physician Holden—but remains faithful to the raid's basic history, with some exceptions: Holden eliminates sick troopers before the mission—in fact, Grierson sent them galloping home on April 20 to confuse the rebels. Based on Harold Sinclair's novel.

Recommended Reading:
Stephen Z. Starr, *The Union Cavalry in the Civil War.*

Ironclads ★★

(1991) 100 Minutes

Director: Delbert Mann

Cast: Virginia Madsen, Alex Hyde-White, E. G. Marshall, Fritz Weaver

Historical Background: March 8, 1862—Hampton Roads, Va.: Goggle-eyed lookouts on the USS *Cumberland* watched a distant "floating barn roof" loitering toward them at five knots. It was the CSS *Virginia*—a 262-foot monster combining the salvaged hull of a wrecked Union frigate (the *Merrimack*) with a fully armored 178-foot casemate bristling with heavy guns and an iron ramming lance. Red-hot steel rained on the approaching ironclad by the *Cumberland, Congress,* and *Minnesota* dribbled off her sides "like India rubber balls." The rebels closed in, rammed a seven-foot hole in *Cumberland*'s hull, came about and reduced the *Congress* to splinters, then ran the *Minnesota* aground. At dusk, *Virginia* retired to Sewell's Point.

In three hours, the ironclad had deep-sixed two mighty Union frigates, striking the South's first blow against Northern interdiction of transatlantic supply lanes vital to Richmond's war effort. (On April 19, 1861, Lincoln ordered his navy to blockade 3,500 miles of Confederate coastline. Rebel countermeasures turned on *Virginia*-like ironclads—22 saw action by war's end—designed to control rivers and breach the Union quarantine. Called the "paper blockade" at first, Lincoln's cordon grew tighter each year, and by 1865, desperate shortages crippled the Confederacy, even though many privateers slipped through the blockade.)

At 7 A.M. on March 9, *Virginia* returned to sink the *Minnesota*—but floating beside her was a "shingle . . . with a gigantic cheese box rising from its center." It was the *Monitor*—a Union ironclad designed by John Ericsson and featuring a heavily armored revolving turret housing twin 11-inch rifled cannons. Ordered to protect the *Minnesota*, *Monitor* steamed forward, guns booming. Sailing in 100-yard spirals, the ironclads blasted away at each other for four hours before disengaging. The melee ended in a draw: the *Monitor* had saved the *Minnesota,* winning strategically by securing the harbor; but for the undamaged *Virginia* it was a tactical victory—she had wrecked *Monitor*'s pilothouse, blinding her captain. The ironclads had revolutionized naval warfare, but neither would see the new year: forced to flee Norfolk, Confederate sailors scuttled the *Vir-ginia* in May; on December 31, the *Merrimack* foundered and sank off Cape Hatteras.

Union spy Madsen vamps half the South's intelligence officers for technical specifications on the dry-docked *Merrimack* and its projected launch date. Eliminate all of this (70% of the film—and 100% fatuous nonsense), and you have a factually sound half-hour movie on the two-day Hampton Roads shootout. Highlights include terrific ironclad replicas and some of the best restaged naval warfare on film.

Recommended Reading:
William C. Davis, *Duel Between the First Ironclads.*

The Red Badge of Courage ★★★★

(1951) 69 Minutes

Director: John Huston

Cast: Audie Murphy, Bill Mauldin, Douglas Dick, Royal Dano, Arthur Hunnicutt, Andy Devine

Historical Background: Moments after his first battle, a haggard Confederate volunteer muttered, "I wish the earth would break open and let me drop in." A study in misery and heroic endurance, the average Civil War infantryman stood 5´7´´ tall and weighed 145

pounds. He grew up on a farm or in a small town. He was 20–25 years old, and for four dreadful years, hunger, disease, disfigurement, and death stalked him night and day. His first enemy was sloppy combat training based on archaic offensive tactics: more than anything else, Civil War recruits practiced close-order marching, because they attacked even the most heavily defended bastions *en masse,* aiming to blast out a weak spot with heavily concentrated gunfire, then seize the position at bayonet-point. (Marked by frequent accidents, weapons instruction came late in both sides' training programs and—incredibly—permitted new enlistees only ten practice shots per week.) In battle after battle, hundreds of men packed elbow to elbow in long, serried ranks poured across open fields toward enemy fortifications bristling with 12-pound "Napoleon" howitzers, 3-inch Rodman guns, and angry riflemen.

It was suicide. At 2,000 yards, artillery crews opened up on their attackers; at 500–600 yards, they began firing canister charges designed to spew steel balls in cone-shaped patterns at approaching infantry formations. At 400 yards, marksmen armed with accurate riflemuskets—British Enfields or U.S. Springfields—began picking off surviving assault troops. (Civil War bullets were far more destructive than mid-20th-century military cartridges. Rocketing forward at 2,800 feet per second, WWII-era steel-jacketed .30-caliber slugs passed through targets quickly and cleanly—like pellets from high-velocity air guns piercing a window and leaving neat holes. Conical, hollow-based .58-caliber Civil War minié balls were far messier, smacking their targets like large bricks hurled end over end through a mirror. Poking along at 960 fps, minié balls tumbled on impact, dispersing energy laterally, splintering bones,

and wreaking awful damage on organs and muscle tissue several inches from initial entry wounds.) The carnage was horrific: one year after the 1,177-man 22nd Massachusetts Regiment first rolled into action, its field commanders could muster only 200 combat-ready souls. Even when assault forces modified their tactics—attacking in open order, advancing in short, quick thrusts, and hitting the dirt under heavy fire—casualty rates routinely totaled 30%.

Shattering wounds from rifle and cannon fire were fearsome enough, but for sheer menace they lagged far behind traumatic infection and disease. Bivouacking in filthy rear-echelon camps was far riskier than closing with the enemy in battle. Garbage, open latrines, brackish water, mosquitoes, rats, lice, and flies spread raging pestilence among troopers living in close quarters with thousands of other men and exposed, for the first time, to common childhood illnesses. More than 359,000 Federal soldiers died in the war—a quarter million from malaria, typhus, gangrene, diphtheria, measles, smallpox, and pneumonia. For Confederates it was worse: disease inflicted 75% of the South's military deaths. (Revolting food deepened the nightmare. Endlessly repeated doses of hardtack, bacon, salt pork, and pickled beef—often rancid or crawling with worms, always deep-fried in pools of grease—bred epic-scale malnutrition, dysentery, and diarrhea on both sides.)

Medical procedures straight out of 18th-century voodoo primers helped little (students could master a medical school's full curriculum in one year). Always in short supply, glassy-eyed surgeons spent most of their time amputating mangled limbs. Drug-related therapies amounted to fishing expeditions: physicians took many blind shots, rarely hitting the mark—they successfully battled malaria with quinine, for example, but they also prescribed the medication for high fever, rheumatism, and syphilis. On both sides, ghastly hospital conditions prevailed (Walt Whitman called military clinics the battlefield's "seething hell and black infernal background"). Packed with dying men and swarming with bacteria, infirmaries spread contagion among the sick and infected desperately needed medical staffs: typhoid flattened Louisa May Alcott a few weeks into her first nursing tour in Union hospitals. By war's end, disease, minié balls, and hissing shrapnel had killed more than 600,000 men. Most faced death with extraordinary courage and resolve. "Do not mourn my loss," a mortally wounded private's final letter reads. "I had hoped to have been spared, but a righteous God has ordered it otherwise and I feel prepared to trust my case in his hands." He lies in an unmarked grave near Gettysburg.

Huston's lean, tough adaptation of Stephen Crane's classic tale about cowardice and redemption remains as riveting today as it was a half-century ago. (Civil War survivors praised the film, but audiences stayed away in droves.) Expertly filmed by Harold Rosson to mirror Mathew Brady photographs, the movie is remarkably authentic, right down to period dialogue, pointless pre-combat drills, the chilling rattle of disembodied rebel yells echoing across smoking battlefields, and vintage 1862 Union musketry. Hard-hitting, with terrific performances from Murphy, Hunnicutt, and Devine.

For Further Viewing:
The Red Badge of Courage ★★ (1974) 78 Minutes (Richard Thomas, Michael Brandon, Wendell Burton, Charles Aidman, Warren Berlinger):

Lee Philips' remake falls flat on its face more than once, chiefly through awful historical detail: uniforms and other "period" vestments look like giveaway rags from a bargain-basement sale; even worse, most of the weapons are postbellum breech-loading rifles (soldiers load from the muzzle end anyway, making the anachronism more annoying). And some viewers feel that Philips' version—shot a year before America's withdrawal from Vietnam—mutes Crane's deep respect for the martial virtues (honor, courage, patriotism). Thomas—a bright spot—makes an excellent Fleming, projecting an air of naiveté more convincingly than decorated WWII veteran Murphy.

Recommended Reading:
James I. Robertson, Jr., *Soldiers Blue and Gray*.

Springfield Rifle ★★★

(1952) 93 Minutes

Director: Andre de Toth

Cast: Gary Cooper, David Brian, Lon Chaney, Jr., Phyllis Thaxter, Paul Kelly, Phil Carey

Historical Background: Spring 1861—Oxford (Ohio) Female College: With news of Fort Sumter's fall ringing in her ears (and incensed by her school's all-Unionist staff),

Southern loyalist "Little Miss" Ginnie Moon steamed into the headmaster's office, loudly trumpeting plans to rejoin her mother in Memphis—*immediately*. Out of the question, replied the principal: she was too young to make the long journey alone. With cold fury, Ginnie stormed out of the building, drew a small-caliber revolver, took dead aim at the school's wind-lashed American flag, and shot every single star out of the banner's blue field. Hours later, she was on the road to Dixie. For the next half decade, Ginnie and her older sister put the same brassy nerve more quietly to work for "the Cause," blooming overnight into one of the finest high-level espionage teams of the war. (More readily trusted than men—and less likely to hang if captured— women made topnotch spies and couriers. Confederate and Union intelligence rosters bristled with feminine names—the South's Belle ["la belle Rebelle"] Boyd and the North's Pauline Cushman were national celebrities by war's end.)

Separated by 105 miles of rolling Virginia countryside, both governments had massive informal spy networks in place when war erupted in 1861. Richmond and Washington hummed with enemy sympathizers— author Edwin Fishel puts at least 20,000 loyal Southerners in the Federal capital—but neither side mounted coordinated intelligence efforts at first. Generals built their own spy networks, recruited and trained their own scouts, and devised their own codes. Reconnaissance, combat intelligence, espionage, clandestine communications, and intelligence analysis—undercover activities taken for granted today—were new, mysterious arts for a chaotic swarm of spies, scouts, couriers, and saboteurs.

In July 1861, the war's closest likeness to a professional intelligence bureau formed with Lincoln's appointment of Chicago detective Allan Pinkerton—Union general George McClellan's close friend—to command an 11-man "secret service" team. For 14 months, Pinkerton's sleuths wrote the book on 19th-century American espionage and counterintelligence. But they fell flat at tactical combat intelligence, the most critical clandestine activity in any war: Pinkerton routinely fed McClellan grossly inflated rebel troop-strength reports, deepening the general's legendary torpor in the field. On November 5, 1862, Lincoln sacked McClellan, and Pinkerton resigned. Three months later, General Joseph Hooker created the U.S. Bureau of Military Information (BMI), America's first one-stop independent intelligence corps. A lean, tough outfit numbering 200 spies and scouts, the agency improved forward reconnaissance operations and forged new intelligence-analysis techniques, outpacing Southern espionage efforts through the end of the war. (The rebels excelled at cavalry reconnaissance, but never assigned a high-ranking officer to coordinate intelligence campaigns matching the Federal program's scale. They formed an espionage bureau in November 1864—far too late to alter the war's outcome.)

But the Confederates crafted ingenious secret missions behind enemy lines and launched daring raids into Union territory. Two spectacular forays came five months before war's end. In October 1864, cavalry lieutenant Bennett Young and 20 men—all escaped POWs quartered in Canada—donned civilian clothes, drifted across the border, took rooms in several St. Albans, Vt., hotels, and cased the town.

Decked out in Confederate gray, they reassembled at 3 P.M. on the 19th and galloped into the town square, loudly pronouncing St. Albans the property of the Confederate States of America. They rifled every bank in town, torched several buildings, then thundered toward the border through a hissing curtain of bullets. Three were wounded, but all made it back to Canada. The war's northernmost Confederate land raid netted the South $200,000—and the rebels weren't through. Five weeks later, six Toronto-based saboteurs slipped into New York City, planted several bottles of "Greek fire"—a phosphorus compound ignited by air contact—in 19 major hotels, and waited for the buildings to burn. The bombs flopped (only one caused serious damage), and Union authorities eventually bagged, tried, and executed one raider, Robert Cobb Kennedy. His body lies in New York's Cypress Hill Cemetery under a slab reading "Unknown Confederate Soldier."

Ginnie Moon fared far better: after the war, she opened a Memphis boardinghouse. On a lark—at age 75—she went west, crashed a Hollywood casting office, and demanded an audition for a small part in an upcoming film. She got it, eventually appearing in movies with Douglas Fairbanks and Mary Miles Minter before returning to New York. The raw vinegar so terrifying to Oxford Female College officials never mellowed. A half century after Appomattox, she and some Greenwich Village neighbors drove past Grant's Tomb on Riverside Drive: "Damn him!" she roared, unrepentant—and unconquered—to the end.

In 1864, Union infiltrator Cooper wrecks a rebel horse-theft operation, convincing army brass to create America's first "Intelligence Department." (Using "experimental" breech-loading carbines, the Federals win a climactic shootout with Confederate spies.) De Toth shovels ample nonsense throughout: the action unfolds later than the BMI actually formed; Washington staffers insist that "the Confederates have a well-organized spy system"—a misconception, true only for scattered outfits such as the "Secret Line" (a trans-Potomac courier system); de Toth's weapons plot stinks—the Union bought thousands of breech-loading carbines before 1864 (they were Sharps rifles, not Springfields); and villains kill BMI commander George Sharpe—in fact, Sharpe lived until 1900. Still, this absorbing look at the birth of organized U.S. counterespionage conveys the bold, impromptu quality marking Civil War intelligence. Cooper and Chaney are excellent.

For Further Viewing:

The Raid ★★★★ (1954) 83 Minutes (Van Heflin, Richard Boone, Lee Marvin, Anne Bancroft, Peter Graves, Tommy Rettig): Director Hugo Fregonese peppers his film on the St. Albans raid with insignificant historical distortions and three awful blunders (for no real reason—embellishing the facts could never improve the true story): Young (played by Heflin and rechristened Neil Benton) shoots raider Marvin in church (!) for compromising the operation; townspeople kill two more rebels; and worst of all, Heflin gags on second thoughts about the mission just before H-Hour (nonsense). But Fregonese delivers a crackling, accurate rendition of the raid and sticks to the facts most of the time. Fine performances throughout—especially by Marvin and Boone (a tormented Union veteran).

Recommended Reading:
Philip Van Doren Stern, *Secret Missions of the Civil War;* Harnett T. Kane, *Spies for the Blue and Gray;* Edwin C. Fishel, *The Secret War for the Union: The Untold Story of Military Intelligence in the Civil War.*

Young Mr. Lincoln ★★

(1939) 100 Minutes

Director: John Ford

Cast: Henry Fonda, Alice Brady, Donald Meek, Marjorie Weaver, Richard Cromwell, Ward Bond

Historical Background: Many glowing legends about Abraham Lincoln are true. He really was born in a Kentucky log cabin. Virtually self-educated, he once walked six miles to borrow an English grammar text. He plied a quick, stiletto-sharp wit to deflect pork-barrel requests from political allies. Lincoln mastered a stunning arsenal of marketable skills: before running for president, he'd been a store clerk, postmaster, soldier, flatboatman, carpenter, hog drover, surveyor, blacksmith, railroad lobbyist, state legislator, U.S. congressman, and practicing attorney. (He read the law on his own and won a glittering courtroom victory in 1858,

impeaching eyewitness testimony that William Armstrong killed James Metzker during a late-night melee near New Salem. Lincoln produced an almanac proving that the moon had set before the 11 P.M. brawl, imposing a darkness too murky for witnesses to identify anyone.) Lincoln's early life harbors an odd riddle: his association with Ann Rutledge—a New Salem girl he courted before she died of typhoid fever—remains stubbornly mysterious (not a single letter or journal entry on the romance survives). Her death devastated Lincoln, but speculation that it permanently wrecked his romantic faculties makes little sense: on November 4, 1842, he married Mary Todd; prone to depression, both were tough to live with at times, but their correspondence reveals a warm, solid marriage.

Lanky, ungainly, and self-effacing, Lincoln shambled along flatfooted—like a harrower—but during public speeches, his whole manner could change as if by magic into majestic, irresistible elegance. This odd, fleeting charisma gripped audiences attending his debates with Stephen Douglas during Illinois' 1858 senatorial campaign. Douglas won the election, but Lincoln's performance made headlines, fueling his 1860 drive to the White House. Inaugurated on March 4, 1861, he weathered continuous wartime political crises and a four-year nightmare in the field. From the start, the war was unpopular. Right or wrong, Lincoln's army was the invader—and few Northerners liked this (especially draft-eligible men: a worthy cause, preserving the Union, but chillingly abstract when the drums began to roll). Federal strategic goals—fragment the Confederacy by seizing the Mississippi, Cumberland, and Tennessee rivers, then destroy its armies piecemeal—were sound and simple, but maddeningly elusive. Cursed with a numbing procession of middling commanders (George McClellan, John Pope, Ambrose Burnside, Joseph Hooker, George Meade), Lincoln fumed helplessly as the war went nowhere for three slaughterous years, then saw it end 13 months after he named Ulysses S. Grant supreme Union commander.

On April 14, 1865, five days after Robert E. Lee's surrender, John Wilkes Booth killed Lincoln at Ford's Theater in Washington, broke his left leg during a frantic escape, stopped briefly for treatment at Maryland physician Samuel Mudd's home, then fell to a Union bullet on April 26. Federal troops arrested hundreds of rebel sympathizers, tried eight for Lincoln's murder, and hanged four of them. Completely innocent, Mudd drew a life sentence for setting Booth's leg. During his incarceration, he worked heroically to contain a four-month 1867 yellow fever epidemic, saving many lives and eventually contracting the virus himself. Two years later, President Andrew Johnson pardoned Mudd—one of the long, bloody nightmare's last casualties.

Entertaining Lincoln lore bristling with absurd errors. Lincoln decides to study law because a falling stick points toward Ann Rutledge's grave (go figure). Ford peddles a fictionalized, error-packed version of the Armstrong trial: two brothers stand trial for the murder (Lincoln defended one client), and Fonda's Abe has little courtroom experience (the real Lincoln practiced law for years before defending Armstrong). Ford's murder

weapon is a knife (Metzker died from a beating). Worst of all is Fonda's sentimental tirade at trial's end: "I may not know much law," he bellows, "but I know what's right and what's wrong"—utter nonsense coming from any trial lawyer and especially from Lincoln (he devoured most of attorney John Stuart's legal texts before taking the bar examination). The upside: Fonda's folksy on-target performance and ample low-key comedy throughout.

For Further Viewing:

Gore Vidal's Lincoln ★★★ (1988) 200 Minutes (Sam Waterston, Mary Tyler Moore, Richard Mulligan, John Houseman, Ruby Dee): This tedious chronicle of Lincoln's presidential career and wartime family life sticks with history much of the time. Director Lamont Johnson's look at the Lincoln marriage avoids either exaggeration or understatement of Mrs. Lincoln's emotional problems and collisions with the president. Factually, the film errs badly on two major points: Moore's Mary Lincoln is an ardent abolitionist (way off) and Johnson suggests that Lincoln—guilt-ridden over the war's carnage—willingly embraced the possibility of assassination attempts (absolutely untrue; Lincoln had critical long-term plans for "reconstructing" America as painlessly as possible). Look for fair renditions of shady cabinet intrigue and Lincoln's problems with pre-Grant commanders.

The Prisoner of Shark Island ★★★★ (1936) 95 Minutes (Warner Baxter, Claude Gillingwater, Gloria Stuart, John Carradine, Arthur Byron, Francis McDonald): Director John Ford's riveting film on Samuel Mudd's outrageous conviction and long ordeal in the Dry Tortugas' miasmal Fort Jefferson prison. Highlights include fine performances by

Baxter (Mudd) and Carradine (an evil guard), chilling renditions of Lincoln's assassination and the ensuing hysteria-drenched witch-hunt that rolled over Mudd, and Mudd's heroism during the awful 1867 yellow fever epidemic. Terrific—one of Ford's best—with one minor drawback: McDonald conveys none of Booth's seething fanaticism.

Recommended Reading:
John J. Duff, *A. Lincoln: Prairie Lawyer;* Benjamin Thomas, *Abraham Lincoln: A Biography;* David Herbert Donald, *Lincoln;* Hal Higdon, *The Union vs. Dr. Mudd.*

chapter 4

The American West

(Overleaf)
Union Pacific
(Photofest)

Chronology

1803
APRIL 30: Louisiana Purchase.

1804–1806
Merriwether Lewis, William Clark chart western U.S.

1808
APRIL: American Fur Co. founded.

1810
JUNE: Pacific Fur Co. founded.

1821
NOVEMBER 16: Santa Fe Trail charted.

1836
FEBRUARY 23–MARCH 6: Battle of the Alamo.

APRIL 21: Battle of San Jacinto.

1842–1845
MAY: John C. Frémont explores Rocky Mountains.

1845
MARCH 1: U.S. annexes Texas.

1846–1848
Mexican War: U.S. gains New Mexico, Arizona, California.

1847
JULY 23: Mormons arrive at Great Salt Lake.

1848
JANUARY 24: California gold strike.

1857
MARCH 3: Butterfield Overland Mail opens first stagecoach line.

1859
JUNE 10: Nevada prospectors strike silver ("Comstock Lode").

1860
APRIL 3: First Pony Express ride.

1861
NOVEMBER 18: Last Pony Express ride.

1862
MAY 20: Homestead Act signed.

JULY 1: Pacific Railroad Act signed.

1864
NOVEMBER 26: First Battle of Adobe Walls (Kit Carson and 335 troopers defeat Comanche–Kiowa army).

1866
FEBRUARY 13: First peacetime bank robbery (James gang, Liberty, Mo.).

1867
MARCH 30: U.S. buys Alaska from Russia.

1868
NOVEMBER 27: Custer's 7th Cavalry kills Black Kettle in Washita River battle.

1869

MAY 10: Union and Central Pacific railroads connect in Utah.

1871

APRIL 15: Wild Bill Hickok marshal of Abilene.

1872

JUNE 17: Dodge City founded.

1874

JUNE 27: Second Adobe Walls battle—buffalo hunters defeat Quanah Parker.

1876

JUNE 25: Battle of Little Big Horn.

AUGUST 2: Jack McCall kills Wild Bill Hickok.

SEPTEMBER 7: James gang's Northfield raid.

1877

SEPTEMBER 5: Crazy Horse killed.

1878

FEBRUARY 18–JULY 19: Lincoln County range war.

1881

JULY 14: Pat Garrett kills Billy the Kid.

JULY 19: Sitting Bull surrenders at Fort Buford.

OCTOBER 26: Gunfight at OK Corral.

1882

APRIL 3: Ford brothers kill Jesse James.

1883

MAY 17: First performance of Buffalo Bill's Wild West Show.

1884

AUGUST: Doc Holliday wins last gunfight (Leadville, Colo.).

1885

APRIL: Annie Oakley joins Wild West Show.

1886

SEPTEMBER 4: Geronimo surrenders.

1889

OCTOBER 15: Dalton gang slaughtered in Coffeyville.

1890

DECEMBER 15: Sitting Bull killed.

1896

AUGUST 12: Klondike gold strike.

1899

MAY 30: History's last stagecoach robbery (by Pearl Hart in Arizona).

1904

SEPTEMBER 21: Chief Joseph of the Nez Percés dies.

Broken Arrow ★★★★

(1950) 93 Minutes

Director: Delmer Daves

Cast: James Stewart, Jeff Chandler, Debra Paget, Will Geer

Historical Background: Blessed with unmatched military prowess and diplomatic skills, Cochise was easily the greatest—and least bellicose—Apache chief: his conflict with settlers and soldiers began a full 24 years after the Apache Wars broke out in southern New Mexico. (The first systematic Apache raids in the American Southwest began near Silver City after the 1837 murder of Juan José Compa, a Mimbres Apache, by English immigrant and scalp hunter James Johnson.) Highly regarded for his integrity and reliability, Cochise signed a contract with the Butterfield Stage line to supply wood for its Apache Pass station during the winter of 1860. But peace ended in 1861 with a preposterous blunder by George Bascomb, a second lieutenant based at Fort Buchanan. Inexperienced and utterly without judgment, Bascomb led 54 troopers into Apache Pass to recover a ten-year-old boy kidnapped by an Apache war party. During a February 4 meeting in Bascomb's tent the lieutenant accused Cochise of the abduction, threatening him with imprisonment if he didn't return the boy immediately. Cochise angrily denied the charges, correctly blaming the crime on a band of warlike Pinal Apaches. When Bascomb ordered the chief's arrest, Cochise drew his knife, slashed a gaping hole in the tent wall, and bolted to safety through a hail of army gunfire. Eleven years of the bloodiest warfare ever seen in the Southwest had begun.

In typical Apache fashion (see *Ulzana's Raid*), Cochise's men raged across Arizona in small bands, killing and terrorizing settlers, ranchers, and prospectors. They butchered more than 150 people in March and April, and that was just the beginning. In July 1862, at least 200 warriors—the largest Chiricahua force ever assembled—ambushed 70 soldiers at Apache Pass, killing two men and retreating only after 12-pound howitzers poured a withering barrage into the canyon rocks. Bitter fighting continued until Tom Jeffords, a frontiersman who had befriended Cochise sometime between 1867 and 1870, arranged a meeting between the Apache chief and General Oliver Howard in the fall of 1872. Howard agreed to all of Cochise's terms: in December, the government established a new Chiricahua reservation incorporating all of the land Cochise had asked for, including game-rich areas in the Chiricahua Mountains. Under new Indian agent Jeffords, the Chiricahua enjoyed a degree of freedom unmatched on other reservations. A year and a half later, Cochise died of stomach cancer, and his warriors dropped his body into a deep mountain fissure that remains undiscovered to this day. Growing unrest and dissension gradually tore the Chiricahua tribe apart. Many of them participated in bloody raids along the Mexican border, and the great reservation closed in 1876. The night before their scheduled removal to San Carlos, 700 Apaches led by Geronimo galloped into Mexico and began preparing for the last—and most storied—Apache War.

Based on Elliott Arnold's 1947 novel, *Broken Arrow* focuses on Cochise's friendship with Jeffords (well played by Stewart). The film's one glaring error is a romantic subplot linking Jeffords—who remained a confirmed bachelor all his life—with an Apache maiden. (The film also ends on a note of sentimental optimism, omitting the eventual failure of the reservation.) Otherwise, the movie is a colorful, reasonably accurate account of events that ended Cochise's long war against the army.

Recommended Reading:
Dan L. Thrapp, *The Conquest of Apacheria;* Robert M. Utley, *A Clash of Cultures: Fort Bowie and the Chiricahua Apaches;* David Roberts, *Once They Moved Like the Wind: Cochise, Geronimo, and the Apache Wars.*

Butch Cassidy and the Sundance Kid ★★★

(1969) 112 Minutes

Director: George Roy Hill

Cast: Paul Newman, Robert Redford, Katharine Ross, Cloris Leachman, Ted Cassidy

Historical Background: Road-weary in rural Michigan, a late arrival booked the last room in Mancelona's only hotel and retired early. At 1 A.M., the innkeeper woke him with news that a sheriff hounding "some bandit named Cassidy" would share his room for the rest of the night. The man went back to sleep, rose before 6 A.M., glanced at the snoring policeman, then quit the hotel (and Mancelona) forever: Robert Leroy Parker, alias George Ingerfield, Jim Ryan, Santiago Maxwell, and Butch Cassidy, had left another lawman empty-handed and inches away from a collar worth front-page headlines throughout America.

Born in April 1866, Parker learned horsemanship and a taste for banditry from Johnson County range war veteran Mike Cassidy. (He later took the old rustler's surname as an outlaw sobriquet.) Intelligent and charming, Parker launched a lifetime criminal career in 1889 with bank heists in Denver and Telluride. Imprisoned for rustling in 1894 and paroled in 1896, Parker fled to Brown's Hole, an outlaw stronghold near the Utah–Wyoming–Colorado borders. (His fabled "Hole-in-the-Wall" hideout was a remote Wyoming bastion accessible only through a narrow pass.) By year's end Parker had forged the hard, larcenous core of his legendary Wild Bunch: Elza Lay, Will Carver, Harry Tracy, Ben Kilpatrick, Harvey Logan, George Curry, and Harry Longbaugh (the Sundance Kid). (Tracy and Logan, the gang's coleaders, were hard-eyed, vicious killers. A latecomer to the outfit, Longbaugh saw few holdups and became Parker's friend just before the gang disbanded.)

With military precision, the Wild Bunch robbed banks and trains at will, stealing a fortune in cash and government bonds. Their biggest railroad heists came at Wilcox and Tipton in Wyoming, Castle Gate in Utah, and Malta in Montana. In 1901 it ended—horse-bound desperadoes simply couldn't outpace

20th-century machines: telegraph networks enhanced law-enforcement communications enough to put posses several days closer to bandits on the run, and Union Pacific had unleashed a souped-up train loaded with horses and Pinkerton agents able, now, to run Parker and his gang into the ground. Accompanied by Longbaugh's girlfriend Etta Place, Butch and Sundance sailed for Buenos Aires in 1902. (Shrouded in mystery, Etta might have met Longbaugh at Fannie Porter's Fort Worth brothel. "Place" was a sobriquet, and she used at least four different first names. In 1907, she returned to Denver for medical treatment, then vanished from history.) Parker and Longbaugh looted banks, trains, and mining commissaries in Argentina, Chile, Bolivia, and Peru. In 1909, Bolivian authorities finally trapped them in San Vicente. An all-night gun battle left both men dead, and eyewitnesses swore that at least one, Parker, had committed suicide. Many Wild Bunch cultists believe the two survived and returned to the States, but no hard evidence supports the theory.

A joy to watch, *Butch Cassidy* scores C-minus for accuracy. Hill makes the hardworking Pinkertons flint-hearted killers and the outlaws carefree harmless rogues. He gives no sense of their gang's great size (100-plus, at least) or the homicidal character of many Wild Bunch outlaws. An early segment pits Logan against Parker in combat for solo command (utter nonsense), then Parker insists that the gang stick to robbing banks, not trains—Cassidy actually hated bank heists (too dangerous), naming his crew "The Train Robbers Syndicate" in 1897. Lousy history—but terrific moviemaking, thanks to great performances and William Goldman's crackling script.

Recommended Reading:
Larry Pointer, *In Search of Butch Cassidy;* Anne Meadows, *Digging Up Butch and Sundance.*

Cheyenne Autumn ★★★

(1964) 154 Minutes

Director: John Ford

Cast: Richard Widmark, Gilbert Roland, Ricardo Montalban, Carroll Baker, Karl Malden, Dolores Del Rio, Edward G. Robinson

Historical Background: November 27, 1868—Washita River, Indian Territory: Jolted awake by four thundering columns of the 7th Cavalry, groggy warriors reeled from their lodges to repulse George Armstrong Custer's predawn attack on Chief Black Kettle's winter camp. Brawling troopers rode them down one by one in the opening salvo of Philip Sheridan's scorched-earth campaign to end murderous Cheyenne raids on Kansas and Colorado settlements once and for all. It was over in minutes: tipis, food, weapons, clothing—everything necessary for weathering the long winter—went up in smoke before looming counterattacks from downriver camps sent Custer packing. Black Kettle, his wife, 20 troopers, and 100 Southern Cheyennes died in the raid. (During the 1830s, the Cheyenne Nation split into northern and southern bands, one remaining in the Powder River country, the other heading for Colorado to kill buffalo and deal hides for rifles with white traders.)

For veterans on the Indian frontier, the snarl of mutual incomprehension and explosive crosscurrents surrounding the Washita affair was grimly familiar. Like the elders of most Plains tribes, Black Kettle favored peace and compromise with the whites. Like other leaders, he signed many agreements. But none of the chiefs could ensure treaty compliance by all of their braves: strictly an advise-and-consent affair, tribal government elevated individual liberty to near-anarchic levels, leaving hotheaded young men free to ignore their leaders and raid white settlements at will. The Washita engagement followed barbarous atrocities inflicted on white civilians by marauding Cheyennes, many from Black Kettle's camp. In July 1868, 200 warriors, angered by the Indian Bureau's refusal to give them guns, attacked settlements on the Solomon and Saline rivers, raping five women, killing 15 men, burning several farms, and stealing precious livestock. During the Washita fight, troopers found the mutilated bodies of Clara Blinn and her child, both kidnapped months earlier in Colorado. (Cheyenne noncombatants died in Custer's attack, but it wasn't a Sand Creek–style massacre: Custer himself gave orders to spare women and children, quartering them in a large tipi flanked by guards. John Chivington's lawless, freelancing 1864 slaughter at Black Kettle's Sand Creek camp broke sharply with military policy. A U.S. Army regiment in name only, Chivington's "3rd Colorado Cavalry" was a short-term unit manned by hard-drinking thugs recruited from Denver saloons—under normal combat conditions a well-armed ROTC cadet corps could have

swept them from the field. Sand Creek appalled white Americans everywhere and prompted Congressional bills leading, eventually, to a government peace policy toward the Indians.)

After Washita, grim, fiercely contested engagements flared across the southern Plains, with momentum swinging completely to the army after the June 1874 Adobe Walls battle (see *The Searchers*). Two months later, Col. Ranald Mackenzie overran a huge Indian village in Palo Duro Canyon, torched a mountain of winter supplies, and scattered or killed 1,500 horses, ending forever the conflict between whites and Southern Cheyennes. But the stiff-necked northern band fought on, joining Sitting Bull at the Little Bighorn, then losing one melee after another to Sheridan's tough, seasoned troopers. On November 25, 1876, Mackenzie and 1,100 cavalrymen sacked the winter camp of Dull Knife—a reflective Cheyenne leader blessed with copious diplomatic skills and backed by wily, pugnacious war chief Little Wolf. Five months later, Dull Knife and 970 Northern Cheyennes surrendered at Fort Robinson, Nebraska, then marched southward to the Cheyenne–Arapaho reservation near Fort Reno in Indian Territory. For the Cheyennes, Fort Reno was a steaming, poisonous hellhole of the first rank (each month, many fell to the sweltering climate's robust strains of malaria and influenza). Agency superintendent John D. Miles' humanitarian efforts to return the Indians to the Northwest went absolutely nowhere, and on September 9, 1878, Dull Knife, Little Wolf, and 297 Cheyennes jumped the reservation, launching a 1,500-mile run for the Powder River. Harried all the way by 10,000 cavalrymen, the Indians won four pitched battles, forded seven major rivers, and crossed three heavily patrolled railroad lines undetected, making headlines from Omaha to Boston and winning legions of white sympathizers.

Six weeks into their grueling exodus, the Cheyennes split into two ragged bands. More than 100 slogged on with Little Wolf, finally surrendering on March 25 to his old friend W. P. Clark at Fort Keogh, Montana. (Allowed to remain there, they eventually formed the Northern Cheyenne Tongue River Reservation.) Dull Knife led 124 exhausted men, women, and children to Fort Robinson, living comfortably there until Commandant Henry W. Wessells locked them in an unheated barracks for refusing to march back to Fort Reno. On January 9, 1879, the Cheyennes reassembled several rifles that they'd dismantled and concealed before their surrender, shot their way out of the fort, and bolted for a line of bluffs two miles away. By the 21st, Wessells' troopers had shot or recaptured everyone but Dull Knife, his wife, their son and daughter-in-law, and two small children. Incredibly, all of them made it to the Pine Ridge Agency and eventually joined Little Wolf on the new reservation, where both leaders died—Dull Knife in 1883 and Little Wolf 21 years later.

Roland (Dull Knife) and Montalban (Little Wolf) dominate this long, rambling epic chronicling the Cheyennes' pilgrimage from Oklahoma to the Powder River country. At midpoint, the film falls flat on its face with a strange, gratuitous Dodge City barroom segment aiming at "comic relief." Striving too hard for sixties-style "relevance," Ford makes Wessells a Nazi-like martinet ("I'm an instrument of orders with which I don't agree") and tinkers needlessly with historical facts: Robinson's Interior Secretary Carl Schurz misses the mark badly—though friendly toward the Indians, Schurz whimsically opposed them on several occasions

and never mounted a prolonged crusade to help the Cheyennes. Still, Ford's last western is highly entertaining and true to the spirit of the Cheyennes' spectacular long march.

Recommended Reading:
George Bird Grinnell, *The Fighting Cheyennes;* Robert M. Utley, *Cavalier in Buckskin: George Armstrong Custer and the Western Military Frontier.*

Conagher ★★★★

(1991) 117 Minutes

Director: Reynaldo Villalobos

Cast: Sam Elliott, Katharine Ross, Barry Corbin, Billy Green Bush, Ken Curtis, Buck Taylor, Dub Taylor, Daniel Quinn, Anndi McAfee

Historical Background: A 19th-century British tourist—tame, spruce, and utterly lost on his host's Wyoming ranch—approached an ancient cowhand perched atop a hitching rail and asked, "I beg your pardon, where can I find your master?" According to cowboy lore, the old drover hit the ground walking, sauntered toward his employer's guest, stopped a whisker's width from the man's chin, and replied, "Mister, the son of a bitch ain't bin born yit."

Tough, resourceful, independent, and proud, American cowboys and their exploits crowned a 345-year tradition launched in 1519 by Gregorio de Villalobos' introduction of cattle into New Spain. By 1529, so many herds roamed the Mexicalzimgo Valley's rich grasslands that Mexico City's town council founded La Mesta—history's first stockgrower's association—to regulate a growing, chaotic livestock industry. A century later, large haciendas worked by freewheeling vaqueros stretched all the way to the Rio Grande River. (Vaqueros developed clothing styles, equipment, working methods, and roundup techniques later adopted and refined by 19th-century American cowboys. Early vaqueros, for example, dropped their *lazo* loops over steers' heads from extended cavalry lances, learning later to "rope" cattle with long, well-aimed throws. American cowboys developed an incredible array of sophisticated roping techniques, or "catches": the heeling catch, the Hoolihan catch, the forefooting slip catch, the underhanded head catch, and several others sent the drover's lasso loop snaking through the air in a vertical or horizontal position toward his target's horns or hooves. Some throws required dazzling quickness, timing, and arm strength: only a top hand could master the tough backhand slip catch to snare calves loping across his path at right angles—behind his galloping horse.)

By 1800, Texas rangelands groaned under the weight of so many wild, tough longhorn cattle that only profligate theft by Indians kept the animals from becoming worthless. But ranching there grew slowly until postbellum railroad expansion (see *Union Pacific*) and waves of European immigrants created huge demands for beef on the Atlantic Coast. In 1867, Chicago entrepreneur Joseph G. McCoy built a 250-acre labyrinth of cattle pens near the Union Pacific railhead in tiny Abilene, Kan. (the West's first great cow town), creating an eastbound delivery system for longhorn cattle and opening a hungry market for Texas cattlemen.

Within weeks, the first roundups began. For a quarter century, "open-range" ranching prevailed in the U.S.: millions of cattle roamed unfenced public lands throughout the West, with neighboring ranchers' herds grazing huge common ranges. "Line riders" rode the outskirts of each ranch, turning cattle about to drift into nervous sodbusters' carefully tended fields. Isolated and utterly bored, the riders circled their ranch's entire periphery, sleeping in cabins or primitive dugouts placed ten miles apart along the line. Spring roundups staged to gather cattle and group them by individual ranchers' brands keyed the industry, creating seasonal work for at least 40,000 cowboys between 1867 and 1890. Anchored by five to ten widely spaced chuck wagons—each the mobile headquarters and main camp for a ten-man range crew—major roundups were triumphs of teamwork and iron discipline. Cowboys in a typical crew rode away from camp in all directions, following evenly spaced lines stretching outward like a wagon wheel's spokes. At fifteen miles they stopped, reversed course, and drove the cattle within their ever-tightening circle back toward camp, concentrating a sizable herd by nightfall. At dawn, top hands on nimble, highly trained cutting horses isolated darting, jittery longhorns and maneuvered them to the herd's perimeter. After branding new calves and grouping market-ready cattle, range crews repeated the process—again and again—until they'd scoured every inch of the open range for strays and runaways.

Then came the cowboys' toughest, most

dangerous work: driving their herds to market over great cattle trails—the Goodnight-Loving Trail to Pueblo; the Shawnee Trail to Kansas City and St. Louis; the Western Trail to Dodge City; and the old Chisholm Trail between Wichita and San Antonio. (Hard-riding Texans pushed the Chisholm northward—via "McCoy's Extension"—all the way to Abilene. The short Texas Cattle Trail linked Wichita and Ellsworth.) Led by the trail boss, two wranglers driving extra horses (the "remuda"), and two trail-wise point riders charged with setting the herd's pace, 2,500 bawling cattle began the 900-mile journey north in early April. Swing men and flank riders on both sides of the herd "squeezed the cattle down" and strung them out into a tapered, triangular mass, holding them in tight formations up to three miles long for the entire drive. Eating dust every inch of the way, new hands rode "drag" behind the herd, forcing calves and laggard cattle to match the lead steers' rigorous pace (15–20 miles per day). It was tough, grueling business, demanding long hours and permitting little rest. Every day in the saddle meant 12 to 18 hours of jolting monotony, broken only by quickly wolfed meals (beans, bacon, canned tomatoes, biscuits, and coffee), the ever-present threat of stampedes, and—worst of all—many perilous river crossings.

After three months of this, every hand was ready to sprint to the wide-open, beckoning cow town at trail's end. There they drew wages ($35–$38 per month), bathed, and headed for saloons offering industrial-strength liquor and compliant "nymphs du prairie" with colorful professional sobriquets—topping many lists were Hambone Jane, Cuttin' Lil Slasher, Fatty McDuff, Squirrel Tooth Alice, Lady Jane Gray (!), and Roaring Gimlet. A day or two later the adventure ended. Most trail hands moved on after one drive, and few worked for more than a decade. It was just as well: by 1890, waves of settlers, new railheads in Texas, consolidation of most spreads into ranching conglomerates, and widespread use of barbed wire (patented by Joseph Glidden in 1874) ended the great cattle drives and the golden age of the cowboy. But to no one's surprise, cowhands became instant folk heroes, not relics of history: well before the open-range era ended, they fascinated and mystified their city-bound contemporaries. According to legendary drover and artist Charles Russell, an "Eastern girl" once asked her mother if cowboys ate grass: "No, dear," the woman replied, "they're part human."

Produced by Ross and Elliott and beautifully directed by Villalobos, *Conagher* matches—or tops—Hollywood's best westerns, including *High Noon* and John Ford's epic-scale productions. Stranded with two children on a remote homestead after her husband dies in an accident, Ross (at her very best) struggles to scratch out a living and fend off "those south-of-the-border Apaches" in the wild American Southwest. Top cowhand and straight shooter *par excellence* Con Conagher (Elliott, in a magnificent, understated performance) drifts into and out of her life, helping her get by and meeting the tough ethical standards of the Cowboy Code ("I take a man's money, I ride for the brand—I don't know no other way"). Visually stunning, with super work from a veteran ensemble cast—especially by Corbin (stage driver Charley McCloud) and Curtis (a grizzled rancher fighting outlaws determined to take his spread). Based on the Louis L'Amour novel.

For Further Viewing:

Lonesome Dove ★★★★ (1990) 372 Minutes (Robert Duvall, Tommy Lee Jones, Robert Urich, Danny Glover, Diane Lane, Frederic Forrest, Rick Schroeder, D. B. Sweeney): Director Simon Wincer's beautifully realized adaptation of Larry McMurtry's novel about retired Texas Rangers (Duvall and Jones, in knockout performances) abandoning their Rio Grande Valley homestead, stealing a herd of Mexican cattle, and driving it north to start Montana's first cattle ranch. Great supporting performances, especially by Urich, Sweeney, and Forrest (as terrifying renegade half-breed Blue Duck), accurate period detail right down to Duvall's huge .44-caliber "Walker" Colt revolving pistol, and a terrific script deliver a powerful, authentic look at life on America's frontier during the late 1870s.

Monte Walsh ★★★★ (1970) 106 Minutes (Lee Marvin, Jeanne Moreau, Jack Palance, Mitch Ryan, Jim Davis): Well-scripted and well-performed—but relentlessly downbeat—story of veteran cowboys steamrolled by conglomerate buyouts and blanket "downsizing" in America's late-19th-century cattle industry. Marvin is excellent in the title role, scrambling to stay afloat financially and watching everything he cares about die or disappear. A grimly realistic film, authentic in every detail, with one drawback: though she tries gamely, Moreau is miscast and unconvincing as an aging saloon girl.

Will Penny ★★★★ (1968) 108 Minutes (Charlton Heston, Joan Hackett, Donald Pleasence, Ben Johnson, Anthony Zerbe): Middle-aged cowboy Heston takes an off-peak job riding line on a large ranch, then falls in love with Hackett after finding her squatting for the winter with her young son in an isolated mountain cabin. An accurate, absorbing rendition of cowboy life and the line rider's isolated, enervating work—marred only by Pleasence's ranting performance as a scripture-quoting but thoroughly unchristian patriarch bent on murdering Heston for killing his son in self-defense. Easily Heston's finest performance.

Recommended Reading:

David Dary, *Cowboy Culture: A Saga of Five Centuries*; Charles M. Russell, *Trails Plowed Under: Stories of the Old West.*

Drum Beat ★★★

(1954) 111 Minutes

Director: Delmer Daves

Cast: Alan Ladd, Charles Bronson, Audrey Dalton, Marisa Pavan, Robert Keith, Rodolfo Acosta, Elisha Cook, Jr.

Historical Background: In the spring of 1873, one of the saddest chapters in U.S. history peaked when Kintpuash—leader of the Modocs, an obscure California Indian tribe numbering fewer than 300 souls—murdered Edward R. S. Canby, the only general ever killed in the field during the 400-year conflict between white and Native Americans. (Custer was a lieutenant colonel when he died fighting the Sioux.) Long feared by neighboring tribes, the Modocs were a bellicose, fiercely independent people. During the 1850s, they preyed on immigrants taking the Applegate Trail to Oregon, until California militia sent them packing to a reservation in southwestern Oregon. But the Klamaths, a larger tribe living in the same area, made life there miserable for them. In 1865, a small Modoc faction led by Kintpuash—also called Captain Jack by settlers and soldiers—jumped the reservation and returned to the eastern foothills of California's Cascade Mountains, barely sustaining an uneasy seven-year truce with the settlers there. Nothing, it seemed, could persuade the Indians to return to Oregon. On November 29, 1872, a cavalry troop rode into the Modoc camp to force the issue. Shots rang out. In the confusion, Kintpuash and 50 warriors fled south, killing 20 settlers before stopping at the Lava Beds—a moonlike 120-square mile chaos of scattered pits, intersecting ravines, and underground caves near Tule Lake. Called "the land of burned-out fires" by the Modocs, it was a perfect natural fortress for Captain Jack and his men.

They soon faced a force of 800 troopers under Canby's command, and an eight-month siege called the Battle of Captain Jack's Stronghold began. On January 16, 1873, the soldiers mounted an attack in heavy fog, losing 37 men to Modoc sharpshooters before falling back in a rout. A government peace commission—eventually chaired by Canby—arrived in February. It resolved nothing, and the siege dragged on. Then, on April 11, a Modoc delegation met with Canby and other commissioners halfway between the warring camps, and Kintpuash drew a hidden pistol and shot the general to death. The murder proved tragic for both sides: a Modoc girl had warned Canby of the coming treachery, but he attended the meeting out of sympathy for the Indians; and Kintpuash, against killing Canby from the start, had acted under severe pressure from other chiefs con-vinced that murdering the general would destroy U.S. Army morale. Ravaged by hunger and dissension, the Modocs held out until mid-May, when they fled the Lava Beds. The army soon captured most of them, finally seizing Kintpuash on June 1. He and three of his men were hanged for murder on October 3, 1873, and 150 Modocs—the last of their tribe—retired to a reservation in the "Indian Territory" (now Oklahoma), hundreds of miles from their famous stronghold.

Bronson completely dominates *Drum Beat* with his terrific performance as a menacing Captain Jack. Treatment of the actual Lava Beds siege is attenuated, but historically accurate. The film is at its best when it focuses on the pugnacious Modocs, but its bickering whites (divided in their views on how to deal with the Indians) grow tiresome very quickly. Throw in an absurd ending—with a strapping, knife-wielding Bronson subdued by the tiny, unarmed Ladd—and *Drum Beat* becomes, at best, a strangely uneven movie.

Recommended Reading:
Richard H. Dillon, *Burnt-Out Fires: California's Modoc Indian War;* Arthur Quinn, *Hell with the Fire Out;* Erwin N. Thompson, *Modoc War: Its Military History and Topography.*

The Far Country ★★★★★

(1955) 97 Minutes

Director: Anthony Mann

Cast: James Stewart, Walter Brennan, John McIntire, Ruth Roman, Corinne Calvet

Historical Background: America's mad rush for Klondike gold began in July 1897, when a pair of Alaskan schooners carrying a fortune in ore and bullion from northwestern Canada steamed into San Francisco Bay and Seattle's Puget Sound, igniting a frenzied stampede of would-be prospectors to the Pacific Northwest. (Few of them knew anything about mining, and enterprising swindlers saw them coming: one outfit, the Trans-Alaskan Gopher Co., hawked vouchers for nonexistent gophers "trained" to claw their way through the Yukon's rock-solid permafrost to rich gold deposits below.) Most stampeders boarded ships that took the "inside passage" from Seattle, a narrow slot between the coast of British Columbia and a line of islands extending to the province's northern border. They docked at Dyea or Skagway, wide-open boomtowns on the tidal flats of Alaska's southeastern panhandle. (Skagway was legendary for its lawlessness and corruption. Sam Steele, one of Canada's first mounted policemen, called it "little better than a hell on earth—the roughest town in the world.")

Things would get rougher. From Skagway, Klondikers had to cross White Pass, a chaos of muddy quagmires, fallen trees, and huge boulders that sourdoughs renamed Deadhorse Trail because so many pack animals died there. Just outside of Dyea lay Chilkoot Pass, a gap in the mountains ending with a glacier so steep that many climbers had to claw their way to its summit on their hands and knees. Those who made it through the passes faced a harrowing 600-mile journey down the raging Yukon River—usually on makeshift boats and rafts—to Dawson and the mining camps. Awful hardship and drudgery awaited them there. They lived in one-room cabins just large enough to store supplies and house a bunk, two chairs, a stove, and a table. Many sourdoughs worked even when temperatures reached 20° below zero. Some stood knee-deep in half-frozen streams, panning the bottom for placer gold. Others built huge fires over their claims to thaw the ground, then hacked out ten feet of permafrost before hitting bedrock and pay dirt. They measured their progress in inches, hauling frozen earth to the surface with windlasses and dumping it near sluice boxes, where they "washed" it for gold when spring arrived. Miners took more than $200 million in gold out of the Klondike, an enormous sum in an era when fine apartments rented for $5 per month. But gold production began to drop steadily by 1900. The stampede ended, and the last great adventure of the American West passed into history as abruptly as it had begun three years earlier.

A cynical loner (Stewart) and his garrulous sidekick (Brennan) drive a herd of steers from the U.S. to Dawson, hoping to sell them for a tidy profit to beef-starved Klondikers. As soon as they hit Skagway the fireworks begin. Fine performances by all, authentic portrayal of mining camps and boomtowns, breathtaking location filming, and remarkable historical accuracy make *The Far Country* a must for anyone who likes Westerns.

Recommended Reading:
William Bronson with Richard Reinhardt, *The Last Grand Adventure: The Story of the Klondike Gold Rush and the Opening of Alaska;* Delia Ray, *Gold! The Klondike Adventure.*

Geronimo: An American Legend ★★★

(1993) 115 Minutes

Director: Walter Hill

Cast: Jason Patric, Robert Duvall, Gene Hackman, Wes Studi, Matt Damon, Rodney A. Grant

Historical Background: An average military tactician—by Apache standards—and possessing no diplomatic skills, Geronimo remains noteworthy for leading the last organized resistance to the U.S. government's reservation system. His most distinctive qualities were ferocity in battle and a bilious, volcanic personality. Lt. Britton Davis, commander of scouts at the San Carlos reservation, called him "thoroughly vicious, intractable, and treacherous." His fellow Apaches found him ill-tempered and utterly without humor ("a true wild man, devoted entirely to warfare," according to one Sonoran Chiricahua). More than anyone else, Geronimo's adversaries

in northern Mexico felt the force of his wrath: in 1851, 400 Sonoran soldiers killed his wife and three children, filling him with a hatred for Mexicans extraordinary even for a Chiricahua. (A 250-year tradition of implacable hostility between Mexicans and Apaches began in the 1630s, when Spanish colonial governors sold many Indians into slavery.) For the rest of his life in the Southwest, Geronimo killed Mexican men, women, and children wherever he could find them.

He rode with Cochise in Arizona and Mexico until 1872, then lived on the thriving Chiricahua Reservation until it closed in 1876 (see *Broken Arrow*). A year of raiding in Mexico and four bitter years at San Carlos followed. Thanks to a politicized agency, living conditions on the reservation deteriorated until Apache rancor escalated into open revolt in 1881. That August, hundreds of San Carlos Indians made unauthorized pilgrimages to Cibecue Creek on the Fort Apache reservation to hear the declamations of a fiery, militant shaman named Nakaidoklini. The rowdy meetings alarmed agency officials. They ordered the shaman's arrest, and on August 30 a detail of soldiers and Apache scouts took him into custody at Cibecue Creek. As they led the holy man away, swarms of heavily armed Apaches suddenly surrounded them. Shots rang out (no one really knows who fired first), the scouts mutinied, and a sergeant killed Nakaidoklini. Led by Geronimo, 74 Chiricahuas bolted for Mexico, igniting a sporadic five-year war. For 23 months the renegades raided along the border, at one point invading San Carlos and forcing hundreds of reservation Apaches to follow them back to Mexico.

On May 15, 1883, General George Crook and Charles Gatewood, a cavalry lieutenant trusted by Geronimo, persuaded the Indians during a series of meetings to return to San Carlos. Chafing under agency regulations (especially galling to them was the rule against wife-beating), 42 warriors and their families fled to Mexico again in May 1885. Ten months later—exhausted by their constant flight from Mexican and U.S. cavalry—they met with Crook a second time. All but Geronimo and 33 holdouts capitulated. Crook soon retired, and his replacement, Nelson A. Miles, sent Gatewood into the Sierra Madres with orders to find Geronimo and persuade him to give up. They met on August 25, and Geronimo surrendered for the final time on September 4. He spent his last years at Fort Sill, Oklahoma, where—unpredictable to the end—he died a Dutch Reformed Christian in 1909.

Beautifully filmed and brimming with fine performances—especially by Patric (as Gatewood)—*Geronimo* falls flat on its face just often enough to dilute its reliability as a chronicle of the Geronimo wars. Most of its flaws are polemical distortions of history. Studi plays a pensive, deliberate Geronimo very well, but also absurdly, since Geronimo was about as pensive and deliberate as a vial of nitroglycerine. All of Hill's Apaches are innocent victims, a silly notion utterly discredited by history, and Geronimo's psychotic feud with the Mexicans goes unmentioned. Throw in Damon's solicitous Britton Davis and you have an interesting—but very messy—film.

Recommended Reading:
Dan L. Thrapp, *Al Sieber, Chief of Scouts;* Jason Betzinez, *I Fought with Geronimo.*

The Grey Fox ★★★

(1982) 92 Minutes

Director: Phillip Borsos

Cast: Richard Farnsworth, Jackie Burroughs, Wayne Robson

Historical Background: When Bill Miner first entered San Quentin in 1866, it was one of the grimmest places on earth. Two convicts shared each tiny unheated cell, sleeping on straw ticks and protected from the cold by two flimsy blankets. Recalcitrant prisoners were flogged, beaten with rubber clubs, or hung by their wrists until they lost consciousness. None of this was forbidding enough to reform Miner. During his squalid career he committed at least 27 major crimes—including armed robbery, smuggling, horse theft, and burglary—in Canada and the American West. He robbed more stagecoaches than the James and Younger brothers combined. On September 10, 1904, he staged the first train robbery in Canadian history, and by February 22, 1911—the date of his last arrest—he had stolen a grand total of $370,000 in cash and securities. He landed in prison eight times (including five terms in San Quentin) and spent 37 years behind bars. As his biographer Mark Dugan notes, Miner was very good at getting caught.

But he enjoyed great celebrity during his own lifetime. Blessed with charisma and a folksy sense of humor, he passed himself off as an aging, good-natured free spirit incapable of harming anyone. Everybody, especially the press, took the bait: the day after his death, a newspaper described him as "a kindly, lovable old man . . . whose manner was that of a friend to all humankind." The manner and the man were exact opposites. Miner grew up in a middle-class family, turning to crime because he simply didn't like the pressures or self-discipline associated with productive work. He was appallingly hypocritical: a self-proclaimed socialist, he lived like a king in 1880 while his mother sank into poverty after his father's death—Miner never gave her a cent. But he fooled everyone: he died a major folk hero on September 2, 1913, after swallowing rancid swamp water during a failed attempt to escape from the Milledgeville prison farm in Georgia. A week later, some of the town's most prominent businessmen served as pallbearers at his funeral.

The Grey Fox is great entertainment—thanks to Farnsworth's performance—but awful history. Distorting and omitting many facts, it amounts to a glowing endorsement of Miner's way of life and portrays him as a criminal genius. ("I'm just no good at work planned by other heads," he remarks at one point, which is pure hokum: Miner never planned much of anything, leaving tactics to his accomplices.) Borsos even implies that he died a free man in Europe. If you're looking for the truth about Miner, forget the film and read Dugan's fine biography.

Recommended Reading:
Mark Dugan, *The Grey Fox: The True Story of Bill Miner, Last of the Old Time Bandits.*

Heaven's Gate ★★

(1980) 149 Minutes

Director: Michael Cimino

Cast: Kris Kristofferson, Christopher Walken, Isabelle Huppert, Jeff Bridges, John Hurt, Sam Waterston

Historical Background: July 20, 1889 Johnson County, Wyoming: Prostitute Ella Watson went down swinging—before her lynching by wealthy cattle barons, "she exhausted a blasphemous vocabulary upon [her hangmen], who essayed to stop the vile flow, but found the task too great" (*Cheyenne Daily Leader*). Watson's lover, saloonkeeper Jim Averill, "begged and whined and protested innocence" when his turn came. The cattlemen's ropes silenced both of them and ignited the West's final, most murderous range war. Averill had publicly insulted the cattle barons many times, and Ella had antagonized them by accepting stolen calves for her services from cash-poor cowboys—not hanging offenses, but infinitely foolish behavior in Johnson County, a 12,000-square-mile ocean of the world's finest grazing land that cattle barons aimed to keep wide open despite efforts to fence it in by small ranchers and immigrant settlers from the East. Johnson County hadn't even existed ten years earlier, but everyone knew that northern Wyoming's lush, rolling terrain was perfect for raising livestock. By 1879, great cattle companies had formed in the East. Wealthy men bought huge herds in Texas and

Nebraska, drove them to Wyoming, and turned them loose on the vast open range. Cattlemen formed the Wyoming Stock Growers' Association and so prospered that by 1886 the county's teeming rangeland groaned under the weight of 4 million cattle.

Then came the horrific winters of the "Great Die-up" (1886 and 1887). Temperatures dropped past –50° and stayed there for weeks. In 1887, a two-month windstorm howled without letup across Wyoming, blowing trains off their rails and killing wranglers determined to rescue freezing cattle. On January 6, the first of many ten-day blizzards erupted. Unable to venture outside for firewood, people froze to death in their houses. By March 30, 75% of Wyoming's cattle—3 million head—lay dead on the range. Many cattle companies failed, forcing unemployed cowboys to start their own modest spreads with mavericks—unbranded calves that anyone could rope and claim. (Rustling—stealing branded cattle and altering their marks with running irons—increased sharply.) Settlers followed suit, and fuming cattle barons faced the galling spectacle of shrinking ranges and dwindling herds. Something had to give. The cattlemen had gotten there first, they had fought off the Sioux and Cheyenne, and they had built the young territory's fledgling economy. But the land they worked was public land, and every homesteader was entitled to 160 acres under the 1862 Homestead Act. (Since each steer needed 40 acres of grazing land to survive, 160 acres was too little for the homesteaders—and too much for the cattlemen to give up.)

The Stock Growers Association began hiring high-priced gunmen called "stock detectives" or "regulators" and compiled a death list bearing 70 names. They hired ex-outlaw Frank Canton to lead their Cheyenne-based army, and "rustlers" such as Averill and Watson began leaving the area—or turning up dead. On April 5, 1892, 46 regulators rode into Johnson County from Casper, determined to seize control of the range once and for all. They assaulted a cabin owned by small rancher Nate Champion, immediately shooting two men and killing Champion after 12 thunderous hours of non-stop gunfire. Word of the raid spread. Terrified homesteaders formed their own army, tracking the regulators to a deserted ranch and surrounding them on the evening of April 11. A savage battle raged through the 13th, when cavalry dispatched by Wyoming's acting governor arrived and took the gunmen into custody. Though none of the cattle barons went to prison, huge legal fees and the three-year cost of maintaining their army broke their iron grip on Johnson County. Wyoming finally saw the opening of the cattle industry—and the end of an era.

Gorgeous location filming and meticulous period detail make Cimino's lumbering epic worth a look for amateur historians. But *Heaven's Gate*—a floundering, incoherent mix of accurate history and ridiculous error—makes sense only if you understand the Johnson County War. Cimino makes Champion a stock association foreman. Averill (Kristofferson) escapes the hangman's rope, and Ella Watson leads settlers in the final shoot-out that actually took place three years after her death. Awful tedium reigns throughout: at one point, a stationary camera remains nailed to Kristofferson for 30 empty seconds as he ambles across a barnyard. On the plus side: Bridges' fine performance and the grandly orchestrated final battle.

For Further Viewing:

The Big Country ★★★ (1958) 166 Minutes (Gregory Peck, Charlton Heston, Jean Simmons, Burl Ives, Carroll Baker, Charles Bickford): This sprawling epic has former sea captain Peck moving west to marry Baker, whose tough cattleman father (Bickford) festers at crude small rancher Ives' refusal to sell out and move on. A good companion piece for *Heaven's Gate* and historically accurate: disputed water rights—a constant, explosive issue in the Old West—fuels the feud between Bickford and Ives.

Recommended Reading:

Helena Huntington Smith, *The War on Powder River.*

I Will Fight No More Forever ★★★★

(1975) 100 Minutes

Director: Richard T. Heffron

Cast: James Whitmore, Ned Romero, Sam Elliott, Nick Ramus

Historical Background: October 1877—northern Montana: Chief Joseph (the younger) faced the end of a spectacular 1,700-mile fighting retreat that had begun more than three months earlier near Wallowa Lake in northwestern Oregon. Ordered in May to move to a government reservation, Joseph and 800 Nez

Percés had fled across the Bitterroot Mountains, followed their eastern slopes to Wyoming, turned northward into Montana, and launched a breathtaking run for the Canadian border. Along the way they had fought seven major engagements with the U.S. Cavalry, winning five of them and killing 180 troopers. Their long odyssey remains one of the most remarkable feats in military history, but it ended in bitter defeat in Montana's Bear Paw Mountains.

The large faction of Indians led by Joseph—and commanded in battle by his brother Ollokot, a brilliant tactician—had seceded from a tribe numbering 4,000. Occupying eastern Oregon and western Idaho, the Nez Percés first came in contact with American pioneers through Presbyterian and Jesuit missionaries in 1836. By 1855 two-thirds of the tribe had become Christians and farmers, and all of them had agreed to live on a large Idaho reservation incorporating most of their traditional homeland. But eight years later, gold strikes within their sanctuary led to a tribal split: an 1863 treaty opened "mineral districts" on the original reservation to waves of prospectors from the East. The Nez Percés whose homes lay within the boundaries of the new reservation—by far the largest faction—signed the treaty and remained where they were. But Chief Joseph's father (who died in 1871) refused to sign and led 300 warriors and their families back to Oregon's Wallowa Valley. In 1873 the government declared part of the area a reservation for Joseph's "Non-treaty" Indians, only to reverse its decision two years later under furious protest by settlers and farmers in the valley. (Vivid memories of a long, bitter war against the Cayuse tribe—ignited by the Indians' unprovoked massacre of 15 civilians in 1847—had left the settlers with precious little sympathy for Oregon's Native Americans).

Joseph's three-month war began with an awful incident beyond his control. On June 13, 1877, four young braves inflamed on stolen whiskey killed four white civilians. Several other intoxicated warriors went on a two-day rampage, murdering a settler named Chamberlain, his two children, and his pregnant wife (whom they disemboweled). At least 19 settlers died before Joseph regained control. Certain that the army would seek bloody revenge on the whole tribe, the Nez Percés ambushed 100 cavalrymen at White Bird Canyon on June 17 and fled for the Bitterroot Mountains. General Oliver Howard and more than 400 soldiers took the field in hot pursuit, and the long race for Canada was on. Three hundred Nez Percés eventually slipped through the soldiers' lines and escaped, but Joseph and the rest of the fugitives, cut off by cavalry attacking from all directions, fell 40 miles short of their goal. On October 5, Joseph faced a sympathetic General Howard in the bitter autumn cold and surrendered with stirring eloquence: "Our chiefs are killed. The old men are all dead. It is cold, and we have no blankets. The little children are freezing to death. From where the sun now stands, I will fight no more forever." At first sent to sanctuaries in Kansas and Oklahoma, the Nez Percés eventually moved to Washington State's Colville reservation, where Joseph died in 1904.

I Will Fight *No More Forever* is a fine film that needlessly distorts or omits a few messy facts out of sympathy for the Nez Percés. Heffron downplays the awful atrocities inflicted on settlers by drunken Nez Percé warriors, for example, and he gives Joseph, not Ollokot, credit for the brilliant tactics that almost carried the tribe

to Canada and freedom. Still, this is a very good movie, and Heffron's portraits of Howard, his aide, and the cavalrymen who fought the war are accurate and fair-minded.

Recommended Reading:
Mark H. Brown, *The Flight of the Nez Percé: A History of the Nez Percé War.*

Jeremiah Johnson ★★★★
(1972) 107 Minutes

Director: Sydney Pollack

Cast: Robert Redford, Will Geer, Stefan Gierasch, Allyn Ann McLerie, Charles Tyner, Josh Albee

Historical Background: Mountain men were the toughest characters ever produced by the American West: on one occasion, a hermit-like trapper named Tom Smith amputated his own shattered leg with a skinning knife to prevent gangrene. So perilous were the hazards of a two-year tour in the High Rockies that fewer than 150 souls survived the entire 18-year era of the American trapper. Those who didn't make it died of smallpox, tetanus, bacterial infection, animal attacks, drowning, dysentery, food poisoning, snakebites, accidental gunshot wounds, and long falls from cliffs or precipitous mountain trails. Many perished at the hands of the hated Blackfeet and Arikara Indians.

All of this to supply whimsical Atlantic Coast and European clothing markets with pelts for fashionable $10 beaver-skin hats. (John Jacob Astor's American Fur Co. and W. H. Ashley's Rocky Mountain Fur Co. built fortunes on the trappers' annual haul.) Money—not misanthropy or thirst for adventure—impelled men to head for the mountains. A competent trapper could average 125 pelts and a hefty $1,000 profit per season; the best of them caught 350 beaver each year, and legendary Jedediah Smith once harvested 665 skins. In 1822, the first trapping expedition left St. Louis and sailed up the Missouri River for the Rockies. During the next 18 years, hundreds of men followed in canoes, keelboats, log rafts, and dugouts, usually completing their journeys in four months. Most of them hauled the same basic outfit: one buckskin suit with an extra pair of leggings, a year's supply of coffee, tea, and salt, a dozen knives, a clay pipe and tobacco, several beaver traps, a pair of pistols, and—most important of all—a single-shot .60-caliber Hawken rifle, accurate at 250 yards and powerful enough to put a grizzly bear flat on its back. Along with his rifle each man packed extra flints, 20 to 30 pounds of black powder, and plenty of lead. (Trappers took little or no food on their expeditions, surviving instead on fish and wild game.)

Mountain men camped and hunted in groups called "brigades" or set up shop on their own. Some built cabins, but most lived in primitive three-sided "shantees" made from dried animal skins stretched over wooden frames. As soon as streams, ponds, and marshes began to thaw, the trapper went to work, anchoring his traps far enough beneath the water's surface to drown struggling beaver once they were caught. The trapping season ended five or six months later, when waterways froze over. Once a year (usually in early July) the trappers packed their skins—dried, stretched, and scraped—to an annual month-long rendezvous. There they sold pelts and bought supplies for the coming year, then spent most of their money on liquor and Indian girls before returning to the wilderness, where the process began all over again.

In 1840, the last great rendezvous ended everything. The beaver population had dwindled, but that mattered little, since silk hats had become fashionable on the Atlantic Coast and overseas. Most trappers moved on to a variety of other trades: some became army scouts, others signed on as guides for settlers moving to Oregon or prospectors headed for the California goldfields. Few of them left the mountains with money in their pockets, but they had charted the American wilderness from the eastern slopes of the Rockies to the Pacific Ocean, leaving historians with one of the Old West's most colorful legacies.

Well crafted and beautifully filmed, *Jeremiah Johnson* paints a grimly realistic picture of the trapper's perilous, solitary existence in a supremely hostile environment. Redford performs admirably in the title role, and Geer is wonderful as a grizzled old trapper who wanders through the movie, appearing at key points to palaver with Redford and offer tips for survival in the high country. The film's intermittent chronicle of the fragile truce between trappers and Indians is first-rate.

For Further Viewing:
Man in the Wilderness ★★★★ (1971) 105 Minutes (Richard Harris, John Huston, John Bindon,

Ben Carruthers): Based on a true incident in the life of mountain man Hugh Glass, who crawled 90 miles to safety after being mauled horribly by a grizzly bear and left for dead by his companions. A very good movie, well directed and acted by a fine cast.

The Mountain Men ★★ (1980) 102 Minutes (Charlton Heston, Brian Keith, Victoria Racimo): Heston plays an aging trapper battling Blackfeet and scratching out a meager existence during the final years of the fur trade. Not Hollywood's best film on the mountain men, but not as awful as many critics insist, either. Period detail alone makes this worth a look.

Recommended Reading:
Paul C. Phillips and J. W. Smurr, *The Fur Trade;* Dale L. Morgan, *Jedediah Smith and the Opening of the West;* Robert M. Utley, *A Life Wild and Perilous: Mountain Men and the Path to the Pacific.*

The Last Command ★★★★

(1955) 110 Minutes

Director: Frank Lloyd

Cast: Sterling Hayden, Ernest Borgnine, Richard Carlson, Arthur Hunnicutt

Historical Background: Winter 1835–36: For foot-slogging privates in Mexican dictator Santa Anna's army, just getting from Mexico City to San Antonio de Béxar and the Alamo was a terrible ordeal. There was never enough to eat. Clad in thin cotton uniforms, many soldiers died of hypothermia in the damp central Texas winter. Long marches over rocky terrain shredded sandals and flimsy shoes, and many men finished the 950-mile journey on lacerated bare feet. There were no medical supplies or surgeons: soldiers weakened by dysentery fell to the ground and died from sheer neglect. During the siege, inferior weapons cost many Mexican lives. Poor gunpowder rendered Santa Anna's artillery wildly inaccurate. His infantry carried obsolete, notoriously unreliable smooth-bore muskets, effective only when fired simultaneously from tight formations—a frightening procedure, according to author Jeff Long. On one occasion, the sulfurous concussion from a young draftee's musket knocked a nearby man to the ground, his hair aflame. "I [was] made a sergeant," the conscript said, "to prevent me from firing any more guns." Small wonder that nine Mexican soldiers fell for every defender they killed. (Long understates Mexican losses at 600; the figure given by Santa Anna's secretary, 1,544, may be too high, but it is probably closer to the truth.)

Drawn to the northern Mexican province of Tejas by generous government land grants, the "Texians" holding the Alamo and most of their fellow colonists had grown to loathe Mexico's capricious, increasingly repressive federal government. (Some established landowners and immigrants connected in Mexico by marriage or business activities were more ambivalent toward the central government.) Civil liberties had disappeared. Taxes were too high. By 1832, the Texians were spoiling for a fight, and on June 26 a group of colonists infuriated by federal moves to impose martial law routed the small Mexican garrison at Anahuac. Stephen F. Austin's pleas for provincial democratic reform drew 11 weeks of thundering silence from Mexico City, and three years later a full-scale insurrection was on. The 1836 Alamo siege was the fifth engagement in Texas' short, bloody war of independence. In June and October 1835, rebel volunteers and Mexican troops clashed at Anahuac, Gonzales, and Goliad. Then, after five days of bitter fighting, 300 Texians led by Benjamin Milam drove 1,400 federal troops from San Antonio on December 9. About 180 rebels occupied the Alamo, and Santa Anna began building an expeditionary force.

Originally called the Mission of San Antonio de Valero, the Alamo opened in 1757 as a center for teaching Indians how to farm and raise livestock. Without protective bastions for its 12-foot walls or gunports to shield riflemen and cannoneers, it made a poor fortress. The mission was too large for prolonged defense by the small band of rebels: its three-acre plaza spread their ranks and made concentrated firepower throughout their perimeter impossible, ensuring a breach if attackers assaulted from four sides at once. Supreme commander Sam Houston wanted to destroy the fort and fight an aggressive, hit-them-hard-and-run guerrilla war. But William Travis, sharing command of the San Antonio militia with Jim Bowie, wouldn't budge. As Santa Anna's legions began closing in, the Texians worked feverishly to bolster the Alamo's defenses.

The Mexicans occupied San Antonio on February 22. Fighting erupted the next day, when Travis answered Santa Anna's surrender demands with a booming shot from an 18-pound howitzer. Steady bombardment by Mexican artillery and probing infantry attacks began, and by March 4, Santa Anna's 5,000-man

army surrounded the Alamo, severing it from reinforcement or resupply. The final assault came at 5 A.M. on March 6. Four thousand Mexicans simultaneously blitzed the old mission's east wall, its heavily fortified south wall, and its two northern corners. Sharpshooting rebels cut the Mexicans to pieces as they advanced, but the attackers were relentless. Travis fell almost immediately, struck in the head by a musket ball after emptying his double-barreled shotgun into a clot of enemy troops scaling the north wall. Ill with pneumonia (or tuberculosis), Bowie died in bed from multiple bayonet wounds. Furious disagreement persists about Davy Crockett's fate: some historians insist that he surrendered and pleaded for mercy before his execution by firing squad; others believe that he fought to the bitter end, killing 20 Mexicans before falling. Ninety minutes after the assault began, the Alamo's last defenders died in the barracks built into the mission's east wall. (A handful of women and children survived the battle.) The siege had little strategic effect, but it gave Sam Houston time to consolidate his forces and strengthened his commitment to mobile offensive warfare. At 4:30 P.M. on April 21—six weeks after the Alamo fell—800 raging Texians surprised Santa Anna at San Jacinto, slaughtering 650 federal soldiers and ending Mexican rule north of the Rio Grande.

Easily the best film about the legendary siege—and the only one that examines the choices facing colonial families with relatives and business associates on the Mexican side. It distorts history in places (creating, for example, a familiarity between Bowie and Santa Anna that never existed), but its portrait of early Texas and its account of events preceding the Alamo fight are remarkably accurate. Hayden's understated Bowie—torn by old loyalties to Mexico's aristocracy and new sympathy for democratic colonials—is a bull's-eye. Hunnicutt is perfect as a folksy, opportunistic Crockett, and Lloyd's re-creation of the siege is the best on film.

For Further Viewing:

The Alamo ★★★ (1960) 161 Minutes (John Wayne, Richard Widmark, Laurence Harvey, Chill Wills, Ken Curtis): Hollywood's best-known film on the legendary battle. *The Alamo* is reasonably accurate, even though it inflates the characters of Bowie (Widmark) and Crockett (Wayne). Harvey's pugnacious rendition of Travis would be perfect if it weren't so florid, and Wills is wonderful as one of Crockett's rambunctious, hard-drinking Tennesseans. Rousing battle scenes are expertly done.

The Alamo: 13 Days to Glory ★★ (1987) 145 Minutes (James Arness, Brian Keith, Raul Julia, Alec Baldwin): Based on Lon Tinkle's *13 Days to Glory,* this torpid version of the Alamo saga seems to drag on longer than the actual siege did. Arness, Keith, and Baldwin are well-cast, but they can't overcome a trite, ponderous script. Julia performs well as a fuming, grandiose Santa Anna, and director Burt Kennedy's sweeping battle scenes are excellent—but they can't offset more than an hour of long-winded tedium.

Recommended Reading:
Jeff Long, *Duel of Eagles: The Mexican and U.S. Fight for the Alamo;* Lon Tinkle, *13 Days to Glory.*

The Last Day ★★★★

(1975) 100 Minutes

Director: Vincent McEveety

Cast: Richard Widmark, Robert Conrad, Christopher Connelly, Richard Jaeckel, Tim Matheson, Barbara Rush, Tom Skerritt

Historical Background: October 12, 1892—Coffeyville, Kan.: At 9:45 A.M. an odd spectacle unfolded in Coffeyville's business district—several men milling about on the street abruptly dropped what they were doing and headed for the town's two hardware stores. Moments later, many were outside again. Packing brand-new shotguns, rifles, and pistols, they walked into shops on both sides of the street and took positions at every window on the block. Bob, Grat, and Emmett Dalton—supported by Bill Powers and Dick Broadwell—were robbing both of Coffeyville's banks at the same time. But the outlaws had made two fatal errors: the Daltons had once lived in Coffeyville, and they were wearing preposterous fake mustaches and beards that drew startled looks from at least two bystanders who instantly recognized them. Worse still, street workers had removed the hitching rails from Coffeyville's main thoroughfare, and instead of canceling the raid, the gunmen left their horses in an alley (known today as Death Alley) two blocks from the banks—a very long walk for bandits hauling away every cent in town. (A few historians believe that lawman Chris Madsen had warned

Coffeyville's authorities that the Daltons were coming, but the only evidence for this theory came in 1942 from secondhand reports of Madsen's recollections of the raid.)

Moments after their arrival, Powers, Broadwell, and Grat Dalton took the Condon Bank, while Bob and Emmett Dalton struck the First National across the street. The Condon trio, believing a bank officer's phony story that an impenetrable time lock protected his vault, walked away empty-handed. Emmett and Bob Dalton rifled $30,000 from First National's coffers, but as soon as the gunmen hit the street, withering gunfire poured in on them. Somehow they all managed to sprint back to their horses, but they got no farther: Coffeyville's raging ad hoc army shot them down one by one as they tried to bolt from Death Alley, and—just like that—the most elusive band of outlaws ever seen in the West ceased to exist. Broadwell, Powers, and Bob and Grat Dalton were dead on the ground, while Emmett Dalton—riddled with 20 gunshot wounds—lay barely breathing next to his older brothers. In fifteen thunderous minutes, Coffeyville, a nowhere town, had carved itself a permanent niche in the American West's storied history by exterminating the Daltons and bringing the era of the outlaw gangs to a close.

The Daltons' blunders remain incomprehensible. No one thought they'd ever be arrested or killed: they were former lawmen, and they never made mistakes. For 18 months they had stolen horses and robbed trains with impunity, eluding countless manhunts because they knew exactly how the law would react and pursue them. (The brothers had turned outlaw after discovering that a U.S. marshal was routinely pocketing federal payroll money belonging to them.) Details of the gang's legendary exploits should have died with them, but Emmett made a miraculous recovery. Pardoned after a 14-year stretch in prison, he joined the fledgling motion picture industry as an adviser (and, occasionally, an extra) for westerns. He died in 1937. Today, more than a century after the Daltons' last ride, the Condon Bank still prospers in Coffeyville.

A solid, entertaining documentary-style account of the Daltons' last raid and the three days preceding it. Conrad's tough Bob Dalton and Skerritt's burned-out, alcoholic Bill Powers are the best of many excellent performances by a fine ensemble cast. McEveety includes some highly speculative material—such as the mysterious common-law marriage of Bob Dalton and Daisy Bryant—but everyone who writes about the Daltons speculates about something. (Reputedly the sister of outlaw Charley Bryant, Daisy Bryant may actually have been real-life female bandit Flo Quick, who had a long affair with Dalton.) *The Last Day* also assumes that Coffeyville knew the Daltons were coming, thanks to Will Spence (Widmark)—a purely fictional character.

Recommended Reading:
Robert Barr Smith, *Daltons! The Raid on Coffeyville, Kansas;* David S. Elliott, *The Last Raid of the Daltons;* Nancy B. Samuelson, *The Dalton Gang Story.*

The Lawless Breed ★

(1952) 83 Minutes

Director: Raoul Walsh

Cast: Rock Hudson, Julia Adams, Hugh O'Brian, Dennis Weaver

Historical Background: August 23, 1877—Pensacola, Fla.: Texas Ranger John Armstrong stepped into a railroad car and looked straight at John Wesley Hardin, the man he'd ridden 900 miles to arrest. The pistoleer was heavily armed and easily provoked: Hardin had killed his first man—at age 15—for refusing to yield the right-of-way on a narrow road. Three years later he had poured a fusillade of pistol shots through a hotel-room wall, killing a stranger whose snoring had disturbed his sleep. In ten short years Hardin had slain 44 men, including nine soldiers, two Pinkerton detectives, five cowboys, a trail boss, at least five lawmen, and a carnival roustabout who had asked to see his admission slip. As soon as he spotted Armstrong, Hardin drew a nickel-plated Colt Thunderer from his cross-draw shoulder holster, but the pistol's hammer snarled in his suspenders. According to a deputy, the most dangerous man on earth "almost pulled his breeches off over his head" as he thrashed wildly about to dislodge his weapon. He didn't make it. Armstrong's gun barrel smashed into his head, driving him to the floor. Five weeks later, a jury in Comanche, Tex., sent him packing to Huntsville State Prison on a 25-year sentence for murdering a deputy sheriff.

During his internment, Hardin underwent a stunning character change. He studied law books, theological texts, and the Bible. He became captain of the prison debating team and head of the Sunday school class. So complete was his transformation that he received a full pardon in March 1894, and moved with his son and two daughters to a friend's ranch near Gonzales, Tex. (His wife, Jane, had died in 1892, a tragedy that haunted him for the rest of his life.) After passing the Texas bar examination, Hardin moved to El Paso and opened a law office. His practice went nowhere, and he began drinking heavily. On August 19, 1895, he joined a dice game in the Acme Saloon, where John Selman—a constable who had drawn threats from Hardin by arresting his girlfriend for loitering—spotted him through a window. Selman stormed into the bar and shot Hardin behind his left ear. For two hours, the legendary gunman lay dead on the floor while everyone in town filed by to view his body. The following day, El Paso's newspaper printed the 42-year-old killer's photograph above an undertaker's remark: "Except for being dead, Hardin appeared to be in remarkably good shape."

The high point of Walsh's dull portrait of Wes Hardin as an unjustly persecuted victim comes with a Ranger captain's unintentionally funny appraisal of the gunman's character: "John Wesley Hardin has made the name of Texas stink in the nostrils of justice." Loosely based on Hardin's autobiography, *The Lawless Breed* falsifies virtually everything about his bloody ten-year killing spree. It implies that lawmen charged him with many unsolved murders to cover their own incompetence. Walsh kills the woman Hardin actually married—Jane Bowen—before he goes to prison and marries him off to buxom Julia Adams, who spends most of her screen time in frilly bloomers. Instead of practicing law after his pardon, Walsh's Hardin settles down with Adams on a horse farm. Forget this one—read Lewis Nordyke's fine biography instead.

For Further Viewing:

The Gunfighter ★★★★ (1950) 84 Minutes (Gregory Peck, Helen Westcott, Millard Mitchell, Jean Parker, Karl Malden): Superb chronicle of an ex-gunfighter's last hours—and a more realistic look at reformed outlaws suffering the consequences of earlier mistakes than *The Lawless Breed.* Peck (the gunfighter) and Mitchell (a lawman who once rode with him) perform flawlessly in a film set almost entirely in a saloon, where Peck waits for a meeting with his estranged wife. The town, meanwhile, broils with gossip and speculation about who will finally kill the aging gunman. One of the first—and best—examples of a new type of film called (in 1950s parlance) the "adult western."

Recommended Reading:

Lewis Nordyke, *John Wesley Hardin, Texas Gunman;* John Wesley Hardin, *The Life of John Wesley Hardin as Written by Himself;* Dale Schoenberger, *The Gunfighters;* Joseph G. Rosa, *The Gunfighter.*

Lawman ★★★★

(1971) 98 Minutes

Director: Michael Winner

Cast: Burt Lancaster, Robert Ryan, Lee J. Cobb, Robert Duvall, Sheree North, Richard Jordan

Historical Background: August 14, 1889—Lathrop, Calif.: Onlookers in the local train station sat spellbound by a two-man spectacle almost as incongruous as it was volatile. David Terry—a hulking 6′2″ mesomorph who had just assaulted Supreme Court Justice Stephen Field—stood motionless as Deputy U.S. Marshal David Neagle stepped into his path. Neagle was five feet tall. Pointing his right index finger straight at Terry's nose, he ordered the big man out of the room. With a bellowing roar, Terry went for his knife. The steady, hard-eyed lawman drew a revolver from his left hip pocket and shot his adversary cleanly through the heart. Chalk one up for the law.

Justice Field was lucky—25 years earlier Neagle might not have been there to protect him. The mid-century West was a confused jumble of safe havens and regions utterly without law. Local police forces, if they existed at all, were no match for growing waves of people seeking land, silver, and gold. Vigilance committees thrived, especially in boom towns: between 1863 and 1864 the "Vigilantes of Montana" hanged 25 outlaws in Virginia City. (Since there were no prisons in western Montana, acquittal and execution were a suspect's only possibilities.) West of the Mississippi, U.S. marshals were in high demand.

Appointed by the president to enforce federal law, each marshal usually patrolled an entire state or territory. By the 1870s, many were administrators, dispatching squads of deputies into the worst areas. The "Indian Territory" (now Oklahoma), a 74,000-square-mile wilderness infested with squalid criminals, was a graveyard for lawmen: 25% of all the deputy marshals killed between 1789 and 1989 died during a 24-year bloodbath that began there in 1872. (In the end, the deputies were too tough to lose the war. Legendary Texan Heck Thomas once arrested 32 prisoners—by himself—in Oklahoma and hauled them to a Fort Smith jail.) As time passed, pressure on the deputies eased: more elected sheriffs policed counties, and "town marshals" brought the law to mining camps and cow towns. Even so, the names of federal lawmen and their deputies still resonate the loudest in chronicles of the American West: Wild Bill Hickok, Heck Thomas, Ben Daniels, Bill Tilghman—and tough, pint-sized David Neagle, who blasted his way into history almost exactly 100 years after George Washington appointed Nathaniel Ramsey America's first U.S. marshal.

Lancaster is a taciturn, tough-as-nails U.S. marshal pursuing several louts who accidentally gunned down an old man during a drunken revel. After tracking them to a dreary little town, he discovers that one is married to old flame North, while others work for a popular—and powerful—local rancher (Cobb). Ignoring the crime's loose ends (as he must), Lancaster soon stands alone against everyone else in the area. From start to finish, *Lawman* is a fine chronicle of the isolation and danger facing 19th-century U.S. marshals. Jordan's hotheaded cowhand almost steals the show, and Ryan is excellent as an aging, overcautious sheriff caught between unyielding forces that seem destined to clash despite everyone's best efforts to keep them apart.

For Further Viewing:

The Tin Star ★★★★ (1957) 93 Minutes (Henry Fonda, Anthony Perkins, Neville Brand, Betsy Palmer, John McIntire): Tough bounty hunter and former lawman Fonda visits a small Western town to collect reward money for killing a notorious outlaw. Waiting for the cash to arrive, he drifts into friendship with green—but winsome—new sheriff Ben Owen (well played by Perkins) and schools him in pistoleer/law-enforcement techniques. Brutal slimeball "Bogardus" (Brand, in a show-stealing performance) soon puts the rookie sheriff's new skills to the test. A fine, low-keyed examination of law-enforcement psychology and social dynamics in small frontier towns from director Anthony Mann *(The Far Country, Winchester '73, Bend of the River)*.

High Noon ★★★★ (1952) 84 Minutes (Gary Cooper, Grace Kelly, Thomas Mitchell, Lloyd Bridges, Katy Jurado): Deserted by his new bride (Kelly) and an entire town when vengeful ex-cons come to kill him on his wedding day, Cooper (Marshal Will Kane) and Jurado (his former mistress) dominate director Fred Zinnemann's legendary story of loyalty and courage under fire. Zinnemann scores two bull's-eyes for historical accuracy: for many years, Western towns had to defend themselves against outlawry (no FBI or state troopers to help), and—like Will Kane—local lawmen occasionally found themselves fresh out of friends when trouble rode into town. Gregory Peck refused the role played well enough by Cooper to win the Best Actor Oscar.

Recommended Reading:
Frederick S. Calhoun, *The Lawmen;* Robert Sabbag, *Too Tough to Die: Down and Dangerous with the U.S. Marshals.*

The Long Riders ★★★★

(1980) 100 Minutes

Director: Walter Hill

Cast: David, Keith, and Robert Carradine, Jim and Stacy Keach, Dennis and Randy Quaid, Christopher and Nicholas Guest, Pamela Reed.

Historical Background: 2 P.M., September 7, 1876—Northfield, Minn.: Turning to mount his horse, gunman Clell Miller took a full load of pepperlike birdshot—smack in the face at close range—from an angry townsman's light shotgun. Medical student Henry Wheeler quickly shattered Miller's sternum with a well-aimed rifle shot, and the first outlaw casualty in 19th-century America's sorriest high-crime snafu was history. Seconds later, blacksmith Anselm Manning catapulted Bill Chadwell from his galloping horse with a shot through the heart. Cole Younger fell

next, hit in the thigh as he sprinted to Miller's aid. Inside the First National Bank, Frank James decapitated Joseph Heywood with a pistol shot after the cashier gamely slammed a vault door on the pistoleer's outstretched arm. Jesse James broiled hotly near a lobby window as his gang's final heist unraveled at warp speed.

Hopelessly checkmated, the James brothers and Bob Younger bolted into Northfield's roaring streets, mounted their horses, and galloped away, through withering gunfire, with Charlie Pitts, Jim Younger, and Cole. On September 17, they split up near Mankato, riding in different directions to confuse hundreds of pursuing lawmen. Four days later, Sheriff James Glispin and six deputies killed Pitts and captured the Youngers near Madelia, S.D. (Riddled with 11 gunshot wounds, Cole Younger rose flamboyantly to his feet in a clattering wagon and tipped his hat to townspeople cheering the returning posse.) Sharpshooting lawmen and outraged civilians had killed three outlaws and wounded four others. Only Frank and Jesse had escaped, taking with them their total haul from bloody Northfield: $26.70.

The legendary bandits never recovered. For ten years they'd scored coup after coup, robbing banks in Liberty (1866), Savannah (1867), Richmond (1867), and Gallatin (1869), Mo. They rifled Corydon, Iowa's treasury office in 1871, then robbed the town's biggest bank a day later; in 1872, they stole $10,000 at the Kansas City State Fair; two years after that, they robbed trains and banks in Arkansas, Iowa, and Missouri. They were unstoppable. As hard-riding killers for William Quantrill's Bushwhackers during the Kansas–Missouri border wars (see *Dark Command*), the James–Younger steamroller had written the book on knocking off small-town banks: chart the city layout and split your force; strike targets quickly and hard while half your men wreak diversionary chaos in crowded streets; take the money and ride out before lawmen and residents can regroup and fight back. The gang's blitzkrieg tactics had prevailed in at least 20 holdups, but Northfield—a "secondary target" loaded with Civil War veterans trained and willing to use firearms—was different. Jesse had canceled a well-planned raid on Mankato (the gang's first choice) because he believed residents had recognized him during a reconnaissance run. On Chadwell's impulsive recommendation he decided to hit Northfield. Worst of all, the First National Bank fiasco had marooned the outlaws in alien country, far from compliant ex-rebels eager to protect them from stalking lawmen.

After their arrest, the Youngers landed in Minnesota's Stillwater State Penitentiary (Bob died there; Cole and Jim left on parole in 1901). On April 3, 1882, fellow outlaw Bob Ford murdered Jesse James in his St. Joseph home. Five months later, Frank James surrendered to Missouri governor Thomas Crittenden and weathered four years of grueling, inconclusive criminal trials. He and Cole Younger spent their last years packing lecture-circuit halls, telling rapt audiences that crime doesn't pay—and collecting fat appearance fees for their time and trouble.

Reaches, Carradines, Quaids, and Guests perform well as the brothers James, Younger, Miller, and Ford in this crackling version of the outlaw saga. Hill's history misfires occasionally: the real Cole Younger probably never touched Belle Starr (well played by Reed), but Hill locks them in a steamy long-term affair. The film's worst blunder has Frank and Jesse deserting the ravaged Youngers—to Cole's fury—immediately after Northfield, a popular notion denied vehemently by the real Youngers in interviews. Still, a fine film and an accurate, detailed portrait of the harsh postbellum world of the 1870s.

For Further Viewing:

The Return of Frank James ★★ (1940) 92 Minutes (Henry Fonda, Gene Tierney, John Carradine, Jackie Cooper): Fonda reprises his 1939 portrayal of Frank James in this Fritz Lang sequel to *Jesse James*. The film's premise—that a reformed Frank James, disillusioned by the law's failure to punish Bob Ford, would seek justice on his own—is loony. But *The Return of Frank James* filled many theaters and remains interesting to history buffs for two reasons: it reflects Hollywood's compulsion to thicken the fictional haze surrounding the outlaw's ugly exploits, and Missouri actually buzzed, during the early 1880s, with half-baked reports that Frank planned to avenge Jesse's death (some people think the rumors drove Charlie Ford to commit suicide).

Recommended Reading:

Marley Brant, *The Outlaw Youngers: A Confederate Brotherhood;* William A. Settle, *Jesse James Was His Name: Or, Fact and Fiction Concerning the Careers of the Notorious James Brothers of Missouri.*

Pony Express ★★★

(1953) 101 Minutes

Director: Jerry Hopper

Cast: Charlton Heston, Rhonda Fleming, Jan Sterling, Forrest Tucker

Historical Background: Summer 1860: Intent on packing the mail to Butte Station, Utah, in record time, Pony Express rider Howard Egan galloped into a narrow canyon, then suddenly reined in his horse. It was dusk, and he had ridden straight to the edge of a Paiute war camp. Unable to ride around the bivouac, Egan never considered retracing his route to Shell Creek Station and safety. Kicking his horse hard in the flanks and screaming at the top of his lungs, he roared through the camp at a pell-mell gallop, firing his Colt Navy revolver in all directions. Certain that they were under cavalry attack, the terrified Indians scattered in all directions as Egan rode on with the mail.

A rousing story, but by company standards little more than routine: no matter what the obstacles, the Pony Express record for speed and reliability was incredible. Its extraordinary riders routinely hauled mail from St. Joseph, Mo., to Sacramento—2,000 miles across endless prairie, wide rivers, and snow-choked mountain passes—in ten days, less than half the fastest time posted by any other mail delivery system. By 1861, 150 relay stations marked the route between Missouri and California, with "home stations" (where riders could rest) positioned at 100-mile intervals along the trail. Changing horses every ten miles, each man rode the distance between two home stations before "relaying" the mail to the next rider. (Circumstances often required longer trips: 19-year-old Jack Keetly once galloped 345 miles in 31 hours, arriving at Fort Kearney ahead of schedule—and sound asleep.) Letters—written on tissue paper because of the exorbitant $5-per-half-ounce rates—rode in four boxlike *cantinas* fixed to the corners of ingeniously designed leather devices called *mochilas*. Resting atop the saddle and held in place by slits fitting over the saddle horn and rear cantle, *mochilas* extended just below the rider's knees on each side of his horse and were impossible to remove—or drop—unless the rider dismounted.

Russell, Majors, & Waddell—a huge freighting company—launched the Pony Express on April 3, 1860, with 80 riders and 500 high-priced Kentucky Thoroughbreds. But horsemen couldn't compete with Western Union's new transcontinental telegraph line. In 1838, Samuel Morse had developed an electromagnetic keying system for transmitting signals to receivers that transcribed dots and dashes on rolls of paper. Eighteen years later, "sounding-key" systems made modern telegraphy possible. Ezra Cornell, underwriter for most of Morse's research, parlayed the new technology into a communications empire by merging many small companies into Western Union Telegraph. In 1860, Western Union lines stretched from Nebraska to the Atlantic. On July 4, 1861, construction gangs in Sacramento and Omaha began stringing wire toward each other through inclement weather and rugged terrain. They met in Salt Lake City on October 24, linking Western Union offices in New York and San Francisco and dealing a death blow to the Pony Express: Russell, Majors, & Waddell officially discontinued their grand enterprise on October 26, 1861. During its brief 18-month existence, the Pony Express had logged more than 150 round trips, totaling 650,000 miles, between St. Joseph and Sacramento. By 1866, meanwhile, Cornell's expanding juggernaut had strung 75,000 miles of wire around the U.S., making Western Union America's first corporate monopoly.

Buffalo Bill (Heston) joins Wild Bill Hickok (Tucker) to push the famous mail route past ruthless saboteurs and surly Indians to Sacramento. Colorful, entertaining, and thoroughly inaccurate historically. Absurd fictions abound: Hickok never got close to an Express pony, and Cody worked in Kansas as a boy messenger for Pony Express offices four miles apart; Heston buys Indian ponies for the fledgling mail service, which really purchased most of its horses from army quartermasters; in a loony subplot, Fleming and cohorts sabotage relay stations as part of a scheme to get California to pull out of the Union. Great fun, though: where else can you see Jan Sterling start a mudfight with Rhonda Fleming?

For Further Viewing:
Western Union ★★★★ (1941) 94 Minutes (Robert Young, Randolph Scott, Dean Jagger, Virginia Gilmore, John Carradine, Slim Summerville, Chill Wills): Entertaining film version of Zane Grey's novel has Young working feverishly to complete the telegraph circuit linking the two coasts. Scott is perfect as a reformed outlaw working on the project. The main plot element, Confederate renegades dressed as Indians sabotaging the wire, is fictional; just one war-related incident seriously hampered

Western Union's transcontinental project: in June 1861, Missouri governor Claiborne Jackson ordered the Jefferson City line torn down. Western Union's main concerns at the time were bad weather and rough terrain on its western leg. Still, an excellent movie: many consider the famous "barbershop gunfight" Hollywood's best shootout.

Recommended Reading:
Raymond W. Settle and Mary Lund Settle, *Saddles and Spurs: The Pony Express Saga;* Phil Ault, *Wires West;* Robert Luther Thompson, *Wiring a Continent: The History of the Telegraph Industry in the United States, 1832–1866.*

The Searchers ★★★★★

(1956) 119 Minutes

Director: John Ford

Cast: John Wayne, Jeffrey Hunter, Vera Miles, Ward Bond, Natalie Wood, Harry Carey, Jr., Henry Brandon, Lana Wood.

Historical Background: March 19, 1840—Bexar Council House, Texas Republic: With cold fury, three government commissioners, several local ranchers, and a squad of Texas Militia gazed at the ravaged countenance of 16-year-old Matilda Lockhart, kidnapped years earlier and brought for ransom to the Bexar Peace Council by Penataka Comanche chief Maguara. Every inch of the girl's body bore bruises, sores, and scars from beatings and repeated burnings; Comanche squaws had seared her nose off all the way to bone remnants protruding from a ghastly hole in the center of her face. Asked by hard-eyed commissioners for 200 additional captives he'd promised to deliver on the council's opening day, Maguara stupidly demanded more blankets and ammunition in ransom, adding, "How do you like that answer?" as he returned to his seat. A heartbeat later, blazing militia guns shredded the entire Penataka delegation, leaving 65 Indians dead on the floor and declaring total war—with no quarter—until Comanche depredations on the Texas frontier ended forever.

The bellicose Texans couldn't have drawn tougher adversaries: "Comanche" is the Spanish derivative of a Ute term (*komántcia*) meaning "anyone who wants to fight me all the time." Driven from the Snake River region by larger tribes packing European firearms, the Comanches languished militarily until 17th-century Spanish explorers brought horses to the Rio Grande. Many animals escaped, and wild mustangs soon swarmed over the southern Plains, falling into Comanche hands by the thousands. Overnight, the tribe's fighting prowess flowered. Before they were five years old, Comanche boys owned their own ponies. Drilling day after day, they learned to fire arrows and snatch twigs from the ground at a full gallop. Afoot they were nothing, but on horseback Comanche braves were demons—military historians still consider them the finest light cavalry the world has ever seen. By 1719, they were terrorizing settlements in New Mexico. They happily mauled their traditional Ute, Pawnee, and Tonkawa enemies and routed military-trading expeditions from Mexico. For more than a century, they ruled a 450-mile-wide area bordered on the north

by the Arkansas River and reaching 600 miles southward to present-day San Antonio.

Comanche forays against Anglo-Texans began with a savage 1836 raid on Isaac Parker's fort near Waco. (Kidnapped during the raid, Parker's young daughter Cynthia Ann remained with the Indians for a quarter century. In 1850, five years after Texas joined the Union, she gave birth to Quanah Parker, the last—and greatest—Comanche war chief. He fought the army to a standstill for eight years, finally surrendered in June 1875, then turned military defeat into incredible personal triumph, earning a fortune through railroad investments and cagey real estate deals with wealthy cattlemen. Rescued on the Pease River in 1860, Cynthia Ann lived with her brother until her death at age 37.) After the raid on Parker's fort, bitter guerrilla-style warfare between Indians and whites—punctuated by lame treaties and maddeningly whimsical government agendas—raged fitfully for 39 years. (Especially galling to Texans was a futile, short-lived 1869 federal "Peace Policy" depriving them of army protection against Comanche raids launched from reservation sanctuaries and fought with government-supplied hunting rifles.) Hostilities peaked with the legendary 1874 Adobe Walls standoff between 28 sharpshooting white hunters and 700 Comanches and Cheyennes. Their failure to overrun the tiny stronghold—thanks mainly to long-range enemy buffalo guns—wrecked the Indians' morale and triggered a downward spiral ending with Quanah Parker's June 1875 surrender at Fort Sill. The "Red River War" was over, and Comanche raiders would never thunder across Texas again.

Spectacular Monument Valley location filming and knockout performances by Wayne, Bond, and Hunter highlight Ford's most famous western. Snarling with hatred throughout, Wayne dominates the film as a tough Civil War veteran determined to find and kill the Comanche captors of his niece (Wood). Inaccurate in many details—after a decade in Comanche captivity, for example, Wood looks like a 19th-century Gibson Girl, not the broken remnant usually discovered by real-life frontier rescue parties—*The Searchers* still captures beautifully the bitter spirit of the long battle for Comancheria. Based on the Cynthia Ann Parker story and easily Ford's most memorable work. Wayne's performance as Ethan Edwards was his personal favorite.

For Further Viewing:
Two Rode Together ★★★★ (1961) 109 Minutes (James Stewart, Richard Widmark, Shirley Jones, John McIntire, Andy Devine, Linda Crystal): Director John Ford's encore to *The Searchers* teams jaded lawman Stewart with Widmark (a tough cavalry officer on special assignment) in a long, perilous expedition to find and rescue Texas pioneers captured years earlier by Comanches. Inferior to *The Searchers* as entertainment—what western isn't?—*Two Rode Together* paints a far grimmer picture of the toll taken by Comanche bondage on white victims (one of them, a long-term captive in his late teens, is an absolute wild man) and scores slightly higher marks for historical accuracy.

Recommended Reading:
Ernest Wallace and E. Adamson Hoebel, *The Comanches: Lords of the South Plains;* Bill Neeley, *The Last Comanche Chief: The Life and Times of Quanah Parker;* A. C. Greene, *The Last Captive: The Lives of Herman Lehmann.*

Son of the Morning Star ★★★

(1991) 186 Minutes

Director: Mike Robe

Cast: Gary Cole, Rosanna Arquette, Terry O'Quinn, David Strathairn, Dean Stockwell, George American Horse, Rodney A. Grant, Buffy St. Marie

Historical Background: December 21, 1866—Bozeman Trail, northern Wyoming: dispatched to rescue a woodcutting party under Indian attack, Captain William Fetterman and 80 bluecoats came to a halt just outside Fort Phil Kearny's walls as ten howling Sioux warriors bolted into view and rode straight at them. An artillery round from the fort momentarily scattered the attackers, forcing a measured retreat to the north (and away from the wood-train). But one of them—the young Oglala Crazy Horse—hung back, twirling a blanket above his head and taunting the soldiers. Spoiling for a fight, Fetterman and his men charged the war chief just as he wheeled to rejoin his comrades. For the troopers, it was a maddening chase: whenever they began closing on Crazy Horse he managed to pull away, just out of rifle range. Ignoring commander Henry Carrington's orders, Fetterman and his men pursued the Indians across Lodge Trail Ridge into Peno Valley—scant miles from the fort, but completely hidden from its lookouts. At that point, they were dead men. Crazy Horse had executed a brilliant ruse, holding his horse in a three-quarter-speed canter and pretending to quirt the animal furiously on its flanks. As the last troopers entered the valley, 2,000 Sioux and Cheyenne thundered into view from all directions, blackening the sky with arrows (40,000 by battle's end). Minutes later, Fetterman and every trooper in his detail lay dead on the ground. Hundreds of warriors savagely mutilated all 81 bodies, then left for the safety of remote winter camps.

A ghastly preview of Custer's Last Stand, the Fetterman Massacre was the first wholesale slaughter of a major American military force by Plains Indians. With bitter irony for the Sioux, it launched the bloody closing era of a traditional way of life based on violence and rapacity. An arrogant, warlike people, the Sioux were consummate predators: with horses brought to the New World by Spaniards, they became, in effect, a nomadic imperial power, attacking smaller tribes (the Crow, Pawnee, Arikara, and Shoshoni, among others) and plundering their ancestral hunting grounds. By the mid-19th century, six tribes of Teton Sioux—the Brulé, Oglala, Hunkpapa, Miniconjou, Sans Arcs, and Blackfeet—ruled the northern Plains from South Dakota to Montana's Bighorn Mountains. Their bloody collision with white Americans began with a random 1862 conflagration between settlers and the Eastern (Santee) Sioux in Minnesota. Robbed of government funds and provisions by corrupt reservation agents, the tribe split into angry factions—one urging negotiations with the Indian Bureau, the other open warfare. On August 17, 1862, Indian hunters impulsively murdered five innocent farmers, igniting a dreadful uprising by Santee militants. In one bloody month, a riot of killing, rape, and plunder left 800 whites dead. On September 23, a 1,600-man force under General Henry H.

Sibley ended the revolt, crushing 700 warriors at Wood Lake. Three months later, 38 Santee—some convicted unjustly—died on the gallows in Mankato.

Word of the bloodbath raged across the plains, spreading terror among settlers and fanning a smoldering belligerence in Teton leaders (especially Oglala leader Red Cloud) determined to rout small bands of miners taking the Bozeman Trail to Virginia City's goldfields. This they did handily, bringing a Congressional peace commission to negotiations and reaping major concessions in the Fort Laramie Treaty of 1868: forts protecting the Bozeman Trail closed, and all of South Dakota west of the Missouri River—the Great Sioux Reservation—went to the Indians; Sioux braves could hunt buffalo in additional "unceded Indian territory" blanketing the Bighorn Mountains and the Powder River Basin. But the "Nontreaty" Indians or "hunting bands"—3,000 Sioux and Northern Cheyenne led by Sitting Bull, Gall, and Crazy Horse—rejected the treaty, spurned the reservation, and regrouped in the unceded territory. Many Indians drifted between the two worlds, choosing the security of reservation life in winter and returning to Nontreaty camps during the summer.

The whole scheme was hopelessly fragile. Ambiguous on key points and utterly confusing to the Indians, the treaty invited violation by both sides. It authorized railroad construction anywhere in the area, virtually guaranteeing raids on unsuspecting Northern Pacific surveyors by Sitting Bull's braves. Fueled by visiting hunting bands, turmoil prevailed on the reservation: in 1872 and 1873, Nontreaty Indians attacked Fort Lincoln; they murdered ranchers and travelers in Nebraska and Montana; they invaded the Fort Berthold Agency to assault

Mandan and Arikara camps; in 1874, they killed an agency clerk, an army officer, and a corporal. Treaty violations by whites kicked into high gear with Horatio Nelson Ross's July 30, 1874, discovery of gold in the Black Hills. For President Grant, the timing couldn't have been worse. America's economy, still reeling from the Panic of 1873, had no place for thousands of desperately impoverished voters—all viewing the promise of reservation gold as a last-minute reprieve from imminent destitution. They looked to the Black Hills and saw an immense territory held by a handful of Indians indifferent to gold (or any sort of riches), but determined to keep it away from hungry white families. The army couldn't have kept them away with Gatling guns. By February 1876, 15,000 prospectors squatted in the Black Hills, digging for gold and ensuring some sort of showdown between Sitting Bull's growing legions and Grant's weary cavalry.

One peaceful solution—government purchase of the Black Hills—remained, but Grant first had to quell intimidation of Red Cloud's people by hostile Nontreaty warriors (in September 1875, they'd threatened to kill reservation chiefs negotiating sales proposals with the whites). Plains Division commander Philip Sheridan acted quickly: hotly contested melees at the Powder River (March 17, 1876) and Rosebud Creek (in mid-June) ended in narrow Sioux victories and drew more and more fuming Indians toward the Nontreaties' stronghold in the valley of the Little Bighorn. (Between June 18 and 24, the village swelled from 3,000 to 7,000 people—2,000 of them fighting men— in what amounted to a great Sioux–Cheyenne coalition fashioned by Sitting Bull.) On June 21, Brevet Gen. George Armstrong Custer, Gen. Alfred Terry, and Col. John Gibbon met on the Yellowstone River and laid plans to trap the Sioux: Custer would lead the 7th Cavalry Regiment down Rosebud Creek to the upper (or southern) Little Bighorn and strike northwest through the valley, driving the Indians into Gibbon's blocking force at the river's mouth.

On the 22nd, the 7th began its march along the Rosebud, soon picking up an Indian trail discovered earlier during a scouting expedition led by Maj. Marcus Reno. By June 24, the trail had spread out into a huge, much newer track swinging westward toward the lower Little Bighorn. Fearing that the Indians would spot him, Custer decided to launch his attack on the 25th (a day before Gibbon's column arrived). Unsure of his enemy's exact position (or strength) in the lower valley, he divided the 7th into three columns: with orders to rejoin the main force as quickly as possible, Captain Frederick Benteen and three companies swept northward down the left side of the valley to block, temporarily, that course of escape from the valley floor; Reno would attack the southern end of the Sioux village; to his right—across the Little Bighorn—Custer and 210 exhausted riders drove downriver atop a series of high bluffs to hit the camp's northern flank. A sound enough plan—but it began unraveling almost immediately. Reno's diversionary attack never got off the ground: his troops dismounted and formed a skirmish line when Gall and hundreds of Sioux suddenly swarmed forward from a hidden ravine. After 15 bloody minutes, Reno fell back in a rout (not a disciplined retreat) to a stand of cottonwoods near the river, then scrambled up the bluffs on its northern bank— four miles, now, behind the isolated main column.

By then Benteen had scouted the empty upper valley, but instead of rushing to help

Custer, he doubled back, rejoining Reno and the regiment's newly arrived packtrain. Frantically digging shallow trenches along the ridgeline, 368 terrified men waited for a crushing frontal assault. It would come later. Gall had spotted Custer descending the bluffs through Medicine Tail Coulee to ford the river and charge the village. Sensing no aggressive moves by Reno, the Sioux leader and 1,500 braves raced back down the valley and splashed across the water on Custer's left, forcing his troopers to fall back toward the bluff tops. Crazy Horse and 1,000 men were waiting for them. The Oglala chief had executed a complex flanking maneuver, sweeping around the camp's northern edge in a wide arc and storming up the ridgeline's reverse slope behind Custer's column. An ocean of Sioux and Cheyenne warriors rolled over the cavalrymen from all directions. In less than an hour, Custer and 210 soldiers lay dead in the field. Throughout the next day, Benteen and Reno repulsed furious assaults from their formidable hilltop positions above the river. Near sunset on the 26th, Sitting Bull's warriors finally disengaged, setting the prairie grass behind them ablaze and heading west for the Bighorn Mountains.

Controversy over Custer's responsibility for the disaster still rages, partly because no one really knows exactly how the fighting unfolded. Based partly on accounts of the battle distorted by Reno and Benteen to downplay their own mistakes, most familiar indictments of Custer crumble under close scrutiny. Custer, for example, didn't disobey orders by attacking before Gibbon's column arrived. Well aware that no one could predict when or where the 7th would find Sitting Bull's camp, Terry made his instructions discretionary. And Custer's indifference to Sioux numbers was standard procedure for line officers on the Great Plains: warriors there always scattered—searching for their families and fragmenting their fighting strength—during cavalry forays into Indian camps. Custer wanted to surprise the hostiles and keep them in one place: to do this and attack at least two sides of the Indian camp at once, he divided his command. Failures by Benteen and Reno to support Custer or tie down at least part of Gall's force in the upper valley—and, above all, the Indians' surprising resolve to stand and fight—caused the awful mismatch above Medicine Tail Coulee. As fatal as they seem to the historian's backward glance, Custer's decisions didn't really lose the battle: brilliant leadership and flawless tactical decisions by Gall and Crazy Horse won it.

News of the slaughter infuriated whites everywhere and drew a fierce, decisive response from Washington. As Sitting Bull's alliance began falling apart, reinforced cavalry companies flooded the Great Plains, isolating and crushing Indian bands piecemeal. On May 6, 1877, Crazy Horse and more than 1,500 warriors surrendered at Red Cloud Agency. Four months later, the Sioux's greatest war chief lay dead in an army guardhouse, stabbed during a fight with soldiers and Indian policemen. Earlier that year the Hunkpapas had fled to Canada, but barren hunting grounds and hostile northern tribes gradually forced them back across the border, and in 1881 the last of them surrendered at Fort Buford. On December 15, 1890, Sitting Bull fell to a Sioux policeman's bullet at Standing Rock Reservation. Two weeks later, the last major battle between Indians and the army—an awful hand-to-hand brawl punctuated with close-quarter small-arms fire—flared at Wounded Knee Creek in South Dakota. (Neither side wanted or expected a fight—it erupted when a Sioux rifle accidentally went off.) Booming Hotchkiss guns finally ended the melee, leaving 25 troopers and 150 Indians (many of them women and children) dead in the bitter cold. On January 15, 1891, 4,000 runaway Sioux finally surrendered to General Nelson A. Miles, ending the long conflict between white and Native Americans.

Despite its failings, *Son of the Morning Star* (based on Evan S. Connell's best-seller) is the most accurate film on Custer and the bloody struggle for control of the Great Plains. It aims at fairness by framing onscreen action with commentary from two narrators: Buffy St. Marie (the voice of Cheyenne woman Kate Bighead) and Rosanna Arquette (Custer's wife, Libbie) deliver Robe's version of Indian and white perspectives on historical events. On balance, the device works well, and the film is reasonably fair for a product of America's 1991 film industry.

But it stumbles badly in places. A harrowing rendition of Custer's 1868 foray against Cheyenne camps on the Washita River, for example, shows nothing but cavalrymen gunning down helpless Indians (in fact, stunned Cheyenne warriors quickly rallied and fought back gamely). At battle's end, Kate Bighead insists that the attack "was about the land; it was always about the land." Unmentioned is the real reason for Sheridan's winter campaign: throughout the year, militant Cheyenne warriors had attacked homesteads in Colorado and Kansas, murdering and kidnapping innocent settlers, including women and children. Custer found four white captives in the Cheyennes' Washita River camps—the battle was *not* just "about the land" (see *Cheyenne Autumn*).

Still, *Son of the Morning Star* is well worth a

look: its re-creation of the Little Bighorn battle is excellent, its portrait of Custer is easily the best on film (Cole is superb in the title role), and Grant plays a terrific Crazy Horse.

For Further Viewing:
Dances With Wolves (1990) 181 Minutes (Kevin Costner, Mary McDonnell, Graham Greene, Tantoo Cardinal, Rodney A. Grant, Wes Studi): Bent on demolishing vintage stereotypes of American Indians as childish savages, director Costner simply substitutes fashionable New Hollywood platitudes for Old Hollywood's tacky clichés. The plot is simple enough: a Union officer (Costner) wounded during the Civil War and reassigned to the Indian frontier befriends, then joins, a band of Sioux. At this point, cataracts of maudlin, politically correct nonsense drown every trace of the historical Sioux and their dealings with whites and other Indians. Especially other Indians. Costner's chief villains are merciless Pawnee killers intent on slaughtering his new friends and stealing everything they own. (Historically, the reverse was true: the Sioux and their allies outnumbered the Pawnee 25 to one and would have happily exterminated them to seize their land had the need arisen.) During one incomprehensible segment, Costner browbeats reluctant Sioux warriors into using cavalry rifles instead of "traditional" weapons to battle Pawnee raiders. In fact, Plains tribes would do just about anything to acquire guns: at the Little Bighorn, Sioux braves shot Custer's cavalry to bits with repeating rifles and six-shooters, many taken from soldiers killed in earlier fighting. Every white in the film is either insane (the officer who posts Costner to Sioux territory), obnoxious and foolish (the muleskinner who takes him there), or murderous (soldiers and cavalrymen). *Dances With Wolves* excels in places: Wes Studi's fine performance as "the toughest Pawnee" and a beautifully choreo-

graphed, earthshaking buffalo hunt dwarf the rest of the film. But they can't save it: replacing old, distorted notions about Indians with equally warped 1990s cant leaves three hours of pretentious, invincible ignorance on film—not a better understanding of 19th-century Native Americans.

They Died With Their Boots On ★ (1941) 138 Minutes (Errol Flynn, Olivia de Havilland, Gene Lockhart, Arthur Kennedy, Anthony Quinn): Director Raoul Walsh's famous big-budget tribute to Custer and the 7th Cavalry is *Dances With Wolves'* opposite number—a colorful, exciting action film glorifying Custer (Flynn) and virtually ignoring history. The movie's worst inaccuracies come during Walsh's re-creation of the Little Bighorn battle (a swarming banzai charge filmed on the wrong kind of terrain) and peak with an absurd closing scene (Sheridan, of all people, promising Libbie to honor Custer's final request by guaranteeing the Indians' right to live on their own land). If you like Flynn, de Havilland, and vintage Hollywood westerns, you'll enjoy *They Died With Their Boots On.* If you're interested in Custer and the Sioux, skip it.

Custer of the West (1968) 140 Minutes (Robert Shaw, Jeffrey Hunter, Mary Ure, Robert Ryan, Ty Hardin, Robert Hall, Lawrence Tierney): A thoroughly bizarre atrocity, *Custer of the West* plops the 7th Cavalry into terrain resembling the Judean wilderness, combines Crazy Horse, Red Cloud, and Sitting Bull in one nameless chief (Cheyenne, not Sioux), and makes Benteen (Hunter) an enlightened advocate for the Indians. Preposterous dialogue reigns throughout (Sheridan to Custer: "You know, Custer, you could become a living legend—or get yourself killed. Dead men make better legends"). Director Robert Siodmak's awful rendition of the Last Stand has Shaw—a humorless, jaded Custer—warning hordes of Indians (moments before the battle) to return to the reservation or stand and fight. Not available on videotape, but screened more than once by the History Channel (even heaven doesn't know why).

Recommended Reading:
Robert M. Utley, *Cavalier in Buckskin: George Armstrong Custer and the Western Military Frontier* and *The Lance and the Shield: The Life and Times of Sitting Bull;* John S. Gray, *Centennial Campaign: The Sioux War of 1876.*

Stagecoach ★★★★★

(1939) 96 Minutes

Director: John Ford

Cast: John Wayne, Claire Trevor, Andy Devine, Thomas Mitchell, John Carradine, George Bancroft

Historical Background: For people unwilling to journey long distances on horseback, traveling anywhere on the American frontier during the 1860s and 1870s meant traveling by stagecoach. In 1862, a ruthless Missouri entrepreneur, Ben Holladay, bought the Central Overland, California and Pikes Peak Express Co. and turned coaching into big business. He dominated the industry for four years, then sold out to Wells, Fargo & Co.—a commercial monster that "went everywhere and did almost anything for anybody," according to one client.

Founded by Henry Wells and William G. Fargo in 1852 and marked by efficient service, the company monopolized the stagecoach and mail delivery business west of the Mississippi for decades. (Wells Fargo was "innovative" in many ways: to deter highwaymen intent on plundering silver and gold from stagecoach strongboxes, shotgun guards often locked rattlesnakes inside the company's famous green chests moments before departure.)

The Abbot-Downing Co. in Concord, N.H., manufactured the most widely used vehicles and made a fortune selling them both domestically and overseas. An engineering marvel of rugged efficiency, the typical "Concord Coach" stood ten feet high, weighed at least a ton, and carried up to 18 people—nine seated on benches inside the carriage, seven more crowded together on the roof, and the driver and shotgun guard in the "driver's box." The most distinctive feature of the coach was its suspension: the carriage rested on two thick strips of leather—called "thoroughbraces"—attached to spring-steel supports and strung from front to back on either side of the chassis. The design cushioned the worst jolts, but resulted in a rocking movement that caused motion sickness in many passengers.

Teams of six horses, changed every dozen miles, pulled the coaches at an average speed of ten miles per hour over eight major routes running westward from cities in Nebraska, Kansas, Missouri, and Tennessee. For passengers, the journey west was more than rigorous. The 2,795-mile ride from St. Louis to San Francisco on the Overland Mail Route, for example, was a pell-mell, bone-rattling ordeal of dust, noise, and sleeplessness that continued—virtually nonstop—for a month. Conditions were worse for drivers and guards, since they made the en-tire trip exposed to the harsh, fickle weather of the frontier. Food was coarse and expensive: a typical meal of bread, bacon, dried apple pie, and incredibly strong black coffee sold for $1.50. Constant fear of murderous road agents and hostile Indians eventually prompted express companies to line many coaches with bulletproof steel. (The danger was real: in June of 1867, for example, 100 Sioux and Cheyenne warriors attacked a coach near Fort Wallace, Kansas. The driver, one soldier, and five passengers fought well enough to reach safety at Big Timbers Station, but six of the seven men were seriously wounded or killed.) The "era of the stagecoach," one of the most colorful in the annals of the American West, continued through the turn of the century, but began to fade with the expansion of the railroads in the 1880s and 1890s.

Stagecoach made John Wayne a star and set new standards for Hollywood westerns. Ford's Concord Coach provides the perfect arena for a taut, entertaining study of eccentric personalities under the pressures of a long journey across Apache territory. Led by Thomas Mitchell (who won an Oscar for his performance as the drunken doctor), a powerhouse cast scores one bull's-eye after another, creating many character types that still surface in westerns—Devine's jovial stage driver, Bancroft's tough shotgun guard, and Carradine's dapper gambler, among others. Beautifully filmed in Monument Valley, *Stagecoach* is a vivid chronicle of the West that you can watch and enjoy as much today as pre-war audiences did in 1939.

For Further Viewing:
Wells Fargo ★★★★ (1937) 94 Minutes (Joel Mc-Crea, Frances Dee, Bob Burns, Lloyd Nolan, Ralph

Morgan, Johnny Mack Brown, Robert Cummings, Porter Hall): A well-done film chronicling the legendary company's history from its beginnings through its acquisition of the Butterfield Overland Mail and buyout of Holladay's empire. Well researched and historically accurate most of the time—even in its citation of mid-19th-century postal rates (Wells Fargo charged 6¢ per letter, undercutting U.S. Postal rates by a whopping 80%). McCrea is fine as a trusted employee who handles almost every job in the company, from Pony Express rider to vice president. The McCrea–Dee romantic subplot seems intrusive, but only because the historical material is so interesting.

Recommended Reading:
J. V. Frederick, *Ben Holladay: The Stagecoach King;* Noel Loomis, *Wells Fargo: An Illustrated History.*

Tom Horn ★

(1980) 98 Minutes

Director: William Wiard

Cast: Steve McQueen, Linda Evans, Richard Farnsworth, Billy Green Bush, Slim Pickens, Elisha Cook

Historical Background: For Tom Horn—Indian fighter, Pinkerton agent, and bounty hunter—killing was a well planned, long-distance affair requiring infinite patience: he once sat for hours in heavy rain, eating raw bacon and drinking cold coffee, until his victim came within range of his lethal Winchester '73. Born in Scotland County, Mo., on November 21, 1860, Horn is said to have provoked a bar fight with Billy the Kid while they were teenagers. In 1875 he surfaced in Arizona, where he met Al Sieber, legendary Indian fighter and chief of scouts for the San Carlos Reservation. Impressed by Horn's superb marksmanship and fluent Spanish, Sieber hired him on the spot as a scout and interpreter. Horn spent the next decade tracking Geronimo and performing so well that Sieber, disabled by a gunshot wound, gave him temporary command of the scouting force in 1885. (Horn insisted that he arranged Geronimo's surrender to General Nelson Miles the following year, but the claim remains unsubstantiated.)

In 1892, Horn moved to Wyoming and signed on as a "stock detective" for the Swan Land and Cattle Co., an organization of cattle barons embroiled in the Johnson County range war. Horn—who received $500 for every "suspected rustler" he captured or shot—quickly earned a reputation as a cold-blooded killer. His first and final scrape with the law came in 1901, after two shots from a Winchester '73 killed 14-year-old Willie Nickell. Days later, the boy's father (a sheepman and bitter enemy of Horn's employers) also fell to rifle fire. A U.S. deputy marshal named Joe Lefors believed that Horn had killed the boy by mistake while waiting to ambush his father. Lefors tracked Horn to a Denver saloon, struck up a conversation, and got him so drunk that he boasted of the Nickell killings in front of witnesses and a hidden stenographer. Convicted and sentenced to hang on the strength of his "confession," Horn broke out of jail on August 6, 1903, but failed to escape because he didn't know how to operate a German semiautomatic pistol. On November 20, 1903, Tom Horn died on the gallows in Cheyenne. His exploits were so extraordinary—and his execution so controversial—that a Tom Horn cult, of sorts, eventually coalesced around his legend and persists to this day.

Based on Horn's memoirs, McQueen's next-to-last film focuses on the famous frontiersman's final months in Wyoming. The movie is oddly indecisive: it hints that Horn's employers conspired to frame him for Willie Nickell's murder, then abruptly drops the idea. During his trial, Horn absurdly refuses to defend himself, telling the court that he's "not gonna give you the satisfaction" (whatever that means). *Tom Horn* is a strange, lifeless film worth a look only because of fine period detail, beautiful photography, and authentic turn-of-the-century atmosphere.

Recommended Reading:
Chip Carlson, *Tom Horn: "Killing Men Is My Specialty"*; Dean F. Krakel, *The Saga of Tom Horn*; Mark Dugan, *Tales Never Told Around the Campfire: True Stories of Frontier America.*

Ulzana's Raid ★★★★★

(1972) 103 Minutes

Director: Robert Aldrich

Cast: Burt Lancaster, Bruce Davison, Jorge Luke, Richard Jaeckel, Joaquin Martinez

Historical Background: Derived from the Zuni term *apachu,* the word "Apache" means "enemy," and with good reason—history has yet to produce anyone so ferocious or skilled in battle as the average, run-of-the-mill Apache warrior. In the early 1800s, a great Sioux army invaded Apache territory; years later, according to Indian legend, you could trace the Sioux line of retreat by following the skeletons of the dead they left behind during their frantic withdrawal. A loose association of tiny tribes totaling 8,000 people, the Apache fought invading Spaniards to a standstill in Mexico for at least 200 years. They successfully resisted the U.S. government's reservation system far longer than any other group of American Indians.

The source of the Apache's military prowess was their intelligent preparation of young men for war. One well-known Apache drill required apprentice warriors to fill their mouths with water, run several miles, then spit the water out at the feet of an adult brave. The exercise taught discipline and built endurance, but its main purpose was purely practical: it made breathing through the nose an ingrained habit (breathing through the mouth is instinctive for a runner, but it dries his mouth and increases his sense of thirst). By the time an Apache boy turned 15, he automatically clenched his teeth when he ran and could sprint farther than most of his enemies could trot. He fought with every weapon available on the frontier, especially the bow and arrow, and—from the 1850s until Geronimo's surrender in 1886—the rifle. (The Apache often had to make their own ammunition, using spent brass casings and stone, gold, or silver for projectiles—all easier for them to get than lead.) Resourceful, cunning, and tough, the Apache terrorized settlers and prospectors in the American Southwest for 49 years, beginning in 1837 (see *Broken Arrow*). Against them the U.S. Army sent 5,000 troopers, who fought from remote outposts scattered throughout the region's vast mountain ranges and deserts. For soldiers, fighting Apaches meant wearisome small-unit patrols marked by tedium and punctuated with savage skirmishes, usually fought on the Indians' terms.

Typical of the bloody, bitter character of the Apache Wars was a stunning raid led by Ulzana, a Chiricahua warrior known also as Josanie. In early November 1885, Ulzana and ten warriors jumped the San Carlos Reservation, crossed into New Mexico, and killed everyone who blundered into their pell-mell dash for the Florida Mountains. On the 23rd, they returned to Arizona and murdered 12 reservation Indians near Fort Apache, then faded into the hills and disappeared for three weeks. A patrol of ten soldiers and 18 Apache scouts began scouring the area for the raiding party. They found nothing, and on the 27th, 100 additional scouts joined the hunt. A few days later, the renegades bolted out of the mountains and turned south, stealing horses from settlers and killing two homesteaders near

Solomonville. By then they had become national news, infuriating General Philip Sheridan and prompting him to send hundreds of scouts and troopers into the field. On December 19, Ulzana's men ambushed a small cavalry column, killed a surgeon and four soldiers, and slipped away before anyone even saw them. The raid continued until December 30, when the Chiricahuas crossed the Mexican border and disappeared without a trace into the Sierra Madres. In less than two months they had covered 1,200 miles, killed 38 people, and stolen more than 200 horses and mules, losing only one man. The spectacular raid was the last foray of its kind; on March 27, 1886, Ulzana and two other chiefs surrendered to General George Crook. Five months later Geronimo capitulated, ending the Apache Wars in America's desert Southwest.

Ulzana's Raid is the best film ever made about the conflict between American Indians and the U.S. Cavalry. Meticulously researched, it provides a clinic on Apache combat tactics and the cavalry's use of Apache scouts. Aldrich occasionally distorts history, but always for good reasons—in the movie only Lancaster and a few troopers (not hundreds) pursue Ulzana, highlighting the small scale and personal nature of the Apache Wars. Lancaster's Apache scout (beautifully played by Luke and based on a real-life Chiricahua) ends the movie by killing Ulzana, the only fictional element introduced for no obvious reason.

For Further Viewing:
The Stalking Moon ★★★★ (1969) 109 Minutes (Gregory Peck, Eva Marie Saint, Frank Silvera): *The Stalking Moon* views an Apache warrior's ferocity through the eyes of former army scout Peck

and the settler woman (Saint) he rescues from her Apache captor, Silvaje. Director Robert Mulligan highlights Silvaje's terrifying warrior skills by keeping him offscreen until Peck hunts him down, forcing a bloodcurdling hand-to-hand fight that ends the film.

Apache ★★★ (1954) 91 Minutes (Burt Lancaster, Jean Peters, John McIntire): An eccentric film, *Apache* follows renegade Chiricahua Lancaster's escape from a reservation-bound train and his subsequent flight from the U.S. Army. If you can suspend disbelief enough to accept Peters as an Apache girl, the movie is realistic and entertaining.

Recommended Reading:
Keith Basso, ed., *Western Apache Raiding and Warfare;* Frank C. Lockwood, *The Apache Indians.*

Union Pacific ★★★★

(1939) 135 Minutes

Director: Cecil B. DeMille

Cast: Barbara Stanwyck, Joel McCrea, Robert Preston, Akim Tamiroff, Brian Donlevy, Anthony Quinn

Historical Background: April 28, 1869—northern Utah: at 7 A.M. on the nose, a hand-picked Central Pacific section gang rolled into synchronized pandemonium: forty-one wagons loaded with ties swept eastward, flanked by Chinese tie-layers unloading and grounding the supports at perfectly spaced intervals. Behind them, two squads of Irishmen hauled massive rail links from flatcars and positioned them on the moving wooden substructure. Spiker teams followed, pinning the gleaming ribbons in place—three strokes per spike, ten spikes per rail, 400 rails per mile. It was a grand spectacle of disciplined barehanded toil ending ten miles, 200 feet, and 12 sweat-drenched hours from the dawn starting line: in a single shift, ten iron-hearted Irishmen had hauled and placed a staggering 2 million pounds of rail, and Central Pacific's crew had anchored 25,800 ties, driven 55,000 spikes, and tightened more than 14,000 bolts on 7,040 fishplates. They'd smashed a 7.5-mile one-day track-laying record set weeks earlier by crack Union Pacific gangs pounding relentlessly toward them from the east. Twelve days later, crews from both companies met at Promontory Point and joined 1,776 miles of converging tracks, linking Sacramento, Omaha, and the great Atlantic ports by rail.

Central Pacific's rousing marathon crowned a titanic drive to complete America's first transcontinental railroad. Decades earlier, New Yorker Hartwell Carver had proposed building a railway linking San Francisco and New York. Dismissed as lunacy, the notion went nowhere until engineer Theodore Judah convinced California entrepreneurs Collis Huntington, Charles Crocker, Leland Stanford, and Mark Hopkins that men could hack railroad beds through the Sierra Nevada and make a fortune doing it. The "Big Four" formed Central Pacific on June 28, 1861, and Judah headed for Washington to seek federal support for the project. On July 1, 1862, President Lincoln signed the Pacific Railroad Act commissioning the Central and Union Pacific corporations to build the railway. (Created by Congressional charter in 1862, Omaha-based Union Pacific broke ground in December 1863.) Each outfit got a 400-foot-wide right-of-way strip on both sides of the tracks, five 640-acre land sections per mile, and huge low-interest federal loans ($16,000 per mile on flat land, $48,000 in the mountains).

The companies hammered their way toward Utah under different circumstances. Created by federal commissioners and run by corrupt Thomas C. Durant, the Union Pacific faced fiscal and managerial dilemmas from day one. To attract Boston investors, Lincoln convinced Congressman Oakes Ames and his brother to pour money into the underfunded enterprise. It worked, but internal bickering and poor leadership strangled early track-laying operations: during the company's first two years, Union Pacific rails advanced only 40 miles. Then, in 1866, brilliant surveyor Grenville Dodge took over as chief engineer, streamlining field logistics and construction techniques. Between May and December, Dodge's crews laid 293 miles of track, pushing railheads all the way to North Platte. Tough problems still remained: prairie timber (for ties) was scarce and pulpy; alkaline water corroded locomotive engines; and attacks by Sioux warriors threatened to stop construction cold until the Red Cloud War ended in 1868. But Dodge's men had refined track-laying operations so meticulously by then that progress averaged one to three miles per day.

Remarkably free of bureaucratic imbroglios, the Big Four's daily nightmare was tectonics—fording gorges and punching tunnels through the guts of America's wildest mountains. On the Sierra's western edge loomed the first great barrier: a gigantic, diamond-hard granite formation that devoured 500 kegs of blasting powder a day for eight deafening months. (Central Pacific's appetite for explosives caused a black-powder shortage in 1866.) Picks and hammers rang without letup until the "Bloomer Cut"—a fissure 800 feet long—opened the Sierra to Crocker's engineers. By December 1866, they'd battered their way to Donner Pass, and they reached the outskirts of Reno in June; behind them were 15 tunnels hewn inch by inch through solid rock. In five years they'd built 150 miles of track, but they took just 11 more months to drive all the way across Nevada's broiling desert to Promontory Point. There, on May 10, 1869, Stanford drove the ceremonial golden spike home, rendering every other form of transcontinental transport in America obsolete.

Union Pacific troubleshooter McCrea battles payroll thieves, two train wrecks, raging Sioux warriors, and crooks using every available means—including liquor and loose women—to derail heroic section crews pushing the tracks westward. Union Pacific representatives helped Paramount Studios create realistic construction sequences, vintage sets, and authentic costumes. But DeMille stumbles often: dialogue slides into hokey bombast more than once, the McCrea–Preston–Stanwyck romantic triangle is tedious, and the central "conspiracy" story is hokum. Still, a fine cinematic clinic on railroad lore and 19th-century section-gang work—and DeMille's rendition of the "golden spike" ceremony (Stanford's failure to hit the spike, followed by spectator laughter) is accurate.

For Further Viewing:
The Iron Horse ★★★★ (1924) 119 Minutes (George O'Brien, Cyril Chadwick, Madge Bellamy, Fred Kohler): John Ford's silent epic about the transcontinental railroad made train robbery and

track demolition stock elements in Hollywood westerns. Opening credits pronounce the film "accurate and faithful in every particular," an obvious exaggeration: Ford filmed exclusively in Nevada, and he sidesteps Central Pacific's seminal role in the enterprise. Overall, the film is remarkably accurate: in 1867, mounted Indians actually tried to stop a locomotive with a 40-foot hand-held rope, and "Hell on Wheels" saloon/brothels did follow crews westward. Stark realism prevails, with many classic scenes: Ford's rendition of crews building Cheyenne, Wyo., is faithful to history—squatters erected a few huts on company land there, but railroad crews built the real town in 1867.

Recommended Reading:
Robert West Howard, *The Great Iron Trail: The Story of the First Trans-Continental Railroad.*

Wagon Master ★★★★

(1950) 86 Minutes

Director: John Ford

Cast: Ben Johnson, Joanne Dru, Harry Carey, Jr., Ward Bond, Alan Mowbray, Jane Darwell

Historical Background: History had never seen anything like it: in May 1841, the first pioneer wagon train left Missouri for the Pacific Coast, launching an epic pilgrimage that rolled over the Oregon Trail without pause for a full quarter century. Hauling their worlds with them in rugged "prairie schooners," thousands of farmers and prospectors seeking new lives rumbled westward for five months and 2,000 unforgiving miles. They followed the southern bank of the twisting Platte River to Fort Laramie, crossed the Rockies at Wyoming's South Pass—the only route through the mountains—then rumbled on to Oregon's fertile valleys or took the trail's southern branch to California's beckoning goldfields. (The "Mormon Trail" hugged the Platte's northern bank, veering toward Utah's Great Salt Lake from South Pass.)

Death stalked them every step of the way: so terrible were the hazards of the long passage that 20,000 pioneers—one emigrant in 17—died during the "Great Migration." Some perished in towering prairie fires. Others exhausted their provisions or lost them to spoilage, dying of thirst or starvation on the plains. Many fell to accidents. Lightning, hailstorms, and stampeding buffalo often scattered irreplaceable draft animals for miles, forcing long, potentially fatal stops. (Caravans had to cross the mountains before winter snows marooned them—low on provisions and a lifetime away from the nearest town—on the wrong side of the Continental Divide. In 1846, 87 emigrants led by George Donner suffered the migration's darkest horrors because of early delays: trapped by fall blizzards after taking a "shortcut" to regain lost time, the entire party floundered high in the Sierra Nevada until rescuers found 47 starving wraiths more than two months later. To survive, many had eaten stew containing human flesh.) Disease was the long journey's deadliest scourge: countless pioneers fell to smallpox, malaria, pneumonia, tuberculosis, dysentery, food poisoning, measles, and whooping cough. Asiatic cholera—easily the most profligate killer—took 2,500 lives in 1850 alone.

For transport and marginal comfort on the

trail, families relied on solid "outfits": stout, judiciously provisioned wagons—the lighter the better—pulled by tough, powerful, compliant oxen. (Horses—finicky eaters and vulnerable to distemper—made terrible draft animals. Mules were strong and hardy enough, but they wandered at night and lacked humility: trailbreaking them left "many valiant riders . . . in very undignified positions," according to one pioneer.) Built of hickory, maple, or oak, the best rigs featured wide tracks and simple boxes—ten feet long, four feet wide, and two feet deep—fitted with hickory bows supporting waterproof covers of oiled linen or heavy canvas. Wise emigrants chose wagons built for three-ton loads, then limited their cargo to 2,500 pounds: bare essentials included firearms, a cast-iron stove, spare wagon parts, cooking utensils, and 400 pounds of food (coffee, salt, bacon or cured ham, dried fruit, and sugar).

Most overlanders traveled in small groups ordered as rigorously as military fire teams, rotating sentry duty and dust-ravaged rear caravan positions equally among "company" members. (For iron discipline and meticulous planning, Mormon expeditions took top honors. Brigham Young launched Utah-bound trains in ten-, 20-, and 50-wagon waves, each caravan planting crops along the trail to feed the next group.) Guides and elected "captains" sought evening campsites near potable water, circling their wagons to corral animals for the night and pitching tents outside the protective ring. (Indians stole many animals, but mounted few assaults on well-armed wagoners.) Advancing in consecutive four-wagon ranks, caravans merged into single columns only in congested areas such as South Pass. Year by year, they rolled westward in growing legions, their number peaking at 55,000 in 1850. The Great Migration ended officially in 1866, and completion of the first transcontinental railroad four years later sent covered wagons packing to museum showrooms or secondhand outfitting depots. By then, more than 350,000 doughty souls had followed the old trails west.

Freelancing wranglers Johnson and Carey sell Mormon elder Bond a herd of horses, then lead his small wagon train to Utah. Super entertainment from start to finish and historically accurate in many details: Bond's group, for example, is an advance party marking the trail and planting crops for later caravans. But Ford routes them toward Utah's San Juan River, far south of the Mormons' true itinerary. Other Hollywood conventions (single-file trains, for one) elbow history aside, but the film is so good and its look at daily life on the trail so convincing that nobody cares about its historical lapses. Ford's daughter helped edit the movie, and his son cowrote the screenplay.

For Further Viewing:
Bend of the River ★★★★ (1952) 91 Minutes (James Stewart, Arthur Kennedy, Julie Adams, Rock Hudson): After the Civil War, former border raider Stewart leads a wagon train to central Oregon's Columbia River country. One of director Anthony Mann's better westerns, exciting and faithful to history—with occasional lapses: Kennedy (also an ex-raider) implies at one point that the Oregon Trail traversed the Black Hills and Little Bighorn country, both north of its actual course. Tightly scripted, with convincing presentations of the farmers' narrow margin for survival—they were wholly dependent on supply shipments from Portland—during their first year in Oregon. Based on Bill Gulick's *Bend of the Snake.*

Recommended Reading:
Merrill J. Mattes, *The Great Platte River Road: The Covered Wagon Mainline Via Fort Kearny to Fort*

Laramie; James Hewitt, *Eyewitness to Wagon Trains West;* George R. Stewart, *Ordeal by Hunger: The Story of the Donner Party.*

The Westerner ★★★

(1940) 100 Minutes

Director: William Wyler

Cast: Gary Cooper, Walter Brennan, Fred Stone, Doris Davenport, Forrest Tucker

Historical Background: Gazing sadly into newlyweds' eyes, Judge Roy Bean always closed wedding ceremonies with the same earnest plea—"May God have mercy on your souls." Easily the most wildly eccentric jurist in American history, Bean has surfaced in more colorful anecdotes—true and apocryphal—than any other frontier legend, including Davy Crockett. (Many of the quirkiest stories are factual: in February 1892, he fined a carpenter's corpse bearing two $10 bills and a pistol $40 for carrying a concealed weapon.)

Born in 1825, Bean left his native Kentucky at age 16 and wandered the West for decades, compiling a crazy-quilt résumé before landing in Texas' Pecos River country. He raised dairy cattle, hawked fresh beef, and drove an ammunition wagon in the Mexican War. In 1852, he and his brother opened a San Diego saloon. Six years later, Bean killed a man in a duel and left town seconds ahead of a fuming lynch mob. During the Civil War, he fought with an obscure New Mexico–based Confederate outfit called the Free Rovers. In 1882, Bean opened his famous saloon—the Jersey Lily—near a west Texas railroad camp called Eagle's Nest, later renaming the ramshackle community Langtry for the popular British actress, Lillie. (The two corresponded, but never met. She once offered to send him an ornate drinking fountain for his bar: Roy declined, noting that "the only thing the citizens of Langtry never drink is water.")

Infested with squalid criminals, the area was so vast that even the fearsome Rangers finally asked Texas' adjutant general for help. In 1882, they got it: county commissioners appointed Bean justice of the peace on August 2, and his saloon thrived as a legal center and Ranger haunt for two decades. Justice there was often harsh and always swift: Bean told jurors he'd chain them to a tree if they deadlocked, and they knew he meant it—he wasn't about to pull a Ranger from his rounds to escort prisoners to alternate venues hundreds of miles away. The old judge was capricious and overbearing, but he was universally popular among settlers for keeping the peace. He died of pneumonia in 1903—eight months before Lillie Langtry visited his town for the first time.

One of the finest westerns ever—and a hatful of hokum as historical biography. Accused of horse theft, Cooper cons Bean (Brennan) into leniency by offering him a lock of Lillie Langtry's hair, then sides with homesteaders "oppressed" by the judge and area ranchers. All of this is nonsense: no one ever duped Roy Bean, and Pecos County settlers reelected him many times. Wyler's version of his death tops a long list of additional blunders, but Brennan's Oscar-winning performance makes *The Westerner* a must for Western fans.

For Further Viewing:
The Life and Times of Judge Roy Bean (1972) 120 Minutes (Paul Newman, Ava Gardner, Jacqueline Bisset, Anthony Perkins, Tab Hunter, John Huston, Stacy Keach, Ned Beatty, Roddy McDowall): Historically, this bizarre semicomic marathon amounts to first degree homicide, and director John Huston pleads guilty—upfront—in an opening disclaimer: "Maybe this isn't the way it was . . . It's the way it should have been." Newman's Bean is a murderous gunslinger on the run after robbing a bank; fifteen minutes into the film, he's roared through a murky Eagle's Nest saloon/brothel, killed at least twelve men in a single preposterous shootout, and taken over the "business." Crowning himself the Law West of the Pecos, he converts a bumbling, half-starved equestrian gang into his own private army of "marshals" (Huston virtually ignores the Texas Rangers). The movie's nuttiest—and least convincing—fiction casts Bisset as Newman's pistol-packing only child, Rose. (In fact, Bean and Virginia Chavez started a family soon after marrying in 1866—they eventually had five children, including an adopted son.) At film's end, Newman loses control of Langtry to lawyer McDowall, vanishes for two decades, returns in the 1920s (years after the real judge died) and destroys the town with Bisset's help. Just how bad is *The Life and Times of Judge Roy Bean*? One critic labeled the film outlandish enough to convince viewers unschooled in Texas history that Roy Bean and Lillie Langtry were purely fictional char-

acters. Worst of all: the movie is boring, and Huston's sporadic lapses into slapstick and farce fall absolutely flat.

Recommended Reading:
C. L. Sonnichsen, *Roy Bean: Law West of the Pecos.*

Wild Times ★★★

(1980) 200 Minutes

Director: Richard Compton

Cast: Sam Elliott, Ben Johnson, Bruce Boxleitner, Penny Peyser, Timothy Scott, Pat Hingle, Harry Carey, Jr.

Historical Background: May 11, 1887—London: From custom-built seats high above the arena floor, a pop-eyed Queen Victoria gazed at the roaring spectacle below: brandishing war lances and whooping at the top of their lungs, scores of "Noble Red Men" galloped straight at cowering spectators, wheeling away at the last second to attack in another direction; simulated cyclones demolished entire storefront prairie towns; the Deadwood Stage repulsed galloping Indian attacks; and William F. Cody himself blasted countless flying glass balls to bits with his trusty rifle. Buffalo Bill's Wild West Educational Exhibition was the hottest ticket in town, its Command Performance the unmatched highlight of Queen Victoria's Silver Jubilee celebration (she actually stood and bowed as horsemen carried the American flag into the arena), and everyone in London was ready to welcome Cody's upstart Yankee colonials back into the empire.

Inspired by P. G. Barnum's popular circus, small-scale Wild West shows had surfaced in America's entertainment industry before—and all had failed, leaving a huge, wide-open market for Buffalo Bill's brand of glittering spectacle. By 1872, Cody had worked as a sawmill hand, a freighting-firm messenger, a boardinghouse proprietor, an army dispatch rider, a railway grader, a buffalo hunter, and the 5th Cavalry's chief of scouts. For bravery during an Indian attack he'd earned the Congressional Medal of Honor (later revoked because he was a civilian). He was a genuine frontier hero, and his big break came when writer Ned Buntline christened him Buffalo Bill in a series of frothy newspaper stories trumpeting his exploits and vaulting him to instant celebrity.

Encouraged by Buntline, he formed an acting troupe—Buffalo Bill's Combination—and packed East Coast theaters for a decade. On July 4, 1883, his first Wild West spectacle in North Platte, Neb., knocked everyone's socks off. Two years later, Phoebe Anne Moses joined the show as Annie Oakley (America's sensational "Little Sure Shot"), launching a spectacular run that drew more than 50 million spectators over three decades. Cody grew more sophisticated with every show, adding new, exotic acts to outpace a host of competitors (more than 100 impresarios eventually sponsored Wild West exhibitions). His "1893 Programme" listed "Native Dances and Feats of Horsemanship by Russian Cossacks and Racing between Prairie, Arab, Spanish, and Indian Girls." High expenses, fierce competition, and newfangled motion pictures gradually eroded ticket sales, bankrupting the show

in 1913. The American West had long since passed into history, but nobody cared: thanks to Cody and his troupe, the West of the Imagination—available to anyone with a taste for dime novels or silent movies—had taken the world by storm.

On the lam for killing his father's murderer, jack-of-all-trades Elliott takes an alias and rides from town to town, living on odd-job wages and his winnings from professional sharpshooting contests. Eventually he teams with fellow marksman Johnson and dime novelist Hingle to form one of the first Wild West shows. Highly entertaining and accurate, with faithful renditions of Wild West show acts and good work by a large cast of crack character actors. The film's only drawback is a lame, intrusive romantic subplot linking Elliott with a rancher's daughter and an Apache girl.

Recommended Reading:
Helen Cody Wetmore, *Last of the Great Scouts: The Life Story of Colonel William F. Cody;* Isabelle S. Sayers, *Annie Oakley and Buffalo Bill's Wild West.*

Winchester '73 ★★★★★

(1950) 92 Minutes

Director: Anthony Mann

Cast: James Stewart, Shelley Winters, Dan Duryea, Stephen McNally, Charles Drake,

John McIntire, Will Geer, Rock Hudson, Tony Curtis

Historical Background: On September 6, 1868, 600 Sioux and Cheyenne horsemen attacked 50 U.S. cavalrymen armed with seven-shot Spencer carbines and dug in on Beecher's Island in eastern Colorado. The Indians' first assault failed when a wall of lead disintegrated the center of their charging army. Surging past the soldiers' positions, the attackers wheeled and advanced once more, only to be cut to pieces a second time. And so it went—again and again—as Major George Forsythe's outnumbered troopers repulsed mounted assaults for more than a week. When it was over, Forsythe had lost fewer than 20 men. He had also proved what many officers were reluctant to admit: that the repeating rifle was essential for survival on the frontier and that it was there to stay. Spencer's elegant little carbine had its flaws—it wasn't as accurate as the Sharps, and the pull-out tubular magazine running through its stock made reloading cumbersome and slow. Still, it was one of four noteworthy predecessors to Winchester's legendary Model 1873 lever-action rifle.

In the early 1850s, a Smith & Wesson subsidiary made the weapons-design breakthrough of the century: Volcanic Arms' lever-action rifle, featuring a 12-shot tubular magazine positioned below a long, octagonal barrel. The weapon's design was ingenious, but its ammunition was unsound—it fired bizarre, self-propelled "rocket-balls" that proved unreliable. In 1857, Oliver F. Winchester bought Volcanic from Smith & Wesson, renaming it the New Haven Arms Co. and appointing B. Tyler Henry production manager. The firm modified Volcanic's original design, producing the famous 16-shot Henry rifle with its revolutionary two-piece rimfire cartridge—a brass casing filled with primer and black powder and tightly fitted at the top with a lead projectile. The gun was hard-hitting and accurate at 400 yards, but it retained a drawback from its Volcanic predecessor: the magazine had to be loaded at the muzzle end, a slow and occasionally hazardous procedure. Nine years after production of the first Henry repeater, New Haven patented the greatest rifle the world had yet seen—the Winchester Model 1866 (first to bear the former haberdasher's name). It had a much smoother cocking action that produced a one-round-per-second rate of fire. More critically, the new rifle featured a loading port just beneath the cartridge chamber on the right side of its brass receiver. With his 15-shot Model 1873, Winchester perfected the new design, converting the brass receiver to steel and adding a centerfire firing pin; the rifle was chambered for the centerfire .44-caliber cartridges used with the most popular Colt pistols. The magnificent weapon wasn't the only "gun that won the West," but it was certainly the finest. More than a century later, its basic design remains unchanged and just as popular as it was in 1873.

Stewart—a tough, seasoned cowboy—relentlessly tracks three men who steal the signature "One in One Thousand" Winchester '73 that he wins in a shooting contest. An entertaining, gritty, realistic film that enlists fine acting and an excellent script to focus on the key role played by weapons technology in daily life on the frontier. The final shootout is one of Hollywood's best.

Recommended Reading:
Harold Francis Williamson, *Winchester: The Gun That Won the West;* Joseph G. Rosa, *Guns of the*

American West; Charles Workman, *Firearms of the American West.*

Wyatt Earp ★★★

(1994) 195 Minutes

Director: Lawrence Kasdan

Cast: Kevin Costner, Dennis Quaid, Mark Harmon, Michael Madsen, Catherine O'Hara, Bill Pullman, JoBeth Williams, Mare Winningham, James Gammon, Annabeth Gish, Lewis Smith

Historical Background: When Wyatt Earp first rode into Tombstone in December 1879, he saw a restless sprawl of tents and cabins that included 14 casinos, four dance halls, at least 25 saloons, and—according to one prominent citizen—three Bibles. Wyatt loved the place: Tombstone was a city of transients, and he had never lived in one place for very long.

Born in 1848 near Monmouth, Ill., Earp moved steadily westward with his family until 1864, when they settled in Colton, Calif. For the next 15 years, he roamed the chaotic post–Civil War frontier, struggling to survive. His first law-enforcement job came in 1869, when he was elected constable of Lamar, Mo. In 1870, he married a young woman there, but she died of typhus a few months later. Earp began

wandering, again: before moving to Arizona, he had fled Oklahoma as a horse thief, hunted buffalo in Kansas, drifted through a two-year stint as a city policeman in Wichita, and earned a reputation as a tough, hardworking deputy marshal in Dodge City, Kan.—the largest and toughest of the great beef-trading centers.

But law enforcement was seasonal work in cattle towns: every year, lawmen had to scramble for work in saloons and casinos when range-weary cowboys with money to burn finally moved on. Mining towns were a different matter. Seventy miles east of Tucson lay booming Tombstone, with its rich silver deposits and opportunities for aggressive entrepreneurs. When Virgil Earp became deputy marshal there in 1879, Wyatt and his younger brothers Morgan and James headed for Arizona. John ("Doc") Holliday, a tubercular dentist and gambler befriended by Wyatt in Dodge City, quickly followed. The Earps soon prospered through solid investments in silver mines and gambling houses, but trouble loomed in Tombstone's tense political climate.

Barely three years old, the town was central to a factional struggle for control of Cochise County. The two most powerful and antagonistic groups were the town's business community and a band of drifters and gunmen called the Cowboys. Led by the Clanton and McLaury families and protected by county sheriff John Behan, the Cowboys stole and resold cattle on both sides of the Mexican border, dominating affairs in the entire county—but not in Tombstone. One of them, Curly Bill Brocius, had killed Virgil's boss in November 1880. With their growing commercial interests, the Earps backed Mayor John Clum's business group. Wyatt detested Behan, who had defeated him in the sheriff's election to become Virgil's chief political and professional rival. Throw in actress Josephine Marcus—who took up with Behan, then dumped him for Wyatt Earp—and some sort of confrontation seemed inevitable.

It began on October 25, 1881, when Ike Clanton and Tom McLaury capped a night of heavy drinking with a series of robust threats against the Earps. Arrested by Virgil and released the following morning, they met William Claiborne, Wes Fuller, Billy Clanton, and Frank McLaury in an open yard next to the OK Corral. Four of them were heavily armed, and the taunting began again. Virgil—the real leader of the Earp clan—headed for the Corral to disarm the Cowboys. With him came Wyatt, Morgan, and Holliday (who carried two pistols and a 10-gauge shotgun). Within seconds, the ten men faced each other across a dusty no-man's-land barely six feet wide. Gunfire erupted as soon as Virgil demanded the rustlers' guns and continued for 30 seconds. During the exchange, Virgil was hit in the leg and Morgan in the shoulder. Ike Clanton had run away, the McLaury brothers were dead on the ground, and Billy Clanton lay mortally wounded. Charged by Behan with three murders, Wyatt and Holliday were acquitted after a 30-day trial, and a host of fuming Cowboys—led by Brocius and Johnny Ringo—soon retaliated. On the night of December 28, three men with shotguns flattened Virgil Earp on Allen Street, mangling his left elbow and ending his law-enforcement career. Two months later, a pistol shot fired from an alley into Bob Hatch's billiard hall severed Morgan's spine, and he died minutes later. The feud soon escalated into a small range war. Wyatt and Warren Earp, Doc Holliday, Jack Johnson, Sherman McMasters, and Texas Jack Vermillion went after key members of the Clanton gang, hunting them down one by one. They shot Frank Stil-

well in a Tucson railroad yard. They killed Florentino ("Indian Charley") Cruz on a ranch near Tombstone. Wyatt blew Curly Bill Brocius apart with a shotgun blast at Iron Springs. On July 14, 1882, Ringo's body mysteriously appeared in the Chiricahua Mountains (Holliday is often credited with the killing, but he and Wyatt were probably in Colorado at the time).

With Brocius' death, the Cowboys' gang broke up. Many of them, including Ike Clanton, fled to Mexico. Holliday died in a Glenwood Springs sanitarium in 1895. Wyatt drifted from town to town—accompanied by Josephine Marcus—for another decade, finally settling in Los Angeles. As a child, Earp had seen American Indians hunt buffalo with bows and arrows. By the time he died in 1929, airplanes were commonplace and scientists' first efforts to split the atom were a decade away. But despite universal fascination with the OK Corral shootout, authors and publishing houses took little interest in Wyatt's extraordinary story during his lifetime. Today, more than 25 films and countless books preserve his memory.

Wyatt Earp scores decent marks for historical accuracy and Quaid's terrific Doc Holliday, but that's about it: the rest of the movie is lifeless. Obsessed with thoroughness, Kasdan devotes as much screen time to dull conversation during a buffalo hunt as he does to the murder of Morgan Earp. Costner is fine as a dour, wooden Wyatt, but Madsen is badly miscast as Virgil, whose key role in the Tombstone affair the film ignores. Kasdan also skirts the Earps' involvement in local prostitution rings—and the horrible plight of working girls in the West.

For Further Viewing:
Tombstone ★★★★ (1993) 128 Minutes (Kurt Russell, Val Kilmer, Sam Elliott, Stephen Lang, Powers

Boothe): *Tombstone* chronicles the events leading to the famous gunfight (beautifully done in the film) and the ensuing reign of terror inflicted by the Earps on the Cowboys. The film scores a first for historical accuracy by making Virgil Earp—perfectly played by Elliott—the leader of the clan. Russell is fine as Wyatt, but Kilmer's florid Holliday is labored and tedious. An unpretentious, enjoyable film focusing mainly (with no apologies) on the legendary, heroic version.

Gunfight at the O.K. Corral ★★ (1957) 122 Minutes (Burt Lancaster, Kirk Douglas, Rhonda Fleming, Jo Van Fleet): Douglas' lethal Doc Holliday and Van Fleet's burned-out Kate Elder are a joy to watch, but for historical accuracy the film is a disaster. The shootout itself is fairly well done, but bears no resemblance to what really happened at the famous stockyard. Lancaster's Earp is unbearably noble.

Recommended Reading:
Casey Tefertiller, *Wyatt Earp: The Life Behind the Legend.*

Young Guns ★★★★

(1988) 107 Minutes

Director: Christopher Cain

Cast: Emilio Estevez, Kiefer Sutherland, Lou Diamond Phillips, Charlie Sheen, Dermot Mul-

roney, Casey Siemaszko, Terence Stamp, Jack Palance, Brian Keith, Patrick Wayne

Historical Background: During the autumn of 1877, an itinerant 17-year-old killer surfaced at John Tunstall's sprawling ranch 35 miles south of Lincoln, N.M., and signed on as a cowhand. Impecunious and fresh out of friends, Billy the Kid had blundered his way straight to ground zero of the simmering Lincoln County range war—by far the bitterest cattlemen's feud in the annals of the American frontier. Eventually, it would cost him his life.

The West's most famous pistoleer was born in New York City's Irish tenements in 1860. His real name was Henry McCarty—not William H. Bonney (an alias he began using when he introduced himself to Tunstall). Following his father's death in the early 1870s, he moved west with the rest of his family, then drifted to Arizona after tuberculosis killed his mother. McCarty's first killing came in 1877, when he shot an ex-soldier named Windy Cahill to death—probably in self defense—during a saloon brawl in Fort Grant, Ariz. He fled to New Mexico and went to work for Tunstall, one of several English entrepreneurs who built healthy fortunes in the American Southwest. Tunstall and lawyer Alexander McSween were determined to wrest control of Lincoln County from a group of ruthless banker-merchants led by Lawrence G. Murphy and James Dolan. The two men ran virtually everything in Lincoln County, an area the size of West Virginia. In Lincoln itself, they owned the only bank and the only store, controlling prices and credit terms for the entire county. Tunstall threw his gauntlet to the floor in August 1878 by opening a huge general store offering customers easy credit and all sorts of merchandise at low prices. Murphy and Dolan were furious.

As tension between the two factions escalated, both sides began hiring gunmen: Tunstall called his small army the Regulators; the Murphy–Dolan riders were simply "the Boys." All of them were expert marksmen, and Bonney—now called the Kid because of his youthful demeanor and easygoing manner—was the best of the lot. On the evening of February 18, 1878, a "posse" led by Sheriff Bill Brady (a Murphy hireling) murdered Tunstall in open country between his ranch and Lincoln. Billy the Kid and five Regulators—appointed "special constables" by Lincoln's justice of the peace—retaliated on April 1, shooting Brady 12 times in front of Tunstall's store and igniting a full-scale war that would take 29 lives before the year ended. Pitched battles between the two factions raged across the county until a five-day siege in Lincoln peaked with the burning of McSween's house on July 19. Bonney and several Regulators shot their way out of the building and disappeared into the surrounding mountains. The bloody battle had decimated both sides, ending the war before a clear winner emerged.

Billy the Kid—now wanted for Brady's murder—began rustling cattle with Arkansas Dave Rudabaugh and a small gang. In December 1880, newly elected sheriff Pat Garrett—an old gambling friend of Bonney's—finally tracked Rudabaugh, Charley Bowdre, and Billy to an abandoned stone house near Stinking Springs, killing Bowdre and arresting the other fugitives after a three-day siege. Tried, convicted, and sentenced to hang on May 13, 1881, Bonney awaited execution in the Lincoln County Courthouse, guarded by two deputies and manacled to the floor of a second-storey room. A week after the trial, he escaped by shooting J. W. Bell with a pistol concealed in the courthouse privy. He then killed the second deputy with his own shotgun, rode to Fort Sumner, and took refuge at the house of his longtime friend Pete Maxwell.

Three months later, at midnight on July 13, Garrett caught up with Billy the Kid and shot him to death in Maxwell's bedroom. Henry McCarty was 21 years old when he died. Captivated by his story, journalists adorned it with fabrications that refuse to go away. Most people still think that his real name was William Bonney. He killed nine men, at most—not the 21 of legend and fable. Only three known photographs of McCarty still exist; one of them, a full-length portrait of the Kid brandishing a Winchester in his right hand, was originally printed backward, preserving another myth: to this day, most people wrongly believe that Billy the Kid was a southpaw.

Young Guns is the only film on Billy the Kid that gives a detailed and reasonably accurate account of the vicious Lincoln County range war. The movie opens with Billy—perfectly played by Estevez—joining Tunstall's outfit, witnessing his mentor's murder a few weeks later, and leading the Regulators in a bloody vendetta against the Murphy–Dolan gang. Palance is excellent as the rapacious Murphy, and Mulroney's jittery, tobacco-chewing Regulator almost steals the show. The final siege at McSween's house is a knockout.

For Further Viewing:
Young Guns II ★★★ (1990) 103 Minutes (Emilio Estevez, Kiefer Sutherland, Lou Diamond Phillips, Christian Slater, William Petersen): This uneven sequel to *Young Guns* begins with the silly notion that Pat Garrett didn't really kill Billy the Kid,

who—at age 80—dictates the story of his outlaw days after the Lincoln County war to a reporter. Except for its bizarre opening premise, *Young Guns II* is entertaining and faithful to the facts, speculating only where gaps in the historical record exist.

The Left-Handed Gun ★ (1958) 102 Minutes (Paul Newman, Lita Milan, John Dehner): Newman (as the Kid) hunts down four killers who shoot down a friend. Based on Gore Vidal's play (also starring Newman), *The Left-Handed Gun* opens well, but soon deteriorates into a bizarre, silly pop psychoanalysis of Billy. Newman has great screen presence—as always—but he turns the famous pistoleer into a manic-depressive, careening from despair to euphoria and back again. Dull and unconvincing all the way, with precious little historically based material for amateur historians.

Recommended Reading:
Robert M. Utley, *Billy the Kid: A Short and Violent Life;* Pat Floyd Garrett, *The Authentic Life of Billy the Kid.*

chapter 5

World War I

(Overleaf)
All Quiet on the Western Front *(1930)*

(Photofest)

Chronology

1914

JUNE 28: Serb Gavrilo Princip assassinates Austria-Hungary's Archduke Franz Ferdinand and wife.

JULY 28: Austria-Hungary declares war on Serbia.

AUGUST 1–4: Germany declares war on Russia and France, invades Belgium.

AUGUST 4: Britain declares war on Germany.

AUGUST 6–12: Austria, France, and Britain declare war on Russia.

AUGUST 20: Germans take Brussels.

AUGUST 26–31: Russians lose Battle of Tannenburg.

SEPTEMBER 6–9: First Battle of Marne River.

SEPTEMBER 23: Germans take St. Mihiel.

OCTOBER 19–NOVEMBER 17: British win First Battle of Ypres.

NOVEMBER 3–5: Russia, England, and France declare war on Turkey.

1915

FEBRUARY 18: Germans blockade England.

APRIL 22–MAY 9: Second Battle of Ypres.

MAY 7: German submarine sinks British liner *Lusitania*, killing 128 Americans.

OCTOBER 4–16: Russia, England, and France declare war on Bulgaria.

1916

JANUARY 9: British evacuate Gallipoli.

FEBRUARY 21: Germans attack Verdun.

MAY 31–JUNE 1: British win Battle of Jutland.

JULY 1: Allies launch Somme River offensive.

AUGUST 27: Italy declares war on Germany.

OCTOBER 8: German submarine sinks five ships off Nantucket Island, Massachusetts.

NOVEMBER 18: Battle of Somme ends.

DECEMBER 16: French victory at Verdun.

1917

MARCH 8: Russian Revolution begins.

MARCH 15: Russian government collapses.

APRIL 6: U.S. declares war on Germany.

MAY 16: Aleksandr Feodorovich Kerensky becomes Russia's war minister.

JULY 16: Aleksandr Feodorovich Kerensky becomes Russia's provisional prime minister.

JULY 31: British open Third Battle of Ypres.

OCTOBER 24: Italians routed at Caporetto.

OCTOBER 31: Australians take Beersheba.

NOVEMBER 7: British take Gaza.

NOVEMBER 8: Bolsheviks overthrow Kerensky.

NOVEMBER 20: British attack Cambrai.

1918

JANUARY 8: Woodrow Wilson's "Fourteen Points" peace program.

MARCH 3: Brest-Litovsk treaty ends Russia's participation in war.

MAY 1: Germans take Sevastopol.

JULY 15–18: Allies win Second Battle of Marne River.

JULY 21: Allies take Château-Thierry.

AUGUST 30: Germans retreat in Flanders.

SEPTEMBER 26: Allies launch Meuse–Argonne offensive.

OCTOBER 1: British take Damascus.

OCTOBER 5 AND 12: Wilson receives German peace proposals.

OCTOBER 13: British take Tripoli.

OCTOBER 31: Turkey signs armistice with Allies.

NOVEMBER 11: Germany signs armistice.

All Quiet on the Western Front ★★★★★

(1979) 150 Minutes

Director: Delbert Mann

Cast: Richard Thomas, Ernest Borgnine, Patricia Neal, Ian Holm, Donald Pleasence

Historical Background: For three and a half years, ground combat at its very worst rocked the Great War's western front. The typical infantry assault began with deafening state-of-the-art artillery barrages, proceeded with attackers racing across no-man's-land through a curtain of fire from modern repeating rifles and machine guns, then peaked—with satanic irony—in primitive hand-to-hand combat fought on the muddy floors of enemy trenches with weapons straight out of the middle ages—wooden clubs bristling with nails, trench knives resembling miniature cutlasses, and small military shovels, their edges filed razor-sharp. After a few minutes of bloody mayhem, outnumbered assault troops, their ranks decimated in the pell-mell rush across no-man's-land, fell back toward their own lines to repulse the inevitable counterattack, and the mad process began all over again.

Kaiser Wilhelm II's invasion of France opened the slaughter on August 3, 1914: Germany's western army swept southward through Belgium—around and behind enemy fortifications dotting the Franco-German frontier—and straight toward the French capital. Five weeks later, French and British defenders near the Marne River stood fast, fighting wildly for three

days and stopping the German onslaught 20 miles east of Paris. Without pausing for rest, each army raced desperately to skirt the other's flanks, and the front began spreading out laterally from north to south until a fantastic, unbroken S-shaped line of parallel trench systems stretched 400 miles from the North Sea to the Swiss Alps. (Throughout the war, a common infantryman's joke speculated on the fortunes of a whispered message beginning in Flanders and passed from one man to the next all the way to the mountains: what, exactly, would soldiers on the southern flank eventually hear? Author Paul Fussell puts the combined length of Allied and Central Power trenches at 25,000 miles—the circumference of the earth.)

Early trenches were little more than shoulder-deep ditches—quickly dug temporary defensive positions and launching points for counterattacks. But defenders firing machine guns and high-powered rifles shot their attacking adversaries to bits. To further strangle infantry assaults, both sides anchored forests of rolled barbed wire just outside hand-grenade range in no-man's-land. Hoping that rapid-fire artillery would wreck the obstacles, annihilate entire enemy divisions, and break up stout defensive battlements, tacticians massed more and more big guns behind their third-line trenches. The stalemate was building on itself: crashing shellfire drove armies to build deeper, tougher fortifications, their walls buttressed with sandbags, timbers, and steel beams, their floors covered with duckboards, and their trenches bristling with concrete pillboxes and machine guns. (Trenches zigzagged in a series of V-shaped traverses to contain damage from explosions and foil enfilading rifle or machine-gun fire from either end.) More ominous still, advanced artillery technology developed to break the stand-off actually made it worse—millions of high-explosive rounds proved ineffective against barbed wire and churned no-man's-land into a wild, shell-pocked chaos that slowed attacking infantry to a crawl.

By 1915, a stagnant nightmare of unparalleled carnage prevailed on the western front. For three years, neither side advanced more than ten miles—and even if one army had broken the other's defenses the logistics of moving millions of men and thousands of big guns would have limited offensives to 100 miles or less. (The Allies took extraordinary measures to wreck German fortifications: south of Ypres, British miners dug 21 horizontal tunnels under no-man's-land, cramming a million pounds of gunpowder and ammonol beneath German positions on Messines Ridge. Detonation came on June 7, 1917—19 of the 21 mines exploded, rattling windows 130 miles to the east in London. The ensuing attack rolled past empty German trenches, then bogged down in heavy rain.)

Casualty rates throughout the conflict were appalling. On July 1, 1916, for example, 110,000 British soldiers assaulted enemy positions on the Somme River, and the Germans gunned down 60,000 of them before sunset; no-man's-land echoed with the screams of wounded men for days. Whenever the guns fell silent, squalid living conditions made life miserable. Men at the front lived like burrowing animals: they slept during the day, repairing trenches, digging sapper ditches toward enemy lines, repairing barbed wire, fetching rations and mail, and patrolling no-man's-land after dark. Even the best trench complexes were muddy, cold, filthy, lice-infested, and overrun by enormous rats crawling with fleas that spread trench fever among the troops. Standing water bred rotting feet (trench foot) and ulcer-

ated mouths (trench mouth) in epidemic proportions. Stuffed with corpses and body fragments from ground level to depths limited only by the power of high-explosive shells, no-man's-land reeked with a stench spreading for miles behind the trenchlines. Food quality ranged from monotonous to horrible, and there was never enough of it. Worst of all, life remained terribly dangerous, especially for the careless: snipers lurked everywhere along the line, firing at troglodytes who ventured aboveground before sunset.

Privation, squalor, the ever-present horror of coexistence with the rotting dead, inept leadership at the highest levels, and the maddening futility of trench warfare ground steadily away at morale—especially among the French. On April 16, 1917, France's new commander in chief, Robert Nivelle, launched a suicidal northward thrust against 43 crack German divisions dug in near Rheims and Soissons. Two weeks and 250,000 casualties later, Nivelle had advanced 500 yards. On May 3, mutiny erupted in the French army: entire divisions refused to return from rear areas to first-line trenches; others remained at the front, willing to hold their positions, but refusing to assault deeply entrenched German rifle companies and machine-gun teams. Before the crisis passed in mid-June, 120 units in more than 60 divisions joined the revolt. Nivell was sacked on May 15, and courts-martial eventually convicted 23,400 men, condemning 432 to death (55 died, in the end—the rest went to French penal colonies).

Throughout the rebellion, patriotism among mutineers flourished: they had no quarrel with their government, and slinging arms before every single German soldier left France was out of the question. A change of tactics (their stated goal) was long overdue, but the malaise they shared with soldiers on both sides reflected their sense that the war literally would go on forever—or until every European male over the age of 15 lay dead in no-man's-land. Their fear was reasonable: after the 1917 mutinies, a British officer measured the distance on a map from the trenches to Germany's western border, divided the mileage by total Allied real-estate gains during major campaigns such as Verdun, and multiplied the figure by the offensives' combined duration—and according to his calculations, Allied forces would be able to drive the Germans back across the Rhine in 180 years. Even today, traces of the Great War stubbornly linger: remnants of trench sections still show up in aerial photographs, and the last undetonated Messines mine finally exploded near Ploegsteert in 1955.

Many modern viewers enjoy this superb remake more than the original classic pacifist film based on Erich Maria Remarque's novel about German soldiers fighting in the French sector of the western front. (Remarque served in the German trenches during some of World War I's worst fighting.) Mann's sets are meticulously accurate, his battle scenes beautifully filmed and choreographed, and his segments set in French villages and German cities and schoolrooms could stand alone as short period pieces. Richard Thomas (as Paul Baumer), Ernest Borgnine (the wily old veteran Katczinsky), and Ian Holm (as Himmelstoss, the sadistic training officer turned coward at the front) deliver convincing, finely crafted performances. Patricia Neal excels in her small role as Paul's mother.

For Further Viewing:
All Quiet on the Western Front ★★★★★ (1930) 133 Minutes (Lew Ayres, Louis Wolheim, John Wray, Slim Summerville, Russell Gleason, Ben Alexander): Seven decades after winning Oscars for Best Picture and Best Director, Lewis Milestone's masterpiece remains one of the best war movies ever made. It was an extremely effective antiwar film in the U.S. because Ayres and his fellow Germans were blazing away at French *poilus,* not American doughboys. When the movie opened in Germany, Nazi thugs smashed into the theater and released several snakes to terrorize the audience. Hitler and Mussolini banned the movie, and authorities in France—home of the heroes' mortal enemy—didn't authorize its release there until 1962. Modern viewers usually find the dialogue hokey and the thirties-style acting florid, but they still love the film.

Paths of Glory ★★★★ (1957) 86 Minutes (Kirk Douglas, Ralph Meeker, Adolphe Menjou, George Macready, Wayne Morris, Richard Anderson): Director Stanley Kubrick's version of Humphrey Cobb's novel about mutiny in the French army. Staff officers Menjou and Macready order suicidal assaults on a German strongpoint by regimental commander Douglas' veterans. Half the men refuse to attack, and a court-martial condemns three randomly chosen soldiers to execution for cowardice (despite peacetime lawyer Douglas' able defense). Kubrick's fashionable Hollywood iconoclasm waxes and wanes throughout, hauling historical accuracy with it: the film correctly identifies high-level officers as the mutineers' nemesis, but it casts career advancement as the staff's only motive for ordering the attack—a thoroughly wrongheaded notion (murderous frontal assaults prevailed in all armies until more effective tactics surfaced in 1918, and losing too many men led to dismissal—not promotion—in the French army). Still, an excellent film, with super performances by Douglas, Macready, Morris, and Menjou.

Recommended Reading:

Paul Fussell, *The Great War and Modern Memory;* Alan Lloyd, *The War in the Trenches;* Erich Maria Remarque, *All Quiet on the Western Front;* Robert Graves, *Good-bye to All That.*

The Blue Max ★★★

(1966) 156 Minutes

Director: John Guillermin

Cast: George Peppard, Jeremy Kemp, James Mason, Ursula Andress, Carl Schell

Historical Background: On May 19, 1918, American fighter ace Raoul Lufbery jumped onto a motorcycle, roared from his barracks to the Etain airfield, commandeered the nearest Nieuport fighter, and took off in pursuit of a lone German Albatros he'd spotted moments earlier. During his second pass at the Hun triplane, Lufbery's weapons jammed. Incendiary bullets from his enemy's guns struck a fuel line on his plane, igniting its spewing petrol and setting the machine on fire. To escape the torture of a flaming death, Lufbery jumped from the plane. His leap was fatal, because he carried no parachute, even though they'd been available for quite some time (a century earlier, inventors had begun testing primitive chutes by strapping them onto animals and dropping the terrified beasts

from high towers). Like many pilots on both sides, Lufbery still considered hitting the silk a tacit admission of cowardice. For him, aerial combat was a sporting proposition: each of his 17 victories had come in skirmishes behind enemy lines, and the isolated German Albatros provided a welcome chance to run up his score in plain sight of a friendly home-field crowd. Again, Lufbery's attitude was typical. Individual honor remained the first concern of most combat aviators, despite the horrid impersonal slaughter—in the air as well as on the ground—wrought by four years of increasingly efficient technological warfare. (By 1918, accurate rapid-fire machine guns had reduced the typical aircraft's combat life to only a few weeks.)

The airmen's "warrior spirit" was a magnificent anachronism held over from the early days of the war. In contrast to nameless foot soldiers who died by the millions in muddy trenches, the first WWI pilots fought freewheeling individual duels in a limitless arena of battle. Used mainly for observation and reconnaissance, the underpowered aircraft of 1914 and 1915—built by hand from wood, wire, and cloth—were so fragile that sudden violent maneuvering tore their wings apart. Aviators stored small bombs in their cockpits, dropping them by hand with far more hope than accuracy. Early dogfights were clumsy, comic affairs fought with odd assortments of shotguns, pistols, and rifles. Some early planes carried one or two wildly inaccurate rifle-caliber machine guns mounted on upper wings above the propellers.

The brutal demands of mechanized warfare changed all of this. In 1914, all of the belligerents combined could field a grand total of 2,500 primitive planes, and control of air operations lay entirely with army and naval commanders. By 1918, Sir Hugh Trenchard had built the world's first independent strategic air corps in England; he commanded 22,000 military aircraft. Fragile fighters designed for single combat had given way to faster, more durable planes that flew in great formations. Germany boasted long-range Siemens-Schuckert R-VIII bombers with wingspans of more than 140 feet. The first aircraft carriers—converted battleships with launching platforms built atop gun turrets—had appeared. A list of lethal technology used by most belligerents during WWI is staggering: diesel-powered submarines, machine guns, poison gas, modern artillery, tanks, accurate repeating rifles, and military aircraft all made their mark during the Great War. Compared to other new weapons, the airplane did little to bring about the end of the war. But it had given the world a grim preview of what was to come: by 1917, Englishmen were using subways as bomb shelters during German air raids, and aircraft identification posters dotted the walls of most public buildings. A second worldwide conflagration was just 22 years away, and the gateway to total war was wide open.

Peppard plays an ambitious working-class German infantryman who transfers to a fighter squadron during the final months of 1918. His cynicism about the war, born in the trenches and greeted with hostility by his fellow pilots, fuels his determination to win the "Blue Max" (Germany's highest medal for bravery in air combat). War-related footage is excellent throughout, but *The Blue Max* stumbles with an annoying, pointless subplot tracing an illicit romance between Peppard and Ursula Andress, cast as the wife of a German count (played by James Mason, of all people). The consequent low comedy mars what should have been a five-star knockout production.

For Further Viewing:
Aces High ★★★ (1976) 104 Minutes (Malcolm McDowell, Peter Firth, Simon Ward): A tough, realistic look at the 1914–18 European air war. Disillusioned squadron leader McDowell must look out for Firth, a naive rookie who happens to be his sister's fiancé. Simon Ward is excellent as a pilot on the verge of cracking up. Combat sequences and special effects are good as well, but much of the film's antiwar message comes across as clichéd hyperbole.

Recommended Reading:
Captain Eddie V. Rickenbacker, *Fighting the Flying Circus;* Bernard Fitzsimmons, ed., *Warplanes and Air Battles of World War I;* John Lucas, *The Big Umbrella: A History of the Parachute from da Vinci to Apollo.*

A Farewell to Arms ★★★

(1957) 152 Minutes

Director: Charles Vidor

Cast: Rock Hudson, Jennifer Jones, Vittorio De Sica, Alberto Sordi, Mercedes McCambridge

Historical Background: July 8, 1918—near Fossalta, Italy: Moments after distributing candy, coffee, and cigarettes to weary Italian soldiers entrenched near the Piave River, American Red Cross ambulance driver Ernest Hemingway heard the metallic cough of a huge Austrian trench mortar. Seconds later, its whirring five-gallon projectile landed several feet away, exploding on contact and spewing hundreds of junk-metal fragments and sectioned steel rods in all directions. Hurled backward and slammed to earth by the searing concussion, Hemingway glanced numbly toward an Italian sniper screaming in no-man's-land. Staggering to his feet, the dazed American sprinted 150 yards to the wounded man, heaved him over one shoulder, and reeled crazily homeward through withering enemy fire, finally collapsing at the Italian command post. Soldiers witnessing the spectacle gazed in pop-eyed disbelief at Hemingway's battered form—a machine-gun round had smashed his right knee, and deeply embedded in his legs were 227 mortar fragments. (It would take a dozen operations to remove them all.)

Volunteer ambulance drivers were among the bravest men on the western and Italian fronts: exposed to the same artillery and machine-gun fire as troops in deep steel-reinforced bunkers, they sat in high, unprotected cabs, driving at deliberate speeds to spare wounded men life-threatening jolts on the rough roads leading to rear-echelon aid stations. Every day, drivers and stretcher bearers saw the ghastly forms of death and injury inflicted by high technology in the world's first purely industrial war. Fought with stately 18th-century tactics and slaughterous 20th-century weapons (see *All Quiet on the Western Front*), great battles flooded aid stations and hospitals with shattered men in overwhelming numbers. (Forty-eight hours into the Somme campaign, 10,000 groaning soldiers littered every inch of the six-acre grounds surrounding a British casualty station staffed and equipped to treat 1,000 patients. A line of fully loaded ambulances, bumper-to-bumper and one mile long, stretched back toward the front from the facility's gates.) Near-senseless with fatigue, physicians and nurses faced unprecedented clinical problems: shell shock; gangrene from gas-forming anaerobic bacteria infesting northern France's muddy soil; earth and soiled clothing fibers—impossible to find with surgical probes—driven into deep muscle tissue by shell fragments; delirium and virulent skin lesions caused by lice-borne trench fever; lungs charred by phosgene gas; mustard-gas-induced blindness and blisters; feet rotting away from constant immersion in muddy water; and horribly disfiguring facial wounds (more than a quarter million on the western front alone).

At awful cost, physicians learned much from grueling tours in wartime hospitals. Abdominal surgery, shunned as an unsafe procedure during the Boer War, saved many lives. Determined surgeons fresh out of medical school revolutionized chest and brain surgery and developed new skin-grafting techniques. Modern indirect transfusion of stored blood, using sodium citrate as an anticoagulant, began in Great War medical facilities. (Direct transfusion linked donor and patient by tube, relying on the donor's stronger heartbeat to move the blood.) For soldiers, the most critical advances brought new logistical systems (essentially unchanged to this day) for moving casualties in great numbers: borne on stretchers from battlefields to regimental aid posts, wounded men moved toward the rear through a series of facilities, each staffed and equipped to treat more serious injuries than the last. On the western front, evacuation systems and personnel grew remarkably efficient—by war's end they had gathered and transported more than 7 million partially destroyed men.

Producer David O. Selznick canned original director John Huston for refusing to turn *A Farewell to Arms* into a Jennifer Jones showcase. A more compliant Vidor delivered this lumbering, uneven adaptation of the novel based on Hemingway's exploits in World War I Italy. Stunningly photographed and very convincing on the battlefront, the movie occasionally derails during romantic interludes involving Jones (nurse Catherine Barkley) and Hudson (miscast as Lieutenant Henry). Vidor's final product is a handsomely packaged, sadly average version of Hemingway's moving story. Still, excellent period detail and harrowing action sequences make the film worth watching for aficionados of the Great War.

For Further Viewing:
A Farewell to Arms ★★★★ (1932) 78 Minutes (Gary Cooper, Helen Hayes, Adolphe Menjou, Mary Philips, Jack LaRue): Hemingway detested Laurence Stallings' 1930 stage version of *A Farewell to Arms,* mainly because of its contrived happy ending. Film director Frank Borzage shot two endings for this early adaptation of the novel, using the upbeat rendition for test screenings, but keeping the somber version in his final cut. Hemingway still hated the movie, but fans loved it. Cooper (as Henry) and Hayes (Catherine Barkley) make perfect ill-fated lovers in one of Hollywood's great tearjerkers. The film's dreamlike atmosphere lends force to its story about the magical—but temporary—dispersion of a horrifying world by a simple love affair. Hemingway and Cooper eventually became friends.

Recommended Reading:
Guy Emerson Bowerman, Jr., *The Compensations of War: The Diary of an Ambulance Driver During the Great War;* Raymond McLaughlin, *The Royal Army Medical Corps.*

Gallipoli ★★★

(1981) 110 Minutes

Director: Peter Weir

Cast: Mark Lee, Mel Gibson, Bill Kerr, Robert Grubb, David Argue, Tim McKenzie

Historical Background: August 7, 1915—Gallipoli Peninsula: Six hundred men from the Third Australia–New Zealand Army Corps ("Anzac") Lighthorse Brigade crouched in the uppermost trench of their low-lying foothold, a line of bunkers and furrows hacked into the sandy cliffs paralleling Gallipoli's northern shoreline and sprawling wildly upward toward the dominant heights of Sari Bair Ridge. Scant yards behind them lay the Aegean Sea. Ahead of and above them lay their objective—a heavily fortified trench complex in the "Nek" sector on the ridgeline's crest, manned by enemy infantry and backed by artillery that had rained hell on Allied troops and warships since April.

Driven into deep bunkers by Royal Navy gunfire, Turkish defenders sat and waited, hoping that the bombardment would lift before waves of sprinting Anzacs were on top of them. At 4:23 A.M.—a full seven minutes ahead of schedule—the booming guns fell silent: infantry commanders and naval gunnery officers had synchronized their watches with fatal imprecision. In stunned disbelief, fuming Anzacs listened as their adversaries swarmed into defensive positions, doubling their riflemen's firepower by massing two deep in staggered ranks along their trenchline. At 4:30, Col. A. H. White jumped from the forward trench, shouted his attack order, and disintegrated before he'd advanced ten yards. Three hundred Anzacs followed him into a wall of rifle and machine-gun fire, then reeled backward, many of them blown apart before they cleared the trench. It was over in 30 seconds, but grenade detonations and blazing Turkish guns continued to roar along the trenchline. With breathtaking courage, the second wave of Australians—unable to hear whistles signaling the attack—glanced at the officers waving them forward and raced straight to annihilation. When the shooting stopped, 128 Anzacs were still standing. At Suvla Bay to the north, a simultaneous—but chaotic—25,000-man British assault intended to split the Turkish army in two floundered on lightly defended beaches because of imprecise topographical maps, green junior officers, and poorly navigated, botched landings.

With horrible consistency, Gallipoli had devoured yet another well-planned Anzac tactical thrust, bringing the Allies' campaign to seize the Dardanelles Strait one step closer to disaster. In 1915, England had sound reasons for launching a campaign there: the long, narrow waterway separating European Turkey from the rest of the country links the Aegean with the Sea

of Marmara and the Bosphorus, completing the only maritime route from the Black Sea to the Mediterranean. Taking the Dardanelles and the Bosphorus would let the Americans ship vital war matériel to Tsar Nicholas, keeping Russia in the war; it would protect Great Britain's 500,000-man Egyptian force and leave Constantinople wide open to Allied attack; and it might bring Italy—perhaps even the Balkans—into the Allied camp.

For the Allies, the campaign brought a maddening series of near misses—all falling just short of success and leaving a charnel house of terrible waste with little compensating gain. To seize the Dardanelles, for example, an attacker would have to take the Gallipoli Peninsula on the strait's northwest side, and this the Allies could have done had they delayed their initial naval strike until a well-equipped occupying force joined the fleet. They didn't. On February 19, Royal Navy bombardments began leveling the strait's outer forts. On the 25th, marine landing parties—virtually unopposed by two skeletal, poorly equipped Turkish divisions—destroyed every shore battery they found on the peninsula's tip (Cape Helles). Three Allied divisions, at this point, could have taken and occupied all of Gallipoli with minimal casualties, but the troops weren't there. Stage two of the campaign, a drive by French and British ships to force a passage through the strait, failed in mid-March after a tiny, hidden line of 20 enemy mines disabled three Allied ships and sent three more to the bottom of Eren Keui Bay. Fearing bombardment by nonexistent Turkish guns, the fleet retired. Lord Kitchener raised a 72,000-man expeditionary force (most of them Anzacs) for beachfront assaults on Gallipoli.

Gone was the vital element of surprise: by early April, four enemy divisions swarmed over the high ground on both sides of the strait, digging trenches, fortifying artillery positions, laying mines, anchoring forests of barbed wire (some of it underwater), and dotting the area with hidden machine-gun nests. When the first landings came, thousands of deeply entrenched Turks were looking down their adversaries' throats. Short of artillery, unable to communicate with commander Sir Ian Hamilton, and outnumbered six divisions to five, the Allies launched their invasion at 4:20 A.M. on April 25, hurling Sir William Birdwood's Anzacs toward the wide beaches at Gaba Tepe. Minutes later, everything began to unravel. Powerful currents swept the assault boats ashore in a rocky cove well north of their objective. Meeting little resistance on the awful terrain, 8,000 Anzacs clambered ashore and tried to move forward—with nothing to guide them but maps copied from tourist handbooks. A maze of brush-choked ravines and precipitous cliffs scattered the attackers, dispersing the force of their assault. Worse still, Mustafa Kemal—the Turks' finest commander—quickly launched an unauthorized counterattack, stopped the Anzacs cold, then garrisoned Sari Bair Ridge with his crack 19th Division.

Similar confusion—and hideous carnage—reigned at Cape Helles, 15 miles to the south. Incredibly, rookie officers from Britain's 29th Division walked to the top of a high, ungarrisoned ridgeline shortly after hitting the beach: with no orders to take the impregnable position, they returned to the beach and sat there, awaiting instructions. In one sector, a grounded landing ship carrying 2,000 soldiers reeled under the impact of withering Turkish machine-gun and artillery fire. Troops trying to escape died before they hit the water, and pilots in the area said that blood from Allied corpses

had turned a 50-foot-wide strip of ocean stretching along the beach "absolutely red." Ten days later, reinforcements steaming ashore could see hundreds of bodies pinned to the seafloor under 90-pound packs. By nightfall, the Allies held a broken coastal line vulnerable every inch of the way to bombardment and machine-gun fire from superior Turkish positions. For 259 days the two sides slaughtered each other, pouring division after division into the stalemated holocaust. A quarter million Turks fell, and Allied forces lost the same number (many from disease and frostbite) before evacuating the peninsula on January 9, 1916. The tough, resourceful Anzacs went on to fight brilliantly in Europe and Palestine, capturing the key city of Beersheba (and its desperately needed water) on October 31, 1917, with a glorious in-your-face cavalry charge reminiscent of the 19th-century American West. April 25—Anzac Day—remains Australia's most celebrated national holiday.

Gallipoli follows Lee and Gibson from western Australia to the Allied nightmare in the Dardanelles. Worth watching for marvelous period detail and an interesting story (written by Weir), *Gallipoli* is fine entertainment. As film history, it fails terribly: Weir gives no historical background for the long campaign—viewers unaware of the strait's strategic importance and Allied objectives there won't learn about them from the movie. Nor will they know what the Nek is, even though the action unfolds there; Sari Bair goes unmentioned, and Suvla Bay surfaces in one brief, silly remark.

These lapses support Weir's apparent effort to find British villainy behind the Dardanelles catastrophe. During the climactic assault, for example, an Australian insists that "the British are sitting on the beach sipping tea" at Suvla Bay, clearly implying that English sloth and indifference to Australian casualties was par for the course in the Dardanelles. This is utter nonsense: the Suvla Bay failure came from disorganization, inadequate knowledge of inland terrain, and isolated junior commanders who didn't know what to do after landing. Thousands of British soldiers died with the Anzacs at Gallipoli; England's Liberal government fell, and many British heads (including Admiralty Lord Winston Churchill's) rolled because of the Dardanelles disaster. British leaders were guilty of sloppy preparation and bungled logistics—but they weren't apathetic about Australia's sacrifices.

For Further Viewing:

The Lighthorsemen ★★★★ (1987) 111 Minutes (Jon Blake, Peter Phelps, Nick Wateres, Tony Bonner, Bill Kerr, Sigrid Thornton, Anthony Andrews): Anzacs, again—still fighting the Turks, but this time on horseback and victorious in the 1917 desert campaign. The acting could be better in places, but this accurate, sweeping epic about the October 31 Beersheba assault and events preceding it is a delight for lovers of action movies based on meticulous historical research. Director Simon Wincer clearly presents Anzac strategic objectives and delivers great period detail, right down to the Lighthorsemen's mean sword-bayonets and Model 1902 Short Magazine Lee-Enfield rifles (one of the great weapons of all time, developed specifically for mounted troops). The long final cavalry attack on the city of the seven wells ranks with Hollywood's great film spectacles (it is absolutely thunderous in full-sized theaters). Andrews excels as a high-ranking British intelligence officer.

Anzacs: The War Down Under ★★★ (1985) 165 Minutes (Paul Hogan, Andrew Clarke, Megan Williams, Jon Blake): Pre-*Crocodile Dundee* Hogan

and mates josh their way through several Anzac campaigns, beginning at Gallipoli and ending with the 1918 Amiens slaughterhouse. Inferior dramatically (and technically, in spots) to *Gallipoli*, *Anzacs* delivers far superior history (it is remarkably thorough, especially on the Gallipoli fiasco), offering an ongoing clinic on tactical trench warfare and basic WWI weapons. A good overview of Australia's contribution to the Allied war effort, with expertly done battle scenes.

Recommended Reading:
Captain Eric Wheler Bush, *Gallipoli.*

Sergeant York ★★★★★

(1941) 134 Minutes

Director: Howard Hawks

Cast: Gary Cooper, Walter Brennan, Joan Leslie, George Tobias, Stanley Ridges, Margaret Wycherly, Ward Bond, June Lockhart

Historical Background: Almost as soon as he could walk, Alvin C. York began hunting small game in the Cumberland Mountains around Pall Mall, Tenn., to help feed his parents and ten siblings. So precious was each day's quarry that lethal hits below the neck were deemed failures because they destroyed desperately needed meat. By his late teens, York had become an incredible marksman: firing an old revolver from a moving horse, he once killed six turkeys without a single miss—at night. (Incredulous witnesses swore that he was "as drunk as a saloon fly" at the time. Another farmer owned the birds, and York landed in small-claims court the next day.)

A few years later, York blasted his way into military history and American legend on the bloody fields of northeastern France. America's April 1917 declaration of war on Germany left most Tennessee mountaineers ambivalent—at best. All were patriots, but most (including York) belonged to the pacifist Church of Christ in Christian Union, an offshoot of American Methodism modeled on John Wesley's doctrines. (The church's antipolitical notions also appealed to the fiercely independent hilltoppers, and especially to York's father: think of the Germans as federal revenue agents, he said before York shipped out, and gun them down by the hundreds.) Denied draft exemption as a conscientious objector, York lost four appeals after registering for conscription. Assigned after boot camp to a front-line rifle company in the 82nd Infantry Division, he explained his pacifist convictions to battalion commander George Buxton. After long conversations about Biblical passages on just wars, Buxton sent York home for ten days, promising him a noncombat assignment if he still wanted one when he returned.

He didn't. On May 1, 1918, York sailed for France, landing in a front-line trench in the Meuse River–Argonne Forest sector of the Allied line. By late September, the 82nd had moved deep into the Argonne for an all-out assault on elevated, near-impregnable German fortifications shrouded in barbed wire and bristling with hundreds of machine guns. On October 7, York's battalion joined the attack, striking west through a U-shaped valley toward the critical Decauville Railroad (a major German supply route). As two forward platoons reached the valley's center, Germans entrenched on the surrounding heights opened fire, cutting to pieces the Americans ahead of York's squad. It was a nightmare—so desperate that York and Sgt. Bernard Early led three tiny squads up the reverse slope of a hill behind the German perimeter to attack several machine guns pouring fire into the valley below. As soon as they rounded the Germans' right flank, York and 15 Americans stood one and a half miles behind enemy lines, separated from their battalion by a full regiment of the crack 2nd Landwehr Division. Moving toward the ringing clatter of light machine guns, York's patrol stumbled into a large group of German reserves eating breakfast. York shot one of them. Flabbergasted, the rest surrendered seconds before German machine gunners thirty yards away spotted the Americans and opened fire, hitting Early and eight others. York fell to the ground and picked off the Germans one by one as they peered over their parapets to find him. An enraged officer finally spotted him and led a howling six-man bayonet charge straight at the exhausted doughboys: York killed all of them with a Colt .45, shooting the last man first and working his way to the front—just as he'd done with his neighbor's turkeys years earlier. In goggle-eyed terror, the remaining Germans surrendered. Similar scenarios unfolded throughout the day, and by late afternoon York had killed 25 Germans and captured 132—so many that he had to take them all the way to divisional headquarters to find facilities large enough to hold them.

York's 82nd Infantry Division was part of

an American Expeditionary Force needed desperately, in 1917, by battle-ravaged Allied armies. For 33 months, the U.S. had remained neutral—officially, at least—as Europe bled itself slowly to death. In fact, the U.S. was deeply committed to the Allies, even before news of Germany's 1914 Belgian atrocities surfaced in Yankee newspapers. Huge American loans and virtually all of America's overseas trade (including war-related industrial resources) went to England, France, Italy, and Russia. Germany's unrestricted submarine warfare—a vile depravity to everyone but the Germans—infuriated Americans. (After German torpedoes killed 128 Americans aboard the *Lusitania* on May 7, 1915, thousands of men flocked to military training camps for U.S. civilians, prompting the Kaiser to rein in his fleet—but only for a while. By January 1917, his subs were back on the prowl.) In mid-March, Germany sank three more American ships, and the U.S. declared war.

Extraordinary mobilization efforts began. Supreme commander George Pershing faced a staggering weapons shortfall. The army, for example, had only 600,000 Model 1903 Springfield rifles on hand—less than half the number required by a mushrooming AEF. By early 1918, Winchester and Remington, under contract for years to manufacture rifles for England's army, filled the gap with Model 1917 Enfields. On May 18, 1917, Woodrow Wilson signed a conscription bill to mold a peacetime army with just 20 staff officers into a force capable of waging modern technological warfare, and by December more than 500,000 men were in uniform. In six grueling months, 200,000 workers built 32 city-sized military facilities equipped to train and house them all. National Guard units flourished, building remarkable *esprit de corps* by recruiting large groups of young men from the same area, training them together, and leaving their units intact for combat duty. (New York's legendary "Fighting 69th" Irish Regiment was one of them: manned by Irish Catholics from New York City's Catholic Athletic Clubs and Irish County Societies, the 69th terrorized Germans on the battlefield and made headlines for Col. Douglas MacArthur's 42nd "Rainbow" Division.) In early January 1918, more than 176,000 Americans were rehearsing advanced trench warfare tactics in France. Ten months later, the AEF had fought its way into history at Belleau Wood, Château-Thierry, Cantigny, the Argonne Forest, and the St. Mihiel salient. The Meuse–Argonne holocaust—scene of York's heroism—raged intermittently until Allied and German representatives at Versailles ended the war on November 11. By then, 2 million doughboys held 21% of the western front, more than 50,000 Americans had died in battle, and Alvin York—holding the French Croix de Guerre, the Distinguished Service Cross, and the Congressional Medal of Honor—returned to Tennessee America's greatest military hero.

A **dynamite** biography of the backwoodsman, beginning in rural Tennessee and ending with his repatriation after the war. Remarkably accurate, right down to its re-creation of an authentic "blind tiger"—a honky-tonk straddling the Tennessee/Kentucky border and divided by a white line into two halves, one observing Kentucky's liquor laws, the other Tennessee's. Many blind tigers served thirsty Cumberland mountaineers—and kept them out of court. Hawks' most important error makes York's religious conversion instant and dramatic. In fact, York's faith grew slowly, the product of much willpower and very little consolation. Super battle scenes, great performances, and a lyrical account of rural life in turn-of-the-century America make this one of Hollywood's finest films.

For Further Viewing:
The Fighting 69th ★★★ (1940) 90 Minutes (James Cagney, Pat O'Brien, George Brent, Jeffrey Lynn, Alan Hale, Dennis Morgan, John Litel): Ten years before Warner Brothers released *The Fighting 69th,* Lewis Milestone's nihilistic *All Quiet on the Western Front* cast Great War veterans as victims of pointless epic-scale slaughter (and nothing more). Hitler's armored legions rolling across Poland changed everything. Director William Keighley's tribute to the Irish regiment has fiery, undisciplined Cagney—court-martialed for cowardice under fire—making a 180-degree about-face thanks to patient counsel by O'Brien as real-life priest Francis Patrick Duffy. (Lynn plays regimental poet Joyce Kilmer, also a historical figure.) Well-done combat scenes help, but florid performances—especially by Cagney—and too much low comedy mar what could have been a very good film.

Recommended Reading:
David D. Lee, *Sergeant York: An American Hero;* Edward M. Coffman, *The War to End All Wars: The American Military Experience in World War I.*

chapter 6

1920-1940: Gangsters, the Roaring Twenties, and the Great Depression

(Overleaf)
Bonnie and Clyde
(Photofest)

Chronology

1920

JANUARY: Volstead Act enforcing 18th Amendment launches Prohibition era.

NOVEMBER 2: Warren G. Harding elected president, Calvin Coolidge vice president.

1922

FEBRUARY 27: Supreme Court declares women's suffrage constitutional.

1923

AUGUST 2: Harding dies.

AUGUST 3: Calvin Coolidge sworn in as president.

1924

NOVEMBER 4: Coolidge reelected.

1925

JULY 10–21: John Scopes tried, convicted, and fined $100 for teaching evolution.

1927

JANUARY 7: AT&T offers first transatlantic telephone service.

MAY 20: Charles Lindbergh makes first nonstop solo New York–Paris flight.

OCTOBER 6: *The Jazz Singer,* first "talking" motion picture, released.

1928

NOVEMBER 6: Herbert Hoover elected president.

1929

FEBRUARY 14: St. Valentine's Day Massacre.

SEPTEMBER 3: Stock prices hit all-time high.

OCTOBER 24: Sudden stock decline.

OCTOBER 29: "Black Tuesday"—stock market crash.

1930

MARCH 13: Astronomers identify planet Pluto.

DECEMBER 11: Bank of United States closes. More than 1,300 banks fail by year's end.

1931

JANUARY 7: U.S. unemployment 5 million.

SEPTEMBER–OCTOBER: Total of 827 banks close.

1932

Unemployment totals for year reach 13 million. Hoover plans public works programs—most launched months later by Franklin D. Roosevelt.

JANUARY 22: Reconstruction Finance Corporation endowed to aid failing financial institutions, insurance companies, railroads.

JULY 2: FDR coins term "New Deal" in Democratic nomination acceptance speech.

JULY 28: Soldiers remove 2,000 veterans

seeking cash payments for military bonus certificates from tent city near Capitol.

NOVEMBER 8: FDR elected president.

1933

MARCH 4: Bank-failure hysteria peaks, Governor Herbert Lehman of New York declares statewide bank holiday.

MAY 18: Tennessee Valley Authority created.

JUNE 16: Federal Deposit Insurance Corporation, National Recovery Administration, and Public Works Administration established.

NOVEMBER 8: Civil Works Administration established.

DECEMBER 5: Prohibition ends.

1934

JUNE 6: Securities and Exchange Commission created.

JUNE 28: Federal Housing Administration established.

1935

MAY 6: Works Progress Administration created.

AUGUST 14: Social Security Act signed.

1936

NOVEMBER 3: Roosevelt reelected.

1937

MAY 27: Golden Gate Bridge opens.

SEPTEMBER 2: National Housing Act signed.

1938

MAY 26: House Committee to Investigate Un-American Activities created.

JUNE 23: Civil Aeronautics Authority created.

1939

JUNE 28: Pan American Airways starts first transatlantic air service.

1940

SEPTEMBER 16: Congress passes Selective Service Act.

NOVEMBER 5: FDR reelected.

Al Capone ★★★

(1959) 105 Minutes

Director: Richard Wilson

Cast: Rod Steiger, James Gregory, Fay Spain, Martin Balsam, Nehemiah Persoff

Historical Background: September 20, 1926—Cicero, Ill.: Bristling with submachine guns, several thug-heavy roadsters dispatched by Earl Weiss crawled past Alphonse Capone's headquarters and poured more than 1,000 rounds into the building, shredding walls and furniture, wounding a bodyguard, and narrowly missing Capone. Police quickly arrived for a report on the shooting, but the gangster's only remark was "What shooting?" Capone had developed plenty of flair on his bloody ride to Chicago's underworld summit.

In 1917, he was washing dishes at future racketeer Frankie Yale's Coney Island bar. Less than a decade later, Al Capone carried $35,000 to $50,000 ready cash at all times and financed a 700-man private army. He owned 15 gambling houses, ran more than 950 bookie operations and at least five illegal breweries, managed several brothels, and rode everywhere in a bulletproof 16-cylinder automobile. At restaurants and speakeasies he tipped entertainers $1,000. By 1929, he'd bled regular "protection" payments from countless business proprietors and tradesmen throughout the city, raising their overhead and inflating consumer prices by $135 million annually. He bribed everyone immune to muscle: mayors, ward bosses, aldermen, lobbyists, congressmen—and especially policemen (Chicago cops rode shotgun on his beer trucks).

Prohibition made Al Capone. Born in Brooklyn on January 17, 1899, he surfaced in Chicago 21 years later to work with old friend Johnny Torrio and brothel lord "Big Jim" Colosimo. Chicago's first mob kingpin, Colosimo ran a string of bordellos stretching from his upscale Everleigh Club all the way to the South Side's ramshackle Bedbug Row. Colosimo's Café, the hottest nightspot in town, drew a full roster of luminaries—Jim Corbett, George Cohan, Florenz Ziegfeld—every evening. But Big Jim—wealthy and reveling in crime-boss celebrity—vetoed a Torrio-Capone scheme for building new empires on Chicago's titanic thirst for bootleg liquor. On May 11, 1920, Yale killed Colosimo, and his two lieutenants took aim on the liquor market, bringing as many small gangs into the fold as they could and killing bigger, tougher rivals.

Their flashiest hit, North Side Irish boss Dion O'Banion, ignited citywide gang warfare. In 1925, Torrio went down (he survived, then retired), and Capone stood alone, determined to exterminate every hostile crew in town. Chicago quickly spun out of control: for four years, gangsters slaughtered each other (final body count: 530) and at one point notched an average of seven murders and two bombings per week. On Valentine's Day 1929, the massacre peaked: that morning, four heavily armed Capone enforcers splattered seven of "Bugs" Moran's goons all over a North Side garage, appalling everyone. Federal cops turned up the heat, escalating a pincers campaign—featuring Treasury investigator Frank Wilson and Prohibition Bureau agent Eliot Ness—against

Capone's empire. Wilson's task force finally nailed the mobster for federal income tax evasion. (Ness played no part in the IRS assault on Capone, but his team mounted a relentless blitz against gangland bootlegging operations, deflecting attention from Wilson's investigation.) Sentenced to 11 years on October 17, 1931, Capone went home with tertiary syphilis after serving eight years. He died on his Florida estate in 1947.

A decent account of Capone's Chicago career and slide into Alcatraz, despite some awful blunders: a ridiculous romance links bachelor Capone (Steiger) and a naive widow (the real gangster was married); Capone personally murders Colosimo; and the city of Chicago gets more credit than the IRS for Capone's takedown. Still, Wilson scores many bull's-eyes for accuracy, including Capone's partnership with Torrio; O'Banion's assassination in his own flower shop, Weiss' Cicero fusillade, the Capone–Moran feud, and the wide-open competition driving Chicago's underworld. Balsam shines as corrupt journalist Keely—a thinly veiled knockoff of real-life reporter Jake Lingle.

For Further Viewing:
The Untouchables ★★★ (1987) 119 Minutes (Kevin Costner, Sean Connery, Robert De Niro, Andy Garcia, Patricia Clarkson, Billy Drago): *The Untouchables* hums with traditional errors. The whole Capone hunt belongs to model family man Ness (Costner—made a Treasury agent by director Brian DePalma). The real Ness was single during his mob-stalking days, gradually developing a booze problem that sank two marriages; a publicity hound, he alerted reporters before each brewery bust (Costner avoids journalists). At film's end, Ness kills Frank "the Enforcer" Nitti—in fact, Nitti

committed suicide. "Untouchable" flatfoot Malone (Connery) was really a corrupt Philadelphia detective. And Capone's trial is pure pulp fiction. The upside features fine performances, terrific period detail, and great Prohibition-era Chicago atmosphere.

Recommended Reading:
Laurence Bergreen, *Capone: The Man and the Era.*

Bonnie and Clyde ★

(1967) 111 Minutes

Director: Arthur Penn

Cast: Warren Beatty, Faye Dunaway, Michael J. Pollard, Gene Hackman, Estelle Parsons

Historical Background: In April 1933, Bonnie Parker and Clyde Barrow almost sank an extraordinary full-throttle getaway by stopping to take a wild potshot at a wounded deputy. Months later, they murdered a policeman—without provocation—and drove away laughing. Two of history's most squalid criminals, they proved—again and again—that they'd rather kill than live. (Their murderous depravity disgusted John Dillinger: asked to assess their outlaw skills, he called them "kill-crazy" and changed the subject.)

Released after 20 months' imprisonment

for burglary, Barrow joined Parker and Ray Hamilton in Dallas and in April 1932 launched a two-year, 15-murder nightmare for residents in a dozen states. That fall, Michigan police grabbed Hamilton, and Clyde recruited brother Buck Barrow, sister-in-law Blanche, and 17-year-old car thief W. D. Jones. (The gang coerced Jones' participation in killings and bisexual romps with Clyde and Parker.)

Kidnapper Albert Bates called Bonnie and Clyde "cheap filling-station thieves." They were incompetent and fatally impulsive: instead of planning a few big scores separated by long hibernations to reduce their exposure to arrest, they meandered around the country, hitting grocery stores and gas stations whenever cash ran low. (Their biggest haul was $2,000; at one point, the entire gang's financial reserves totaled $8.) They were incredibly foolish: Clyde once bought license plates, then gasoline, under two different aliases at the same garage on the same day. In January 1934 the Barrows snatched Hamilton from a prison work detail, prompting former Ranger Frank Hamer to form a task force and hunt them down; 100 days later, near Gibsland, Louisiana, the five-man team shredded Barrow and Parker in their roadster with withering submachine-gun fire. Given the bad news, Bonnie's once-doting aunt said, "I'm glad she's dead—she is surely in hell."

Bonnie and Clyde is one of the 1960s' least accurate historical films. It glamorizes Barrow (Beatty) and Parker (Dunaway) as Dillinger-style bank robbers revered by common folk: loathed by just about everyone, the real gangsters robbed few banks. Penn makes Clyde impotent, whitewashing his out-of-control sexual aberrations (and later admitting that he fictionalized this side of Barrow's character). Episodes

bringing sympathetic poor people to the gang's aid are fabrications, and Penn's portrait of Hamer is slanderous—he wasn't a vindictive man, and the Barrows never captured him. Fine entertainment—but a factual mess.

Recommended Reading:
E. R. Milner, *The Lives and Times of Bonnie and Clyde;* John Toland, *The Dillinger Days.*

Bugsy ★★

(1991) 135 Minutes

Director: Barry Levinson

Cast: Warren Beatty, Annette Bening, Ben Kingsley, Harvey Keitel, Joe Mantegna

Historical Background: For most of his contemporaries, Benjamin Siegel was certifiably insane. Lapsing capriciously—and often—into ungovernable fury, he earned the hated sobriquet "Bugsy" ("crazy as a bedbug") as a young man and never managed to shake it. Born in Brooklyn in 1906, Siegel helped Meyer Lansky build a Lower East Side juvenile gang specializing in hijacking and burglary. Bootlegger Arnold Rothstein eventually hired them to manage booze-running operations, and by 1926 both were rising mob stars. A prolific, unrepentant killer, Siegel murdered New York

Mafia don Joe Masseria in 1931, launching a Lucky Luciano *coup* and capping his own rise to the top of New York's underworld.

Bugsy's place in history rests on deceptions surrounding construction of the Flamingo Hotel in Las Vegas. Several hotel-casinos were already up and running when he arrived; he didn't launch Las Vegas, but he bought into the gaming-industry boom early, building the Flamingo with Luciano-backed loans in 1945–46. (Creditors ordered Siegel's mistress, Mob insider Virginia Hill, to monitor his building operations from day one. Ruthless, calculating, and treacherous, Hill crashed Chicago's rackets at age 17. For years, she smuggled drugs, laundered money, and slept with Mafia dons from coast to coast. By the time she met Siegel, in 1937, she had enough dirt on the Mob to sink half the crooks in America. Officially ruled a suicide, her 1966 death in Austria was probably a Mob hit.) Siegel constantly delayed the project, wrecking and rebuilding entire sections of the hotel and driving costs to a staggering $6 million by 1946. These were calculated moves enabling him to skim $2 million from creditors by overstating costs, paying the actual (and much lower) bills, then pocketing the difference. He fooled no one. On June 20, 1947, a mob gunman blew Siegel's head apart with a .30–30 carbine in Hill's L.A. mansion. Five people attended his funeral.

Fine entertainment—and little more for history buffs. Bening's Hill is too refined (the genuine article cursed like a longshoreman); a reference to her promiscuity as occasional free-spirited independence surfaces once, but in fact, Hill's depravity was limitless—she once had sex with several men at a party as their girlfriends watched. Bening never spies on Siegel, sticking with him until his murder (Hill left for Europe

before the hit). Beatty's Siegel is a gregarious wheeler-dealer—a volatile flake victimized by bad luck—not history's homicidal nut case. Levinson also peddles the "Siegel made Las Vegas" myth. All of this adds up to shameless glamorization of an ugly, sleazy story.

Recommended Reading:
Andy Edmonds, *Bugsy's Baby: The Secret Life of Mob Queen Virginia Hill;* Robert Lacey, *Little Man: Meyer Lansky and the Gangster Life.*

Dillinger ★★★★
(1973) 96 Minutes

Director: John Milius

Cast: Warren Oates, Ben Johnson, Cloris Leachman, Michelle Phillips, Richard Dreyfuss

Historical Background: November 27, 1934—Barrington, Ill.: Ignoring hundreds of incoming submachine-gun slugs plastering the far side of his stalled roadster, a crouching, homicidal gangster rose to his full height of five foot five and sauntered into the open, his Thompson gun blazing away at FBI agents Herman Hollis and Sam Cowley. Hit a dozen times, George "Baby Face" Nelson (Public Enemy No. 1 and former top gun of the late John Dillinger's defunct gang) wasted both G-men at point-blank range, returned to his car, smiled at his gaping partner, collapsed in the backseat, and surfaced in a ditch—stark naked and dead—the next morning.

Nelson anchored an outfit rebuilt by Dillinger after history's brassiest jailbreak. On January 15, 1934, his first gang rifled East Chicago's First National Bank and bolted for Arizona. Ten days later, Tucson police jailed Harry Pierpont, Charles Makley, and Russell Clark, charged Dillinger with killing East Chicago policeman William O'Malley, and extradited him to Crown Point, Ind. On March 3 he blustered his way through six jailhouse doors with a wooden pistol purchased from corrupt deputy Ernest Blunk. Incarcerating every lawman in the building, Dillinger stole a police car and slipped past more than 100 guards ringing the facility. (For months, his mortified ex-jailers weathered an avalanche of mail addressed to "Clown Point," Ind.)

Crown Point made Dillinger—fame-hungry, handsome, and flamboyant—a top-of-the-charts gangland star. Gutsy, congenial, and even-tempered, he was the stabilizing force in a gang loaded with explosive personalities (Nelson, Homer Van Meter, John Hamilton, Eddie Green, and Tommy Carroll). Meticulous planning and cool precision marked "Dillinger gang" bank heists: the crew cased entire towns, memorized commercial-house floor plans, designed operations inside banks around estimates of police response times, went in strong, grabbed everything they could, and roared away in high-speed roadsters. Sensational getaways quickly became their signature: before each job, they stashed extra gasoline along escape routes and planted tire-busting spikes and nails to waylay pursuing squad cars.

Fuming lawmen hated it. Determined to collar or kill Dillinger, FBI agent Melvin Purvis exploited his adversary's legendary soft spot for females. (Dillinger's wife left after his first stickup—a botched 1924 grocery-store heist—sent him to prison. Released in 1933, he led a parade of girlfriends through 54 weeks of high-octane larceny. His most famous companion, Evelyn "Billie" Frechette, eventually landed in jail for harboring him during police dragnets.) Immortalized as the "Woman in Red," Chicago madam Anna Sage agreed to finger Dillinger for $5,000 and rescision of a pending order deporting her to Romania. Sporting an orange dress (not red) impossible for lurking FBI agents to miss, she accompanied Dillinger and new girlfriend Polly Hamilton to the Biograph Theater's July 22 late show. It worked. Purvis' men and several cops instantly spotted Dillinger leaving the theater and shot him on the spot. (No one really knows whose guns killed the gangster: police and federal agents both demanded credit, but neither could confirm the shooting.) Before going down, Dillinger had emptied at least 12 major banks in seven states, and his gangs had left 15 corpses in their wake.

Mixing Dillinger's original and post–Crown Point gangs, Milius wanders often from the historical record: Oates' surly Dillinger whittles his own wooden breakout gun (a hallowed gangland legend); Johnson's Purvis looks nothing like the short, rail-thin G-man; Milius kills Nelson (Dreyfuss) before Dillinger goes down. Worse still: seconds after their first meeting at a Wisconsin resort (the wrong location), Oates clobbers Nelson and rolls him into a lake—had this really happened, Dillinger wouldn't have lived to see the Biograph. Even so, Milius is on the money much of the time (especially fine are souped-up hoodlum roadsters and a knockout re-creation of Dillinger's Mason City, Iowa, heist and shoot-out). Exciting all the way, with a well-crafted 1930s atmosphere throughout.

For Further Viewing:

Young Dillinger ★ (1965) 102 Minutes (Nick Adams, Robert Conrad, Mary Ann Mobley, Victor Buono): Director Terry Morse kisses history goodbye as soon as his opening credits roll. "Pretty Boy" Floyd (!) kills Nelson during a frantic getaway, and Adams' Dillinger—a ranting, murderous hothead—sticks with fictional wife Mobley for the duration, slaughtering several high-level Chicago racketeers for ridiculing him in an elevator (in fact, O'Malley was Dillinger's only confirmed kill). Despite occasional lapses into historical accuracy, it's all downhill from there.

Recommended Reading:
G. Russell Girardin, *Dillinger: The Untold Story.*

The Front Page ★★★★

(1931) 103 Minutes

Director: Lewis Milestone

Cast: Adolphe Menjou, Pat O'Brien, Mary Brian, Edward Everett Horton, James Gordon, Mae Clarke

Historical Background: In Roaring Twenties Chicago, wealth earned five years ago was old money, and yesterday's triumphs old hat. The modern city rested on the ashes of 1871's terrible fire: Chicagoans rebuilt with metal and stone, inventing the steel-frame skyscraper, expanding core industries (stockyards, slaughterhouses, lakefront shipping, meat-packing plants, steel mills), and drawing waves of northern European immigrants looking for work. The city's population reached 500,000 nine years after the fire and topped 2.5 million in 1920. Chicago seethed with raw energy. The "Chicago Renaissance" saw a parade of household names—Frank Lloyd Wright, Ernest Hemingway, Louis Sullivan, Ben Hecht, Benny Goodman, Walter Howey, Charles MacArthur—design the city's buildings, compose its music, and write or edit eight daily newspapers. By the twenties, Chicago was a gigantic, wide-open commercial-industrial-political engine running on high-order corruption. During his 1927 mayoral campaign, "Big Bill" Thompson accepted more than $300,000—and countless stuffed ballot boxes—from Al Capone and North Side racketeer Bugs Moran. On election night, Thompson openly served contraband whiskey to campaign workers, and after winning he appointed several mob-friendly bureaucrats to important city offices.

More than any other field, journalism reflected Chicago's wild and woolly personality. Throughout the twenties, the news was high-octane business, and reporters formed an integral section of Chicago's "32 feet of intestines." (Some journalists jumped right into the Byzantine snarl of city politics and high crime. On Capone's payroll for years, *Tribune* reporter Jake Lingle lobbied for police chief William Russell's appointment, then built ties between high-level law enforcement and enterprising racketeers. Insiders called Lingle the city's "unofficial police chief.") Legendary author Ben Hecht launched his career at the *Chicago Daily Journal*—as a "picture chaser." Packing a set of burglar's tools, he picked locks, clambered through transoms, and passed himself off as a public-utility worker to crash homes or offices and steal newsworthy photographs from people unwilling to sell them. Hecht's mentor Sherman Duffy spoke French and Spanish, knew the literary classics by heart, and excelled at horticulture—but spent his time reporting the news from Chicago's roaring streets: "Socially, a journalist fits in somewhere between a whore and a bartender," he said, "but he knows the world is round." Hecht became one of America's great reporters before moving on in 1924. Three decades later he wrote that "we were fools to have left . . . this stockyard Athens. We knew the world would turn up nothing better than the frowsy streets and hooligan towers of Chicago."

Milestone's adaptation of the Hecht/MacArthur play features several reporters waiting in Chicago's criminal courts pressroom to cover an execution. Their staccato-paced chatter races through many period issues—Prohibition, anarchism and the "Red Scare," political corruption, newspaper sensationalism, and cops on the take. A clinic on 1920s newspaper operations: reporters, for example, don't write—they root out stories and phone them in to "rewriters." Hecht based many characters on Chicago journalists, including Hilding Johnson, played by O'Brien, in the lead. (Johnson was a wild man: he once taped together a jury's shredded murder-trial ballots, built a story on the information, called it in to his editor, and left a wad of forged, error-packed ballots in the jury room for snooping rival reporters.) Menjou steals the show as editor Walter Burns (based on *Chicago Examiner* editor Howey).

For Further Viewing:

The Front Page ★ (1974) 105 Minutes (Jack Lemmon, Walter Matthau, Carol Burnett, Susan Sarandon, Charles Durning): Director Billy Wilder's limp remake wanders far from the pressroom and wallows in an "updated" script loaded with annoying profanity, copious references to feminine undergarments, and pointless historical errors (a reference, for example, to Hecht's leaving Chicago for Hollywood: in fact, he went to New York). Loud, abrasive, and slovenly clad, Matthau is all wrong as Burns/Howey (always natty, the real Howey "cooed like a dove," according to Hecht). Only Durning is convincing as a street-smart reporter.

Recommended Reading:

William MacAdams, *Ben Hecht: The Man Behind the Legend;* William T. Moore, *Dateline Chicago;* Lloyd Wendt and Herman Kogan, *Big Bill of Chicago;* Ben Hecht, *A Child of the Century.*

King of the Hill ★★★★★

(1993) 109 Minutes

Director: Steven Soderbergh

Cast: Jesse Bradford, Jeroen Krabbe, Lisa Eichhorn, Karen Allen, Adrien Brody, Elizabeth McGovern, Joseph Chrest, Amber Benson

Historical Background: On September 9, 1929, fat American stock prices began a breathtaking 45-day downward spiral, cratering horribly on "Black Tuesday" (October 29): in one trading session, 16.4 million shares changed hands, and by day's end, American finance lay motionless on the NYSE floor. The great mid-twenties boom was history: Americans had bought all the cars, radios, and cloche hats that they wanted, inventories were piling up everywhere, and the U.S. economy had ground to a dead stop. By 1932, 54,650 firms had gone belly-up, and average wages had dropped by 50%. Jobs simply disappeared: five years after the crash, unemployment topped 27%, leaving 35–40 million people with no livelihood.

The hungry and homeless were everywhere. Soup kitchens served countless free meals every day, but it wasn't enough. Gangs lurked in alleys, fighting like animals for scraps of food from garbage dumped by restaurants. Millions of hoboes (true dropouts, men wanting no part of daylight society or regular employment) and transients (people seeking work, but unable to find it) flooded the country, living in city missions, "hobo jungles" near railroad tracks, roadside "ditch camps," and "Hoovervilles"—frightful hovel cities fashioned from cardboard, scrap lumber, and tin. In 1932 alone, the Southern Pacific Railroad caught 683,000 vagabonds riding in boxcars—and of these, nearly a quarter of a million were minors.

During the Depression, children suffered more than anyone else. Many Appalachian kids lived on wild berries and flowers. For years, malnutrition ravaged 20% of New York City's schoolchildren; a year into the Depression, 99% of the students in one Kentucky school were 10% underweight. Even worse: thousands of schools shut down, taking vital lunch programs with them. By 1934, legions of American children without jobs, schools, or families able to feed them hit the road—and the rails—to survive. Wandering in huge packs for self-protection, they frightened many older derelicts, but posed little danger to anyone. Their toughest challenge: replacing shoes and clothing worn to tatters by the rigors of constant travel. Despite massive government relief programs and a brief 1937 economic upturn, the nightmare persisted until massive WWII defense-industry growth put America to work again.

This beautifully realized adaptation of A. E. Hotchner's memoir features Bradford as a young boy forced by his mother's illness and his father's job-on-the-road to survive alone in early-1930s St. Louis. The film incorporates many characters and experiences based on people and events from Hotchner's boyhood—Benson's Ella, Chrest's evil bellboy, Brody's Lester. (And Hotchner really bred canaries for food money.) Soderbergh's faithful picture of Depression-era Americans' daily life is history-based filmmaking at its best. Super period atmosphere and detail, right down to 1930s golfing vernacular ("spoon," "cleek," "midiron," "mashie," etc.).

Recommended Reading:
John A. Garraty, *The Great Depression: An Inquiry into the Causes, Course, and Consequences of the Worldwide Depression;* A. E. Hotchner, *King of the Hill.*

Places in the Heart ★★★★★

(1984) 102 Minutes

Director: Robert Benton

Cast: Sally Field, Danny Glover, John Malkovich, Lindsay Crouse, Ed Harris, Amy Madigan, Bert Remsen

Historical Background: March 3, 1935—Guymon, Okla.. Stretching for miles in all directions, a towering wall of dust boiled up from the earth and rolled like a gigantic tidal wave, pulverizing everything in its path, straight toward Vernon Hopson's house. Locomotives stopped dead on the tracks or remained in terminals until the storm passed, wrecking railroad schedules for the entire day. Aware that headlights could bore no farther than three to five feet into the storm's dark shroud, drivers pulled off of roads, killed their engines, and waited. ("Dirty Thirties" dust storms blocked out the sun completely, sending chickens—wide awake and thoroughly confused—cackling back into barns at high noon to roost for the night.) Hopson headed for cover as a full 55-gallon oil drum rocketed past his window. The storm snapped 50 telephone poles in half on its way to the next town. (So destructive were the worst storms—also called "black blizzards" and "rollers"—that Charles Lindbergh feared flying near them more than he dreaded the risks of solo transatlantic flights. On May 6, 1933, he grounded himself for a day in the Texas panhandle after spotting a roller looming in the distance.)

In 1930, the worst drought in U.S. history ravaged America's heartland, lingering in some areas through 1932. Struck hardest was a 20-million-acre swath blanketing southwestern Kansas, the Texas and Oklahoma panhandles, northeastern New Mexico, and southeastern Colorado: by 1933, the blazing sun had desiccated every single granule of dirt in the area. On January 21, gale-force winds roared across western Oklahoma, whirling the dead, powder-dry topsoil aloft in an enormous cloud. Again and again, monstrous storms raked the five-state area—christened the Dust Bowl in 1935 by journalist Robert Geiger—killing wheat and piling dirt into great drifts on farms and city streets. Dust Bowl residents had seen spectacular rollers before, but nothing like this: 70 black blizzards hit the area in 1933, launching a five-year nightmare that peaked with a staggering 134 storms in 1937.

Rollers uprooted trees and leveled the sturdiest barns and houses. Their choking dust suffocated livestock, destroyed harvests, clogged water pumps, buried farm equipment, and turned stock-tank water into rancid mud. Static electricity sparked by black blizzards killed entire crop sections spared by airborne dirt and wind. Finer than expensive cosmetic talcum powder, the storms' dust penetrated microscopic crevices around sealed windows and doors, powdering floors, walls, and ceilings—even in new buildings—with a noxious black film. Farmers covered half-filled cream pitchers with triple layers of damp cloth, and still the grime seeped through. Virtually everyone in the Dust Bowl contracted dust-related diseases: "dust pneumonia," by far the worst, caused respiratory inflammation ending in gasping suffocation. Incredibly, rollers didn't exhaust nature's fury: between 1933 and 1937, countless tornadoes and storms packing baseball-size hail pounded farms and small towns throughout 17 Dust Bowl counties. Rare torrential thunderstorms flooded creeks and rivers, washing out roads, wrecking farmhouses, and demolishing bridges: in 1935, a series of "killer floods" took more than 150 lives in Dust Bowl states. Worse still, for farm families, were mammoth 1937 grasshopper infestations. In less than a year, Oklahoma's Beaver County poured 175 tons of poison on its rangelands to kill the equivalent of 23,400 grasshoppers per acre. Cars cartwheeled off roads smeared from shoulder to shoulder—for miles—with a thick, greaselike film of crushed insects.

The thirties' breadbasket crisis sired a new American social class, the rural homeless, and launched a great westward pilgrimage from the heartland to California. By 1939, 200,000 penniless homesteaders, unemployed farmhands, and bankrupt storekeepers unable to find jobs had piled into rattling jalopies and left in great caravans for the West Coast, hoping to work on California's legendary "industrialized" farms. When they arrived, jobs were scarce, wages rock-bottom, and living conditions severe at best. Fearing financial ruin themselves, many Californians formed vigilance committees, blocking highways and waging pitched battles against migrants—or "Okies" in 1930s parlance—unwilling to turn back. Most stayed, wandering from one fruit camp to another and surviving on subsistence-level pay. Today, many misconceptions about migrant families, the Dust Bowl, and government policies during the calamity stubbornly persist. Thousands of migrants, for example, came from areas outside the Dust Bowl (humid parts of Texas, Arkansas, Missouri, and Oklahoma), their destitution caused more by newfangled machines and the

Depression than drought and dust storms. In use well before 1935, revolutionary farm technology—combines, more powerful trucks, tractors, and one-way plows—eventually gave America a powerhouse farm system, but it eliminated most agricultural jobs. Traditional family farms simply couldn't produce enough food at competitive costs: agribusiness and economies of scale had arrived, offering small growers and hired hands two choices—get a job or move on.

It was brutal, heartrending business, and New Deal agricultural reform and relief programs made things worse for people needing help the most. Some government programs (the 1933 and 1938 Agricultural Adjustment Acts and the Soil Conservation and Domestic Allotment Act, for example) did pour cash and other resources into the Dust Bowl, saving many farms and deflecting total economic collapse. But prosperous large farms and growers outside the heartland got most of the money: in 1933, the AAA gave $96.8 million to farmers, but only $1.6 million went to desperate small homesteaders under federal wheat-production-adjustment contracts, and most received $100 or less. This was no accident: the government wanted to force homesteaders off of their farms, buy the land, and engineer a new nationwide agricultural system, reserving the Great Plains for ranching and breeding livestock.

New implements for breaking and turning the soil, many invented by local farmers, saved Dust Bowl agriculture over the long haul. (Fred Hoeme of Hooker, Okla., developed an ingenious cultivator—the "Hoeme Chisel"— that scattered furrows with dirt clods large enough to break the wind's erosive power and keep rivulets of precious water from flowing off plowed fields.) By 1940, America's drought-ravaged heartland had recovered, but the great westward migration that began there spread to other states and continued for more than a decade. Countless migrants survived squalid transient camps and backbreaking toil, finally landing in the armaments plants that equipped Allied armies during World War II and fueled California's rise to the top of America's postwar industrial juggernaut. And the Okies—ignored and reviled by just about everybody—had gotten there first, pioneering one of history's greatest demographic revolutions.

Benton's lyrical, understated look at life in a small Texas town at the height of the Depression took Oscars for Best Actress (Field) and Best Screenplay (Horton Foote). Newly widowed Field struggles to keep her family together and raise cotton—for the first time—on uncultivated farmland left by her husband. To make ends meet, she takes in a blind boarder (Malkovich) and a migratory workman (Glover) with years of cotton-farming experience.

Meticulous period detail and episodic subplots focusing on Depression-era community life make *Places in the Heart* excellent fare for students of the thirties. Benton's re-creation of a grueling four-day harvesting marathon to save Field's land from mortgage foreclosure beautifully captures the daily backbreaking hardship faced by people fighting desperately just to get by. Filmed in Waxahatchie, Tex. (Benton grew up there), a small town used frequently for location filming because of its beauty and rustic charm.

For Further Viewing:
The Grapes of Wrath ★★★★★ (1940) 129 Minutes (Henry Fonda, Jane Darwell, John Carradine, Charley Grapewin, Dorris Bowden, John Qualen): Director John Ford's classic adaptation of Steinbeck's novel about the Joad family's grueling odyssey from Dust Bowl Oklahoma to California's orchards and transient camps has lost none of its punch. Sweeping, accurate social history stressing the power of family—and small, improvised communities—to maintain hope in desperate circumstances. The movie's politics fall well left of center and seem hopelessly naive to many viewers aware of economic failures and police-state atrocities marking daily life in Soviet Russia. But radicalism was commonplace throughout Depression-era America, and Ford doesn't push politics as a foolproof panacea for economic and social problems. Fonda (Tom Joad) earned a Best Actor Oscar nomination, but lost to James Stewart. Darwell (Best Actress) and Ford won Academy Awards, but 1940s Oscar for Best Picture went to *The Philadelphia Story*. The legendary Fonda–Darwell closing farewell was unrehearsed and "wrapped" after one take—standard procedure in Ford's films: he thought that rehearsals killed spontaneity, producing mannered, unrealistic performances.

Of Mice and Men ★★★★★ (1981) 125 Minutes (Robert Blake, Randy Quaid, Lew Ayres, Pat Hingle, Cassie Yates, Ted Neeley, Mitchell Ryan, Whitman Mayo): A beautifully realized version of Steinbeck's 1937 novella about two itinerant workers struggling to eke out a living during the Depression and landing, finally, on a ranch where trouble looms from day one. Quaid plays a wonderful Lennie Small—mentally disabled in a childhood accident, but as strong as an ox and better than most at "bucking barley." Executive producer and costar Blake is terrific as George, Lennie's friend and caretaker—thanks largely to his performance, director Reza Badiyi has pulled off a very tough task: conveying without pretense or sentimentality just how contagious virtue can be.

Of Mice and Men ★★★★ (1992) 110 Minutes (John Malkovich, Gary Sinise, Sherilyn Fenn,

Alexis Arquette, Joe Morton, Ray Walston): Director Gary Sinise does a fine job with Horton Foote's lean screenplay and performs well as George. A beautifully filmed movie featuring meticulous period detail and topnotch ensemble acting. Fenn is perfect as ranch foreman Curly's sultry wife. The one problem (incredibly) is Malkovich. Badly miscast as Lennie (Malkovich will never come across as a lumbering dimwit), he wrecks parts of the film with annoying streams of baby talk, drawing attention away from the story. Viewing the movie—in places, at least—is like watching Malkovich play himself in a documentary about making *Of Mice and Men*. Still, an excellent film with a wonderful feel for life during the Depression.

Recommended Reading:
Paul Bonnifield, *The Dust Bowl: Men, Dirt, and Depression;* John Steinbeck, *The Grapes of Wrath* and *Of Mice and Men.*

chapter 7

World War II

(Overleaf)
The Longest Day
(Photofest)

Chronology

1938

MARCH: Germany annexes Austria.

SEPTEMBER: Munich Pact gives Hitler the Sudetenland.

1939

MARCH 15: Germany annexes Czechoslovakia.

AUGUST 23: Nazi–Soviet nonaggression pact signed.

SEPTEMBER 1: Germany invades Poland.

SEPTEMBER 3: England, France, and Australia declare war on Germany.

SEPTEMBER 27: Germans take Warsaw, agree with Russians to divide Poland.

1940

APRIL 9: Germany invades Norway.

MAY 10: Winston Churchill becomes British prime minister.

MAY 29–JUNE 4: Thousands of British and French troops evacuate Dunkirk.

JUNE 22: France surrenders to Germany.

JULY 10: Battle of Britain begins.

AUGUST 25: First RAF Berlin bombings.

SEPTEMBER 27: Japan joins Axis.

OCTOBER 6: German bombing of England ceases, ending Battle of Britain.

OCTOBER 16: America's first peacetime draft begins.

1941

FEBRUARY 11: Roosevelt signs Lend-Lease Act authorizing massive aid to Allies.

MAY 10: Rudolph Hess parachutes into Scotland, tries to negotiate British surrender, is imprisoned for rest of war.

JUNE 22: Germany invades USSR.

OCTOBER 18: Hideki Tojo named Japanese premier.

OCTOBER 19: Germans attack Moscow.

DECEMBER 7: Japan attacks Pearl Harbor.

DECEMBER 8: U.S. and Britain declare war on Japan.

DECEMBER 11: U.S. declares war on Germany and Italy.

DECEMBER 12: Japan invades Burma.

DECEMBER 25: Hong Kong falls.

1942

FEBRUARY 15: Japanese take Singapore.

MARCH 17: Douglas MacArthur takes command of Southwest Pacific forces.

APRIL 9: Bataan falls to Japanese; U.S. and Filipino prisoners driven on 65-mile "Death March" to railway junction.

APRIL 18: James Doolittle leads first American bombing of Tokyo.

MAY 4–8: Battle of Coral Sea.

JUNE 3–6: Battle of Midway.

JULY 1: British victory at El Alamein.

AUGUST 9: Japanese navy wins Savo Island battle.

NOVEMBER 8: Americans invade North Africa.

1943

JANUARY 26: Allies demand unconditional surrender at Casablanca Conference.

FEBRUARY 2: Soviets retake Stalingrad.

FEBRUARY 8: U.S. takes Guadalcanal.

MAY 12: Germans withdraw from North Africa.

AUGUST 17: Allies take Sicily.

SEPTEMBER 3: Allies invade Italy.

NOVEMBER 24: Marines take Tarawa.

NOVEMBER 28: Tehran Conference.

1944

JANUARY 22: Allied Anzio landings.

JUNE 4: Americans enter Rome.

JUNE 6: Allies invade Normandy.

JULY 9: Americans take Saipan.

JULY 20: Failed assassination attempt at East Prussian "Wolf's Lair" injures Hitler.

AUGUST 10: Allies take Guam.

SEPTEMBER 26: Allied troops surrender to Germans in Arnhem.

OCTOBER 23–26: U.S. Navy wins Battle of Leyte Gulf.

DECEMBER 16: Battle of the Bulge begins.

1945

JANUARY 16: Americans win Battle of the Bulge.

JANUARY 17: Russians take Warsaw.

FEBRUARY 4–11: Yalta Conference.

MARCH 7: Americans cross Rhine at Remagen.

MARCH 26: Marines take Iwo Jima.

APRIL 12: FDR dies, succeeded by Harry Truman.

APRIL 28: Italians execute Mussolini and his mistress.

APRIL 30: Hitler and Eva Braun commit suicide in Berlin.

MAY 2: Russians take Berlin.

MAY 7: Germany surrenders.

JUNE 21: Americans take Okinawa.

JUNE 26: UN charter signed.

JULY 5: Allies liberate Philippines.

JULY 16: Americans detonate world's first atomic bomb in New Mexico test.

AUGUST 6: Americans drop uranium bomb on Hiroshima.

AUGUST 8: USSR declares war on Japan.

AUGUST 9: Americans drop plutonium bomb on Nagasaki.

AUGUST 15: Japan surrenders (formal instrument of surrender signed September 2 aboard USS *Missouri*).

Anzio ★★

(1968) 117 Minutes

Director: Edward Dmytryk

Cast: Robert Mitchum, Peter Falk, Robert Ryan, Arthur Kennedy, Patrick Mage

Historical Background: In his 1949 memoir (*To Hell and Back*), Audie Murphy—the most highly decorated combat veteran in American military history—describes a level of fear gripping him (as never before) during heavy fighting at Anzio, a resort town 35 miles south of Rome: "It strikes first in the stomach, coming like the disemboweling hand that is thrust into the carcass of a chicken. I feel now as though icy fingers have reached into my mid-parts and twisted the intestines into knots." Murphy participated in the relatively quick, 38-day Allied drive through Sicily, but his first devastating, prolonged trial-by-battle came at Anzio—and it was an awful test. As soon as the Allies took Salerno on September 18, 1943, they set their sights on Rome. Because a line of rugged mountains extends from Italy's southern tip all the way to the Alps, the Americans and British had confined their initial offensive to the flatter terrain running along both coasts of the peninsula. Crack German divisions commanded by Field Marshal Alfred Kesselring waited for them at the Gustav Line, a formidable series of fortifications beginning at the Adriatic coastal town of Ortona and stretching across Italy to the Tyrrhenian Sea.

By late 1943, Kesselring's troops had stopped the advancing Allies cold. To break the stalemate, two American divisions sailed around the Gustav Line's western flank and mounted an amphibious assault at Anzio. They achieved total surprise, landing unopposed on January 22, 1944. But instead of pushing inland, Gen. George Lucas paused for ten days to consolidate his shallow beachhead, giving the Germans time to regroup. Kesselring rushed several divisions to the area and counterattacked furiously, trapping the Americans in a pocket 12 miles long and seven miles deep. They sat there for four long months, absorbing horrific artillery and infantry attacks (so heavy were the German barrages that several wounded GIs requested early medical releases because frontline positions seemed safer than hospitals in the center of town). By March, Anzio was rubble. Finally, on May 11, the American Fifth and Eighth armies launched massive offensives from Cassino to the mouth of the Garigliano River on the Tyrrhenian coast. Battered U.S. units broke out of Anzio and drove north, reaching Rome on June 4, 1944—two days before the Allies struck across the English Channel and established a second front in northern Europe.

Anzio is the war film equivalent of an all-star spaghetti western. Mitchum, a cynical American war correspondent, accompanies the Anzio invasion force and winds up behind enemy lines with a reconnaissance patrol. Solemn music and lousy dialogue almost sink the film immediately, but *Anzio* is reasonably accurate—even though Dmytryk gets the American commander's name wrong (Leslie instead of Lucas). Epic-scale battle scenes are excellent.

For Further Viewing:
To Hell and Back ★★★ (1955) 106 Minutes (Audie Murphy, Marshall Thompson, Jack Kelly, Charles Drake, Brett Halsey, Gregg Palmer, David Janssen,

Denver Pyle, Rand Brooks, Art Aragon, Susan Kohner): A five-star gem for movie fans, director Jesse Hibbs' crackling adaptation of Murphy's 1949 memoir delivers rousing entertainment, but falls short historically. Hibbs restages many wartime episodes with reasonable accuracy (Murphy's withering tommy gun salvo at his own reflection in a full-length mirror during bitter house-to-house fighting at Montélimar; his relentless slaughter of German machine gunners—with one of their own weapons—after they kill his best friend; his incredible solitary, Medal of Honor–winning stand with a heavy machine gun against six advancing Wehrmacht tanks and at least 200 German troops in France's Colmar Pocket). But *To Hell and Back* also hums with factual errors: Murphy's childhood poverty, for example, was far worse than Hibbs' early segments indicate; Audie was wounded three times, not once—and his hip injury occurred months before the Colmar Pocket heroics; his chance to go to West Point surfaced after the war; and his Medal of Honor award came three weeks before his twenty-first birthday, not "shortly after his nineteenth birthday." Worst of all: the film sanitizes the war—especially Anzio's multiple horrors—and for this reason Murphy hated Hibbs' final cut. Like it or not, amateur historians must vote with Audie: "I don't give a damn if this movie makes 17 million dollars," he told a friend, "we missed by a mile."

Recommended Reading:
Carlo D'Este, *Fatal Decision: Anzio and the Battle for Rome;* William L. Allen, *Anzio: Edge of Disaster;* Don Graham, *No Name on the Bullet: A Biography of Audie Murphy.*

Battleground ★★★★

(1949) 118 Minutes

Director: William Wellman

Cast: Van Johnson, John Hodiak, George Murphy, Marshall Thompson, Denise Darcel, Richard Jaeckel, James Whitmore

Historical Background: Early morning, December 16, 1944—Ardennes Plateau, Belgium: Without warning, a huge sector of the western front—so quiet that Allied troops thought the war might end within weeks—roared to life with the terrible whine and crack of detonating shells from 1,000 German field pieces and railroad guns. Swarming out of fog-shrouded forests, Wehrmacht tanks and infantrymen steamrolled hundreds of flabbergasted Allied troops in the opening salvo of the biggest battle fought on the western front during the entire war.

From day one, the Battle of the Bulge was a bare-knuckle, in-your-face foot soldier's slugfest. Fragmented by impenetrable mist and chest-deep snow, the battleground offered no clearly defined front for classic battles and sweeping armored thrusts: men in both armies were everywhere, fighting small, bitter brawls across a crazy-quilt 2,500-square-mile killing ground so chaotic and fluid that soldiers and local civilians often had no idea which side occupied specific villages. Untempered by the impersonal, machinelike processes of modern industrial warfare, close-quarter combat in the Ardennes escalated more than once into awful battlefield atrocities: in one of the bloodiest, Wehrmacht colonel Jochen Peiper's shock troops slaughtered 100 American prisoners near Malmédy. (When word of the killings spread, scattered American retaliations flared—on a much smaller scale—against surrendering Germans.)

Hitler's lightning thrust through Belgium was a high-risk, last-ditch effort to split the Allied juggernaut at its weakest point, isolate British forces north of Liège, seize Antwerp, and force a separate negotiated peace on Churchill and Roosevelt. Spearheaded by Peiper's tanks and mechanized infantry, three panzer armies launched crushing opening attacks with 550,000 men and 1,500 tanks on an 85-mile front, smashing a V-shaped salient (the "Bulge") more than 50 miles deep in the Allied perimeter. For a week, terrible weather and zero visibility grounded warplanes mobilized to protect battered Allied infantrymen. Everywhere, chaos reigned: English-speaking German infiltrators in American uniforms switched road signs, cut telephone lines, and sabotaged U.S. efforts to destroy bridges logistically vital to Hitler's armored columns.

The onslaught continued for nine days, finally grinding to a halt northwest of Celles on Christmas day and settling into a bloody battle of attrition—the last thing that Hitler's generals wanted. (By then the weather had cleared, freeing 5,000 Allied aircraft to rain hell on enemy armored columns and infantrymen.) More than anything else, a heroic stand by the U.S. 101st Airborne Division at Bastogne—a town commanding the junction of several key roads—threw the battle to the Allies. Outgunned and surrounded, Gen. Anthony McAuliffe's "battling bastards of Bastogne" repulsed furious assaults for a week, holding the town and cutting Wehrmacht supply routes in the heart of the salient. (McAuliffe's legendary reply to German surrender demands—"Nuts!"—baffled enemy commanders.) Racing north with the 4th Armored Division to join the fight, George Patton arrived on the 26th and forced a German retreat. Though fighting raged into January, the Wehrmacht's failure to reach Antwerp and turn the Bulge into a corridor splitting Allied forces completely in two killed Hitler's chances for a negotiated peace in the west. On January 16, the Germans withdrew to the Rhine, leaving 120,000 irreplaceable troops in Allied captivity or dead on the ground.

Director Wellman and scriptwriter Robert Pirosh (an Ardennes-campaign veteran) belted a box-office home run with this high-octane, GI Joe look at the Battle of the Bulge through the eyes of top kick Whitmore, dogface Johnson (perfectly cast), and their wisecracking, hard-fighting buddies. Focusing almost exclusively on the Little Picture, Wellman delivers a knockout chronicle of what the Ardennes holocaust was like for men in the foxholes: cut off and surrounded, Whitmore's small squad weathers cold, snow, confusion, and bitter firefights in a hellish battle for survival. Highly accurate segments on German infiltrators, roaring enemy tanks, the weather's impact on the campaign—all of the battle's key elements—make *Battleground* one of Hollywood's finest war movies.

For Further Viewing:
Battle of the Bulge ★★★ (1965) 163 Minutes (Henry Fonda, Robert Shaw, Robert Ryan, Telly Savalas, Dana Andrews, George Montgomery, Ty Hardin, Charles Bronson): As a movie, *Battle of the Bulge* flops badly—as history, it's a mixed bag. Director Ken Annakin crafts accurate renditions of the Malmédy slaughter, German commando raids,

Allied indifference to reports of a massive pre-assault enemy buildup, and the Wehrmacht's opening attacks. But he blames fuel shortages, alone, for the German defeat, ignoring the pivotal Bastogne siege and decisive late-December Allied air strikes (with no Luftwaffe opposition) against German armor and supply columns. To save money, Annakin shot the movie in Spain (Antarctica would've been better), and most battle scenes unfold under sunny skies in desertlike terrain. Good performances by Ryan, Fonda, Shaw, Bronson, and Hardin (as a clever German infiltrator) are fun to watch, but they can't save this ambitious, floundering potboiler.

Recommended Reading:
Gerald Astor, *A Blood-Dimmed Tide: The Battle of the Bulge by the Men Who Fought It.*

Battle of Britain ★★★★

(1969) 132 Minutes

Director: Guy Hamilton

Cast: Harry Andrews, Michael Caine, Trevor Howard, Curt Jurgens, Kenneth More, Laurence Olivier, Christopher Plummer, Michael Redgrave, Ralph Richardson, Robert Shaw, Susannah York

Historical Background: From day one of Hitler's air offensive against England, women flooded Royal Air Force facilities, serving in offices, planning rooms, frontline fighter bases, and radar communications centers. During the campaign's first month, Tangmere radar station commander Jack Boret fielded several complaints from staid Air Ministry officials about a young radio monitor's "highly colorful language" in conversations with fighter pilots under fire. Finally, Boret summoned the girl to his office. Attractive and demure, she stood at attention, eyes downcast, through his stern homily on good military form. "Have you anything to say for yourself?" he concluded. "Yes, sir," came the instant reply. "Balls!" Shaking with laughter—and fully certain that high mettle would weigh heavily in British efforts to win the war—Boret waved the young woman back to her post.

Months earlier, as Hitler's panzers rumbled toward Paris, Great Britain braced for a German invasion. By August 1940, more than a million men—armed with swords, clubs, spears, and shotguns—had joined the Local Defence Volunteer force. But Hitler hesitated, foolishly thinking that France's collapse would prompt Churchill to sue for peace. Weeks passed as German treaty proposals demanding British recognition of Nazi rule throughout Europe drew thundering silence from London. In mid-July, Wehrmacht commanders began crafting plans for an all-out amphibious assault on England's Kentish coast (Operation Sealion), preceded by massive Luftwaffe sweeps to clear the skies of blazing RAF Spitfires and tough Hawker Hurricanes—both capable of sending cross-Channel invasion fleets to the ocean floor in a single afternoon.

Reichsmarshal Hermann Goering launched the Battle of Britain on July 10, 1940, hurling swarms of Me-109s, Ju-87 "Stuka" dive-bombers, and Do-17Z medium bombers against Churchill's Channel convoys and southern military facilities. Sporadic at first, howling attacks quickly multiplied and raged into August, but Chief Air Marshal Hugh Dowding's RAF—outnumbered three to one—sent two Luftwaffe planes flaming to earth for every British fighter that went down. RAF pilots were flexible, quickly abandoning tightly grouped, triangular formations vulnerable to surprise attack by German fighters. British squadrons began flying in linear four-fighter sections and attacking bombers at close range—150 yards or less—when their return fire proved ineffective. Even worse for German pilots: England's newfangled radar nets and tireless radio controllers gave RAF pilots precise information on the strength, as well as the location and speed, of Luftwaffe formations, allowing commanders to keep many pilots on the ground and out of harm's way. Incredibly, Goering underestimated the power of Churchill's early-warning system, launching few attacks on radar stations. Strategy, for him, meant picking off as many enemy aircraft as he could, but Britain's war industry was churning out plenty of planes by 1940. The RAF lacked pilots, not Spitfires, and downed British airmen—in constant radio contact with command headquarters and battling above their own turf—were far easier to rescue than their German adversaries.

Despite all this, the Luftwaffe nearly prevailed through sheer weight of numbers: by late August, 1,000 German planes roared aloft every day, forcing exhausted RAF pilots to fly 40 missions per week. But Hitler squandered his chance for a knockout blow: enraged by Britain's initial August 26 bombing runs over Berlin, he suspended sorties against English military targets, marshaling the Luftwaffe's full fury for payback raids on London. The great "Blitz" opened on September 7: attacking in waves, 1,200 German aircraft rained high-explosive and incendiary bombs on London's docks, railway stations, and gasworks, killing 500 people and injuring 1,000 more by morning. For 57 consecutive nights, Luftwaffe formations hammered away at the city, targeting civilian neighborhoods as well as government and industrial districts. (Other cities also suffered terribly: in December, a single raid ignited 600 enormous fires in Manchester.)

Throughout the ordeal, England's home front stood fast. With grim tenacity, men and women toiled in armaments factories until they collapsed from exhaustion. Girls in their late teens and early twenties joined women's service branches and volunteered for grueling farmwork. Children served as firewatchers. Older men joined fire brigades, bomb-disposal squads, or the Air Raid Precaution Organization. By 1941, the entire country had mobilized, and no one stood down for four long years. Unable to wreck Britain's air defenses or slow her industrial output, Goering's Blitz withered dramatically in December and ended for good the following summer. More than 23,000 people (including 13,500 Londoners) died in the raids. Losing only 900 aircraft, the RAF gunned down an incredible 2,000 German warplanes—1,500 of them in July, August, and September.

Perfectly cast as Dowding, Olivier leads a knockout ensemble cast in this solid version of England's finest hour. The movie opens in May 1940—with France overwhelmed and Britain on the ropes—then follows an RAF squadron and command headquarters strategists through the great air battle. Director Hamilton worked hard for period accuracy—producers scoured

Europe for WWII warplanes, finally borrowing several vintage Luftwaffe bombers from the Spanish air corps. *The Battle of Britain* drags, in places, and Hamilton skips the Blitz's full horrors, but fine acting, reasonably accurate history, and remarkable air-combat choreography more than offset the film's shortcomings for history bluffs.

For Further Viewing:

Hope and Glory ★★★★ (1987) 113 Minutes (Sarah Miles, David Hayman, Derrick O'Connor, Susan Wooldridge, Ian Bannen, Sebastian Rice-Edwards, Annie Leon): Director John Boorman's marvelous autobiographical chronicle of a family adapting to wartime shortages, breathtaking social change, and the random carnage of Hitler's Blitz. Through the eyes of a London schoolboy (Rice-Edwards), Boorman delivers a lyrical glimpse, packed with period detail, of English daily life between 1939 and 1945: rationing, back gardens studded with tubular bomb shelters, the urgency of wartime romances between youngsters growing up too soon, and the sudden shock of deafening Luftwaffe attacks add up to historical drama so good that cutting 30 seconds of footage would mangle the film. Bannen (Grandfather George) is terrific, but Miles, in a show-stopping performance as Rice-Edward's mother, dominates the movie from start to finish.

Recommended Reading:

Alfred Price, *Battle of Britain: The Hardest Day, 18 August 1940;* Susan Briggs, *The Home Front: War Years in Britain, 1941–1945.*

The Boat (Das Boot) ★★★★★

(1981) 145 Minutes

Director: Wolfgang Petersen

Cast: Jurgen Prochnow, Herbert Gronemeyer, Klaus Wennemann, Hubertus Bengsch, Martin Semmelrogge, Bernd Tauber, Erwin Leder, Martin May

Historical Background: In 1776, rebellious American colonists launched history's first submarine attack against the *Eagle,* a British frigate anchored in New York Harbor. The Yankee submersible—christened the *Turtle*—was a one-man wooden vessel shaped like a hen's egg standing on end. It was powered by two hand-cranked propellers and fitted with an auger for attaching an explosive device to the underside of the English warship. The attack failed because the *Eagle*'s hull had a copper shell that the *Turtle*'s auger couldn't penetrate. But the Americans had changed naval warfare forever, even though their new weapon was dangerous to operate and technologically primitive.

By early 1944, the submarine had become the most efficient, devastating weapons system of World War II—American subs sank 33% of Japan's fighting ships and most of her supply vessels. But it was German Admiral Karl Doenitz who pioneered modern submarine strategy and tactics in order to cripple Allied convoys carrying vital war matériel to England. Against them Doenitz sent large numbers of small, nimble U-boats—the famous wolfpacks—

that attacked from deep within the convoys to protect themselves from Allied destroyer escorts, which risked hitting their own ships if they fired upon the submarines.

Submarine duty was grim, grueling business. If subs remained submerged for more than 12 hours, air became foul, then unbreathable. Men couldn't use the head during battle, since flushing toilets would send bubbles to the surface and give their position away. Officers and crew slept fully clothed—sharing bunks in shifts—and wore the same clothing for weeks on end, since they seldom bathed or shaved. German U-boats sank millions of tons of Allied shipping, but they paid a terrible price. During the final years of the war, the Allies developed remarkably precise tracking devices and broke the Germans' sub-to-sub signaling code. Eventually they sent 785 U-boats to the bottom, killing more than 30,000 of Germany's 40,000 submariners.

Gripping and accurate, Petersen's signature war film delivers superb performances by all, a fine script, and grimly harrowing battle scenes. Based on Lothar-Guenther Bucheim's autobiographical novel, *The Boat* also takes a detailed, realistic look at daily life down below. Crewmen wear the same filthy clothes throughout the entire film (none wear uniforms, and all have beards halfway into the movie). Earlier films showed neat, clean, squared-away submarines; the interior of this U-boat has a dank, barely lit, stinking look. Subtitled original-language versions of *The Boat* are available on videotape, but go for the dubbed version if it's available—the action is so fast and furious and the special effects so splendid that you won't want to miss any of it while reading English subtitles.

For Further Viewing:

The Enemy Below ★★★★ (1957) 98 Minutes (Robert Mitchum, Curt Jurgens, Theodore Bikel): Director Dick Powell's ensemble cast is excellent in this taut chronicle of a duel between an American destroyer and a German sub in the North Atlantic. Both commanders—Jurgens (an anti-Nazi German) and Mitchum (a dour, no-nonsense American)—are cool, experienced veterans tested to the limit by a sudden confrontation forcing each of them to switch from offensive to defensive tactics and back (again and again). A riveting clinic on WWII submarine and destroyer tactics.

Run Silent, Run Deep ★★★★ (1958) 93 Minutes (Clark Gable, Burt Lancaster, Jack Warden, Don Rickles): Aiming to plaster the Japanese destroyer that sank his last boat, submarine skipper Gable goes eyeball to eyeball with hostile executive officer Lancaster (passed over for command of the sub and still smoldering). Critical mass—for both officers and the prowling enemy destroyer—comes in the perilous Bungo Strait. Adapted from the novel by Edward L. Beach, captain of the USS *Triton* during its submerged circumnavigation of the globe (history's first), *Run Silent, Run Deep* delivers a tough, authentic picture of the cramped atmosphere and steadily building pressure on WWII submariners hunting enemy convoys solo in the vast Pacific. One of Lancaster's best performances.

Recommended Reading:
Terry Hughes and John Costello, *The Battle of the Atlantic;* Geoffrey Jones, *Defeat of the Wolfpacks.*

The Bridge on the River Kwai ★★★★

(1957) 161 Minutes

Director: David Lean

Cast: Alec Guinness, William Holden, Jack Hawkins, Sessue Hayakawa, Geoffrey Horne, James Donald, Andre Morell, Ann Sears

Historical Background: Spring 1944—New Guinea: For more than a month, Pakistani POW Hatam Ali had endured backbreaking toil—12 hours a day, seven days a week, no breaks for rest—with a ragtag construction gang hacking Japanese runways through the broiling Indonesian jungle. Most of his comrades were sick, many were badly injured, and all were starving. Fully expecting to die in a matter of weeks, Ali figured that his captors had already exhausted their arsenal of brutality. He was wrong. One day the Japanese took him to an isolated hut well away from the main camp: inside was a fellow prisoner with gaping wounds in his legs and buttocks where guards had cut away—and eaten—great chunks of his flesh. The man was still alive. Mad with fear, Ali smashed one guard to the ground, broke the other's hold on his arms, and bolted into the jungle. Discovered by Australian infantrymen two weeks later, Ali reviewed his horror story in grim detail, surprising none of his rescuers: Australian patrols had found victims of Japanese cannibalism as early as January 1943.

No one knew the extent or precise nature of Japan's prison-camp atrocities until Allied armies liberated the facilities. The Japanese tortured, starved, bayonetted, drowned, and worked to death military and civilian captives. They buried stubborn POWs alive or slowly crushed their heads with carpenter's vises. Kempeitai goons (Japan's military police) forced men to swallow uncooked rice and water, watching them die in agony as the swelling rice distended, then ruptured their stomachs. In eastern Manchuria, a Japanese biological-warfare-development group ("Unit 731") systematically exposed prisoners to syphilis, bubonic plague, and typhoid fever; its research biologists and physicians cut livers, hearts, and kidneys out of living POWs strapped to operating tables. Many grisly medical experiments and some of the war's worst savagery unfolded in mysterious, remote camps unknown for years to most westerners: on Ambon Island in the Moluccas, physicians murdered more than 100 men, injecting them with experimental poisons to see how quickly death came; guards there shot and beheaded hundreds, leaving less than a quarter of Australia's original 1,000-man garrison alive at war's end. Worse still was Sandakan in northeastern Borneo: starvation, disease, forced death marches, and random executions (including horrible crucifixions) killed all but six of the camp's 2,500 Allied prisoners.

(European noncombatants swept into captivity during Japan's opening onslaughts fared better—but not much. In December 1941, Japanese legions sacked Shanghai's International Settlement, capturing hundreds of women and children; their number swelled by 80,000 with the 1942 collapse of Singapore and the Dutch East Indies. Marched to primitive forced-labor camps on rubber plantations and bomb-torn airfields or thrown into dank, crumbling prisons, they lived on tea, fish heads, and rice until Japan surrendered three and a half years later. More than 10,000 of them died from overwork, malnutrition, and disease.)

For America's skeletal Pacific garrison, defeat, confinement, and death began in the Philippines: Japanese infantry landed on Luzon on December 10, 1941, and raced all the way to Manila in less than a month. General Homma Masaharu's forces swept down the island's western quarter in early January, driving its defenders to the Bataan Peninsula's southern tip. There, outgunned, ravaged by disease, low on supplies, their backs to the sea—75,000 Allied troops (including 12,000 Americans) fought like wild men for three months, finally surrendering on April 9. Without rest, food, or medical treatment, they began a nonstop 65-mile forced march into captivity at Camp O'Donnell. Japanese soldiers gunned down sick or exhausted stragglers. Scores died of hunger, thirst, and 110° body temperatures induced by cerebral malaria. At journey's end, more than 10,000 bodies littered the ground between Tobang and San Fernando, and another 40% fell to disease and malnutrition during the next three months. (Homma held the Philippines for three more years, but thanks to American commandos and fierce Filipino guerrillas it was a jittery occupation. Poorly armed and provisioned, the insurgents hammered away fanatically at their enemies, saving many American lives and gathering vital intelligence for the Allied juggernaut rolling toward Japan. On June 5, 1945, Japanese dominion in the Philippines collapsed, and Homma—tried and convicted of war crimes—was executed ten months later.)

One of the war's most notorious horrors, Japan's frenzied drive to complete the Thailand–Burma Railway through 260 miles of steaming, pestilent jungle, thrust 61,000 POWs and civilian slaves into a hellish 13-month nightmare. Logistically vital to Japan's 15th Army in Burma, the railway would greatly reduce delivery time for supply shipments from the home islands to Rangoon. From Three Pagodas Pass, the tracks followed the Khwae Noi ("Kwai") River to its confluence with the Mae Klong, swinging gradually eastward from there to Banpong. In September 1943, labor gangs from 40 camps scattered along the right-of-way began hacking through bamboo groves, felling teak trees, and building railbed embankments. Driven by remorseless Korean and Japanese guards, POWs toiled for 16 hours a day in wildly chaotic insect- and snake-infested terrain. Many lost more than half their body weight in the suffocating 115° heat. Camp "hospitals"—jammed with cadaverous men weighing 70 to 90 pounds—were little more than huts for the dying. Many perished from infected, bone-deep tropical skin lesions the size of baseballs. Pellagra, beriberi, malaria, and cholera killed prisoners every day. Bridging the Mae Klong River—the legendary trestle stood there, not on the Kwai—was a nightmare. Working from makeshift platforms rigged with pulleys, hand-held ropes, and steel weights, POWs slammed away at massive timber beams, sinking them into the riverbed inch by inch. Exhausted prisoners died in accidents every week, and the river's swift current swept scores of men working in chest-deep water to their deaths. On October 17, 1943—just south of Burma on the Kwai River—a few hammer strokes completed work on the railroad. Building it had cost 16,000 Allied lives.

Throughout World War II, Japan's camps were far worse than their German counterparts for Australian, British, and American prisoners:

4% of the Allied prisoners held in Germany—9,345 men—died in captivity; the Japanese killed 35,700 souls—a full 27% of their prison-camp population. After the war, an Allied tribunal executed seven war criminals, including Imperial Army head (and virtual dictator) Hideki Tojo. Local military courts condemned 900 more and sent 3,000 to prison.

Based on Pierre Boulle's novel, Lean's grand spectacle about British POW railroad gangs in Thailand is a cinematic knockout—and pure bunk as history. For starters, Guinness and his fellow prisoners build the bridge across the wrong river (the Kwai), and their push to prove British mettle and competence by building a topnotch bridge is hokum: Allied prisoners sabotaged their work on the railway at every opportunity, causing constant breakdowns and driving Japanese officers crazy. British commandos never tried to destroy the bridge, and Lean overplays the captives' open, all-for-one/one-for-all defiance: fueled by decency (and hatred for the Japanese), prisoner solidarity survived the camps intact, but during the railway project's final months, many starving, desperate POWs stole food from each other and from the sick (considered beyond help). Still, a realistic picture of life in Japan's prison camps, with fine performances by Guinness and Hayakawa.

For Further Viewing:
Empire of the Sun ★ (1987) 152 Minutes (Christian Bale, John Malkovich, Nigel Havers, Joe Pantoliano, Miranda Richardson, Emily Richard): A technically superb—and factually awful—film about an English boy (Bale) separated from his parents in Shanghai and interned by the Japanese. Director Steven Spielberg underplays Japanese brutality and their civilian captives' awful suffering: throughout a long, dull captivity segment, he implies that the prisoners' constant hunger resulted from ration shortages instead of Japanese barbarism—this is unconscionable nonsense; the Japanese always hoarded food and Red Cross medical packages in their prison camps, methodically starving captives until they were too weak to revolt or escape. From start to finish, Japan waged a genocidal war, exterminating 200,000 civilians in Nanking alone. Nothing like this surfaces in *Empire of the Sun.* Adapted from J. G. Ballard's autobiographical novel—and a potboiler all the way.

Back to Bataan ★★★ (1945) 95 Minutes (John Wayne, Anthony Quinn, Richard Loo, Beulah Bondi): Director Edward Dmytryk's rousing tribute to Death March veterans and Filipino guerrillas (organized and led by Wayne) opens and closes with footage of a dozen men actually freed from Japan's infamous Cabantatuan prison camp during a 1945 rescue mission. Not the most accurate WWII film, but great viewing for history buffs interested in America's mood three months (!) after the Cabantatuan raid and four months before Japan's surrender. Wayne & Co.—especially Quinn (as a Jap-hating Filipino insurgent)—deliver a solid, on-target picture of the bitter, no-quarter guerrilla war in the Philippines.

Prisoners of the Sun ★★★★ (1991) 109 Minutes (Bryan Brown, Terry O'Quinn, John Bach, George Takei, Toshi Shioya, Deborah Unger, John Clarke): Director Stephen Wallace's finely crafted drama chronicling Japanese atrocities—in flashback—during local postwar court-martials on Australian-occupied Ambon Island. Never slipping into sentimental pity for Japanese prisoners on trial or ignoring the awful daily pressures that drove them in the mad atmosphere of the camps, Wallace focuses on the difficult task of holding normally decent individuals accountable for committing genocidal acts under orders. Brown's standout performance as a tough—but fair—prosecutor battling red tape and skilled defense attorneys keys the film from start to finish. Riveting stuff, with excellent performances by a fine ensemble cast.

Recommended Reading:
Ernest Gordon, *Through the Valley of the Kwai;* Yuki Tanaka, *Hidden Horrors: Japanese War Crimes in World War II;* William A. Berry with James Edwin Alexander, *Prisoner of the Rising Sun;* Arnold C. Brackman, *The Other Nuremberg: The Untold Story of the Tokyo War Crimes Trials;* Donald Knox, *Death March: The Survivors of Bataan.*

The Court-Martial of Billy Mitchell ★★★★★

(1955) 100 Minutes

Director: Otto Preminger

Cast: Gary Cooper, Charles Bickford, Ralph Bellamy, Rod Steiger, Elizabeth Montgomery, Darren McGavin

Historical Background: A brilliant military theorist blessed with keen practical intelligence, Brig. Gen. William (Billy) Mitchell became America's premier air combat officer of World War I. In July 1918, he flew a near-suicidal solo reconnaissance mission behind enemy lines, spotting and reporting huge German troop concentrations near the Marne River; the Allies launched a flanking attack based on Mitchell's report and won a crushing victory. Two months later, Mitchell led the largest air attack in history—a 1,500-plane bombing run over the St. Mihiel salient that dealt a knockout blow to the German army.

Mitchell's combat experience left him certain that the U.S. should develop a powerful, autonomous air force, an idea dismissed by military leaders equally certain that battleships should remain the backbone of national defense. Nothing, it seemed, could convince his opponents, and with every rebuff, Mitchell grew more determined: on June 13, 1921, Mitchell and several handpicked pilots sank three captured German warships—including a mammoth dreadnought—in a bombing demonstration off the Virginia coast. With cold fury, his high-ranking opponents demoted him to the rank of colonel and exiled him to remote Fort Sam Houston in Texas. Undeterred, Mitchell went public, blasting both service branches for shortsightedness.

By then, his great passion had become an obsession, and reasoned lobbying turned into tactless, combative agitation. Critical mass—and catastrophe—came in 1925, when a naval airship crashed during a public relations flight, killing 13 crewmen (including Mitchell's close friend Lt. Comdr. Zachary Lansdowne). Mitchell attacked without mercy: the general staffs of both service branches, he said, were criminally negligent in their ignorance of air safety and incompetent for not building a stand-alone air force. The generals, the admirals, and President Calvin Coolidge went ballistic. They court-martialed Mitchell in October, convicting and sentencing him to suspension from duty for five years. (Douglas MacArthur cast the only dissenting vote.) Mitchell retired from the army on Feb. 1, 1926. A genuine visionary with a remarkable grasp of technology's potential and its looming presence for 20th-century society, Mitchell made many accurate predictions: he warned that Japan would attack the U.S. fleet at Hawaii on a Sunday; he insisted that German militarism was not dead and that air power would win the next great war; England, he said, would soon be vulnerable to saturation bombing; and he predicted the widespread tactical use of paratroopers. Mitchell died before his prophecies came true (on Feb. 19, 1926), but in 1946 the U.S. Congress presented his son with a medal honoring his memory.

A beautifully understated, thoroughly accurate, engrossing film about Billy Mitchell's crusade for air power and the court-martial that proved his professional undoing. Like many fine fact-based films, *The Court-Martial of Billy Mitchell* steadily builds suspense even though many people know how the story will end before they walk into the theater. As a sincere tribute to Mitchell, the film is rhetorically effective: you can't view it without feeling black fury at everyone's refusal to consider Mitchell's ideas. Steiger plays a superb lead prosecutor, and Cooper (as usual) is great, though he doesn't convey Mitchell's contentious personality as well as an actor such as Steiger might have.

Recommended Reading:
Davis Burke, *The Billy Mitchell Affair.*

Cross of Iron ★★★★

(1977) 119 Minutes

Director: Sam Peckinpah

Cast: James Coburn, Maximilian Schell, James Mason, David Warner, Senta Berger, Klaus Lowitsch

Historical Background: Christmas Eve 1943—Boporoeivska, Ukraine: Mindful only of the shattering cold and icy winds swirling through Russia's endless, rolling steppe, Wehrmacht rifleman Guy Sajer gazed past the minefield ringing his company's trenchline. Suddenly the hair on the back of his neck stood straight up: a thin dotted line stretching from north to south across the horizon was sweeping toward him. The Siberians—hundreds of them—were attacking his tiny sector of the Gross Deutschland Division's forward echelon. Bursting starshells bathed the landscape in eerie blue light as inchoate rumblings from the assault wave swelled to a thundering battle cry—"Ourrah, Pobeida!" As they often did, Soviet commanders had reversed the customary order of attack, sending mobs of sprinting Mongols ahead of their armored columns to detonate mines and preserve their tanks. The howling assault broke under a curtain of mortar and small-arms fire, but the Germans never stood down: they knew the slaughter would continue until their mines were spent, leaving them to repulse waves of Soviet armor with nothing but their ingenuity and a few antitank rifles.

For Sajer and the bleeding Wehrmacht, it was business as usual on the eastern front: in two short years, the merciless war in the east had become a nightmare of death on an unimaginable scale. Operation Barbarossa—the great invasion launched by Hitler in June 1941—had rolled with breathtaking speed across western Russia, then slowed to a crawl in December's paralyzing cold. On December 6, a surprise counterattack by 40 Soviet divisions stopped the German onslaught ten miles from Moscow. To the north, Leningrad lay surrounded—but unconquered. (The city's long ordeal remains history's most terrible siege: by 1942, 4,000 Leningraders were starving to death each day. When the siege lifted in 1944, at least a million civilians—half the city's population—had perished.) Stalled along a line stretching from the Baltic Ocean to the Black Sea, 3 million Germans waited to mount a second thrust against the Red Army. It came on the critical southern front in high summer 1942. On June 28, Hitler hurled 74 divisions—54 of them German, the rest drawn from Romanian, Italian, and Hungarian satellite armies—straight through the Don Bend toward Stalingrad and from there to his main targets in the south: the great oil fields and mineral reserves of the Caucasus, needed desperately by Germany to wage a long war of conquest.

At first, the massive offensive looked like a reprise of Barbarossa's initial 1941 onslaught. Gen. Friedrich Von Paulus' Sixth Army roared eastward from Kharkov at breakneck speed, reaching the outskirts of Stalingrad—a showcase industrial city sprawled along the west bank of the Volga—on August 23. Paulus assaulted the city with unprecedented ferocity. Before sunset on the battle's first day, waves of Stuka dive-bombers and Messerschmitt fighters annihilated 40,000 civilians. At first a secondary target, Stalingrad quickly became the pivotal battle of the entire European theater. Determined to protect Soviet factories and troop concentrations east of the Volga—"not one step back" was Stalin's terse command—the Russians transformed buildings throughout the city into heavily armed fortresses designed to drive enemy units into areas registered for pinpoint artillery fire by batteries on the river's east bank. Soon, rubble-choked alleys and streets rendered tank deployment impossible, and the battle fragmented into hundreds of small, vicious duels for isolated city blocks and individual buildings. Fighting raged from floor to floor and room to room, often moving into cellars and filthy sewers beneath Stalingrad's ravaged streets. Men fought with grenades and submachine guns, then hacked away at each other with knives, entrenching tools, and shovels when ammunition ran out. The mayhem never stopped: long before reaching the city, incoming troops could hear booming shellfire and see towering pillars of black smoke marking the battlefront. At night, the hellish glow of burning rubble was visible from incredible distances.

By October 15, the Germans held 90% of the city, but fanatical Russian defenders stopped them cold at the giant tractor works in Stalingrad's industrial center. The Wehrmacht would advance no farther. Paulus' reserves of food, fuel, and ammunition were desperately low: his overland supply lines, tautly stretched from the beginning, had broken weeks earlier. He had no tactical reserves. Inebriated by the Sixth Army's dazzling race to the Volga, Hitler had foolishly diverted every spare man and much of Paulus' armor to the rugged mountains protecting Stalin's southern oil fields. Worse still, a mammoth Soviet buildup on both German flanks funneled tanks, artillery, and hordes of infantry—assembled and trained deep in Siberia—to staging areas north and south of Stalingrad. On November 19, the twin juggernauts attacked. Four days later the giant pincers met at Kalach, trapping 270,000 battered Germans in Stalingrad. Ravaged by bitter cold and starving to death in the ever-tightening Soviet ring, the Sixth Army held on until Paulus finally surrendered on January 31, 1943. Small units of diehard German veterans, inflamed by amphetamines and alcohol, fought like sewer rats to the bitter end. By mid-February, a deathlike silence had settled over the city. To this day, Stalingrad remains the worst killing ground in military history: its prewar population (500,000) swelled quickly as refugees from the west streamed into Stalingrad ahead of Paulus' onslaught; few of them managed to evacuate, and a census taken at battle's end found only 1,515 noncombatants alive in the city. Military losses were equally staggering: 400,000 Germans, 750,000 Russians, 200,000 Romanians, 130,000 Italians, and 120,000 Hungarians—1.6 million soldiers—were killed or wounded in the Stalingrad inferno. (The Wehrmacht never recovered. That summer, a second catastrophic blow fell during the Kursk salient's epic tank battle, the largest in military history. Russian armor and artillery crushed Hitler's final major offensive in the east, destroying 1,000 tanks and killing 100,000 men by late August.)

After the Volga bloodbath, the Germans began a bitter withdrawal that ended in the rubble of Berlin two years later. Harried all the way by swarming Yak-9 fighters and hotly pursued by Soviet armored divisions, their casualties reached epic numbers before they crossed the USSR's western frontier. Thousands fell to vicious attacks by raw, freelancing guerrilla armies seeking vengeance for atrocities inflicted on civilians by Gestapo and SS thugs. The partisans' savagery exceeded anything yet seen by German troops in Russia: as the retreat dragged on, Hitler's toughest veterans gagged at the increasingly common sight of wounded comrades left to die with their heads bound tightly inside the gaping wounds of disemboweled German corpses.

At war's end, more than 20,000 cities and towns in the USSR lay in ruin, and at least 27 million Russians (new figures released by Russia's post-Soviet historians) had died in the "Great Patriotic War." Of the original 3 million Germans who launched Operation Barbarossa's long eastward march only 300,000 returned to Germany alive. Guy Sajer was one of them, but life as he'd known it had ceased to exist: everyone he'd left behind in 1941, including his fiancée, was gone forever—only his aging parents remained.

A **grim**, realistic look at the Wehrmacht in pell-mell flight across southern Russia in 1943. Stranded in enemy country by his battalion's chaotic retreat, a battle-hardened, cynical German sergeant (Coburn) leads his veteran squad back to friendly lines through a hornet's nest of Soviet tanks and infantry. It's all downhill from there: Soviet attacks multiply, and Schell—a green but ruthless Prussian officer—develops a bitter, unchecked hatred for the highly decorated Coburn. Easily the best film ever made about the Great Patriotic War, thanks mostly to phenomenal action footage featuring swarms of Soviet tanks on the loose and a white-knuckle running battle inside a large shattered factory. Warner is excellent as a disillusioned junior officer attached to German field headquarters.

For Further Viewing:

Stalingrad ★★★ (1993) 150 Minutes (Jochen Nickel, Sebastian Rudolph, Dominique Horwitz, Thomas Kretschmann, Dana Vavrova, Heinz Emigholz): *The Boat* producer Günter Rohrbach's technically superb epic on history's bloodiest battle excels in some spots and stinks in others (there is no middle ground in this odd film). Director Joseph Vilsmaier assembles an incredible array of vintage Wehrmacht vehicles and weaponry, delivering some of the finest combat segments on film—and all are bull's-eyes historically: thunderous street fighting, white-knuckle house-to-house melees, and gruesome small-unit sewer brawls build a convincing, horrifying, picture of what the eastern front's pivotal crucible must have been like for German infantrymen and Russian civilians. But *Stalingrad* craters badly whenever the shooting stops. Vilsmaier provides no historical context for the battle and (like many postwar German filmmakers) wallows in sophomoric pro-left ideology that quickly grows ludicrous: a noncom, for example, responds to his lieutenant's warning that the Soviets were murdering POWs with "Do we deserve any better?"—a laughably preposterous line for anyone familiar with frontline WWII Russia. Great fireworks, but very little else for teachers and students of the Great Patriotic War.

A Time to Love and a Time to Die ★★★★ (1958) 132 Minutes (John Gavin, Lilo Pulver, Don De-Fore, Keenan Wynn): Director Douglas Sirk's gritty film brackets a grim look at war-torn Berlin with realistic segments following an exhausted Wehrmacht in full retreat on the eastern front. In 1944, after two years of nonstop fighting in the USSR (nightmare #1), tough veteran Ernst Graeber (Gavin) returns to Germany on furlough. He arrives in Berlin and finds his family gone, civilians starving, and most of the city, including his own house, leveled by Allied carpet bombing (nightmare #2). He meets and marries Pulver, then rejoins his old unit—more battered than ever—three weeks later. A perfect companion piece for *Cross of Iron* and *Stalingrad:* together, the three films deliver a solid, grindingly bleak view of the only prospects facing Wehrmacht veterans in the east—fighting the Soviets was bad enough; weathering B-17 raids in Berlin was almost as dangerous, and living under postwar Soviet occupation would be bitterly severe at best. Hard-hitting and realistic, one of the 1950s' best war movies. Based on the novel by Erich Maria Remarque (who appears in the film briefly as Graeber's old professor).

Recommended Reading:
Guy Sajer, *The Forgotten Soldier;* William Craig, *Enemy at the Gates: The Battle for Stalingrad;* Willi Heinrich, *Cross of Iron.*

The Desert Fox ★★★★

(1951) 88 Minutes

Director: Henry Hathaway

Cast: James Mason, Cedric Hardwicke, Jessica Tandy, Luther Adler, Everett Sloane, Leo G. Carroll, George Macready, Richard Boone, Robert Coote

Historical Background: The familiar stereotype of lemminglike Wehrmacht robots is nonsense, thanks in large measure to Erwin Rommel. A half-century ago, Rommel practiced "empowerment" with breathtaking success on WWII battlefields: "I give orders only when necessary," he wrote in his desert journals, continuing, "The commander must keep his troops abreast of all the latest tactical developments and insist on their practical application." The Wehrmacht's ratio of enlisted men to line officers was very high: German lieutenants and captains commanded many more men than their Allied counterparts, so the Germans formally trained every noncommissioned officer and enlisted man to do the job of his immediate superior—if a German lieutenant fell, any sergeant in the area could replace him, and his piece of war machine rolled on without a hitch. Corporals and privates could replace sergeants in the same fashion. This gave German soldiers a double advantage: they were resourceful and made quick, imaginative tactical decisions under severe pressure. And they trained intensively in small-unit tactics and leadership, the main reason that Wehrmacht platoons and companies routinely defeated much larger enemy units—with fewer than 15,000 men, Rommel captured 33,000 British soldiers at Tobruk in June 1942.

Born in Heidenheim on November 15, 1891, Erwin Johannes Eugen Rommel fought on three fronts in World War I, earning the Iron Cross for valor in France. After the armistice he remained in the army and took command of a panzer division in February 1940, when the second European conflict expanded westward. He'd had no training in armored warfare, but he roared across France in three months. He was a born tank commander, and Hitler posted him to North Africa at the head of three elite armored divisions—the Afrika Korps—when Mussolini's army collapsed in the deserts of Libya. On March 24, 1941, one week after his arrival, Rommel launched an all-out offensive, driving the British out of El Agheila, Mersa Brega, and Benghazi.

The rout continued until July 1, 1942, when the Afrika Korps reached El Alamein, a rail depot just east of the Libyan Plateau. After 16 days of bitter fighting, Sir Claude Aukinlek and various battered British units retreating from Tobruk finally stopped Rommel's onslaught. In August, Bernard Montgomery took command of the Eighth Army and prepared for a second, decisive battle on the same ground. Flanked by the Mediterranean on the north and an impassable rocky canyon called the Qattara Depression on the south, El Alamein formed a narrow static front: Rommel's principles of mechanized warfare—sweeping end runs, sudden flanking moves, stunning counterattacks—were irrelevant. Worse still: by fall 1943, British tanks outnumbered Rommel's by five to one, the Afrika Korps was almost out of fuel, and the RAF enjoyed total control of the air. Montgomery attacked on October 23, pushing the Germans back almost 700 miles in two weeks. With the war in the desert virtually over, Rommel returned to Germany to oversee Wehrmacht forces defending the 3,000-mile "Atlantic Wall" against an anticipated Allied invasion. For six months, 250,000 men built huge bunkers, anchored thousands of underwater obstructions, flooded rear areas to impede tanks, and laid more than 6 million mines along the coastline. When the Allies smashed their way inland, Rommel vainly urged Hitler to end the war. Thoroughly disillusioned, he supported the July 20 attempt on Hitler's life at a staff meeting in East Prussia. The conspirators were captured and executed, but Rommel—by then Germany's greatest military hero—was allowed to commit suicide in exchange for his family's safety. He died on October 14, 1944, and received a hero's funeral.

Mason is excellent in the title role of this moving account of Rommel's final weeks in North Africa, his return to Germany, and his grimly coerced suicide. Based on Desmond Young's biography, the film portrays Rommel as a wise, dedicated, and fatally apolitical military genius who recognizes Hitler's madness far too late. Initially, U.S. veterans' organizations boycotted *The Desert Fox,* but its audiences grew; today it is considered Hollywood's best biography of Rommel.

Recommended Reading:
Desmond Young, *Rommel, the Desert Fox;* B. H. Liddell Hart, ed., *The Rommel Papers.*

The Desert Rats ★★★★★

(1953) 88 Minutes

Director: Robert Wise

Cast: Richard Burton, James Mason, Robert Newton, Chips Rafferty

Historical Background: The world had never seen anything like the 1940–43 North African campaign. It was warfare on an enormous scale, fought over flat desert terrain that offered tank crews and infantrymen no visual landmarks: armies had to find their way from one place to the next as sea captains did, using the stars as reference points and navigating with compasses. It was mechanized, lightning warfare that ran on precious gasoline and the fleet machines of death that it fueled. It was thrust-and-parry warfare marked by grand offensives covering hundreds of miles, followed by sudden counterattacks and equally long retreats—during Erwin Rommel's 14-month tenure in Africa, for example, Benghazi changed hands five times. More than anything else, it was grueling warfare that created a rough camaraderie between soldiers on opposing sides—no North African veteran thought it strange that the British Tommies' favorite song, "Lili Marlene," was also the favorite song of Germany's Afrika Korps, where it originated.

The campaign began in September 1940, when Mussolini hurled 250,000 Libya-based troops across the Egyptian border at Britain's 30,000-man Army of the Nile. The British fought and fell back—again and again—until December 9, when they wheeled abruptly and counterattacked, driving the stunned Italians 500 miles westward and capturing the critical Libyan port of Tobruk. With the collapse of Mussolini's East African Empire a certainty, Hitler sent the Afrika Korps to the rescue. Rommel hit the ground running, launching a major offensive on March 24, 1941, that drove the British back into Egypt. The Germans recaptured every city occupied by the British except Tobruk, and as long as Tobruk held out, the Afrika Korps had no first-class natural harbor to receive supplies—a circumstance made doubly critical by England's determination to hold

Malta. (The small island lay due south of Sicily and well within striking distance of Tunisian ports to the west: RAF Spitfires and Royal Navy warships based there were perfectly positioned to interdict German convoys carrying precious gasoline to Hitler's North African legions.)

For Germany to prevail in North Africa, Rommel had to take Tobruk and its vast stores of food, water, and gasoline. Cut off and surrounded 100 miles behind enemy lines—with their backs to the sea—15,000 untested men of Australia's 9th Division prepared to defend the city. Tobruk bristled with more than 200 field guns. Concentric circles of minefields, antitank ditches, and trench lines protected by barbed wire stood between Rommel and the embattled harbor's wharves. On April 14, Rommel's 5th Light Division mounted a full-scale assault on the city's outer perimeter. The Australians held. Between the 15th and the 24th, they repulsed five more German attacks, each more furious than the last. Australia's tenacious infantrymen—the "diggers" and "Desert Rats" of North Africa—simply wouldn't let go. Throughout the summer and early fall, the Luftwaffe flew more than 1,000 raids against them, and still they held out. In November, a British offensive drove the Germans back and relieved the exhausted Australians. For months, bitter fighting raged back and forth across the desert until Rommel finally forced the British out of Tobruk on June 21, 1942.

But it made little difference, thanks in part to an enormous blunder by Hitler: he called off a meticulously planned invasion of Malta, and Britain continued to rule the Mediterranean. On October 23, Bernard Montgomery's Eighth Army attacked Rommel at El Alamein, and by November 6 the Afrika Korps was in full retreat. German resistance in North Africa ended on May 12, 1943, less than a year after Rommel's triumphant capture of Tobruk. The consequences of the Desert Rats' tenaciousness at Tobruk spread far beyond the shores of North Africa. They kept Hitler's finest general out of the European and Russian theaters during the most critical year of the war—a maddening state of affairs for the Germans, who had no interest in conquering all of Egypt or occupying huge desert tracts east of the Suez Canal: they were in Africa to protect Fortress Europe's southern flank, to tie up as many British divisions as they could, and to seize at least some of the oil fields on the Persian Gulf. Their miserable failure on all three counts cost them the war in the west.

The Desert Rats delivers a riveting, authentic, suspense-filled view of the Tobruk siege through the eyes of a small Australian commando squad led by Burton and hanging on for dear life against the Afrika Korps. Fine performances and many harrowing moments—including a gut-wrenching raid on a German ammunition dump and a last-ditch Australian defensive stand behind enemy lines—make this one of Hollywood's finest World War II films. Mason makes a cameo appearance as Rommel.

For Further Viewing:
Tobruk ★★★ (1967) 110 Minutes (Rock Hudson, George Peppard, Nigel Green, Guy Stockwell, Jack Watson): An odd, uneven movie about the efforts of a group of English commandos (led by Green) and a squad of highly trained German Jews (under Peppard's command) to blow up Rommel's fuel dumps at Tobruk during the final months of the North African campaign. Packed with explosions and gruesome combat scenes, *Tobruk* will appeal mainly to students of the desert war interested in the rigors it imposed on individual infantrymen.

Five Graves to Cairo ★★★★ (1943) 96 Minutes (Franchot Tone, Anne Baxter, Eric von Stroheim, Akim Tamiroff): Von Stroheim struts and sneers his way to Olympic Gold as the most Prussian Erwin Rommel on film (in a scene that must be incomprehensible for today's younger viewers, he tells Baxter that he hates the company of women in the morning!). The plot turns on Tone's impersonation of a dead German spy—with Baxter's help he discovers logistical secrets of German tank units in North Africa, making the Allied victory at El Alamein possible. Highly entertaining, even though the film is dated.

Recommended Reading:
George Forty, *Desert Rats at War.*

Escape from Sobibor ★★★★★

(1987) 150 Minutes

Director: Jack Gold

Cast: Alan Arkin, Rutger Hauer, Joanna Pacula, Jack Shepherd, Dijana Krzanic

Historical Background: September 29, 1943—eastern Poland: Eight months after landing in Sobibor death camp, Leon Feldhendler knew that the Germans aimed to murder every single Jew in Europe. Ghettos in Kraków, Warsaw, and Bialystok, the last pockets of unin-

terned Jews in Poland, lay in smoking, blood-soaked ruin. On August 23, 200 Jews at Treblinka had revolted—killing several Ukrainian guards and one SS officer—only to be shot or recaptured days after fleeing the camp. Now, Treblinka was gone (800,000 men, women, and children had died there). The last 500 Jews at Belzec had fallen to German guns after disinterring 600,000 murdered comrades and burning them on towering pyres to rob marauding Red Army legions of Holocaust evidence. (Belzec's stunned liberators found only one living prisoner in the camp.) Clearly, Feldhendler and Sobibor's 599 surviving prisoners were next.

On the 29th, Feldhendler and Alexander Pechersky, a fearless Soviet officer, began plotting an escape. Small breakouts from Sobibor and other camps had always failed. Their only chance was a mass exodus, sudden, violent, and sufficiently pell-mell to disorient and overwhelm their captors. If they could quietly isolate and kill enough German guards just before the break, the remaining Ukranians—always undisciplined and often drunk—wouldn't recover quickly enough to stop all of them. On October 14, they were ready. By late afternoon, a team of tough, steady men had lured ten guards into tool sheds and tailor shops, splitting their skulls with makeshift axes or slicing them to ribbons with contraband knives. Informed of the escape minutes before evening roll call, prisoners jammed the main yard, barely able to restrain themselves. At 5:10 P.M., Pechersky climbed atop a small table and launched the breakout. In concert, more than 400 souls with half a decade of searing hatred to vent stormed the main gate and its flanking fences, escaping on two sides of the compound. At least 100 prisoners fell to machine-gun fire and land mines, but 300 made it, completing history's only successful mass escape from a Nazi death camp. On the 15th, German death squads murdered Sobibor's remaining prisoners and obliterated the camp.

Between 1933 and 1945, the Third Reich built more than 1,600 concentration camps and 900 slave-labor facilities. Two months after seizing power, Hitler opened the first camp at Dachau (near Munich), launching his genocidal campaign against Jews and other "undesirables." A state-sponsored two-year euthanasia facility in Brandenburg slaughtered 90,000 "incurably insane" Germans before folding in 1941. During Operation Barbarossa, mass-murder battalions—the Einsatzgruppen—trailed combat outfits into the USSR and the Baltics, relentlessly stalking Soviet Jews, gunning them down in huge numbers, and burying the bodies in mass graves. By 1943, more than a million had died in Lithuania, Latvia, and the Ukraine.

For SS colonel Adolf Eichmann, overseer of the vast killing program, Einsatzgruppen sweeps were expensive, hit-and-miss affairs. To kill all 8.85 million Jews under Nazi rule, the SS began building huge extermination mills in Poland. Equipped with crematoria and death chambers using hydrogen cyanide gas (Zyklon B), Sobibor, Treblinka, Chelmno, Belzec, and Maidanek were built specifically for systematic, epic-scale slaughter. Auschwitz-Birkenau was a forced labor camp as well as an extermination facility. Designed to kill most Jewish prisoners within 24 hours of their incarceration, all six facilities were up and running in 1942. Rounded up, stripped of all their possessions, and shipped to the camps in filthy boxcars without food, water, or sanitary facilities, Jews from every city in Europe died immediately in gas chambers or perished slowly from overwork

and starvation (the maximum labor-camp life expectancy was three months). Incomprehensible cruelty prevailed throughout the system: guards beat prisoners to death—for no reason—every day; caged dogs, intentionally underfed and mad with hunger, tore pregnant women to pieces; SS goons forced mothers to watch their children tortured and murdered; in Auschwitz, Josef Mengele directed ghastly medical experiments—without anesthesia—on prisoners. At war's end, Hitler's bloody nightmare had consumed 5,934,000 Jews—about one-third of the world's total Jewish population.

The "Final Solution" was Hitler's centerpiece program from the beginning, and virtually everyone in Germany knew about it well before the Allies landed at Normandy. By early 1943, great prison trains packed with Jews rolled eastward through major population centers around the clock; hundreds of Germany's top industrial firms (Krupp, BMW, and I. G. Farben among them) used slave laborers from Dachau and other facilities; more than 800,000 Germans served in the SS, and the railway network employed another 1.2 million—far too many to keep the camps' existence and function secret. In a totalitarian state where the government and secret police controlled all the means of violence, open opposition to the camps undoubtedly would have been suicidal and futile, but most Germans knew what was happening to the Jews, and so did the Allies.

(A number of Germans took great personal risks to protect as many Jews as they could. By far the most prominent, entrepreneur Oskar Schindler, ran a Kraków-area enamelware plant employing 370 Jewish workers to produce mess-kit gear for the Wehrmacht. A dedicated Nazi during the late thirties—and at one point an intelligence agent in Czechoslovakia—Schindler remade himself after witnessing German governor-general Hans Frank's brutal 1943 liquidation of Kraków's Jewish quarter. Filled with revulsion and electrifying contempt—in a postwar interview, he called the Nazis "pigs"—Schindler launched a personal crusade to rescue hundreds of Jews. Lying about untrained workers' skills to keep them out of the gas chambers, he began hiring more prisoners. He fed them well and allowed them—illegally—to bring hungry relatives to his factory for hot meals. He provided basic medical care—again illegally—and bribed SS officers to leave sick prisoners off execution lists. At least 800 men and 297 women survived the Holocaust because of Schindler's extraordinary efforts to protect them. After the war, his financial and business affairs hit rock bottom, but Jewish groups granted him generous stipends, extending the payments to his wife, Emilie, after his death in 1974.)

On November 20, 1945, the Holocaust's full horrors began unfolding publicly during trials before a four-power tribunal in Nuremberg. (It's remarkable that the Allies extended any sort of due process to Hitler's apes: Churchill himself favored summary execution of the worst criminals; U.S. Treasury secretary Henry Morgenthau, Jr., went further: shoot Nazi "archcriminals" now, he insisted, then wreck every Ruhr Valley factory and abolish heavy industry in Germany forever.) The court set many precedents. It was history's first international tribunal and the first to treat waging aggressive war, violating the rules and customs of war ("war crimes"), and mass murder of civilians ("crimes against humanity") as felonies punishable by death. With great practical foresight, authors of the tribunal's charter combined two judicial approaches: the Anglo-Saxon system based on adversarial prosecution and defense teams and the Continental practice of charging multiple judges—instead of juries—with hearing evidence and reaching verdicts. On October 1, 1946, the court acquitted three German civilians, sentenced 12 political and military leaders to death, sent three to prison for life, and gave long jail terms to four others. A dozen more major trials (the "Subsequent Proceedings") followed, ending in more than 175 convictions and 12 death sentences. For five more years, the Allied occupying powers held their own trials, convicting thousands of Nazis and putting more than 450 to death. (Many German industrialists landed in prison, but a U.S. Clemency Act freed most of them in 1951.)

Many Holocaust architects and henchmen vanished from history or escaped prosecution, but Adolf Eichmann wasn't one of them. (Jewish groups began stalking him before Israel became an independent nation.) High drama marked his capture in San Fernando, Argentina—a Buenos Aires suburb—by Israeli Mossad agents fourteen years after he escaped from an American holding camp in Bavaria. At 8:05 P.M. on May 11, 1960, Peter Malkin and three handpicked members of a large task force waylaid Eichmann near a Garibaldi Street bus stop, hauled him to a safe house an hour's drive away, and held him there for nine days. (Israeli commandos attached to the team went after Mengele as well, but he'd disappeared months earlier. Most experts believe that he suffered a massive stroke and drowned while swimming off the Brazilian coast in 1979.) On May 21, the Israelis drugged Eichmann, hustled him aboard a special El Al passenger jet, and left for home. Charged with 15 specific war crimes, he went to court in Jerusalem on April 11, 1961. One hundred Holocaust survivors testified against him during a long, sensational trial ending with "guilty" verdicts on all counts. On May 31, 1962, Eichmann died on the Ramla Prison gallows. Less than three hours later, Auschwitz survivor Michael Giladi hurled his ashes into the Mediterranean Sea from the stern of an Israeli police launch. To this day, Eichmann remains the only criminal ever executed in the state of Israel.

Adapted from Richard Rashke's book, *Escape from Sobibor* is as accurate as any movie based on an actual historical event. Producers and writers cleared every line of dialogue, every character name, and every action-packed detail of the suspenseful escape with Rashke and survivors of Sobibor; after many interviews, they ruthlessly trashed several unconfirmed portions of the script's first draft. The final product is terrific all the way—a deliberately paced, chilling delivery of the camp's horrors with very little graphic violence (at least by today's standards). History Channel screenings feature interviews with Rashke and Esther Terner Raab, a Sobibor survivor played beautifully by Krzanic in the film. A treat for movie fans and history buffs.

For Further Viewing:
Judgment at Nuremberg ★★★★ (1961) 178 Minutes (Spencer Tracy, Burt Lancaster, Marlene Dietrich, Richard Widmark, Maximilian Schell, Judy Garland, Montgomery Clift): Director Stanley Kramer's riveting—but flawed—film about the prosecution of several German judges charged with war crimes by an American tribunal. (Lancaster plays the most prominent defendant, Tracy the presiding judge.) Throughout the film Kramer insists that patriotism and the Great Depression drove ordinary Germans to support Hitler. This is absurd:

the worldwide depression ravaged England and struck the U.S. harder than it did Germany, but neither country tried to exterminate the Jews. (And both were loaded with patriots.) Another error, the notion that Churchill ignored the Holocaust while Roosevelt opposed it, surfaces twice. In fact, the reverse was true: Churchill, a lifelong Zionist, was the only Allied leader who consistently urged some sort of military strike against the camps. With incredible cynicism, Roosevelt lectured the prime minister in 1943 on the "understandable complaints that the Germans bear towards the Jews in Germany." Still, a fine film with super performances and an on-target portrait of the spirit of the Nuremberg trials.

Schindler's List ★★★★ (1993) 195 Minutes (Liam Neeson, Ralph Fiennes, Ben Kingsley, Jonathan Sagalle, Caroline Goodall): Neeson is excellent in the title role, and *Schindler's List* (based on Thomas Keneally's best-selling "nonfiction novel") is a very good film—but not the flawless historical "document" (director Steven Spielberg's self-serving term) lavishly touted by most critics hours after its release. Neeson's mawkish closing monologue, for example, is pure fiction, and Spielberg's contrived ending offended many Jewish viewers. The film portrays Holocaust Jews as perfectly submissive, helpless victims—but this was not the case in Schindler's Kraków: young Jewish resistance fighters killed several Germans there before Frank's barbarous ghetto sweep. Spielberg also mutes the force of Schindler's "conversion" and his electrifying contempt for the Nazis. (See Philip Gourevitch's review in *Commentary* magazine, February 1994, for a dissenting view of the film. A mixed bag, the review drew many furious letters from *Schindler* fans.) Spielberg does deliver a sound, accurate version of the Schindler story, but omits—or changes—too many details to deserve the number-one ranking among Holocaust filmmakers.

The House on Garibaldi Street ★★★ (1979) 100 Minutes (Martin Balsam, Topol, Janet Suzman, Leo McKern, Nick Mancuso): Based on Isser Harel's book—the first authoritative account of "Operation Eichmann"—director Peter Collinson's talky film chronicles the Mossad's pursuit of Hitler's top murderer, the meticulously executed kidnapping in San Fernando, and the long wait for secret transport back to Israel. Harel, the Eichmann mission commander, altered several details of the operation and used pseudonyms throughout his book because some of the historical material was still classified in 1974. Collinson adds his own fictional twists for dramatic effect: the most egregious comes at film's end with a last-minute escape-plane takeoff delay caused by a local police inspector's efforts to board the airliner and search for Eichmann. The episode is pure hokum—there was a takeoff delay, but a botched flight plan caused it. Still, a very accurate "quick-study" film on the daring operation.

Operation Eichmann ★★ (1961) 93 Minutes (Donald Buke, Werner Klemperer, Barbara Turner, John Banner, Ruta Lee): Director R. G. Springsteen covers Eichmann's role in the Holocaust, follows him to Argentina, and closes with his capture there. The film hums with conjecture because its release came before Eichmann's execution, when heavily censored newspaper stories were the only sources of information on Harel's top-secret mission. Springsteen's researchers also made several historical errors: at one point, Eichmann (played by Klemperer) suggests building crematoria in the death camps after the USSR's 1943 Stalingrad victory—in fact, Treblinka installed crematoria several months earlier. Worse still, Klemperer gives Eichmann far too forceful a personality (the real-life devil was a drab, boring, unimaginative bureaucrat). Not a bad film, but no match for *The House on Garibaldi Street*—especially for history instructors.

Recommended Reading:
Richard Rashke, *Escape from Sobibor;* Martin Gilbert, *Final Journey: The Fate of the Jews in Nazi Europe;* Benjamin B. Ferencz, *Less than Slaves: Jewish Forced Labor and the Quest for Compensation;* Telford Taylor, *The Anatomy of the Nuremberg Trials;* Thomas Keneally, *Schindler's List;* Elinor J. Brecher, *Schindler's Legacy: True Stories of the List Survivors;* Peter Z. Malkin, *Eichmann in My Hands.*

Fat Man and Little Boy ★★

(1989) 126 Minutes

Director: Roland Joffe

Cast: Paul Newman, Dwight Schultz, Bonnie Bedelia, John Cusack, Laura Dern, Ron Frazier, Natasha Richardson

Historical Background: In September 1944, America's massive effort to build a plutonium separation plant in Hanford, Wash., stalled because of a walkout by 750 bored, drunken plumbers. Within 24 hours, project director Franklin T. Matthias settled the strike and returned to work, thoroughly exhausted. Clearly, drudgery and shot nerves—not glamour—made the daily diet of 125,000 souls who won America's furious dash to build history's first atomic bomb. This was inevitable, thanks to the colossal scale of the program and its obvious potential for ending the war quickly. Called "gadgets"—for secrecy's sake—by the scientists who created them, Fat Man (a plutonium bomb) and Little Boy (the uranium device dropped on Hiroshima) cost the U.S. $2 billion, a staggering figure in 1945. Construction costs devoured most of the money: the architectural firm of Skidmore, Owings & Merrill built an entire city from scratch (Oak Ridge, Tenn.) to house and support three plants for separating U-235 from uranium ore.

America's drive to build the bombs began in August 1939, when physicists Albert Einstein and Leo Szilard sent a letter urging Franklin Roosevelt to begin funding work on an atomic bomb before the Germans' lead in nuclear research became insurmountable. But plans for an atomic weapons program languished in Washington's impenetrable bureaucracy until the U.S. declared war on Germany and Japan. By September 1942 the Manhattan Project, named for the Corps of Engineers' Manhattan District that built its research and testing facilities, was well under way. Directing the program was Lt. Col. Leslie R. Groves, who picked physicist Robert J. Oppenheimer to manage the daily work of a large group of American and European scientists. Their task was twofold: build a weapon that worked, then make it small enough for delivery by American bombers.

They knew from the beginning that they could build a uranium bomb based on nuclear fission. Little Boy's mechanism for triggering a chain reaction was simple: conventional explosives near the bomb's tail fired a subcritical "bullet" of U-235 through a gun barrel into a second block of uranium in the bomb's nose, creating a critical mass and igniting a huge explosion. Because U-235 extraction was a slow process requiring gigantic amounts of uranium ore, the

physicists used plutonium to make Fat Man. Refining plutonium was relatively easy, but its fission rate was so high that the gun-barrel mechanism caused it to "fizzle" instead of exploding. A process of sudden compression achieved critical mass in the second bomb: an outer shell of high explosives, wrapped around a hollow plutonium sphere and focused inward, "imploded" the sphere into a small solid core, triggering the devastating blast that leveled Nagasaki. (No one was sure that implosion would work until the Los Alamos team exploded a prototype plutonium device in the famous "Trinity" test near Alamogordo, N.M., on July 16, 1945. Less than a month later, Little Boy and Fat Man fell on Hiroshima and Nagasaki, ending the war.)

Development and production of the bombs had taken three and a half years. It had ended one scientist's life—accidental exposure to lethal gamma rays killed Louis Slotin in May 1946. At war's end, America was the only nuclear power on earth, but not for long. Despite Groves' near-fanatical security measures, Klaus Fuchs, an employee in the Los Alamos implosion group, passed classified information to the Soviets, who detonated their first nuclear device in September 1941. Fuchs was arrested in 1950, but it was far too late: Pandora's box was wide open.

Fat Man and Little Boy should have been a fine film, but thanks to an underlying antinuke agenda it often plays like a smug, tired sermon against all things military. The script is embarrassingly vapid. ("You know, I wonder," asks a glassy-eyed Laura Dern, "if it's instinct to save a man, what is it that makes us want to kill one? Is that instinct?") Far worse are key distortions of documented historical facts. A fictional character based on Louis Slotin, for example, dies of radiation sickness before the Trinity test takes place, falsely implying that the U.S. fully understood the multiple horrors of the bomb's aftereffects when the *Enola Gay* took off on August 6. Joffe's Oppenheimer is a pure altruist whose decision to work on the bomb comes after agonizing moral scrutiny. In fact, the ambitious Oppenheimer once advised Groves to irradiate Germany's food and water supplies. Joffe's distortions trivialize the terrible necessities behind Harry Truman's decision to drop the bombs, implying that the devastation suffered by innocent civilians in Hiroshima and Nagasaki was merely absurd, not tragic.

Recommended Reading:
Leslie R. Groves, *Now It Can Be Told: The Story of the Manhattan Project;* Rachel Fermi, *Picturing the Bomb: Photographs from the Secret World of the Manhattan Project.*

5 Fingers ★★★★

(1952) 108 Minutes

Director: Joseph L. Mankiewicz

Cast: James Mason, Danielle Darrieux, Michael Rennie, Walter Hampden

Historical Background: The career of a drab, mercenary little fellow named Elyesa Bazna typifies the spectral, murky quality of

WWII intrigue. Code-named Cicero by British intelligence (MI-6), Bazna was the Yugoslavian-born valet of Sir Hughe Knatchbull-Hugessen, British ambassador to Turkey. In October 1943, Bazna approached German embassy official Albert Jenke and offered to sell him photographs of top-secret documents stored by the ambassador in his bedroom safe (they included lists of MI-6 agents in Turkey, the key to England's diplomatic code, initial plans for the Allied invasion of Europe, and bombing plans for the Balkans).

Jenke took the offer to German ambassador Fritz von Papen. Skeptical at first, the Germans eventually paid Bazna $1.2 million for his services. But the British, who penetrated virtually all of Hitler's espionage networks early in the war, learned all about Cicero from German defector Ewart Seager. MI-6 began feeding Bazna detailed "plans" for the coming invasion of France and a simultaneous Allied strike in the Balkans. The Germans took the bait: as the largest amphibious force in history stormed ashore at Normandy in 1944, 25 full-strength German divisions waited on the Balkan peninsula for an assault that never came. Fearing discovery, Bazna quit his job and disappeared—only to discover that more than 90% of his new wealth was counterfeit money forged by the Germans for use in a bizarre plan to devalue English currency. "Cicero" eventually married a woman 20 years his junior, fathering four children before he died in 1971.

Set in wartime Ankara and Istanbul, *5 Fingers* drips with a creepy sense of menacing intrigue. Mason is terrific as the cynical Cicero, gleefully keeping two warring nations off-balance while he steals top-secret documents right under Knatchbull-Hugessen's nose. Against him the film pits Michael Rennie—superb as a British agent—and a taut spy hunt begins. *5 Fingers* is excellent throughout—a fictional romantic sub-plot works well enough to justify its inclusion in the movie. (Mankiewicz actually found and interviewed Bazna following the war. After helping the director with some of the film's historical details, Bazna demanded payment for his services. Mankiewicz refused.)

Recommended Reading:
James T. Rogers, *The Secret War: Espionage in World War II;* Elyesa Bazna, *I was Cicero;* Fitzroy Maclean, *Take Nine Spies.*

The Great Escape ★★★★

(1963) 168 Minutes

Director: John Sturges

Cast: Steve McQueen, James Garner, Richard Attenborough, James Donald, James Coburn, Charles Bronson, Donald Pleasence

Historical Background: February 1944—Stalag Luft III, Sagan, Poland: Stepping as gingerly as greenhorns trapped in a minefield, several German "ferrets" (guards trained and equipped to probe for tunnels) ambled around the North Compound yard of Hitler's showcase prison camp in a tightly packed huddle. A griz-zled old man walked point, sweeping the ground with an "authentic" divining rod that would—he swore—pinpoint the deepest POW escape shafts as well as neighboring oil deposits. Bewildered at first, 300 Allied "stooges" (prisoners assigned to monitor ferrets around the clock) soon grasped the bizarre procession's mission. Hysterical laughter erupted, drawing other prisoners out of their huts and quickly swelling into a chorus of hoots and catcalls that engulfed the acrimonious ferrets and rattled the air well after their retreat through the compound's inner gate.

Between 1940 and 1945, hordes of Allied troops locked in Reichmarshal Hermann Goering's stalags took multiple shots at going over, under, and through the wire in every conceivable type of holding facility. (One Englishman launched 15 different breakout tries in less than two years.) By 1942, the Germans had taken a bellyful: in April, they gathered thousands of Allied prisoners with extensive escape-attempt histories (most were airmen), hauled them to Sagan, and dumped them in Stalag Luft III (SL 3)—the final word in state-of-the-art, high-security POW camps. Two ten-foot barbed-wire fences ringed the facility. Just inside the first barrier lay a 30-foot-wide swath of soft earth separated from the inner yard by a single warning wire and registered for saturation fire by "goon-box" (guard-tower) machine guns dotting the outer fence. A few feet beneath the camp lay tons of sandy yellow dirt—impossible, the Germans believed, to haul out of tunnels-in-progress and conceal in the compound's dark topsoil. Buried microphones rigged to detect digging noises ringed the entire camp.

On paper, SL 3 was a great idea. In practice, it was a nightmare for the Germans. In one camp they had concentrated 10,000 insolent, ruthless, resourceful, combat-hardened, thoroughly fearless Anglo-American loose cannons, most of them oozing contempt for their rear-echelon German adversaries (especially the Americans) and all of them itching to break out no matter how high the cost (especially the British). Collectively they had decades of experience in escape strategy and tactics. And because the Germans couldn't risk sending them to work outside the wire, they had absolutely nothing to do but discuss their favorite subject—how to get out of SL 3 and back into the war. Attempted breaks literally began on day one: minutes after their arrival at the camp, ranking British officer Harry ("Wings") Day and two airmen donned RAF uniforms altered to resemble Luftwaffe dress grays and strutted brazenly toward SL 3's main gate. Guards stopped them and—laughing uncontrollably—marched the three men straight to isolation in the camp "cooler."

Less than a year later, Day and Spitfire pilot Roger Bushell launched the most extraordinary breakout project of the war, marshaling the talents of 600 men (the "X-organization") to dig three massive tunnels—"Tom," "Dick," and "Harry"—and outfit 200 prisoners for survival outside the wire. The tunnels were engineering marvels: all were 30 feet deep (below the range of subterranean listening devices) and so elaborate that discovery of one shaft would, Bushell reasoned, convince the Germans that no additional excavations existed. Conduit pipes fashioned from old milk cans and secured to makeshift canvas pumps ventilated the shafts, and lighting systems feeding off the camp's power supply illuminated them. To haul excavated sand ("spoil") out of the tunnels, Bushell's diggers laid wooden rails—covered with noise-muffling blankets—for rope-drawn

trolleys used later to shuttle escapees down the narrow shafts. (Stunning ingenuity marked trolley-system engineering: the carts, for example, featured wooden ball bearings lubricated with margarine from Red Cross parcels.) To move 100 tons of spoil to the compound for dispersal, prisoners suspended woolen tubes filled with sand and closed at the bottom with straight pins inside their trousers.

By September, tunnel Tom's two-man digging teams had burrowed well outside the wire, but ferrets discovered the shaft's entrance and dynamited the tunnel. Bushell suspended digging for four months, then threw all his resources into pushing tunnel Harry an incredible 335 feet from hut 104 to the woods north of camp. On March 24, 1944, excavation stopped and 200 men—packing makeshift compasses, four-color maps, forged travel permits and identity cards, civilian clothing, fake Wehrmacht uniforms, and oatmeal-based escape rations—began rolling down tunnel Harry's two-foot-square corridor toward freedom. Then, before a single man traversed the tunnel, a series of catastrophes sandbagged the getaway for more than two hours: oversized survival kits dislodged shoring boards, causing minor cave-ins; a Berlin air raid cut the power supply, blackening the tunnel for 40 minutes; icy snow jammed the exit door shut. Worst of all: diggers had missed the forest's edge by ten feet, forcing men to exit in the open—15 yards from a goon-box—and bolt for cover between searchlight sweeps.

At 4:55 A.M., seconds after the 76th escapee had vanished into the woods, a sentry wandered away from his post, stumbled over the exit hole, and stopped the breakout cold. The fugitives' toughest work, getting out of Germany and safely home, had barely begun.

(Grindingly difficult for Allied POWs held in Germany, post-breakout repatriation was all but impossible for Axis prisoners interned in 21 Canadian camps and 500 U.S. facilities. Against incalculable odds, a few German prisoners actually made it back to the Reich. By far the most famous—fighter pilot Franz von Werra—jumped from a speeding POW train near Lake Ontario in 1941, stole a boat, crossed the St. Lawrence River to the still-neutral U.S., and crashed the German embassy in New York. From there he sailed to Germany, only to die in an airplane accident over Holland in 1945.) Bushell's SL 3 break launched one of the century's great manhunts. Three men eventually made it back to England, but German patrols recaptured the others and murdered 50 of them—including Bushell—on Hitler's orders. (After the war, Allied tribunals tried and hanged 14 Germans implicated in the killings.) To this day, great escape survivors insist that the breakout was a rousing Allied victory, and simple numbers bear them out: a staggering total of 5 million Germans left critical war-related jobs for two weeks to recapture Bushell's runaway loose cannons.

Sturges' colorful epic about the legendary breakout distorts history more than once, but always for good reasons. He uses fictional names throughout, combining several historical figures into a few characters; two key exceptions are Attenborough's Bartlett (a dramatic version of Bushell) and Donald's Ramsey (Wings Day). Garner's post-escape airplane hijacking never happened: several Allied prisoners tried to steal enemy planes, but none succeeded. McQueen's "hotshot pilot" Hilts is terrific film fiction: before the breakout, all of SL 3's American prisoners transferred to a new compound—none

participated in the great escape, though many served in the X-organization. But the escape's essential details, including Sturges' compressed rendition of the POWs' meticulous year-long preparations, are on the money all the way. One of Hollywood's greatest history-based films.

For Further Viewing:

The Captive Heart ★★★★ (1946) 108 Minutes (Michael Redgrave, Basil Radford, Mervyn Johns, Jack Warner, Gordon Jackson): The first feature film (riveting and super-accurate all the way) about life behind the wire in a WWII German prison camp. Embattled Czech Redgrave escapes from Dachau, makes his way to France during the 1940 Calais–Dunkirk debacle, takes the uniform and identity papers of a British casualty, then falls into German hands again. Confined in a POW camp, he answers letters from the dead man's unsuspecting widow (Rachel Kempson) to maintain his masquerade. Cutting from "Stalag 27" to POW family activities in Britain and back again, director Basil Dearden develops several ongoing POW–home-front epistolary "stories" into a power-packed chronicle of the war's effect on marriage and friendship. Shot on location at Malag Nord, a real Third Reich prison camp.

49th Parallel ★★★★ (1941) 107 Minutes (Anton Walbrook, Leslie Howard, Laurence Olivier, Niall MacGinnis, Eric Portman, Raymond Massey, Glynis Johns): Director Michael Powell's taut chronicle of escape maroons a small foraging detail of German submariners in Canada after their boat goes down in Hudson Bay. Reaching and crossing neutral America's northern border (the 49th parallel) is their one chance to escape prison-camp internment, and they barrel across Canada with a vengeance—burning books, mocking religion, and shoveling Hitlerite rant at German-Canadians every step of the way. Pursuers take them down, one by one, until only Portman remains. A unique look at challenges facing Axis fugitives trying to cross the parallel before America entered the war—and one of the era's first and finest Allied propaganda films.

Recommended Reading:
Paul Brickhill, *The Great Escape;* David A. Foy, *For You the War Is Over: American Prisoners of War in Nazi Germany;* Arnold Kramner, *Nazi Prisoners of War in America.*

The Halls of Montezuma ★★★★★

(1950) 113 Minutes

Director: Lewis Milestone

Cast: Richard Widmark, Jack Palance, Robert Wagner, Jack Webb, Karl Malden

Historical Background: June 28, 1944—Mariana Islands: Most of Saipan's 32,000-man Japanese garrison lay dead. Survivors of the U.S. Marines' fierce onslaught, including 17-year-old Yamauchi Takeo, were in pell-mell retreat toward the island's northern tip. Racked with dysentery, the starving, dehydrated Takeo survived by lapping rainwater off tree trunks. The Americans chased him through a long valley bristling with fragmented, stinking, blackened corpses hanging from tree limbs where artillery fire had blown them a day earlier. Finally surrounded by Marines imploring them to give up, a few soldiers and 4,000 civilians committed suicide rather than surrender. Only Takeo survived.

The war with Japan pitted American fighting men against the most tenacious enemy on earth and featured the war's most savage, pitiless combat. Two kinds of action marked the Pacific war: extended campaigns on large islands such as Guadalcanal—taken on January 8, 1943, after six months of bitter fighting—and briefer battles of nonstop, horrific intensity such as the three-day Tarawa bloodbath. But regardless of each island's size or terrain, fighting conditions and the order of battle remained the same. First came deafening naval gunfire and aerial bombardments, then head-on beachfront assaults by Marines storming ashore from naval landing craft. Furious Japanese counterfire often erupted before the Americans landed (Iwo Jima); occasionally, assault troops hit the beaches unopposed, only to draw withering artillery and machine-gun fire as soon as they pushed inland (Guadalcanal).

Preassault bombardment seldom killed large numbers of enemy soldiers. Protected by blockhouses of five-foot-thick, steel-reinforced concrete encased in flexible, spongelike palm tree logs, Japanese riflemen, artillery crews, and machine gunners took their posts when the American guns fell silent. Deep, interlocking fortifications, configured so that attackers fighting past one bunker advanced into a crossfire from two or three others, blanketed each island. (Enemy defenses on Betio, a one-square-mile dot in the Tarawa Atoll, featured hundreds of fighting holes and trenches connected by tunnels: when a position fell, surviving Japanese defenders simply vanished and reappeared in another place. One sector of the tiny island bristled with 500 machine-gun nests.) And worst of all, taught from childhood that they belonged to the emperor, Japanese soldiers never surrendered: they died fighting or committed suicide. Transport ships often left them, with no hope of reinforcement or resupply, to fight and die on isolated island strongholds. Thus, a grisly pattern, unparalleled in the annals of warfare, persisted throughout the Pacific campaign: entrenched defenders died in far greater numbers than their attackers. Only 17 men from a Japanese garrison of 4,500 survived the fight for Tarawa. They killed 1,000 Americans before the battle ended on October 24, 1943.

Tarawa and Guadalcanal opened a unique "island-hopping" strategy fashioned by Gen. Douglas MacArthur and Adm. Chester Nimitz to prevail in a theater of unprecedented size. MacArthur pushed northward from the Solomons toward the Philippines. From Pearl Harbor, Nimitz struck west, taking islands in the Gilbert, Marshall, and Mariana chains. Huge task forces combining assault troops, battleships, cruisers, and aircraft carriers flanked by nimble destroyers took key islands and bypassed others in a relentless advance toward Japan. The giant pincers finally met at the Philippines in October 1944. Iwo Jima fell five months later, and from there—on June 22, 1945—the Americans took Okinawa, the last stop before a massive invasion of Japan itself. It never came. On August 6 and 9, 1945, atom bombs vaporized Hiroshima and Nagasaki, ending the war and heaving the world into an ominous new technological age.

Great action sequences, fine performances, and excellent directing highlight one of Hollywood's best World War II films. Milestone skillfully weaves actual combat film and his own footage into a grim look at life in a U.S. Marine rifle company under fire (it isn't a pretty picture). Former chemistry teacher Widmark—a lieutenant who's seen so much action that corpsman Malden keeps him going with painkillers for fear-induced "psychological migraines"—leads the attack on a large Pacific island. His assignment: find and destroy Japanese rocket and artillery positions so well camouflaged that their deadly unopposed fire threatens to stall the entire operation. An exciting, realistic, meticulously accurate portrait of combat hell—no student of World War II should miss it.

For Further Viewing:

The Thin Red Line ★★★ (1964) 99 Minutes (Jack Warden, Keir Dullea, James Philbrook): Director Andrew Marton's adaptation of James Jones' novel views the long campaign for Guadalcanal through the eyes of Warden, a tough infantry sergeant, and Dullea, a green infantryman. Jones took his title from the familiar aphorism "There's just a thin red line between the sane and the mad," and Marton's subject is the "thin red line" separating the kind of fighting required of every soldier from the precipitous descent into utter barbarism that beckons more strongly with each new battle. As the Americans push farther into the island's interior, all of them draw closer to the line. A well-done movie with good performances and convincing combat scenes.

The Thin Red Line (1998) 171 Minutes (Nick Nolte, Sean Penn, Ben Chaplin, Elias Koteas, Woody Harrelson, Jim Caviezel, George Clooney): Director Terrence Malick's pretentious film embeds about 40 minutes of competently staged combat choreography in an eternity of awful historical distortion smothered, throughout, with dime-store "philosophical" narration. (Many voice-over lines are clichéd—and occasionally meaningless: "Are we all part of the same great face?"; "War poisons the soul!"; "Where does war come from?"; "Love—where does it come from?"). Even worse are Malick's occasional revisions of Jones' book to misrepresent American and Japanese behavior during the island-hopping campaign: at novel's end, for example, GIs overrun fanatically defended, heavily fortified Japanese positions near Boola Boola village, killing many enemy troops and watching most of the others commit *harakiri* to avoid the humiliation of surrender; but Malick's version of the fight ends with Japanese soldiers sitting passively (in the lotus position!) or falling to their knees and begging for mercy after GIs break through their defensive ring (the Americans summarily execute most of them). In fact, Japanese soldiers seldom showed signs of weakness under fire and virtually never surrendered voluntarily during the war's early years.

An American survivor's remark at film's end reflects the indifference to history underpinning *The Thin Red Line:* "Life ain't supposed to be that hard when you're young," he mumbles—apparently oblivious to a nightmare of suffering borne by thousands of American children during the worst depression in modern history. Worst of all: from start to finish, *The Thin Red Line* patronizes and insults America's World War II veterans. In one appalling segment, whining frontline stretcher-bearers try to beg their way out of recovering wounded men under fire; in fact, American medics and stretcher-bearers were among the war's bravest soldiers, routinely exposing themselves to withering enemy fusillades—and suffering high casualty rates—to treat injured men in the field. *The Thin Red Line* is awful history—and tedious viewing most of the way.

Battle Cry ★★★★ (1955) 149 Minutes (Van Heflin, Aldo Ray, Tab Hunter, Anne Francis, Raymond Massey, James Whitmore, Nancy Olson): A formulaic, much-copied classic, *Battle Cry* remains as entertaining today as it was 40 years ago. Focusing on Marine Corps boot camp, advanced combat training, and wartime romance, it follows a single outfit—commanded by Heflin—through a series of frustrating sideline assignments that lead to awful frontline fighting on Saipan. Realistic and well acted, with a standout performance by Ray.

Recommended Reading:
John W. Dower, *War Without Mercy;* Donald T. Regan, *For the Record;* Eugene Sledge, *With the Old Breed at Peleliu and Tarawa.*

Hiroshima: Out of the Ashes ★★★★
(1990) 100 Minutes

Director: Peter Werner

Cast: Max von Sydow, Judd Nelson, Mako, Tamlyn Tomita, Stan Egi, Pat Morita, Kim Miyori

Historical Background: August 9, 1945, 11:02 A.M.—Nagasaki, Japan: Growing impatient with skeptical colleagues' reluctance to believe his account of a new American bomb capable of destroying an entire city with a single blast, ship designer Tsutomu Yamaguchi suddenly stopped in midsentence and flung himself to the factory floor in disbelief. For the second time in three days he had seen the same unearthly, silent amber flash that preceded double atomic shock waves of crushing force. And for the second time in three days, he survived a nuclear conflagration inflicted on his dying—but still belligerent—homeland. Yamaguchi was one of 21 Nagasaki residents on holiday in Hiroshima when the first bomb fell. All of them had weathered the blast and labored mightily for more than a day to get back to their families in Nagasaki. All of them again faced nuclear annihilation, and all but one of them lived to tell the tale. Three days after its birth, the "Atomic Age" had produced what will surely remain the least probable statistic in recorded history.

By the summer of 1945, the Japanese had suffered terribly at the hands of Allied bombers. In July alone, huge B-29 Superfortresses based in the Marianas flew more than 1,000 missions per week against Japan's home islands. Conventional bombs had killed 500,000 Japanese civilians before the nuclear attacks of early August. American pilots had destroyed virtually all of Japan's fighter aircraft, and the *Enola Gay*—a B-29 stripped of all its weapons but the tail gun to accommodate "Little Boy," its five-ton atomic payload—would attack Hiroshima unopposed. (Located on the southwestern tip of Honshu Island, Hiroshima was the Second Army Group's regional headquarters, a staging area for troops assigned to foreign battlefields, and a manufacturing center for Japan's weapons industries.)

The *Enola Gay* took off from Tinian Island at 2:45 A.M. on August 6, 1945. At 8:15, bombardier Tom Ferebee released Little Boy over his aiming point—the T-shaped Aioi Bridge on Hiroshima's Ota River—and pilot Paul Tibbets wrenched the Superfortress into a sharp 155° evasive turn. Forty-three seconds later, the bomb detonated at an altitude of 1,850 feet, releasing a blast equaling the explosive force of 12,500 tons of TNT. In less than a second, two-thirds of the city disappeared. Shock waves roared outward from ground zero at the speed of sound, flattening 48,000 of Hiroshima's 76,000 buildings. Hundreds of survivors were blown out of their clothes. Ground-level temperatures reaching 5,400°F. turned stones and granite blocks within a three-quarter-mile radius from the hypocenter into glass. The heat flash literally boiled away nearby victims' internal organs and burned their bones to charcoal. Thousands of small fires ignited by overturned lanterns and charcoal stoves produced white-hot thermal waves and wind velocities of 500 miles per hour, fueling a hellish citywide firestorm. Many survivors described huge bluish-green fireballs that rolled down streets throughout the city, consuming countless victims unable to outrun them. Hours after the explosion, most survivors were still unable to speak or cry out. Little Boy instantly killed at least 80,000 Japanese; by the end of the year, 60,000 more had died from injuries and radiation sickness. Incredibly, the Japanese high command waited until August 15—six days after a second atomic bomb had killed 70,000 civilians in Nagasaki—to surrender.

A **fine,** fact-based film about the Hiroshima bombing and its immediate effects on three Japanese families, a German missionary, and three American POWs who survived Little Boy's initial blast. Von Sydow excels as real-life Roman Catholic priest John Siemes, but Mako steals the show as a crusty old Japanese infantry sergeant who takes a young survivor under his wing. Special effects are grimly realistic, and historical accuracy prevails throughout—except for one politically correct distortion of the facts: halfway through the film, Japanese soldiers rescue three American POWs staggering through Hiroshima's blasted streets from an angry mob. In fact, three of the five Americans who survived the bombing were killed by vengeful Japanese soon after Little Boy fell. The other two died horribly from radiation sickness weeks later.

Recommended Reading:
Michihiko Hachiya, *Hiroshima Diary;* John Hershey, *Hiroshima;* Adrian Weale, ed., *Eyewitness Hiroshima.*

The Longest Day ★★★★★

(1962) 180 Minutes

Director: Ken Annakin, Andrew Marton, Bernhard Wicki

Cast: John Wayne, Robert Ryan, Henry Fonda, Robert Mitchum, Richard Burton, Jeffrey Hunter, Eddie Albert, Curt Jurgens, Gert Frobe, Red Buttons

Historical Background: Midnight, June 6, 1944—southern England: Ramming a full carton of cigarettes down the inside of each trouser leg, Cpl. Frank Brumbaugh waited for takeoff with a mob of jittery paratroopers assigned to protect the western flank of the Allies' D-Day invasion force. Less than an hour later, he was drifting earthward through crackling antiaircraft fire over Normandy's northwestern coast. Arcing upward like bursts from a million Roman candles, multicolored tracers converged on the 508th Parachute Infantry from what had to be—by Brumbaugh's reckoning—every heavy machine gun west of the Rhine River. Suddenly, two white-hot projectiles straightened their course and rocketed straight for his groin. One ripped into the inseam of his right trouser leg, caught the outside corner of the cigarette carton stashed there, veered crazily away from his thigh, and vanished into the darkness behind him. Incredibly, the second tracer repeated the process exactly, smashing the cigarettes cradled against his left leg and blasting a huge, smoking exit hole in the seat of his pants. Seconds later, he touched down—completely intact and delighted to be the most ridiculous looking paratrooper in northern France.

Brumbaugh was one of 176,475 troops hurled against Hitler's "Atlantic Wall" on the first day of history's greatest amphibious assault. Preliminary schemes for a cross-Channel Allied invasion first surfaced in December 1941 (far too late for Winston Churchill: in June 1940, he'd promised that the British would heave the war right back into Hitler's lap—"alone, if necessary"—as quickly as they possibly could). It took three long years to marshal enough men and resources to launch Operation Overlord, tentatively scheduled at the Tehran Conference for May 1, 1944. Like everyone else in Europe, the Germans knew that France's northern coastline—well within range of warplanes based in England—would be the Allied target. Because Pas-de-Calais lay much closer to

Britain's southern coast than Normandy, Hitler figured the assault's main blow would fall there and concentrated his best troops, most of his armor, and his heaviest fortifications in the area. As Allied convoys turned all of England into a vast supply depot and staging area, German commanders Erwin Rommel and Gerd von Rundstedt expanded Wehrmacht coastal defenses, peppering every foot of ground between Brittany and the North Sea with machine-gun nests, heavy artillery, mortar positions, forests of barbed wire, fortified trenches overlooking beachfront landing areas, and death zones bristling with booby traps and antitank mines. Submerged "hedgehog" obstacles, capable of ripping the keels out of most landing craft, clogged approaches to the coastline.

Delayed for 24 hours by the worst Channel weather in a quarter century, supreme Allied commander Dwight Eisenhower's mammoth invasion fleet weighed anchor before dawn on June 6, 1944. (Making the initial trip were 5,000 ships, 3,000 field guns, 10,000 combat aircraft, more than 2,000 transport planes, 1,500 tanks, 15,000 support vehicles, and two artificial "Mulberry" harbors to quarter supplies and reinforcements for the gargantuan operation.) Covered by booming naval gunfire, the U.S. 1st and 4th Infantry Divisions hit Utah and Omaha beaches on the Allies' western flank, opening the long-awaited European second front. To the east, British and Canadian infantry slammed into Gold, Juno, and Sword beaches, fighting like wild men to fan out and consolidate the five landing zones into a continuous lodgment.

Four sectors fell quickly to the Allied battering ram, but Rommel's crack 352nd Division stood fast at Omaha, raking American troop carriers and amphibious tanks with machine-gun, artillery, and mortar fire before they cleared the water. Within minutes, the beach became a ghastly charnel house littered with corpses and burning equipment. Only a fraction of Eisenhower's shock troops floundered ashore, taking cover behind a low shingle shelf within spitting distance of the sea. As naval guns and unopposed Allied air sorties poured withering fire into German hilltop positions, Omaha's weary GIs slowly brawled their way inland. By nightfall, 150,000 Allied soldiers ruled more than 80 square miles of provincial Normandy—a slippery foothold, but crushing Allied air superiority (the Luftwaffe had fewer than 175 planes in all of France) saved the landings, easily severing reinforcement and supply lines to Hitler's reeling coastal defenders.

Two days later, American infantry and British forces from Gold Beach converged, nailing down Eisenhower's right flank and pushing the Allies' western perimeter 20 miles inland. For six weeks they fought savagely, measuring progress in yards and inches, through an endless snarl of fortresslike hedgerows blanketing Normandy's *bocage* country. On July 9, Field Marshal Bernard Montgomery's Second Army took Caen from fanatical German defenders. St. Lô fell on the 18th, and by August, George Patton's legions were driving battered Wehrmacht remnants toward Paris in a 40-mile-per-day rout. Nine months later, Nazi Germany was history.

More than 50 top actors, thousands of NATO soldiers, three directors, and several consulting D-Day veterans weave many colorful vignettes into a sprawling spectacular on the great invasion. High drama occasionally shoves historical accuracy aside. One error sends an American demolition team sprinting across Omaha Beach (under withering fire) to blast a passage through cement and barbed-wire obstacles with bangalore torpedoes; they finally succeed, and thousands of infantrymen pour through the breach. A few men from the 1st Infantry Division did blast through the wire in this fashion, but the main exits from Omaha opened after American soldiers skirted the flanks of German fortifications on beachfront bluffs and attacked them from the rear.

Despite this and various minor lapses, Zanuck's presentation of the invasion is a hard-hitting, reasonably accurate, and remarkably entertaining masterpiece. For D-Day—and aftermath—carnage, *Saving Private Ryan* is fine, but for comprehensive overviews (from different players' perspectives) *The Longest Day* remains the cinematic standard version.

For Further Viewing:

Breakthrough ★★★★ (1950) 91 Minutes (John Agar, David Brian, Frank Lovejoy, William Self): Praised for accuracy by D-Day veterans, but often confused with an identically titled sequel to *Cross of Iron, Breakthrough* opens at an amphibious-assault school in England weeks before D-Day. Commander Brian whips platoon leader Agar and his GIs into shape, then leads them from Omaha Beach all the way to St. Lô. Great supplementary viewing for Zanuck's more celebrated epic: director Lewis Seiler covers the entire Normandy campaign, not just the initial "longest" day, focusing (unlike Zanuck) on pressure-packed, in-your-face combat tactics. Especially realistic are segments on the fighting in Normandy's hedgerows—rock-solid four-foot-high earthen walls covered by hedges and bound together by the shrubs' densely woven root systems. A super little film for students of the western war's final months.

Saving Private Ryan ★★★ (1998) 168 Minutes (Tom Hanks, Tom Sizemore, Edward Burns, Matt Damon, Jeremy Davies, Adam Goldberg, Van Diesel): On D-Day, Captain Miller (Hanks) and eight rangers assault Omaha Beach, then head inland to find and pull Pvt. Ryan—the only survivor of four soldiering brothers—from combat. Spielberg's combat scenes are the finest ever—hands down. But *Saving Private Ryan* isn't the definitive D-Day feature-film history trumpeted by pre-release advertisements. For one thing, the invasion just happens, with no historical overview. And Spielberg doesn't get the weapons right. At one point, Hanks orders his squad to "ignore the Tiger tanks. Go for the panzers." But the word "panzer" referred to any armored vehicle—Tigers included—or to armored units (panzer divisions; "Panthers" were Germany's bread-and-butter tanks). Damon calls P-51 Mustangs "tank busters," but Mustangs were long-range bomber-escort fighters; P-47s were used as antitank fighter-bombers. One Spielberg GI can't define the acronym FUBAR (as if it were obscure GI slang: in fact, most WWII-era Americans, including Rosie the Riveter, knew it meant fouled up beyond all recognition"; it was an escalation of SNAFU).

But Spielberg blunders worst with his presentation of the soldiers' perspectives on the war: from start to finish they moan about the unfairness of their "chickens-hit" (tactically pointless) mission. All soldiers gripe, but this is carefully orchestrated whining, peaking with a democratic discussion on whether to continue or turn back—all with Hanks' blessing (he actually gives one man permission to bug out). A number of journalists have echoed film historian Neal Gabler's complaint that "this falsifies the sentiments of the soldiers of that time by having them declare that they're fighting only to get back home, when in reality they were avowedly fighting to stop Adolf Hitler." (Hence Spielberg's omission of context—and purpose—for D-Day: it lends force to Sizemore's remark that saving Ryan is "the only decent thing we can pull out of this whole shitty mess.") This is fiction, not history: many WWII veterans were volunteers, convinced that some things—a world without Nazi Germany, for one—were actually worth dying for. Spielberg clearly admires them, but *Saving Private Ryan* suggests, perhaps unintentionally, that they were mistaken.

The Big Red One ★★★★ (1980) 113 Minutes (Lee Marvin, Robert Carradine, Mark Hamill, Bobby Di Cicco, Kelly Ward, Siegfried Rauch, Stephane Audran): Formed in mid-1917, the U.S. Army's 1st Infantry Division—called the "Big Red One" because of its shoulder insignia (a bright red "1")—remains one of the most distinguished fighting outfits in modern military history. Between November 1942 and May 1945, Big Red One infantrymen fought on several of World War II's most celebrated battlegrounds: Kasserine Pass (North Africa), Sicily, Omaha Beach (Normandy), and the Ardennes, among others. The division saw so much action that by war's end 50,000 men—three times its normal, full complement—had served in its ranks because of high casualty and replacement rates.

Director Samuel Fuller's fine semiautobiographical account of his harrowing experiences with the division follows a single rifle squad—Carradine (a would-be author and Fuller clone), Di Cicco, Hamill, and Ward—through some of the war's bloodiest campaigns. Led by their tough veteran sergeant (nameless throughout the film and well played by Marvin), they survive bitter fighting in North Africa and Sicily, storm ashore on Omaha Beach, then drive through Europe all the way to Falkenau concentration camp in Czechoslovakia. Fuller proceeds episodically, depicting war the way soldiers experience it—as a series of bloody brawls with no end in sight. Terrific action sequences open less than 15 minutes into the film and include nightmarish restagings of the Kasserine Pass debacle (an awful Allied defeat) and the Omaha Beach bloodbath. An excellent war movie—one of Fuller's finest.

Recommended Reading: Stephen E. Ambrose, *D-Day June 6, 1944: The Climactic Battle of World War II* and *Pegasus Bridge: June 6, 1944;* Russell Miller, *Nothing Less Than Victory: The Oral History of D-Day;* Blythe Foote Fink, *No Mission Too Difficult;* Gerald Astor, *June 6, 1944: The Voices of D-Day;* Cornelius Ryan, *The Longest Day;* John Keegan, *Six Armies in Normandy;* Roger J. Spiller, "War in the Dark," *American Heritage,* Feb. 1999.

The Man Who Never Was ★★★★

(1956) 103 Minutes

Director: Ronald Neame

Cast: Clifton Webb, Gloria Grahame, Robert Flemyng, Josephine Griffin, Stephen Boyd

Historical Background: One of Britain's most spectacular WWII intelligence coups was Operation Mincemeat, a macabre project to deflect German attention from the 1943 invasion of Sicily. A product of Royal Navy intelligence officer Ewen Montagu's inflamed musings, the plan was fanciful and outrageous: Montagu would acquire an anonymous corpse, dress it in a Royal Marine officer's uniform, load it with phony documents pointing toward an Allied invasion of Sardinia and Greece (instead of Sicily), float it to a beach in southern Spain, and hope that Spanish officials would turn everything over to German agents.

(Finding a body without tipping his hand became Montagu's biggest problem. St. Pancras coroner William Purchase finally supplied one, dubbing it "Major Martin." To lend authenticity to the ruse, Montagu placed a bank overdraft and a steamy photograph of the major's fictional girlfriend in the corpse's wallet.) A Royal Navy submarine launched Major Martin—"the man who never was"—toward the Spanish coast in April 1943. Incredibly, the plan worked. After reading Montagu's phony documents Hitler spread his Mediterranean defenses over so wide an area that the Allies' July landings on Sicily were virtually unopposed.

Dating from the mid-16th century, England's intelligence service has included two major divisions since 1918: MI-5 (internal security and counterintelligence) and MI-6 (foreign espionage). Led by Sir Stewart Menzies, British agents performed every kind of covert activity conducted during the war. In 1940, MI-5 identified every Nazi spy based in Great Britain by cracking the key to Enigma, Germany's radio transmission encoding device. Especially critical was MI-9's work with French resistance groups to smuggle highly trained RAF crews downed during bombing runs back to England. (The standard escape plan routed fugitives southward from German-occupied northern France to the Vichy Zone and across the Pyrenees into Spain.) A stunning MI-5 "war story" supports arguments that England's 1940–45 bureau was the finest intelligence outfit ever assembled: Felipe Fernandez, an MI-5 double agent, spent the entire war feeding phony information to Germany's top espionage group. So thoroughly did Fernandez fool his Nazi "colleagues" that he received the Iron Cross for valorous service to the Reich. Rule, Britannia.

A witty, crackling adaptation of Montagu's best-selling book about Operation Mincemeat,

The Man Who Never Was features Webb (as Montagu) at his best and fine work by a top-notch supporting cast. (Grahame is wonderful as a hot-blooded, warmhearted "Lucy the languishing librarian," Neame's rendition of the young woman who penned the phony love letter planted on "Major Martin.") Like Montagu's book, the film focuses more on devising instruments of deception—letters, photos, secret documents—than on the larger problem of finding the corpse of a man dead from pneumonia (to simulate death by drowning). Neame includes speculative material imputing more prudence to the Germans than they really exercised.

For Further Viewing:

One Against the Wind ★★★★ (1992) 100 Minutes (Judy Davis, Sam Neill, Denholm Elliott): Director Larry Elikann's superb chronicle of aristocratic English expatriot Mary Lindell's heroic work with British agents and French resistance units to guide downed Allied pilots and other fugitives to the southern frontier of occupied France. Dominating wire-to-wire are terrific low-keyed performances by Davis (Lindell) and Neill (a composite character—"Guardsman" James Ligget—and, in the film, Davis' first wartime rescue. In fact, Lindell's initial underground efforts came earlier than the film implies, and her first British fugitive was a woman.) Elikann tells Lindell's elaborate story by mixing history (her imprisonment in Fresnes and eventual internment in Ravensbrück concentration camp) with complex, fact-based fictions. (Davis personally drives Neill to the frontier, for example, picking up a Luftwaffe hitchhiker along the way and charming the socks off his grateful commandant at Châteaudun. The basic story is true, but Lindell's real-life cargo was Captain Jimmy Windsor Lewis, later a brigadier general. Neill resurfaces as Davis' main contact in England, then finds her during Ravensbrück's liberation.) The film's main interest for history buffs is its on-target rendition of the danger, ingenuity, complex organization, and teamwork among many players marking underground efforts to return pilots to England.

Recommended Reading:
Richard Deacon, *A History of the British Secret Service;* M.R.D. Foot, *S.O.E. in France;* Ewen Montagu, *The Man Who Never Was;* Robert Jackson, *Coroner: A Biography of William Bently Purchase;* Barry Wynne, *No Drums . . . No Trumpets: The Story of Mary Lindell.*

Memphis Belle ★★★

(1990) 101 Minutes

Director: Michael Caton-Jones

Cast: Matthew Modine, Eric Stoltz, Tate Donovan, D. B. Sweeney, Billy Zane, Sean Astin, Reed Edward Diamond, David Strathairn, John Lithgow, Jane Horrocks

Historical Background: By September 1942 the Royal Air Force and America's Eighth Air Force had transformed southern England into an enormous military airbase. British bomber groups had smashed Cologne, Hamburg, and Leipzig in a series of "saturation raids" launched at night, when Luftwaffe fighter planes couldn't fly. Having seen his Spitfires sweep German bombers from the sky during the Battle of Britain, RAF commander Sir Arthur Harris insisted that night area bombing, even though it was imprecise and killed civilians indiscriminately, was the only prudent course for a long-term strategic campaign. American commander Carl Spaatz disagreed. He argued that U.S. bombers—armed with revolutionary Norden bombsights that gave bombardiers control of their planes during bomb drops—would wreck Germany's transportation network and industrial centers quickly enough to shorten the war. On September 8, 1942, Allied leaders struck a pivotal compromise: both air forces would pound Germany around the clock—the British by night, the Americans by day—in a nonstop, all-out blitz.

As critical as the RAF's role proved to be, there is no doubt that the bombing campaign's crushing results flowed mainly from high-altitude daylight precision bombing—and central to the Eighth Air Force's success was its B-17 Flying Fortress, one of the finest combat aircraft of all time. The plane's greatest strength was its sheer toughness; veterans have often insisted that unless a Fortress took massive hits it usually would not go down. They weren't exaggerating: films and archival photos show B-17s returning to England after sustaining dreadful damage over Germany—some with huge portions of horizontal stabilizers shot away. During the early stages of the campaign, U.S. fighter aircraft lacked the range to escort bombers all the way to their targets and back, a problem partially solved by armaments and flight tactics. Each Fortress carried at least 13 .50-caliber machine guns placed in six different positions on the plane. To make the most of each B-17's bristling firepower, the Americans developed an original concept, "daylight formation flying," that grouped bombers in tight "closed-box formations." Each box included three 18-plane groups flying in coordinated three-level "stacks," producing interlocking fields of fire in every direction. The new tactic proved devastating: many American gunners were skilled enough to pick off German fighters from distances of 1,000 meters, and as a group B-17 marksmen were so good that they shot down more German planes over Europe than all other U.S. aircraft combined—fighters included.

But the Luftwaffe developed a harrowing countermeasure: assault each formation head-on and shoot down the lead plane, spreading out the remaining bombers just enough for attacking fighters to penetrate the box and pick off individual bombers at will. (German pilots also attacked from above, dropping bombs set to detonate near the center of the formations.) As the campaign ground on, American losses mounted: during the heaviest raids, entire squadrons occasionally went down. Then, in December 1943, swarms of revolutionary American long-range fighters flooded the skies over Germany and turned the tide of the air war: the high-performance P-51 Mustang, fitted with "drop-tank" extra fuel containers and capable of flying twice as far as any other fighter on the same amount of fuel, began protecting the B-17s for the duration of each raid. The results were horrific: by the close of 1944, Allied bombers had destroyed more than 70% of Germany's factories, and at war's end every large city in the country lay in ruin.

Memphis Belle would have made a great 70-minute movie. Segments on the ground are clichéd and poorly done, but Caton-Jones exploits modern film technology to produce beautifully crafted, panoramic footage of B-17 formation flying and spectacular aerial combat scenes, highly praised for their realism by WWII veterans (and justification enough for viewing the film). *Memphis Belle* chronicles the legendary bomber's final mission, deftly embellishing the crew's ordeal to capture the horror of air battles over Germany: at mission's end, for example, two crewmen lie wounded, and the crippled plane barely survives touchdown. In fact, the actual mission went smoothly, and the bomber returned undamaged to England. But Caton-Jones adds one purely fictional—and inexcusably inaccurate—episode: the terrified navigator (well played by Sweeney) tries to release the plane's bombs prematurely to avert a near-suicidal second run over the primary target (obscured by smoke on the first pass). The incident never happened and pointlessly insults the bomber's real-life navigator, Vincent Evans, who won the Distinguished Flying Cross for heroism under fire.

For Further Viewing:

Twelve O'Clock High ★★★★ (1949) 132 Minutes (Gregory Peck, Dean Jagger, Paul Stewart): The perfect companion piece for *Memphis Belle*. Used by the U.S. Navy in a senior officers' leadership training seminar during the 1980s, *Twelve O'Clock High* focuses on the emotional toll on commanders who sent so many young men to their deaths in the great B-17 raids over Germany. Gregory Peck and Dean Jagger are superb in the lead roles. Low-keyed, but riveting and accurate all the way.

Recommended Reading:

Marshal Cavendish, Ltd., *Target Germany: The Air Assault on Germany*; Philip Makanna, *Ghosts of the Skies: Aviation in the Second World War*; Max

Hastings, *Bomber Command;* Thomas Childers, *Wings of Morning.*

Midway ★★★

(1976) 132 Minutes

Director: Jack Smight

Cast: Charlton Heston, Henry Fonda, James Coburn, Glenn Ford, Hal Holbrook, Robert Mitchum, Cliff Robertson, Toshiro Mifune, Robert Wagner, Edward Albert, Christopher George

Historical Background: By May 1942, the Japanese had won victory after victory in ten years of bitter fighting throughout Asia: they had occupied much of mainland China; they had attacked Guam, Wake Island, the Philippines, Malaya, Burma, and Singapore; two weeks after the Pearl Harbor debacle they had taken Hong Kong; in February, a Japanese submarine had surfaced off the California coast and shelled an oil refinery. It was the first assault on the continental U.S. since the Treaty of Ghent ended the War of 1812, and to the rest of the world Japan's war machine seemed invincible. The Americans were determined to prove that it wasn't—and six months after they entered the war, they stopped the Japanese onslaught cold near the island of Midway, handing the Imperial Navy its first defeat since 1592.

Paving the way for the stunning victory was the less celebrated Battle of the Coral Sea. After Lt. Col. James Doolittle's April bombing raid on Tokyo, Japan moved to extend her defensive perimeters in the Central and South Pacific. She struck southward first. Hoping to isolate the U.S. from Australia, the Imperial Navy sent a huge invasion fleet, led by three aircraft carriers, steaming toward Port Moresby, New Guinea. An American task force commanded by Vice Adm. Frank Fletcher and anchored by two big flattops (the *Yorktown* and the *Lexington)* sailed north to intercept the Japanese in the Coral Sea. The engagement took place on May 7–8, when—for the first time in naval history—carrier-based planes did all of the fighting: except for antiaircraft fire, the surface vessels' guns remained silent throughout the battle. American planes sank one enemy carrier and damaged another, while Japanese pilots sank a tanker, a destroyer, and the *Lexington;* they also crippled the *Yorktown,* but American engineers repaired the carrier in 48 hours, enabling her to fight in the coming Midway battle. Technically, the battle was a draw: America lost more ships, but destroyed more enemy planes.

Japan's southern strategy had failed. The course of the Pacific war now turned on the outcome of Adm. Isoroku Yamamoto's eastward strike against the American garrison at Midway Island. His objective was twofold: first, to take and hold the island as a base for attacking Pearl Harbor again, driving the Americans back to their own Pacific coast and putting Japan's home islands beyond the range of U.S. bombers; and second, to lure Adm. Chester Nimitz's Pacific Fleet westward, then ambush and destroy it as it raced to defend Midway. On May 25, a huge strike force under Adm. Chuichi Nagumo, spearheaded by 11 battleships and four carriers, sailed for the small island. Yamamoto's complicated plan began with an elaborate diversionary assault on Alaska's Aleutian Islands. But American cryptographers had broken the Japanese signaling code, and Nimitz didn't take the bait. Sending a token force toward the Aleutians to mask his own trap, he dispatched two carrier groups— led by Fletcher and Raymond Spruance and built around the carriers *Hornet, Enterprise,* and *Yorktown*—to surprise the unsuspecting Nagumo. By June 2, the American fleet lay 250 miles northeast of Midway, but during the next 48 hours its scout planes were unable to spot Nagumo's strike force. The first Japanese assault on Midway came before dawn on June 4. Seventy-two planes hit the airfield hard, destroying most of the U.S. aircraft on the ground but leaving the runways intact. Now Nagumo had to order a second strike, but he'd armed his remaining planes with torpedoes to defend his armada from possible attack by the elusive U.S. fleet. At this point, a dizzying sequence of unplanned events threw victory toward the Americans, who seized it and put it away.

Sighting no American warships anywhere in the area, Nagumo decided to unload all of his torpedoes and rearm his shipboard aircraft with bombs for a decisive attack on the Midway airbase. With unarmed aircraft from the first Midway strike clogging Nagumo's flight decks, 41 unescorted American torpedo planes suddenly stumbled upon his fleet. Knowing that they faced impossible odds without fighter protection, the U.S. pilots attacked. Within 40 minutes, scrambling Japanese Zeroes destroyed 35 of the torpedo planes, killing 68 American airmen. But their sacrifice turned the tide of battle for the U.S.: as the Zeroes landed to refuel, 55 American dive-bombers appeared—by sheer luck—above the Japanese carriers. In an improvised coordi-

nated attack lasting only five minutes, they sent Japan's three biggest flattops and all 250 of their aircraft to the bottom. The fourth they damaged so badly that it sank the next day. Nagumo's pilots managed to disable the *Yorktown,* but it didn't matter: the Allies, not Japan, would be on the attack in the Pacific from then on.

Midway will appeal to amateur historians for the same reason that many critics panned it: Smight uses footage from WWII documentary films to lend authenticity to his chronicle of the great sea battle. The film's presentation of the battle is solid and accurate. *Midway*'s biggest drawback is a banal subplot tracing the romantic entanglement of an American pilot and a young Japanese girl—it's dull, clichéd, and intrusive, needlessly interrupting the main story's continuity.

For Further Viewing:

In Harm's Way ★★★ (1965) 165 Minutes (John Wayne, Kirk Douglas, Patricia Neal, Burgess Meredith): Not director Otto Preminger's best work, but this long epic does convey the taut "we're hanging on by our fingernails" atmosphere felt by most Americans during the first four months of the war, when a decimated U.S. fleet stood alone between the marauding Japanese navy and America's West Coast.

Recommended Reading:

Edwyn P. Hoyt, *Blue Skies and Blood: The Battle of the Coral Sea;* Gordon W. Prange with Donald M. Goldstein and Katherine V. Dillon, *Miracle at Midway;* Thomas R. Buel, *The Quiet Warrior: A Biography of Admiral Raymond A. Spruance.*

Mission of the Shark ★★★★

(1991) 100 Minutes

Director: Robert Iscove

Cast: Stacy Keach, Richard Thomas, Don Harvey, Bob Gunton, Steve Landesburg, Carrie Snodgress, Andrew Prine, Stacy Keach, Sr.

Historical Background: July 30, 1945: Exhausted, burning with thirst, and chin-deep in the Pacific Ocean, 850 terrified men from the USS *Indianapolis* fought desperately to stay afloat. The water was alive with predators. Sharks and barracuda circled small groups of survivors, brushing against the screaming men's legs and torsos. Some crewmen had already been torn apart and eaten after swells had carried them a few yards away from their tightly grouped comrades. Sick with fear, many men fought savagely for places on crowded life rafts, while others, terribly wounded, gave their life jackets to shipmates and drifted away to isolation and certain death.

At 11:45 P.M. on July 29, 1945, the *Indianapolis* had taken broadside hits by three Japanese torpedoes. The heavy cruiser plowed forward as she gradually sank, leaving men strung out for miles in the vast waters of the Pacific. Though none of the survivors knew it, they had just delivered components of the first atomic bomb to the American airfield on Tinian Island. After a two-day layover there, Capt. Charles B. McVay III gave the order to weigh anchor and sail to the Philippines. Less than 48

hours later, his ship was on the bottom and his men in the water. Their ordeal peaked after sunset on August 1. Horribly dehydrated, some of the men drank large quantities of seawater. They grew delirious and began hallucinating. Some of them saw islands scant yards away populated with women who looked like Rita Hayworth. Others thought that Japanese soldiers had infiltrated their groups and began stabbing each other to death in the eerie moonlight. Worst of all, they were aware that no one knew they were missing—the Navy never reported warships' arrivals in port, since fighting vessels usually sailed in large task forces and recorded their own losses.

On August 4, a PBY navigator spotted several men thrashing about in the water below, and the last survivors were rescued by nightfall. Of the original 1,196-man crew, 316 remained alive. It was the worst disaster in U.S. naval history. That December, McVay was court-martialed for not ordering a zigzag course on the night of the 29th and for failing to issue orders to abandon ship quickly enough. He was convicted on the first charge, even though Mochitsura Hashimoto, commander of the Japanese submarine that sank the *Indianapolis*, insisted that zigzagging would have changed nothing. The court-martial suspended McVay's sentence, and he remained in the Navy until 1949. Nineteen years later, he shot himself to death in his own front yard.

A riveting account of the *Indianapolis'* final days and the ordeal of the men who survived the Japanese torpedo attack. Wonderful performances by Keach (as McVay) and Thomas highlight first-rate work by a fine ensemble cast. The film is thoroughly accurate except for its inclusion of a meeting between McVay and

Hashimoto that never took place but that adds resonance to its re-creation of McVay's court-martial and its aftermath.

Recommended Reading:
Dan Kurzman, *Fatal Voyage: The Sinking of the USS* Indianapolis.

Objective, Burma! ★★★★

(1945) 142 Minutes

Director: Raoul Walsh

Cast: Errol Flynn, William Prince, James Brown, George Tobias, Henry Hull, Warner Anderson

Historical Background: March 1944—northern Burma: Flanked on three sides by Japanese infantry, Lt. Logan Weston's battered veterans waited for a final banzai charge. For four hours they had repulsed probing assaults so furious and continuous that they'd been unable to disengage and cross the Numpyek River behind them. They were low on ammunition and out of water. No one had eaten in 30 hours, many had dysentery, and all were exhausted. Suddenly the howling attack came. But Weston's perimeter was so small and the surrounding enemy so near that waves of sprinting Japanese fired across the American lines and into their own comrades attacking from the other side. The Americans shot many enemy soldiers in the back after they had dashed all the way through the tiny defensive ring. In the confusion, Weston's men slipped across the river to safety. Famished, dehydrated, and spent, they ate, slept, and went into action again two days later.

Burma was a fetid, sweltering, malarial green hell. Insects swarmed everywhere, and the climate—six months of steam heat and six months of torrential rain—bred virulent diseases that killed 100 men for every combat fatality in 1943. The topography, an endless series of precipitous, jungle-choked mountain ranges separated by narrow lowlands, was worse. In the bitterly contested Hukawng Valley, only one road was suitable for military use; troops walked everywhere, single-file, hacking their way through forests of seven-foot kunai grass and measuring their progress in inches. (Bamboo was worse: packed with silica, its resilient stems dulled machete blades after a few strokes, flinging them back in the faces of exhausted men who fell to the rear after a few minutes' work.) In that kind of terrain, numerical superiority meant little: an experienced platoon could suddenly appear from nowhere, guns blazing, and shoot a rifle company to bits without taking a single casualty. Battling Japan in Burma, said Churchill, was "like going into the water to fight sharks."

No one really wanted the place, but no one could afford to let it go. By taking Burma the Japanese could better protect their Southeast Asian conquests, interdict supply lines to Allied armies in China, and seize huge reserves of oil and rice. For England and America, the logical overland route for flanking moves against Japanese armies in China lay through Burma, which also protected British forces on India's eastern border. In December 1941, the Japanese attacked, driving the Allies out of the country in four breathtaking months. By late 1943, the British had fought their way back in after three bloody offensives, and U.S. general Joseph W. Stillwell's Chinese and American composite force began to drive eastward from Ledo, hacking out a highway toward the country's only major supply route to China (the Burma Road). In March and April 1944, Gen. Frank Merrill's "Marauders"—3,000 tough American volunteers known also as the Galahad Force—completed two extended missions, disrupting Japanese communication and supply lines throughout the Hukawng Valley. On August 3, they won a bitter campaign for Japan's critical Myitkyina airfield. Stillwell's most charismatic leader, Merrill suffered a heart attack and retired after the Myitkyina victory. The Marauders disintegrated as an autonomous unit, but they had helped deliver the knockout blow that routed the Japanese from Rangoon and opened the Burma Road to China in January 1945. Surrounded and cut off from resupply, gaunt remnants of Japan's Burmese Army starved in the jungle mud until Fat Man and Little Boy ended the Pacific War.

The enemy gets little sympathy in Walsh's epic about the Pacific theater's brutal "sideshow." Released before the war ended, *Objective, Burma!* opens with aerial views of an endless wilderness identified as "Burma, a Jap-infested jungle and the toughest battlefield in the world!" Minutes later, Flynn and 50 Americans parachute 180 miles behind enemy lines to destroy a communications center before the reinvasion of Burma begins. This they do handily, but their airborne escape plan fails. Then an ambush destroys their radio, forcing them to fight their way back to American lines on their own. Despite excessive jungle-slogging, *Objective, Burma!* is an entertaining, accurate account of the rigors endured by Allied sol-

diers in Burma. Well acted and packed with character types copied in later films.

For Further Viewing:
Merrill's Marauders ★★★★ (1962) 98 Minutes (Jeff Chandler, Ty Hardin, Peter Brown, Claude Atkins): Excellent chronicle of the Galahad Force's tour in Burma. Historically accurate throughout, featuring fine combat simulations and—better still—focusing without letup on the terrible toll taken by the heat and mountainous jungle on Merrill's volunteers. Chandler and Hardin both excel in a movie without frills: no grueling boot camp, no sweethearts back home—just the Japanese and all you'll ever want to know about wartime Burma.

Recommended Reading:
Charlton Ogburn, Jr., *The Marauders;* Winston Churchill, *Closing the Ring;* Ian MacHorton, *The Hundred Days of Lieutenant MacHorton.*

O.S.S. ★★★

(1946) 107 Minutes

Director: Irving Pichel

Cast: Alan Ladd, Geraldine Fitzgerald, Richard Webb, Don Beddoe, Patric Knowles

Historical Background: Confronted in Normandy by Gestapo agents, Office of Strategic Services operative Narcisse Bouchardon spat in one German's face and kicked another in the groin before taking a bullet in the thorax. Feigning death, Bouchardon lay motionless as his enemies loaded him into a car and sped away. Seconds later he drew a pistol, shot the Germans, exited the car after it careened into a ditch, and strolled to a friend's house. He then returned to England, and four months later parachuted into France again. There were no wallflowers in America's wartime OSS.

In 1942, William J. Donovan began building the OSS around three basic divisions: Research and Analysis, Secret Intelligence, and Morale Operations (the bureau's propaganda arm). Aspiring agents learned surveillance techniques, weapons maintenance, cartography, code-breaking, signature forgery, and hand-to-hand fighting. Their high-tech equipment included the first wireless telephones, diversionary firecrackers that sounded like falling bombs, and potassium cyanide capsules (lethal when chewed, but harmless if swallowed whole). By midyear, OSS agents were active in major countries around the world. In Europe, their main theater of operations, they provided such accurate information on German oil refineries that Allied saturation bombing destroyed 90% of Germany's oil production before 1945. (Many OSS spies in Germany were POWs—captured Wehrmacht volunteers trained in espionage techniques by the OSS and clandestinely repatriated to gather information on troop movements, potential bombing targets, and production schedules for large factories.)

The agency's toughest test came in pre-invasion France, where support missions for the Normandy landings proved critical to Operation Overlord's success. In May 1944, more than 900 OSS agents roamed the country, many of them working in three-man groups called "Jedburgh teams" that included at least one Frenchman. By D-Day they had demolished more than 100 war-industry plants. (Plant administrators often allowed them to destroy vital factory equipment at night to avoid civilian casualties from saturation bombing.) Jedburgh teams trained, equipped, and led a powerful guerrilla army—the Maquis—that hammered away at enemy troop concentrations and assaulted German convoys headed for Normandy and Pas-de-Calais. They also disabled more than 1,000 German locomotives. (Bouchardon invented the "phantom train" tactic: he and his men removed engineers from inbound trains, set the engines at full throttle, and sent them roaring into their home stations, where they crashed and put several lines out of action for weeks.) A catalog of vital OSS wartime activities would fill volumes, but despite its glittering record, America's first intelligence agency died before its fourth birthday: in October 1945, President Truman disbanded the organization, and two years later Congress passed the National Security Act creating the CIA.

The first screening of *O.S.S.* electrified America with the longest kiss in movie history, a smoldering 21-second clinch between Knowles and Fitzgerald. Moments later, the film kicks into high gear and never slows down. Ladd—a former PR executive—and Fitzgerald join the OSS and parachute into northern France to blow up a railroad tunnel in a heavily guarded German military zone. The Germans kill their team leader almost as soon as they touch down, and the fireworks start. Caught up in the chaos following D-Day, the three remaining agents try to stay one step ahead of the Gestapo until their getaway rendezvous. A good film all the way, with early segments showcasing several espionage gadgets (including a pistol that looks exactly like an expensive briar pipe).

For Further Viewing:

Decision Before Dawn ★★★★ (1952) 119 Minutes (Gary Merrill, Oskar Werner, Hildegarde Neff, Richard Basehart): An accurate, gritty adaptation of George Howe's autobiographical novel about German POWs who volunteer for espionage forays ("tourist missions") behind Wehrmacht lines. Merrill is outstanding as the American officer running the tourist program, and Werner excels as an idealistic German volunteer. A fine suspense yarn and study of ambivalent U.S. attitudes toward the heroic—but traitorous—German prisoners.

Recommended Reading:
R. Harris Smith, *O.S.S.: The Secret History of America's First Central Intelligence Agency;* William Casey, *The Secret War Against Hitler;* James T. Rogers, *The Secret War;* Milton J. Shapiro, *Behind Enemy Lines: American Spies and Saboteurs in WWII;* George Howe, *Call It Treason.*

Patton ★★★★

(1970) 169 Minutes

Director: Franklin Schaffner

Cast: George C. Scott, Karl Malden, Stephen Young, Michael Strong, Frank Latimore, James Edwards, Lawrence Dobkin, Tim Considine, Michael Bates

Historical Background: May 14, 1916—northern Mexico: Seven years after graduating near the bottom of his West Point class, 1st Lt. George S. Patton, Jr., won an obscure engagement in John Pershing's futile expedition to seize Chihuahuan bandit Pancho Villa. (Two months earlier, raging Villistas had raided Columbus, N.M., stealing all they could carry and murdering 17 Americans.) During a routine supply run, Patton noticed several rough-looking characters galloping away from a hacienda outside Saltillo. On a hunch, he picked ten troopers and roared back to the ranch in three Dodge sedans; within seconds, he divided his force, cut the hacienda's escape routes, surrounded the building, and flushed three jittery horsemen, their carbines blazing, out of a nearby corral. With five pistol shots, Patton brought down the first rider. A sixth blast sent bandit number two cartwheeling to the ground. Seconds later, soldiers stationed near an exit road killed the last Villista. History's first glimpse of Patton's freewheeling genius on the attack was over in a heartbeat.

Two years later, the same vigor marked Patton's first WWI armored assault—a rousing sneak preview of the swashbuckling, headstrong drive that won battle after battle between 1943 and 1945. It came in September 1918 with an American drive to reduce the St. Mihiel salient. At great cost, British commanders had learned that massed infantry assaults on fortified positions always decimated attacking formations (see *All Quiet on the Western Front*). Newfangled tanks, they thought, would throw a decisive edge back to the offense. But they spread their armor thinly on a broad front, diffusing the force of mechanized thrusts and isolating machines slowed by engine trouble or mechanical breakdowns. Patton—a colonel by then—spotted the tactical flaw instantly. On September 12, he massed the 304th Armored Brigade's tanks in tight formations on the salient, breached the German line (crushing absolutely everything in front of him), smashed his way to the village of Pannes, and routed the Germans there. A few days later, he drew a reprimand from his immediate superior for leaving his command post to lead the attack—and a letter of commendation from U.S. commander George Pershing for his spectacular performance.

Twenty-two years before Hitler's *Blitzkrieg* swamped France and Poland, Patton had put basic maneuver-warfare tactics to the test—but WWI ended two months later, and nobody cared. After the war, Patton's blueprints for larger, faster tanks (remarkably similar to Germany's WWII panzers) drew yawns from FDR and most high-level American military officers. But Hitler's African and European conquests changed everything. Promoted to major general in 1942 by Eisenhower, Patton led America's Western Task Force ashore during the Allied invasion of North Africa. In March 1943, he rebuilt the disheveled U.S. II Corps and smashed Germany's 10th Panzer Division near El Guettar. A month later, he took command of the Seventh Army, directing U.S. preparations for a July 10 Anglo-American invasion of Sicily. Slated to protect British commander Bernard Montgomery's left flank, Patton landed on the island's southern coast, drove all the way to its northwestern tip in 12 days, and captured Palermo. Wheeling to his right, he led a breathtaking eastward run along Sicily's northern shoreline, mounted two amphibious assaults to block the Germans' seaward escape routes (missing narrowly both times), and took Montgomery's objective, Messina, hours before the British arrived on August 17. It was an

incredible performance, but Patton lost command of the Seventh Army after slapping two shell-shocked GIs (he considered them cowards) in evacuation hospitals before the campaign ended. Ike pulled him out of the line, ordered him to apologize publicly, and exiled him to career limbo on the island while Mark Clark led American troops up the Italian peninsula.

Five months later, Eisenhower brought Patton to London, ordering him to sit out the June Normandy landings, but promising him command of the Third Army in August. (Convinced by his presence in England that Patton would lead some sort of assault on France's northern coast, Hitler held 17 divisions at Pas-de-Calais while bitter fighting raged along Normandy's shoreline on D-Day; see *The Longest Day*). Posted to Omaha Beach in July, Patton joined 12th Army Group commander Omar Bradley's breakout from France's hedgerow country on the 27th. Five days later, Third Army was up and running, and Patton roared forward, slashing 440 miles across northern France all the way to Troyes in four breathtaking weeks. (His tactics dazzled everyone: at one point, individual Third Army units launched simultaneous smoking attacks in four different directions.) On December 26, he relieved the U.S. 101st Airborne Division at Bastogne after a grueling forced march, then drove toward the Rhine frontier—fuming hotly every time he ran out of gas—in a series of sweeping armored thrusts. By March 21, 1945, he had wrecked Hitler's Seventh Army, killing or capturing 120,000 Wehrmacht troops and losing fewer than 10,000 of his own. When Germany surrendered on May 7, Third Army units straddled the Czechoslovakian border, and George S. Patton was the most celebrated fighting general in the world. Almost immediately, his career took an ugly tailspin. Appointed military governor of

Bavaria, Patton publicly criticized Allied de-Nazification policies, prompting Eisenhower to fire him. On December 9, a freak automobile accident near Mannheim fractured the third and fourth vertebrae in his neck, transecting his spinal cord and paralyzing him from the neck down. Twelve days later, Patton died in Heidelberg of pulmonary edema and congestive heart failure.

Schaffner's blockbuster epic on Patton's spectacular exploits from 1943 to 1945 took seven Oscars, including Best Picture, Screenplay, Director, and Actor (Scott asked the Academy to withdraw his nomination). Neither pro-war nor pacifist—remarkable for a 1970 movie—*Patton* focuses on the military mind and Patton's high-octane personality by giving ample play to Omar Bradley's perspective on his friend's military decisions and flamboyant behavior. Historical accuracy suffers in places because of this: Schaffner puts too many stars and medals on Patton's uniform for his opening speech (he got his fourth star at war's end)—but Patton loved gaudy military outfits loaded with decorations, and that, for Schaffner, was more important than perfect period detail. Action-packed and riveting, with great performances by all, especially Malden (perfect as Bradley) and Bates (an absolute knockout as Montgomery).

For Further Viewing:
The Last Days of Patton ★★★★ (1986) 150 Minutes (George C. Scott, Eva Marie Saint, Murray Hamilton, Ed Lauter): In a muted performance, Scott skillfully augments his 1970 portrayal of Patton, completing a personal film biography of the old warhorse. Director Delbert Mann covers almost everything that Schaffner omitted, including a series of brief vignettes on Patton's early life and long extramarital affair with his wife's half niece (she committed suicide two weeks after Patton's death). Based on Ladislas Farago's books and scrupulously accurate, with one glaring exception—Mann soft-pedals a raft of anti-Jewish remarks made by Patton during a bizarre ten-week stretch in his tenure as Bavarian military governor.

Recommended Reading:
Martin Blumenson, *Patton: The Man Behind the Legend;* Curt Anders, *Fighting Generals;* Ladislas Farago, *Patton: Ordeal and Triumph* and *The Last Days of Patton.*

The Sands of Iwo Jima ★★★★

(1949) 110 Minutes

Director: Allan Dwan

Cast: John Wayne, John Agar, Adele Mara, Forrest Tucker, Arthur Franz, Julie Bishop, Richard Jaeckel, Wally Cassell, Richard Webb

Historical Background: Between August 1944 and mid-February 1945, the U.S. Navy and Seventh Air Force ravaged Iwo Jima—a barren volcanic island 775 miles from Japan—with 6,800 tons of high-explosive bombs and more than 22,000 5- and 16-inch shells. It was the most massive pre-assault bombardment in history, and everyone in the American invasion force assumed that U.S. Marines would hit the beach on February 19 and walk unopposed to the summit of Mt. Suribachi, an extinct volcano rising 550 feet from the island floor. Instead, Iwo Jima became the bloodiest slaughter in Marine Corps history, claiming 7,000 lives and 14,000 other casualties. In return, the Americans killed all but 216 of the island's 21,000 Japanese defenders. The cost was terrible, but American strategists knew that capturing Iwo Jima would shorten the war and in the end save lives. For months, Japanese Zeroes based on the island had decimated the ranks of U.S. B-29 Superfortresses flying from the Marianas to bomb Japan's cities and military installations. More critically, Iwo would be a perfect emergency landing field for crippled B-29s and a forward base putting Japan well within range of America's new P-51 long-range fighters, enabling them to escort B-29s throughout their bombing missions. The Americans had no choice—they had to take Iwo Jima.

At 9 A.M. on the 19th, Lt. Gen. Holland Smith sent his 10,000-man invasion force steaming toward its landing areas. Assault troops reached the beaches and began fanning out, unhampered by Japanese artillery or machine-gun fire. Amphibious tanks, half-tracks, jeeps, and guns churned ashore, then began floundering in the loose volcanic cinders and ash that covered the island. Marines sank knee-deep into the black sand, unable to sprint up the 20-foot-high natural seawall a few yards in from the shoreline. Within an hour, the entire landing area was a densely packed, chaotic snarl of men and equipment. Suddenly, Japanese field guns on Mt. Suribachi began to roar, raining steel and high explosives down on the logjammed beaches. The American bombardment had done nothing, because for months, enemy engineers had hacked away at the volcano, building an intricate system of bombproof caves, bunkers, and connecting tunnels that even the heaviest naval guns couldn't destroy. Three hundred yards from the beach, camouflaged machine guns hammered away at Marines foolish enough to peer out of hastily dug, shallow foxholes.

For two full days the Americans lay motionless on their narrow beachhead. On the third day, artillery spotters began locating Japanese cannon and machine-gun positions for naval gunnery officers. A thunderous rolling barrage began, driving enemy gunners back into their caves and allowing the Marines and a few tanks to scale the seawall. Using demolished U.S. vehicles and the bodies of fallen comrades for cover, the Americans smashed their way toward Mt. Suribachi inch by inch. Hundreds of pillboxes, minefields, and snipers' nests stood in their way, and the battle broke down into countless savage little brawls. On February 23, 40 Marines burned and blasted their way up Mt. Suribachi and planted an American flag on its summit, but the fighting continued until March 26. Badly damaged B-29s began landing on Iwo Jima as early as March 4, and by war's end more than 2,200 American bombers carrying 24,761 men made emergency landings there. The last Japanese soldier on the island surrendered in 1965.

Wayne—who earned an Oscar nomination for his performance as a tough-as-nails Marine sergeant—and Agar, an enlisted man who loathes the military, are at their best in this grim, realistic film that inspired countless spin-offs and inferior imitations. Once the troops hit the beaches (first on Tarawa, then on Iwo Jima), the action is entertaining and thoroughly realistic. Dwan expertly blends footage of actual combat with his own battle scenes, one reason that *The Sands of Iwo Jima* remains a perennial favorite of WWII enthusiasts.

Recommended Reading:
Richard F. Newcomb, *Iwo Jima;* Richard Wheeler, *Iwo;* James S. Vedder, *Surgeon at Iwo: Up Front with the 27th Marines;* Eugene Sledge, *With the Old Breed at Peleliu and Tarawa.*

Sink the Bismarck! ★★★★

(1960) 97 Minutes

Director: Lewis Gilbert

Cast: Kenneth More, Dana Wynter, Carl Mohner, Laurence Naismith, Geoffrey Keen, Karel Stepanek, Michael Hordern

Historical Background: On May 24, 1941, a huge projectile fired by the *Bismarck*—pride of the German fleet—crashed through the HMS *Hood*'s main deck and exploded near her magazines, igniting an enormous blast amidships. A 15-inch-gun turret weighing thousands of pounds flipped end over end like a threepenny coin as it sailed upward from the *Hood*'s smashed deck. In less than seven minutes, the largest warship in the world disappeared, leaving three survivors from its full complement of 1,417 men. The Royal Navy had a problem.

It could have been worse: though WWII historians focus mainly on Germany's U-boats, Hitler's navy had the nucleus, in the late 1930s, of an effective—though undersized—surface fleet.

Despite Versailles Treaty sanctions, Germany began building submarines and heavy cruisers (also called "pocket battleships") soon after the Great War ended. In 1938, Hitler ordered construction of a dozen battleships, two carriers, and 15 cruisers to battle the Royal Navy and enhance his U-boats' striking power against Atlantic convoys steaming for England. Fortunately for Britain, war came too soon for Germany's shipyards to meet Hitler's demands. Grand Adm. Erich Raeder, head of Hitler's navy, had to patrol the Atlantic with 200 submarines, a small fleet of destroyers and cruisers, and two formidable heavyweights: the *Graf Spee*, a swift, powerful pocket battleship, and the newly commissioned *Bismarck,* easily the mightiest warship afloat.

In late 1939, the *Graf Spee* raged across the South Atlantic, sinking nine Allied freighters and forcing England to respond with a sudden, deadly ambush by three battle cruisers. The *Achilles,* the *Ajax,* and the *Exeter* chased the *Graf Spee* all the way to Montevideo and into the mouth of the River Plate. Unable to break out into the Atlantic, the German captain scuttled the great ship on December 17 and shot himself to death three days later. With relentless tenacity, the Royal Navy went after the *Bismarck* as soon as she hit the water. Escorted by a squadron of submarines, the battleship slipped through a British blockade in the Baltic Sea on May 18, 1941, and steamed toward the North Atlantic in search of Allied convoys. But British scout planes soon spotted her, and an eight-day running battle that swept across the entire North Atlantic began. By May 23, 42 British warships, including five battlewagons and two aircraft carriers, were hounding the German dreadnought. On the 26th, several Royal Navy torpedo planes attacked the *Bismarck* and delivered what would prove to be a fatal blow: somehow, a single torpedo found the great ship's rudder and froze it solid. A day later, circling British warships poured withering fire into the *Bismarck*'s upper decks and gun turrets, inflicting damage so severe that the Germans had to scuttle her.

The Royal Navy had swept Hitler's greatest weapon from the high seas, leaving Germany's U-boats virtually on their own. They continued to sink Liberty ships until the end of the war, but a grand tradition remained intact—England ruled the Atlantic, and during the next four years she would send 75% of Germany's submariners to their deaths.

Fine performances by More and Wynter highlight this superb film. Based on C. S. Forrester's novel, *Sink the Bismarck!* gives a thorough, accurate, and remarkably lean account of the great 1941 sea chase. Gilbert cuts back and forth from action on the warships to taut planning sessions in the underground headquarters of the British Admiralty, producing a genuine white-knuckle wartime thriller. Highly entertaining—a joy for Anglophiles, aficionados of action, and students of World War II.

For Further Viewing:
Pursuit of the Graf Spee ★★★ (1956) 119 Minutes (Anthony Quayle, Peter Finch, John Gregson, Patrick Macnee): A very well done documentary-style film on the great pocket battleship's final days. Good production values and expert direction by Michael Powell and Emeric Pressburger keep the story interesting, but fine performances by Quayle and Finch (as the staunch, anti-Hitlerite German captain) dominate the movie from start to finish.
In Which We Serve ★★★★★ (1942) 115 Minutes (Noel Coward, John Mills, Celia Johnson, Bernard Miles, Joyce Carey, Richard Attenborough): Coward and David Lean co-directed this knockout,

flashback-style chronicle of a British destroyer's tour of duty from its initial launching to its destruction by German dive-bombers off the coast of Crete. With their ship (the HMS *Torrin*) on the bottom, a dozen survivors—including skipper Coward—cling to a life raft, weather relentless attacks by German aircraft, and review their past lives and service in the Royal Navy. Loosely based on Lord Louis Mountbatten's real-life wartime exploits aboard the HMS *Kelly*, riveting all the way, and on the money in its rendition of stiff-upper-lip British toughness in the face of Nazi Germany's onslaught. Attenborough's movie debut; well acted by all and expertly filmed by Ronald Neame.

Recommended Reading:
Dudley Pope, *Graf Spee: The Life and Death of a Raider;* Ludovic Henry Coverly Kennedy, *Pursuit: The Chase and Sinking of the Bismarck;* Theodore Taylor, *HMS* Hood vs. Bismarck: The Battleship Battle; Peter Kemp, ed., *History of the Royal Navy;* Nathan Miller, *War at Sea: A Naval History of World War II.*

Tora! Tora! Tora! ★★★★★

(1970) 143 Minutes

Directors: Richard Fleischer, Toshio Masuda, Kinji Fukasuku

Cast: E. G. Marshall, Soh Yamamura, Joseph Cotten, Jason Robards, Tatsuya Mihashi, James

Whitmore, George Macready, Wesley Addy, Leon Ames

Historical Background: With few natural resources, little arable farmland, and a huge population for its size, Japan's position grew increasingly weak after the Pacific settlement of World War I. During the 1920s, various patriotic societies began to press for aggressive expansion. Their voices were heard, since the Japanese military machine—especially the Imperial Army—had the prime minister's blessings and great influence on the country's conduct of foreign policy. World War II may in fact be said to have begun in 1931 when the Japanese seized Manchuria. In 1933, Japan withdrew from the League of Nations, and four years later a full-scale war broke out in China. (The bulk of Japan's army remained in China throughout the war, never firing a shot at U.S. troops during the Pacific island-hopping campaign.) The Japanese occupied major Chinese cities, attacked and occupied Indochina, then targeted the Dutch East Indies and other colonies in the Pacific sea-lanes.

By late 1941, Japan looked invincible. During ten years of bitter fighting it had won victory after victory throughout Asia. But there were problems. The occupation of China and Indochina had strained relations with the U.S. to the breaking point. An American export embargo and other sanctions against trade with Japan threatened to cut off most of her precious oil supply. Thus, on December 2, 1941, Japan's huge naval task force sailed east to attack the U.S. Pacific Fleet, which had left San Diego and redeployed at Pearl Harbor. Led by Vice Adm. Isoroku Yamamoto, the attack force included ten aircraft carriers and eight state-of-the-art battleships.

With newly developed long-range Zero fighters, high-altitude dive-bombers, and deadly torpedo planes—all in the hands of highly trained pilots—Yamamoto would attack an American fleet of four carriers, two heavy cruisers, and nine older battleships. The two-pronged assault began around 8 A.M. on December 7, and, incredibly, took the Americans completely by surprise. Virtually all U.S. aircraft on the ground were destroyed. Seven American battleships were sunk or badly damaged. More than 2,400 Americans were killed and more than 1,000 wounded. The Japanese lost 30 planes and five midget submarines. It was a spectacular victory, but Yamamoto hadn't destroyed his real targets, the American carriers. Six months later, he would pay dearly for that failure near Midway Island in the pivotal battle of the Pacific theater. The war was on. It would end in Tokyo Bay—on the decks of the USS *Missouri*—four bloody years later.

Dynamite. One of the best war movies ever made—historically accurate and riveting all the way, made more remarkable by the film's steady buildup to a state of gut-wrenching suspense even though everyone over age ten who sees it probably knows all about the Pearl Harbor story anyway. The long segment covering the attack is beautifully orchestrated—and guaranteed to knock your socks off.

For Further Viewing:
From Here to Eternity ★★★★ (1953) 118 Minutes (Burt Lancaster, Montgomery Clift, Frank Sinatra, Deborah Kerr): A perfect complement for *Tora! Tora! Tora!* and one of the finest period films ever made. From start to finish, it conveys flawlessly the atmosphere prevailing in the U.S. just before

the Pearl Harbor attack (staged effectively as the film's closing segment). Also one of the very few movies focusing on army life during the period. Fine work by a superb ensemble cast.

Recommended Reading:
Haruko Taya Cook and Theodore F. Cook, *Japan at War;* Stephen Badsey, *Pearl Harbor;* James Jones, *WWII;* Gordon Prang, *At Dawn We Slept.*

A Walk in the Sun ★★★★★

(1945) 117 Minutes

Director: Lewis Milestone

Cast: Dana Andrews, Richard Conte, Sterling Holloway, John Ireland, Herbert Rudley, Lloyd Bridges

Historical Background: September 13, 1943—Salerno, Italy: Shooting continuously and reloading as quickly as he could, Sgt. Chuck Kelly melted the firing mechanisms of three Browning Automatic Rifles before he began flinging live 60mm mortar shells with his bare hands at the Germans assaulting his position. Before the day ended, Kelly—later awarded the Congressional Medal of Honor—killed 35 enemy soldiers.

A nightmare from start to finish, the September 9 Anglo-American amphibious landing

at Salerno ignited one of the most savage battles of the war. Gen. Mark Clark's Fifth Army disembarked at 3:30 A.M. with no preliminary naval barrage, hoping to surprise German commander Alfred Kesselring's powerful defense force—a foolish notion, since Salerno was the only port on the Italian peninsula within range of Allied aircraft based in Sicily. Kesselring knew exactly where the assault would come, and GIs began dying as soon as their landing craft approached Salerno's beachfront. German guns blew many assault boats out of the water. The Americans who managed to clamber ashore faced barbed-wire obstacles, minefields, heavy-machine-gun fire, and enemy tanks.

Four days after American and British troops established a tiny beachhead, Kesselring counterattacked savagely, almost splitting the Allied force in two. But massive U.S. bombing runs and withering gunfire from Allied warships slowed the assault just enough for Clark's men to regroup. On the 14th, they began smashing their way toward the high ground surrounding Salerno. (Every man on shore joined the fight to break out, including members of a military band who assaulted a rocky hill christened Piccolo Peak by other GIs.) The Germans began falling back toward Naples, 25 miles to the northwest, the next day. When the battle officially ended on September 18 the combined Allied force had sustained 7,000 casualties; by then, most of the survivors realized that the bloody fight for Italy would only get worse (see *Anzio*).

Milestone's best work (along with *All Quiet on the Western Front*), *A Walk in the Sun* focuses on the basics: there are no barroom brawls, no girls back home, no basic training exercises—just the savage fighting and terrifying atmosphere surrounding the Salerno battle. During the first minute, assault boats roaring ashore explode, a platoon leader and his ranking sergeant die, and the men left alive—led by Dana Andrews, the only surviving noncom—begin walking toward their objective, a farmhouse six miles inland. Grim and tough all the way, a must-see film for WWII enthusiasts.

Recommended Reading:
Eric Morris, *Salerno: A Military Fiasco;* Carlo D'Esto, *World War II in the Mediterranean, 1942–1945.*

chapter 8

Korean War

(Overleaf)
Pork Chop Hill
(Photofest)

Chronology

1950

JUNE 25: North Korean People's Army (NKPA) invades South Korea.

JUNE 28: Seoul falls.

JUNE 30: President Truman orders U.S. forces to Korea.

JULY 7: Douglas MacArthur named supreme UN commander.

JULY 13: NKPA occupies half of South Korea.

AUGUST 4: Pusan perimeter established.

SEPTEMBER 15: Inchon landings.

SEPTEMBER 26: Allies recapture Seoul.

OCTOBER 1–7: ROK, American forces cross 38th parallel.

OCTOBER 12: Chinese troops enter Korea.

NOVEMBER 21: Americans reach Manchurian border.

NOVEMBER 27: Chinese attack U.S. Marines at Chosin Reservoir.

DECEMBER 1–11: Marines retreat to Hungnam.

1951

JANUARY 1: Communists drive toward Seoul.

JANUARY 25: UN counteroffensive begins.

APRIL 3: Eighth Army crosses 38th parallel.

APRIL 11: Truman relieves MacArthur for opposing American foreign policy. Matthew Ridgway succeeds him.

APRIL 22: Chinese spring offensive.

MAY 23–JUNE 13: American counterattack reaches 38th parallel.

JULY 10: Truce talks open in Kaesong.

AUGUST 1–OCTOBER 31: Americans win Bloody Ridge and Heartbreak Ridge battles.

AUGUST 23: Communists boycott talks.

OCTOBER 25: New talks open in Panmunjom.

1952

MAY 12: Ridgway succeeds Eisenhower as NATO commander. Mark Clark replaces Ridgway.

OCTOBER 8: Deadlocked negotiations recess.

DECEMBER 5: President-elect Eisenhower visits Korea.

1953

FEBRUARY 22: Allies suggest exchanging sick and wounded prisoners.

APRIL 20–26: Prisoner exchange in Panmunjom.

MAY 1–JUNE 30: Communists launch attacks along stalemate line.

MAY 28: Allies threaten to break off armistice talks.

JUNE 8: Chinese agree to UN peace proposals.

JULY 27: Armistice signed in Panmunjom. More than 33,600 Americans dead, 103,250 wounded (1950–53).

The Bridges at Toko-Ri ★★★★

(1954) 103 Minutes

Director: Mark Robson

Cast: William Holden, Grace Kelly, Fredric March, Mickey Rooney

Historical Background: Fall 1950—central Korea: Climbing out of a low-level bombing run, Ensign Edward Jackson felt two violent jolts microseconds before his F9F Panther Jet's canopy imploded into his visor, blinding him completely. Jackson had roared into a North Korean cable trap (mazes of steel cordage strung across narrow mountain valleys), wrecking a fuel tank and mangling his starboard wing. Incredibly, wingman Dayl Crow led him back to their carrier and talked him through a perfect touchdown on the *Philippine Sea*'s pitching flight deck.

It was history's first "blind" carrier landing, the signature coup of an aggressive American air campaign loaded with celebrated milestones: on November 7, 1950, F-80 Shooting Star pilot Russell Brown flamed a MiG-15 in air combat's first jet fighter duel; Korea saw the first use of carrier-launched jet fighters; warfare's first rescue helicopters—Sikorsky H-5s, H-19s, and HO3Ss—routinely "extracted" wounded soldiers from battlefields and rescued pilots downed in the sea or behind enemy lines. And for the first time, a militarily decisive air war belonged almost exclusively to "fighter jocks" and a tiny cadre of light-bomber pilots.

U.S. Air Force (USAF) pilots flew 60% of the Allies' logistic-interdiction raids and fought nearly all of America's air-to-air dogfights. (Throughout the war, superior pilot performance achieved U.S. air supremacy: China had far more planes, and only our F-86 Sabre Jets, a fraction of America's total fighter force, matched the Communists' MiG-15s—but by war's end, American pilots had gunned down their adversaries at a smoking 12-to-1 ratio.) The 3rd Bombardment Wing's swashbuckling B-26 light-bomber pilots performed brilliantly, especially on night raids against Communist convoys and trains. Seventy-two twin-prop B-26s flew more than 55,000 deck-level sorties during the war (an incredible 44,000 after sundown), wrecking 35,000 railcars, 168 bridges, and 400 locomotives.

For many reasons, naval aviation took center stage in Korea. During the war's early phase, carrier-launched sorties prevented the annihilation of UN and ROK infantry divisions unprotected by tanks or artillery. (Foreign-based USAF fighters were out of range.) Korea was a ground-combat theater flanked by oceans on three sides, and carrier-based tactical aircraft—especially tough F9F fighters—were perfect infantry-support planes, shredding thousands of enemy soldiers in strafing and low-level bombing onslaughts. Many Navy and Marine pilots had built remarkable air-to-ground fighting skills during World War II's long Pacific island-hopping campaign. (They were so good that during the Chosin Reservoir retreat, Marine Corsairs flew air cover so close that their shell casings fell on embattled Marines.) Because of ever-shifting fronts on the peninsula, USAF commanders occasionally moved endangered planes to Japan, but American flattops could follow the action, steaming close to battlefields and putting fighters above enemy troop concentrations in a heartbeat.

Swiftly dispatched carrier planes also demolished many Communist trains, marshaling yards, power plants, and bridges. (Yalu River causeways were the toughest targets: forbidden to violate Chinese airspace, pilots couldn't fly in from the south to attack the trestles lengthwise; instead, they followed the river, approaching bridges at right angles and firing only at their southern sections.) America's crushing multiservice air campaign wrecked Chinese battlefield logistics, limiting troop and equipment convoys to night runs and eventually strangling the flow of supplies to enemy combat units. More important: U.S. pilots killed enough Communist soldiers to gut their war-of-attrition strategy, forcing the Chinese to Panmunjom's negotiating tables and keeping them there until they gave in to every UN peace proposal.

Robson's pensive, hard-hitting adaptation of Michener's novel yanks naval reservist Holden—skeptical about the war's purpose—from home and family, plopping him into the cockpit of a carrier-based Panther. Authentic props and great aerial footage feature blazing F9Fs, plenty of flak, and hair-raising Sikorsky helicopter rescues. Highly accurate; for some Americans, Korea was the "wrong war," and many air force and naval reserve pilots performed brilliantly, but resented their recall to active duty.

For Further Viewing:
Men of the Fighting Lady ★★★★ (1954) 80 Minutes (Van Johnson, Walter Pidgeon, Louis Calhern, Dewey Martin): Director Andrew Marton's documentary-style clinic on life aboard a U.S. aircraft carrier operating off the Korean coast is made to order for history buffs. An accurate, nuts-and-bolts film—based on Michener's magazine article "The Forgotten Heroes of Korea"—with well-done aerial sequences featuring Panther attacks on North Korea's railroad infrastructure. Marton includes a gripping fictionalized version of Eddie Jackson's 1950 blind miracle-landing (Johnson = "Lt. Howard Thayer" = Dayl Crow; Martin = "Ensign Kennie Schechter" = Jackson). Pidgeon (playing Michener) visits the carrier and narrates parts of the film.

Recommended Reading:
Richard P. Hallion, *The Naval Air War in Korea;* Richard C. Knott, *A Heritage of Wings: An Illustrated History of Navy Aviation;* Robert F. Dorr and Warren Thompson, *The Korean Air War.*

The Manchurian Candidate ★★★★

(1962) 126 Minutes

Director: John Frankenheimer

Cast: Frank Sinatra, Laurence Harvey, Janet Leigh, Angela Lansbury, Henry Silva, John McGiver, Khigh Deigh

Historical Background: American soldiers captured during China's 1951 spring offensive faced a terrible ordeal. Driven relentlessly northward for two months, they survived on a diet of seaweed, raw sorghum, and rancid water. Men died from exhaustion and untreated wounds. If they collapsed, Chinese guards shot their throats out and left them to die. Many prisoners froze in high mountain passes, and some lost both feet to frostbite after Communist guards forced them to walk barefoot across half-frozen creeks littered with sharp stones and refuse. Their 400-mile march ended in the infamous Yalu River camps—clusters of squalid, unheated mud huts divided into closet-sized rooms housing a dozen men each.

Without exception, appalling living conditions and criminal brutality prevailed in the camps. Chinese and North Korean troops usually destroyed captured Allied medical supplies, allowing disease to spread unchecked throughout the camps—POWs died from untreated wounds, pneumonia, hepatitis, bacterial infection, malaria, bone fever, beriberi, and dysentery. Systematically starved on 500 grams of millet and corn per day, many prisoners lost half their body weight and died. Savage beatings and submersion in water followed by exposure to bitter cold killed many others. (Hated and feared the most by Communist personnel were Allied priests—major threats to relentless ideological campaigns against recalcitrant POWs: Sgt. Charles Schlichter, captured in December 1950, told interviewers that guards murdered every military chaplain brought to the camps between 1951 and 1953.)

"Reeducation" campaigns to convert POWs to Marxism supplemented torture and starvation-induced confusion with hundreds of dull, droning four-hour lectures. Systematic efforts to extract confessions of U.S. "germ warfare" began, in part, to deflect world attention from a small typhus epidemic spread during the massive 1950 invasion by infected Chinese sol-diers. Though some POWs made defamatory statements—often to let families know they were still alive—China's clumsy attempts at thought reform failed: of all the Americans taken by the Communists, only 14 faced courts-martial in the end. (Many prisoners resisted their humorless captors ingeniously. At one Yalu camp mired in the germ-warfare propaganda campaign, American officers killed a rat, tied its tail to a miniature parachute fashioned from handkerchiefs, and heaved it over their compound's wire fence. Baffled by raucous POW laughter, Chinese guards and physicians wearing surgical masks gingerly retrieved the ripening carcass and carried it at arm's length to a military lab for analysis.)

On September 4, 1953, prisoner exchanges began in Panmunjom. Though Chinese commanders often forced prisoners to haul their dead across the Yalu, burying them there and making a precise UN death count impossible, historians believe that the Communists captured 7,140 Americans. At least 2,701 of them—40%—died in captivity. (During World War II, less than 4% of the Americans held in Nazi prison camps died.) Of the 132,000 Communist troops captured by the Allies, 90,000 chose to repatriate at war's end. Among them were more than 400 North Korean women carried by rail to Panmunjom; en route, they removed their "imperialist-made" prison uniforms, urinated and defecated in the aisles of their coaches, and walked—stark naked and howling Marxist slogans at the top of their lungs—across the demarcation line. The 20th century has seen many wars larger than the Korean nightmare, but none more bitter.

In 1959, novelist Richard Condon coined the term "Manchurian Candidate"—any American

POW "brainwashed" to return home and kill on coded commands from former captors. (Many Allied POWs reported periods of disorientation and amnesia during their tenure in the camps, but brainwashing—personality destruction and "replacement" with new, easily manipulated "identities"—was beyond Communist capabilities.)

Frankenheimer's film follows decorated Manchurian Candidate Harvey from his homecoming reception to a climactic assassination attempt. Fellow POW and tormented amnesiac Sinatra works with Pentagon officials investigating Communist brainwashing campaigns, and the race against time is on. A dated—but entertaining—movie. Lansbury (Harvey's sinister mother) rewrites the book on female film villainy, and Gregory creates a perfect comic/baroque parody of Sen. Joseph McCarthy. Sinatra broke the little finger on his right hand training for Hollywood's first-ever martial arts fight.

For Further Viewing:

The Rack ★★★ (1956) 100 Minutes (Paul Newman, Wendell Corey, Walter Pidgeon, Edmond O'Brien, Lee Marvin, Anne Francis): Director Arnold Laven's brooding adaptation of Rod Serling's screenplay puts Korean War vet Newman on trial for making anti-American statements during his two-year stay in a brutal POW camp. Newman, O'Brien (his defense attorney), Corey (the prosecutor), and Marvin (in a knockout performance as Newman's fellow prisoner and accuser) are excellent. Unfortunately, a silly ending involving Newman's father (well played by Pidgeon) and reeking of yahoo pop psychology deflates what could have been one of the best Korean War–era movies.

Sergeant Ryker ★★★★ (1968) 85 Minutes (Lee Marvin, Bradford Dillman, Vera Miles, Lloyd Nolan): Marvin (Ryker) plays an American soldier convicted and condemned in 1951 for collaborating with the Chinese. Army prosecutor Dillman, troubled by blunders marring the sergeant's courtroom defense, risks his career to fight for a new court-martial and investigation of Ryker's claim that he was on a secret mission—authorized by a recently killed colonel—behind enemy lines. Director Buzz Kulik's remake of *The Case Against Paul Ryker* (a made-for-television movie) delivers a convincing account of the fierce passions and loyalties generated by the war's ideological dimension—completely new for Americans during the conflict's early days.

Recommended Reading:

Larry Zellers, *In Enemy Hands: A Prisoner in North Korea;* Rudy Tomedi, *No Bugles, No Drums: An Oral History of the Korean War;* Donald Knox, *The Korean War: Uncertain Victory.*

Men in War ★★★★★

(1957) 104 Minutes

Director: Anthony Mann

Cast: Robert Ryan, Aldo Ray, Vic Morrow, Robert Keith, James Edwards

Historical Background: July 20, 1950—Taejon–Kongju Road, South Korea: Feigning madness as victorious North Korean People's Army (NKPA) troops approached, Lt. Charles Payne sat straight up in a ghastly heap of mangled American corpses, ranting wildly and foaming at the mouth. Incredibly, thoroughly spooked enemy riflemen left him alone—at dusk, Payne joined remnants of several American rifle companies and slogged back to the 1st Air Cavalry's defensive perimeter. Three weeks earlier, 96,000 NKPA regulars escorted by Soviet T-34 tanks had swarmed southward into the Republic of Korea (ROK) through six invasion corridors dotting the 38th parallel (several east-coast amphibious landings completed North Korean dictator Kim Il Sung's pulverizing assault). Opposing them were 500 stupefied American advisers and an anemic eight-division ROK army without tanks, heavy artillery, or combat aircraft.

It was a breathtaking military fiasco. On July 1, Far East commander Douglas MacArthur hurled America's 24th Infantry Division into the meat grinder, but NKPA columns continued hurtling toward Pusan (a logistically vital southeastern port). Payne's nightmare recurred continually along the shrinking, fragmented Allied perimeter: again and again, Communist tacticians froze isolated US/ROK battalions with massive frontal assaults, then swept around both flanks and struck from the rear, blocking every avenue of retreat. One by one, ROK cities fell: Uijongbu (June 26), Seoul (June 28), Osan (July 5), Taejon (July 21), Kochang (July 29). But U.S. ground-force commander Walton Walker persevered, leapfrogging surviving units southward—fighting small, vicious engagements every step of the way—and buying time for Allied transports ferrying men and equipment to Pusan.

By August 4, Walker's legendary Pusan perimeter—a rectangular pocket slicing 50 miles inland from Pusan and stretching 100 miles from Yongdok to the Korea Strait—had formed, stopping the invaders cold and winning the frantic race against time. Hungry, ragged, and mired at the wrong end of overextended supply lines, NKPA

veterans hammered away at increasingly robust American defenses for six weeks. In mid-September, MacArthur launched a daring amphibious assault at Inchon (20 miles west of Seoul) and roared eastward, cutting Communist forces in two, smashing their Seoul-based communications hub, and fueling a ferocious Eighth Army breakout from the Pusan perimeter. The Allied offensive rolled into North Korea, scattering everything in its path and bagging more than 100,000 NKPA prisoners. By late November, Americans near the Yalu River could see southern Manchuria's barren wastes—and an end to the UN's bloody "police action." But days later, waves of howling Chinese invaders brought the conflict's darkest hour—and the U.S. Marines' most harrowing ordeal since Iwo Jima—to the frozen Chosin Reservoir (see *Retreat, Hell!*). The real war was just beginning.

Marooned in enemy territory two weeks into the war, Ryan leads 19 battered survivors toward America's new forward perimeter. Philip Yordan's screenplay incorporates many details peripheral to his story, but is historically on the money: Mann's NKPA troops, for example, risk death to steal American small arms—in fact, Communist units and South Koreans pressed into their ranks occasionally went into battle unarmed, cannibalizing weapons from isolated GIs (or corpses) in their line of march. An accurate, realistic, wire-to-wire nail-biter stressing the terrifying, naked isolation endured by Allied troops during the war's early days. Ray is terrific as a tough sergeant shepherding his shell-shocked colonel to safety.

For Further Viewing:
The Steel Helmet ★★★★ (1951) 84 Minutes (Gene Evans, Steve Brodie, Robert Hutton, Richard Loo): Director Samuel Fuller's cut-off-and-surrounded saga features a single GI facing circumstances similar to

Charles Payne's: during the war's opening weeks, rugged "Sgt. Zack" (Evans) survives an NKPA execution-style massacre, slogs doggedly (with a young Korean refugee) toward an ever-receding Allied perimeter, joins several heavily mauled Americans along the way, captures a propaganda-spewing NKPA infiltrator, and defends a Buddhist temple under heavy enemy attack. A realistic, accurate film (though it sounds incredible): infiltrators and refugees—400,000 during the war's first two weeks—flooded southward in 1950; NKPA atrocities identical to Fuller's opening nightmare flourished; and small-scale brawls flared everywhere before the Pusan perimeter solidified. Fuller filmed the entire movie in two weeks.

Recommended Reading:
Donald Knox, *The Korean War: Pusan to Chosin;* Michael Langley, *Inchon Landing: MacArthur's Last Triumph.*

Pork Chop Hill ★★★★★

(1959) 97 Minutes

Director: Lewis Milestone

Cast: Gregory Peck, Harry Guardino, George Peppard, Woody Strode, Rip Torn, Robert Blake, Gavin McLeod, Martin Landau.

Historical Background: April 1953: For 18 months, peace talks in Panmunjom had gone nowhere while bitter fighting raged continuously along an extended stationary front, splitting the devastated Korean peninsula in half at the 38th parallel. A mid-century "police action" had begun to resemble World War I's awful stalemate. The entire theater of battle lay within a desolate, narrow no-man's-land separating two massive trench systems. More and more, progress at the negotiating table hinged on the West's readiness to defend strategically worthless ground against massive assaults launched by the Chinese to break the will of their adversaries.

Some of the worst fighting during this stage of the war took place on Pork Chop Hill, a steep, rocky uplift west of the village of Ch'orwon and just south of what soon would become the cease-fire line. In March, Chinese assault troops had seized "Old Baldy," a low peak overlooking Pork Chop Hill from the southwest. They went after Pork Chop on April 16, mounting furious night attacks that trapped a 96-man U.S. garrison there. By 2 A.M. on the 17th, the Communists held most of the hill. Desperate American survivors fought on from isolated bunkers and revetments that dotted a broken trenchline ringing the high ground. At 4:30 A.M., Lt. Joe Clemons led King Company—a tough, veteran outfit—in a counterattack up the hill's reverse slope. For four hours the assault reeled forward through a chaos of shellholes, collapsed trenches, shattered bunkers, loudspeakers blaring Chinese propaganda, and withering fire from Communist positions near the hill's crest. A trail of dead and wounded men marked every step of the advance. By 8 A.M., King Company had smashed its way through the enemy's defensive center, finally taking—and barely holding—the high trenches.

Fifty-five weary Americans now faced hundreds of Chinese soldiers across 15 short yards of blasted, treeless earth. For Clemons, the fight to retake Pork Chop Hill had become a nightmare in slow motion. He was outflanked. His lines of communication with rear-echelon groups had broken down. He sent message after message requesting more men and supplies, but he hadn't had time to count and report his casualties. Assuming that King Company had taken minimal losses and driven the Chinese off the hill, regimental headquarters dispatched a public relations officer to photograph the aftermath of a grand American victory. Clemons sent him packing with another plea for help. (A surreal coincidence illustrates the battle's horrible dreamlike quality: a company of desperately needed reinforcements eventually arrived, only to be recalled by battalion HQ as soon as they showed up—and they were led by Clemons' brother-in-law, who wasn't even thought to be in Korea at the time.)

At 4 P.M., the exhausted Americans regrouped, moved back, and dug in around Pork Chop Hill's highest promontory. Only 25 of them were left. They waited—without food or water, their ammunition almost spent, glassy-eyed with fatigue—but still grimly determined to take out as many Chinese as they could when the final human wave assault came. Small-arms fire poured in on them throughout the afternoon. Tough and disciplined to the bitter end, they shot back—one round at a time—whenever a likely target appeared beyond their perimeter. (Clemons himself killed at least two snipers from distances of 100 yards.) As night fell, the Chinese began to close in. Then, at the very last minute, orders to relieve Clemons' tiny detachment came down from regimental headquarters. Attacking from both flanks, two reinforced rifle companies rolled over the stunned Chinese,

sweeping them from Pork Chop Hill and securing it for good. (The Communists tried to recapture the hill many times, but they never advanced beyond the Americans' first-line trenches.) At 9:30 P.M., Clemons and his battered survivors began the long walk back to the rear. Of the 135 men who had begun the murderous journey up the slopes of Pork Chop Hill, 14 were still standing. A half-century later, few people remember their heroic stand, but it wrecked Communist bargaining power in Panmunjom's peace negotiations: three months after Clemons' ordeal, the guns fell silent along the 38th parallel.

This grim account of the brutal struggle for Pork Chop Hill focuses entirely on the battle's critical second day. Gregory Peck's elegant, understated portrait of Joe Clemons equals or surpasses any other performance of his long career. Almost as outstanding are Guardino, Strode, Torn, Blake, McLeod, and Fell—at the time a cast of unknowns. As history, the movie is unfailingly accurate, delivering a powerful account of Clemons' harrowing 18-hour trial by fire. Veterans lavish unmixed praise on *Pork Chop Hill* as the most realistic film presentation of infantry combat that they've ever seen. It is the one movie to view for a concise, powerful look at what the bloody Korean War was really like.

Recommended Reading:
S.L.A. Marshall, *Pork Chop Hill: The American Fighting Man in Action;* Max Hastings, *The Korean War.*

Retreat, Hell! ★★★★

(1952) 95 Minutes

Director: Joseph H. Lewis

Cast: Frank Lovejoy, Richard Carlson, Russ Tamblyn, Anita Louise

Historical Background: November 27, 1950—western arm, Chosin Reservoir: Without warning, hordes of Communist Chinese (CCF) regulars converged from all compass points on Pfc. Raul Rendon's U.S. Marine rifle company. Blazing rifle fire tore into Rendon's legs, catapulting him down a short slope into another Marine's foxhole. Offered a cigarette by the stunned rifleman, Rendon thought hard, then refused: smoking, he'd decided, was bad for his health. Temperatures hovering at –25° had finally strangled even the toughest Marines' reasoning processes. (Equipment fared worse: air-cooled machine guns froze solid—oil, moving parts, everything—and only early-WWII guns, their water jackets loaded with antifreeze, saved the Americans from annihilation.)

Incredibly, China's onslaught surprised Allied leaders completely. In October, Eighth Army and X Corps troops had consolidated near Seoul after MacArthur's Inchon landings, forming huge columns and slicing northward through mountain valleys toward the Yalu River (see *Men in War*). On the 24th, three CCF divisions had attacked South Korean (ROK) and U.S. forces along a sprawling, discontinuous front stretching from Unsan (west) to the Hung-

nam Road (east). It looked like a major offensive aimed at driving the Allies southward to the Korea Strait, but on November 7 the Chinese vanished, leaving ghastly tiers of CCF dead scattered along the UN perimeter. Noting the carnage, Allied strategists pronounced the convulsion a rousing win.

But the assault was just an overture—a series of strategic probes designed to register Allied positions for artillery fire and the irresistible "human sea" attacks that soon flattened Raul Rendon and his buddies. Sleeping by day, marching by night, and shooting careless stragglers, CCF field commanders covertly slipped 200,000 men into Korea by late November. They attacked in the west on the 25th, steamrolling Eighth Army veterans toward the 38th parallel. On the 27th, they surrounded thousands of Marines on the Chosin Plateau, 35 miles from Manchuria. Fighting like wild men for 72 hours, the Marines stood fast, repulsing continual assaults and inflicting horrific losses on the swarming Chinese.

On November 30, General O. P. Smith ordered a 78-mile withdrawal to the port city of Hungnam. Hauling all of their dead and wounded with them, 10,000 Marines launched a ferocious, perfectly disciplined drive to the sea. (Smith's remark "We're not retreating; we're attacking in another direction" was literally true: the CCF cordon made the American withdrawal a continuous assault against enemy infantry dug in along the Marines' line-of-march.) Heroics bordering on madness unfolded round the clock: at Toktong Pass, a single rifle company battled two Chinese regiments to a standstill for six days, preserving a vital gap in the CCF ring and allowing the American column to pour through. On December 10, the column's point reached Hungnam.

Groaning with troops and North Korean refugees, the last ships left the shattered city on December 24. Eight days later, a huge Chinese offensive rolled into South Korea. In February, UN defenders held the line at Chipyong-ni, gradually drove the Chinese back to the 38th parallel, and the war sank into awful stalemate (see *Pork Chop Hill*). The bloody deadlock floundered on for two more years.

Lewis' blend of newsreel footage and scripted action delivers a first-rate account of the 1st Marines' Korean tour, from Inchon through the Chosin retreat. Dramatically weak in spots—thanks mainly to Tamblyn's gung-ho 17-year-old (he welcomes the attack at Chosin because he doesn't want to rotate home)—but scrupulously accurate renditions of the Inchon landings, street fighting in Seoul, and the withdrawal to Hungnam make *Retreat, Hell!* a must for Korean War aficionados. Lewis' title incorporates the inaccurate popular version of Smith's famous description of the retreat.

For Further Viewing:

Fixed Bayonets ★★★★ (1951) 92 Minutes (Richard Basehart, Michael O'Shea, Gene Evans, Craig Hill): Led by Evans and Basehart, 48 hand-picked infantrymen fight a vicious rearguard action to protect their reeling division's pell-mell retreat during the January 1951 Chinese offensive. Snipers and mortar teams start picking them off until only a few remain, determined to hold until their assigned "bug-out" hour. One of director Samuel Fuller's finest films, realistic all the way (including an impromptu clinic—GI-style—on diagnosing and preventing frostbite!). Hill fighting—authentic and grim—begins minutes into the film and never lets up.

Recommended Reading:

Eric Hammel, *Chosin: Heroic Ordeal of the Korean War*; Harry Middleton, *The Compact History of the Korean War*.

chapter 9

Unity and Upheaval:
USA, 1950–1975

(Overleaf)
American Graffiti
(Photofest)

Chronology

1950

FEBRUARY: Sen. Joseph McCarthy claims State Department employs 205 Communists.

1951

FEBRUARY 26: The 22nd Amendment limits presidents to two terms.

1952

NOVEMBER 4: Eisenhower elected president.

1953

JUNE 19: Julius and Ethel Rosenberg executed for atomic espionage.

1954

DECEMBER 2: Senate censures McCarthy for conduct during public hearings.

1955

MAY 31: Racial segregation in schools banned.

1956

NOVEMBER 6: Eisenhower reelected.

1957

SEPTEMBER 9: Eisenhower signs first civil rights bill.

OCTOBER 4: USSR launches *Sputnik.*

1958

JANUARY 31: U.S. launches first unmanned satellite.

JULY 28: NASA created.

1959

JANUARY 3: Alaska becomes 49th state.

AUGUST 21: Hawaii becomes 50th state.

1960

SEPTEMBER 26: First television debate between presidential candidates Nixon and Kennedy.

NOVEMBER 7: JFK elected president.

1961

MAY 5: Alan Shepard makes first American manned spaceflight.

1962

FEBRUARY 20: John Glenn becomes first American to orbit the earth.

SEPTEMBER 30: U.S. marshals escort James Meredith, University of Mississippi's first black student, onto campus.

1963

JUNE 12: Civil rights leader Medgar Evers murdered.

NOVEMBER 22: JFK assassinated; suspect Lee Harvey Oswald arrested.

NOVEMBER 24: Jack Ruby shoots Oswald.

1964

JULY 2: LBJ signs 1964 Civil Rights Act.

NOVEMBER 3: LBJ reelected.

1965
FEBRUARY 21: Malcolm X assassinated.

1966
JUNE 6: James Meredith killed.

1967
JULY 12–17: Newark race riots kill 26.

JULY 23–27: Detroit race riots kill 43.

1968
FEBRUARY 1: Richard Nixon announces candidacy for Republican presidential nomination.

MARCH 31: LBJ announces he will not seek reelection.

APRIL 4: Martin Luther King killed by James Earl Ray.

APRIL 11: LBJ signs 1968 Civil Rights Act.

JUNE 5: Sirhan Sirhan assassinates Robert Kennedy.

AUGUST 29: Democratic National Convention in Chicago nominates Hubert Humphrey for president. Police and antiwar demonstrators clash.

NOVEMBER 5: Nixon elected.

1969
JULY 20: Neil Armstrong walks on moon.

1970
MAY 4: Kent State shootings.

JULY 4: Thousands gather in Washington to support Nixon's Vietnam war policies.

1971
APRIL 20: School busing ruled constitutional.

1972
JUNE 17: Five men arrested for burglarizing Democratic National Headquarters in Watergate apartments.

NOVEMBER 7: Nixon reelected.

1973
MAY 17: Senate opens hearings on White House involvement in Watergate.

AUGUST 6: Justice Department announces investigation of Spiro Agnew for taking kickbacks as governor of Maryland.

OCTOBER 10: Agnew resigns. Nixon replaces him with Gerald Ford.

1974
JULY 30: Three articles of impeachment against Nixon approved.

AUGUST 9: Nixon resigns, Ford becomes president.

1975
SEPTEMBER 5: Lynette Fromme tries to kill Ford in Sacramento.

SEPTEMBER 22: Sara Jane Moore wounds Ford in San Francisco.

American Graffiti ★★★★★

(1973) 110 Minutes

Director: George Lucas

Cast: Richard Dreyfuss, Ron Howard, Paul LeMat, Cindy Williams, Charles Martin Smith, Candy Clark

Historical Background: In 1957, the biggest bomb ever dropped on North America—Ford Motor Co.'s high-tech Edsel—hit the ground limping, rolled over quietly, and died unmourned. During the late fifties, engine efficiency meant nothing to U.S. consumers. They wanted longer-lower-wider, and they got it: most 1958–59 General Motors models sported 55-inch heights, road-to-roof, and blinding chrome body trim. More than any other index, Detroit's automobiles reflected America's mammoth power and wealth during the fifties and sixties.

It was a dazzling, unprecedented spectacle: still shackled by post-Armageddon rationing to strict allotments of meat, cheese, and sugar, mid-1950s Europeans could only gape in wonder as two-car American families averaged one new model every other year. Most Americans owned television sets. Many purchased air-conditioned houses featuring all-electric kitchens and automatic washing machines. Virtually everybody went to high school, and by 1962, millions enrolled in college. America's golden age was cruising—in high gear—and it would continue through the early 1970s.

Part of it was luck—U.S. cities never felt WWII's awful fury—but it was no accident: postwar America built unheard-of prosperity and social unity through business savvy and judicious public policy. Bankrolled by the GI Bill, more than 2 million veterans joined a growing pool of college graduates and earned degrees between 1946 and 1962. They chased career opportunities all over the country, giving the U.S. an evenly distributed white-collar population and the most highly educated workforce in history. Americans invented transistors, put telephones in most households, launched the computer age, pioneered private-sector commercial aviation, and built a 42,000-mile interstate highway network unifying a single nationwide economic market. By 1960, New York stockbrokers and California investors were practically next-door neighbors.

And their neighborhoods were probably similar. During the fifties, 30 million Americans moved to the suburbs and started families, building a huge middle-class subculture with all the trimmings (PTA, drive-in restaurants, Little League baseball). By 1960, industries serving a novel American subspecies, suburban teen consumers, banked stupefying profits: baby boomers enjoyed unchaperoned "car dates," for example, prompting high school girls to spend more than $20 million a year on lipstick. Boomers dressed, talked, behaved, and—above all—danced differently. On average they each burned a cool $375 a year on clothes, movies, stereos, and new tunes from Elvis, Little Richard, the Platters, the Everly Brothers, Buddy Holly, Ritchie Valens—the list is endless, and it represents a way of life still resonant in the American memory. It wasn't perfect, and it began unraveling in 1967—but millions of people spanning two generations still miss it.

An exuberant, high-voltage flip side to *Blackboard Jungle* (Lucas' opening credits roll to "Rock Around the Clock"), featuring a fine, star-making performance by Dreyfuss. A small-town Class of '62 cruises the Friday-night strip together for the last time, building a comprehensive portrait of an entire era in less than two hours. Meticulous period detail—music, clothes, hot rods, drive-in waitresses on roller skates—and a muted sense that all of this will end (very soon, and not just for the graduates) add up to near-perfect fictional history.

Recommended Reading:
Michael Elliott, *The Day Before Yesterday: Reconsidering America's Past, Rediscovering the Present.*

Apollo 13 ★★★★★

(1995) 139 Minutes

Director: Ron Howard

Cast: Tom Hanks, Ed Harris, Kevin Bacon, Bill Paxton, Gary Sinise, Kathleen Quinlan

Historical Background: July 20, 1969—*Apollo 11* Lunar Excursion Module (LEM): A half-mile above the moon's surface, *Apollo 11*

commander Neil Armstrong reeled at the view rushing toward his plummeting LEM *(Eagle).* NASA's Sea of Tranquillity landing site was a gigantic crater ringed with towering boulders. Mounting a desperate search, Armstrong finally found a flat spot and touched down—with 16 seconds' worth of fuel left in his descent engine.

Potential catastrophe loomed large for astronauts of the late sixties and early seventies. Ignition, lift-off, and reentry spooked NASA's toughest customers—including John Glenn, the first American to orbit Earth. On February 20, 1962, he climbed into *Friendship 7*—a tiny space capsule fixed atop an enormous Atlas rocket—and waited for oceans of liquid oxygen to detonate beneath him; 150 vertical miles later, he was streaking around the world at 18,000 mph. Five hours after liftoff he blazed back into Earth's atmosphere, his heat shield burning away one layer at a time, as designed. Then, seconds after he'd spotted sheets of flame crackling outside his porthole, malfunctioning alarm lights prompted ground controllers to warn him of a possible shield failure. Even though cabin temperatures remained rock-steady, Glenn believed that *Friendship 7* had become an inferno certain to incinerate well before splashdown. Only after hitting the Atlantic's icy waters did he breathe easy: unjettisoned retrorocket straps and normal 5,000° heat-shield temperatures had caused the harmless fire.

On May 5, 1961, Alan Shepard had piloted America's first manned spaceflight, a 15-minute suborbital pop-up followed by Gus Grissom's identical July 21 mission. Gordon Cooper's spectacular 22-revolution voyage capped NASA's orbital-flight program in May 1963. Stalked all the way by Soviet cosmonauts,

America won a fiercely contested sprint for the moon with Armstrong's *Apollo 11* voyage. (The USSR had taken early "space-race" heats with two unmanned *Sputnik* launches in 1957 and Yuri Gagarin's historic April 1961 orbital flight.)

November 1969 *Apollo 12* lunar-walks went so smoothly that bored Americans began channel-surfing after liftoff, but the next moon-shot sent wake-up calls to NASA engineers and television audiences worldwide. On April 11, 1970, a bloodcurdling jolt rocked *Apollo 13*'s command module *(Odyssey)*, terrifying its crew (Jim Lovell, John Swigert, Fred Haise). At first they thought something had struck their hull (more than anything else, astronauts fear random hits by space flotsam—in the airless heavens, a BB-size ice fragment packs the destructive force of a cannonball smacking a car at 65 mph). In fact, soaring temperatures caused by a bad thermostat switch had melted Teflon wiring insulation in a service-module oxygen tank, sparking an explosion, cutting *Odyssey*'s power supply, and crippling its primary engine. (The same blast 24 hours later would have marooned *Apollo 13* in lunar orbit or on the moon's surface.)

A four-day nightmare was on: their water and oxygen dwindling, the crew piled into the LEM *(Aquarius),* transferred guidance-program data to its computer, and rigged duct tape, cardboard, and storage plastic to house lithium hydroxide for "scrubbing" their carbon dioxide exhalations. Rounding the moon, they used lunar gravity and *Aquarius'* descent engine to fling them out of orbit and back toward Earth. On their return trip, they spent the LEM's two-day battery charge like misers (cabin temperatures plunged to 40°, humidity remained near 100%). Nearing reentry on April 17, they moved back to *Odyssey,* jettisoned *Aquarius* and the wrecked service module, adjusted their approach angle manually, and hit Earth's heavy atmosphere at 25,000 mph. Within minutes, they splashed down in the South Pacific—143 hours after liftoff. Thirty-two months later, the Apollo program closed with a 75-hour stopover on the surface of the moon.

Apollo 13 is the toughest kind of movie to make, because everyone knows how the story ends. But it succeeds spectacularly: riveting, technically accurate, and on-target historically, this ultra-suspenseful blockbuster will floor demanding movie fans and amateur historians. Howard's main fictional embellishment, a Haise–Lovell–Swigert argument to heighten dramatic tension just before reentry, is palatable (but unnecessary). Best of all: top performances, great early-seventies period detail, and an approach/reentry segment that will keep sensitive souls out of airplanes forever.

For Further Viewing:

The Right Stuff ★★★★ (1983) 193 Minutes (Sam Shepard, Ed Harris, Scott Glenn, Dennis Quaid, Fred Ward, Pamela Reed, Barbara Hershey): Director Philip Kaufman's adaptation of Tom Wolfe's tribute to legendary test pilot Chuck Yeager and NASA's original "Magnificent Seven" astronauts is great stuff most of the way. Highly accurate in places: NASA, for example, actually considered using acrobats for early launches, and nature called Shepard—loudly—seconds before his historic liftoff. Kaufman occasionally distorts or omits important facts: he makes James Webb a superfluous publicity hound, for example—in fact, the talented NASA administrator's fund-raising and managerial skills were indispensable for America's space program. Another minus: Kaufman's satiric tone flops badly, killing the wonder and elation felt by Americans during early space-race days.

Recommended Reading:
T. A. Heppenheimer, *Countdown: A History of Space Flight;* Jim Lovell and Jeffrey Kluger, *Lost Moon: The Perilous Voyage of* Apollo 13.

Blackboard Jungle ★★★★

(1955) 101 Minutes

Director: Richard Brooks

Cast: Glenn Ford, Anne Francis, Vic Morrow, Sidney Poitier, Richard Kiley

Historical Background: America's first juvenile-crime wave came during World War II: fathers overseas and mothers staffing war-industry plants gave thousands of teenagers too much empty, unsupervised time, losing many to a nationwide subculture of "wild children" living at the bottom of the rules. War-era delinquency's high noon came in June 1943 with a week-long brawl pitting L.A.'s flamboyant "zoot-suiters"—a Mexican-American crew decked out in peg-legged pants, broad-shouldered jackets, and heavy shoes—against servicemen from local bases.

During the 1950s, adolescent crime rates zoomed off the charts: between 1952 and 1957, FBI files showed a 60% rise in teen arrests and a new, chilling taste for mayhem reflected in escalating gang violence and random, pointless savagery. Small gangs penetrated many communities. Battalion-size, highly disciplined city outfits run by formal chains of command flourished, fighting huge "rumbles" fueled by turf disputes and race hatred. Warring gang leaders often set rules governing weapons—chains, knives, tire irons, bats, bricks—for upcoming face-offs in deserted slums.

All of this begged for media hype, and booming television sales drove a nationwide collective fret over delinquency to near-hysteria. In 1953, a Senate delinquency subcommittee formed, igniting an airmail avalanche blaming the crime epidemic on spaceships, hostile conspiracies, fluoridated water, and—above all—comic books: "Our two boys," wrote one mother, "behave as if drugged in the presence of comic books and will not speak when spoken to. . . . If we cannot stop [this], what chance is there for mankind to survive longer than one generation?" A hot 60-million-copy-per-month sales pace stoked cross-country comic-book burnings by "incensed groups amidst elaborate ceremonies." At the crusade's peak, Safeway dropped comics from all of its supermarket magazine racks. It didn't help—nothing did, even though Senate investigations dragged on for years: in 1965, police pinned half the car thefts, burglaries, and armed robberies in the U.S. on juveniles; a decade later, 106,000 known American gangs incorporated 1.7 million members;

and a 550% violent-crime rise between 1960 and 1990 came mainly from children—the fastest-growing niche in America's outlaw community.

First-year teacher Ford scrambles to maintain classroom discipline, then life and limb, in a tough mid-fifties New York high school cowed by a small, sullen core of delinquents. Brooks' landmark hit set new standards for crime-movie grit and realism—but enraged many contemporaries with its graphic schoolhouse rape attempt and harsh view of inner-city school administrators. An extraordinary early picture of America's brand-new "generation gap" percolates throughout. Poitier's first top role, but Morrow—magnificent as chief hooligan—dominates the movie.

Recommended Reading:
James Gilbert, *A Cycle of Outrage: America's Reaction to the Juvenile Delinquent in the 1950s;* Charles P. Cozic, ed., *Gangs: Opposing Viewpoints.*

JFK

(1991) 188 Minutes

Director: Oliver Stone

Cast: Kevin Costner, Tommy Lee Jones, Sissy Spacek, Jay Sanders, Laurie Metcalf, Gary Oldman, Joe Pesci, Donald Sutherland

Historical Background: In a 1978 television interview, JFK assassination fiend Delphine Roberts claimed temporary past custody of a dead pigeon sent as a veiled threat to JFK, insisted she'd "read the sacred scrolls that God himself gave to the Hebrews for placing in the Ark of the Covenant," and hawked an in-progress assassination study that would "also tell the story of the Creation." Incredibly, many "Warren Commission critics"—including Oliver Stone—swear by Roberts' crackpot ruminations on assassin Lee Harvey Oswald and a vast plot to kill JFK.

A fanatical Roberts apologist, New Orleans district attorney Jim Garrison fell from grace after a 1967 NBC exposé documented continual bribery and witness intimidation during his campaign to nail French Quarter renovator Clay Shaw for plotting JFK's murder. Garrison concocted a conspiracy theory based on flaky lawyer Dean Andrews' testimony that an obscure attorney, "Clay Bertrand," had offered to defend Oswald. No one could find Bertrand, and Garrison decided that Shaw was really Bertrand because the first names were identical, Shaw was gay, and "homosexuals always change their last names, but never their first names." The JFK murder "was a homosexual thrill-killing," Garrison told journalist Jim Phelan. "Look at the people involved: Clay Shaw, homosexual. Dave Ferrie, [a pilot falsely accused of planning Oswald's getaway], homosexual. Jack Ruby, homosexual. And then there's Lee Harvey Oswald. A switch-hitter who couldn't satisfy his wife."

Relentless vendettas against Shaw peaked with Garrison staffer Louis Ivon's threat (at gunpoint) to kill teenager Alvin Beauboeuf for witnessing—and taping—an attempted bribe. (A jury quickly acquitted Shaw in 1969. Andrews eventually admitted that Clay Bertrand never existed, blaming the hoax on drugs: "I was smoking weed. You know, sailing on cloud nine. . . . I would swear to anything.") Undeterred, Garrison broadened his conspirator list, eventually including the Pentagon, neo-Nazis, White Russians, the CIA, Texas oilmen, the FBI, and anti-Castro Cubans. He believed that plotters might have killed Oswald assassin Jack Ruby with cancer-cell injections (medically impossible).

Garrison's zaniness infuriated reputable scholars baffled by loose ends surrounding JFK's assassination, but new interviews, recently discovered files, better technology for analyzing evidence, and eyewitness Abraham Zapruder's computer-enhanced film of the assassination have closed the door on conspiracy theories. In *Case Closed,* for example, assassination expert Gerald Posner scuttles multiple-killer notions in a remarkable chapter on the Warren Commission's famous "single bullet" argument. Most conspiracy theorists omit critical information—especially statistics. All of them, for example, insist on more than three shots—the number Oswald fired from the Texas School Book Depository's sixth floor—and at least two gunmen, one behind Kennedy and one in front. Of the 200 witnesses interviewed by investigators, one in 20 heard more than three shots, and only four heard shots from different places—remarkably low numbers for a well-known outdoor echo chamber so confusing that 78 "earwit-

nesses" had no idea where the shots originated. At least 28 people near the Depository placed the killer there, and three workmen viewing the motorcade from a fifth-floor window (directly beneath Oswald's sniper's nest) described three shots and the double click of a bolt-action breech—before investigators found Oswald's Carcano rifle.

Allegations that gunsmoke hung in the air motionless near the notorious grassy knoll quickly collapse, wrecking notions of a second assassin hidden there: 6.5mm Carcano cartridges used smokeless cordite propellant, but even a black-powder flintlock charge wouldn't have produced lingering smoke in the steady 20-mph winds lashing Dealey Plaza. (Stone used a bellows to pump smoke from the knoll—he couldn't find ammunition that produced enough, even on a still day. Zapruder filmed the killing from the knoll's crest, saw no smoke, and heard only echoes. Witnesses might have seen heavy vapor from a nearby steampipe.)

More critical still: Oswald opened fire from Kennedy's rear, but Zapruder's film clearly shows JFK's head snapping backward, convincing lay viewers that shots came from the front. In fact, a split second after impact, Kennedy's head moved forward 2.3 inches, then whipped back—precisely the reaction a rear head shot would cause: the projectile destroyed JFK's cerebral cortex and caused neck-and-back-muscle contractions, throwing him upward and to the rear. The exiting bullet, brain tissue, and bone also had a "jet effect," generating momentum greater than the bullet's original impact and thrusting the head backward. (Physician John Lattimer's examination of Kennedy's autopsy X-rays and photographs confirmed this, and other forensic experts concur. "People have no conception of how real-life bullet wounds work," notes Dr. Michael Baden. "It's not like Hollywood, where someone gets shot and falls over backwards.") Most eyewitnesses and virtually all the evidence point overwhelmingly to Oswald as JFK's killer, but the assassination supports a morbid entertainment industry certain to add new volumes to the 2,000 books already written on the Dallas nightmare.

According to *JFK*, LBJ and a cast of hundreds killed Kennedy to keep America in Vietnam. Packed with similar harebrained nonsense, Stone's genuflection to Jim Garrison mangles history throughout, beginning with its vignette of a dying prostitute—Rose Cheramie—warning emergency-room physicians about a plot to murder JFK. The real Cheramie said nothing to doctors (she was in shock from heroin withdrawal), but on November 20 she'd threatened—in a drug-induced haze—to kill Kennedy herself.

Another Stone falsification: the summary of Oswald's marksmanship by Ivon (Sanders): "Zapruder's film establishes three shots in 5.6 seconds. . . . He tried to hit a target at 88 yards, and Oswald was at best a medium [sic] shot. The guy couldn't do the shootin'. Nobody could." In fact, taking 4.1 to 5.6 seconds each, 11 volunteers averaged two out of three cranial hits in assassination reconstructions for a 1975 CBS documentary (for average marksmen with high-powered rifles, 88 yards is point-blank range); Oswald scored a Marine Corps sharpshooter rating (using open sights, he placed eight of ten shots in ten-inch bull's-eyes from 200 yards—his NCO called him "an excellent shot").

More compelling still, repeated digital tests of Zapruder's film recorded 8.0 to 8.4 seconds between Oswald's first and third shots. Overlong, overacted, and overpriced ($50 million), *JFK* makes *Cinderella* look like a BBC documentary.

For Further Viewing:
Fatal Deception: Mrs. Lee Harvey Oswald (1993) 96 Minutes (Helena Bonham Carter, Frank Whaley, Robert Picardo): Carter's critically acclaimed lead performance is the only plus in this creepy conspiracy film. Scriptwriter Steve Bello's Oswald (Whaley) is a fall guy: "Somebody very powerful must have been pulling the strings," according to conspiracy buff and *Best Evidence* author David Lifton (well played by Picardo; the real Lifton met Marina Oswald in 1981). Picardo surfaces continually to hawk vague conspiracy theories—but Bello omits the governing premise of *Best Evidence:* according to Lipton, conspirators stole Kennedy's body from its sealed *Air Force One* casket (Mrs. Kennedy, LBJ, his staff, and Secret Service guards saw nothing), removed his brain, surgically altered his wounds to look like rear-entry hits, returned the body to *another* casket, and replaced the brain during JFK's autopsy (honest). Lucy, you got some *'splaining* to do.

Recommended Reading:
Gerald L. Posner, *Case Closed: Lee Harvey Oswald and the Assassination of JFK.*

Medium Cool ★★★★

(1969) 110 Minutes

Director: Haskell Wexler

Cast: Robert Forster, Verna Bloom, Peter Bonerz, Marianna Hill, Harold Blankenship

Historical Background: More than anything else, discord over the Vietnam conflict made the 1960s post-WWII American history's most tortured decade. According to a 1969 Harris survey, most Americans supported the war until Lyndon Johnson and bureaucratic advisers from the Kennedy years mired America's expeditionary force in vacillation and strategic discontinuity (despite clear, solid advice from the U.S. military: get out of Indochina, or win—quickly). Worse still: Vietnam was an undeclared war fought by draftees—not volunteers—and as head counts rose, body bags proliferated. By 1968, 15,000 American troops had died—60% of them in 1967, half of them draftees—and conscripts garrisoned more than 85% of America's line outfits. To diffuse the draft's immediate impact, Selective Service policy, considered unfair to everyone but deferred college students, conscripted recruits individually from communities around the country instead of raising whole units en masse, WWII-style, from each town. It didn't work: rancor at the draft boiled hotly and spread—mainly on university campuses. Worst of all: hamstrung by dithering civilian leadership,

America's military seemed unable to draft a cogent strategic plan for winning the war by a realistic projected date.

As fighting floundered through 1966 and 1967, isolated demonstrations escalated into a full-blown nationwide convulsion of antiwar protests. Divided by ideological differences, diverse antiwar elements never coalesced into a unified "movement," falling, instead, into three broad groups: liberals and "left-liberals" (SANE, for example, committed first to antinuke agitation, then to peace activism); pacifists (opposed to violence, intent on reforming individuals, suspicious of ideological systems); and the radical left (Students for a Democratic Society, or SDS—hard-core Marxists determined to "revolutionize" American society, often provoking violent collisions with authorities). Between 1967 and 1970, protesters staged several antiwar rallies, most notably in New York City (April 1967); Washington, San Francisco, and Boston (October 1969); Washington and San Francisco again (November 1969); and Washington (May 1970). National demonstrations attracted large, diverse crowds—professional organizers, representatives from campus antiwar groups, ordinary college students, faculty members, curious onlookers—often numbering 100,000-plus.

But the most notorious rally—a volcanic debacle engulfing Chicago's 1968 Democratic National Convention—was also one of the smallest and least diverse. Organized by MOBE (Mobilization to End the War in Vietnam) under the leadership of Tom Hayden and Rennie Davis, Chicago drew just 10,000 demonstrators—mostly radicals "prepared to shed blood" (Hayden's words: he predicted that 25 people would die before August 29).

Citywide chaos and violent attacks on "night-clubs, stores, theaters, and restaurants where the bourgeoisie live their lives" were the goals. On Saturday, August 24, protesters began drifting into Chicago. The first violence erupted Sunday night in Lincoln Park: hurling rocks and obscenities at a police security line, hundreds of demonstrators scattered wildly as fuming officers broke ranks, mauling all the dissidents they could catch, then re-forming—weirdly—within seconds.

Similar melees erupted again and again, building fury on both sides and peaking on the 28th with a long brawl raging around the Conrad Hilton Hotel. Shedding badges—and discipline—police went ballistic, attacking 10,000 demonstrators, motorists, and gawking bystanders with nightsticks, mace, and tear gas. It was a rock-bottom lowpoint in post-WWII American history, and sensationalist television coverage made the most of it, intercutting hours-old riot footage with live convention proceedings and leaving 90 million viewers with the impression that the mayhem lasted much longer than it actually had. (The networks drew heavy fire from all quarters. Columnist Joseph Kraft, for example, asked, "Don't we, as Mayor [Richard] Daley and his supporters have charged, have a prejudice of our own? Most of us in the communications field are not rooted in Middle America. . . . It seems wise to exercise caution in pressing our claim to be at all times the agent of the sovereign public." Viewers agreed—by 11 to one, according to thousands of post-convention letters received by CBS.)

Hayden pronounced the spectacle "a 100% victory in propaganda," but most Americans supported the police: in Survey Research Center polls, more than half the an-tiwar respondents censured the protesters, and 23% were extremely hostile. The protesters' radical wing had fatally damaged the antiwar campaign: "As unpopular as the war had become," writes former radical Todd Gitlin, "the antiwar movement was now detested still more—the most hated political group in America, disliked even by most of the people who supported immediate withdrawal from Vietnam." Historian Stephen Ambrose agrees, adding that peace demonstrations, in the end, had little effect on American policy: "I was part of the antiwar movement. . . . [Its] permanent influence was not to shorten the war but to extend the boundaries of the counterculture." And in fact the largest crowd of the decade (450,000) assembled almost exactly one year after Chicago for a music festival (Woodstock)—not an antiwar rally. Woodstock wouldn't have happened without Vietnam, but it was a gigantic private gathering—the counterculture celebrating itself: "There's people out there that really don't dig it," said one spectator, "but very few of them are here. This really is just family, man." Antiwar demonstrations continued, but after Woodstock, protesters gradually drifted into other movements (gay rights, feminism, environmentalism, Puerto Rican independence), and many changed politically: in the 1980 presidential election, Neil Young voted for Ronald Reagan, igniting a fit of perplexity in rock-music circles that persists to this day.

A left-leaning, eccentric film following television reporter Forster and sound man Bonerz on news junkets covering civil rights marches, the 1968 Los Angeles primary, Robert Kennedy's funeral, and Chicago's

Democratic National Convention. Wexler nails the sixties social and political climate, adding a masterful subplot: newly arrived West Virginia widow Bloom struggles to support herself and her son in a marginal Chicago neighborhood. Her story's gut-wrenching immediacy keeps Wexler's political material at arm's length, highlighting the antiwar movement's strange, invasive impact on ordinary, mystified working people. One calculated historical distortion: at film's end, Wexler absurdly implies that many Chicago business proprietors supported the SDS after August 28's street war.

For Further Viewing:

Woodstock ★★★★ (1970) 184 Minutes (Joan Baez, Richie Havens, Jefferson Airplane, Joe Cocker, Janis Joplin, Jimi Hendrix, Arlo Guthrie, The Who): Whether you view *Woodstock* as a riveting chronicle of the counterculture's high-water mark or as three hours of tedium punctuated by wacky kids dancing to industrial noise, director Michael Wadleigh's documentary of the three-day festival is *de rigueur* viewing for students of the late sixties. Wire-to-wire coverage includes pre-festival preparations, interviews with musicians, and commentary from pilgrims-in-attendance (much of it idiotic: "I don't want to become president: I just want to maintain the Hamlet trip, you know—'To be or not to be' "). A fine documentary, even though Woodstock didn't pack the earth-shaking significance remembered by many baby boomers.

Easy Rider ★ (1969) 94 Minutes (Dennis Hopper, Peter Fonda, Jack Nicholson, Karen Black, Luke Askew, Robert Walker): You'd have to have a heart of stone to watch this movie without laughing (many thanks, Oscar Wilde)—except for Nicholson's knockout performance as a hard-drinking lawyer, that's how dated and pretentious director Dennis Hopper's incoherent, seat-of-the-pants classic looks from the 1990s. After a lucrative cocaine deal, Fonda and Hopper motorcycle from L.A. to New Orleans, with stopovers at two bedrock counterculture "institutions" (a commune and a Kafkaesque acid trip). Packed with infantile symbolism—Fonda dumps his watch before departing (he's not into 9-to-5 time, get it?)—but a vivid look at the counterculture hurtling at warp speed toward the burned-out seventies (and meltdown).

The Graduate ★★ (1967) 105 Minutes (Dustin Hoffman, Anne Bancroft, Katharine Ross, Murray Hamilton, Elizabeth Wilson, William Daniels, Norman Fell): If you can ignore director Mike Nichols' silly governing assumption—all white Americans over thirty and living well are dense, hypocritical, and hopelessly encumbered with cheating spouses—you'll enjoy his well-crafted, funny look at naive Hoffman, fresh from college, ready to drop out, weathering tackles by Mrs. Robinson (Bancroft) and her daughter (Ross), and trying to figure out what he's going to do in the real world. The apparent answer, at film's end, is "nothing, for now."

Recommended Reading:

Adam Garfinkle, *Telltale Hearts: The Origins and Impact of the Vietnam Antiwar Movement;* David Farber, *Chicago '68;* David Horowitz, *Radical Son: A Generational Odyssey;* Todd Gitlin, *The Sixties.*

Mississippi Burning ★★

(1988) 125 Minutes

Director: Alan Parker

Cast: Gene Hackman, Willem Dafoe, Frances McDormand, Brad Dourif, R. Lee Ermey

Historical Background: The early civil rights movement's pivotal events unfolded in America's most segregated state: in 1964, only 5.3% of Mississippi's black electors had registered to vote (the figure for Virginia was 45.7%). By then, racial tension in Mississippi had boiled hotly for more than two years, and throughout the harrowing summer Ku Klux Klan voter-intimidation raids escalated, leveling black homes (30 in all) and churches (37 by early fall).

In June 1964, the Council of Federated Organizations (COFO) sent 1,000 recruits, mostly white college students, on a drive to register Mississippi's black voters. On the 21st, three volunteers (black Mississippian James Chaney and white New Yorkers Andrew Goodman and Mickey Schwerner) suddenly vanished after visiting a black church in Neshoba County. A few days later, searchers found their station wagon, gutted and torched, near Philadelphia. LBJ poured FBI agents into an areawide search, drafting hundreds of Meridian Naval Base sailors, at one point, for a gruesome swamp drag that unearthed corpses of several long-dead lynching victims, but no COFO volunteers. Finally, on August 4, investigators dug

the three men's bodies from an earthen dam. In 1967, a federal jury convicted Deputy Sheriff Cecil Price and seven Klansmen of violating the volunteers' civil rights—the first civil rights conviction by an all-white jury in Mississippi history.

Extremist terror had backfired, launching a high-profile nightmare for the Klan. Swarming television crews had electrified viewers everywhere, flooding the airwaves day after day with sensational stories and graphic search-and-murder footage. Worse still for the Klan, moderate Southern whites (especially business leaders) were furious: unprecedented postwar economic growth had brought tantalizing opportunities for highlighting the region's minimal taxes and rock-bottom living costs to draw new industries from the North and Midwest. A cracker image was the last thing the New South needed during the early sixties.

Launched by wartime demographic, economic, and social changes, sweeping public-opinion shifts on racial issues had finally surfaced in 1964's anti-Klan backlash. As important as federal legislation was, the civil rights movement was a grass-roots campaign locally orchestrated by blacks and their white allies—not a government dole hatched in Washington during the sixties (the first "Freedom Rides" came in 1947) and driven from the top down. It began on December 1, 1955, with middle-aged seamstress Rosa Parks' refusal to move to the Negro section of a Montgomery, Ala., bus: her arrest sparked a 381-day boycott—led by Baptist minister Martin Luther King, Jr.—ending with a court order integrating Montgomery's buses.

In 1957, King and several NAACP and Congress of Racial Equality (CORE) leaders formed the Southern Christian Leadership Conference (SCLC), launching a national antisegregation movement based on nonviolent demonstrations. In 1960, sit-ins opened Woolworth's all-white lunch counter to African-Americans in Greensboro; in 1961–62, Freedom Riders helped integrate transportation facilities dotting highways between New Orleans and Washington, D.C.; in Birmingham, massive spring 1963 demonstrations drew national publicity and support from local newspapers, black organizations, and the white Chamber of Commerce. King's popularity peaked on August 28 with his rousing "I have a dream" oration before a huge audience—250,000 strong—at the Lincoln Memorial. Less than a year later, LBJ signed the 1964 Civil Rights Act into law.

As the sixties reeled forward, factionalism eroded King's national coalition, and racial violence increased—thanks partly to ex-convict and Black Muslim convert Malcolm Little (Malcolm X). A charismatic near-crackpot, Little believed an apocalyptic, Allah-ignited firestorm would one day sweep the earth and rage for 310 years, killing only "white devils." He spewed appalling racist pronouncements covering many topics. (On the Holocaust: "Why is everybody wet-eyed over a handful of Jews who brought it on themselves?" On 120 white passengers killed in an airline crash: "A very beautiful thing has happened. . . . We call on our God and He gets rid of 120 of them at one whop.") Expelled by Black Muslim leader Elijah Muhammad in 1964, Malcolm formed his own militant black-separatist organization. Apparently, a 1964 trip to Mecca tempered his views, but he'd made too many enemies by then: on February 21, 1965, three Black

Muslims blew him apart with shotgun blasts in Harlem's Audubon Ballroom. His successors Stokely Carmichael and H. Rap Brown launched the "Black Power" movement in 1965–66. They flourished briefly, but after widespread rioting gutted America's inner cities between 1965 and 1968, their coarse rhetoric and appetite for violence alienated virtually all of the black American mainstream. With King's 1968 assassination in Memphis, the national civil rights movement fragmented, and black leaders began exploiting its hard-won gains, seeking—and winning—public office in unprecedented numbers.

Based on the 1964 Philadelphia murders, *Mississippi Burning* is well acted, well intentioned—and far too fictional. Many errors and omissions embellish Parker's central fabrication: clean-Gene FBI man Dafoe and savvy local agent Hackman solve the Chaney-Goodman-Schwerner killings all by themselves. (In fact, FBI "detective" work solved nothing—reduced sentences and highly publicized cash rewards eventually loosened a few suspects' tongues, blowing the case wide open.)

All of Parker's white Southerners are rednecks, and his blacks do nothing but stand around, mute, helpless, and terrified. He omits J. Edgar Hoover's resistance to LBJ's order dispatching agents to Mississippi, casting the civil rights movement as a benevolent Big Brother project orchestrated from Washington. Limiting the story to a few individuals also misrepresents the three murders as isolated incidents without resonance in a vague civil rights movement unfolding somewhere else. Fine for film buffs, but X-rated for amateur historians.

For Further Viewing:

Malcolm X (1992) 201 Minutes (Denzel Washington, Angela Bassett, Albert Hall, Al Freeman, Jr., Delroy Lindo, Theresa Randle): Director Spike Lee's pedantic film version of *The Autobiography of Malcolm X* is little more than fact-starved hagiography. Malcolm X radiated personal magnetism and delivered galvanic orations, routinely holding listeners spellbound for hours. But Washington (in the lead) is affable, laid-back, void of the fuming anger driving the real Malcolm. Lee's idealization of Malcolm's abusive father and his sentimental rendition of 1930s Harlem as a golden-age Mecca are absurd. Even sillier is his suggestion that the CIA backed Malcolm's murder. Worst of all, *Malcolm X* drones endlessly with bumper-sticker Black Muslim ideology, often delivered lecture-style ("Black men were a race of kings when the white man crawled around on all-fours. . . . The true nature of the original man, the black man, is righteousness, so the true nature of the white man is wickedness"). A major-league disappointment: frivolously distorted history and (incredibly, considering its subject) wire-to-wire tedium.

Recommended Reading:

Stephan and Abigail Thernstrom, *America in Black and White: One Nation, Indivisible;* Shelby Steele, *The Content of Our Character: A New Vision of Race in America;* George Breitman, ed., *Malcolm X Speaks;* Malcolm X with Alex Haley, *The Autobiography of Malcolm X.*

Nixon

(1995) 190 Minutes

Director: Oliver Stone

Cast: Anthony Hopkins, Joan Allen, Ed Harris, Powers Boothe, E. G. Marshall, Bob Hoskins, James Woods

Historical Background: August 6, 1974 the White House. Glancing at Richard Nixon during his last cabinet meeting, Caspar Weinberger whispered to Defense Secretary James Schlesinger, "All that talent; all those flaws." One quality or the other surfaced at every major turning point of Nixon's career. In 1968, 43.2% of the popular vote barely put him into the Oval Office. By 1972, he'd wrought a stunning turnaround: the greatest numerical landslide in presidential-election history returned him to the White House for a second term. Twenty months later, Watergate drove his Gallup Poll ratings through the floor (17% at one point), forcing his resignation and retreat from public life.

For a decade, Nixon relaxed, wrote books, and lectured occasionally. Then, at a celebrity-packed 1992 Georgetown conference, he delivered a riveting keynote address on America and the post–Cold War Soviet Union, drawing thunderous applause and rave reviews from the same news organizations that had pummeled him mercilessly during the seventies. The old war-horse was back, and most of his ancient enemies were delighted to have him: it was pure Americana, a remarkable comeback echoing revisionist trends in historical accounts of his presidency.

Nixon built a glittering foreign-policy record. During his first term, he cut U.S. forces in Vietnam by 526,000, then ended America's involvement with 1973's Paris Peace Agreements. He engineered spectacular moves toward rapprochement with China and the USSR: to mute Soviet saber-rattling, Peking hosted a historic visit by Nixon in February 1972, igniting a media spectacle (at one point, Chairman Mao's Red Army Band played "Home on the Range" as diplomats toasted each other on worldwide television). His China triumph launched Nixon's "triangular diplomacy" strategy, further splitting the Communist giants and bracing America's bargaining position at the May 20 Moscow summit. Thanks to his hard-line views on Communism and America's robust atomic arsenal, the Soviets feared Nixon—at first. But his summit performance surprised everybody. A fiercely tenacious negotiator, he also was flexible—an approach the Russians understood: Soviet policy adviser Dimitri Simes called Nixon "tough but never polemical. He didn't preach at top men in the Politburo. He spoke . . . a language they understood, of national self-interest and realism—and always with respect." Summit payoffs included history's first nuclear-arms-control agreement (SALT I) and several lesser treaties forming Soviet-American trade relationships and scientific/technological research projects.

During international crises Nixon was at his best. In 1973, with Watergate nearing critical mass, Egypt and Syria wrecked 20% of Israel's air force and destroyed 220 tanks in a shattering surprise attack. Resisted by Schlesinger and anti-Israeli Pentagon heavyweights, Nixon directed a 32-day, 6,400-mile airlift, delivering tons of equipment to Tel Aviv. Elbowing political expediency aside, he saved one of America's loyal allies from probable annihilation, a performance indispensable for a fair assessment of his presidency: Nixon had little to gain by intervening so forcefully and much to lose by turning his attention from the ruinous Watergate mess. It was his finest hour in the White House—and it's all but forgotten today.

Watergate dealt awful wreckage to Nixon's reputation: few remember America's 1973 Paris peace-treaty signatory (William Rogers), but Watergate's key players (John Haldeman, Sam Ervin, John Dean, Gordon Liddy, John Erlichman, E. Howard Hunt) remain household names. Washington police opened the can of worms on June 17, 1972, arresting five men—including three Cuban expatriates and Committee to Reelect the President employee James McCord—for burglarizing Democratic Party National Headquarters in the Watergate building. (A late-May burglary had unfolded without incident.) Early newspaper stories on the break-in read like low-budget "007" knock-offs, and linking the burglars (or "plumbers") to the White House seemed absurd with Nixon's reelection virtually guaranteed. (No one has produced a reasonable motive for the burglaries, but recent theories implicate former White House counsel John Dean in a series of freelance break-ins—"Operation GEMSTONE"—fishing for proof of Democratic ties to a Washington call-girl ring. Evidence supporting the notion is compelling, and some historians take it seriously, but a quarter-century of heavy digging still hasn't revealed a proven rationale for the burglaries.)

Despite countless articles by *Washington Post* reporters Bob Woodward and Carl Bernstein, the story languished nationally until Judge John Sirica handed the plumbers provisional life sentences to force their cooperation with a Senate committee investigating Watergate. Everyone but Liddy complied. A Congressional inquest rolled forward, but floundered without evidence confirming Dean's charges that Nixon had whitewashed administration collusion with the burglars. Then, on July 13, former aide Alexander Butterfield testified that Nixon had recorded his Oval Office conversations. Ten days later, special prosecutor Archibald Cox subpoenaed incriminating tape transcripts, and Nixon's presidency was history. (Especially damning was the famous "smoking gun" recording of Nixon weighing plans to impede Watergate investigators. Another tape contained an 18$\frac{1}{2}$-minute gap—secretary Rose Mary Woods testified that she might have erased the material accidentally, but her attorney Charles Rhyne demolished later efforts to prove this. To this day, no one knows who altered the tape.) On June 30, 1974, the House Judiciary Committee adopted three impeachment articles against Nixon. He resigned on August 9. Vice President Gerald Ford succeeded him, and a month later pardoned him for crimes he may have committed as president.

Watergate still bristles with mysteries, but most recent histories concur on two points. First: Nixon didn't order the burglaries. No one—prosecutors, Congress, the FBI—produced evidence linking him to the actual break-ins. Confirmed by many witnesses, his initial reaction to the burglaries was derision laced with surprise (he dismissed the plumbers as pranksters). More convincing is Haldeman's mixed testimony in *The Ends of Power:* certain that White House involvement really was news to Nixon, he also insisted that "the President was involved in the cover-up from Day-One." Fired by Nixon and eventually imprisoned, Haldeman had no reason to lie about one issue in a frequently unfriendly book (he and Nixon didn't reconcile until 1990). Second: Nixon sank himself by orchestrating the cover-up. For months, he lied about the break-ins. He never considered finding and firing the plumbers' White House connections. He sought to turn the Cubans' involvement against electioneering Democrats by resurrecting JFK's Bay of Pigs fiasco. He authorized a $120,000 payoff to silence Hunt. Throughout the nightmare, Nixon's judgment faltered: he considered using CIA contacts to derail FBI investigations (this never happened, but his taped ruminations on the idea frosted most of his Congressional support), and he thoroughly misread the American electorate's exasperation and disillusionment with politicians.

Without exonerating Nixon, it's fair to say that just about everyone involved—the president, the media, the Senate committee—behaved badly much of the time. Sen. William Proxmire, a liberal Wisconsin Democrat, believed that Nixon was "buried up to his ears" in Watergate, but insisted that reporters and many Committee members were mounting a "witch-hunt of McCarthyistic destruction," especially against innocent players such as Rose Woods. Europeans have always considered the break-in trivial, but 24 years after President Nixon's resignation, Watergate still evokes volcanic, conflicting opinions from Americans old enough to remember it.

Loaded with absurd distortions and outright lies, *Nixon* is historical biography at its very worst. (Historian Stephen Ambrose panned the movie—and Ambrose freely states in his Nixon biography that he once "held negative feelings about" Nixon and that he still didn't "claim to have attained a position of neutrality.")

Stone's nuttiest "theory" implicates Nixon (Hopkins) in a Castro-assassination attempt leading, somehow, to JFK's murder. The film's sick version of Nixon's marriage is near slander, and Hopkins' overwrought Nixon-as-drunken-obscenitor rests on notions discredited many years ago. (Nixon's "drinking problem" is a media myth built around John Erlichman's offhand remark that "one drink can knock him galley-west if he's tired." For this reason, Nixon was a remarkably temperate drinker. Hopkins' scurrilous cursing is a legacy of the Watergate-tape transcripts: peppered with "expletive deleted" excisions, they made Nixon look like a world-class trashmouth, but Ambrose reports that presidential statements on the unedited tapes contain only "Sunday-school" swearing, "words like 'Hell' and 'damn,' used in an embarrassed sort of way.") Fine biographers on both sides of the aisle—Aitken and Ambrose, for example—have written solid books on Nixon: their opinions vary widely, but they never disguise speculation or venomous fantasy as fact. You can't ask more than this from a historian—and from a filmmaker aiming to be taken seriously, you certainly shouldn't ask less.

For Further Viewing:

All the President's Men ★★ (1976) 138 Minutes (Robert Redford, Dustin Hoffman, Jason Robards, Martin Balsam, Jack Warden, Hal Holbrook): Director Alan J. Pakula's adaptation of the Woodward/Bernstein best-selling book delivers fine entertainment and re-creations of nuts-and-bolts newsroom operations, but grossly inflates the *Post*'s role in bringing Nixon down—"Woodstein" certainly kept the story alive, but the media didn't erode Nixon's core-constituency support until the "smoking gun" tape surfaced. More important—and underplayed, here—were Butterfield's testimony and the committee's 200 lawyers and assistants. Other fictions/distortions: Pakula's assertion that their digging endangered the reporters' lives is ridiculous; and the *Post* crusade wasn't pure altruism: editor Ben Bradlee believed the White House had blocked *Post* broadcast-license petitions, later citing this as his reason for pursuing the Watergate story fanatically.

Kissinger and Nixon (1995) 100 Minutes (Ron Silver, Beau Bridges, George Takei, Kenneth Welsh, Ron White): "Kissinger's apotheosis and the wholesale slaughter of history" makes a better title for this lamebrained rant on the 1972–73 Paris peace talks—nothing but an occasional date squares with the facts. Kissinger, for example, intimidates Gen. Alexander Haig throughout (the reverse was true). Director Daniel Petrie's North Vietnamese negotiators dominate in Paris, but historically the Communists were desperate for a treaty by late 1972: thanks to triangular diplomacy, the USSR and China had virtually stopped military shipments to North Vietnam, limiting their aid to food only. Petrie gives Kissinger full credit for the 1973 accord, but in fact, his erratic behavior and reckless pre-election television grandstanding compromised negotiations, infuriating Nixon and Haig. Nixon's policy mix of flexibility in Paris and hard-nosed bombing in the field, not Kissinger's bargaining skill, kept Communist negotiators off-balance. A dull, silly film, wire-to-wire.

Recommended Reading:
Jonathan Aitken, *Nixon: A Life;* Len Colodny and Robert Gettlin, *Silent Coup: The Removal of a President;* Stephen E. Ambrose, *Nixon.*

Quiz Show ▲▲▲▲

(1994) 130 Minutes

Director: Robert Redford

Cast: John Turturro, Rob Morrow, Ralph Fiennes, Paul Scofield, David Paymer, Elizabeth Wilson, Mira Sorvino, Griffin Dunne, Timothy Busfield

Historical Background: On October 14, 1954, the living-room audience for *Name That Tune* totaled 45–50 million Americans—staggering numbers in a country unable to boast (as it can today) at least one TV set for virtually every household. Night after night, during the 1950s, television quiz show mania held countless glassy-eyed Americans hostage. *Twenty-One* (NBC), *The $64,000 Question* (CBS), and *The $64,000 Challenge*—all top-rated entries in network schedules littered with game shows—became the most celebrated casualties of a sen-

sational 1958–59 scandal. Official rumblings of high-stakes chicanery first came in August 1958, with allegations from would-be actor Edward Hilgemeier, Jr., that he'd witnessed *Dotto* MC Jack Narz give reigning champion Marie Winn a list of answers just before airtime three months earlier. Manhattan assistant DA Joseph Stone took Hilgemeier's statement, then filed it away as a crank stunt. Stone soon changed his mind. The story surfaced in an August 18 *New York Post* article—written by Hilgemeier's friend Jack O'Grady—revealing that CBS had canceled *Dotto* after the actor filed a formal complaint with the FCC on July 31. Still uncertain of Hilgemeier's reliability, Stone and DA Frank Hogan launched a cursory investigation, quickly uncovering enough dirt at CBS to convince them that the actor was telling the truth.

Then, on August 27, a surprise jackpot fell into Stone's lap from deep left field: prompted by O'Grady's article, Herb Stempel—a grating eccentric *par excellence*—barreled into the DA's office, swearing that *Twenty-One* producer Daniel Enright had bribed him with promises of a game-show panelist's job to throw the December 5, 1956, game to Columbia University English instructor Charles Van Doren. Enright wanted a new champion to boost ratings and settled on the charming, witty Van Doren, son of prize-winning poet Mark Van Doren (also at Columbia) and well-known writer and editor Dorothy Van Doren. Stempel agreed to dive, but he didn't like it. Especially galling was the give-away question (name the Oscar-winning best picture for 1955) that Enright ordered him to flub: the film was *Marty,* and Stempel had seen it three times. Exiting the studio after his loss, Stempel overheard a network employee call him "a freak with a sponge memory," and the remark rang mercilessly in his ears for weeks. Cursed with a genius IQ (170) and great intellectual pride, Stempel watched *Twenty-One* week after week, fuming hotly as Van Doren's jackpots and phenomenal popularity quickly topped his own. Every day he gagged on news of Van Doren's abundant fan mail, his gracious rejection of Hollywood film-role offers, and reminders of his $1,000 weekly fee for regular stints on NBC's *Dave Garroway Show*. The Garroway business was worst of all: by early 1957 Stempel had frittered away most of his $49,500 winnings, and Enright's promised job offer hadn't come. The ex-champ jumped at the chance to nail Enright & Co. as soon as Hilgemeier's story broke in the *Post*.

On August 28, 1958, Stempel's story made the front page of the *Journal-American*. Livid with rage, Enright steamed into Stone's office with countercharges of blackmail against his former champion, and Hogan launched a nine-month, 60-session, 200-witness grand jury probe of all the television quiz shows. It went nowhere: there were no laws regulating the content of television programming, and most contestants and producers stonewalled the proceedings, derailing potential indictments and leaving investigators with fragmentary evidence of industry corruption. With no trials looming, Judge Mitchell Schweitzer sealed and impounded the jury's findings to protect the reputations of various people named in the report. But the imbroglio's foul bouquet lingered—especially for Stone, Congressman Oren Harris, and Richard Goodwin, a special consultant to Congress' subcommittee on legislative oversight. Irked by Schweitzer's closed presentment, Harris kept digging and eventually managed to get his hands on the

sealed grand jury minutes. He opened a Congressional investigation on October 6, 1959, with Stempel the lead witness.

On November 2, a tormented Van Doren read prepared remarks admitting that NBC producers had fed him answers before each of his appearances on *Twenty-One*. The can of worms was wide open: a parade of witnesses, including many celebrities, came forward, 13-year-old Patty Duke and Dr. Joyce Brothers among them (both had won big on *The $64,000 Challenge*). Brothers denied receiving any kind of help, even though she'd missed several grand-jury "test" questions that she'd answered correctly on television. "I dismiss everything [from memory] that I possibly can," she explained, insisting that "the more you try to hold in mind, the less you can learn." The quiz shows were over, in other words, so she just dumped the data. People believed her, and the scandal that wrecked many television careers launched hers. Fired by Columbia, Van Doren wrote books (pseudonymously) for years and edited for *Encyclopaedia Britannica*. During the 1980s he began writing under his own name, never returning to academic life. A second grand jury (June–November 1960) convicted several contestants of lying under oath during the first investigation, then suspended their sentences. In 1960, amendments to the Communications Act tightened the rules for television game shows, outlawing undisclosed prearranged outcomes on quizzes and games of skill.

Based on Goodwin's brief account of the *Twenty-One* scandal in his book *(Remembering America: A Voice from the Sixties)*, *Quiz Show* focuses on Stempel and the events leading to the 1959 Harris investigations. Redford exaggerates Goodwin's role in the affair, ignoring

Hilgemeier, Stone, Hogan, and players from other game shows embroiled in the mess—minor defects, at worst, in a film clearly aiming to deliver basic information about the scandal and a fair assessment of Van Doren, Enright, and Stempel. Scofield (as Mark Van Doren) and Turturro (at his near-maniacal best as Stempel) perform brilliantly in one of the finest movies ever made about the fifties. The script crackles with memorable one-liners ("Herbie Stempel—now there's a face made for radio") and show-cases many vintage automobiles—polished to a high shine—from the period.

Recommended Reading:
Joseph Stone and Tim Yohn, *Prime Time and Misdemeanors: Investigating the 1950s TV Quiz Scandal;* Thomas A. DeLong, *Quiz Craze: America's Infatuation with Game Shows.*

chapter 10

Vietnam War

(Overleaf)
The Deer Hunter
(Photofest)

Chronology

1847
France invades Indochina.

1887
France unifies Laos, Cambodia, Cochinchina, Annam, and Tongking.

1930
Ho Chi Minh forms Indochinese Communist Party.

1949
OCTOBER 1: Communists win Chinese civil war.

1954
MARCH 13–MAY 7: Dien Bien Phu siege.

JULY 21: Geneva Accords divide Vietnam. More than a million refugees flee south.

1955
OCTOBER 26: South Vietnam becomes independent republic under Ngo Dinh Diem.

1960
DECEMBER: Hanoi forms National Liberation Front (NLF).

1961
JANUARY–MAY: JFK posts 7,000 troops to South Vietnam.

1963
NOVEMBER 1–2: Coup topples Diem government. Diem murdered.

1964
AUGUST 2: North Vietnamese torpedo boats attack USS *Maddox* in Tonkin Gulf.

AUGUST 7: Congress adopts Tonkin Gulf Resolution authorizing military action against North Vietnam.

1965
OCTOBER–NOVEMBER: Americans mount war's first massive helicopter assault, defeat NVA in Ia Drang Valley.

1966
MIDYEAR: U.S. commander Westmoreland builds several strongpoints, including Khe Sahn firebase, along DMZ.

1967
SEPTEMBER 3: Nguyen Van Thieu elected South Vietnam's president.

DECEMBER 31: Total of 500,000 American troops in Vietnam.

1968
JANUARY 20–APRIL 7: Battle of Khe Sahn.

JANUARY 30–FEBRUARY 25: Tet Offensive.

MARCH 16: My Lai massacre.

MAY 14: U.S. and North Vietnamese negotiators meet in Paris.

1969

JUNE 8: President Nixon announces first American troop withdrawals.

1970

DECEMBER: Senate rejects Tonkin Resolution, reduces aid to Cambodia.

1972

MARCH: NVA mount major offensive, peace negotiations collapse.

DECEMBER 18: Talks resume after 11-day U.S. bombing campaign.

1973

JANUARY 27: Henry Kissinger and Le Duc Tho sign treaty ending U.S. involvement in war.

MARCH 29: Last Americans leave Vietnam.

1974

DECEMBER: North Vietnam launches final offensive in South Vietnam.

1975

APRIL 17: Khmer Rouge capture Phnom Penh, begin genocide campaign.

APRIL 30: Saigon falls.

MAY–AUGUST: NVA begin extermination campaign against Laotian hill tribes.

1976

JULY: Hanoi disbands NLF, takes control of South.

1978

MARCH: Hanoi begins sending thousands of Vietnamese to "reeducation" camps.

CHRISTMAS DAY: Vietnam invades Cambodia.

1979

DECEMBER: Hanoi diverts medical aid and food from refugees fleeing Cambodian death camps.

1983

JUNE: Vietnamese use of chemical weapons in Cambodia confirmed.

1984

Every month, 4,000 defectors leave Vietnam. More than a million Vietnamese held in camps.

1990–1993

With disintegration of Soviet Union, Vietnam's war-driven economy collapses. Deprived of massive Soviet aid, Hanoi solicits aid from various "capitalist" governments.

1994

President Bill Clinton lifts long-standing trade embargo on Vietnam.

Bat 21 ★★★★

(1988) 105 Minutes

Director: Peter Markle

Cast: Gene Hackman, Danny Glover, Jerry Reed, Clayton Rohner

Historical Background: During the Vietnam War, the U.S. developed a complex, sophisticated process for recovering downed airmen. The array of personnel and high-tech equipment used in each rescue operation was stunning: OV-10 propeller planes located survivors, instructing them by radio throughout each mission; computer-equipped jet fighters capable of hitting camouflaged targets attacked nearby enemy troops and missile installations; radar-equipped aircraft reported enemy troop movements to ships in the Tonkin Gulf for analysis and relay to rescue teams; two helicopters, flanked by six propeller-driven fighters, recovered survivors.

It was the most successful air rescue system the world had ever seen, and on April 2, 1972, Lt. Col. Iceal Hambleton, an electronics and missile expert, needed all the resources it could muster. A SAM missile had blown his surveillance plane apart, killing everyone else on board. Using "BAT-21" (the call letters of his aircraft) as his radio call sign, Hambleton bailed out just south of the DMZ, landing smack in the middle of a major North Vietnamese logistical hub during the biggest NVA offensive of the war. He spent a week hiding from enemy troops, who had found his wrecked plane. They had his name and rank. They understood his military function, and they knew that he had a skullful of valuable classified information. The Americans had to get Hambleton out, but it wouldn't be easy. The nearest practical rendezvous point was the Song Cam Lo River, several miles to his east. He faced a dangerous journey through mountainous jungle with hundreds of NVA—who could find him by monitoring his radio transmissions—in hot pursuit.

But Hambleton had a fighting chance, thanks to an ingenious plan devised by his commander and an old golfing buddy. The two of them printed an imaginary golf course, using holes familiar to Hambleton, on a piece of clear plastic and placed the layout over an aerial photo of the area he would traverse to reach the river. Each of the holes ran east by northeast, routing him around enemy camps and strongpoints. Using golf terminology—mere gibberish to the NVA—OV-10 pilots could safely talk Hambleton to the Song Cam Lo. After four harrowing days he made the river, where a sampan picked him up and carried him to safety. Eight Americans lost their lives during the recovery operation. At great personal risk, Hambleton had reported NVA gun and missile positions to U.S. fighter-bombers several times during his ordeal. He received the Silver Star and eventually left the Air Force. Today he lives near a golf course in Tucson.

Bat 21 is a solid, exciting adaptation of William C. Anderson's book about Hambleton's 12-day odyssey. With two exceptions, it is faithful to the facts: for simplicity's sake the film incorporates the rescue operation's many OV-10 pilots into one fictional character

(Glover), and Markle credits Hambleton—not his commander and golf partner—with devising the ingenious 18-hole escape route.

Recommended Reading:
William C. Anderson, *Bat 21.*

Flight of the Intruder ★★★★

(1991) 113 Minutes

Director: John Milius

Cast: Brad Johnson, Willem Dafoe, Danny Glover, Rosanna Arquette, Tom Sizemore

Historical Background: Before leaving office in 1969, President Lyndon Johnson and his White House advisers squandered American airmen, resources, and credibility in a bizarre carrot-and-stick bombing campaign "derived," according to historian Walter Boyne, "more from Dr. Spock than Clausewitz." Continual air strikes began after Communist mortar barrages on the U.S. Pleiku compound killed eight Americans in early February 1965. A week after the attack, LBJ authorized his "Rolling Thunder" air offensive against North Vietnam, and the first American aircraft roared across the DMZ on March 2. From the beginning, Rolling Thunder belly-flopped, because Johnson was deaf to advice from his Joint

Chiefs of Staff (JCS) and other high-level aerial-warfare experts. America's top military minds hammered the point home every day: hit the enemy hard, quickly, continuously, and without restraints—"flatten every war-making facility in North Vietnam" (Adm. Ulysses S. Grant Sharp)—and air strikes would pay off.

Incredibly, Johnson ignored them, allowing civilian bureaucrats dominated by Defense Secretary Robert McNamara to isolate him from the military, control the air war, and press a ridiculous "graduated-response" strategy of steadily intensified air raids—a "slow squeeze" punctuated by bombing halts (16 in all) "timed" to lure the North Vietnamese into peace negotiations. The JCS, CIA, Defense Intelligence Agency, and Bureau of Intelligence and Research warned LBJ that Hanoi would view his restrained air-war policy as a lack of conviction and resolve. That is precisely what happened. In interviews, the North Vietnamese openly ridiculed Washington's dithering efforts to bring them to the bargaining table: "Wars aren't fought for cease-fires," sneered one official, "but for victories." The Communists happily used bombing pauses to repair facilities wrecked by previous U.S. sorties: during one lull, they built 40 surface-to-air missile (SAM) installations in Hanoi.

Even worse than Washington's strategic blindness was its death grip on daily tactical operations. Every Tuesday, Johnson, McNamara & Co. met for lunch and pored over maps, picking targets, ordnance loads, formation sizes, flight patterns, even approach directions for bombing runs. Frontline commanders couldn't launch strikes without White House approval. (Their targeting requests had to clear bureaucratic snarls at five different headquarters—including the National Security Council—before gaining approval. By then, tactical requirements had usually changed.) If sudden bad weather prevented in-progress missions, pilots ordered not to seek targets of opportunity jettisoned their armed bombs in the sea. Worst of all were preposterous "rules of engagement" hamstringing U.S. airmen: they couldn't attack SAM installations under construction; they couldn't destroy MiG aircraft on the ground; they couldn't bomb antiaircraft batteries until fired upon.

It was madness, causing countless American casualties, protecting enemy combat personnel and weaponry, and landing hundreds of U.S. airmen in dreadful Communist prisons. (Most infamous was the old Hoa Lo compound, christened the Hanoi Hilton by American POWs. Starved, tortured, buried interminably in solitary confinement, some prisoners endured captivity for nearly a decade. Occasionally, they made fools of their jailers: under torture, two POWs told interrogators that Ben Casey and Clark Kent had incurred courts-martial for refusing to fly sorties north of the DMZ. Their "confession" made worldwide headlines, mortifying Hanoi PR officers briefed later about American TV programs and comic-book heroes.)

Rolling Thunder ended on November 1, 1968. No bombs fell north of the DMZ until Richard Nixon's crushing 1972 Linebacker I and II campaigns scattered NVA offensive thrusts in the South and flattened antiaircraft installations in Hanoi and Haiphong, forcing Communist negotiators to sign peace accords a month after Linebacker II's initial sorties. By then, North Vietnamese air defenses had destroyed more than 900 U.S. warplanes and killed 820 American airmen. On January 27, 1973, the first of 591 POWs boarded C-141

transports at Hanoi's Gia Lam Airport and headed for home. A quarter-century later, more than 2,100 American names—many of them undoubtedly downed pilots—fill missing-in-action lists from the Vietnam War.

Crack A6 Intruder pilot Davis and bombardier Dafoe lead missions against nothing targets, watch fellow airmen die pointlessly, mount an unauthorized attack on Hanoi, then—at film's end—join early Linebacker sorties across the DMZ. (The Intruder, a two-seat, twin-engine carrier-based attack plane, was a phenomenal combat aircraft. An all-weather plane, it could deliver 15,000-pound bombloads at night with remarkable precision.) An intrusive Davis/Arquette romantic subplot and too much off-duty horsing around flop badly, but Milius delivers a clinic on A6 capabilities and tactics—right down to bomb types, ordnance loads, and early computerized navigation/targeting gear—and a super re-creation of Hanoi's bristling antiaircraft defense system. Perfect for Vietnam air war aficionados.

For Further Viewing:
The Hanoi Hilton ★★★★ (1987) 130 Minutes (Michael Moriarty, Paul LeMat, Stephen Davies, Jeffrey Jones, Gloria Carlin, Aki Aleong): Many critics on the left hated director Lionel Chetwynd's tribute to American POWs because of Carlin's gullible reporter (a merciless Jane Fonda sendup) and because Chetwynd geographically restages North Vietnam's criminal treatment of captured U.S. pilots. (Fonda called the POWs "liars and hypocrites" after hearing their accounts of Communist barbarism.) Overlong and soporific in places, *The Hanoi Hilton* draws an appalling, scrupulously accurate picture of prison life in the North (Chetwynd used several former

POWs as technical advisers), including grisly interrogation sequences. Aleong is excellent as a brutal Communist officer.

Recommended Reading:
Jack Broughton, *Going Downtown: The War Against Hanoi and Washington;* Sam Johnson and Jan Winebrenner, *Captive Warriors: A Vietnam POW's Story;* Stephen Coontz, *Flight of the Intruder.*

Full Metal Jacket ★★★

(1987) 116 Minutes

Director: Stanley Kubrick

Cast: Matthew Modine, Arliss Howard, Dorian Harewood, Vincent D'Onofrio, Lee Ermey, Adam Baldwin, Ed O'Ross, Kevyn Major Howard

Historical Background: Twenty years after America's withdrawal from Vietnam, the terrible price paid by Communist soldiers to resolve the war is clear: former North Vietnamese Army commander Vo Nguyen Giap has admitted that between 1964 and 1968, Communist forces suffered 600,000 battle deaths. An equivalent U.S. casualty rate (proportional to its population) would have totaled 7 million fatalities. The massacre peaked

in 1968 with a huge Viet Cong offensive launched on the traditional Tet holiday. Giap based plans for the massive operation on the ludicrous notion that South Vietnam's "proletariat" would rise spontaneously, striking American and ARVN troops everywhere as soon as his guerrilla army mounted its nationwide attack. On January 30, Communist forces attacked Nha Trang. Within 24 hours they had assaulted five major cities, 36 provincial capitals, 64 district capitals, and countless villages throughout South Vietnam. In Saigon, they occupied part of the American embassy.

The suddenness and enormous scale of the offensive took everyone by surprise, but after absorbing the initial shock of the assault, American and South Vietnamese troops regrouped and counterattacked, slaughtering Viet Cong guerrillas everywhere and winning one of the most lopsided victories in military history. By February 25 the offensive was completely broken. The South Vietnamese Army had fought bravely, and Gen. Nguyen Van Thieu's government still stood. Having suffered at least 85,000 battle deaths, the Viet Cong army was virtually destroyed. For the Communists, the catastrophe was so severe that they were never again able to fight a conventional offensive war against the Americans on so large a scale.

Incredibly, the American press—especially television journalists—portrayed the offensive as a Communist victory. Peter Braestrup, *Washington Post* bureau chief in Saigon in 1968, insists that some media reports amounted to outright suppression of the truth: "A lot of reporters in Vietnam . . . showed edited images of isolated events, and nothing lies better than a camera." After Tet,

America's efforts in Vietnam began to unravel. By November 1968, furious disagreement about the war had toppled the Johnson presidency and opened the White House to Richard Nixon, who soon announced the first phase of U.S. troop withdrawals from Vietnam. The last American soldiers left Southeast Asia on March 29, 1973. Two years later, Saigon fell to the North Vietnamese.

The first half of *Full Metal Jacket* rehashes every conceivable cliché on the rigors of Marine boot camp, adding a cataract of profanity that we've all heard before—in junior high school locker rooms. But the film is worth watching because its second half, set in Hue during the bloody battle for the city, delivers a powerful account of the terrible fighting that marked the Tet Offensive. Otherwise, *caveat emptor:* from beginning to end this is an annoying, pretentious movie. The final scenes, for example, follow an American rifle squad through pluperfect hell: a booby trap decapitates one GI; a sniper brutally kills four others; the remaining Americans then hunt down their adversary (a pretty Viet Cong girl), shoot her several times, and watch her die slowly in the rubble of a blasted building. Then, in a triumph of incoherent nonsense, Kubrick cuts to the film's closing sequence—a rolling shot of the same soldiers gaily singing the "Mickey Mouse Club Anthem" as they march to the Perfume River. What this is supposed to "mean" is unclear—but who cares?

Recommended Reading:
Peter Braestrup, *The Big Story: How the American Press and Television Reported and Interpreted the Crisis of Tet 1968 in Vietnam and Washington;* Don Oberdorfer, *Tet!;* Charles A. Krohn, *The Lost Battalion: Controversy and Casualties in the Battle of Hue.*

Go Tell the Spartans ★★★★★

(1978) Minutes

Director: Ted Post

Cast: Burt Lancaster, Marc Singer, Craig Wasson, Jonathan Goldsmith, Joe Unger, Dolph Sweet, James Hong

Historical Background: During the early years of the war, virtually all of the fighting pitted Viet Cong guerrillas against highly motivated U.S. Special Forces (SF) volunteers who trained and led Montagnard tribesmen on small, quick-hitting operations throughout the Central Highlands of South Vietnam. (The basic SF tactical unit, or "A-team," included 12 men: a captain, a first lieutenant, a sergeant, two radio operators, an intelligence expert, two medics, one or more demolitions men, and two or more weapons specialists. Green Berets had to speak at least one foreign language, and some were fluent in as many as five. They knew basic medical procedures. They taught civilians the concepts and tactics of small-unit counterinsurgency warfare. A crack A-team could attack its enemies on their own turf, disappear, and survive alone in the field for months.)

Between 1960 and 1965, Green Berets ran the Civilian Irregular Defense Group (CIDG) program in South Vietnam, concentrating their activities among twelve Montagnard tribes in the Central Highlands. (Indochina's "Montagnards"—French for "mountaineers"—are Malaysian, not Vietnamese. The term *viet nam* means "moving toward the south" and originally denoted the invading ancestors of today's Vietnamese, who drove the Montagnards into remote mountain strongholds 1,000 years ago.) The CIDG program aimed to convert several strategically located villages into fortified defensive outposts, isolating the Viet Cong by severing their contact with South Vietnam's rural population. The typical "strategic hamlet" had a meticulously planned defense system. Traverse trenches five to six feet deep ringed the entire village. Mortar pits protected the hamlet's perimeter, and machine guns with interlocking fields of fire covered all four sides of the compound. A swath of bare earth, dotted with mines and ringed with concertina wire, circled the entire village.

Despite a promising debut, the CIDG program eventually failed. After the 1965 Ia Drang Valley campaign, NVA regulars began concentrating in Central Highlands strongholds. The guerrilla war was ending. A conventional war fought over tropical terrain was on, but the Green Berets' initial successes prompted U.S. commanders to use them for "small unit saturation patrolling" from 1967 until the end of the war. One SF reconnaissance scheme called Project Delta flooded an 800-square-mile area with small, mobile A-teams commanding massive artillery support from firebases in secure areas. By calling in sudden air strikes and fire missions, Project Delta tied up the entire 325th NVA Armored Division—a total of 10,000 men—for months. Vietnam veterans who stayed in the service after the war refined small-unit techniques into the lightning "maneuver tactics" used by America's all-volunteer forces to smash Iraq's huge, ponderous army during Operation Desert Storm.

Many veterans consider *Go Tell the Spartans* the best film ever made on the Vietnam War. Lancaster dispatches (then joins) a CDIG team led by American advisers to refortify an abandoned village threatened by gathering VC forces. All goes well until the guerrillas launch a furious night assault on the hamlet. Dialogue and battle scenes are first-rate, and the team's effort to establish rapport with rural villagers rings true. Based on Daniel Ford's novel *Incident at Muc Wa*.

Recommended Reading:
Douglas S. Blaufarb, *The Counter-Insurgency Era;* Col. Francis J. Kelly, *U.S. Army Special Forces, 1961–1971;* Shelby L. Stanton, *Green Berets at War: U.S. Army Special Forces in Southeast Asia, 1956–1975.*

Hamburger Hill ★★★★

(1987) 110 Minutes

Director: John Irvin

Cast: Michael Patrick Boatman, Don Cheadle, Anthony Barrile, Don James, Michael Dolan,

Dylan McDermott, Tim Quill, Courtney B. Vance, M. A. Nickles, Steven Weber

Historical Background: By 1969 the Vietnam conflict had become a full-scale conventional war between U.S. forces and North Vietnamese Army troops based in fortified mountain camps. American commander William Westmoreland welcomed the change. Fighting in remote areas would reduce civilian casualties, he reasoned, and the bloody war of attrition would edge closer to an American victory with every engagement pitting massive U.S. firepower against large enemy troop concentrations. Rifle companies began sweeping the Central Highlands, attacking every Communist stronghold they could find. On May 10, 1969, the 101st Airborne Division's 3rd Brigade began searching the rugged A Shau Valley for NVA supply dumps and infantry camps. One arm of the sweep, led by Lt. Col. Weldon Honeycutt, began near the base of Ap Bia Mountain. Within 24 hours the Americans were fighting what would become the most famous battle of the war, a savage ten-day brawl up the slopes and along the summit of the mountain—soon renamed Hamburger Hill by battle-weary GIs.

Fortified North Vietnamese positions were incredibly strong, surviving relentless, deafening air and artillery strikes day after day. The Communists had also set up elaborate interlocking fields of fire covering every foot of the hill's forward slopes, where two American companies fought their way steadily upward throughout the day on May 12, only to fall back to their previous positions by nightfall under a hail of machine-gun and mortar fire. As the battle raged on, U.S. spotters located more and more enemy bunkers, calling in mur-

derous AC-47 gunship strikes around the clock. The North Vietnamese repelled a second assault on the 13th. Two days later the Americans attacked again, advancing yard by yard against fanatical NVA resistance. They reached the crest of the hill. Suddenly, one of their own attack helicopters began pouring fire into their right flank, and the assault disintegrated. Another attack bogged down in the mud on the 18th, but the 101st finally prevailed on May 20, clearing the last enemy bunkers by late afternoon. The Americans—who abandoned Ap Bia Mountain a week later—had sustained 60 battle deaths. They had killed at least 633 enemy soldiers, winning an overwhelming victory.

But Americans back home didn't care. Their response to the fight for Hamburger Hill reflected the fatal flaw in Gen. Westmoreland's strategy of attrition: a reasonable military plan—given the nature of the war and the restrictions imposed on the American high command—had produced disastrous political effects. U.S. civilians couldn't understand and would not accept the notion of spending lives to gain real estate, only to walk away at battle's end. They were tired of the war, and they just wanted out. By 1970, the same malaise had penetrated American frontline ranks in Southeast Asia—*GI Says,* an underground army newspaper in Vietnam, offered a $10,000 reward to anyone who killed Honeycutt. The war would drag on for six more years, but it was already lost.

One of the best movies about the Vietnam conflict. Many film critics with inflexible political agendas tried mightily to damn *Hamburger Hill* with faint praise. Their reasons were obvious. For one thing, the movie doesn't strain to portray NVA soldiers as patriotic souls fighting for their freedom against long odds. In *Hamburger Hill,* the North Vietnamese are just a bunch of unlucky stiffs trying to stay alive in a terrible battle that their side is losing. Some writers complained about the thin plotline, but a complicated plot would get in the way of the film's simple and obvious goal—to deliver a realistic, accurate history of the battle. Audiences watching *Hamburger Hill* couldn't care less about plot: they don't ask, "What happens next?" They *do* ask, "How much more can these guys take?" That kind of audience response signals success for any war movie.

The cast includes no big names—only journeyman actors—and that, too, is a plus: in *Hamburger Hill* you see soldiers, not last year's Oscar winners. Murderous, chaotic action on the screen has your full attention throughout the film; for this reason, *Hamburger Hill* comes as close as a movie can to putting you smack in the thick of things during a real battle. This is a remarkable accomplishment, and it makes up for whatever real flaws you might spot in the movie. *Hamburger Hill* won't interest people looking only for an ideological approach to the war. But history lovers and movie fans who want to understand the rigors of combat in Vietnam a bit better will love it.

Recommended Reading:
Samuel Zaffiri, *Hamburger Hill: May 11–20, 1969.*

Indochine ★★★

(1992) 155 Minutes

Director: Régis Wargnier

Cast: Catherine Deneuve, Vincent Perez, Jean Yanne, Linh Dan Pham, Henri Marteau, Carlo Brandt

Historical Background: In December 1953, a group of Algerian prostitutes (listed in French military records as "the Medical Field Battalion") joined France's doomed garrison at Dien Bien Phu and remained with the Legionnaires throughout the entire siege. This extraordinary footnote to the famous 1954 battle typifies the chimerical arrogance that marked a century of French colonial rule in Southeast Asia. France's war of conquest in Indochina began in 1847 with a battle at the city of Tourane (modern Da Nang) and continued for 40 years as the Foreign Legion fought mulishly to control Laos, Cambodia, and the three regions of Vietnam known at that time as Cochinchina, Annam, and Tonking. As quickly as they could, French civilians called *colons* hustled into safe areas to sell supplies to the Legionnaires. Soon a governing bureaucracy staffed by hordes of third-rate officials flourished.

Free to broaden their political influence, the *colons* controlled all of Vietnam by 1879, launching a 75-year period of unfathomable, myopic barbarism. Vietnam's system of universal education disappeared: 80% of precolonial Vietnamese were literate, but by 1926 only one in 12 Vietnamese boys could read, and one girl in 100 attended school. Massive 19th-century public works projects consumed thousands of lives. Accidents and disease, for example, killed 25,000 Vietnamese forced to work on one 300-mile stretch of the Trans-Indochinese Railroad. Hunger was rampant, since the *colons* allowed cultivation of only 25% of the country's arable farmland. Many Vietnamese starved because salt producers had to sell the mineral to the government, then buy it back at an 800% markup to preserve their food. A pall of degradation shrouded urban life—in Hanoi, Frenchmen raced one another to bordellos in separate rickshas, prodding the Vietnamese who pulled them until they collapsed.

Though the French had created a powder keg in Southeast Asia, Vietnamese resistance was chaotic and diffuse until the 1920s and 1930s, when an opportunity for revolt began taking shape. An obscure radical named Nguyen Ai Quoc—later known as Ho Chi Minh—intended to make the most of it. He attended the 1920 Paris Conference of the French Communist Party, then moved to Moscow to study the techniques of espionage and guerrilla warfare. In 1930, he formed the Indochinese Communist Party, and during the next 18 months the group launched several small, violent insurrections in Vietnam—all crushed by the Foreign Legion. But the long insurgency had begun. Vietnamese hatred of the French made it easy for the Communists to begin organizing the Viet Minh army by seizing control of diverse nationalistic movements that had fermented for years in Vietnam. (Most nationalists knew little about Ho, thinking that he was another patriot just like them. No one dreamed that once in power he would prove as ruthless as Stalin.)

Despite the *colons'* open collaboration with Japan's occupation force during World War II, President Harry Truman supported temporary French occupation of Vietnam to contain the chaos that erupted throughout Indochina when the Japanese surrendered. Fighting broke out between French and Communist forces in December 1946, but the Legionnaires now faced a large, well-equipped Viet Minh army that bore little resemblance to the ragged terrorists of the 1930s. The First Indochina War dragged on for seven more years—ending with France's defeat at Dien Bien Phu in 1954—and by the end of the decade Ho's forces were poised to begin their drive to dominate all of Southeast Asia.

Indochine won the 1992 Oscar for best foreign film, even though its principal plot is little more than daytime television for the big screen. Still, many history lovers will enjoy it: set in Vietnam during the turbulent 1930s, it offers fine period detail of life on a large rubber plantation and a guided tour of colonial Saigon's bistros, sidewalk cafés, and casinos. Plot elements framing the main love story—brutal conditions at a railway work camp, the formation and early activities of the Indochinese Communist Party, and life with a nomadic theatrical troupe—also are well done.

Recommended Reading:

Tom Boettcher, *Vietnam: The Valor and the Sorrow;* Tela Zasloff, *Saigon Dreaming: Recollections of Indo-China Days;* Nguyen Phut Tan, *A Modern History of Viet-Nam 1802–1954);* Christie Dickason, *Indochine: An Epic Novel of Vietnam.*

277

The Iron Triangle ★★★

(1989) 91 Minutes

Director: Eric Weston

Cast: Beau Bridges, Haing S. Ngor, Johnny Hallyday, Liem Whatley, James Ishida

Historical Background: History's first large-scale victory by a guerrilla force came in 512 B.C., when phantomlike bands of Scythian horsemen hammered away at the army of Darius I, driving the Persians eastward across the Danube once and for all. More than 2,400 years later, Communist insurgents in South Vietnam used similar hit-and-run tactics against their American adversaries. In 1955, Viet Minh veterans of the war against France began building a guerrilla army in the South. Directed by Hanoi, they stocked huge weapons caches with American M1 rifles, Chinese machine guns, mortars, and assault rifles, and 130mm Soviet field guns. To discredit the Diem regime by proving its inability to protect its own people, the Viet Cong waged barbarous murder campaigns against government officials, health-care workers, and teachers. Their political arm, the National Liberation Front, recruited thousands of peasants by promising to give them land. In May 1961 the Communists launched massive attacks across South Vietnam's Central Highlands and northern provinces. At the end of the year, they boasted a guerrilla army of 17,000 men capable of mounting hundreds of attacks every month.

In classic guerrilla style, the Viet Cong relied on mobility, superior intelligence-gathering techniques, and intimate knowledge of local topography. They peppered trails, highways, and arterial roads throughout the countryside with antipersonnel mines. They combined small diversionary assaults on U.S. strongpoints with sudden attacks in force against weaker American units in nearby areas. The NLF concentrated its forces in large, secure sanctuaries—staging areas for small, widespread ambushes designed to scatter U.S. rifle companies over a large area, where they could be attacked piecemeal. One of the oldest of these sanctuaries was the "Iron Triangle," a 60-square-mile snarl of dense jungle and isolated villages located just north of Saigon and long used by the Communists as a staging area for terrorist attacks on the capital. In 1967, two U.S. divisions, one armored regiment, and 70 attack helicopters assaulted the sanctuary from all four sides. The Americans killed 800 Viet Cong, swept the remaining guerrillas from the area, and leveled huge swaths of jungle to make troop movements impossible to conceal. The Iron Triangle was no longer a secure staging area for the Communists in South Vietnam, and a few months later the guerrilla army perished in the Tet Offensive's awful bloodbath.

Bridges, captured in the Iron Triangle by a young Communist guerrilla, learns what life is really like in a Viet Cong infantry battalion (it stinks). The film is inaccurate in places: it's set in 1969—long after the Communists were routed from the area—and it places the sanctuary west of its true location. But *The Iron Triangle* is worth a look for its effort to paint a detailed picture of daily life among the VC.

Recommended Reading:
Douglas Pike, *Viet Cong: The Organization and Techniques of the National Liberation Front of*

South Vietnam; David Chanoff and Doan Van Toai, *Portrait of the Enemy: The Other Side of the War in Vietnam;* Michael Lee Lanning and Dan Cragg, *Inside the VC and the NVA.*

The Killing Fields ★★★★

(1984) 141 Minutes

Director: Roland Joffe

Cast: Sam Waterston, Haing S. Ngor, John Malkovich, Bill Paterson

Historical Background: A vestige of the ancient Khmer Empire, present-day Cambodia has had many hated foreign masters, but none of them matched the murderous spectacle inflicted during the 1970s by Cambodian Communists on their own people. The holocaust's architects were middle-class elitists who deemed themselves intellectuals (all of them had studied Sartre in Paris). They numbered eight—five secondary-school teachers, a college professor, a government bureaucrat, and an economist—and they led a ruling clique called the "higher organization" that orchestrated the countrywide slaughter anonymously. (Pol Pot, the supreme dictator, was obsessed with anonymity: he kept many houses in Phnom Penh, moving surreptitiously from one to another on a daily basis for four years.) Though all

of them were city dwellers who had never held jobs requiring manual labor, they aimed to create a rural "workers' utopia" by exterminating everyone with reasons for maintaining Cambodia's traditional way of life.

The nightmare began after Khmer Rouge guerrillas, winners of a four-year civil war, took Phnom Penh on April 12, 1975. On the 17th, they began driving the city's 3 million residents into the countryside, starting with 25,000 hospital patients. By June, urban Cambodia was gone: virtually the entire population filled prisons and rural concentration camps, where the killing began. Guards tortured and murdered thousands of people who had no idea why they had been arrested. Teachers, high school and university students, civil servants, and the terminally ill were bludgeoned to death or suffocated with plastic bags. Many victims were crucified—some nailed to trees, others fixed to large wooden frames resembling football goal posts. At Tuol Sleng Prison, a special extermination center in Phnom Penh, pregnant women were disemboweled, forced to watch their unborn babies hanged, and left to die where they lay. (Professional classes were prime targets for extermination, so the country's medical network collapsed. The Communists replaced murdered physicians with "people's doctors," some of them so ignorant that they dispensed tablets and capsules according to their shape and color.) The killing began to wane when Vietnam invaded Cambodia in December 1978. Estimates of the final death toll vary, but it is virtually certain that at least one-third of the population perished, making Cambodia's holocaust the worst, proportionally, that the world has ever seen.

Cambodian refugee Haing S. Ngor won an Oscar for his performance as Dith Pran, the film's main character and real-life assistant of *New York Times* reporter Sydney Schanberg (Waterston). Based on Schanberg's award-winning magazine article, *The Killing Fields* re-creates Pran's ordeal, beginning with his arrest by the Khmer Rouge and eventual escape. *The Killing Fields* is fine film history that occasionally bogs down in silly polemics: at one point, for example, a television reporter asks Schanberg if journalists had underestimated the Khmer Rouge's brutality; his casuistic reply, "Maybe we underestimated the insanity that $7 billion worth of bombing would produce," could be used by Nazis to justify the Holocaust, since Allied bombers reduced every city in Germany to rubble.

Recommended Reading:
Haing Ngor, *A Cambodian Odyssey.*

Platoon ★★★

(1986) 120 Minutes

Director: Oliver Stone

Cast: Charlie Sheen, Tom Berenger, Willem Dafoe, Forest Whitaker, Francesco Quinn, Kevin Dillon

Historical Background: Steve Fredrick paid a heavy price for leaving school: drafted in 1967, he landed in Vietnam the following year. Once after a typical patrol he covered his head

with a gas-mask bag, submerged his entire body except for his face in a flooded rice paddy, and—protected, at last, from Indochina's swarming, ever-present mosquitoes—caught two hours of uninterrupted sleep. Only 10–15% of the Americans posted to Vietnam fought in the field, but the misery they endured was staggering. Fredrick's exhaustion was par for the course among "grunts": few of them ever really slept, dozing in brief "fits," instead. At one point, Fredrick stayed awake for 21 hours, nonstop, every single day for three consecutive months. Leaning against trees, he napped on his feet for five minutes whenever he could. One sergeant said that sleep deprivation kept many men sane during protracted, murderous combat: "They're so damn tired, they don't give a shit anymore."

Heavy gear, alone, guaranteed instant fatigue on patrols: typical kits included eight to 15 hand grenades, a steel helmet, four canteens, an entrenching tool, C-4 plastic explosive, three days' worth of canned food, field glasses, a first-aid kit, claymore mines, a six-pound M16 rifle (light) with 200–600 rounds (heavy—to accommodate the weapon's blistering rate of fire), and extra machine-gun ammunition. Many packed 40mm M79 grenade launchers and Remington shotguns firing lethal miniature darts. Individual loads totaled 85–135 pounds. Soldiers slogged through awful terrain—lacerating eight-foot-tall elephant grass, mountainous jungle, and sucking, knee-deep lowlands mud—in atrocious weather. Vietnam's dry season, May through September, brought choking dust and steady 90–105° temperatures with suffocating 90% humidity; in two days, heatstroke could easily level half the men in a 140-man rifle company. Violent monsoons followed—for months—bringing rain so heavy that men in foxholes opened firefights relatively dry and fired final solvoes neck-deep in rising water. Many developed trench foot and ringworms from the constant moisture and 30-day intervals between hot baths.

Because Vietnam was a "nonlinear" war—the front literally was everywhere—patrols made huge circular "sweeps," searching out hidden adversaries waiting in ambush. Indiscriminate death and disfigurement lurked everywhere: mines and booby traps inflicted almost 25% of U.S. soldiers' combat fatalities and 15% of their nonlethal wounds. In "hot" areas, villages were an infantryman's nightmare. Enemy guerrillas built hidden fortifications and tunnel complexes beneath countless "combat hamlets" designed for ambushing American soldiers. Even friendly villages were dangerous. Communists shadowing U.S. patrols often raced from jungle hideouts, planted mines on hamlet perimeters, then vanished, barely ahead of the approaching Americans. One soldier called searching villages for weapons caches and hidden guerrillas "the military equivalent of Chinese water torture."

Small wonder that most combat-related atrocities by Americans came in or near rural *villes*. By far the most highly publicized incident raged at My Lai hamlet in the "Pinkville" sector, a heavily mined Communist stronghold near Quang Ngai. Led by Lt. William Calley, an American platoon approached My Lai on March 16, 1968. Inexperienced and frightened (they'd already taken many casualties), several GIs opened fire on villagers bolting from straw huts. The slaughter continued until Warrant Officer Hugh Thompson intervened—by then, 178 villagers lay dead (some estimates put the final body count at 347). Calley, apparently, was thoroughly out of control—soldiers had twice threatened to kill him that morning. Court-martialed and convicted, he got a life sentence (later reduced to 20 years).

For a ten-year conflict incorporating thousands of part-time "civilian" (Viet Cong) adversaries, similar atrocities were remarkably few. (Courts-martial convicted 278 Americans for crimes against noncombatants: of the 122 homicides, only 30 came in the field—the rest happened in rear-echelon areas and cities.) South Vietnamese noncombatants suffered terribly during the war, but maily at the hands of Communist guerrillas and NVA regulars: during the 1968 Tet Offensive, for example, Communists murdered 6,000 residents in Hue alone. Even though the U.S. took unprecedented measures to protect noncombatants, misconceptions about American policies and civilian casualty rates persist today: the media, for example, falsely reported that America's practice of clearing "free-fire zones" increased civilian fatalities. In fact, the Geneva Convention mandated creation of free-fire zones to protect noncombatants by evacuating them from combat areas, and free-fire zones saved thousands of lives in Indochina: 300,000 South Vietnamese civilians died war-related deaths between 1963 and 1973; more than three times as many South Korean civilians—a million—lost their lives in the conflict there, even though it lasted only three years and raged for 12 months, near war's end, along a stationary front far from population centers. To this day, the United States remains the only country that has ever observed Geneva's free-fire-zone rule.

Stone's best movie is half terrific and half awful, with no middle ground. Military details (uniforms, weapons, base camps, jungle sets, and small-unit tactics) are scrupulously accurate, and only *Saving Private Ryan* tops *Platoon* for gut-wrenching, authentic combat scenes. (The first, a night ambush in heavy jungle, is absolutely terrifying.)

But Stone politicizes everything with a

heavy hand, skewing his presentation of individual soldiers and the U.S. military. His core drama, a protracted, open conflict between morally upright Sgt. Elias (Dafoe) and morally corrupt Sgt. Barnes (Berenger) is absurd: line officers would have ended it quickly, court-martialing Barnes or moving one of the men to another outfit. Worst of all—and highly offensive to Vietnam veterans—Stone's good guys all smoke dope and hate the war; his bad guys swill whiskey instead, and revel in opportunities to kill enemy soldiers, prisoners, and civilians. Former veteran and platoon leader Michael Lanning calls this "a shame for misled viewers and an insult to every Vietnam veteran—poor, extremely biased history." No surprise there—especially if you've seen *Nixon* and *JFK*.

For Further Viewing:
Casualties of War ★★ (1989) 113 Minutes (Michael J. Fox, Sean Penn, Thuy Thu Le, Don Harvey, John C. Reilly, Ving Rhames, Dale Dye): Brian De Palma's fact-based, oddly inconsistent account of an American squad's abduction, gang rape, and murder of a Vietnamese girl. One man (Fox) refuses to participate, eventually turning the others in. The film's hard-hitting, concise summary of the pressures, exhaustion, and constant fear igniting the atrocity is excellent. De Palma is perfectly fair to the NCO instigating the incident (Penn). But *Casualties of War* implies that similar crimes happened often in the field (they didn't) and that many of them were premeditated (virtually all were spontaneous). De Palma's officers are either half mad and morally blind (Rhames) or cynical, indifferent bureaucrats (Dye). Well-intentioned, but packed with blunders (one of the worst: VC resupply squads operate in broad daylight).
The Deer Hunter ★★★★ (1978) 183 Minutes (Robert De Niro, Christopher Walken, John Savage, Meryl Streep, George Dzundza): Michael Cimino's epic follows three Pennsylvania men from their jobs in roaring steel mills through the Vietnam cauldron and its aftermath. The film's re-creation of blue-collar Russian-American social life is wonderful and historically on target: most Vietnam recruits came from working backgrounds, not college campuses. For accuracy, Cimino's Vietnam segments are mixed: his brief picture of the war's savagery and Communist soldiers as the real day-to-day menace for rural villagers is accurate, but veterans panned scenes of ambushed rescue helicopters abandoning De Niro and Savage under fire. The calamitous turmoil engulfing Saigon just before its fall is perfectly drawn, but Cimino's professional Russian-roulette matches in back-alley saloons are bunk. Oscar winner for Best Picture and Best Supporting Actor (Walken).
A Rumor of War ★★★ (1980) 200 Minutes (Brad Davis, Brian Dennehy, Keith Carradine, Michael O'Keefe): Director Richard T. Heffron's film version of Philip Caputo's memoir detailing his Vietnam tour and court-martial for murdering Vietnamese civilians excels—in places: white-knuckle helicopter insertions, radio-directed artillery fire, ambushes by enemy machine-gun and mortar crews, and a constant focus on Vietnam's awful heat and terrain get top marks. But Heffron demonizes all things military (especially Marine Corps officers), thoroughly downplaying Caputo's guilt and faltering leadership in the field. Grim, entertaining—but highly biased and tendentious. Also released in a severely edited 106-minute video version.
Apocalypse Now ★ (1979) 150 Minutes (Martin Sheen, Robert Duvall, Marlon Brando, Albert Hall, Frederic Forrest, Dennis Hopper, G. D. Spradlin, Sam Bottoms, Larry Fishburne, Harrison Ford, Scott Glenn): U.S. Army captain Willard (Sheen) travels by river from South Vietnam's central coast to Cambodia with orders to find and kill renegade

Green Beret colonel Kurtz (Brando) for deserting, forming his own army, killing ARVN officers suspected of treason, and waging a bloody private war. For history lovers, Vittorio Storaro's Oscar-winning cinematography and Duvall's eye-popping helicopter assault are the only bright spots in director Francis Ford Coppola's pedantic, loose adaptation of Joseph Conrad's *Heart of Darkness*.

Factual blunders—some of them famous, by now—and occasional nonsense surface throughout the film. The Mekong River links Cambodia and South Vietnam's southern tip, for example, but Sheen's boat weighs anchor far north of Saigon, and no rivers traverse the country there. Nung tribesmen form the bulk of Brando's renegade band—but the Nungs were mountain people (originally from China) occupying the highlands of North Vietnam. Some marched south to work with American Special Forces outfits, but they didn't launch raids from semipermanent Cambodian sanctuaries. And the spectacle of Kurtz hanging corpses and severed heads from trees in and around his stronghold is absurd—the stench would be unbearable, and carrion-bred pestilence would probably infect his entire garrison. But the real rap against Apocalypse Now—often voiced by Vietnam veterans—is its trivialization of the war through continual, overdone satire and its portrayal of U.S. soldiers as ignorant pawns (Sheen's riverine crew), cold-blooded killers (Duvall's Lt. Colonel Kilgore), or hopeless clowns (Army brass).

Recommended Reading:

James R. Ebert, *A Life in a Year: The American Infantryman in Vietnam, 1965–1972*; Eric M. Bergerud, *Red Thunder, Tropic Lightning: The World of a Combat Division in Vietnam*; Lt. Gen. W. R. Peers, USA (Ret.), *The My Lai Inquiry*.

chapter 11

Cold War

(Overleaf)
The Hunt for Red October
(Photofest)

Chronology

1945

JULY 3: U.S. and Britain occupy Berlin.

1947

MARCH 12: Truman Doctrine "supporting free peoples . . . resisting subjugation by armed minorities" announced.

1948

JUNE 24: Berlin blockade begins.

NOVEMBER 2: Truman reelected.

1949

MAY 12: Berlin Blockade ends.

SEPTEMBER 21: Federal Republic of Germany (West Germany) founded.

OCTOBER 7: German Democratic Republic (East Germany) proclaimed.

1952

NOVEMBER 4: Eisenhower elected president.

1953

MARCH 5: Stalin dies.

SEPTEMBER 3: Khrushchev becomes Communist Party first secretary.

1954

APRIL 8: U.S. and Canada build 3,000-mile early-warning radar net across northern Canada.

1955

MAY 14: Warsaw Pact signed.

1956

OCTOBER 23–NOVEMBER 4: Hungarian revolt against Communist government.

NOVEMBER 6: Eisenhower reelected.

1957

AUGUST 26: First Soviet ICBM test.

DECEMBER 17: U.S. fires its first ICBM.

1958

MARCH 1: Khrushchev named Soviet premier.

1959

FEBRUARY 6: Fidel Castro becomes Cuban premier.

1960

MAY 1: Soviets shoot down American U-2 intelligence plane.

1961

APRIL 17: Bay of Pigs invasion by Cuban expatriates. It collapses April 24.

1962

OCTOBER 22–NOVEMBER 20: Cuban Missile Crisis.

1963

AUGUST 30: Moscow–Washington telephone "hot line" operational.

1964

OCTOBER 15: Khrushchev deposed. Leonid Brezhnev becomes party chief, Alexei Kosygin premier.

NOVEMBER 3: China detonates its first atomic bomb.

1966

APRIL 18: China's Cultural Revolution begins.

1967

JUNE 5–9: Israel wins Arab–Israeli "Six-Day War."

1968

JANUARY 3: Alexander Dubcek becomes first secretary of Czechoslovakian Communist Party, liberalizes Czech government.

AUGUST 21: Warsaw Pact forces invade Czechoslovakia.

1970

MARCH 5: U.S. and USSR sign Nuclear Nonproliferation Treaty.

1971

OCTOBER 25: Communist China admitted to UN, Nationalist China expelled.

1972

FEBRUARY 21–28: Nixon visits China.

MAY 22–30: Nixon visits Moscow.

OCTOBER 3: SALT treaty limiting antiballistic missiles signed.

1973

JUNE 16–25: Brezhnev visits U.S.

1974

JUNE 25–JULY 3: Nixon and Brezhnev sign agreement curbing nuclear-weapons testing.

1975

MAY 12: Cambodia seizes U.S. merchant ship *Mayaguez*. Fifteen U.S. soldiers killed in May 14 rescue.

1976

MAY 28: U.S. and USSR sign agreement limiting underground nuclear tests.

1977

JUNE 30: President Carter stops B-1 bomber production.

1978

SEPTEMBER 6–17: Carter, Egypt's Anwar el-Sadat, and Israeli prime minister Menachem Begin hold Middle East peace conference.

OCTOBER 16: Karol Wojtyla becomes 263rd Roman pontiff as John Paul II.

1979

MARCH 26: Begin and Sadat sign treaty ending hostilities between Israel and Egypt.

JUNE: Pope's first pilgrimage to Poland.

NOVEMBER 4: Iranians seize U.S. embassy and 65 hostages in Tehran.

DECEMBER 17–25: The USSR invades Afghanistan.

1980

JUNE: Solidarity trade union organized in Gdansk.

NOVEMBER 4: Ronald Reagan elected president.

1981
JANUARY 20: Iranians release U.S. hostages.

1982
NOVEMBER 10: Brezhnev dies.

NOVEMBER 12: Yuri Andropov succeeds Brezhnev.

1983
SEPTEMBER 1: Soviets shoot down KAL Flight 007, 269 passengers die.

OCTOBER 23: Truck bomb kills 241 Americans at U.S. Marine headquarters in Beirut.

OCTOBER 25–NOVEMBER 2: U.S. forces invade Grenada after pro-Cuban Marxists stage coup, murder government leaders.

1984
FEBRUARY 7: Marines evacuate Beirut.

FEBRUARY 9: Andropov dies.

FEBRUARY 13: Konstantin Chernenko succeeds Andropov.

APRIL 26–MAY 1: Reagan visits China, signs economic agreements.

NOVEMBER 6: Reagan reelected.

1985
MARCH 10: Chernenko dies. Mikhail Gorbachev succeeds him.

DECEMBER 27: Libyan-backed terrorists kill 18 in Rome and Vienna airports.

1986
JANUARY 7: Americans in Libya ordered home.

APRIL 2: Arab terrorists bomb TWA jet, killing four Americans.

APRIL 5: Libyan terrorists bomb West Berlin discotheque.

APRIL 14: U.S. aircraft attack Libyan military bases and terrorist camps.

1987
JUNE: Third papal visit to Poland.

1988
NOVEMBER 8: George Bush elected president.

1989
FEBRUARY 15: Soviets leave Afghanistan.

APRIL–JUNE: Antigovernment demonstrations in Peking's Tiananmen Square. Chinese troops kill 2,600 demonstrators.

AUGUST 24: Poland forms first Soviet-bloc non-Communist administration.

NOVEMBER 4: Czechoslovakia opens border to East German refugees.

DECEMBER 3: East German Politburo falls.

DECEMBER 10: Non-Communist Czechoslovkian cabinet takes office.

DECEMBER 21: Secret police attack Romanian demonstrators in Bucharest.

DECEMBER 22: Fighting between Ceauşescu's army and Romanian demonstrators erupts.

DECEMBER 25: Ceauşescu and wife killed.

DECEMBER 29: Vaclav Havel becomes Czechoslovakian president.

1990

MAY 1: Anti-Gorbachev demonstrators disrupt Red Square May Day parade.

AUGUST 2: Iraq invades Kuwait.

OCTOBER 3: Germany reunifies.

1991

JANUARY 15–16: Operation Desert Storm begins.

FEBRUARY 28: Gulf War ends.

MARCH 31: Warsaw Pact dissolved.

JUNE 12: Boris Yeltsin elected Russian Republic president.

AUGUST 24: Ukraine declares independence from USSR.

DECEMBER 22: USSR dissolved, Commonwealth of Independent States created.

DECEMBER 25: Gorbachev resigns. Russian tricolor raised over Kremlin.

The Beast ★★★★

(1988) 109 Minutes

Director: Kevin Reynolds

Cast: Jason Patric, George Dzundza, Steven Bauer, Stephen Baldwin, Erick Avari

Historical Background: January 16, 1988—northern Afghanistan: To punish Kolagu villagers suspected of harboring mujahedin rebels, Red Army troops hauled seven small children from their homes, bound them hand and foot, flung them into the town mosque, and burned them alive. Horrific barbarism marked official state policy from day one of the USSR's Southwest Asian venture: for a full decade, systematic carpet bombing leveled communities throughout Afghanistan; mass executions were commonplace; worst of all, Communist troops turned the entire country into a ghastly 252,000-square-mile minefield. By 1988, the Soviets had planted 30 million mines designed primarily to kill Afghan civilians and their children: made of cleverly camouflaged plastic, Soviet mines were undetectable or designed to look like toy watches, fountain pens, and rag dolls. On their own, reasoned the Soviets, people would fight, but they'd submit if you began slaughtering their children.

It was meticulously planned genocide on an appalling scale ("depopulation" was the official Communist euphemism for "extermination"). By 1987, Soviet forces had killed 1.25 million Afghans—a higher percentage of Afghanistan's population than the USSR lost of its own population during World War II. The slaughter opened on December 25, 1979, with a full-scale, 80,000-man Red Army invasion to tighten puppet "revolutionary" Babrak Karmal's shaky grip on his country's presidency. But ponderous Red Army legions floundered badly in Afghanistan's wild, rugged countryside. Trained to wage World War III on the open plains of central and eastern Europe, Soviet armored divisions proved virtually useless against rebel attacks launched from rocky gorges, narrow valleys, and precipitous mountain strongholds. The mujahedin were cunning, implacable, and incredibly tough. Soviet line officers, to their surprise and horror, couldn't counter the rebels' primitive, chaotic, freelancing guerrilla methods. For the mujahedin, there was no "big picture": they had no grand strategy, no formal command structure, and no tactical consistency. Unlike the Viet Cong, they'd formed no national organization the Soviets could infiltrate or monitor. Sophisticated surveillance technology was useless because the rebels—again, unlike the Viet Cong—didn't use radios or telephones. They were thoroughly unpredictable, and they had only one "objective"—hit the Communists whenever they could and deal bloody death until their enemies regrouped and began fighting back.

For the Red Army it was a nightmare. Their one consistently effective weapon, the Hind helicopter gunship, became an airborne deathtrap the minute the U.S. began supplying rebel units with Stinger missiles in 1986. By then, *glasnost* and *perestroika* made Russia's presence in Afghanistan pointless. (And it was less popular at home than the Vietnam War was among Americans, even though Soviet leaders shrouded the debacle in total secrecy: until 1985, Russian civilians believed their soldiers were building roads, schools, and hospitals for Karmal's new socialist state. Moscow even banned televised weather reports from Kabul.) On May 15, 1988, the Soviets began withdrawing from Afghanistan. Nine months later the last Soviet troops pulled out, leaving devastation, death, and a raging civil war in their wake. (In 1992, mujahedin rebels finally overthrew the Communist government in Kabul.) Afghanistan's towns and villages lay in rubble, its economy was destroyed, and half the refugees in the entire world—6 million souls—were Afghan civilians. The Soviet Union paid a high price for the war, as well: ten years of futile high-tech warfare kicked Russia's sputtering economy into a breathtaking downhill slide, hastening the USSR's collapse. The effects linger, with drab tenacity, to this day.

The "beast" is a Russian tank isolated and stalked through desert foothills by vengeful mujahedin rebels after its Soviet commander (Dzundza) levels their village, indiscriminately killing many civilians. Accurate all the way, with one colossal blunder: Reynolds' only Afghan Communist militiaman (well played by Avari) is a humane idealist interested only in "bringing Afghanistan into the 20th century"—in fact, Karmal's "soldiers" were little more than mass murderers; in January 1980, they strangled a dozen farm children to death in front of their parents, and similar atrocities continued throughout the war. Some prints retitled *The Beast of War*.

Recommended Reading:
Robert D. Kaplan, *Soldiers of God: With the Mujahidin in Afghanistan.*

The Big Lift ★★★★

(1950) 120 Minutes

Director: George Seaton

Cast: Montgomery Clift, Cornell Borchers, Paul Douglas, O. E. Hasse

Historical Background: April 21, 1945—Berlin: Marlena Eberhardt, a ghostlike survivor of Dresden's phosphorescent holocaust, sat slowly starving to death in a dank, stinking basement room as the battle for Berlin raged without letup from street to street. Clenching a knife in her teeth, she dragged herself upward into the street and slithered forward—rolling corpse after corpse aside—until she reached her objective: the carcass of a horse killed by shell fragments just moments earlier. Eberhardt tore several chunks of flesh from the animal's flanks and crawled back to her basement, thinking that things couldn't get worse.

She was wrong. Ten months later, it was much worse—the roaring shellfire and dry clatter of machine guns were gone, but so were the horses, dogs, cats, and every other edible creature in the city. Things were so grim that Gen. Lucius Clay, U.S. military governor of Germany, called Berlin "the city of the dead." Reeling from the coldest winter in more than 100 years, Berlin was one of the worst places on earth to be. Streets ringing its suburbs crawled with wolves, driven by hunger from nearby forests, and seeking warmth and prey. Infant mortality rates were staggering. All of the city's water mains had frozen and burst. Every day, scores of Germans without gas, electricity, or coal froze to death in their apartments. Throughout Germany, conditions were equally bad. There was no one to do the heaviest cleanup and reconstruction work because the war had destroyed an entire generation of young German men: only women, young children—including 2 million orphans—and people too old to fight remained. Critically disabled Germans numbered 1.6 million. Every city in the country lay in rubble. Habitable shelter in the industrial Ruhr, for example, measured five square yards per person (prison cells are larger). Everywhere, electricity, running water, natural gas, telephone service, and postal facilities were gone. As winter retreated, conditions improved, but not much: divided into four sectors (American, British, French, and Russian), Berlin lay in Soviet-occupied eastern Germany, and the Russians limited Allied passage through their zone into the city to one narrow highway and a single rail line—well below minimum logistical margins for supplying a population the size of Berlin's.

The wartime alliance between the USSR and the West had begun unraveling in late 1944, when the Soviets refused to share details of experimental U-boat technology harvested from Germany's abandoned Gdynia submarine station. Three years later, Stalin had devoured Poland, Hungary, Romania, Czechoslovakia, Bulgaria, and the Balkans. Clearly, he wanted the Allies out of Berlin—and out of Germany if he could manage it. He blocked their proposals for reunifying Germany and mulishly opposed America's $12 billion Marshall Plan for returning Europe to prosperity and economic independence. By 1947, the Western powers had seen enough: ignoring Stalin, they authorized formation of provisional state parliaments for the Western occupation zones; the British and American zones merged, and on June 18, 1948, the Allies issued a new West German currency to quell runaway inflation. Six days later, Russia cut off Berlin's electricity and blockaded land and river routes into the dying city.

Great Britain and the U.S. countered with the largest—and longest—continuous airlift in history. For 11 months, British and American pilots flew cargo planes packed with food, fuel, medical equipment, clothing, and building materials from the Western Zone to Berlin and back. Before the airlift ended, they logged 272,000 missions and hauled 2,325 million tons of supplies to Berliners. Round-the-clock flight schedules were grueling: pilots and crews labored to the point of exhaustion, stood down and slept for a few hours, then went to work again. (The aviator on one return flight tripped his automatic-pilot switch and fell asleep—when he woke up, he and his glassy-eyed crew were halfway across the English Channel.) Operations officers kept huge cargo planes airborne until they began coming apart: one weary pilot flew his rattling C-47 until deafening vibrations drove his crew to the point of mutiny; ground personnel inspecting the plane discovered that every single rivet on the aircraft was loose—or gone. The "Big Lift" was a stunning, but costly, success: when the Russians finally lifted their blockade on May 12, 1949, inclement weather, fog, and harassment by Russian fighter planes had killed 78 Allied airmen—35 of them Americans.

At year's end the Cold War was in high gear, with separate administrations governing East and West Berlin and Germany partitioned into two states—the Federal Republic of Germany (West) and the German Democratic Republic (East). West Germany began a surging recovery (now called "the economic miracle"), but East Germany floundered into an agonizing downward slide. On June 17, 1953, labor strikes erupted in East Berlin, spread throughout the GDR, and escalated until Russian troops and tanks crushed the uprising, killing more than 250 demonstrators in the process. After that, everyone wanted out. Between 1945 and 1961 nearly 4 million Germans (equaling the entire population of Norway) had left the Communist zone, producing a bizarre, humiliating statistic: birth rates in the GDR rose every year, but every year its population shrank dramatically. Berlin hosted most of the defections—in July 1961, 1,000 people per day fled to the city's Western sector. The exodus bled East Germany's already feeble economy even more, and on August 13, Soviet and East German authorities desperate to stop the debacle began to close the border. First came barbed wire, ditches, and berms. Within weeks the Communists had built a permanent 28-mile wall of concrete and steel, bristling with machine guns, watchtowers, and searchlights, through the center of Berlin. A 200-yard-wide minefield skirted the barrier's eastern side from end to end. Barbaric though it was, it turned the cascade of defections into a trickle, rescuing the East German economy. During the 28 years that followed, more than 5,000 people found a way to breach the Berlin Wall, and hundreds died trying. (Mass escapes were always by tunnel: the longest, dug directly beneath the feet of soldiers guarding a small row of deserted apartments, measured 360 feet and conveyed 29 refugees to freedom in 1962.) On November 9, 1989, with Communist governments disintegrating throughout central and eastern Europe, the Wall finally came down. Eleven months later, Germany and the two Berlins officially reunified.

During the airlift, U.S. Army flight engineer Clift meets, falls in love with, and plans to marry a German widow. He gradually learns that she's carrying a dark secret to the altar. An excellent film, made remarkable by location filming in rubble-choked Berlin a few months after Stalin lifted the blockade. Except for Clift and Douglas, all of the movie's "military" characters are real U.S. Armed Forces personnel stationed in Berlin during the filming. Airlift operations, including an edge-of-your-seat emergency landing on a fogbound runway, are so authentic that a good editor could use them to make a first-rate documentary. Douglas steals the show as a bitter Polish-American air traffic controller who logged time in a German POW camp.

For Further Viewing:

Berlin Tunnel 21 ★★★★ (1981) 150 Minutes (Richard Thomas, Jose Ferrer, Horst Buchholz, Ken Griffith, Nicolas Farrell, Jacques Breuer): Based on a novel by Donald Lindquist, *Berlin Tunnel 21* is the best film ever made on the ingenious schemes, titanic efforts, and enormous risks taken by East Berliners determined to breach the divided city's infamous wall. Thomas plans and leads a mass escape from the Communist sector through a tunnel designed and built by Buchholz, a structural engineer. The film begins slowly enough, gradually builds suspense as construction of the tunnel progresses, and turns at midpoint into a riveting thriller. Excellent performances by all and beautifully directed by Richard Michaels.

Recommended Reading:

Richard Collier, *Bridge Across the Sky: The Berlin Blockade and Airlift, 1948–1949;* Ann and John

Tusa, *The Berlin Airlift;* Peter Wyden, *Wall: The Inside Story of Divided Berlin;* Jerry Bornstein, *The Wall Came Tumbling Down.*

The Falcon and the Snowman ★★★

(1985) 131 Minutes

Director: John Schlesinger

Cast: Timothy Hutton, Sean Penn, David Suchet, Lori Singer, Pat Hingle, Dorian Harewood, Chris Makepeace

Historical Background: January 1977: Exhausted, dehydrated, terrified, and awash in his own excrement, Andrew Daulton Lee sat—each wrist shackled tightly to its opposing ankle—on the floor of a lice-infested closet in Mexico City's Metropolitan Police Headquarters. For six days, Lee had taken frightful punishment from interrogators highly skilled at bulldozing confessions from suspects. Convinced that he was a murderer working with Marxist terrorists to topple Mexico's government, they had spent hours immersing his head in a revolting, fully filled toilet bowl until bursting lungs forced him to exhale. They had beaten him on the ears until he suffered continual intense headaches. By the evening of the 14th he'd had enough: hoping for extradition, Lee told U.S. embassy attachés intervening on his behalf that he was a Soviet spy.

A heroin-addicted drug dealer with limitless ambition and powerful radar for quick, easy money, Lee was the weak link in a two-man espionage operation so oddly conceived and sloppily executed that on paper it resembles the subplot of an unpublished Cold War potboiler. But according to FBI officials, Lee and Christopher Boyce—architect, director, and intelligence source for the venture—did more damage to U.S. national security than any agents since Julius and Ethel Rosenberg. After dropping out of three colleges and drifting through seven jobs in two years, Boyce took a clerical position at TRW Systems Group—a Redondo Beach satellite manufacturing firm under contract with the CIA—on July 29, 1974. Incredibly, he got top intelligence clearances from the CIA and Defense Department and a high-level crytographic clearance from the National Security Agency on September 24. A few months later, Boyce was relaying classified information to CIA headquarters and two Australian bases from TRW's "Black Vault," a communications center at the heart of America's most critical intelligence operation—White House–directed international satellite espionage. Most of his transmissions came from top-priority *Rhyolite* and *Argus* spacecraft monitoring Russian ICBM installations and collecting data on military activity in mainland China.

Boyce wasn't impressed—he was bored. Disappointed that he couldn't buy a Triumph roadster on his $140 weekly salary, he got a second job tending bar, often working until 2 A.M., and began taking amphetamines to stay alert through long, smothering days in the vault. Morose and exhausted, Boyce finally launched his espionage scheme after a full night of partying at Lee's house. (Sharing a passion for the obscure, ancient sport of falconry, the two had been close friends since childhood.) Through a sleep-starved, cocaine-induced haze, Boyce showered Lee with details of TRW's business and his own work in the vault, finally suggesting an arrangement to sell state secrets to the Russians: Lee would take highly classified documents—photographed and smuggled out of the vault by Boyce—to the Soviet embassy in Mexico City, find a Russian intelligence officer, and make a deal. Lee accepted the offer, flew to Mexico in April 1975, and quickly came to terms with Soviet agents there. For 21 months, he and Boyce sold the Russians countless government secrets, including technical data on America's electronic intelligence-gathering capabilities and precious encryption ciphers for decoding CIA messages.

The operation's long-term success remains incomprehensible. Cursory, uncommonly poor planning by Boyce marked the whole sorry affair: Mexico seemed a perfect theater of operations, for example—Lee's drug business took him across the border often, and his presence in Mexico City was unlikely to raise anyone's suspicions. But the Soviet embassy there was notorious for harboring disgruntled, traitorous Americans (Lee Harvey Oswald among them), and the CIA had been watching the place around the clock for decades. Choosing Lee as a partner was lunacy. Arrested for drug trafficking more than once and closely watched by police, he spent more time sampling his product than selling it—especially before meetings with the dour, probing Russians. (At one rendezvous, he actually tried to recruit eminent middle-aged KGB agents as partners in a drug deal.) He was garrulous and bragged openly about his "CIA" exploits and his ties to the Mexican Mafia. Worst of all, he was overconfident and impulsive: though the

Russians often warned him to avoid the embassy, Lee slipped into the compound unannounced several times. Police arrested him for throwing notes through the iron gate there—exactly the same method for passing messages used by an antigovernment terrorist group under constant surveillance by Mexican agents. Extradited, tried separately from Boyce, and convicted of espionage, Lee began serving a life sentence at California's Lompoc Penitentiary on August 4, 1977.

On January 16, 1977, the FBI nabbed Boyce during a falcon-trapping excursion on a Southern California ranch. Three months later, a jury took less than four hours to convict him on eight counts of espionage and conspiracy, but he got a lenient 40-year sentence (also at Lompoc) for cooperating with prosecutors. On January 21, 1980, he escaped and remained at large for 19 months. U.S. marshals and FBI agents finally arrested him at a Port Angeles, Wash., drive-in restaurant in August 1981. (Shortly before his arrest, he'd called 20th Century Fox from a public phone to ask about the studio's progress in filming *The Falcon and the Snowman*; thinking that Boyce was an unemployed actor looking for work, a secretary hung up on him.) Authorities added 25 years to his sentence, transferring him to a high-security unit of the Federal Correctional Institution in Marion, Illinois—America's "New Alcatraz."

According to CIA officials, the security breach wrought by Boyce and Lee amounted to a "national calamity," and for American intelligence the debacle would get worse: in 1984, Barbara Walker, former wife of a petty officer in the U.S. Navy, called the FBI to report another spy ring—far more sophisticated and damaging than Boyce's operation—run by her ex-husband for 18 years. Racked by debt from his side business (a small bar in Ladson, S.C.) and miserable in his marriage, John A. Walker, Jr., had contacted KGB officers at the Soviet embassy in December 1967. For $2,000 he sold them encryption-code keylists for the U.S. Navy's KL-47 cipher machines, enabling their experts to track U.S. nuclear submarines on patrol. The Soviets agreed to pay him $1,000 per week for further information, and Walker made a small fortune selling detailed intelligence on new American weapons, secret military ventures, U.S. warship locations, nuclear-war contingency plans, and CIA counterintelligence activities. After leaving the navy in 1976, he brought his son Michael, his brother Art, and naval communications specialist Jerry Whitworth into his operation. Incredibly, Barbara Walker's tip gathered dust for three months in a Boston field office file before the FBI acted, finally nailing Walker at a Rockville, Md., Ramada Inn in May 1985.

Though Walker and Boyce seemed to have little in common, they shared three convictions making treason an irresistible route to quick, easy money. The USSR, for them, was an abstraction—an outline on a map, thousands of miles away—not a mortal enemy capable of putting the U.S. into an ashtray with massive ICBM launches. They considered state secrets nothing more than rooks or pawns in a huge, international board game played for no real stakes. And (with fatal naiveté) they assumed that they were smarter than everyone else—a mistake they'll both regret for the rest of their lives.

Strung-out and howling all the way, Penn makes a marvelous Andrew Daulton Lee and walks off with the movie. *The Falcon and the Snowman* could have been superb biographical

history—and a first-rate dramatic thriller—but Schlesinger waxes politically correct just often enough to send credibility packing, especially in his effort to make Boyce—well played by Hutton—an altruistic, pensive, tragic figure (certainly not the Boyce who committed five armed robberies after escaping from Lompoc prison). Still, most of the facts are there, and the film is well worth a look. Hingle's rendition of Boyce's father (a retired FBI agent who, in real life, put his son in the Black Vault through TRW contacts) is outstanding.

For Further Viewing:
Family of Spies ★★★★ (1990) 200 Minutes (Powers Boothe, Lesley Ann Warren, John M. Jackson, Graham Beckel, Jeroen Krabbe, Gordon Clapp): A very long, but remarkably thorough and accurate, account of the Walker family spy ring, beginning with John Walker's first contact with the Russians in 1967. Boothe, in top form, plays a reptilian, manipulative Walker, and Warren's portrait of the tormented, alcoholic Barbara is a knockout. Director Stephen Gyllenhaal's treatment of Walker's children (especially younger daughter Laura, who cooperated with federal agents hot on her father's trail) is first-rate all the way.

Recommended Reading:
Robert Lindsay, *The Falcon and the Snowman: A True Story of Friendship and Espionage* and *The Flight of the Falcon;* Pete Earley, *Family of Spies: Inside the John Walker Spy Ring;* John Ranelagh, *The Agency: The Rise and Decline of the CIA.*

Gulag ★★★★

(1984) 120 Minutes

Director: Roger Young

Cast: David Keith, Malcolm McDowell, David Suchet, John McEnery, Warren Clarke

Historical Background: In 1932, hordes of innocent Soviet citizens began descending into history's worst earthly hell—the gold mines of Communist Russia's Kolyma Region Arctic death camps. Six times the size of France, the vast 120-camp area was a frozen, desolate nightmare sprawling across far northeastern Siberia. Prisoners worked 16-hour days, seven days a week. Temperatures dropped to -60° and stayed there for weeks during bitter eight-month winters, but operations never stopped. In 1937, the Communists banned winter clothing: guards replaced confiscated felt boots with sackcloth-and-rubber *burki;* commissaries issued cotton underwear, caps, and mittens, tattered secondhand trousers and tunics, flimsy puttees (instead of socks), and thin coats fashioned from discarded blankets. Housing was atrocious. Lucky prisoners lived in drafty, lice-infested barracks and slept on bare boards in three- or four-tiered bunks. (Virtually all of them developed incontinent bladders from the intense cold and would do just about anything to avoid sleeping on the bottom pallets.) "Trotskyites" and other ill-favored political prisoners lived in tents riddled with holes and lashed by angry, round-the-clock polar winds. Allowed two baths each year, prisoners developed raw skin lesions and festering sores.

Worst of all was the work. Men entered the mines through small surface holes, riding ancient, rickety hoists to tunnels 3,000 feet below ground. Every day, scores died in accidents. Mineshafts so narrow and low that prisoners crawled through them single-file often caved in, burying entire labor gangs alive. Grease candles, the only light source, ignited volatile gases seeping from tiny crevices in floors and walls. Frantic to make "norms" (everyone had to hack eight cubic meters of rock per day from frozen tunnel walls), exhausted men regularly maimed or killed themselves with faulty explosive drills and ammonal-packed cylinders. Surface mining—digging up and hauling away tons of frozen soil and peat—meant prolonged exposure to subzero temperatures and bitter Siberian winds.

Failure to meet quotas brought reductions in starvation-level rations: the heartiest gulag diets totaled 1,500 daily calories per person—on average 1,000 less than POWs received in Japan's WWII Kwai River camps and far too low for prisoners performing hard labor in cold weather. To survive, prisoners ate anything that wouldn't kill them: birch-tree sap, houseflies, moss, grass mixed with salt, cockchafer beetles, even industrial petroleum jelly. So horrible was *katorga* (hard penal servitude) that many prisoners wrought terrible punishment on themselves to escape certain death: they slashed open their own abdomens or injected kerosene into their forearms; they hacked off fingers and wrapped feet with damp rags to induce frostbite; some amputated limbs by placing them on railroad tracks just ahead of oncoming trains. Most miners perished anyway: those not shot or beaten to death by guards died of starvation, hypothermia, polyavitaminosis, tuberculosis, typhus, or pellagra.

Kolyma was one of many regions supporting massive Soviet slave-labor concentrations. Weeks after Lenin seized power in 1917, his secret police (the Cheka) began running labor camps in areas controlled by Communist armies. By 1933, a vast network of facilities stretched from Kiev all the way across Soviet Central Asia to northeastern Siberia. Building railroads and canals and producing lumber, anthracite, coal, and precious metals, slave-labor camps drove the entire Soviet economy. From 1933 to 1960, annual gulag headcounts averaged 10–12 million souls—every year, a million of them died. Soviet camps also held countless foreign nationals, including many Americans: two repatriated survivors, Victor Herman and Alexander Dolgun, have written books on the gulag. During the late 1930s, state psychiatric prisons also began devouring Russian dissidents (almost always "diagnosed" as schizophrenics with "reformist delusions" caused by "persistent mania for truth-seeking"). "Orderlies" beat inmates senseless and wrapped them in wet canvas sheets that shrank as they dried, inflicting hours of intense pain. Feared the most by inmates were frequently "prescribed" punitive medications inducing insomnia, 105° temperatures, agonizing pain, and uncontrollable trembling and agitation. So terrible was Dnepropetrovsk's psychoprison that several thieves sent there in 1973 asked for transfer back to labor camps. (Exiled in 1980 to the closed city of Gorky for protesting Russia's Afghanistan invasion, physicist Andrei Sakharov endured chemical torture peaking, at one point, with 25 subcutaneous injections per day. His legs swelled to twice their normal size.) The world may never know the full extent of Russia's Communist terror: Boris Yeltsin has resealed vast KGB archives opened to historians for the first time shortly after the Soviet Union's collapse.

Framed for espionage during Moscow's 1980 "Pre-Olympic track and field games," American sportscaster and former Gold Medalist Keith lands in a Siberian labor camp for political prisoners and foreign nationals. (The plot isn't as far-fetched as it sounds—Victor Herman was a well-known parachutist and athlete at the time of his arrest.) Accurate in every detail, including Russian conversational slang terms such as *tufta*—common parlance for shoddy work done only to meet government quotas. Grimly realistic all the way; especially harrowing is a nightmare sequence in Lubyanka prison's deepest dungeons, ending, after several weeks, with Keith's signature on a phony confession.

For Further Viewing:
Sakharov ★★★ (1984) 118 Minutes (Jason Robards, Glenda Jackson, Nicol Williamson, Frank Finlay): A dated, uneven, but well-intentioned chronicle of the physicist's political activities and arrest, *Sakharov* bogs down in scriptwriter David Rengels' polemical dialog and lifeless rendition of Sakharov's relationship with Elena Bonner (Robards and Jackson). Ever-present but oddly tame, KGB goons generate no terror. Also missing is the drab monotony of life in Soviet Russia (director Jack Gold's dissidents live in tastefully decorated, spacious apartments and wear fashionable clothes). Still, reasonably accurate, worthwhile viewing for viewers who stick with it. Released two years before Sakharov's exile ended.

Recommended Reading:
Harvey Fireside, *Soviet Psychoprisons*; Robert Conquest, *Kolyma: The Arctic Death Camps*; Alek-

sandr Solzhenitsyn, *The Gulag Archipelago;* Andrei Sakharov, *Memoirs;* Alexander Dolgun, *Alexander Dolgun's Story: An American in the Gulag;* Victor Herman, *Coming Out of the Ice: An Unexpected Life.*

The Heroes of Desert Storm ★★★

(1992) 93 Minutes

Director: Don Ohlmeyer

Cast: Daniel Baldwin, Angela Bassett, Michael Alan Brooks, William Bumiller, Marshall Bell, Michael Champion, Maria Diaz

Historical Background: February 23, 1991—southern Iraq: Hurtling northward at 150 mph and flying low enough to shred his rear wheel on a sand dune, a freewheeling Blackhawk helicopter pilot crossed the Euphrates River, dropped an eight-man Special Forces team into the vast Ar Rihab desert, and roared away. Charged with monitoring enemy troop movement along Highway 8 before the Allied Coalition's ground offensive began, Richard Balwanz and his men had landed in an irrigation canal slicing toward a farming village (missing on area maps) less than a mile away. At first light, civilians flooded the area. Spotted immediately and reported to Bedouin militia, the luckless commandos radioed for evacuation helicopters and

braced for battle. Thoroughly drilled in close-quarter defensive tactics, they repulsed furious head-on assaults and flanking attacks throughout the day, killing 40 Iraqis without taking a single casualty. At sundown, the same Blackhawk chopper (still minus its rear wheel) returned and carried them to safety. Virtually lost in Desert Storm's high-tech stealth and smart-bomb light show, U.S. infantry operations produced plenty of crackling suspense at the rock-bottom, individual GI level.

Five and a half months before Balwanz's baptism of fire, Iraqi dictator Saddam Hussein had hurled 100,000 soldiers across his southeastern border into Kuwait. (A crackpot megalomaniac of the first rank, Saddam grabbed the tiny emirate to protect Iraq from an imaginary U.S.-led "conspiracy" to reduce crude-oil prices.) Killing, looting, and raping every step of the way, Iraqi troops raced all the way to Saudi Arabia's Kuwaiti frontier in 24 hours. Despite worldwide UN trade embargoes, warnings from other Arab governments, and several Soviet "peace initiatives," Saddam wouldn't budge, feverishly garrisoning Kuwait's southern border, but—incredibly—leaving his entire right flank wide open.

On January 17, a precision Allied air blitz howled aloft and continued nonstop for 39 days. Radar-proof F-117 stealth aircraft put laser-guided ordnance smack in the middle of enemy command-and-control, air-defense, and communications facilities, beheading and fragmenting Iraq's gigantic occupation army. Infrared night-targeting gear illuminated enemy armor—blinded and immobilized by impenetrable darkness—for swarming AH-64 Apache gunships and Allied warplanes. (American tank crews used the same sighting technology, destroying 200 Iraqi tanks in one night battle without taking a single hit.) Blazing F-16 fighters—so fast and agile that they could actually outmaneuver low- and heat-seeking missiles—wrecked enemy radar sites, antiaircraft batteries, and tank formations on the move. All of this—and much more—pulverized Iraq's infrastructure and knocked Saddam's troops senseless well before Allied columns rolled through their border fortifications.

Norman Schwarzkopf's ground campaign was a masterpiece of meticulous planning and on-the-spot pre-assault training. U.S. tactical experts studied detailed satellite photographs of Iraqi defensive positions throughout the Gulf theater, built identical fortifications in U.S. desert areas, and filmed letter-perfect assault exercises by American shock troops. Again and again, commanders screened copies of the films for combat teams, then walked their soldiers through similar drills so many times that line officers said their men could have marched all the way to Baghdad blindfolded and backward. On February 24, Coalition forces struck northward from Saudi Arabia along a huge 300-mile front. Near the Persian Gulf on the offensive's eastern flank, U.S. Marines and Saudi infantry smashed through enemy battlements and raced straight toward Kuwait City. To their left, Allied units drove into Iraq just west of Kuwait's border and wheeled east, cutting off withdrawal routes for Iraqi troops in the area. Still farther west, the 101st Airborne Division rolled all the way to the Euphrates River, trapping most of Saddam's Republican Guard in a massive blocking maneuver. The mortal blow came with a lightning-like American armored sprint from the Allied left flank—an incredible 125 miles west of Kuwait and behind the entire Iraqi army—sealing the most decisive large-scale victory in modern military history.

By February 27, only two of 42 Iraqi divisions (both in pell-mell retreat toward Baghdad) remained intact. The next day, President Bush declared a cease-fire. In 100 hours of air and ground fighting, Coalition forces had sustained 300 battle deaths, killing 50,000 to 100,000 enemy soldiers and capturing 175,000 more. With Saddam's defeat, several popular antigovernment uprisings flared throughout Iraq: all failed, and Coalition troops occupied northern areas of the country to protect refugees—most of them Kurds—from Republican Guard vengeance. The Allied assault's speed and power prompted Jordan's King Hussein and PLA head Yasir Arafat to sign peace accords with Israel, but Saddam's saber-rattling continues.

History buffs will enjoy this accurate—but wildly uneven—docudrama re-creating several Americans' real-life exploits during the Gulf War. (Film purists will find it tough going.) Ohlmeyer opens with the Iraqi invasion, skillfully mixing live CNN combat footage with dramatized vignettes of U.S. military personnel preparing to ship out. But the film quickly loses its focus, adding episode after episode in an effort to catalog every phase of the war (Iraqi missile attacks on Tel Aviv, the bombing campaign, infantry engagements, enemy units surrendering en masse, tank battles—it's all here). The good news: Ohlmeyer stages ground fighting very well and chooses knock-your-socks-off aerial footage of cutting-edge Allied warplanes in action.

Recommended Reading:
Norman Friedman, *Desert Victory: The War for Kuwait;* Al Santoli, *Leading the Way: How Vietnam Rebuilt the U.S. Military, an Oral History;* Richard

P. Hallion, *Storm over Iraq: Air Power and the Gulf War;* James Turner Johnson and George Weigel, *Just War and the Gulf War.*

The Hunt for Red October ★★★★★

(1990) 135 Minutes

Director: John McTiernan

Cast: Sean Connery, Sam Neill, Alec Baldwin, Scott Glenn, Richard Jordan, Joss Ackland

Historical Background: Today's nuclear submarines represent the most spectacular triumphs of 20th-century technology, carrying men on top-secret missions to remote depths of the world's great oceans. Easily the most effective and terrifying weapons systems of all time, America's largest ballistic missile subs—called "boomers"—stand more than four storeys high, measure the length of two football fields from bow to stern, and displace more than 18,700 tons of water when submerged. They are at least as large as vintage aircraft carriers from World War II, and Russia's Typhoon-class submarines are larger still. Boomers are, in effect, mobile missile platforms designed during the Cold War to provide strategic deterrence. Their nuclear-tipped missiles—with ranges of 4,000 to 5,000 miles—pack more than 1,000 times the explosive power of the bombs dropped on Hiroshima and Nagasaki. Once submerged, boomers can patrol for months without resurfacing, and they are capable of launching their deadly ordnance from the ocean's surface or at depths approaching 200 feet. They can sail undetected beneath the frozen Arctic Ocean, smash their way upward through the ice, and rain atomic death on any target in the world. Because they never remain stationary on patrol, boomers aim their weapons with computerized inertial targeting systems that use gyroscopes and data from navigational satellites to feed missile guidance equipment continuously recalculated information linking the subs' depth, speed, and direction to the earth's rotation. With their machinery mounted on sound-absorbing bases and their hulls silenced by anechoic coating to quell the reflection of sound waves, boomers become virtually "invisible" to surface vessels and aircraft once they leave port.

Against them, modern navies send smaller, swifter attack submarines—lethal "hunter-killers" that prowl the seas with orders to find and shadow their larger counterparts (and to destroy them with sonar-guided torpedoes should war break out). A single reactor, fueled by one pellet of enriched uranium 1.75 inches in diameter, can propel a modern attack submarine at incredible submerged speeds of 40 knots, or 46 miles per hour. Hunter-killers must search out their prey in an environment crackling with the chaotic noise produced by surface vessels, thousands of fish and marine mammals, and other submarines. Attack subs do this with electronic detection systems that use intricate configurations of sensitive microphones to collect the ocean's sounds and translate them into detailed visual images on the boat's sonar display screen. A good con-sonar operator can view thousands of glowing bluish-green dots on his screen and find the exact pattern produced by an enemy submarine. At that point, he can usually count the blades on his adversary's propeller.

For a full quarter-century preceding the Soviet Union's collapse, Warsaw Pact and NATO subs, always on alert, stalked one another around the globe in elaborate cat-and-mouse games. The Cold War is over—at least for now—but the world's navies have yet to decommission a single state-of-the-art atomic submarine. They're still out there . . . waiting and listening.

In rousing fashion, McTiernan combines an exciting plot and several compelling character studies with a fascinating clinic on the technology and combat tactics of the latest American and Soviet nuclear subs. Renegade Soviet skipper Connery commandeers a new ballistic missile submarine rendered completely silent by a top-secret, revolutionary power plant. He intends to defect and present the boomer—a purely offensive weapon "with only one purpose"—to the U.S. military. But the Soviets tell the Americans that he's a mad fanatic determined to fire his missiles at New York and Washington. The taut game is on for keeps when Glenn, a crack U.S. attack sub commander who finds and communicates with the fleeing Russians, must decide exactly what Connery's real intentions are and act accordingly.

Based on Tom Clancy's novel, *The Hunt for Red October* re-creates a theater of the Cold War that remains, for the most part, shrouded in mystery.

Recommended Reading:
Tom Clancy, *Submarine: A Guided Tour Inside a Nuclear Warship;* Thomas S. Burns, *The Secret War for the Ocean Depths;* Clay Blair, *The Atomic*

Submarine and Admiral Rickover; Edward Latimer, *Around the World Submerged: The Voyage of the* Triton; Sherry Sontag and Christopher Drew, *Blind Man's Bluff.*

Stalin ★★★

(1992) 170 Minutes

Director: Ivan Passer

Cast: Robert Duvall, Maximilian Schell, Julia Ormond, Jeroen Krabbe, Joan Plowright

Historical Background: October 1961—Moscow: Eight years after Joseph Stalin's death, memories of his fiendish reign still shrouded the USSR, poisoning the air wherever his heirs gathered to wish away their terrified complicity in a 25-year nightmare of depraved, epic-scale murder. Desperate to move on, First Secretary Nikita Khrushchev closed the Soviet Union's 22nd Party Congress with the strangest staged event in modern political history. On cue, Dora Abramovna Lazurkina—an ancient Bolshevik with gleaming, witchlike eyes—tottered to her feet and disclosed frequent invocations of Lenin's ghost: "Comrades, I survived my most difficult moments because I always consulted Lenin on what to do. Yesterday . . . he was standing before me, and he said, 'How unpleasant to be buried next to

Stalin, who did so much harm to the party.' " Thunderous applause erupted, and workmen soon hauled Stalin's mummy from Red Square to an obscure gravesite away from the Kremlin wall.

It was high voodoo *par excellence,* a lurid exorcism of demons unshackled the moment Lenin crowned Stalin general secretary of the party in 1922. Two years later the aging Lenin died, freeing Stalin to steamroll his rivals for the party's empty throne (major contenders included Leon Trotsky, Lev Kamenev, Grigori Zinoviev, Alexei Rykov, and Nikolai Bukharin). Quietly provoking furious ideological disputes, Stalin fractured Russia's new monolithic ruling elite into small, quarreling factions. Always he took the middle ground. Siding covertly with one group and then another, he isolated and destroyed his enemies one by one, quickly replacing them with loyal allies. By 1928, he ruled the Soviet Union.

The process moved quietly—by stealth—and peaked without warning: nothing in Stalin's personality, appearance, or background augured his rise to power. Born in Gori on December 9, 1879, and christened Joseph Vissarionovich Dzhugashvili, he seemed cursed with humiliating adolescent calamities: smallpox blanketed his face with ugly scars; he stopped growing at 5′4″; an accident shortened and withered his left arm. In 1899, authorities at Tiflis Theological Seminary expelled him, and he began to drift. He joined the Bolsheviks in 1903, took the pseudonym "Stalin" in 1912, and gradually impressed Lenin with his plodding diligence and willingness to do just about anything for the party. Utterly without flair, he conducted meetings with sullen indifference, seldom speaking to or looking at anyone, and doodling nonstop with red crayons.

Determined to build a modern industrial state overnight, Stalin launched a series of "five-year plans" requiring massive food stores for workers in urban factories and plenty of grain for lucrative foreign export deals. In 1928, he ordered Russia's peasants ("kulaks") to surrender their entire harvest—keeping only enough to feed themselves—for transport to industrial centers. The kulaks resisted, especially in the Ukraine, and Stalin mounted a campaign to exterminate every peasant in the region ("Liquidate the kulaks as a class!" became an official party slogan). Backed by legions of party thugs, Red Army troops sealed the Ukraine's borders in 1929 and launched five years of nonstop genocide. Carpet bombing and artillery barrages demolished entire towns. Armored divisions patrolled highways and back roads, shooting everyone without an official internal passport. Crammed like cattle into filthy boxcars, hauled eastward for days, then dumped without food or shelter in chest-deep snow, thousands of kulaks vanished in the vast Siberian wilderness. Soviet troops surrounded villages, confiscated every morsel of food they could find, and forced families to stay in their homes and starve. Horrors inconceivable to westerners were routine: cannibal gangs dragged solitary pedestrians into alleys, killed them, butchered their bodies, and ate them. In a 1942 meeting, Stalin told Winston Churchill that 10 million kulaks had died by 1935, and historians believe that Communist goons murdered 3.3 million more in prisons and death camps. (Horrified by the carnage, Stalin's second wife, Nadezhda Alliluieva, committed suicide on November 8, 1932.)

Stalin had turned Russia into a slaughterhouse. By 1936, his secret police (NKVD) had murdered Kirov, Kamenev, and Zinoviev, igniting a campaign of extermination (the "Great Terror") against veterans of the 1917 revolution, their families and friends, members of Stalin's own government, and "enemies of the state," a heading vague enough to include Russia's entire civilian population. In 1938, NKVD death squads dispatched by new director Lavrenti Beria widened Stalin's Red Army purge, killing more than half its officers and leaving Russia virtually defenseless at the outbreak of World War II. (A degenerate, homicidal monster, Beria routinely arrested teen-age girls, hauled them to his chambers, and raped them.) Russia's second full-blown holocaust consumed millions of lives before the Wehrmacht rolled across Stalin's western frontier in 1941. Two years after Germany's surrender, with his country still reeling from 27 million war deaths, Stalin launched a new witch-hunt against writers, musicians, geneticists, physicists, and chemists. In January 1953, he announced a "Doctors' Plot" by Jewish physicians to kill Communist leaders in the Kremlin. Flattened by a sudden, massive stroke on March 2, he died three days later—before his new terror campaign got off the ground. By then he had murdered at least 25 million people.

Names, places, correct dates, the Stalin–Trotsky feud, Nadezhda Alliluieva's suicide—Passer includes most of the facts in his lumbering chronicle of the 1917–53 Bolshevik cauldron. But he stumbles badly with portrayals of Stalin's cronies (Bukharin, Lenin, even Trotsky) as cerebral, well-meaning victims of the dictator's political skill and manipulation of Beria's bloodlust. This is unconscionable, fatuous nonsense: all were murderous gangsters—including Trotsky and especially Lenin, the inventor of totalitarian concentration camps

(Stalin modeled his own extermination centers on Lenin's paradigms, and Hitler studied them both; see *Gulag* and *Doctor Zhivago).* Well acted—especially by Ormand as Nadezhda Alliluieva—with one problem: Duvall's heavy makeup and studied accent focus viewer attention on his performance instead of on Stalin.

For Further Viewing:
Burnt by the Sun ★★★★ (1994) 135 Minutes (Oleg Menchikov, Nikita Mikhalkov, Ingeborga Dapkounaite, Nadia Mikhalkov): Director Nikita Mikhalkov plays Sergei Kotov, a Red Army colonel and hero of the 1917 revolution vacationing at a rural family dacha in 1936. From absolutely nowhere, his wife's former lover (now an NKVD goon) arrives to ask Kotov a few questions. Knockout performances, super period detail, and languid pacing build a powerful feel for Russian country life during the thirties and exude a heavy, deep-in-the-sticks atmosphere—all calculated to show just how far Stalin's tentacles reached (virtually to the ends of the earth) during the great purges. Landslide Oscar winner for Best Foreign Film.
The Inner Circle ★★★★ (1991) 134 Minutes (Tom Hulce, Lolita Davidovich, Bob Hoskins, Feodor Chaliapin, Jr.): Director Andrei Konchalovsky's finely wrought look at Russia's postrevolutionary nightmare through the eyes of a young projectionist drafted in 1935 to screen movies for Stalin and his "inner circle" thugs. (Stalin was a rabid, eccentric film buff.) Well played all the way by Hulce, protagonist Ivan Sanshin battles to survive an 18-year career that carries him from starstruck naiveté through gut terror to shattered melancholy at film's end. A riveting movie, based on the life of Alexander Ganshin (Stalin's real-life projectionist) and scrupulously faithful to history. Ghosts of Hoskins' lethal, licentious Beria will haunt you until your dying breath.

Recommended Reading:
Robert Payne, *The Rise and Fall of Stalin;* Richard Lourie, *Russia Speaks: An Oral History from the Revolution to the Present;* Andrei Sergeevich Mikhalov-Konchalovskii, *The Inner Circle: An Inside View of Soviet Life Under Stalin.*

Strategic Air Command ★★★★

(1955) 114 Minutes

Director: Anthony Mann

Cast: James Stewart, June Allyson, Frank Lovejoy, Barry Sullivan, Rosemary DeCamp

Historical Background: In late 1944, WWII aviation technology peaked when scores of Messerschmitt Me-262 jet fighters roared aloft to ravage Allied bomber formations hammering German cities into rubble. Stunned by the planes' blazing speed, goggle-eyed B-17 gunners didn't know what the fighters were, calling them "rocket-planes" and hoping that German industry was too far gone to produce them in quantity (it was). Before the decade ended, U.S. warplanes would make Hitler's nimble little jets look like sputtering Model T Fords. Piloting a Bell XS-1 prototype, Chuck Yeager crashed the sound barrier on October 14, 1947. Three years later, American F-86 Sabres were chasing down North Korean MiG-

15s at smoking full-throttle speeds of 687 mph (150 mph faster than the hottest Me-262 could fly), and B-52 Stratofortresses packing 60,000-pound bombloads could reach 650 mph—a remarkable feat, considering the bomber's size: B-52 hangars were so huge that indoor weather systems, including small rain clouds, occasionally formed near the buildings' rafters.

All of this because of Soviet barbarism and naked aggression in Europe. As soon as WWII ended, chilling news of mass arrests and executions by Communist secret police in Poland, Hungary, and Bulgaria began pouring into President Truman's office. Throughout 1946, the USSR tightened its hold on every Soviet-occupied European state and laid the groundwork for a worldwide "cold war" (Bernard Baruch coined the term in 1947). Truman, commander in chief of a skeletal postwar military force, played his only trump: on March 21, 1946, an all-out push for total U.S. air superiority began with General Carl Spaatz's restructuring of the Army Air Corps into three new groups—Air Defense Command (ADC), Tactical Air Command (TAC), and Strategic Air Command (SAC, charged with building a powerful offensive nuclear strike force). Sixteen months later, the National Security Act established an independent U.S. Air Force. (In 1949, amendments to the law created a new Department of Defense incorporating all three military branches and headed by a cabinet secretary.)

Just like that, SAC—the only branch capable (in theory) of winning an all-out war against the Soviet Union—was America's first line of defense against Stalin's juggernaut. In fact, SAC could brandish only a phantom atomic monopoly, its dozen bombs existing in various states of partial assembly and its delivery systems anemic at best. For Truman and everyone else who knew the real odds, it was a terrifying scenario: facing the Allies were 2.9 million Red Army troops and security officers backed by Soviet armor and conventional weapons in overwhelming numbers; and with no European airfields capable of supporting SAC's B-29 heavy bombers, America could launch nothing but one-way "kamikaze" air strikes against the Soviet Union. But Stalin knew none of this, and his futile 1948 Berlin Blockade (see *The Big Lift*) actually bought time for Truman to build a heavyweight nuclear strike force: SAC's brilliant performance during the airlift ripened into a flamboyant nuclear bluff if scores of fully loaded U.S. cargo planes could pack supplies to West Berlin around the clock for 11 months, the Communists had to assume that American bombers could easily haul untold numbers of A-bombs straight to Moscow.

On October 19, 1948, airlift director Curtis E. LeMay became SAC's commander in chief; in less than nine years, he turned a chaotic, undermanned, poorly equipped organization into history's most powerful global strike force. When LeMay took over, SAC had 486 WWII-era B-29s, 35 B-36 heavy bombers, and 35 B-50s (B-29s with upgraded engines). In 1957, he became vice chief of staff, leaving SAC with 1,367 Boeing B-47 Stratojet bombers, 380 B-52s, and 22 B-36s. (His most critical work may have been producing the elegant, revolutionary Stratojet in great numbers, then managing its development as a platform for B-52 Stratofortresses. A remarkable aircraft, the B-47 was also Boeing's prototype for several civilian airliners, including the legendary 707.) Under LeMay, SAC launched America's modern fighter program with the introduction of

Sabre jets in war-torn Korea and teamed with Boeing to pioneer flying-boom aerial refueling techniques. All of this underpinned Truman's successful push to "contain" postwar Soviet expansion and opened a big U.S. lead in sophisticated weapons technology.

In August 1949, America's atomic monopoly died with the USSR's first nuclear detonation, and the full-blown arms race that gradually deepened fractures in Russia's artificial, centralized economy began a year later. Before China's 1950 Korean invasion, Truman's push for a nuclear-based U.S. military had gone nowhere; three years later, America spent more than $50 billion—a huge figure in those days—on national defense. SAC maintained LeMay's commitment to research and development for 40 more years, gradually replacing early Atlas missiles with "smart" bombs, MIRV ICBMs, and cruise missiles. By the 1970s, massive U.S. and Soviet nuclear arsenals virtually guaranteed a jittery reciprocal deterrence based on the grim certainty of "mutual assured destruction" (MAD) during any sort of nuclear exchange. Today, that imperfect stability is history: many experts think the chances of random nuclear strikes by terrorists and Third World dictators able to buy atomic ordnance are higher now than the chances of nuclear warfare were when two superpowers jealously guarded nuclear technology.

Recalled to active duty in the early fifties, major league ballplayer and former B-29 pilot Stewart fumes all the way to his new post, then learns to love his new job—phasing in SAC's racy new Stratojets—under LeMay-like commander Lovejoy. A B-47 *tour de force* with exhaustive nose-to-tail clinics on the sleek bombers and their gigantic B-36 predecessors,

Strategic Air Command beautifully captures the Cold War atmosphere of early 1950s America. (Mann realized that the U.S.–USSR deepfreeze would last for decades: his opening credits end with a salute to active bomber pilots and "the young men of America who will one day take their places beside them.") Realistic and accurate—right down to SAC's long hours—with an expert restaging of history's first nonstop transpacific flight by jet bombers.

For Further Viewing:
By Dawn's Early Light ★ (1990) 100 Minutes (Powers Boothe, Rebecca DeMornay, James Earl Jones, Martin Landau, Darren McGavin, Rip Torn): Renegade Russians nuke Donetsk, and the Soviet president, assuming that Americans fired the ICBM, launches a retaliatory strike. Hospitalized American president Matthau and Russian officials try to stop the escalating holocaust, but McGavin, as acting president, opts to continue the war. B-52 pilot Boothe and copilot DeMornay spend most of the film aloft, waiting for final attack orders. A silly, badly flawed movie: director Jack Sholder makes superpower missile-silo security lax enough to permit freelancing nuclear attacks—killed by the Cold War's end, this possibility obviously never existed. Even worse, most of Sholder's high-ranking officers are bumbling incompetents, an absurd notion taken seriously by no one familiar with the U.S. military (ask Saddam Hussein). DeMornay, Boothe, and Jones excel, but the movie craters after the first 15 minutes.

On the Beach ★★★★ (1959) 133 Minutes (Gregory Peck, Ava Gardner, Fred Astaire, Anthony Perkins): After nuclear war devastates the earth, American submarine skipper Peck docks in Australia (one of civilization's last outposts), falls in love with Gardner, and waits for radioactive fallout to reach the hemisphere. He later sails for the U.S. to see if anyone there survived the war. Dated—like *By Dawn's Early Light*—by the USSR's collapse and the success of nuclear deterrence (while both superpowers still existed, at least), this quiet, apolitical film's grim backdrop supports a series of wonderful character studies (its real subject). Based on Nevil Shute's novel.

Recommended Reading:
Walter J. Boyne, *Beyond the Wild Blue: A History of the U.S. Air Force, 1947–1997.*

To Kill a Priest ★★★★

(1988) 117 Minutes

Director: Agnieszka Holland

Cast: Ed Harris, Christopher Lambert, David Suchet, Joss Ackland, Tim Roth, Joanne Whalley

Historical Background: In late 1966, Poland's "Great Novena"—a continual nationwide vigil launched in 1957 and marked by regular gatherings for public worship—would end with celebrations of Polish Christianity's 1,000th anniversary. That summer, Roman Catholic churches began displaying banners heralding "Poland's Sacred Millennium," prompting Communist authorities to retaliate: soon, pennants proclaiming "A Thousand

Years of the Polish State" draped hundreds of buildings in Warsaw, Gdansk, Gdinya, and other cities. Amused parishioners raised new banners—"For God and Country"—and watched in near-disbelief as the commissars responded with "Socialism and Fatherland." Days later, "The Nation Is with the Church" drew "The Party Is with the Nation," and the game was on: Poland's churches turned into pennant factories, pushing the government's hot buttons as often as possible and sending its apoplectic slogan smiths scurrying to their drawing boards again and again. Despite constant state harassment, millennium celebrations swept the country, setting a precedent—and a national mood that would peak with Pope John Paul II's first pilgrimage to Poland, the rise of Solidarity, the great revolution of 1989, and the end of Communist rule from Berlin to Vladivostok.

Russia's conquest of central and eastern Europe turned on Franklin Roosevelt's trifling performance at Yalta and his frothy naiveté—despite copious Allied admonitions—about Stalin: "If I give Stalin everything I can and ask nothing in return," he told a fuming, incredulous Churchill, "he won't try to annex anything and will work with me for a world of democracy and peace." FDR then signed away Poland, Romania, Czechoslovakia, Bulgaria, and Hungary (along with untold thousands of lives) and promised to withdraw all U.S. troops from Europe in two years. Eight weeks later, Roosevelt was dead and Harry Truman was president. In late 1945, Stalin's summary arrest of 16 Polish legislators and his treaty-breaking ban on free national elections there split the world into two hostile camps. For the next four decades, Poland would be ground zero of the Cold War.

But ruling the Poles meant obliterating the Roman Catholic Church in Poland, and no one had ever been able to do that. (The Nazis had tried mightily: during their Polish occupation, they murdered more than 2.5 million Catholics, including 2,000 priests, 850 monks, and 300 nuns.) Of Poland's 35 million souls, 32.9 million (a full 94%) were Roman Catholics, most of them determined—with stubborn ferocity—to practice their faith no matter who held the reins in Warsaw. Open assaults on the Church began in 1947, gaining momentum as the Cold War deepened: the government seized Church properties, declared Catholic schools illegal, closed Catholic hospitals, orphanages, and nursing homes, and banned Church newspapers. Polish primate Stefan Wyszynski resisted openly, attacking the regime in sermons and episcopate memoranda as often as he could. On September 25, 1953, state police arrested him, and by 1955 more than 2,000 priests, nuns, bishops, and lay activists languished in Communist jails. But a year later, Nikita Khrushchev's 20th Communist Party Congress speech denouncing Stalin ignited riots in Hungary and massive demonstrations in Poland. Desperate to avoid open revolt and keep Soviet tanks from rolling across his eastern frontier, party chief Vladyslaw Gomulka persuaded Wyszynski to return to Warsaw and help keep the lid on, promising to restore religious education and grant amnesty to imprisoned Catholics.

As soon as the crisis passed, Gomulka renewed his anticlerical assaults, and for more than a decade Wyszynski sidestepped or ignored every government move to legislate, frighten, or tax the Church out of existence. During the 1970s, he built a triple alliance of intellectuals, factory workers, and local priests—the social and political foundation of the Solidarity independent trade union formed in 1980. Throughout the seventies, Poland simmered with unrest. Its artificial economy, driven for 25 years by bureaucrats oblivious to the realities of supply and demand, was running on empty. On December 16, 1970, army troops killed 28 Gdansk workers striking for lower food prices, wounding 1,200 more and throwing another 3,000 in jail. It was a PR disaster, and—with Soviet blessings—the party canned Gomulka. Silesian *apparatchik* Edward Gierek replaced him, but the economic slide worsened, and rowdy countrywide demonstrations erupted again in June 1976. The SB (*Sluzba Bezpieczentswa,* Gierik's secret police) retaliated violently, arresting thousands and restoring a fragile state of order.

Then, on October 16, 1978, everything changed. In a stunning move, Rome's College of Cardinals elected Kraków archbishop Karol Józef Wojtyla Bishop of Rome, electrifying Catholics throughout the Soviet bloc. John Paul II, Cardinal Wyszynski's staunchest ally, was history's first Slavic Pope, and for Soviet-bloc Communists he was an absolute nightmare: now everything they did would fall under Rome's closest scrutiny and the cold, glaring light of international media attention. In January 1979, the Pope publicly informed Gierek that, like it or not, he would be coming to Poland before the year ended. Gierek agreed, and five months later John Paul toured the country, urging Poles to struggle—nonviolently—for "the right to self-determination and the right to one's own culture." The response was incredible: in Czestochawa alone, 3.5 million people—the largest gathering for any event in recorded history—congregated for his homily at the Jasna Góra monastery. For nine days, he hammered away at Europe's Commu-

nist overlords, delivering 32 addresses attended by more than 13 million Poles.

It was a knockout blow. A year later, Catholic electrician Lech Walesa—dressed in a jacket sporting a prominent Black Madonna logo—led a 17,000-worker strike at the Lenin Shipyards in Gdansk, winning state recognition for Solidarity in August, 1980. Solidarity and the "Resistance Church" kept agitating for further reform until the government struck back, banning the union and declaring martial law in December 1981; new party head Wojciech Jaruzelski actually declared a "state of war" to "restore order" in Poland. Backed by the Church, Solidarity went underground. In 1984, three SB officers—Waldemar Chmielewski, Leszek Pekalka, and Grzegorz Piotrowski—killed Father Jerzy Popieluszko (his antigovernment sermons had consistently drawn huge crowds in Warsaw) and flung his body into the Vistula River. The regime murdered five more priests—making martyrs of them all—in 1988–89. By then, the government and the economy, mired in constant labor unrest, were coming apart. On February 6, 1989, Jaruzelski opened roundtable negotiations with union leaders, and on June 4 the first free elections in Soviet-bloc history put Solidarity candidates in 260 of 261 contested seats of Poland's parliament. Shock waves rolled through central and eastern Europe all the way to Moscow. On October 23, Hungarian lawmakers declared the country a republic. Erich Honecker's East German regime had already collapsed, and thousands of Germans began whaling away at the Berlin Wall with picks, axes, and hammers on November 4. Communist governments fell in Czechoslovakia (November 24), Bulgaria (December 16), and Romania (Christmas Day), and in 1990 all three

Baltic states declared their independence from the USSR.

By then, the Soviet Union was unraveling at warp speed. Under Mikhail Gorbachev (named Communist Party secretary in 1985) an awful economic system grew worse: for 35 years, the Soviets had spent at least 13–15% of the USSR's annual GNP on defense, putting enormous strains on every sector of their economy. Blessed with vast areas of fertile soil, they still had to import 15–30 million tons of grain annually. Almost half the food produced by Soviet farmers never reached shops and markets, rotting in warehouses because of the system's inefficient distribution processes. Shortages deepened every year: after 1985, only special outlets for top party officials in Moscow sold meat and eggs. Despite all of this, Gorbachev remained an orthodox Marxist committed to extremely limited—and thoroughly ineffective—economic and political reform (*perestroika* and *glasnost*). He dismissed suggestions of a multiparty Russian political system as "nonsense" and did nothing to encourage political or economic changes in Russia's European satellites. (Throughout 1990, in fact, he fought German reunification tooth and nail.) To his credit, he didn't send tanks to crush demonstrators in 1989 (as Brezhnev had done in 1968), but that would have been suicidal to a regime desperate for massive aid from the U.S. and its allies.

By 1990, Gorbachev was one of the least popular men in the USSR: on November 7, a Leningrader took two potshots at him with a shotgun during the Revolution Day parade in Red Square. Six months later, Communist Party defector Boris Yeltsin won the Russian Republic's first popular presidential election, splitting the system's power structure and pushing the government toward collapse. Critical mass came that August: on the 18th, Communist hard-liners backed by the KGB seized Gorbachev at his Crimean dacha, launching an armed *coup*. Tanks surrounded Moscow's city hall, newspaper offices, television stations, and the president's official residence. But Yeltsin managed to rally many rebel soldiers and anti-putsch Muscovites to his side—at day's end, 25,000 of them had gathered around his "White House"—and the *coup* fell apart on August 21. Gorbachev returned to Moscow, but his career was over. He resigned on Christmas Day 1991, and at 7:30 P.M., the Russian tricolor flew over the Kremlin for the first time in 74 years. The USSR had ceased to exist.

To Kill a Priest is a fictionalized account of events in Poland during the early 1980s, based on the political activities, persecution, and murder of Father Popieluszko (Lambert's "Father Alek") by SB officer Harris and his cronies. Highly accurate in spirit and most of the facts—especially in its account of the priest's murder and the Church's key role in keeping Poland's anti-Communist resistance on track during the 1981–83 government crackdown—the film is oddly sympathetic to Harris' "Stefan," a character based on SB goon Piotrowski (in real life, a totalitarian personality driven by limitless personal ambition). Ackland—at his evil best—dominates from start to finish as an anonymous SB colonel subtly (and constantly) pressuring Harris to silence Lambert without giving a specific order to kill him. Released a year before the "annus mirabilis."

For Further Viewing:
Crisis in the Kremlin ★ (1992) 85 Minutes (Theodore Bikel, Robert Rusler, Denise Bixler,

Stephan Danailov, Boris Loukanov, Stoycho Maz-galov, Svetoslav Petkov): Director Jonathan A. Win-frey's oddball, confused film about a retired KGB agent (Bikel) and a CIA rookie (Rusler) teaming up to hunt a Lithuanian freedom fighter bent on assassinating Gorbachev. The movie captures Lithuanians' intense hatred for all Russians—matched only in Estonia, Latvia, Afghanistan, and the Ukraine—but its nutty premise and mangling of history (including an early assassination attempt that never took place) are incomprehensible: all of the facts about the failed coup were on record before Winfrey's cameras started to roll, and half the population of Moscow witnessed the botched attempt on Gorbachev's life. Filmed in Bulgaria and interesting mainly as a bizarre by-product of the dying Cold War.

Recommended Reading:

George Weigel, *The Final Revolution: The Resistance Church and the Collapse of Communism;* Jack F. Matlock, Jr., *Autopsy on an Empire;* John Moody and Roger Boyes, *The Priest and the Policeman: The Courageous Life and Cruel Murder of Father Jerzy Popieluszko.*

chapter 12

Social History,
Period Pieces, and
Biography

(Overleaf)
A Man for All Seasons
(Photofest)

Chronology

1525
William Tyndale translates New Testament into English.

1534
Anglicans break with Rome, name Henry VIII head of English church.

1535
JULY 6: Sir Thomas More beheaded.

1536
MAY 19: Anne Boleyn beheaded.

1558
NOVEMBER 17: Elizabeth Tudor crowned queen. She rules Britain for 45 years.

1648–1879
European Enlightenment.

1712
Rob Roy MacGregor launches outlaw career spanning at least a decade.

1756
JANUARY 27: Mozart born in Salzburg, Austria. He completes several concertos, symphonies, and sonatas at 13; dies in poverty at 35.

1789
JULY 14: French Revolution begins.

1793
APRIL 6: France's "Reign of Terror" begins.

1794
JULY 27: Robespierre falls, Reign of Terror ends.

1799
NOVEMBER 9–10: Napoleon Bonaparte stages coup d'état, proclaims end of Revolution.

1815
JUNE 12–18: Wellington wins Waterloo campaign, ending 23-year Napoleonic Wars.

1845
SEPTEMBER: Great Potato Famine begins, ravages Ireland for four years.

1853–58
Crimean War. (October 25, 1854: Charge of the Light Brigade.)

1858
FEBRUARY: Sir Richard Burton and John Speke reach Lake Tanganyika.

JULY 30: Speke discovers Lake Victoria.

1885
JANUARY 26: Gordon killed at Khartoum.

1899
Stalin expelled from Tiflis Theological Seminary.

OCTOBER: South African Boer War begins. Winston Churchill captured by Boers, escapes, wins Parliamentary seat in 1900.

1902

MAY 31: Peace of Vereeniging Treaty ends Boer War.

1903

Douglas MacArthur graduates from West Point.

1905

JUNE: Battleship *Potemkin* crew mutinies in Odessa Harbor, joining Russian uprising.

1912

APRIL 14–15: *Titanic* sinks.

1915

Eisenhower graduates 61st in a class of 164 from West Point. He ranks 125th in "discipline."

1916

OCTOBER: T. E. Lawrence and Sir Ronald Storrs confer with Faisal al Husein. Lawrence joins Faisal's army as liaison officer, becomes leader in revolt against Turks.

1917

C. S. Lewis wounded in British trenches on western front.

1917–20

Russian Revolution and Civil War.

1918

JULY 16–17: Tsar Nicholas II and family murdered by Bolsheviks in Yekaterinburg.

1919

AUGUST 31: Communist Labor Party of America formed.

1922

Stalin named general secretary of Russian Communist Party.

1927

MAY 20–21: Lindbergh makes history's first nonstop flight from New York to Paris in *Spirit of St. Louis.*

1928

Stalin launches plan to collectivize Soviet farm system.

1929–41

Great Depression in U.S.

1931

C. S. Lewis reconverts to Christianity.

1934

Stalin begins great terror campaign.

1936–39

Spanish Civil War.

1940

MAY: Neville Chamberlain resigns as British prime minister. Churchill succeeds him as head of coalition wartime government.

1948

JANUARY 30: Gandhi assassinated.

MAY: Eisenhower leaves U.S. Army, becomes president of Columbia University.

1949

OCTOBER: Communists take Peking, ending China's revolution.

1954–62

Algerian revolution.

1976

JULY 3–4: Israeli commandos rescue hostages at Entebbe Airport.

1977

NOVEMBER 19–20: Egypt's Anwar Sadat outlines Egyptian-Israeli peace plan (signed March 26, 1979) on floor of Israel's Knesset. Sadat assassinated October 6, 1981.

The Age of Innocence ★★★★★

(1993) 133 Minutes

Director: Martin Scorsese

Cast: Daniel Day-Lewis, Michelle Pfeiffer, Winona Ryder, Alec McCowen, Geraldine Chaplin, Sian Phillips, Alexis Smith

Historical Background: During the 19th century's final three decades, New York City's social elite demanded sheer tonnage—not just stylish elegance—from high-fashion Manhattan clothiers. At Mrs. William K. Vanderbilt's fabulous March 6, 1883, ball, Sarah Cooper Hewitt's outfit included gold-embroidered chamois gloves studded with precious stones, a cumbersome full-length satin robe and heavy pink silk skirt, a gold-net turban, maroon velvet shoes embroidered with gold thread, and a belt sagging with two daggers and a huge broadsword. (Gilded Age interior decoration featured the same teeming overload: rooms littered end to end with ornately carved furniture, overstuffed chairs, bric-a-brac and whatnot shelves groaning under the weight of ceramic knickknacks, and windows smothered by multi-layered curtains. Social arbiters considered rooms with floor space exceeding narrow walking paths underfilled.)

In an 1897 letter to architect Ogden Codman, novelist Edith Wharton consigned the Vanderbilts and their peers to "a Thermopylae of bad taste, from which apparently no force on earth can dislodge them." Wharton's formative years—she hated them—came during the 1870s with the first stirrings of the Gilded Age in "Old" New York. Life was slow, comfortable, and dignified. Elaborately codified social usages and rituals marked middle-class and "old money" patrician living in America's Eastern cities. People spent copious hours going to the opera (a social, not musical, activity for many), paying calls, and attending balls. Small, solemn dinner parties repeated themselves endlessly and identically: guests arrived at seven, drank port or Madeira, and wore standard evening attire (women—ankle-length, whaleboned silk gowns; men—top hats and white waistcoats with gardenia boutonnières). After dinner, men smoked cigars at the dining table, women massed in parlors or drawing rooms to gossip, then everyone reassembled for tea at 10 o'clock sharp. Tomorrow evening, more of the same. Early December brought long evening walks along Fifth Avenue, tobogganing, and ice skating in Central Park. Picnics, boating, and lawn tennis filled the summer months. People lived honorably, worked hard, went to church, and married for life—it was a slow, comfortable, dignified life with few surprises.

During the late 1870s, old American money held its nose and gaped as industrial and commercial families elbowed their way into polite society with vast new fortunes, signaling more than three decades of unprecedented technological, industrial, and social change. America's 1870–1900 industrial boom launched an enormous population shift to cities with service-industry and manufacturing jobs: by the late 1890s, 25 million souls lived in cities and towns with at least 8,000 residents, a staggering increase of 20 million people over four decades. During the 1870s alone, New York City's census rocketed to 1,165,000—an average rise of 22,240 new residents every year.

European immigrants—400,000 a year by 1890—poured into major cities, settling in crowded tenements festering mere blocks from towering skyscrapers and comfortable townhouses. Slum life was horrible, but many enterprising families moved upward and out—some within weeks or months, others within a generation—into a middle-class world of telephones, electric irons and lights, gas stoves, Sears Roebuck mail-order catalogs, department stores, iceboxes, mass-produced clothing, electric trolleys, and brand-name advertising. In three decades, the quaint, leisurely world of Old New York had all but disappeared—and even Edith Wharton missed it. Years later, the Great War's horrors barely extinct, she told old friend Sara Norton why she'd started a new novel, *The Age of Innocence:* "I am steeping myself in the nineteenth century, a blessed refuge from the turmoil and mediocrity of today—like taking sanctuary in a mighty temple."

Engaged to vapid ingenue May Welland (Ryder), old-money attorney Newland Archer (Day-Lewis) meets American expatriate Countess Ellen Olenska (Pfeiffer)—separated from her Polish husband, seeking a divorce in the States, and way too hot for Fifth Avenue. He falls in love with the countess and struggles to stay afloat in his suddenly capsizing world. Scorsese's beautifully crafted adaptation of Wharton's novel on social life and barely strangled illicit passion in late-1870s New York is one of the finest period pieces ever. Great period accuracy—sets, costumes, manners, polite dinner conversations—and remarkably faithful to Wharton's masterpiece from scene one (a languid review of social buzz at the opera, with box-seat audiences paying attention to everything—especially each other—but the music).

Great performances by the leads and a fine ensemble cast.

Recommended Reading:
R.W.B. Lewis, *Edith Wharton: A Biography;* Fon W. Boardman, Jr., *America and the Gilded Age: 1876-1900;* Oliver Jensen, ed., *The Nineties: Glimpses of a Lost but Lively World;* Edith Wharton, *The Age of Innocence* and *The House of Mirth.*

The Bounty ★★★★★

(1984) 130 Minutes

Director: Roger Donaldson

Cast: Mel Gibson, Anthony Hopkins, Laurence Olivier, Edward Fox, Daniel Day-Lewis, Liam Neeson

Historical Background: Winter 1740—Cape Horn: Just off the southernmost point of South America the waters of the Atlantic and Pacific meet with terrifying ferocity. Lashed by 50-mph winds and unchecked by intervening landmasses until they reach Antarctica, mountainous swells roll outward toward the bottom of the world. In 1740, Adm. George Anson and 1,900 seamen tried to "round the Horn" in seven British warships. Raging seas pounded the stout vessels as they strained toward the crests of towering waves, then plummeted at terrifying speeds into the boiling troughs below. Men crashed into gun carriages, breaking necks and severing spinal cords. Some fell overboard. Everything that wasn't tightly secured flew through the air like shrapnel. Anson lost three ships before clearing the Cape, and inboard conditions on his surviving craft—septic from the beginning—were appalling. Seawater was everywhere, fouling provisions, drenching bunks and clothing, and rendering the air below decks unbreathable. Slime coated each ship from bow to stern. Beer and drinking water stored in wooden kegs bred surface encrustations that returned no matter how often thirsty men ladled them away. Scurvy, the terror of seamen everywhere, soon raged through the tiny fleet. Men's gums began to bleed, swelling grotesquely over their teeth and eventually disintegrating. Awful subcutaneous hemorrhaging followed. When Anson limped back to Portsmouth in 1744, only 600 officers and crewmen remained alive.

Though long excursions remained dangerous and naval service harsh, living conditions for seamen in the Royal Navy improved during the 1780s, thanks to England's great explorer James Cook. Cook ran a tight ship. He ordered seamen to bathe regularly and launder clothing often. His crews swabbed lower decks with gunpowder-laced vinegar and fumigated the ship with smoke to exterminate vermin. Familiar with contemporary medical theory linking scurvy to diet, Cook stocked his galley with dried vegetable soup, lemon juice, citrus fruit, and shredded greens marinated in vinegar. He replaced the navy's grueling two-watch duty rotation (four hours on, four hours off) with a three-watch system that gave all hands eight hours of rest every day. Cook's changes brought stunning success. His crews performed brilliantly, helping him to orchestrate spectacular navigational feats and chart vast, trackless maritime areas for the first time.

In one of history's grand ironies, Lt. William Bligh, the reviled ogre of Britain's most celebrated mutiny, trained under Cook and put most of his enlightened principles to work during the *Bounty*'s notorious final voyage. On December 23, 1787, Bligh set sail from Spithead, England, with orders to make port at Tahiti, secure more than 1,000 breadfruit trees, and transport them to England's starving West Indian colonies. Two built-in problems handicapped Bligh before he weighed anchor. Converted by the Royal Navy from a cargo ship into a maritime nursery, the *Bounty* was short on living space—even for a complement severely reduced to expand shipboard "greenhouse" areas. And diminished manpower meant more rigorous duty rotations and harder work for the skeletal 47-man crew: the *Bounty*'s Pacific voyage would be a long, difficult haul.

Happily, Bligh seemed eminently qualified to lead the mission. He was a skilled shipboard manager, a remarkable navigator, and an avid amateur botanist. By 18th-century standards his reputation as a sadistic monster is nonsense. (On the passage to Polynesia, he had one crewman flogged: Matthew Quintal took 12 lashes for insolence—easy punishment, in those days, for so grave an offense.) But flaws in Bligh's temperament aggravated the daily strain already vexing his overtaxed crew. He was vain and thin-skinned. When pressure mounted, minor lapses in discipline drew furious tongue-lashings. Prudent and reasonable at first, his insistence on shipboard cleanliness gradually become a fanatical obsession. In late March 1788 the *Bounty* approached Tierra del Fuego, and Bligh—fully aware of Anson's terrible ordeal—tried in vain for four shattering weeks to round the Horn. He finally reversed course on April 22, sailing eastward from Tierra del Fuego all the way to Australia and beyond. Shipboard tension mounted steadily as the self-assured, dignified Bligh slowly ripened into a petty, caviling Miss Grundy. By the time the *Bounty* dropped anchor in Tahiti's Matavai Bay on October 25, 1788, every sailor on board was ready to swim ashore.

On April 4, 1789, the *Bounty* weighed anchor and embarked for the West Indies with a hold full of breadfruit and a thoroughly disgruntled crew. After 23 weeks of pristine beaches and compliant Tahitian women, the return to tight quarters, iron discipline, and Bligh's grating behavior proved too difficult for many of the men. The captain grew more and more vindictive, especially toward his master's mate Fletcher Christian. A family friend scarcely mentioned in Bligh's journal (and leaving no diary of his own), Christian remains a mysterious character. Like most of the crewmen, he smoldered under the captain's tirades until April 27, when Bligh publicly accused him of stealing coconuts from the ship's stores. The next day he led a mutiny, seizing the *Bounty* and casting Bligh adrift in the ship's launch with charts, navigating gear, food, and 18 other men. Without delay, the 28 mutineers returned to Tahiti, where 16 chose to remain indefinitely. (Two years later, the Royal Navy captured and hanged ten of them.) Christian, his tiny crew, and 12 Tahitian women eventually sailed from Polynesia to Pitcairn Island, burned their ship, and started a colony that survives to this day. Incredibly, Bligh piloted the *Bounty*'s small lifeboat across 4,000 miles of dangerous, uncharted ocean to Timor. He remained in the Royal Navy and fought bril-

liantly with Nelson in the 1801 Battle of Copenhagen, then served for three years as governor of New South Wales in Australia. Bligh retired a rear admiral and died in England on December 7, 1817.

Gritty, realistic, and remarkably accurate in its presentation of Bligh, this is easily the best of Hollywood's three movies on the legendary 18th-century mutiny. *The Bounty* comes as close as historical information permits to showing us what Fletcher Christian and his captain were really like. In one of his best performances, Hopkins judiciously avoids Hollywood's customary presentation of Bligh's disciplined self-control as pathetic Freudian "repression." Instead, we get an intelligent, confident, tough-minded skipper—strengths taken for granted in every officer who lasted for more than a year in the 18th-century Royal Navy.

Gibson's taciturn Fletcher Christian is a bull's-eye: fleet-level junior officers kept their mouths shut and relayed their captain's orders to the crew—period. (This was doubly true on smaller Royal Navy ships, where master's mates had fewer peers.) The real Fletcher Christian, denied familiarity with the seamen as well as with Bligh, undoubtedly stood isolated between the two simmering extremes: with whom, exactly, would he make conversation? Excellent performances, accurate period detail, ample footage on the rigors of shipboard life, and a gut-wrenching rendition of Cape Horn's monstrous horrors combine to make *The Bounty* one of Hollywood's finest chronicles of the sea.

For Further Viewing:
Mutiny on the Bounty ★★ (1962) 179 Minutes (Marlon Brando, Trevor Howard, Richard Harris, Richard Hayden, Gordon Jackson, Hugh Griffith):

This expensive, overlong, and badly bloated remake of the 1935 masterpiece is well worth passing up. Horribly miscast, Brando Method-acts his way to a silly, mannered rendition of Fletcher Christian—you almost expect him to scream "Hey, Stella-a-a!" with each new outrage from Bligh. Brando's age—he was pushing 40 in 1962—makes things worse: angst-ridden, middle-aged mutineers don't ring true (Christian was 23 when the *Bounty* sailed for Polynesia). Howard is very good as an unbalanced Captain Bligh, but he can't carry the entire film.

Mutiny on the Bounty ★★★★ (1935) 132 Minutes (Charles Laughton, Clark Gable, Franchot Tone, Eddie Quillan, Donald Crisp, Henry Stephenson): As impossible as it sounds, Laughton's screen presence completely dwarfs Gable—his Fletcher Christian snagged an Oscar nomination—in this first movie version of the book by Charles Nordhoff and James Norman Hall. Laughton's tyrannical, sadistic, explosive Bligh makes Vince Lombardi look like a psychiatric social worker. It's an irresistible performance, even though the character bears no resemblance to the *Bounty*'s actual skipper. A glaring factual blunder mars the film's ending: Captain Edward Edwards actually led the punitive expedition to capture mutineers in Tahiti, but the movie puts Bligh in command. Still, this is moviemaking at its best—good enough to win the Oscar for Best Picture.

Damn the Defiant! ★★★★★ (1962) 101 Minutes (Alec Guinness, Dirk Bogarde, Anthony Quayle, Maurice Denham, Richard Carpenter, Nigel Stock): Set aboard a frigate sailing from Spithead to join Britain's Mediterranean fleet during the Napoleonic Wars, this gem from director Lewis Gilbert packs colorful, accurate detail—right down to the color of deck planking on 18th-century warships—into a riveting *tour de force* of life in Lord Nelson's navy. Guinness is terrific as the ship's captain, but Bogarde steals the show as a predatory, sadistic first officer scheming to undermine Guinness' authority, take over the frigate, and advance his own career in the process. Dockside press gangs, grandly choreographed battle scenes, training programs for midshipmen (boys in their mid-teens preparing for service as commissioned officers)—every element in the film reflects meticulous research. Lean, mean, and exciting: easily Gilbert's finest work and a must for aficionados of tall ships and the great age of sail.

Recommended Reading:
James Dugan, *The Great Mutiny;* Kenneth S. Allen, *That Bounty Bastard: The True Story of Captain William Bligh;* Patrick O'Brian, *Men-of-War: Life In Nelson's Navy.*

Cal ★★★★★

(1984) 102 Minutes

Director: Pat O'Connor

Cast: Helen Mirren, John Lynch, Donald McCann, John Kavanagh, Ray McAnally, Kitty Gibson

Historical Background: The implacable malice driving extremists on both sides of Northern Ireland's guerrilla-style civil war dates from the Great Potato Famine of the mid-19th century. By 1840, Ireland's moldering one-crop agricultural system—built around thousands of single-family tenant farms—virtually begged for catastrophe. Seventy percent of the country's farmers worked plots of five acres of less, and everyone grew potatoes: they were easy to plant, easy to harvest, and remarkably prolific—a small plot of land could produce them abundantly. By 1841, more than one-third of Ireland's population lived on potatoes and buttermilk. Disaster came in September 1845, with potato-blight spores borne by wind and insects from England and the Continent. In October, the country's entire potato harvest lay rotting in the fields, and serial crop failure continued to ravage Ireland for four awful years. Hundreds of thousands starved to death. Malnutrition bred grisly epidemics of dysentery, typhus, yellow fever, and scurvy.

Slow to discern the famine's full horrors, the British government and private charities in England were providing food for 5 million famine victims by 1848. (Ireland had a right to all the aid England could muster: in January 1801 the Act of Union bound the two countries into a single United Kingdom.) By 19th-century standards, British relief efforts were prodigious, but they came too late: at least 1.4 million people perished during the four-year nightmare, and many survivors blamed England for the staggering death toll. To qualify for government aid, thousands of families abandoned their farms and moved to cities, taking with them unemployment, malaise, and—above all—searing hatred for Britain. At famine's end, another 1.5 million people had left Ireland for good, launching a tradition of emigration that halved the population to 4.5 million by 1900.

Most expatriates—3 million by 1890—sailed for America. Too poor to leave the great debarkation ports, many remained in New York or Boston, working on commercial docks and in street construction-repair gangs, textile mills, and shoe factories. (In the 19th century, more than half the immigrants from Ireland were women: at first they became nurses, maids, cooks—anything to put food on the table—but by 1885 at least 30% of all schoolteachers in New York and 25% in Boston were Irish.) First-generation families lived in crowded tenement apartments, sleeping, eating, and sitting on rented furniture and working 12-to-14-hour days just to get by. Gradually, they fanned out across the continent—many worked their way west in America's booming transportation industry, helping build the Union Pacific and Illinois Central railroads. Through backbreaking toil and plain old-fashioned guts, the Irish—more than any other group—walked point for countless Europeans flooding the U.S. through the early 1920s.

And, like Ireland's new urban poor, most of them hated England. Irish-Americans helped establish the Irish Republican Brotherhood, Ireland's first paramilitary anti-British organization, in 1858. Nine years later, the IRB disbanded after a raid to free prisoners from London's Clerkenwell Jail killed 30 people, horrifying everyone in Ireland. (Not a single prisoner escaped.) But pressure by Roman Catholics for independence from Britain—or at least an all-Irish "home rule" government directing the country's internal affairs—continued to grow, setting a head-on collision course for Catholics and Ireland's Protestant minority. Protestant support for continued union with Britain predates the famine and persists to this day for economic (more than religious) reasons. Concentrated in the northern province of Ulster, Protestant unionists had forged a distinct cultural identity by the early 1830s. They built a prosperous urban economy based on linen manufacturing; by 1800, linen products formed 75% of Ireland's overseas sales. During the 1880s, full-throated southern nationalism stirred Protestant fears that Irish independence would drain away whatever political power they had, gradually diluting their influence and even their participation in Ulster's shipbuilding, banking, and linen industries—all heavily reliant on British markets.

Despite British prime minister Gladstone's endorsement, home-rule bills introduced in 1886 and 1893 died in England's House of Lords. A third bill did not: with King George V's signature, home rule formally passed into law on September 15, 1914, six weeks after Great Britain declared war on Germany. The timing couldn't have been worse. Since all of the United Kingdom's resources went into its war effort, executing the law's provisions would have to wait, and Ireland's last chance for peaceful transition to limited self-government passed: after two years of mechanized warfare on the Continent had annihilated thousands of British soldiers, the IRB—revived by Patrick Pearse and James Connolly—mounted an armed "rising" on Easter Monday 1916. Seizing the General Post Office and other key buildings in Dublin, the rebels proclaimed a "new Irish Republic" and fought off counterattacking British troops for five days, finally surrendering on April 29. At first, public opinion lay with the British, but summary executions of 14 IRB leaders antagonized thousands of Irish moderates.

Ireland quickly drifted into a bloody cycle of homicidal terrorism and barbarous reprisal, as the IRA, created from remnants of the IRB and other republican groups, rejected home

rule for outright independence. In January 1919, IRA gunmen ignited the Anglo-Irish War by killing two members of the Royal Irish Constabulary (the "Black and Tans"), a paramilitary group manned by Irish unionists and British World War I veterans. Bitter guerrilla fighting set off a dizzying skein of events still reverberating in Northern Ireland. Leading guerrilla/terrorist activities were former Irish expatriate and British civil servant Michael Collins and American-born Eamon De Valera: both rose quickly through IRB ranks after the 1916 bloodbath (De Valera was the last guerrilla leader to surrender), and both changed the trajectory of Ireland's history. Imprisoned in Frongoch Camp (Wales) after the Easter rising, Collins began crafting another rebellion the minute British prime minister Lloyd George ordered his December 1916 release. Talented, efficient, a brilliant organizer—and homicidally violent—Collins soon took over strategic and tactical direction of the IRA, directing bloody attacks on British forces despite Irish Constituent Assembly (Dail Eireann) orders to stop the mayhem.

The Government of Ireland Act partitioned the country in 1920, establishing interim parliaments for Southern Ireland (including three of Ulster's nine counties) and Northern Ireland (Ulster's remaining six counties). On December 6, 1921, British and IRA representatives, led by Collins, signed a treaty ending the war and creating in the south an Irish Free State with dominion status in the United Kingdom. (Sick of the killing, most people welcomed the treaty, but De Valera and hard-core separatists rejected it.) Exactly one year later, Protestant Ulster chose to remain part of the UK as a separate 5,452-square-mile province—the Northern Ireland of today. Few citizens of the new state believed anything was settled: by 1922, more than 50,000 policemen—one for every six households—patrolled the streets of Northern Ireland. Ulster needed every one of them: fractured by conflict over the 1921 agreement, IRA factions fought a bloody internecine war pitting "Irregulars" (adamantly opposed to the treaty) against the pro-treaty Free State Army. On August 22, 1922, Collins died in an ambush in west Cork. Free State forces finally prevailed in 1923, but the Irregulars regrouped, rearmed, and rebuilt the hard, unyielding core of today's Irish Republican Army.

In December 1948, the Irish Free State's reconstitution as an independent republic—the Republic of Ireland—with no ties to Great Britain fired new IRA efforts to reunify the two Irelands. Sporadic conflict in Ulster saw a breathtaking increase in June 1969, with huge riots—set off by student civil rights demonstrations—in Londonderry. IRA assassination teams mounted widespread attacks on British government offices, prompting England to dispatch 3,000 troops to Belfast and Londonderry. By December, the futility of escalating violence and rising body counts appalled many IRA regulars, splitting the organization into two factions: a Provisional wing determined to end union with Britain through terrorism, and an Official wing equally bent on unifying Ireland through political negotiation. (Unionist radicals sharing the "Provos'" taste for violence litter the fringes of paramilitary organizations such as the Ulster Volunteer Force [UVF], a group implicated in the murder of many Catholics.)

By 1970, 12,000 British soldiers occupied Northern Ireland, hoping to prevent an all-out civil war. The slaughter peaked in 1972 with 467 deaths—321 of them innocent bystanders—then tapered off after Westminster imposed direct rule. But the killing continued: between 1969 and 1990, gunfire and bombings in Northern Ireland killed 2,800 and wounded 32,000 more. In 1993, Great Britain and Ireland opened talks on Northern Ireland's future, offering to include the IRA in negotiations if terrorist attacks in Ulster ceased. Sinn Fein, the IRA's political arm, rejected the offer, but reconsidered its position eight months later and declared a cease-fire on August 31, 1994. The armistice was all too brief, ending in February 1996 when IRA truck bombs killed two Londoners. On September 24, London antiterrorist squads impounded hundreds of automatic weapons and more than ten tons of IRA explosives in a citywide sweep that left one IRA saboteur dead in his West End flat. It was the largest illegal-arms seizure in British history, but Scotland Yard insisted that the IRA arsenal was large enough to last well into the 21st century.

One of the best period films ever made, and easily the best on Northern Ireland's convulsive history, *Cal* chronicles the chilling story of two ordinary people swept into 1984 Belfast's turbulent guerrilla underworld despite their best efforts to escape it. Persuaded (and then coerced) by Provo killers to serve as a driver on several dangerous operations, Lynch (in the title role) drifts into an affair with the Catholic widow of a Protestant policeman. To his horror, he gradually realizes that he might have participated in her husband's murder. Excellent performances all around, especially by Lynch, Mirren, and Kavanagh (as an intractable IRA officer). A quiet, scrupulously evenhanded film—for every fuming IRA fanatic there is a violent UVF thug—*Cal* is a must for everyone interested in Northern Ireland's ongoing nightmare.

For Further Viewing:

Shake Hands with the Devil ★★★★ (1959) 110 Minutes (James Cagney, Don Murray, Dana Wynter, Glynis Johns, Michael Redgrave, Richard Harris): Wrongly accused by Black and Tan interrogators of grenading a troop carrier in 1921 Dublin, apolitical American medical student Murray breaks out of jail and joins an IRA unit commanded by his fanatical surgery professor (Cagney, in a chilling performance). Opening with apparent pro-IRA sympathies, this fine film ends at ground zero, with Murray standing between two violent extremes senselessly bent on exterminating each other. Johns steals the show as a barmaid and part-time "working girl."

Far and Away ★★★★ (1992) 140 Minutes (Tom Cruise, Nicole Kidman, Thomas Gibson, Barbara Babcock, Robert Prosky): In 1892, tenant farmer Cruise and wealthy aristocrat Kidman leave Ireland for America, land in New York's Gaelic slums, then work their way west. Director Ron Howard's middle and closing segments make this a must for Irish-American history buffs. His meticulous, authentic re-creation of Irish life in New York's tenements and Cruise's sweat-soaked toil on westbound railroad labor gangs are on the money. Howard closes with the legendary 1893 Land Run in Oklahoma Territory's Cherokee Outlet: on September 16, more than 100,000 settlers packing initialized stakes thundered into a sprawling area dubbed an "overrated cow ranch" by the *Arapahoe Bee*. It was lawless, bloody—and glorious: one woman wrapped herself in a feather mattress and jumped from her son's speeding wagon at her chosen spot, freeing him to race toward his own 160-acre section without losing a second. Howard's version of the run is one of Hollywood's great spectacles. One drawback: overdone and overlong romantic bickering between the leads. Otherwise, a fine period film, scrupulously researched and beautifully photographed.

Michael Collins (1996) 132 Minutes (Liam Neeson, Aidan Quinn, Alan Rickman, Julia Roberts, Ian Hart): Loaded with embarrassing clichés and awful writing (Collins: "I hate myself. I hate the British for making hate necessary"), director Neil Jordan's hagiographic biopic belongs in Fantasyland's cartoon vaults, not in history lovers' video libraries. All of Jordan's English and pro-union Irish are genocidal totalitarians (the prevailing fashion in today's Hollywood). And Neeson's sanitized Collins is an idealistic, politically naive, reluctant killer manipulated by de Valera into signing the 1921 treaty. In fact, Collins was politically shrewd, had few qualms about murdering his enemies, and suffered no manipulation during "the Troubles"— least of all by de Valera. Rickman's demonized, slimy de Valera is an oversimplified caricature (absurdly implicated in Collins' assassination): despite a thuggish streak, the real de Valera—not Collins— first believed constitutional pressure the right path toward independence (he favored disbanding the IRB after the Easter rising). Jordan wrongly makes the main source of Collins' estrangement from friend Harry Boland their competition for Kitty Kiernan (Roberts), trivializing their conflict over the treaty (before his death, the historical Boland wrote, "I'm certain we cannot be defeated even if Collins and his British Guns garrison every town in Ireland"). Errors and distortions drone endlessly on, leaving little more than simple-minded propaganda and wasting a great cast.

Patriot Games ★★★★ (1992) 116 Minutes (Harrison Ford, Anne Archer, Patrick Bergin, Thora Birch, Sean Bean, Richard Harris, James Earl Jones): Former CIA agent Ford foils an attack on British Royal Family members, wounding Bean—a terrorist too fanatical even for IRA Provisionals— and killing his brother in the process. Bean soon escapes from prison and goes after Ford and his family. A gripping thriller and an evenhanded portrait of the modern IRA, including reasonable "Official" members (Harris) as well as obsessively homicidal factions (Bean and his mates). Especially fine is a segment on CIA efforts—enhanced by 21st-century high technology—to locate and wipe out a Middle East terrorist camp and training facility. Based on Tom Clancy's best-selling novel.

In the Name of the Father (1993) 127 Minutes (Daniel Day-Lewis, Emma Thompson, Pete Postlethwaite, Corin Redgrave): A shamelessly distorted account of the arrest, trial, imprisonment, and controversial release of petty thief Gerry Conlon for killing five people in the 1974 bombing of a Guilford, England, pub. The film falsifies many documented, critical facts of Conlon's case, making him look like a helpless, innocent victim: writer-director Jim Sheridan concocts a fictional alibi for Conlon; he insists that prosecutors withheld a homeless man's testimony from Conlon's attorneys (the opposite, in fact, is true); the film turns on an IRA officer's confession that he, not Conlon, planted the Guilford bomb, but the character and his confession are fictional. Sheridan ignores a public statement by Pat Maguire (Conlon's uncle) that his nephew should be "put back in prison." Even Conlon's attorney called *In the Name of the Father* ham-fisted propaganda. Watch the movie—but read Robert Kee's book *Trial and Error,* for solid history, instead.

Recommended Reading:
John O'Beirne Ranelagh, *A Short History of Ireland;* Maria McGuire, *To Take Arms: My Year with the IRA Provisionals;* Robert Kee, *Trial and Error;* Michael Coffey and Terry Golway, *The Irish in America.*

The Charge of the Light Brigade ★★
(1968) 130 Minutes

Director: Tony Richardson

Cast: David Hemmings, Vanessa Redgrave, John Gielgud, Harry Andrews, Trevor Howard

Historical Background: October 25, 1854—Crimean Peninsula: Around 7 A.M., advance elements of a 25,000-man Russian army routed countless shell-shocked Turks from artillery redoubts dotting the "Causeway Heights" ridgeline north of Balaclava. (According to eyewitnesses, only a camp-following Scottish wife stood fast at the redoubts, plastering wild-eyed runaways with a broom to turn them back into the Russian stampede.) Round one in the bloody battle producing one of military history's grandest events, the Charge of the Light Brigade, belonged to Tsar Nicholas I.

Seven months earlier, England and France had declared war on Russia, aiming to roll back Nicholas' forays against the sprawling Ottoman Empire. (His objectives: to protect Eastern Orthodox Slavs under Turkish rule and seize the Dardanelles Strait, opening the Mediterranean Sea to Russian shipping.) On September 20, 1854, invading Allied forces crushed Russian armies near the Alma River and—a month later—attacked Russia's great naval base at Sebastopol. The Crimean War, a nightmare of bloody assaults against heavily fortified defensive positions, was in high gear.

The Russian thrust at Balaclava, a logistically vital Black Sea supply port, stunned commander in chief Fitzroy Lord Raglan and British troops suddenly in harm's way. Russia's battering ram rolled up the "North Valley" between Causeway Heights and the Fedioukine Hills, dispatching a 3,000-man cavalry force toward Balaclava's docks. Smack in the middle of their line of march stood Sir Colin Campbell's isolated 550-man 93rd Highland Infantry Brigade. With perfect discipline, the Scots assembled a two-line volley-fire formation atop a small hill, blasting away at the thundering Russians from 600, 350, and 150 yards. Incredibly, the huge mounted formation broke up, wheeling back across Causeway Heights toward the valley.

Pandemonium engulfed both armies. Raglan dispatched Capt. Lewis Nolan with ambiguous written orders for cavalry commander George Lucan to retake the weakly defended Causeway Heights redoubts bracketing the Balaclava–Sebastopol Road. Nolan and Lucan hated each other: asked to clarify the garbled order, Nolan threw a tantrum, waved toward the valley, and rode away. Fuming hotly, Lucan mistakenly—and reluctantly—sent James Lord Cardigan's 673-man light cavalry brigade into the teeth of Russia's main artillery position. It was the worst blunder in a battle marked on both sides by high-command snafus: shot to bits during their 20-minute up-valley approach, Cardigan's heroes breached the enemy defenses, killed the Russian gunners, wheeled 180°, and galloped home. Littering the valley behind them were 247 British casualties. The English held Balaclava, but Russian troops controlled the six-mile supply route to Sebastopol. In mid-September 1855, Allied shock troops finally took the huge port and forced a February armistice, ending the war and containing Russia's westward expansion.

Richardson warps countless Balaclava facts in this strange, pompous, anti-British screen rant. He makes Nolan (Hemmings) a hero, for example, absurdly blaming the catastrophic charge on Lucan and Cardigan. The upside: a thunderous charge, immaculate period detail (military-fashion expert John Mollo directed historical research), and an accurate, chilling segment on the awful pestilential wastage of Allied troops (of the 18,058 British war deaths, disease caused an incredible 16,297—a greater mortality rate than the great plagues inflicted in 14th-century England). Richardson also includes one of the war's strangest features, civilian camp followers—including wives—accompanying expeditionary forces and wandering freely around battlefields. Lovely to look at, but tedious and heavy-handed all the way.

For Further Viewing:

The Charge of the Light Brigade ★ (1936) 116 Minutes (Errol Flynn, Patric Knowles, Olivia de Havilland, Henry Stephenson, David Niven, Nigel Bruce, C. Henry Gordon): Flynn romances de Havilland, follows satanic Muslim prince Surat Khan (exterminator of a surrendering British garrison) from India to the Crimea, finds him with the Russians at Balaclava, personally engineers the light brigade attack—strictly for vengeance—and spears his man at the height of the charge. So much for history. (Director Michael Curtiz weirdly bases the only consistently accurate segment of his film, Surat Khan's murderous rampage in northern India, on an incident from a historical event unrelated to the Crimean War—the siege of Cawnpore, one of many bloody brawls and genocidal massacres distinguishing the 1857–58 Sepoy Mutiny by Indian colonial troops.) Too entertaining to dislike, too full of fantasy for history buffs.

Recommended Reading:
Philip Warner, *The Crimean War: A Reappraisal;* Leo Tolstoy, *The Sebastopol Sketches.*

Citizen Kane ★★

(1941) 119 Minutes

Director: Orson Welles

Cast: Orson Welles, Joseph Cotten, Agnes Moorehead, Everett Sloane, Dorothy Comingore

Historical Background: William Randolph Hearst never took Harvard University seriously—and made no bones about it. He once hung a placard reading "Now There Are Two of You" on a jackass' neck, then left the animal in a professor's room. During his junior year (1885), Harvard gave him the boot for stenciling faculty names on chamberpots and sending them by personal messenger to professors' homes. But university wasn't completely wasted on him. He discovered his real talent there, turning the *Lampoon*—Harvard's somnolent, debt-ridden humor magazine—into a lively, impressive money-maker backed by serious advertisers.

Hearst understood Gilded Age commercial

(read "sensational") journalism. In 1887 he took over his father's reeling San Francisco *Examiner,* unlimbered his bankroll, and went to work. He added pages. He mixed serious, hard-hitting investigative reporting with racy fluff (the latest dirt from local divorce courts, for example) and put sports stories on page one. To give the paper a sophisticated, worldly flair, he bought hot-off-the-wire dispatches from the New York *Herald.* By 1889, the *Examiner* was raking in the cash. Six years later Hearst took dead aim on New York City.

For $180,000 he bought the floundering New York *Morning Journal,* loaded it with long-hitting journalists (Stephen Crane, Julian Hawthorne), and ignited an all-out circulation war with Joseph Pulitzer's muscular New York *World* by stealing his top talent (editor Arthur Brisbane, magazine-section head Morrill Goddard, and color-comics pioneer R. F. Outcault). Hearst cut prices to 1¢ per copy, plastered billboards with the new rate, and mailed pennies to registered voters. The race was on: using the Cubans' 1895 revolt against their Spanish overlords as raw material, Pulitzer and Hearst reeled off a series of sensational (and often manufactured) front-page stories, riling Americans coast to coast and feeding ignition of the 1898 Spanish–American War. (Hearst's most outrageous article—headlined "DOES OUR FLAG PROTECT WOMEN?"—had drooling Spanish police boarding an American ship, disrobing three lovely Cuban girls, and searching them for rebel documents. Days later, the girls insisted that matrons—not leering Iberian cops—had searched them, legitimately, in a stateroom. With copious help from Pulitzer, Hearst had invented "yellow journalism.")

Soon the *Journal*'s sales rocketed off the charts, and Hearst began building his nationwide newspaper chain. By the mid-1920s he owned newspapers in 17 U.S. cities, selling a whopping 5 million copies each day. He bought magazines— *Cosmopolitan, Harper's Bazaar, Good Housekeeping*—and telegraphic news networks. In 1919 he reorganized and expanded his Cosmopolitan Productions film company, mainly to promote the career of Marion Davies, a beautiful, lively Ziegfeld Follies performer with middling acting skills; she met Hearst in 1917 and they soon began an affair that continued for more than three decades. Hearst influenced American politics significantly. A radical Democrat until the mid-1930s, he represented New York (Manhattan) in the U.S. House from 1903 to 1907; backed by more than 150 newspapers, he sought (unsuccessfully) the 1904 Democratic presidential nomination and narrowly lost a 1905 New York City mayoral election. In 1932, his clout on the West Coast helped land FDR in the White House. (Disillusioned with the New Deal, he changed parties in 1936.)

By 1935, Hearst was one of the wealthiest men in the world, but two years later he almost lost everything. The prototype big spender, he frittered away staggering sums: on a 240,000-acre San Simeon, Calif., ranch he built his legendary $30 million mansion, loading it (and several warehouses) with priceless antiques and European art; he once hosted a picnic served by 16 mules carrying food, champagne, caviar, and sleeping bags. In 1937, tax problems, lavish spending, and lousy real-estate investments brought financial problems so severe that he gave temporary control of his publishing empire to old friend Clarence Shearn. (It took WWII's business boom to put Hearst back on top.)

Always controversial, Hearst combined a wild array of strengths and weaknesses beneath a quiet, courteous manner. Biographer W. A. Swanberg calls him "Caesar, Charlemagne, and Napoleon combined"—an eccentric jumble of determination, courage, daring, industrious-ness, ruthlessness, near-megalomania, and a relentless, intense need to get exactly what he wanted. The only person he couldn't dominate was Davies: "She held his peace of mind in the hollow of her hand," a friend once noted; "she knew it, but she never took advantage of it." And she remained loyal to Hearst until his death in August 1951.

Driven by lust for political power, thinly disguised Hearst clone Charles Foster Kane (Welles), publishing tycoon, art collector, and builder of a gigantic mansion (Xanadu), divorces his wife and marries meagerly gifted diva Comingore, an obvious counterfeit Davies, even though Hearst and the actress never married (his wife, Millicent, wouldn't grant a divorce). A political flop, Kane works to make his new wife a star, driving her mercilessly—and, in the end, futilely. She becomes a heavy drinker addicted to solitary jigsaw-puzzle assembly in Xanadu's cavernous gloom. His dreams shattered, Kane dies in misery with his money and a big, dark, drafty house. (All of this surfaces during a long quest to decipher the riddle of his dying utterance: "Rosebud.")

Welles and his cast of virtual unknowns labored mightily on the set, often reshooting the same segment 100 times before wrapping. Six decades after its premiere, many critics praise *Citizen Kane* as the greatest American movie ever. But if you're interested in accurate biography, it's a film easily forgotten. In many places it amounts to slander, and Welles knew it: post-premiere fury (from many quarters) almost deep-sixed Welles' career permanently, even though he denied any premeditated Kane–Hearst connection (lamely: leading many obvious parallels are several Kane one-liners matching documented Hearst remarks almost word for word).

Welles' worst falsification is Comingore's

ill-tempered, dull-witted, selfish Davies knock-off (driven to attempted suicide by the domineering Kane). In fact, Davies was perfectly happy with Hearst; she was full of fun, warm-hearted, thoroughly winsome, and incredibly generous (she lavished expensive birthday and Christmas gifts on studio carpenters and electricians, paid for an office boy's eye surgery, and covered all of a talented, impecunious newsboy's military-school expenses for four years). Highly intelligent, she talked shop constantly with Hearst, gaining a thorough understanding of his business affairs: he often asked her advice—and often followed it. *Citizen Kane* is a fine film, but earns abysmal marks for accuracy.

Recommended Reading:
W. A. Swanberg, *Citizen Hearst: A Biography of William Randolph Hearst.*

Doctor Zhivago ★★★★

(1965) 197 Minutes

Director: David Lean

Cast: Omar Sharif, Julie Christie, Geraldine Chaplin, Tom Courtenay, Alec Guinness, Ralph Richardson, Rod Steiger

Historical Background: May 27, 1905— Tsushima Strait: Fifteen months into the Russo-Japanese War, Admiral Togo Heihachiro's small, modern armada opened fire on Tsar Nicholas II's napping 30-ship Baltic fleet, deep-sixing an incredible 22 warships in two awful days. The crushing loss ended the tsar's push to seize Korea and fueled simmering discontent at home. (Four months earlier, on Sunday, January 22, St. Petersburg's garrison had fired into huge crowds demonstrating for various reforms and an end to the Asian war, killing 100 and launching imperial Russia's bloody slide into oblivion.) For the first time, citizens broke ranks with the tsar: wartime shortages, military blunders, excessive casualties, and stinging memories of "Bloody Sunday" ignited a 12-year political nightmare for Nicholas. In October, strikes paralyzed the entire country, and by year's end Nicholas had endorsed a constitution and an elected legislature (the Duma).

But smoldering malaise hung in the air and festered for a decade. Critical mass came with Russia's floundering WWI performance. Hurling his entire army into the meat grinder instead of mobilizing gradually, Nicholas guaranteed near-collapse at the front. Russian trenches swarmed with unarmed soldiers ordered to cannibalize their fallen comrades' weapons: by 1915, the entire 6-million-man army had only 650,000 rifles. Desertions surfaced, then multiplied. Foolishly, Nicholas took personal command of the army, leaving imperial authority with Tsaritsa Alexandra—a fatal error. Convinced that he could cure her hemophiliac son Alexis, Alexandra took political counsel from vice-driven "holy man" Grigori Rasputin, replacing countless capable officials with third-rate hacks. In December 1916, conspirators poisoned, shot, and clubbed Rasputin, then flung him (still breathing) into the Neva River.

It was too late: bureaucratic waste and ravenous military demands had leveled Russia's economy, driving countrywide coal and food shortages. On March 8, 1917, hungry, freezing St. Petersburg unraveled: 7,000 textile workers poured into the streets, drawing 250,000 riotous supporters within four days. On March 15, Nicholas abdicated, and Communist goons killed him and his family a year later. (Lenin ordered the murders partly because Russians considered their tsars mystical liaisons with God. "It's very high up to God! It's very far to the tsar!" reads a popular proverb. Grasping their hostility to Bolshevism, Lenin hated Orthodox Christians: killing the Romanovs, he thought, would take religion completely out of the new Russian order of things.) Many bromides framing Nicholas' reputation collapse under close scrutiny. Obviously, he was no great tsar: he was fatally injudicious, at times; he could be arrogant; he underrated the stinging wallop of revolutionary ideas pouring into Russia from the West. But Nicholas wasn't stupid, shallow, or weak. He was an average administrator overwhelmed by a job thrust upon him under awful circumstances, and he wasn't alone: the Great War undid other emperors—Germany's, Austria-Hungary's—as well.

During the March riots, the Soviet ("workers' council") of Workers' and Soldiers' Deputies convened, opposing liberal Aleksandr Kerensky's Duma-appointed provisional government. The new regime had foolishly insisted on continuing the war, quickening a rush to economic meltdown. In July, St. Petersburg ordered Russia's peasants to surrender their surplus and market-bound crops. Searing acrimony swept the countryside, most crops remained there, and urban hunger rocketed. By October, mutinies and riots—widespread pandemonium—reigned. Russia was up for grabs, and Vladimir Ilyich Lenin, newly arrived in Petrograd from Swiss exile, knew how to take it. In 1903, he'd formed a rigidly organized cadre of Marxist fanatics—the Bolsheviks—and on October 24–25, they resurfaced, taking Petrograd in a brilliantly timed "nonmilitary" coup.

Six weeks into the revolt (and five months before Russia's WWI disengagement), launching the Cheka—Lenin's secret police—dominated Bolshevik agendas. By 1921, 250,000 Cheka goons were murdering 1,000 people per month and sending countless others to concentration camps. Christened "former people" and "insects" by Lenin, victims' punishments turned on social rank and occupation—priests, schoolteachers, trade-union leaders, the "bourgeoisie"—not criminal activities. Lenin devoted enormous resources to his swelling chain of gulags throughout a bitter civil war pitting Reds (Bolsheviks) against counterrevolutionary Whites (Tsarists). Throughout 1918, highly motivated White armies flourished: Bolshevik desertion rates averaged 40–50%, even though war commissar Leon Trotsky routinely ordered machine-gun units to shoot stragglers. But the Reds controlled Russia's industrial heartland. Based in peripheral areas, White leaders shunned political organization and ignored strategic coordination, fighting an endless series of isolated, bloody brawls throughout a huge geographic area. Incredibly, they fumbled away military support from the west, refusing to promise postwar elections and practicing murderous anti-Semitism in some areas. In 1921, the Bolsheviks finally prevailed, quickly building a gigantic, bureaucratic apparatus of centralized control throughout Russia. Ravaged by a series of strokes, Lenin died in Gorki on January 21, 1924. Many historians believe that Stalin hastened his predecessor's agonizing death with small, incremental doses of poison.

Despite occasional sentimentality and Sharif's overcooked Zhivago, Lean's blockbuster is fine fare for history buffs: *Doctor Zhivago* delivers excellent period vignettes of prerevolutionary Russian life and chilling segments on WWI and the civil war. Lean's treatment of the wars covers most of the basics: Bolshevik "plants" did incite WWI army revolts, killing as many Tsarist officers as they could in the process; Zhivago's awful rail journey eastward from Moscow traverses many isolated civil-war combat theaters; and fluid, widely separated battlefronts marked the 1918–21 holocaust from the start, making railroads logistic musts. The movie highlights all these things, and Lean's images of the multiple horrors inflicted on civilians by the war will linger long for most viewers.

For Further Viewing:

Nicholas and Alexandra ★★★★ (1971) 183 Minutes (Michael Jaston, Janet Suzman, Roderic Noble, Tom Baker, Harry Andrews, Laurence Olivier, Curt Jurgens): Director Franklin Schaffner's adaptation of Massie's classic book delivers a long, detailed look at tsar and tsaritsa—warts and all—drowning in Russia's immense 1905–17 tragedy. Hyper-accurate on most counts. Schaffner composes many scenes from Romanov family photographs; one of the most famous places a languid Alexandra (Suzman) on the antique divan in her mauve boudoir; another replicates the family photo taken just before the Romanovs' murder. Noble is magnificent as Alexis, but Baker's odd, low-keyed Rasputin falls flat—dramatically and historically—in a rare lapse. Terrific history, for Hollywood.

Recommended Reading:

Oliver H. Radkey, *The History of the Russian Revolution*; Robert Payne, *The Life and Death of Lenin*; Robert K. Massie, *Nicholas and Alexandra*; Richard Luckett, *The White Generals.*

The Duellists ★★★★★

(1977) 101 Minutes

Director: Ridley Scott

Cast: Keith Carradine, Harvey Keitel, Diana Quick, Edward Fox, Tom Conti, Christina Raines, Albert Finney

Historical Background: July 19, 1721—an elegant fete on the grounds of the Grand Palace at Versailles: furious upon learning that the Countess de Polignac had become her rival for the affections of a rakish Duc de Richelieu, the Marquise de Nestle disrupted a grand evening by summarily flinging a corsage of roses in the face of her astonished adversary. An eminent chronicler of duels recorded the ensuing skirmish. The countess "threw off all restraint and flew at Lady de Nestle with unbridled fury. . . . In the next few moments jewels, flowers, ribbons, feathers, and laces strewed the ground, and it is not difficult to imagine that these fighting ladies would have torn the clothes from each other had not the Marquis de Malbuisson . . . intervened." Almost immediately the countess issued a challenge, Lady de Nestle accepted, and the two met on the field of honor—dueling pistols in hand—two days later. Both took aim, fired, and missed. Still inarticulate with rage, the ladies insisted on reloading and taking second shots. This time the countess didn't miss, wounding Lady de Nestle seriously and escaping unscathed except for a small nick in one ear. Equal opportunity regardless of sex, it seems, was taken for granted throughout the long, sanguinary history of the duelist's lost art.

Despite the slapstick aura surrounding melees such as Lady de Nestle's affair of honor, dueling endured as a grim, legitimate institution of European society for centuries, passing into history only after the carnage of World War I had exhausted the Continent and ended an entire way of life. The earliest duels on record took place in Burgundy under King Gundobad, who established the "Trial by Battel"—or "judicial" duel—more than 1,300 years ago to rid statutory proceedings of widespread perjury. In 1066, William the Conqueror brought judicial dueling to England, where it remained the chief means of settling legal disputes until Henry II introduced the trial by jury as a voluntary alternative a century later. "Chivalric" dueling between armored knights—a medieval version of judicial dueling—began in the mid-ninth century under French sovereign Charles the Bald and continued without decline until English archers rendered the mounted knight obsolete at the Battle of Crécy in 1346. Trials by "battel" did not fade away with the age of chivalry, however, and they often involved more than two adversaries: one famous encounter took place in Scotland in 1395, when a total of 64 men from two warring clans hacked away at one another until fewer than 15 combatants—all members of the same family—remained standing.

Though formal dueling began as a public institution, the private affair of honor has always

fascinated novelists, biographers, and historians more. Private duels first flourished in Italy, the birthplace of modern fencing techniques, during the early 1500s. From there the practice spread to other European countries, gaining unmatched popularity in France—between 1590 and 1610, more than 8,000 duelists died there. (They fought with double-edged rapiers, less cumbersome foils and triple-edged epées, dueling sabers, even billiard balls on one occasion. Eighteenth-century duelists often chose matched pistols that fired lead balls of .45 to .60 caliber and had a lethal range of 45 yards.) During France's postrevolutionary period, private duels were so commonplace that even Napoleon, who considered the affair of honor a grave breach of military discipline, acknowledged the futility of banning the practice and ignored it altogether in his Military Code of 1810.

History has proved him right: edicts against dueling surfaced in European courtrooms on many occasions, but they were usually ignored and invariably dropped from law books until quite recently. A bizarre form of dueling called the *Mensur,* fought from stationary positions by heavily padded opponents intent on pummeling each other about the forehead with basket-hilted swords, still persists in German universities. Once a prominent feature of college life, the rough-and-tumble brawls still take place covertly even though German authorities outlawed all forms of dueling, including student dueling corps, many years ago.

Scott's dazzling adaptation of Joseph Conrad's fact-based story follows two Napoleonic officers through a series of ferocious duels in early-19th-century Europe. The movie begins in 1800, chronicles 14 years of bitter European warfare, includes a harrowing segment on

Napoleon's retreat from Moscow, and ends with a long, running pistol fight—the last of six expertly choreographed, bloodcurdling duels. Other highlights: a detailed look at 18th-century courtship and arranged marriages, glimpses of Enlightenment political intrigue and professional life, a parlor soirée hosted by the redoubtable Madame de Léon, and a well-crafted character study of camp follower Quick. Scott's immaculate period detail—carriages, apartments, uniforms, civilian clothes, weapons, changing military hairstyles—is extraordinarily comprehensive. A riveting, visually stunning movie that sets very high standards for period films.

For Further Viewing:

Barry Lyndon ★★★ (1975) 183 Minutes (Ryan O'Neal, Marisa Berenson, Patrick Magee, Hardy Kruger, Steven Berkoff, Gay Hamilton): Irish prevaricator Redmond Barry (O'Neal) duels and gambles his way around Europe, marries into big-time aristocratic money, then comes to a sorry end. Director Stanley Kubrick's perfectly mounted Age of Reason "look" makes his adaptation of Thackeray's novel worth viewing: Oscar-winning designers modeled costumes on 18th-century portraits, all filming was on location (no sets), and a beautifully choreographed Seven Years War battle will impress. But great period detail is the whole show for amateur historians. Kubrick's duels fall flat, except for the closing combat fought under obscure "cool-and-alternate-firing" rules used occasionally during the 1780s: a coin flip gives Barry's adversary "first fire," but his weapon discharges too soon, and O'Neal magnanimously shoots into the ground. Honor-code experts detested the system's incorporation of luck, and most duelists left nothing to chance, always looking for an edge—hair triggers, bores rifled from breech to midbarrel, then smooth to the muzzle (only for the dishonorable: rules forbade rifling). Kubrick's "philosophical" assumptions—including reduction of life-and-death matters to chance—are anachronistic 19th-century notions distorted by trendy Hollywood nihilism: Barry, for example, "was destined to be a wanderer." The 18th century produced fine travel stories, but no relentlessly dark chronicles of aimless wandering, without purpose and marked by serial, meaningless fresh starts (new jobs, new towns, new spouses, etc.). Kubrick also mangles Thackeray, changing countless details, including the ending. The result: fair entertainment, hit-or-miss history, and an awful botch of classic fictional satire.

Recommended Reading:
Robert Baldwick, *The Duel: A History of Duelling;* John A. Atkinson, *Duelling Pistols and Some of the Affairs They Settled;* William Makepeace Thackeray, *The Luck of Barry Lyndon.*

Fire Over England ★★★

(1937) 89 Minutes

Director: William K. Howard

Cast: Laurence Olivier, Flora Robson, Raymond Massey, Vivien Leigh, Leslie Banks

Historical Background: August 7, 1588—English Channel: At midnight, Spanish lookouts near Calais Roads spotted eight blazing hulks gliding toward their lightly moored fleet through the sullen, black Channel night. English volunteers had coated the vessels with pitch, loaded them with explosives, and sailed them straight into the Grand Armada, torching and abandoning them at the last second. Anticipating fiery attacks by small tar-boats, Spanish commandant Duke Medina-Sidonia had screened his perimeter with pinnaces rigged for towing fireships clear of his fleet. But England's Howard of Effingham and top lieutenant Francis Drake had launched towering "hellburners"—tall-masted, 100–200-ton infernos—at Spain's fleet, scattering its ships seaward in pandemonium. For Medina-Sidonia, it was the latest installment of a ghastly two-month nightmare slated to haunt King Philip II of Spain forever.

Philip had flexed his muscles worldwide for decades, colonizing the Philippines, invading the Low Countries, mining gold in Mexico, and dotting the New World with outposts from Argentina to Louisiana. In 1571, his brawny fleet plastered the Turks at Lepanto, and nine years later he annexed Portugal. Tension between England and Spain had simmered furiously for years. Philip's growing might and death grip on New World mining areas rankled everybody—especially Queen Elizabeth: her privateers regularly plundered gold-heavy Spanish ships, and many Englishmen fought shoulder to shoulder with Low Country rebels. In July 1588, Medina-Sidonia weighed anchor at Corunna, aiming to sail through the Channel, escort a 30,000-man Spanish-Netherlands occupation force through the Dover Straits, and invade England. Manned by 8,350 seamen, 19,290 men-at-arms, and 2,080 slaves, the 130-ship Armada bristled with 2,630 guns.

Medina-Sidonia's ordeal began on July 31. Probing the lower Channel in a crescent-shaped knot, his Armada ran smack into Effingham's 54-ship in-line battle formation near Plymouth, falling victim for the first time to modern naval warfare. (For Spain, war at sea was ground combat afloat, fought with muskets and swords by soldiers deployed on wide, ponderous, high-castled galleons designed for one tactic: close with hostile ships, board them in overwhelming numbers, and take them hand-to-hand. But Elizabeth's brilliant John Hawkins built revolutionary midsized ships—low-slung, narrow, and much longer—gaining speed, dazzling agility, and deck space for many long-range cannon.) Drake's "race-built" men-of-war sped straight for Medina-Sidonia's flank, turned with breathtaking precision, slipped behind the Armada, and unlimbered their booming guns.

Unable to turn into the wind, Medina-Sidonia tried to run—but his floating forts couldn't outpace Elizabeth's swift men-of-war. Up the channel they went, the English hanging well out of Spanish cannon range, raining white-hot ordnance on Philip's galleons in engagements off Portland Bill and the Isle of Wight, and forcing the Armada's calamitous Calais Roads anchorage. The end came near Gravelines after the fireship debacle: his defensive formation broken, Medina-Sidonia hurled four galleons into a desperate, last-ditch brawl with two swarming English squadrons. Sailing rings around their adversaries, Drake and fellow skipper Martin Frobisher poured withering fire into the Spaniards, gradually reducing their vessels to splinters.

By day's end, three galleons lay on the bottom, one was crippled, countless smaller ships were lost, and Armada ammunition was low.

Medina-Sidonia disengaged, sailed around Scotland, and ran for home. Dreadful Atlantic storms punctuated the long voyage: by the time survivors made Spanish ports in October, 44 ships and 15,000–20,000 men were history. Effingham reported 100 battle deaths—and every English ship survived. (Eight months later, Elizabeth sent Drake—the first Englishman to circumnavigate the globe and her finest New World raider—to destroy Armada remnants in Spain's northern ports. Hungry for booty, he sacked Corunna instead, then sailed for wealthy Lisbon. But awful weather pummeled his 126-ship fleet, returning him to England empty-handed. With regal fury, Elizabeth frosted Drake, shelving him and his globe-trotting zeal for more than five years. He knew he had it coming, and waited patiently until 1595 for another royal commission.)

The most critical week in English history had brought glorious triumph to Elizabeth. At precisely the right moment, personal strengths forged during her harrowing adolescence had paid off handsomely. At 14, she saw her guardian executed for treason, dodging the block herself through quick wits and icy self-control under repeated interrogation. On Edward VI's death (July 6, 1553), England shook with factional quarrels among multiple claimants to the throne. One designated heir, Elizabeth's cousin Lady Jane Grey—reigned for nine days. John Dudley and Jane's parents—the Duke and Duchess of Suffolk—forced her to marry Dudley's son Guilford, then persuaded Edward to make her his successor, bypassing rightful heir Mary Tudor. Jane acceded on July 10. But most Englishmen demanded Mary's return (defiantly: many powerful nobles proclaimed her queen, galloping to join her in Suffolk). Jane abdicated on July 19 and fell to the headsman's axe in February 1554.

Thanks to high intelligence, iron-disciplined prudence, and cold nerve, Elizabeth had become an unmatched virtuoso at survival by then. Crude efforts to implicate her in Thomas Wyatt's 1554 rebellion went nowhere, and by late November 1558 she held the throne. She chose talented ministers—the most able was Secretary of State Lord Burghley—and delegated brilliantly. (Effingham is the perfect example: a fine administrator, he picked top sea captains and turned them loose, with very long leashes, on poor Medina-Sidonia.) Elizabeth's legendary frugality kept England solvent and her subjects unvexed by excessive taxes—a key advantage over Spain's debt-ridden Philip. She hated fanaticism, refusing to persecute ordinary Catholics (priests—especially Jesuits—were fair game during the long struggles against Spain). She had favorites, but fondness never skewed her judgment. Walter Raleigh's intellectual and worldly talents, for example, fascinated her. Handsome, witty, and flamboyant, Raleigh also was arrogant and tactless—an unpopular loose cannon—and Elizabeth never considered giving him high office. Her last minion—the impudent, injudicious Earl of Essex—left his post (against her orders) in rebellious Ireland, returning to England with long explanations for his botched performance during the insurrection. Elizabeth fired him, put him under house arrest, then executed him for trying to ignite a revolt in London. Two years later, on March 24, 1603, Elizabeth died. During her 44-year reign, she'd never removed her coronation ring: it had fused with her finger, literally becoming part of her hand.

Flora Robson's towering portrait of Elizabeth dwarfs other dream-cast performances in Howard's chronicle of Renaissance intrigue and the great naval battle. Accurate in places: Robson's Elizabeth and Massey's Philip are bull's-eyes, and a fire-beacon invasion-warning system dotted England's coast. Thanks to cost overruns, Howard limited his Channel fighting to Effingham's fireship raid, blundering twice: his hellburners are Elizabeth's idea, and most strike anchored galleons—in fact, none of Effingham's terror-weapons found their mark. Other errors: Elizabeth's Tilbury speech wasn't a pep talk—it came after the Armada debacle; prebattle segments imply stout English onshore defenses—historically, they were anemic.

More critical for history lovers: Robson's anti-Catholicism reflects modern misunderstanding of the Inquisition and religion's place in medieval and Renaissance secular affairs. Throughout Europe, two juridical schemes, civil and ecclesiastic, intertwined, forming a comprehensive legal system (see *Becket*). Attacks on the church were always potential attacks on social order, and every European government occasionally persecuted religious minorities. Unlike Robson, Elizabeth wasn't interested in dictating beliefs: she was bent on keeping Philip out of England—period.

For Further Viewing:
The Sea Hawk ★★★★ (1940) 127 Minutes (Errol Flynn, Brenda Marshall, Claude Rains, Flora Robson, Henry Daniell, Alan Hale): Swashbuckling Drake clone Geoffrey Thorpe (Flynn) and his rollicking mates drive Philip's tarheels crazy, doing everything sailors can do for queen (Robson, in top form) and country. Director Michael Curtiz is remarkably faithful to history, in places: Robson's commission to Flynn, "You go with the disapproval of the queen . . . but take with you . . . the affection of Elizabeth," accurately highlights England's desperate need for "privateers"—semipirates raiding with unofficial state sanction, then returning their loot (minus a fat fee) to the crown. Elizabeth faced awful pressure to impede Spanish expansion without provoking all-out war (skeletal English ground forces couldn't match Philip's army), and civilian privateers did the job. Drake was one of the best: in 1580, he hauled bounty worth $300 million back to England. Terrific maritime sets and Flynn's Panama foray—loosely based on Drake's 1572 expedition—vividly mirror the "spirit of the age."

The Virgin Queen (1955) 92 Minutes (Bette Davis, Richard Todd, Joan Collins, Herbert Marshall): Halfway into director Henry Koster's soap opera, Elizabeth (Davis) knights Raleigh (Todd) in her bedroom—just because she likes him—and both agree that "honors are as empty as air" (Davis dispenses them like lollipops). In fact, Raleigh's knighthood came after ample proof of his military and administrative skills, and Elizabeth hoarded state honors, creating only two peers after 1574 (this bred political stability; England's complement of knights actually shrank under Elizabeth). Todd's sanitized Raleigh is way off, but Davis's frivolous, whimsical, undignified queen is the worst of many blunders. Others are ludicrous: Raleigh and Elizabeth Throckmorton (Collins) marry themselves in a hotel room. Koster focuses hard on Raleigh's undercover romance, falsifying virtually all of it. Tedious, lousy history.

The Private Lives of Elizabeth and Essex (1939) 106 Minutes (Bette Davis, Errol Flynn, Olivia de Havilland, Vincent Price, Donald Crisp, Henry Daniell): Thoroughly moonstruck, Elizabeth (Davis) reluctantly sends Essex (Flynn) to fight Irish insurrectionists. He never writes, and in a snit, she withholds vital supplies, ensuring his defeat. Furious, he returns to London and rebels victoriously, but Elizabeth tricks him into disbanding his army. In fact: Essex's incompetence wrecked the Irish campaign; his rebellion—a Keystone Kops fiasco—counted 200 supporters; he and the queen had no final audience. Far worse: Essex and Elizabeth weren't linked romantically—his senior by 34 years, she knew his goals were political and financial and considered him a pleasant diversion, at most. Serious historians dismiss notions of a promiscuous Elizabeth anyway. Mary Stuart's letter detailing lurid accusations (later retracted) by the harebrained Countess of Shrewsbury hatched the first rumors of Elizabeth's unchastity. A dull film—and awful history.

Elizabeth (1998) 124 Minutes (Cate Blanchett, Geoffrey Rush, Richard Attenborough, Christopher Eccleston, Joseph Fiennes, Kathy Burke, John Gielgud): Film critic Janet Maslin labeled this lurid potboiler "historical drama for anyone whose idea of history is back issues of *Vogue*." Give her two bull's-eyes: *Elizabeth* did, in fact, win the Academy Award for best makeup (its only Oscar), and anyone familiar with the great queen's career will cringe at the movie's muddled jumble of anachronisms and glaring historical falsifications. Many distortions come stealthily, in the form of clichéd half-truths: throughout the film, for example, director Shekhar Kapur presents torture and judicial murder as common practices in sixteenth-century England—and this is not true. British common law forbade torture in ordinary circumstances. Government agents did torture suspected political assassins and insurrectionists, but only after getting special warrants—reluctantly granted, in many cases—from the Queen's Council.

Worse still, for history buffs, is Blanchett's Elizabeth, a panting cauldron of lust wary of marriage, but revolted even more by the prospect of chastity—especially when Fiennes' moonstruck Earl of Leicester shows up. We first see Elizabeth—barely out of her teens—lurching into a steamy clinch with Leicester moments before her arrest by Mary Tudor's police for interrogation about the Wyatt Rebellion. This is absurd: historians don't even know precisely when the two first met, and "historical"

accounts of their affair are speculation based on idle court gossip. Worst of all: Kapur cuts the queen's story short, rolling his final credits after the Duke of Norfolk's execution and ignoring the conflict with Spain and Drake's defeat of the Armada (omitting Lee Harvey Oswald from a documentary on John F. Kennedy's presidency would make more sense). *Elizabeth* delivers fine location filming and excellent period costumes, but its "history"—from start to finish—is tabloid fodder, at best.

Lady Jane ★ (1985) 142 Minutes (Helena Bonham Carter, Cary Elwes, John Wood, Sara Kestelman, Jane Lapotaire, Patrick Stewart): Director Trevor Nunn includes a few historical facts in *Lady Jane*, but you'll need a gumshoe army to find them. His silliest fictions cloak the Grey (Carter)–Dudley (Elwes) marriage. Apathetic at first, they quickly fall in love (and into bed—constantly), then start building a kinder, gentler England: "I demand a world where the comfort and happiness of a few aren't borne by the misery of many," rants Elwes; Jane donates her wardrobe "to warm the wretched and clothe the comfortless." In fact, Jane loathed spoiled-brat Guilford, refusing to sleep with him—or even see him after her arrest. As for the clothes, she treasured every scrap of royal finery, keeping much of it on display because it raised her spirits. Great period detail, too much teenage romance, and rail-thin history.

Recommended Reading:

Peter Padfield, *Armada;* Paul Johnson, *Elizabeth I;* James A. Williamson, *The Age of Drake;* Robert Lacey, *Robert, Earl of Essex* and *Sir Walter Raleigh;* Alison Plowden, *Lady Jane Grey and the House of Suffolk.*

Gandhi

(1982) 188 Minutes

Director: Richard Attenborough

Cast: Ben Kingsley, Candice Bergen, Sir John Gielgud, Trevor Howard, Edward Fox, John Mills, Rohini Hattangandy, Martin Sheen, Geraldine James, Michael Hordern, John Ratzenberger

Historical Background: "It costs a great deal of money to keep Gandhi living in poverty": telling words indeed, since they came from the earthy Sarojini Naidu, one of Mohandas K. Gandhi's most devoted apostles. The hypocrisy suggested by Naidu's casual remark was the very least of Gandhi's fatal shortcomings, obscured for years—especially in England and the United States—by a haze of cliché and hagiographic platitude.

Gandhi's reputation as a visionary leader rests mainly on half-truths about his wildly inconsistent and often senseless views on nonviolence. While German panzers rolled virtually unopposed toward the English Channel in June 1940, he published an open letter advising the British government to surrender to the Nazis and oppose them later by organizing huge public demonstrations. (Gandhi's domestic agenda reflected the same oblivion to harsh reality: his scheme to close India's textile mills—the country's only large-scale employers—would have created staggering job losses and hunger on a scale massive even by Third World standards.)

The success of his nonviolent campaign for Indian independence hinged almost entirely on British forbearance—England, in fact, had resolved in 1942 "to give up India to the Indians after the war" (Churchill's words), and many historians believe that transition to Indian rule would have come sooner without Gandhi's disruptive activities.

Throughout his life, Gandhi wrestled with personal demons that surfaced more than once under pressure. Cracks in his facade of respect for all living things were not rare: in a fit of rage he once bellowed that he "would not flinch from sacrificing a million lives for India's liberty." Indian poet Rabindranath Tagore noted Gandhi's "fierce joy of annihilation" and predicted the fratricidal violence that tore India apart after Britain's 1947 withdrawal. Gandhi's fuming disgust with sex revealed powerful totalitarian impulses in a 1936 conversation with birth-control advocate Margaret Sanger, stunned by his "ruthless determination to destroy pleasure wherever he saw it." Even sex within marriage amounted to adultery, he argued, insisting that lovemaking between husband and wife should cease altogether once they had three or four children: "If the social informers cannot impress this idea on people," he concluded, "why not a law?"

Gandhi's behavior as a husband and father was appalling. He refused to educate his sons and insisted that his wife, Kasturbhai, remain illiterate, even though he had financed his own education by selling half of her family jewels. On February 19, 1944, he forbade doctors to treat her pneumonia with penicillin: "If God wills it, He will pull her through," he said. She died on the 22nd. (A few months later, Gandhi took large doses of quinine after contracting malaria.) On January 30, 1948, Gandhi was assassinated in Delhi by a Hindu opposed to his conciliatory attitude toward India's Muslim population. His impact on Indian history was enormous, but a mountain of evidence insists that Gandhi was no candidate for sainthood.

Financed largely with public funds from the Indian government, *Gandhi* is a propaganda debacle of the first rank. It's attractive propaganda, thanks to beautiful photography, ample period detail, and an Oscar-winning performance by Kingsley (no surprise there). Attenborough sanitizes the historical Gandhi to a scandalous degree, leaving out his eccentric behavior, his cranky disposition, his shabby treatment of Kasturbhai and their sons, and his nasty collisions with westerners such as Margaret Sanger. Not even the staunchest Anglophile could suggest that England conquered and governed India—or any of her former colonies—with silks and bonbons, but *Gandhi* would have us believe that the SS staffed the British colonial army with its most fanatical troops. This film is a good example of ideology's ham-fisted tendency to present historical figures and events in tidy little boxes with no gray areas and in terms exaggerated enough to make many viewers suspicious minutes after the opening credits have faded from the screen.

Recommended Reading:
Robert Payne, *The Life and Death of Mahatma Gandhi.*

Ike: The War Years ★★

(1978) 196 Minutes

Director: Melville Shavelson, Boris Sagal

Cast: Robert Duvall, Lee Remick, Wensley Pithey, Dana Andrews, J. D. Cannon, Darren McGavin

Historical Background: During World War II's final two years, steamy fallout from Allied supreme commander Dwight Eisenhower's private life strained his marriage and his steady disposition around the clock. Titillating rumors of an extramarital romance with Irish driver Kay Summersby hummed hotly between late 1942 and 1945, devastating Ike's wife, Mamie, leading her to drink excessively at parties, and launching a spin-off whispering campaign that she'd become a problem drinker. (Inner-ear problems caused her to stumble frequently, fueling the rumor mill. She resumed her normal one-drink limit when family members mentioned the gossip.) Gradually, the scuttlebutt died, but Harry Truman—embittered by Ike's criticism of his Korean War policies—resurrected them in remarks (published posthumously in 1973), insisting that an acrimonious note from Chief of Staff George Marshall had threatened "to bust [Eisenhower] out of the Army" and make his life "a living hell" if he pursued alleged plans to divorce Mamie and marry Summersby. In her memoirs (*Past Forgetting*, crafted by a ghostwriter and published in 1976), Kay writes that Ike tried to seduce her, but insists that he never mentioned marriage—an absurd lapse, on his part, if the rest of Truman's story was true.

In fact, the rumors are wildly embellished—and probably false. Only Truman claimed to have seen the damning letter. Marshall aide C. S. George kept copies of all high-level reprimands in a Pentagon cabinet (Truman said he found Marshall's note there); George alone knew the lock's combination and swears that the letter never existed. Summersby's wartime confidante Anthea Saxe dismissed the gossip, noting that Eisenhower never had more than five minutes to spend alone with anybody (Eisenhower biographer Stephen E. Ambrose concurs). In fact, no one—clerks, servants, high-ranking officers, bodyguards, journalists—working with Eisenhower every day believed an affair took place. Cover-up notions assume a 50-year conspiracy of silence by countless people—all potential candidates for fat tell-all book contracts in a country historically eager for stories about presidential affairs. An indiscretion might have occurred, but not a long-term romance. Many friends believe Summersby authorized publication of *Past Forgetting* to pay huge hospital bills before she died in 1975.

A mix of fact and wild speculation: *Ike*'s versions of Summersby's love affair with fiancé Richard Arnold and her remarkable courage after German torpedoes deep-sixed a ship taking her to North Africa are perfect bull's-eyes. But the film focuses almost exclusively on the Eisenhower–Summersby story—and flops badly even if you accept its assumption of a long-term romance: Shavelson makes Summersby Eisenhower's only chauffeur (he had many, simultaneously, throughout the war; his chief driver was Sgt. Leonard Dry). Remick doubles as Duvall's secretary (nonsense: she couldn't even type—and Ike had three full-time secretaries). And Remick absurdly makes Summersby a strident, insubordinate, late-seventies-style feminist. Also available on video: a 269-minute version released in 1979.

Recommended Reading:
Stephen E. Ambrose, *Eisenhower;* Lester and Irene David, *Ike and Mamie: The Story of the General and His Lady.*

Khartoum ★★★

(1966) 134 Minutes

Director: Basil Dearden

Cast: Charlton Heston, Laurence Olivier, Richard Johnson, Ralph Richardson

Historical Background: During the summer of 1881, Muhammad Ahmad—a fanatical mystic and self-ordained Mahdi (the "expected one" or "guide")—organized an army of Islamic rebels and called for a holy war to drive Egyptian colonists and their British allies out of central Africa's Sudan region. Before the year ended, the rebels smashed an Egyptian infantry company near their stronghold on the Nile River and launched a two-year rampage across the country that carried them to the gates of

Khartoum, a fortified army town and colonial administrative center.

In 1884, British prime minister William Gladstone sent eccentric Gen. George Gordon to the Sudan with orders to evacuate the city if the military situation there was as precarious as it seemed. (It would be Gordon's second trip to the region. Ten years earlier, he had mapped the upper Nile River—one of several feats that had made him a celebrity in England: he had fought bravely with Great Britain's expeditionary force in the Crimean War. In 1863, he'd commanded an Anglo-French detachment quartered in Shanghai to protect European citizens during the Taiping Rebellion, earning the popular nickname "Chinese Gordon" that stuck for the rest of his life.)

As far as Gordon was concerned, evacuating Khartoum was a remote option at best. He was determined to rescue Britain's Egyptian allies, but by the time he arrived in the city its only link to the outside world was a single telephone line to Cairo. Despite Gordon's meticulous, exhaustive work to bolster Khartoum's defenses, including a moat and numerous minefields, a 317-day siege ended in disaster for Khartoum's defenders. The rebels' final assault carried them into the city, where Gordon died fighting on January 26, 1885. Troops sent by Gladstone to rescue him arrived two days later. The victorious Mahdi established an independent Islamic state in the Sudan, only to die of typhus a few months later. In 1898, British troops reoccupied Khartoum, and the Sudanese would have to wait 58 years for independence. When it came, they designated Khartoum their capital city.

Khartoum's workmanlike presentation of Gordon's extraordinary story is definitely worth a look. Heston is fine as Gordon, and Richardson's pensive, suspicious Gladstone is excellent. (Less convincing is Olivier's florid performance as a wild-eyed, lunatic Mahdi.) Highlights include excellent segments on Gordon's final days in Khartoum, spent drilling his 13,000 Egyptian troops and planting land mines around the city's walls. Dearden crafts knockout renditions of 19th-century desert warfare and bends facts, occasionally, to heighten his drama (Gordon and the Mahdi corresponded during the siege, for example, but never met face to face). Still, great entertainment and close to the mark historically.

Recommended Reading:
Charles C. Trench, *The Road to Khartoum.*

Land and Freedom

(1995) 109 Minutes

Director: Kenneth Loach

Cast: Ian Hart, Iciar Bollain, Rosana Pastor, Tom Gilroy, Marc Martines, Frederic Pierrot, Angela Clarke

Historical Background: For sheer savagery, Spain's civil war has few equals. Between 1936 and 1939, Republican Loyalists slaughtered 12 bishops, 5,255 priests, 2,492 monks, and 283 nuns. *Checas* (leftist murder squads) often buried victims alive and raped many nuns before killing them. By war's end, Republicans had butchered at least 55,000 civilians. Their enemies (in rebellion under Gen. Francisco Franco) matched them kill for kill: by 1939, 50,000 noncombatants had fallen to rebel guns. The Nationalists' most infamous atrocity, the carpet bombing of Guernica, flattened 70% of the town's buildings and killed 1,000 people.

Conditions begging for civil war had simmered fitfully on the peninsula for decades. Industrially and economically, Spain lagged far behind northern Europe. Spanish agriculture chaotically jumbled thousands of *minifundia*—farms too small to support even single families consistently—with *latifundia,* huge, sloppily managed, absentee-owned plantations. Farm labor dwarfed demand, flooding Spain with 3 million itinerant, landless peasants barely surviving on seasonal work. As world depression loomed in 1929, Spain's critical mining industry faltered, exports fell, and unemployment rocketed. Politically, Spain split into two hostile blocs—conservative Nationalists (businessmen, Roman Catholic groups, landowners, the army) and the Republican left (peasants, industrial workers, many educators, and highly unified political factions including socialists, anarchists, and Communists). Regional crises surfaced and multiplied: in 1934, general strikes paralyzed Zaragoza and Valencia, Madrid and Barcelona shook with bitter street fighting, and 50,000 miners seized villages throughout Asturia, burning churches and murdering Civil Guards and property owners (Franco crushed the revolt after weeks of bloody fighting).

On February 16, 1936, a fractious leftist coalition, the Loyalist "Popular Front," won a cliffhanging national election, then fumbled its way to catastrophe with a farcical, bureaucratic agrarian-reform program hated by everyone (in-cluding new peasant landowners), an April 5 power grab by Republican Communists, and furious Marxist attacks on churches and convents in major cities. The Loyalists couldn't control violent anarchist/revolutionary Marxist Party (POUM) street gangs thirsting for battle with equally violent fascist Falange Española hooligans. Wherever they looked, Nationalists saw raging chaos, and on July 17, 1936, Franco launched a highly disciplined revolt in regional military towns, taking western Spain and most of the territory north of the Guadarrama Mountains by August.

Spain's fratricidal nightmare was the first of many 20th-century proxy brawls—vicious conflicts between local forces supported by larger, ideologically hostile sponsor nations. The belligerents' alliance management proved critical. Franco bought weaponry from Germany and Italy on long-term credit, giving them vested interests (they wanted their money back) in a Nationalist victory. But the Russian-backed Republicans foolishly handed the Soviets 65% of their huge gold reserve—up front—for arms and equipment. Stalin had his money, a Republican defeat would cost him nothing, and Loyalist leaders had only high-level political clout to swap for further military aid. Just like that, Spain's Communist Party gained extravagant power, provoking vicious internecine conflict in 1937 and—supported by Soviet agents—killing thousands of anarchists and POUM Republicans.

Under these circumstances, Franco's unified coalition and solid military skills guaranteed a Nationalist victory (Soviet aid and the "International Brigades"—thousands of volunteers from more than 40 countries—extended the Republic's life considerably). Ruthless, ambitious, and aloof, Franco was absolutely "unreadable," even for seasoned politicians (Hitler said he'd rather have teeth pulled without anesthesia than negotiate with Franco). Few people realize that Franco wasn't a fascist; politically, in fact, he was "nothing": he detested politicians, diplomats, and statesmen, dismissing all political philosophies—including democracy—with electrifying contempt. Franco believed in the army—period. As commander in chief, he was a merciless—but fair—disciplinarian and ahead of his time tactically: small-unit maneuver warfare (rain ordnance on small enemy sectors, then overrun them with sudden, furious battalion-sized assaults) marked most of his field operations. By October 1937, he'd taken Cádiz, Málaga, and Granada and controlled most of Spain's southern coast. Nine months later, Nationalist armies drove east to the Mediterranean, cutting the Republic in two between Tarragona and Castellon. They took Barcelona on January 28, 1939, and heavily besieged Madrid fell in late March, finally ending the carnage. Between 500,000 and 1,000,000 Spaniards died during the war.

A sluggish propaganda load packed with featherheaded clichés about the war. All of Loach's Nationalists, including the clergy, are fascists—a preposterous fiction: fascists were only one element of Franco's coalition, and most clerics didn't join its ranks until anti-Catholic Republican atrocities reached appalling levels. Other gaffes are ludicrous: drawing thunderous cheers from his buddies, an old Loyalist shouts, "We must keep the revolution alive!"—apparently unaware that the establishment was Republican and the revolution Nationalist (this reversal persists throughout the film). Even worse, Loach sanitizes the bitter war, presenting life in frontline Loyalist trenches as a Boy Scout Jamboree with wineskins, campfire songs, and compliant women. A talky, boring stinker.

For Further Viewing:

For Whom the Bell Tolls ★★★ (1943) 130 Minutes (Gary Cooper, Ingrid Bergman, Akim Tamiroff, Arturo de Cordova, Joseph Calleia, Katina Paxinou, Vladimir Sokoloff): If you're looking for feature-film history, forget this famous adaptation of Hemingway's novel. Director Sam Wood focuses entirely on the Maria (Bergman)–Robert Jordan (Cooper) romance and the war's moral issues, ignoring some of the most "filmable" passages in Hemingway's fiction (activities at Soviet mission headquarters in Madrid's Gaylord Hotel, for one). But the film does convey Hemingway's merciless candor about the war—Wood balances Cooper's early all-for-the-Republic monologue, for example, with a dreamlike rendition of Republican atrocities at Ronda (they murdered 512 civilians there in 1936): the open arena of the world, for Hemingway, was the wrong place to look for virtuous, unbloodied hands. For this reason, Communists worldwide railed loudly against the novel, despite its endorsement of the Republic. Authentic period detail—weapons, uniforms, Spanish saddles—and fine action sequences near film's end.

Recommended Reading:
Hugh Thomas, *The Spanish Civil War;* George Orwell, *Homage to Catalonia.*

The Last Emperor ★

(1987) 160 Minutes

Director: Bernardo Bertolucci

Cast: John Lone, Joan Chen, Peter O'Toole, Ying Ruocheng, Victor Wong, Dennis Dun

Historical Background: On December 2, 1908, two-year-old Manchu prince Henry Pu-Yi became China's last emperor in history's strangest sanctuary—the 8,900-room Imperial Palace, an endless sprawl of interconnected ramparts, towers, courtyards, and kiosks in the heart of Peking's multiple-walled Forbidden City. Strange shades of violet, purple, and scarlet formed a visual riot dominated everywhere by yellow, China's official imperial color. (Childhood memories "filled my head with yellow mist," noted Pu-Yi.)

The huge complex housed an outlandish population: Pu-Yi, 1,000 concubines, 150 cooks, the imperial tutor (Englishman Reginald Johnston), and 1,500 greedy, power-hungry eunuchs. Long-term, epic-scale looting of imperial storehouses and privy purses had made many eunuchs wealthy. In 1923, after an inventory exposed their larceny, Pu-Yi sacked all but 100 of them. It was a stunning blow: for centuries, eunuchs had transmitted imperial decrees, managed financial accounts, staffed the library, guarded Pu-Yi's art collection, processed official documents, drafted daily court schedules, arranged audiences, and run the fire department. Above all, they'd served the emperor, dressing him, cutting his hair, tying his shoes, and squeezing toothpaste onto his toothbrush. Trailing him everywhere, they carried extra clothes, medicines, water, tea, food, umbrellas, even toilets and chamberpots.

Their labors produced a sadistic monster. Capricious, lazy, cowardly, frequently seized by fits of ungovernable rage, Pu-Yi had innocent eunuchs and servant girls flogged with split bamboo canes every day. He tested their obedience by ordering them to eat dirt—literally (they did). His homosexuality provoked legendary quarrels with first wife Wan Jung, often driving her from their chambers howling—at the top of her lungs—"You eunuch!" (He'd planned to escape marriage by fleeing to England in late 1922; Johnston convinced him to stay. In June 1946, Wan Jung died in jail from severe opium withdrawal.)

Forced by the Republican Revolution to abdicate in 1912, Pu-Yi remained in the Forbidden City for a dozen years, then fled to Tientsin. A bizarre string of captivities followed. Bellicose Manchu clans with historic claims to Manchuria—and fanatically loyal to Pu-Yi—dotted the strategic, hotly contested Sino-Soviet frontier: controlling the last emperor meant holding the gateway to Manchuria and military bases in Peking's backyard. In 1932, invading Japanese enthroned Pu-Yi atop a puppet Manchurian government (he happily cooperated, deeming this a step toward regaining his throne). The Russians also wanted him: after WWII, Stalin captured and held him in Siberia, hoping to build an independent Soviet-dominated Manchurian state "legitimized" by Pu-Yi's support.

But Mao Tse-tung's civil-war victory changed everything. Returned to China in 1950, Pu-Yi spent nine years in Communist jails and the Harbin Thought Control Center. Bloody Sino-Soviet border skirmishes prompted Mao—hungry for loyalty from 2.4 million Manchu—to pardon the last emperor in 1959 and personally arrange his 1962 marriage to a 40-year-old Hangchow nurse, symbolically uniting China and Manchuria for the first time. Pu-Yi joined a local militia, attending protests—in front of the Forbidden City (!)—against a Japanese-American Security Treaty; eventually, officials appointed him to two national political committees. He died in October 1967, of kidney cancer and heart failure, according to some biographers—others insist that Red Guards tortured him to death during Mao's Cultural Revolution.

Hamfisted—but beautifully crafted—propaganda bankrolled by Communist China (high-level officials poured $25 million into Bertolucci's coffers and "reviewed" every second of his final cut). Parts of the film are accurate: Pu-Yi's Japanese collaboration, for example, and the eunuchs' burning of imperial stores to undercut the 1923 inventory leading to their expulsion.

But Bertolucci fictionalizes and falsifies much of the time. In the film, Wan Jung's heroin habit wrecks the imperial marriage—in fact, she turned to drugs because of Pu-Yi's sadism and homosexuality (ignored in the film). Lone's conscientious, scholarly Pu-Yi-as-victim—saved, finally, by his conversion and commitment to Communism—is awful. Loyal to no one but himself, the real emperor served anyone capable of increasing his comfort (he lived like a king under Stalin). Pu-Yi's "service" to Mao merely mimicked his collaborations with Japan and the USSR. Worst of all, Bertolucci sanitizes the Cultural Revolution's horrors. The upside:

phenomenal period detail and atmosphere and great first-time footage of the Forbidden City.

Recommended Reading:
Arnold C. Brackman, *The Last Emperor;* Stuart Schram, *Mao Tse-tung;* Colin Thubron, *Behind the Wall.*

Lawrence of Arabia ★★★★

(1962) 216 Minutes

Director: David Lean

Cast: Peter O'Toole, Alec Guinness, Anthony Quinn, Jack Hawkins, Anthony Quayle, Arthur Kennedy, Omar Sharif, Jose Ferrer

Historical Background: In April 1935, from the stairwell of a Paris hotel, Thomas Edward Lawrence staged his last ambush: spotting staid British dignitaries David Lloyd George and Charles Hardinge several floors below, Lawrence collected all the lavatory tissue he could carry and mercilessly bombarded the two into pell-mell retreat. (Hardinge later remarked, "There is nothing funny about toilet paper.") Long famous for nutty behavior, Lawrence at age 46 remained one of history's colossal flakes. At university he skipped meals, snacking constantly on raisins, apples, and cake. Late at night, he prowled Oxford's deserted thoroughfares—no one knows why—and explored the town sewers by canoe, firing pistols to rattle street-level pedestrians. At parties and dinners he sat on the floor in lotuslike positions for hours, listening attentively, saying nothing, and smiling weirdly.

But during the 20th century's early decades, no one in the world matched his bristling arsenal of wide-ranging skills. He translated Homer's *Odyssey* into English. He wrote a number of books (*Crusader Castles, The Mint, Seven Pillars of Wisdom*) and published articles in the *Royal Engineers' Journal,* the *Spectator,* the *Times,* and the *Daily Express.* His diplomatic finesse united a mob of fiercely independent sheiks under Prince Feisal of Mecca in a shattering WWI campaign against Turkey. He was a crack intelligence agent and a talented archaeologist.

His signature legacy still flourishes in the hellish world of "low-intensity" proxy wars: during the 1916–18 Arab-Turkish campaign, Lawrence of Arabia wrote the book on modern guerrilla warfare. By 1917, Britain's desert high command had written off its Arab allies as brave but hotheaded rabble incapable of disciplined, large-scale tactical warfare. Lawrence agreed, but viewed Arab "short-comings" differently. Desert warriors had always viewed battle as a series of quick, aggressive, small-unit explosions—perfect tactics against enemies with superior weapons, more men, and a crushing edge in the means for large-scale troop annihilation. Lawrence's principles of guerrilla warfare, still followed by "irregulars" everywhere, read like incantations from Mao's long march. Win the civilian population's sympathy. Hit quickly, suddenly, and hard. Attack only weakly manned hostile outposts (just often enough to force

continued enemy troop and supply expenditure). Take no casualties and forget about killing Turks: wreck them logistically, instead, plastering traffic along their one supply line—the Beirut-Medina Hejaz Railway—every single day. Above all, keep the railway—a gluttonous siphon for enemy troops and supplies—up and running (barely).

In 1917, Lawrence's theories met their first test at Aqaba, a Red Sea harbor 60 miles west of the railway—and a perfect base for guerrilla operations. That summer, Lawrence hurled 500 raging Arabs against a 1,500-man Turkish army based in and around the port city. The crippling blow came on July 2 near Bir el Lasan (just north of Aqaba) with ferocious night attacks against a large enemy relief column. By daybreak only 90 Turks out of 600 remained standing. Terrorized by news of the debacle, Aqaba's garrison surrendered meekly on July 6. Lawrence usually didn't care about taking and holding enemy garrisons: he wanted to assault them furiously, briefly, and often, always disengaging with victory mere seconds away. The continuous threat of further attack mired tons of enemy field guns, small arms, rations, medical supplies, and thousands of hostile troops—all desperately needed for huge European battles—in a miserable backwater theater. It was strategic brilliance, and it worked, earning Lawrence the *Croix de Guerre,* Britain's Distinguished Service Order, a Companionship of the Bath, a Victoria Cross nomination, and an invitation to join the official Allies' grand entry into Jerusalem in December 1917. After the war, Lawrence lobbied for Arab independence and creation of a Jewish state, then withdrew from public life, joining the RAF and, later, the Royal Tank Corps under phony names. He died in Dorsetshire on May 19, 1935, six days after a motorcycle accident.

O'Toole (Lawrence), one of the most eccentric personalities ever produced by England's movie mills, was Lean's fifth choice for the title role, an odd ranking since Lawrence, himself, was so eccentric. The movie delivers on-target versions of Lawrence's impact on the Aqaba operation and the desert campaign's brutality, severe fighting conditions, and epic geographic scale. But Robert Bolt's script bristles with omissions and distortions: wise, educated, and pensive, Guinness' Feisal bears little resemblance to the real prince (vain, weak, ignorant, and timid); Lean ignores Arab participation in the 1918 offensive against Syria; the Arabs didn't take Damascus on their own—Britain helped them; Lawrence once executed an Arab, but he never told Allied commander Edmund Allenby (Hawkins) that he enjoyed it; and Lean's hints at Lawrence's sadomasochistic homosexuality rest on popular, unproved allegations (he never intentionally burned his fingers with matches, for example, and his beating by Turks in Deraa remains unconfirmed). Still, a walloping masterpiece, faithful in spirit to Lawrence's character and exploits.

Recommended Reading:
Stephen E. Tabachnick, ed., *The T. E. Lawrence Puzzle;* Lawrence James, *The Golden Warrior: The Life and Legend of Lawrence of Arabia;* Robert Graves, *Lawrence and the Arabs;* T. E. Lawrence, *Revolt in the Desert.*

Lost Command ★★

(1966) 130 Minutes

Director: Mark Robson

Cast: Anthony Quinn, Alain Delon, George Segal, Michele Morgan, Claudia Cardinale

Historical Background: On August 20, 1955, Algeria's insurrectionist FLN (National Liberation Front) launched a carefully planned genocidal campaign to murder every French civilian, including pregnant women and their fetuses, in the entire country. That morning, four 20-man FLN death squads raged through Ain-Abid village, severing men's limbs, vivisecting ten teenagers, disemboweling pregnant women and stabbing their unborn babies, and bludgeoning small children to death. Ordered to kill every area Arab in reprisal, French paratroopers moved in, guns blazing, and slaughtered 1,273 civilians. It was business as usual in the 1954–62 French-Algerian War, a bloodbath infamous for criminal butchery by both sides against soldier and civilian alike.

European homesteaders (*pieds noirs*—Spaniards, Italians, but predominantly French) began colonizing Algeria in 1830, most simply moving from the Mediterranean's northern shore to its southern coast (sparsely populated by 1.5 million Arabs). For decades, colonizing efforts served everyone well: settlers got a fresh start; France built ports, railways, a productive agricultural economy, nationwide road systems, and a first-rate medical network (gradually ending typhoid and malaria epidemics, lowering infant death rates—and opening the door for breathtaking population growth among non-Europeans). By 1954, Algerian Muslims numbered 9 million, but most lagged far behind *pieds noirs* politically and economically: only 20% of Algeria's Muslim boys and one girl in 15 enrolled in school, and more than 90% were illiterate in French; countless Muslims couldn't find work; Algerian farm hands earned just 22¢ a day, working, on average, 65 days per year; typical Muslims earned 30 times less than their French counterparts. Worst of all, a revoltingly corrupt political machine (*pied noir* authorities rigged most elections) killed all hope for reform. Incredible government myopia wrecked chances for incorporating both groups into a larger Algerian culture sought by many *pieds noirs* and thousands of reasonable Muslim moderates. On May 8, a ghastly preview of the coming civil war erupted in Sétif: guerrillas slaughtered 103 *pieds noirs,* then weathered a holocaust of French reprisals (1,300 Arabs died).

Muslim rebels fired the French-Algerian War's opening salvo on November 1, 1954, with small-arms and bomb attacks on public facilities, French officials, and Muslim loyalists, killing seven people by midnight. Reacting swiftly, the French arrested 2,000 guerrillas and suspected terrorists, then sent the 25th Airborne Division to sweep the hills around Arris. On November 29, they captured 18 FLN and killed 23 more, including celebrated terrorist Belkacem Grine. For hard-core rebels, the attacks had flopped horribly: they drew no popular support, and journalists in France ignored them, lavishing ink on America's Congressional elections instead. Guerrilla leaders—Ahmed Ben Bella, Saadi Yacef, Bachir Chihani, Ram-

dane Abane—escalated, ordering an all-out murder campaign against Algeria's Islamic moderates, designed to ignite French reprisals and draw ordinary Muslims into the rebel camp: "Kill all the *caids* [local Arab governors] and their children," read a 1955 order from Chihani. "Kill all those who pay taxes. Burn the houses of Muslim NCOs away on active service. Kill any person attempting to deflect the militants." Algeria's peasants suffered horrifically: at Mélousa village alone, FLN death squads left 301 dead from knife and pickax wounds.

The war's monstrous cycle of atrocity and reprisal spun wildly out of control, and by 1956 French men-at-arms posted to Algeria numbered 500,000. On September 30, Yacef's bombs killed three and wounded more than 50 in the heart of the city's European sector, opening the Battle of Algiers—a 12-month terrorist bloodbath aimed at paralyzing the city and bringing down its harried administration. FLN operatives planted bombs at funerals and other gatherings, then quickly vacated the streets, leaving only innocent Muslims open to savage French reprisals. In January 1957, Governor-General Robert Lacoste gave 10th Airborne Division commandant Jacques Massu carte-blanche dominion in the city, authorizing unlimited force—including torture—to liquidate the FLN there. Eight months later, the army's draconian methods had won the Battle of Algiers—but crippled wider war efforts—for France. Military interrogators tortured many innocent Muslims, eventually wrecking morale among Massu's 4,600 paratroopers. Outraged voters in France turned against the war: in Paris, two administrations fell, leaving France without a government for 22 days (1957) and 37 days (1958). In March 1962, the nightmare ended with a cease-fire (followed by a July 1 referendum making Algeria an independent state). Between 300,000 and 1 million Muslims died in the war; France sustained 82,330 casualties, including 17,436 battle deaths.

Three survivors of the French Indochina War—Legionnaire colonel Quinn, Algerian Legionnaire Segal, and division historian Delon—choose different sides (Segal joins the FLN) during the Algerian insurrection. A beautifully photographed, hard-hitting rendition of the war's brutality and a bizarre contortion of history—in both directions. *The Lost Command* whitewashes FLN savagery: rebels protect Muslim civilians throughout, attacking only *pieds noirs;* historically, the reverse was true—during the war's first two years, FLN terrorists murdered 1,035 Europeans, slaughtering at least 6,500 Muslim civilians (a rock-bottom figure disputed by most historians; some estimates top 20,000). But Robson also shifts responsibility for widespread torture from *pied noir* civil authorities: Quinn & Co.—French militarists—seize unlimited police powers on their own (France later brings criminal charges against them for reprisals!). Another blunder: weapons pour into FLN arsenals from Tunisia—in fact, French troops sealed the Algeria-Tunisia frontier with double fences and trigger-happy patrols. Absorbing—but weird and historically unreliable.

For Further Viewing:
The Battle of Algiers (1966) 125 Minutes (Yacef Saadi, Jean Martin, Brahim Haggiag, Tommaso Neri, Samia Kerbash): Director Gillo Pontecorvo's annoying propaganda rant absurdly unfolds documentary-style after its opening screen proclaims, "This dramatic reenactment of the Battle of Algiers contains NOT ONE FOOT of Newsreel or Documen-

tary film"—assuming, apparently, that viewers will be dumb enough to mistake the next two hours for history or journalism. Peppered with voice-over FLN "communiqués" (always preceded by a number—as if they've been archived for posterity), each new segment embellishes FLN righteousness. (Communiqué #2, for example, states that the FLN "takes responsibility for the physical health and mental well-being of the Algerian people.") For two years, Pontecorvo's rebels kill only Legionnaires—usually with guns, not explosives. (A high-level French cop plants the film's first bomb in a crowded Muslim apartment complex—a laughable Pontecorvo fantasy fabricated to justify Yacef's milk-bar massacre the next day.) An awful movie—pompous, inaccurate, and boring throughout.

Recommended Reading:
Alistair Horne, *A Savage War of Peace: Algeria, 1954–1962.*

MacArthur ★★★★★

(1977) 130 Minutes

Director: Joseph Sargent

Cast: Gregory Peck, Dan O'Herlihy, Ed Flanders, Sandy Kenyon, Dick O'Neill, Art Fleming

Historical Background: Most Americans find no middle ground for Douglas MacArthur.

His critics see a demon happily routing hungry, protesting WWI veterans (the "Bonus Army") from their ramshackle Washington, D.C., shanty camp in 1932. For admirers, he was a near-saint holding 15 high decorations—including the Medal of Honor and seven Silver Stars—and blindsided, in the end, by petty politics. But if you view the facts of MacArthur's career without emotion (it's not easy), you'll find a maddening, incongruous riddle—and a life stunning for its decisive impact (lingering to this day) on world events.

Clearly a military genius—even old foe George Marshall called him "our most brilliant general"—MacArthur worked miracles with skeletal resources during the 1941–45 Pacific campaign, changing the conduct of war forever (for specific battles see Chapter 7). To press the Allied advance from New Guinea to Japan's home islands, he invented "triphibious warfare": meticulous coordination of air, sea, and ground forces in crushing, lightning thrusts against enemy strongpoints, bypassing strategically insignificant areas and cutting hostile supply and communication lines to ribbons—unprecedented, at the time, and precisely the same doctrine followed by the Allied Coalition throughout the Persian Gulf War. Half a decade later, his brilliant amphibious assault behind enemy lines at Inchon saved the UN "police action" in Korea. But he was capable of colossal lapses and blunders: in May 1944 he ordered costly, unnecessary frontal assaults against Japanese fortifications on Biak Island; hours after learning of the Pearl Harbor debacle, he left most of his Philippine warplanes unprotected, and Japanese sorties destroyed them on the ground.

MacArthur's biography hums with baffling contradictions. Gregarious, considerate, and—at times—self-effacing in private matters, professionally he was imperious, flamboyant, insubordinate, and stubborn enough to infuriate superiors and peers equally. In Korea, MacArthur waged a ferocious, nonstop *blitzkrieg*, drawing dismissal from command in April 1951 for criticizing President Truman's refusal to bomb Manchurian staging areas—but in 1964, even though his fuming hostility toward Communism still flourished, he urged Lyndon Johnson to get out of Vietnam. Incredibly courageous under fire (the sobriquet "Dugout Doug" was truly unfair), he was terrified (at age 52!) that his mother would discover his early-1930s affair with a Scottish-Filipina girl. Most important: supremely conservative, he rolled into postwar Japan the stern, conquering overseer, then rammed thoroughly liberal reforms—women's suffrage, labor unions, a stupefying array of civil liberties—through mountains of bureaucratic red tape, turning Hirohito's battered imperial relic into a state-of-the-art democracy destined to shake world finance and economics during the late seventies and eighties. MacArthur spent his final 13 years in seclusion and died—at age 84—in 1964. Most biographers agree that no one will ever figure him out.

Peck—a perfect MacArthur—and Flanders—magnificent as Truman—highlight this near-perfect chronicle of the general's career from early 1942 to his moving 1964 West Point address ("Duty, Honor, Country"). Remarkably concise and thorough, featuring great combat choreography, excellent performances, and scrupulous accuracy (including military dress and weaponry), with one exception—Sargent crafts a knockout rendition of the widely accepted popular fiction that MacArthur, in a fit of one-upmanship, arrived 45 minutes late for a 1950 Wake Island meeting with Truman. It never happened; Truman (in his 1956 memoirs) and staff members all say that MacArthur greeted the president as soon as his plane touched down.

Recommended Reading:
D. Clayton James, *The Years of MacArthur;* Charles Andrew Willoughby, *MacArthur, 1941–1951;* William Manchester, *American Caesar.*

A Man for All Seasons ★★★★★

(1966) 120 Minutes

Director: Fred Zinnemann

Cast: Paul Scofield, Robert Shaw, Leo McKern, Wendy Hiller, Orson Welles, John Hurt, Susannah York, Nigel Davenport, Vanessa Redgrave

Historical Background: Sir Thomas More's genial wit took center stage moments before his execution for refusing to recognize Henry VIII as head of the Anglican Church. Weakened by his long imprisonment, More tottered on the scaffold steps, turned cheerfully to the Tower Hill lieutenant, and said, "I pray you see me safe up, sir, and for my coming down let me shift for myself." Then, kneeling calmly at the block, he went to his death completely unafraid. That More died so well surprised no one. A man of unshakable faith, he had always put his religious convictions ahead of everything else, including creature comforts and financial security: at one point, his many acts of charity so strained his income that the Church offered him a stipend to defray some of his professional expenses. More politely refused the grant.

As a young man, he considered a clerical career, but chose instead to practice law as a lay Christian in London. He won distinction in an extraordinary range of vocations. Many London companies profited from his deft negotiation of commercial contracts. His speaking skills and glittering record at the bar prompted Henry VIII to send him on a diplomatic mission to the Low Countries. Before completing the assignment, More finished his classic literary work, *Utopia.* His *History of King Richard III (1518),* published in Latin and English, is a masterpiece of early British historiography. In 1529, More became the first layman ever appointed lord chancellor of England—a stunning break with British tradition: he was a commoner and couldn't join the same House of Lords that he chaired as holder of the realm's highest office.

His row with Henry VIII began in 1530 with More's refusal to sign a letter pressuring the Pope to annul the king's marriage to Catherine of Aragon. (By then, Henry considered the union theologically unlawful—Leviticus forbade marriage to widowed sisters-in-law—and, because Catherine didn't produce a male heir, dynastically catastrophic. On May 23, 1533, Archbishop of Canterbury Thomas Cranmer declared the marriage invalid.) In 1532, England's bishops ratified a document giving

Henry effective control of the church in England. Unwilling to declare war on the Pope, More returned the chancellor's Great Seal—a dangerous move implying opposition to government policy. More wouldn't take an oath rejecting papal authority in England, and king's minister Thomas Cromwell imprisoned him in the Tower of London on April 17, 1534. Perjured testimony from Cromwell ally Richard Rich convicted him, guaranteeing his execution at Tower Hill on July 6, 1535. Five years later, Cromwell fell to the headsman's axe, and More—canonized by Pius XI in 1935—remains one of Christendom's most celebrated saints.

To this day, litanies of misconception about Henry persist. He was no great monarch, but he wasn't the catastrophe of popular legend. Like other European royals, he had extramarital affairs, but he wasn't a cauldron of lust. He was a great builder. Decorous and almost Puritanical, at times, he detested swearing and profanity. He brought efficient government to Britain and forged the core of a great navy. But all of this groans under the weight of More's murder and Henry's six farcical marriages. After Catherine of Aragon came Anne Boleyn (1533–36—executed); Jane Seymour (1536–37—died in childbirth); Anne of Cleves (1539–40—divorced); Catherine Howard (1540–42—executed); and Catherine Parr (1543–47—widowed).

Anne Boleyn, mother of Elizabeth I, remains Henry's most celebrated wife. A talented dancer, witty, graceful, and handsome, she drew courtiers like a magnet (gaining an unmerited reputation for licentiousness). She was highstrung, with a volcanic temper, and unpopular in many circles because of her arrogant manner. Infatuated with Jane Seymour—and still seeking a male heir—Henry sent Anne to the Tower on May 2, 1536, executing her for treason and adultery (charges trumped up by Cromwell) 17 days later. The king died in 1547—from pneumonia or tuberculosis, not syphilis (a common misconception launched by a speculative 1888 magazine article).

A Man for All Seasons is historical biography at its very best. Scofield's Oscar-winning More is one of many fine performances; Shaw makes a superb Henry, full-throated and menacing enough to convince you that here indeed is a man who could behead one of his oldest friends and forget about it moments later; McKern is wonderfully loathsome as Cromwell; Hiller (Lady Alice More) almost steals the show; and Davenport excels as the short-fused Duke of Norfolk. Robert Bolt's beautifully scripted presentation of the reasoning behind each agonizing, increasingly fatal choice by More is riveting.

Throughout the film, witty conversation and verbal duels lend great force to period detail and atmosphere ("The nobility of England would've snored through the Sermon on the Mount," More remarks at one point, "but they'll labor like scholars over a bulldog's pedigree"). *A Man for All Seasons* dominated the 1966 Oscar competition, and the film industry has yet to produce a better movie.

For Further Viewing:
The Private Life of Henry VIII ★★ (1933) 97 Minutes (Charles Laughton, Robert Donat, Binnie Barnes, Merle Oberon, Elsa Lanchester, Miles Mander): Fine period detail and top-notch acting make half the story here. Director Alexander Korda's masterpiece flops as historical biography, even though it's faithful to many facts: his king aims to strengthen England's navy, for example, and commissions a French swordsman to behead Anne

Boleyn (the British axe was less humane). But Laughton's Oscar-winning Henry is a ridiculous caricature, ranting, petulant, childish—a near-moronic slob—and sufficiently unlike the real king to wreck the film for history lovers. Grand entertainment, but failing marks for accuracy.

Anne of the Thousand Days ★★★ (1969) 145 Minutes (Richard Burton, Genevieve Bujold, Irene Papas, Anthony Quayle): Director Charles Jarrott's stunning period detail builds irresistible Renaissance atmosphere, and Bujold—a dead ringer for famous Anne Boleyn portraits (one attributed to John Hoskins)—makes a high-spirited, intelligent queen. But Jarrott replaces many facts with Hollywood whimsy: a disgusted Anne rejects Henry furiously at first, insulting him publicly at least twice—then suddenly reverses course and drags him to bed (rubbish); Henry's affair (ca. 1520–25) with Anne's sister Mary is historical, but didn't produce a child; Henry saw Anne for the last time at a May Day tournament, but Burton crashes Bujold's trial, terrorizing reluctant witnesses—and later offers her clemency if she'll "annul the marriage" (whatever that means). High drama—but biographical fluff.

Recommended Reading:
R. W. Chambers, *Thomas More;* E. E. Reynolds, *The Field Is Won: The Life and Death of St. Thomas More;* J. J. Scarisbrick, *Henry VIII;* Alison Weir, *The Six Wives of Henry VIII.*

A Night to Remember ★★★★★

(1958) 123 Minutes

Director: Roy Baker

Cast: Kenneth More, David McCallum, Jill Dixon, Laurence Naismith, Frank Lawton, Honor Blackman, Alec McCowen, George Rose

Historical Background: April 15, 1912—New York: Hours after taking reports that the RMS *Titanic* had plowed into an iceberg, losing countless passengers and spiraling straight to the North Atlantic's dark floor, the *Evening Sun's* banner headline—ALL SAVED FROM TITANIC AFTER COLLISION—trumpeted a lead story praising Canada's *Virginian* for towing the crippled liner to Halifax. Aboard the *Titanic,* stubborn faith in hyperbole pronouncing the great vessel "unsinkable" led many passengers to doubt that she really was foundering, even as her bow groaned relentlessly downward—and some didn't panic until they hit the ocean's bitter, 28° waters. No one on earth thought a floating ice fragment could deep-six the most gigantic man-made moving object in history.

Hopelessly naive confidence, to us—but perfectly reasonable in 1912: the *Titanic* weighed 46,328 tons, displaced 66,000 tons of water, and sprawled the length of three football fields bow to stern. She was 11 storeys high. Her rudder alone weighed a staggering 100 tons (it was taller than a large house). Full-size twin locomotives could rocket through each of her four towering smoke-stacks—easily. Powered by two four-cylinder reciprocating-engine systems—four storeys high and capable of generating 50,000 horsepower—she could reach 25-knot speeds in open water, an incredible feat for a ship that size. She housed a full-sized gymnasium, four passenger elevators, eight massive cargo cranes, a regulation squash court, a Turkish bath with cooling rooms, and a 50-phone switchboard. The *Titanic* was an absolute monster, and her architecture provided state-of-the-art disaster protection: fitted with automatic doors for sealing flooded areas, steel bulkheads reaching upward from the keel divided the *Titanic*'s lower-hull into 16 watertight compartments (five decks high fore and aft, four decks high amidships).

But the *Titanic*'s builders used Scottish rolled steel—the best of its day, but peppered with impurities (sulfur, phosphorus) rendering it brittle in extremely cold water. Eighty-three hours into her maiden voyage, ship's lookouts spotted a towering iceberg, dead ahead and almost in their laps. Thirty-seven seconds later, helmsmen turned hard aport, but it was too late: at 11:40 P.M., April 14, the *Titanic*'s starboard hull struck a glancing blow along the knifelike edge of a submerged shelf, plowing ahead 250 feet before clearing the sullen blue mountain of ice. In a heartbeat, the Atlantic Ocean began pouring into the *Titanic*'s forward watertight holds—at eight tons-per-second—through a gaping 12-square-foot wound. (It wasn't the 300-foot gash expected to appear in 1985 photographs of the recently discovered hulk—the ice shelf had loosened seams between many hull plates along a 250-foot scar, instead. Had helmsmen simply rammed the iceberg head-on, the *Titanic* probably would have remained seaworthy enough for towing to Halifax.)

Set low in the hull, some third-class ("steerage") cabins filled to ankle depth almost instantly. (Steerage fares suffered more than any group but the crew. Unassisted below decks, baffled by mazelike corridors leading through upper-deck sections to lifeboats, and barred briefly from a quick exit route by crewmen holding berths for women and children, the steerage group lost at least 65% of its complement—all because there was no maritime-law policy, fair or unfair, on steerage rescue. The *Titanic* disaster drove legislation mandating fair treatment of third-class passengers on foundering liners.) With terrifying speed, water rose in the forward watertight holds, breaching bulkhead tops, cascading steadily aft into adjacent compartments, and pulling the bow ever downward. Once the sixth hold submerged, 25,000 tons of water filled the hull, and the *Titanic* was history.

The great ship's lifeboats had 1,178 seats—more than maritime law required, but far too few for the *Titanic*'s 2,224 souls. Captain Edward Smith ordered a women-and-children-first policy (followed with remarkable selflessness by most passengers and crew). Many men and women heroically surrendered seats in the boats to older, weaker, and younger late arrivals. Occasional cowardice and terror drove much early activity: some lifeboats rowed away only half full (one carried just 12 people). By 2:10 A.M., the last boat had pulled away from the foundering leviathan, and the *Titanic*'s plunging bow had dragged her stern out of the water, compressing the keel and producing tremendous strain amidships. She soon broke in half just forward of number-three funnel, freeing the bow to separate and slide quickly away. Nearly vertical by now, the hull's after end sank relentlessly, finally disappearing at 2:20 A.M. Hundreds of people clinging to the stern dove into the freezing sea, dying of hypothermia within minutes. (Throughout the ordeal, another liner, the *Californian,* lay motionless ten miles to the north, ignoring a holocaust of blinding distress flares fired every five minutes from the *Titanic*'s port bow. Fifty-eight miles southwest of the wreck, the *Carpathia* responded to the *Titanic*'s wireless SOS barrage and began rescuing survivors at 4:10 A.M.) Between 675 and 712 survived—British Enquiry, American Inquiry, and British Board of Trade records vary—leaving more than 1,500 dead in the North Atlantic.

Based on Walter Lord's fine history, this documentary-style, nuts-and-bolts account of the legendary disaster remains unsurpassed for historical accuracy and gut-wrenching suspense. Baker spends little time on peripherals—shipboard romances, social gatherings, on-board melodrama—focusing instead on grueling efforts by captain and crew to fill and launch lifeboats and contact nearby ships for help. Especially well done are segments on the *Carpathia*'s full-throttle, perilous, heroic race to the rescue through seas bristling with icebergs (the maritime equivalent of driving into oncoming traffic on the wrong side of an expressway). Baker's rendition of the steerage-fare nightmare is heartrending—and perfectly fair. Excellent history, super filmmaking, and top-notch entertainment.

For Further Viewing:
Titanic ★★★ (1997) 194 Minutes (Leonardo DiCaprio, Kate Winslet, Frances Fisher, Kathy Bates, David Warner, Billy Zane, Gloria Stuart): History's costliest film (producers spent at least $200 million—many times the real *Titanic*'s construction costs) hangs its chronicle of the catastrophe on a te-

dious fictional romance between steerage passenger DiCaprio and first-classer Winslet. Historically faithful renditions of events leading to the disaster and a knockout, superaccurate restaging of collision and aftermath make the film worthwhile for amateur historians. But shallow pulpitry intrudes far too often. With preposterous class-conscious overkill, writer-director James Cameron makes every third-classer valorous and almost everyone on the top five decks scatterbrained, selfish, cowardly, or malevolent (Warner's fictional Lovejoy, for example, is a patrician Hitler–Bugs Moran hybrid). Surely ample heroism unfolded below decks—even though no historical records survive—but giving steerage its due doesn't require ignoring courageous acts by other passengers and demonizing A Deck's upper crust. Worse still: Cameron's silly portrait of Captain Smith as indecisive and useless throughout the disaster contradicts every eyewitness account of his behavior during the 160-minute interval between collision and submersion. Great pyrotechnics—mediocre history.

Titanic ★★★★ (1953) 98 Minutes (Clifton Webb, Robert Wagner, Barbara Stanwyck, Richard Basehart, Audrey Dalton, Brian Aherne, Thelma Ritter): A fine companion piece for *A Night to Remember,* emphasizing passenger interplay more than disaster and death. *Titanic*'s main plot is a moral fable examining the crumbling marriage of Stanwyck and Webb (so crushed by news that his young son isn't really his that he virtually disowns the boy—also on board—a day before the *Titanic* sinks; after the collision it's a whole new ballgame, beautifully orchestrated by director Jean Negulesco). A fictional story with historical merit because it unfolds at formal shipboard dinners and balls, building a fascinating, faithful period canvas of British Edwardian society and manners. (One caveat: well-done collision segments whitewash the steerage tragedy, making third-classers too frightened and confused to head for the boats.) Crackling dialogue and fine, understated performances throughout (Webb is terrific in the lead).

Recommended Reading:
Walter Lord, *A Night to Remember;* Wyn Craig Wade, *Titanic: End of a Dream.*

Raid on Entebbe ★★★★★

(1977) 150 Minutes

Director: Irvin Kershner

Cast: Peter Finch, Charles Bronson, Horst Buchholz, Martin Balsam, Jack Warden, Sylvia Sidney, Yaphet Kotto

Historical Background: History will surely remember Uganda's Idi Amin as the 20th century's most depraved dictator. He murdered and dismembered his first wife and their son. Agents of his secret police force moonlighted as contract killers. During his eight-year reign he massacred 300,000 Ugandans, storing body parts of murdered enemies in his refrigerator. Openly anti-Semitic, Amin made international headlines in 1976 by granting sanctuary to a group of PLO terrorists who had hijacked a French airliner with 103 Israeli passengers on board. When the plane landed at Entebbe airport on June 28, the Palestinians moved 258

hostages into the old terminal building, demanding the release of 52 terrorists imprisoned in Germany, Switzerland, France, and Israel.

Reluctant to endanger non-Israeli passengers, Yitzhak Rabin's cabinet planned no rescue attempt until the hijackers unexpectedly released most of their non-Jewish hostages. Gen. Dan Shomron, director of Israel's elite commando forces, crafted a daring airborne recovery plan based in part on newly freed passengers' descriptions of the terrorists, their weapons, and the airport's physical plant and security system. On July 3, 200 commandos boarded four C-130H cargo planes (each carrying a single assault team) and left for Uganda. Two Boeing 707s—one a command center, the other an improvised hospital—followed. The plan turned on split-second timing and perfect coordination among the four groups, and it succeeded spectacularly. So flawlessly did the commandos execute the operation that the C-130 carrying the first strike team flew the 2,500 miles to Entebbe and landed just 30 seconds behind schedule. The Israelis touched down and attacked in waves, stunning everyone in the terminal, killing seven terrorists, and destroying a dozen Ugandan fighter planes on the ground. Within an hour, the hostages and their rescuers were flying back to Israel. The commandos lost one soldier, and three hostages died on the ground—one murdered a few days after the rescue in a Ugandan hospital.

As accurate as a documentary and highly entertaining, *Raid on Entebbe* is one of the best films ever made on late-20th-century terrorism. Kershner packs an enormous amount of information and detail into the film and gets fine performances from everyone, especially Finch (in his last film, as Rabin) and Kotto (Amin). Superb action sequences recount the actual rescue.

Recommended Reading:
Yeshayahu Ben Porat, Eitan Haber, and Zeev Schiff, *Entebbe Rescue.*

Rob Roy ★★★★

(1995) 139 Minutes

Director: Michael Caton-Jones

Cast: Liam Neeson, John Hurt, Jessica Lange, Tim Roth, Eric Stoltz, Brian Cox, Andrew Keir

Historical Background: Every 24 hours, 17th-century Scotland's capital city temporarily became the biggest sewer in the world. At 10 P.M. sharp, seven days a week, Edinburgh's "night-drum" sounded, and 30,000 lodgers clogging a one-square-mile snarl of buildings flung cataracts of kitchen slop and chamberpot waste out their windows into the open thoroughfares below. So horrific was the lingering stench (dubbed "the Flowers of Edinburgh") that locals torched huge paper wads to fumigate houses and apartments. Twice each year, Rob Roy MacGregor braved the city's pestilent olfactory hell to secure credit and pay bills, and twice a year, he counted the slowly dwindling hours separating him from his Highland home 30 miles north of Glasgow—even though life there was brutish by today's standards.

Born in February 1671, Rob Roy flourished in a society promising an average life expectancy of 26 years (65% of its children died before reaching puberty). Highlanders built sod houses with few windows, four-foot front doors, straw roofs, and peat-burning hearths with thatch holes (no chimneys) for ventilation. (During rainstorms, porous roofs splattered occupants with water darkened by soot-caked ceilings.) Heavy mists and drizzle turned dirt floors to slimy mud and front yards into quagmires. For this reason, Highlanders wore kilts (or "plaids"), not trousers: rinsing bare legs was easier than laundering trousers every day. (Ingeniously designed plaids also served as sleeping bags—and sometimes tents—during long, frequent treks through rugged terrain.) Highlanders bathed with lye soap, slept on straw-stuffed ticks, ate with their fingers, and guzzled colorless industrial-strength whiskey from wooden bowls.

At age six, boys began military training under their fathers' close supervision, whacking away at each other with stout wooden swords. Endless drills made slashing onslaughts from seven attack angles and deft parries from seven defensive positions automatic and instantaneous. Rob Roy probably got a real blade—long, basket-hilted broadswords were popular—and made his first annual muster by age 15. Broad-shouldered and blessed with incredibly long, powerful arms for his size, he was a born swordsman—maybe the best in Scotland: during 35 years of dueling and campaigning, he sustained one minor arm wound, at age 63, against a younger neighbor in a sporting duel.

But his true vocation and genius lay in cattle trading. Most Highlanders worked 25-to-100-head herds, but master drover MacGregor routinely took 1,000 cattle—many bought with loans from wealthy investors—all the way to English markets. (He also prospered from cattle-rieving—or rustling, an ancient Highland custom practiced by all classes, especially small farmers flattened by stock loss from harsh winters. Most Scots considered rieving legal, but many paid chieftains "black rent" to guard their herds.) Then, in 1712, Rob Roy's reputation, financial security, and social standing, built on 18 years of hard work, suddenly collapsed. That April, he employed a man named MacDonald to buy a huge herd (for spring fattening) with money borrowed from the first Duke of Montrose. But Mac-Donald unloaded the herd for £1,000, pocketed the cash, and vanished without a trace. Hungry for Rob's land and its attendant political parity with the second Duke of Argyll, Montrose refused MacGregor's offer to pay the debt in installments, seizing his property and declaring him an outlaw. Rob bolted for the mountains, raised a 65-man fighting force, and spent the next decade on the run, raiding Montrose holdings—and taking time off to fight for Jacobite armies (they lost) during the 1715 rebellion against England's George I. (The Jacobites supported restoration of England's throne to the house of Stuart, overthrown and exiled by William of Orange in the 1688–89 "Glorious Revolution." Between 1715 and 1746, dirty intrigue and four major Jacobite risings rocked England and Scotland. In 1746, the Duke of Cumberland crushed Charles Edward Stuart at Culloden, ending the Jacobite movement.) In 1722, Argyll mediated a fragile reconciliation between MacGregor and Montrose. Fully pardoned four years later, Rob Roy spent the rest of his life on a new farm at Balquhidder, dying there on December 28, 1734.

Neeson shines as Clean Gene MacGregor in this terrific truth-and-fantasy jumble covering several catastrophic months—in 1713—of the legendary Highlander's life. Caton-Jones ignites the fireworks with a factual reversal: instead of stealing the £1,000, Stoltz's true-blue MacDonald loses it—and his life—in a bushwhack by Argyll's deadly, dandified henchman Archibald Cunningham (Roth). Roth keeps the cash, frames Neeson for theft, and chases him all over Scotland, destroying his home and raping his wife, Mary (Lange), just for fun. (In fact, Grahame of Killearn really led Argyll's posse, evicting Rob's family and seizing the house—not burning it. Balladeers probably invented the arson and Mary's rape to embellish MacGregor's legend.)

A bloodcurdling—and fabricated—Cunningham–MacGregor duel at film's end finally settles everything. Roth's fictional Archibald Cunningham is based loosely on the foppish Henry Cunninghame of Boquhan: in 1701, Boquhan's superb fencing skills stunned an overconfident MacGregor, routing him from the field in a farcical bloodless duel. Other errors (obviously intentional: scriptwriter Alan Sharp read W. H. Murray's biography) include Killearn's murder by Mary MacGregor and her son, Argyll's Jacobinism, and a pat ending implying that all of Rob's troubles ended in 1713. But Caton-Jones' meticulous re-creation of 18th-century Scottish life and Highland period atmosphere dwarf his factual errors and distortions. A fine film—and excellent fare for amateur historians.

Recommended Reading:
W. H. Murray, *Rob Roy MacGregor: His Life and Times.*

Shadowlands ★★★★

(1985) 90 Minutes

Director: Norman Stone

Cast: Joss Ackland, Claire Bloom, David Waller, Rupert Baderman, Rhys Hopkins

Historical Background: One of the great Christian apologists of all time, Anglo-Irish author and Cambridge professor of literature C. S. Lewis still converts thousands of discerning, well-educated people to traditional Christianity through a series of remarkably lively, lucid books—*The Screwtape Letters, Mere Christianity, The Problem of Pain*—on complex issues especially vexing to modern readers. The key to his enduring popularity is his insistence that faith begins with clear, rigorously reasoned intellectual assent: "Lewis," wrote Anthony Burgess, "is the ideal persuader for the good man who would like to be a Christian but finds his intellect getting in the way."

A confirmed atheist until 1931, Lewis embraced Christianity after a meticulous, systematic scrutiny of positivist assumptions revealed deep logical flaws and ample nonsense. Nihilists, for example, insist that there are no absolutes and therefore no universal moral laws—an absolute (and therefore absurd) principle: if it's true it's false. (In *Christian Reflections,* Lewis equates nihilists with the stranger warning you to trust no one in the office, but expecting you to trust him.) Lewis builds the case for his faith in the same fashion—not offering to "prove" anything, only to explain his conviction that the Christian story is not only possible, but probable (doubt and mystery form part of the equation). He doesn't convince everyone—but few people take his books lightly.

Lewis also wrote fiction and now-classic critical works on medieval, Renaissance, and 17th-century literature. During the late 1940s, American writer Joy Davidman read most of his books, converting to Christianity in 1948. On January 10, 1950—her marriage to philandering novelist William Gresham virtually over—she opened a long correspondence with Lewis. Two years later, she visited a friend in London, made a lunch date with Lewis, and—with no idea what to expect—finally met him. His attire was a world-class catastrophe: "He had an extraordinary knack," wrote his brother Warren, "of making a new suit look shabby the second time he wore it." Lewis was witty, sportive, gracious, and thoroughly happy ("The world," he once remarked, "is divided into those who like happiness and those who, odd as it seems, really don't"). He loved risqué, late-night conversations fueled by oceans of warm English beer. Possessions—even books—meant little to him (he lived in libraries and avoided bookstores). Incredibly generous, Lewis gave away two-thirds of his income and would have given more had British taxes been lower.

Davidman went back to America, divorced her husband (gaining custody of their two sons), returned to England in 1954, and built a solid friendship with Lewis. In 1956, a year after her health began to fail, Britain's Home Office rejected her residence-permit renewal application. On April 23, she and Lewis married—a formality securing British nationality for her and the two boys. Diagnosed with advanced bone cancer in 1957, she moved into

Lewis' house (expecting to die there), then went into miraculous remission. She and Lewis gradually fell deeply in love (both were astonished), spending three happy years together before her death in June 1960. The loss devastated Lewis, testing his faith—then strengthening it, in the end, and evoking one of his finest books *(A Grief Observed)*. Three and a half years later (on November 22, 1963—the afternoon of John Kennedy's assassination), Lewis died of heart and kidney failure. Weeks earlier, fully aware of death's nearness, he'd written, "Think of yourself just as a seed waiting to come up in the Gardener's good time. . . . We are here in the land of dreams, but cock-crow is coming."

There's no room for improvement in Stone's beautifully realized adaptation of Brian Sibley's classic, concise Lewis biography. In a finely nuanced, understated performance, Ackland brilliantly re-creates virtually every crucial feature of Lewis' personality—his sense of humor, his massive intellect, his generosity, and his witty thrust-and-parry dealings with fellow Cambridge faculty members pronouncing his Christian faith archaic and incomprehensible. But Stone's real subject is Lewis' growing friendship and three-year marriage to Joy Davidman (Bloom, in a knockout performance)—a presentation so moving and faithful to the facts that you have to wonder why Richard Attenborough remade the film less than a decade later. Available on video—many local libraries carry it—and an absolute must for Lewis fans.

For Further Viewing:
Shadowlands (1993) 130 Minutes (Anthony Hopkins, Debra Winger, Edward Hardwicke, Michael Denison, Joseph Mazzello, Peter Firth): Director Richard Attenborough's gloomy dirge falsifies or

severely distorts countless aspects of Lewis' personality, Christianity's impact on his daily life, and the long-term effect of Joy Davidman's death on his beliefs. (William Nicholson's silly script gives Winger, badly miscast as Gresham, nothing to work with. The low point comes in Lewis' study: "So whaddya do awl day," she asks in a labored brogue, "sit in yeh chayuh an' think great thawghts?") Even worse is Hopkins' dull, sullen rendition of Lewis as a cloistered, humorless bachelor unversed in suffering and bent on avoiding women: describing one of his many female friends for a longtime neighbor, the real Lewis once remarked, "Just watching her walk across the room constitutes a liberal education." (For high-spirited Joy Davidman, this kind of impishness was one of his most winsome qualities.) And Lewis endured ample suffering: in 1917–18, he saw some of the Great War's bloodiest action, sustaining a severe shrapnel wound during the Battle of Arras. Attenborough's worst fabrication has Lewis losing his faith after Joy's death: in fact, he publicly reaffirmed his belief in the resurrection less than a month after her funeral. A well-intentioned, sympathetic, but awful film biography.

Recommended Reading:
Brian Sibley, *C. S. Lewis: Through the Shadowlands;* Clyde S. Kilby, ed., *A Mind Awake: An Anthology of C. S. Lewis;* W. H. Lewis, ed., *Letters of C. S. Lewis.*

The Spirit of St. Louis ★★★★

(1957) 138 Minutes

Director: Billy Wilder

Cast: James Stewart, Patricia Smith, Murray Hamilton, Marc Connelly

Historical Background: At age 14, Charles Lindbergh clambered up a 60-foot elm, stood teetering on its brittle top limbs, and trumpeted imminent plans to jump (his mother—enraged—talked him down). Lindbergh believed that confronting his fears would kill them, and isolated heights frightened him—of all people—more than anything else. For years, dreams of falling from skyscrapers jarred him awake, terrified and soaked with sweat. His phobia vanished with a near-fatal aerial stunt near Lincoln, Neb. Packing two parachutes, Lindbergh leaped from barnstormer Charlie Hardin's plane at 2,000 feet, cut the first canopy's harness after it opened, went into a breathtaking free fall, and pulled his second ripcord. The parachute malfunctioned, opening at the last second and—strangely—ending his nightmares forever.

Lindbergh loved machines—he once took his parents' Model T apart, then reassembled it perfectly—and airplanes fascinated him. In May 1922, he joined aviator Erold Bahl's barnstorming tour, performing incredible stunts—wing walks during barrel rolls, plane-to-plane airborne jumps—and earning enough money to start his own tour. By 1926, Lindbergh was flying airmail runs between Chicago and St. Louis. (His parents hated it. In the early twenties, everyone considered aviators reckless oddballs at best, and at worst over-the-top maniacs. Flying was supremely perilous; one study guaranteed at least one serious accident for every 900 hours in the air.)

Preparations for his historic transatlantic solo excursion began with French-American Raymond Orteig's $25,000 offer for the first nonstop flight between New York and Paris. Several St. Louis businessmen financed custom construction of a single-engine aircraft—the *Spirit of St. Louis*—with oversized wings and a gas tank mounted in front of the cockpit to prevent pilot entrapment between the engine and reservoir in a crash. On May 20, 1927, Lindbergh roared aloft from Long Island's Roosevelt Field, riding an ocean of extra fuel. His greatest in-flight challenges: dead-reckoning navigation (without landmarks for course correction, Lindbergh traversed the dark Atlantic waters with magnetic compasses and charts) and fatigue (by journey's end, he'd gone without sleep for more than 40 hours). Traversing Ireland 28 hours after takeoff, he crossed the English Channel, banked left above the Seine River, followed it all the way to Paris, and landed at Le Bourget airport on May 21 at 10:24 P.M.

Lindbergh was the most famous person on earth, but during the next decade tragedy and controversy stalked him relentlessly. In 1929, he married Anne Morrow. Three years later, a kidnapper abducted, then killed their two-year-old son. But the kidnapper collected a fat ransom. Authorities arrested Bruno Hauptmann in 1934, executing him—after a long, circuslike trial—in April 1936. (Some experts believe that Hauptmann was innocent.) In 1940–41, Lindbergh's speeches endorsing American neutrality and soft-peddling Nazi Germany's obvious menace drew fire from everyone, permanently stigmatizing him (even though he eventually flew 50 combat missions against the Japanese). Lindbergh died in 1974 in Detroit.

Except for several composite characters and Stewart's fluffy encounter with a pesky fly buzzing his cockpit over the Atlantic, Wilder's absorbing adaptation of Lindbergh's memoirs remains perfectly faithful to history. Highlights include Lindbergh's harrowing, muddy Roosevelt Field takeoff (he barely clears a forest of telephone cables) and barnstorming orgies featuring wing walks, double-chute jumps, and midair plane-to-plane leaps. Three vintage near-replicas of the *Spirit of St. Louis* crown a glittering riot of perfect period detail. Beautifully staged all the way and drowning in the wild-and-woolly atmosphere radiating from America's first Air Age heroes.

Recommended Reading:
Leonard Mosley, *Lindbergh: A Biography;* Joyce Milton, *Loss of Eden: A Biography of Charles and Anne Morrow Lindbergh.*

A Tale of Two Cities ★★★★★

(1935) 128 Minutes

Director: Jack Conway

Cast: Ronald Colman, Elizabeth Allan, Edna May Oliver, Reginald Owen, Basil Rathbone, Blanche Yurka, Isabel Jewell, Walter Catlett, Henry B. Walthal, Donald Woods

Historical Background: By 1787, France— the most powerful state in western Europe— was in financial, administrative, and political chaos. For years, the royal treasury's bright-red bottom line obsessed the monarchy. Endless European warfare had drained royal purses, forcing France's kings into extraordinary—and, eventually, politically fatal—measures simply to stay afloat financially. They levied new ("extraordinary") taxes—poll taxes, taxes on salt, tobacco, wine, property, income. It wasn't enough. During the Thirty Years War (1618–48), Louis XIV literally began selling political clout to private creditors, trading government administrative and judicial offices, special privileges (tax exemptions, for one), and even ennoblement to wealthy commoners in return for hefty loans, many of them renegotiated years later. Fighting the disastrous Seven Years War (1756–1763) and backing American colonial revolutionaries (1776–1783) virtually devoured King Louis XVI's treasury.

The glittering splendor of Louis' court activities—many of them legitimate state functions—sparked and fueled public resentment of royal extravagance and waste. Worse still: popular contempt for Queen Marie Antoinette escalated daily. Married to Louis at age 15, poorly educated, stolid, and ill prepared for the high visibility of queenship, the former archduchess of Austria was a public-relations disaster from the start. False rumors of the "Austrian Messalina's" promiscuity flared in Louis' hostile court, slithered into Paris' streets, and rocketed through provincial France. The queen drifted into isolation, eventually taking costly private apartments, surrounding herself with a small circle of friends, and thoroughly wrecking, for ordinary Frenchmen, the monarchy's public image.

Critical mass came in 1787: spiraling inflation, a huge deficit, and the refusal of the *parlement* of Paris—France's most powerful regional high court—to approve new taxes and other reforms proposed by the king prompted Louis to summon an Assembly of Notables (144 government, clerical, and aristocratic delegates), hoping for an endorsement prestigious enough to ram his programs past *parlement*'s opposition. Sick of Louis' financial mismanagement and the specter of ever-looming political and social crises, the Assembly voiced a thundering "no." The country's judicial elite and most influential men had stood belligerently against the government, launching France's "aristocratic revolution" (May 1787–August 1788). Pressured by his nobles, Louis called for elections to reinstitute—for the first time since 1614—the French national parliament, or "Estates-General." (Delegates would represent France's three "estates," or classes: the clergy, the aristocracy, and the "Third Estate"—by far the largest—incorporating commoners ranging from rural peasants to middle-class merchants.) Ominous demonstrations marked the election period (January–April 1789): an awful 1788 harvest had left many farm workers unemployed and many commoners hungry. Foraging rural gangs drifted into cities from the provinces. Food riots flared in many places. In May 1789, the Estates-General convened, and instant, heated strife over voting procedure split the assembly: the first two estates (300 deputies each) favored bloc voting (one vote per estate), but 600 Third Estate deputies—soon supported by many clerical and aristocratic allies—demanded strict ballot by headcount, proclaim-

ing themselves France's National Assembly on June 17, convening at a tennis court on the 20th (the government locked them out of their assembly hall at Versailles), and resolving to draft a national constitution for France. (Festering popular unrest continued: rising food prices, Louis' sacking of popular financial director-general Jacques Necker, and rumors of a royal plot to crush the Third Estate ignited the "Paris Mob's" violent seizure of the hated Bastille prison on July 14, 1789.)

Louis gave in, directing the three estates to form a National Constituent Assembly. With the Constitution of 1791, legislators completely restructured the French state, aiming for a constitutional monarchy guaranteeing individual liberty, an elected judiciary, and separation of powers. To reduce France's financial deficit, revolutionaries also seized and sold property of the Roman Catholic Church. Then, in July 1790, the Assembly passed the Civil Constitution of the Clergy, ordering election of bishops and priests and virtually severing relations with the papacy. It was a fatal mistake, infuriating many peasants and working commoners and turning them against the new government. (Many Frenchmen—the *émigrés*—had already left France, building armies on its northeastern border and asking jittery European governments for help. Louis tried to join them in June 1791, but failed.) France's first elected Legislative Assembly cleared the decks for a second revolt by declaring war on the Hapsburg monarchy (sympathetic to counterrevolutionaries) on April 20, 1792. The War of the First Coalition ignited more than two decades of continual conflict between France and Austria (backed by various allies): of the five wars fought during the turmoil, Austria lost four. During the conflict's first two weeks, Austro-Prussian forces plastered the French, opening the country to invasion and convincing radicals that Louis had somehow collaborated with the enemy. On August 10, insurgents stormed the Tuileries palace, arrested the royal couple, and replaced the Paris Commune (the city government) with an insurrectionist commune. On September 20, France stopped an Austro-Prussian advance in a major battle at Valmy, and the next day Paris militants established a new revolutionary National Convention. Just like that, the Assembly was history, the monarchy fell, the French Republic was born—and a door opened for a group of ruthless martinets to launch one of Europe's bloodiest spectacles.

The Convention tried and convicted Louis of treason, executing him on January 21, 1793 (a Revolutionary Tribunal guillotined Marie Antoinette in October). Louis' death, anticlerical legislation, and a national conscription act following renewed Austrian offensives sparked a March 19 guerrilla-style Royalist rebellion by peasants in the Atlantic coast's Vendée area. Montagnards (the assembly's extreme left wing) seized control of the Convention, expelled their moderate Girondin colleagues, formed the dictatorial 12-man Committee of Public Safety dominated by Maximilien Robespierre, and launched a murder campaign targeting suspected Royalists and other enemies of the state. In September 1793, Jacobin fear of sedition—stoked by a Paris bread shortage and discovery of a conspiracy to free Marie Antoinette from captivity—prodded conventioneers to pass the "law of suspects," igniting a ten-month nationwide Reign of Terror. (A powerful political society with 5,500 local chapters, the Jacobins were virtually a Montagnard/Robespierre interest group by 1793.)

During the Terror, Robespierre and his committee arrested at least 300,000 French citizens. Throughout the nightmare, victims in Paris faced the same ordeal: hauled from frightful cells in the Conciergerie Prison—necks shaved and hands bound behind them—they clattered in tumbrels through jeering mobs lining the *Rue St. Honoré* all the way to the guillotine in the *Place de la Concorde.* In a mesmerized collective frenzy, spectators packing the square shoulder-to-shoulder roared approval with every decapitation. (Crashing blades drew many true grotesques to the scaffold's edge: among the creepiest were the *tricoteuses,* or "knitters," women convening near the platform—every single day—to view the mounting carnage. Taunting newly arrived victims and knitting away placidly until the day's slaughter closed, they quickly earned a famous sobriquet: "Furies of the Guillotine.")

But many Parisians revolted by the massacre avoided the awful plaza, and others—in chilling oblivion—went to market, dined at cafés, visited bookstores, and ambled casually through narrow, winding streets as if nonstop judicial homicide in the heart of town were normal routine. Paris saw more than 2,500 heads roll during the long bloodbath—and in provincial France the butchery was worse. Directed by local Jacobin clubs, "watch committees" relentlessly stalked suspected enemies of the Revolution by the thousands, shrouding the countryside in terror and waging all-out war on the Church. They robbed and desecrated churches, jailed priests and other clerics, and drove 130,000 people—mostly peasants—across France's borders in horrified flight. Between 35,000 and 45,000 died before popular unrest and the July (Thermidor) 27 Thermidorean Reaction in the Convention ended with Robespierre's arrest and summary execution.

(France's June 26 victory at Fleurus carried French occupation troops into Belgium, ending rationales for tyranny—even though the war continued—and leading to the *coup d'état*.)

In 1795, the Convention drafted a new constitution creating a bicameral legislature and a five-man executive branch (the Directory). It was another experiment in representative government—and it never had a chance. Inflation, bankruptcies, wildly unstable currency, and food shortages flourished. Bitter divisions between Royalists and former radical insurrectionists lingered and deepened, and both sides took constant aim on the government. In October, Corsican artillery captain Napoleon Bonaparte routed thousands of disenfranchised Royalists marching on the Tuileries Palace. An infuriated Directory cracked down, deporting or arresting many enemies and drastically reducing civil liberties. On November 9, 1799, Bonaparte led a *coup* abolishing the Directory and establishing a three-man ruling Consulate—in fact, a front for one-man rule: in 1802, Napoleon became "consul for life," and in 1804 he declared himself emperor of the French.

He ruled France for 12 years, launching wars against Austria, Britain, Sweden, Russia, and Prussia (his greatest victory came at Austerlitz, on December 2, 1805, against the Austrians and Russians). By 1812, he'd redrawn the map of Europe, ruling an empire stretching from the Pyrenees to Hamburg and from the English Channel to Rome. (French satellites included Spain, the kingdoms of Naples and Italy, Switzerland, and the Grand Duchy of Warsaw.) On June 24, Bonaparte hurled his 449,000-man *Grande Armée de Russie* into Russia and drove the Tsar's legions all the way from the Niemen River to Moscow, taking and occupy-

ing the city on September 14. But Russian civilians—all of them—had evacuated, burning most of Moscow's buildings and leaving no provisions for foraging French troops. By late October, hunger and bitter cold forced the legendary, catastrophic French withdrawal (and merciless Russian pursuit), leaving only 94,000 of Napoleon's troops alive by New Year's Day 1813. (Bonaparte had deserted the army on December 5, barreling by sledge for Russia's western border and France—to raise new armies.) In mid-October 1813, 340,000 British, Swedish, Austrian, and Prussian troops grouped into three armies smashed Napoleon's 195,000-man force at Leipzig, hammered their way toward France, captured Paris on March 31, 1814, and restored Bourbon King Louis XVIII to the throne. Napoleon abdicated in April, accepting Allied-imposed exile—with his own 600-man guard—on Elba Island (between Corsica and northern Italy). He knew that demobilized *Grande Armée* troops hated the new government and that France's peasants believed the Bourbons would reverse the Revolution's land reforms. Bonaparte escaped from Elba and returned to France, landing near Cannes on March 1, 1815. Nineteen days later, he entered Paris and began mobilizing an army.

For more than three months (the "Hundred Days" restoration) he ruled France. By late March, huge Allied armies prepared to march against him. Napoleon mobilized 125,000 troops and drove north, hoping to seize Brussels. In his line of march, two Allied armies—led by the Duke of Wellington and Prussian marshal Gebhard von Blücher—dotted a 90-mile front near the Belgian frontier. On June 18, major elements of the opposing armies—about 72,000 French troops and Wellington's 68,000 men—collided near Waterloo on a tiny battlefield (about three square miles) nine miles southwest of Brussels. Finesse and sophistication never surfaced at Waterloo—the battle was pure attrition, an awful, barbaric brawl beginning around 11:25 A.M. and featuring massive frontal assaults hurled by Bonaparte against Wellington's elevated defensive positions. (Throughout much of the battle, Napoleon directed his legions from a wooden observation tower; Wellington commanded on horseback, remaining in the saddle throughout the engagement.) By late afternoon, 35,000 Prussians finally arrived at the battlefield and began pressuring Bonaparte's right flank. Around 8:30 P.M., Napoleon left the field in a carriage, his army scrambling after him in chaotic retreat. The British captured Bonaparte at Rochefort on July 13, imprisoning him on St. Helena Island in the South Atlantic. "A man like me cares little for the lives of a million men," Napoleon once told Austrian statesman Klemens von Metternich. "I may lose my throne. But I shall bury the whole world in its ruins." He died on May 5, 1821, ridding the whole world of the Revolution's last, supremely violent force.

Many literary critics rank *A Tale of Two Cities* below several other Dickens novels, but Conway's film adaptation (the first sound version) is a fine *tour de force* of pre-Revolutionary and early-insurrectionist France—with a few shortfalls for history buffs. The film ignores completely the 1787–88 aristocratic revolution and its roots in France's financial crisis, for example, leaving the impression that all nobles backed Louis XVI and the status quo—complacently or malevolently (aping Rathbone's superbly evil Marquis St. Evremonde: "Pity is a diseased variety of sentimentality"). *A Tale of Two Cities* also vaguely implies that a long, carefully planned conspiracy of Third Estate Parisians orchestrated the storming of the Bastille. Conway's spectacular restaging of the legendary assault features nearly 18,000 full-throated extras storming huge Bastille replicas, one of many gigantic sets built for the film. Remarkably authentic period detail, from costumes and serpentine streets to dishes and tablecloths, builds an accurate picture of turbulent late-1870s Paris. Best of all: Conway's marvelous orchestration of a perfect Dickensian atmosphere throughout. Super performances—especially by Yurka, radiating evil as the awful Madame Defarge (the actress learned knitting to prepare for the role).

For Further Viewing:

The Scarlet Pimpernel ★★★★ (1982) 150 Minutes (Anthony Andrews, Jane Seymour, Ian McKellen, James Villiers, Eleanor David, Malcolm Jamieson): Pretending to be a trifling, frothy fop, English aristocrat and master of disguise Andrews risks life and limb rescuing French prisoners (often at the last minute) from the guillotine and smuggling them to safety in England. Along the way, he marries Seymour and manages to stay a step ahead of the evil Chauvelin ("Robespierre's most trusted agent"). Highly fictional, with one colossal falsification: the "Pimpernel League" rescues Louis' son (the "Dauphin") from Paris' squalid Temple Prison—in fact, the boy died in captivity on June 6, 1795. No historical Pimpernel existed, but director Clive Donner's adaptation of two novels (the second title: *Eldorado*) by the Baroness Orczy—minus the fictional rescue—isn't as outrageous as it sounds. Less than a year into the Revolution, visions of new-order France crawling with English spies obsessed high-level Revolutionary officials in Paris. By 1793, English secret service networks were, in fact, up and running in France. Agents ran guns, maintained coastal safe houses for fugitive émigrés, tried to ignite provincial insurrections, and held money for bribing key port authorities to ignore in-transit contraband weapons. The movie was made for television, but you won't notice: it's more highly produced and beautifully-photographed than most feature films. Meticulous period detail and terrific performances—a fine re-creation of Robespierre's bloody ten-month nightmare, even though Donner launches the official Terror in 1792 (a year early).

Waterloo ★★★★ (1971) 123 Minutes (Rod Steiger, Christopher Plummer, Orson Welles, Jack Hawkins, Virginia McKenna, Dan O'Herlihy, Michael Wilding): The first half of this chronicle of the Hundred Days barely crawls forward, even though director Sergei Bondarchuk manages some fine, authentic segments—Marshal Michel Ney, for example, promising Louis XVIII to deliver Bonaparte (back from Elba) in an iron cage, then changing sides as soon as he meets Napoleon marching northward from Cannes. Plummer excels as Wellington (the Iron Duke really did call his men "infamous rabble" and "the scum of the earth"—even though he valued their lives); and Steiger nails many of Napoleon's personal qualities: his hypnotic power over the troops; his surface calm, punctuated by sudden, volcanic outbursts of rage. But the real star is Bondarchuk's tactically accurate, brilliantly authentic re-creation of the Waterloo slugfest: it is absolute Armageddon, a murky chaos of rifle fire, galloping cavalry, deafening artillery bombardments, blinding smoke, and appalling carnage (all historically correct—Napoleonic engagements were pure bedlam). A must-see for amateur historians.

Recommended Reading:
François Furet, *Revolutionary France;* Richard Cobb and Colin Jones, *Voices of the French Revolution;* Gregor Dallas, *The Final Act: The Roads to Waterloo.*

Zulu ★★★★

(1964) 138 Minutes

Director: Cy Endfield

Cast: Stanley Baker, Michael Caine, Jack Hawkins, Ulla Jacobson, Nigel Green, James Booth

Historical Background: January 22, 1879—Isandhlwana Mountain, Zululand. As the final moments of British history's worst battlefield catastrophe unfolded, pistol-packing Lt. Wallie Erskine, hotly pursued by swarming Zulu braves, galloped furiously for the Buffalo River and colonial Natal (to the southwest), blasting away at warriors lunging for his bridle. Seconds after his mount belly-flopped into the water, Zulus were all over him: one hurled a short assegai stabbing spear into his thigh. From nowhere, a fearsome-looking brave surfaced, firing a gun at Erskine's head. He missed. Outraged, the tattered lieutenant bellowed—crazily—in Zulu, "Who the hell do you think you're shooting at?" Thoroughly spooked, the warrior gaped at Erskine as he pounded forward up the Natal bank to safety.

Historians love Erskine's getaway, because it highlights the six-month Zulu War's ferocious, up-close-and-personal quality: massed volley fire from Britain's .45-caliber Martini-Henry rifles gutted huge Zulu attack formations, but many warriors usually got through to British fortifications (Rorke's Drift) and infantry squares in open country (Isandhlwana), forcing blood-curdling hand-to-hand combat. (Conflicts among Europeans and native tribes over well-watered pastureland ignited the war: by 1870, many grassy tracts traditionally occupied by Zulus had grown pestilential, leveling their cattle with redwater fever and lung disease. Great swaths of pasturage humming with deadly tsetse flies—and severe droughts in 1876 and 1877—launched a land-and-water nightmare for 350,000 Zulus. They began moving on fertile Transvaal areas between the Blood and Buffalo rivers, prompting Britain to seek confederation—diplomatically—of the Zulus, other mutually hostile tribes, and colonial Europeans.)

Isandhlwana was the war's first major engagement. In January 1879, colonial governor Sir Henry Bartle Frere grouped 16,800 soldiers into five huge columns under Lord Frederic Chelmsford. On the 11th (against London's wishes), Frere hurled three of them across the Buffalo River into Zululand. Chelmsford accompanied the middle column, and eleven days into the war, he split the formation: riding eastward with six companies to reinforce a cavalry detachment near the Nqutu Plateau, he left 1,800 men with Col. Anthony Durnford in a huge, sprawling camp near the mountain's eastern flank. That morning, British gallopers found a steep-walled ravine concealing Zulu king Cetshwayo's main force and galloped back to warn Durnford. Chanting their sibilant war cry *("Zhi-Zhi-Zhi"),* 20,000 braves rose in unison, bolted from the ravine, and headed for Isandhlwana. Incredibly, British troop deployments violated every basic rule of tactical defensive warfare. Packing 500,000 rounds of ammunition, Durnford should have repulsed the Zulus: had he positioned his men—shoulder-to-shoulder—a few yards up the steep moun-

tainside's base, their bristling Martini-Henrys would have shredded Cetshwayo's legions. Instead, he moved away from the mountain, scattering troops along a paper-thin 2,000-yard perimeter with his rear unprotected and his left flank wide open. Worst of all, huge gaps left by Chelmsford's six marching companies broke the line at several points. The engagement was over in 90 minutes, even though British marksmen took a terrible toll. Thousands of Zulus struck in their traditional crescent-shaped "buffalo horns" formation, sending waves of shock troops (the "chest") on a massive frontal assault, with great pincer columns (the "horns") swinging outward from each flank and around Durnford's defenders, encircling the camp, engulfing widely separated companies, and annihilating them.

At least 3,300 slaughtered men (2,000 Zulus, 1,300 British and African colonial troops) littered the ground for miles in all directions—and the massacre wasn't over. Three hours after Cetshwayo's triumph, 4,000 battle-hungry Zulus led by Prince Dabulamanzi assaulted Chelmsford's forward supply depot at Rorke's Drift, 12 miles southeast of Isandhlwana in Natal. Outnumbered 50 to one, Lt. John Chard and first officer Gonville Bromhead converted the depot—in peacetime, Swedish evangelist Otto Witt's mission station—into a compact two-building fortress. With 200-pound mealie bags and cumbersome hardtack boxes they built a high wall incorporating the fortified stone houses (one a makeshift infirmary) in a 350-yard perimeter, bisecting its eastern end with an eight-foot pile of boxes—their last line-of-defense. They cut loopholes through the hospital's walls, armed Surgeon Major James Reynolds' 36 patients—and waited for Armageddon. It came at 5 P.M.

with furious attacks supported by musket fire from Zulu marksmen on a steep uplift beyond the back wall. Volley-firing from triple-rank formations, Chard's troopers shot Dabulamanzi's sprinting braves to bits, burying wide-open killing zones under ghastly, bloody heaps of enemy corpses. With breathtaking courage, warriors reaching the walls impaled dead comrades on British bayonets, giving their encumbered enemies no time to recover before spearing them. More than 20 pell-mell onslaughts pushed the soldiers back to their inner defensive wall, carrying many warriors into the hospital: fanatical British defenders drove them back again, goring so many that several Martini-Henry bayonets broke—or bent at 90° angles. Ten hours later, around 2 A.M., Dabulamanzi withdrew to the northeast, leaving at least 1,000 braves dead on the ground. Fifteen of Chard's men had died—and an incredible eleven won Victoria Crosses. Five more major engagements flared. The last, fought in July at Ulundi, decimated Cetshwayo's army and ended the conflict.

The Zulu War crowned two centuries of global colonial activity bringing 25% of the earth's dry land under British control. In 1661, England's first African colonists founded the James Island settlement on the Gambian River, and by 1793, Great Britain had seized Capetown (from the Netherlands) to host maritime resupply stations and protect Cape of Good Hope sea-lanes for British traders sailing to India. For 50 years, this remained England's main African interest, but during the 19th century's final five decades, British activities on the dark continent ignited a second war (far dirtier than the Zulu conflict) and produced one of history's most brilliant, versatile, eccentric explorers—Sir Richard Francis Burton.

At age 29, Burton had learned French, Italian, Greek, Latin, Multani, Hindi, Arabic, and Punjabi, eventually mastering 25 languages. He served with Britain's Bombay Native Infantry in Sind (modern Pakistan) and trained Turkish guerrillas in the Crimean War. He became a skilled diplomat and wrote more than 40 books on travel and exploration, translating countless more—including *The Arabian Nights* and the *Kama Sutra*. (Burton's sexual appetite was exotic—and occasionally bizarre. In 1847, he engineered the abduction of a pretty, coquettish, and apparently willing Latin teacher from a convent at Goa in southwest India. After two weeks' plotting, he and a servant slipped into the convent at midnight, crashed one of the cells, and abducted—by mistake in the murky darkness—a grim, dozing, extremely hostile subprioress. Outside, a full moon illuminated the blunder. Burton jettisoned his cargo and left Goa as quickly as he could.)

Above all, Burton was an adventurer. He went to Iceland, Italy, Karachi, Utah, Mecca (extremely dangerous for a European), Paraguay, El-Medinah—and Africa. Burton was obsessed with Africa: in 1855, he and John Hanning Speke became the first white men to penetrate Somaliland. (Burton paid dearly for the distinction, taking a native javelin through the cheek in an attack near Berbera.) Determined to find the source of the Nile, he and Speke returned to East Africa in late 1857 and headed inland from Zanzibar. They endured awful hardships: a black beetle crawled into Speke's ear and bored through his tympanum; both men suffered intermittently from virulent fevers and infections; eye inflammations temporarily blinded Speke, and Burton's legs at one point swelled to twice their normal size; smallpox ravaged many of their porters. On February 13, 1858—after slogging more than 800 miles through the most dangerous terrain on earth—they discovered Lake Tanganyika. It wasn't the Nile's source, and they doubled back; at Tabora, Speke struck north, alone (Burton had malaria), walking straight to the world's second-largest body of fresh water (250 miles long, 200 miles wide) on August 3. He named it Lake Victoria, correctly pronouncing it the major source of the Nile. Burton wasn't convinced, publicly rejecting Speke's claims at Royal Geographic Society presentations. Their friendship disintegrated, and Speke died in a hunting accident (it may have been suicide) in September 1864. A quarter-century later, Burton died in Trieste.

By century's end, mineral wealth—more than exploration or trade—drove Britain's activities in Africa. An 1870 diamond stampede to Kimberly (Cape Colony) and a gold-rush in the Transvaal 16 years later scrambled southern Africa's political and social configurations, igniting the bitter 1899–1902 Anglo-Boer War. (In 1657, several families—mostly Dutch, a few French Hugenots and Germans—left Table Bay colony, near Cape Town, struck north along Africa's western coast, and moved inland. New immigrants occasionally joined them. They built enormous farms and intermarried for a century, literally starting a new race: the Boers. They raised cattle and sheep, grew cereals, and spread out, eventually settling the Transvaal and Orange Free State.) Completely cut off from other cultures and incorporating ranches isolated from each other by their great size, Boer society was a huge, loose confederation of self-sufficient, fiercely independent clans.

Nursing white-hot hatred for any sort of government, Boers fumed at British demands that English prospectors mining Transvaal goldfields receive full citizenship. The Boers balked and began hoarding weapons. England posted battalion after battalion to the Cape, driving an Orange Free State–Transvaal military alliance and—on October 12, 1899—a Boer declaration of war. Big, well-equipped Boer legions scored early wins at Colenso, Stormberg, and Magersfontein. Heavy crown reinforcements struck back, taking Johannesburg (May 31, 1900) and Pretoria (June 5). But the Boers persisted, launching furious guerrilla ("commando" in Boer War parlance) raids against isolated British outposts and railroads and murdering many English and Australian prisoners (crown troops responded in kind). In November, Herbert Lord Kitchener took command for Great Britain and began blanketing huge rural areas with manned blockhouses linked by barbed wire. From these bases he methodically razed the countryside, killing cattle and sheep and removing thousands of Boer families to disease-infested refugee camps. On May 31, 1902, the Treaty of Vereeniging finally sealed a British victory, but the war stirred hot controversy in England, signaling a looming rollback of Great Britain's ventures in colonial Africa. In 1910, the Transvaal and Orange Free State united, forming the Union of South Africa—the first independent country on the entire continent.

Caine's first starring role (Bromhead) came in *Zulu,* one of the most exciting historical films ever made—popular enough to run continuously in London theaters for years. Endfield's first hour faithfully chronicles military life at Rorke's Drift, building excruciating suspense the minute Caine and Baker (Chard) hear about Isandhlwana and start fortifying the tiny outpost. Then Dabulamanzi's legions (played by Zulu reenactors) arrive, and the fireworks—

beautifully choreographed with near-perfect accuracy—begin. Endfield's few errors are minor—with one puzzling exception: Hawkins' drunken, whining Witt. In fact, the evangelist left Rorke's Drift long before the Zulus arrived (though he later claimed he was there; another clergyman, George Smith, participated in the battle as an ammo runner).

Other lapses: Endfield's Zulus carry captured Martini-Henrys—not muskets (a common misconception). The real Bromhead never said he felt "ashamed" after the battle, nor did he and Chard nurse any professional rivalry. And Endfield's stirring conclusion (retiring Zulus salute their haggard British adversaries) is ancient, popular myth. Otherwise, *Zulu* is accurate enough to be a documentary. Expertly directed, with fine performances by all.

For Further Viewing:

Zulu Dawn (1979) 121 Minutes (Burt Lancaster, Peter O'Toole, John Mills, Simon Ward, Denholm Elliott, Bob Hoskins, Anna Calder-Marshall): Thanks to a heavy-handed anti-British slant driving much factual distortion, director Douglas Hickock's *Zulu* prequel chronicling the Isandhlwana battle flops badly. Hickock opens with a vaguely sinister Frere (Mills) describing his plan to invade Zululand (without explaining the circumstances behind the decision). Minutes later, we learn that Frere simply wants to make Cetshwayo "change his customs," and then, just before Chelmsford (O'Toole) launches the invasion, Hickock absurdly equates England with Nazi Germany: "Let us hope that this will be the final solution to the Zulu problem," Mills remarks—and it's all downhill from there. British military discipline (so critical in the Rorke's Drift defense) comes off as juvenile playing at war. And Hickock's final battle—technically superb filmmaking all the way—is appropriately terrifying, in spots, but its presentation is muddled, leaving the impression that 20,000 Zulus just showed up and swamped the Brits. A major disappointment.

Mountains of the Moon ★★★★ (1990) 135 Minutes (Patrick Bergin, Iain Glen, Fiona Shaw, Richard E. Grant, James Villiers): A great film with a few factual blunders: in a serious lapse, for example, director Bob Rafelson makes Isabel Arundell (married to Burton in 1861) a closet bohemian and female carbon copy (in outlook and personality) of the great man; at one point, she says, "If I were a man, I'd *be* Richard Burton." In fact, Isabel (Shaw) was Burton's perfect foil: scatterbrained, superstitious, and prim, she burned many of his erotic writings, including *The Perfumed Garden,* when he died. All of this, and other errors, pale beside Rafelson's wonderful study of Victorian England, his faithful restaging of key Burton–Speke exploits and their final estrangement, and his presentation of Africa as the Victorians saw it: an immense, fascinating, savage enigma without law or pity and capable of swallowing anyone—leaving no trace behind—in a microsecond.

Breaker Morant ★★★★★ (1979) 107 Minutes (Edward Woodward, Bryan Brown, Jack Thompson, John Waters, Charles Tingwell): In August 1901—during the Boer War's bitter "commando" phase—six officers of the Bush Veldt Carbineers (an elite Australian antiguerrilla force) ordered a dozen captured Boers shot in the field for murdering Australian prisoners. All six faced courts-martial, and two—Peter Handcock (Brown) and "Breaker" Morant (Woodward)—died by firing squad in February 1902, angering civilians Down Under and infuriating Australia's military. Director Bruce Beresford builds his terrific film on the war around the incident, anchoring his story in the courtroom, filling in details via hard-hitting flashbacks, and delivering a vivid, accurate picture of the Boer conflict. Australians still believe that Kitchener lobbied for the Carbineer executions to placate the Germans (Boer sympathizers and potential battlefield allies) during delicate peace negotiations, and Beresford pushes this view throughout—he lands a solid anti-British punch, but his real "villain" is the yawning, weirdly impersonal (and ultimately unbridgeable) gulf dividing soldiers trapped in awful battle and civilians or rear-echelon military personnel forced to judge actions they can't possibly understand. One of the best war films ever made, accurate and riveting all the way. Thompson is brilliant as the defendants' attorney.

Recommended Reading:
Donald R. Morris, *The Washing of the Spears: A History of the Rise of the Zulu Nation Under Shaka and Its Fall in the Zulu War of 1879;* Byron Farwell, *Burton: A Biography of Sir Richard Francis Burton* and *The Great Anglo-Boer War;* Thomas Pakenham, *The Boer War.*

Acknowledgments

I owe copious thanks to many people whose interest and advice have made *History Goes to the Movies* a better book: to Elias Crim for suggesting that I write it, for reading much of the manuscript, and for invaluable help with research on topics in several sections of the book; to Jenny Roquemore Taylor for her Internet research on current film criticism; to John Allen for reading many reviews and for long, informative conversations about his service as a World War II combat infantryman in the Pacific theater; to Vietnam veteran Jim McClure for sharing his wartime experiences and his exhaustive knowledge of U.S. military history; to Geoff Potter for reading parts of the manuscript and providing much encouragement for the project; to Ken Martin and Stewart Josselyn for discussing (at great length) the history behind many films included in the book; to John Botsis and Angela Condos, proprietors of Video House in Wheaton, Ill., for finding and acquiring many vintage films for me at token prices; to John Thornton for his helpful suggestions and continuing interest in the book; to the Wheaton Public Library's hardworking, patron-focused staff (with special thanks to reference librarians Ursula Ulrich and Kathleen Mallon); and, finally, to my editor Gerald Howard for encouraging and supporting a long, demanding project.

Joseph Roquemore
is a speechwriter and corporate communications specialist
who holds a Ph.D. in English literature and is an avid
reader of history. He lives in the Chicago area.